**1986**
**YEAR BOOK OF**
**SPORTS**
**MEDICINE**®

# The Year Book Series

**Anesthesia:** Drs. Miller, Kirby, Ostheimer, Saidman, and Stoelting

**Cancer:** Drs. Hickey, Clark, and Cumley

**Cardiology:** Drs. Harvey, Kirkendall, Laks, Resnekov, Rosenthal, and Sonnenblick

**Critical Care Medicine:** Drs. Rogers, Allo, Dean, Gioia, McPherson, Michael, Miller, and Traystman

**Dentistry:** Drs. Cohen, Hendler, Johnson, Jordan, Moyers, Robinson, and Silverman

**Dermatology:** Drs. Sober and Fitzpatrick

**Diagnostic Radiology:** Drs. Bragg, Keats, Kieffer, Kirkpatrick, Koehler, Miller, and Sorenson

**Digestive Diseases:** Drs. Greenberger and Moody

**Drug Therapy:** Drs. Hollister and Lasagna

**Emergency Medicine:** Dr. Wagner

**Endocrinology:** Drs. Schwartz and Ryan

**Family Practice:** Dr. Rakel

**Hand Surgery:** Drs. Dobyns and Chase

**Hematology:** Drs. Spivak, Bell, Ness, Quesenberry, and Wiernik

**Infectious Diseases:** Drs. Wolff, Gorbach, Keusch, Klempner, and Snydman

**Medicine:** Drs. Rogers, Des Prez, Cline, Braunwald, Greenberger, Wilson, Epstein, and Malawista

**Neurology and Neurosurgery:** Drs. DeJong, Currier, and Crowell

**Nuclear Medicine:** Drs. Hoffer, Gore, Gottschalk, Sostman, and Zaret

**Obstetrics and Gynecology:** Drs. Pitkin and Zlatnik

**Ophthalmology:** Drs. Ernest and Deutsch

**Orthopedics:** Dr. Coventry

**Otolaryngology—Head and Neck Surgery:** Drs. Paparella and Bailey

**Pathology and Clinical Pathology:** Dr. Brinkhous

**Pediatrics:** Drs. Oski and Stockman

**Plastic and Reconstructive Surgery:** Drs. McCoy, Brauer, Haynes, Hoehn, Miller, and Whitaker

**Podiatric Medicine and Surgery:** Dr. Jay

**Psychiatry and Applied Mental Health:** Drs. Freedman, Lourie, Meltzer, Nemiah, Talbott, and Weiner

**Pulmonary Disease:** Drs. Green, Ball, Menkes, Michael, Peters, Terry, Tockman, and Wise

**Rehabilitation:** Drs. Kaplan and Szumski

**Sports Medicine:** Drs. Krakauer, Shephard, and Torg, Col. Anderson, and Mr. George

**Surgery:** Drs. Schwartz, Jonasson, Peacock, Shires, Spencer, and Thompson

**Urology:** Drs. Gillenwater and Howards

**Vascular Surgery:** Drs. Bergan and Yao

1986

# The Year Book of
# SPORTS MEDICINE®

Editor-in-Chief

**Lewis J. Krakauer, M.D., F.A.C.P.**
*Adjunct Professor of Health, Oregon State University;*
*Assistant Clinical Professor of Medicine,*
*University of Oregon Medical School*


Editors

**Col. James L. Anderson, PE.D.**
*Director of Physical Education,*
*United States Military Academy*

**Frank George, A.T.C., P.T.**
*Head Athletic Trainer,*
*Brown University*

**Roy J. Shephard, M.D., Ph.D.**
*Director, School of Physical and Health*
*Education and Professor of Applied Physiology,*
*Department of Preventive Medicine and Biostatistics,*
*University of Toronto*

**Joseph S. Torg, M.D.**
*Professor of Orthopedic Surgery and Director,*
*Sports Medicine Center, University of Pennsylvania*
*School of Medicine*

**Year Book Medical Publishers, Inc.**


**Chicago • London**

The editor for this book was Linda H. Conheady and the production manager was H. E. Nielsen. The Editor-in-Chief for the YEAR BOOK series is Nancy Gorham.

# Table of Contents

The material covered in this volume represents literature reviewed through February 1986.

# Journals Represented

Acta Endocrinologica
Acta Medica Scandinavica
Acta Neurologica Scandinavica
Acta Oto-Laryngologica
Acta Paediatrica Scandinavica
Acta Physiologica Scandinavica
Age and Ageing
American Journal of Cardiology
American Journal of Clinical Nutrition
American Journal of Epidemiology
American Journal of Medicine
American Journal of Obstetrics and Gynecology
American Journal of Physiology
American Journal of Sports Medicine
American Journal of Surgery
Annales de Chirurgie Plastique
Annals of Allergy
Annals of Emergency Medicine
Annals of Internal Medicine
Archives of Environmental Health
Archives of Orthopedic and Traumatic Surgery
Archives of Physical Medicine and Rehabilitation
Arthroscopy
Athletic Training
Australian Journal of Science and Medicine in Sport
British Heart Journal
British Journal of Sports Medicine
Canadian Journal of Applied Sports Sciences
Canadian Journal of Ophthalmology
Chest
Circulation
Clinica Chimica Acta
Clinical Endocrinology
Clinical Orthopaedics and Related Research
Clinical Pharmacology and Therapeutics
Clinical Science
Cruising World
Contemporary Orthopedics
Drug Therapeutics
Deutsche Medizinische Wochenschrift
European Journal of Applied Physiology and Occupational Physiology
European Journal of Clinical Pharmacology
Foot and Ankle
Fortschritte Auf Dem Gebiete Der Rontgenstrahlen Und Der Nuklearmedizin
General Dentistry
Hospital Practice
Injury
International Journal of Sports Medicine
Journal of Adolescent Health Care
Journal of Allergy and Clinical Immunology
Journal of the American College of Cardiology

9

Journal of the American Medical Association
Journal of the American Osteopathic Association
Journal of Applied Physiology: Respiratory, Environmental and Exercise
   Physiology
Journal of Biomedical Engineering
Journal of Bone and Joint Surgery (American vol.)
Journal of Bone and Joint Surgery (British vol.)
Journal of the Canadian Association of Radiologists
Journal of Cardiopulmonary Rehabilitation
Journal de Chirurgie
Journal of Applied Sports Science
Journal of Clinical Endocrinology and Metabolism
Journal of Computer Assisted Tomography
Journal of Orthopaedic Research
Journal of Orthopaedic and Sports Physical Therapy
Journal of Pediatric Orthopedics
Journal of Pediatrics
Journal of the Royal College of General Practitioners
Journal of the Royal College of Surgeons of Edinburgh
Journal of Sports Cardiology
Journal of Sports Medicine and Physical Fitness
Journal of Sports Sciences
Journal of Trauma
Lancet
Medecine Du Sport
Medicine and Science in Sports and Exercise
Metabolism
Military Medicine
Nephron
Neurology
New England Journal of Medicine
New Zealand Medical Journal
Obstetrics and Gynecology
Orthopedics
Otolaryngology and Head and Neck Surgery
Physical Therapy
Physician and Sportsmedicine
Postgraduate Medical Journal
Quarterly Journal of Experimental Physiology
Quarterly Journal of Medicine
Radiology
Research Quarterly for Exercise and Sport
Scandinavian Journal of Clinical Laboratory Investigation
Schweizerische Medizinische Wochenschrift
South African Medical Journal
Sports Medicine
Thorax

# Drugs in Sports

John A. Lombardo, M.D.

*Medical Director, Sports Section, Cleveland Clinic Foundation*

Drug use has become a serious problem in society. The National Institute on Drug Abuse surveys have shown significant use of alcohol, nicotine, marijuana, cocaine, and other drugs in all age groups from high school seniors to older adults. (*National Survey on Drug Abuse-Main Findings, 1982.* DHHS Publication No. 83–1263 (Adm)). Regularly the media report an overdose, arrest, or investigation of someone involved in drug use. There was a myth, which formerly flourished, that the athletic arena "protected" people from drug use. "Athletes are never drug users." This belief has been disproved by numerous accounts of athletes at all levels who use drugs. Corder et al. have shown similar patterns of drug use in the athlete and nonathlete in the high school population (*Arizona Journal of Health, Physical Education and Recreation* 19:10–11, Fall, 1975), and Toohey et al. had similar findings at major universities (*Journal of School Health* XL:464–468, November 1971). The athlete is not immune from recreational drug use.

The athlete is exposed to a second drug problem, the use of ergogenic aids to improve performance. Competitive athletes are always searching for an edge to make them more successful. Some utilize a special piece of equipment, others have a special training regimen, and others utilize drugs, such as anabolic-androgenic steroids, stimulants (amphetamines or caffeine), or growth hormone, in order to attain their edge.

When discussing drug use in sports, it is important to separate the types of drug use into three categories: (1) therapeutic drugs—including anti-inflammatories, analgesics, antibiotics, and other drugs used in the treatment of injuries or illness; (2) performance aids—including growth hormone, amphetamines, anabolic-androgenic steroids, etc., used by athletes in training or competition to improve performance; (3) recreational (entertainment-escape) drugs—including cocaine, marijuana, alcohol, etc., used by athletes in the same manner as by others in society. This division facilitates a systematic discussion of the problems associated with the various types of drugs.

## Therapeutic Drugs

The therapeutic drugs are used to assist athletes in recovering from an illness (e.g., penicillin for a strep throat), to resolving disabilities (aspirin or a nonsteroidal anti-inflammatory for a soft tissue injury), or to control a chronic problem so that athletes can perform safely (anticonvulsants for a seizure disorder). The use of therapeutic medication in our society is great, as verified by the report of Baum et al. (*JAMA* 253:382–386, Jan. 18, 1985).

The abuses of therapeutic drugs have been anecdotally related in the media, in the locker room, at the cocktail party, and in the courtroom. The story of the injury "shot up" before the game so that the injured athlete can play has often been heard. The use of analgesics (local anesthetics or systemic medication) to kill the pain of a potentially serious injury can place the athlete at risk for exacerbating the existing problem or developing a new problem. This problem has been dealt with legally in the courtroom either through the prosecution of those not licensed to prescribe the medication or through lawsuits against physicians by former athletes.

These abuses can be minimized by informing the medical team of the effects and potential hazards of certain treatments as well as the potential gains with the use of these treatments. This information can be processed weighing the risk versus the benefit and an intelligent decision can be made regarding the use of the medication. If a certain medication or treatment is decided to be beneficial but with risks, then the athlete should be included in the decision-making process and should receive an explanation of the risks and benefits.

## Performance Aids

The use of performance aids poses a different problem from that of therapeutic drugs. These drugs are used either as an adjunct to training—e.g., anabolic-androgenic steroids—or during competition—e.g., amphetamines—for the sole purpose of improving performance. If the athlete were not involved in the event, the drug would not be taken. In a strict medical sense, performance enhancement is not an indication for any of these drugs.

Performance is a multifactorial entity that can be affected in a number of ways. Health, conditioning (training, sleep, diet), psyche, opponent, skill level, environment and, most importantly, genetic composition, all influence performance. This multi-variable nature of performance makes research on this topic complex and also makes it difficult to attribute success to any one factor, e.g., a drug or other performance aid.

When discussing the performance aids, three questions should be asked:

1. Do they give the desired benefit? By examining the scientific evidence and knowing the anecdotal reports, an objective answer to this question may be available. However, a paucity of research can reduce the available scientific evidence necessary to ensure the validity of this information.

2. What are the adverse effects? These drugs not only give the effect that the athlete desires but also can cause undesirable side effects. Side effects of drugs are mentioned in reports of therapeutic trials, case studies, and reports of these effects in athletes who are using the drugs.

3. Is the use of this drug or substance legal and/or moral/ethical? This can be the most difficult of the three questions because the different individuals involved (coaches, athletes, administrators, and the medical team) all have different goals and codes by which they function.

Using anabolic-androgenic steroids as an example, the first question refers to the efficacy of these drugs in the desired areas—increasing lean body mass, increasing strength, and enhancing performance. The literature is contradictory, but a close review of the summary statement of the American College of Sports Medicine Position Stand on Anabolic-Androgenic Steroids reveals that this paper accurately states several conclusions. This paper states that anabolic-androgenic steroids can contribute to increases in body weight in the lean body mass compartment and that, when added to a high-intensity progressive resistance strength training program and with proper diet, anabolic-androgenic steroids can also contribute to increases in strength over the gains in weight and strength in similar circumstances without the use of the drug (*Sports Medicine Bulletin* 19:13–18, July, 1984).

The next question refers to the adverse effects of these drugs. The potential adverse effects of anabolic-androgenic steroids include the following:

1. In the liver: changes in metabolism, association with liver tumors, and development of peliosis hepatis (blood-filled cysts).

2. In the cardiovascular system: decreases in serum HDL-C, development of glucose intolerance, and increases in blood pressure.

3. Psychological changes: frequent mood swings, increases in aggressiveness, and changes in libido.

4. In the male reproductive system: decreases in sperm production, testicular atrophy, impotence, and prostatic hyperplasia.

5. In the female reproductive system: masculinization and menstrual changes.

6. Among children: premature growth plate closure and early maturation.

7. Miscellaneous effects: weakening of connective tissue, acne, alopecia, and gynecomastia.

Some of these effects are reversible when the drug is removed and some are irreversible (*Sports Medicine Bulletin* 19:13–18, July, 1984).

The final area to be discussed is the legal and moral or ethical question. There is presently no law prohibiting a physician from prescribing anabolic-androgenic steroids for an athlete. Nor is there any law prohibiting an athlete from taking the drugs with a prescription, and, without a prescription, athletes can obtain these drugs on the black market.

An athlete who is competing in the Olympics (thereby agreeing to follow the Olympic Code of behavior) or competing under the auspices of the National Collegiate Athletic Association is bound by the rules of the organization not to take anabolic-androgenic steroids. If an athlete has positive test results for steroid use when tested by any of these organizations, this represents an infraction of the rules and penalties may be imposed.

The moral or ethical question surrounding performance aids is an interesting one. Morals or ethics are defined as a code of behavior and therefore are a very individual matter. Many allow their goals to dictate their code of behavior (an end justifies the means philosophy). To these the use of ergogenic aids is not wrong. Some athletes, coaches, administrators, and medical personnel espouse this philosophy; they regard winning as the end and believe any aid to training for that end—be it a drug, herb, or blood—is justified. Athletes and coaches are also faced with the problem of the public's demand for a winner and the public's desire for "purity" (drug cleanliness) in the athletes. Some athletes and coaches believe that these two situations cannot coexist.

The medical team's goal should be the health and safety of the athlete.

With this as a primary aim, allowing the use of drugs with known potentially serious adverse effects in the absence of any illness or injury seems contrary to this aim. Some rationalize that by allowing drug use in a regulated fashion athletes will be safer and healthier than if they administer drugs on their own. Others rationalize that the opposition is using drugs and that their athletes will be at an unfair disadvantage if they do not receive drugs. "Oh what a tangled web we weave" with these rationalizations. By prescribing these drugs, the physician becomes part of the problem and can be one of many suppliers in some instances.

The administrators, especially those of the major governing bodies, are faced with the task of helping their institutions remain competitive and survive financially while maintaining the standards of fair play and a clean competitive arena. In order to complete this task some type of policing of drug use, such as drug testing, is necessary.

When one discusses drug testing for performance aids, it is a situation in which a person breaks the rules to gain an unfair advantage. Drug tests should result in punishments deemed consistent with the severity of the infraction, and they should include disqualification from athletic competition and some type of suspension. In most instances, this is the case.

In addition to conducting drug testing, governing bodies also have responsibility for assisting in the education of the athletes, coaches, administrators, and medical personnel about the drugs. The governing bodies should also support the development of improvements in training, diet, and equipment to help athletes achieve their potential without the need for drugs. The United States Olympic Committee, in their present program, includes these parts.

Athletes have been trying to obtain a competitive edge since ancient times, when activities such as eating the heart of a worthy opponent to increase valor were reported. To suggest that the practice of taking ergogenic aids will be universally abandoned would not be reasonable. However, if competition on the field of sport is a microcosm of life in general, then the philosophy of the end justifying the means should be avoided in both arenas lest it lead to a chaotic situation with disregard for rules.

## Recreational Drugs

The third area of drug use is the recreational (an ironic description) drugs, which can also be referred to as entertainment or escape drugs. These include alcohol, cocaine, marijuana, stimulants, and sedatives.

Chemical abuse and chemical dependency are diseases that have invaded every part of society. National Institute on Drug Abuse surveys have followed the patterns of drug use in all age groups and report high percentages of regular users—especially of alcohol and nicotine—in each of these groups (*National Survey on Drug Abuse. Main Findings, 1982*. DHHS Publication No. (Adm) 83–1263). The list of chemically dependent athletes reported by the media seems to be ever-growing. Professional athletes are at risk for chemical dependency resulting from recreational drug use because of their high income, frequent travel, amount of leisure time, macho image (also associated with drug use), and lack of accountability (they often receive special treatment because of athletic ability) (*Cleve. Clin. Q.* 51:485–492, Fall, 1984). If the problem of recreational drug use and subsequent chemical dependency is to be attacked, a better understanding of the enemy by the public is necessary. It is important that chemical dependency be accepted as a disease if a successful war is to be waged on all fronts (producers, sellers, buyers, users).

The identification of the chemically dependent athlete can be aided by the knowledge of the symptoms. These include the following:

1. Sudden, noticeable personality changes.
2. Severe mood swings.
3. Changing peer groups.
4. Dropping out of extracurricular activities.
5. Decreased interest in leisure time activity.
6. Worsening grades.
7. Irresponsible attitudes toward household jobs and curfews.
8. Depressed feeling much of the time.
9. Dramatic change in personal hygiene.
10. Changes in sleeping or eating habits.
11. Smell of alcohol or pot.
12. Sudden weight loss.
13. Tendency toward increasing dishonesty.
14. Trouble with the law: driving while intoxicated, possession of drugs, theft, etc.
15. Truancy from school.
16. Frequent job losses or changes.
17. "Turned off" attitude if drugs are discussed.
18. Missing household money or objects.
19. Increasing isolation (time alone in room).
20. Deteriorating family relationships.
21. Drug use paraphernalia, booze, or empty bottles found hidden.
22. Observations by others of negative behavior.
23. Obvious signs of physical intoxication.
24. Missed appointments.
25. Sleeping during meetings.
26. Financial problems.
27. Missed assignments.
28. Decreasing productivity.

There are many questionnaires available to help identify those with chemical dependency problems. The initial identification requires a high index of suspicion. Drug testing is an option that should be investigated to aid in identifying an individual with a problem. Care must be taken to ensure accuracy of the test and confidentiality of the results.

Drug testing for recreational drugs should be performed for similar reasons as all other laboratory screenings—to identify potential and present problems. If the primary goal of the program is the treatment of the chemically dependent and not the punishment of the individual, it should be acceptable to all involved. This requires cooperation and support of the administration (whether it be management as in the professionals, or the athletic director and school administrators in high schools and colleges, the athletes and their organizations, and the medical team.

The testing procedures (collection and handling) must be performed in a manner that ensures confidentiality and confidence in the system. The laboratory test must be both sensitive and specific. There should be a second sample saved for a re-test if necessary. The athlete whose test result is positive should be evaluated by a drug counselor and the severity of the problem ascertained with appropriate treatment initiated. Punishments, if included, should be consistent with the severity of the problem and with the previous history of the individual so that they do not add to the problem.

Is drug testing legal? Is it ethical? What is the cost of drug testing? Who should bear this financial burden? The teams? The leagues? The schools? How accurate are the different testing procedures? Which ones should be used? These questions must be addressed prior to the widespread acceptance of mandatory testing.

Just as the goals of treatment of a diabetic, asthmatic, or emphysemic patient are control of the disease, improved quality of life, and return to normal life-style, so also are the goals of the treatment of the chemically dependent. Some diseases carry the burden of social stigma (leprosy, syphilis, AIDS) and make the attainment of the second and third goals more difficult if confidentiality is lost. Chemical dependency carries such a stigma. The success rate of many programs, including the Cleveland Browns Inner Circle program, is due in part to the confidentiality that is maintained. The treatment program consists of identification and acceptance of the program, withdrawal of the drug, ongoing therapy including individual therapy, group therapy, family therapy, and development of a support group such as Alcoholics Anonymous. It is occasionally necessary, because of the notoriety of some athletes, that the support group for some athletes remain closed, such as in the Inner Circle Program (*Cleve. Clin. Q.* 51:485–492, Fall, 1984).

Drug testing for freedom from drugs is an integral part of the therapeutic plan. Education about the drugs and their effects is necesary for high school, college, and professional athletes.

The problem of recreational drug use is significant in society as well as in sports. Inroads can be made in the problem only if a concerted effort is made by all involved groups (athletes, coaches, administrators, medical personnel, fans) to understand the problem and if there is a willingness to combat it.

## Waging the War

In order to address the problem of drug abuse in athletes, the following areas should be developed.

1. Education: athletes, coaches, parents, administrators, and medical personnel should attain knowledge about the different drugs and their effects.

2. Research: in order to adequately educate, research is necessary to expand the fund of knowledge, especially in the area of performance aids.

3. Program development: with regard to performance, improvements in training through developing new techniques, making facilities available, and obtaining quality coaching should be sought. Programs for chemically dependent athletes should aim at giving the individual an opportunity to return to a full life and must be a part of any drug detection program.

4. Detection: if rules are to be made then detection testing is necessary, lest the rules have no "teeth." Detection testing is important in identifying the chemically dependent early in the disease process.

5. Philosophical change: if winning is the measure of success, only one team or athlete can be successful. If winning is the only end, then a "win at all costs" attitude is risked. If doing one's best, competing, and adhering to the rules are stressed, sports can be a solid developmental ground for life and the pressures that result in the use of performance aids or lead to escape via drug abuse can be minimized.

The issue of drug use and abuse in sports is a complex one. We hope there will be an increased awareness of the problems so that successful programs can be initiated in areas where none exist and continue in areas where they already exist. In this way the war can become more intense, with more battles won by the people in the white hats.

# 1 Exercise Physiology and Medicine

## Cardiovascular Physiology

### Effects of Strenuous Exercise on Myocardial Blood Flow

A. A. Bove (Mayo Clinic and Found.)
Med. Sci. Sports Exerc. 17:517–521, October 1985          1–1

The regulation of myocardial blood flow remains incompletely understood, but exercise is an important stimulus of increased flow. Myocardial blood flow is the chief means of increasing oxygen delivery to the myocardium. Perfusion may be inadequate at greatly elevated cardiac work loads, although this has not been demonstrated in humans. Coronary flow during extreme exercise may be limited by α-adrenergic-mediated coronary constriction. Cardiac responses to extreme exercise can be modified by adaptations through exercise training; coronary flow reserve is not altered by chronic endurance exercise in trained animals. There is evidence that the blood pressure response to exercise is reduced by training. Catecholamine changes from training reduce the stimulus for oxygen utilization by the myocardium. Improved myocardial contractility after exercise training remains controversial.

Adenosine infusion studies suggest that chronic endurance exercise does not produce major changes in myocardial flow reserve (Fig 1–1). In humans, coronary flow usually is estimated by indirect methods such as exercise stress testing. Nuclear methods that demonstrate global cardiac performance, such as gated blood pool imaging, can be used to evaluate myocardial performance during exercise. Such studies have established a relation between myocardial function and oxygen delivery. Flow reserve is reduced in cardiac hypertrophy, because resting flow is increased in proportion to the increased mass induced by chronic overload. Regional blood flow distribution between the endocardium and epicardium is an important limiting factor in exercise, especially under pathologic circumstances.

Better methods of understanding myocardial blood flow both at rest and on exercise are needed, so that persons with inadequate coronary flow reserve can be encouraged to avoid exercising beyond their maximal capacity for myocardial perfusion.

▶ Oxygen extraction by the myocardium is near maximum in the resting state. It is for this reason that myocardial blood flow is the major determinant of oxygen delivery to the myocardium. The regulation of blood flow during exercise is dependent upon local metabolic factors and is, to a small extent, dependent on autonomic tone. Maximum flow of 5 to 6 times the resting has been noted in reactive hyperemia experimentation. Of the physiologic stimuli

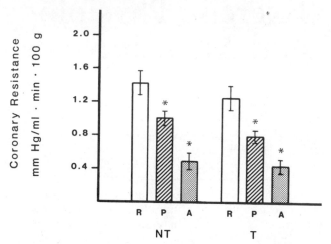

**Fig 1–1.**—Coronary vascular resistance at rest *(R)*, with pacing *(P)*, and with adenosine *(A)* in nontrained *(NT)* and trained *(T)* dogs. *$P < .05$ compared to resting state. (Courtesy of Bove, A.A.: Med. Sci. Sports Exerc. 17:517–521, October 1985. Copyright 1985, the American College of Sports Medicine. Reprinted by permission.)

that increase myocardial blood flow, the most important is exercise. This includes the mildest form of physical activity, such as walking, as well as the entire spectrum from that point to competitive activity of significant vigor, and anaerobic activity of significant vigor.

Practical sense of this study: The increased demand imposed by exercise is not a problem for the normal heart. It is only when limitations are imposed on myocardial blood flow by coronary artery disease or cardiac hypertrophy that risk factors intrude, such as arrhythmia or acute ischemic disease.—Lewis J. Krakauer, M.D., F.A.C.P.

---

**Myocardial Injury After Exercise: A Diagnostic Dilemma**
Arthur J. Siegel (Hahnemann Hosp., Brighton, Mass.)
J. Cardiopulmonary Rehabil. 5:415–420, September 1985                    1–2

Elevations of the MB isoenzyme of creatine kinase (CK-MB) in the serum of endurance-trained athletes may quantitatively resemble findings in patients with AMI. This creates a diagnostic dilemma when certain endurance-trained athletes (e.g., runners) are evaluated for cardiorespiratory symptoms or heat injury during or after races. Serum CK-MB levels in such individuals are not specific for myocardial injury, analogous to ECG findings otherwise suggestive of myocardial ischemia.

The presence of elevated cardiac enzyme levels, including CK-MB, has been confirmed in endurance-trained athletes after competition. The demonstration of elevated serum CK-MB levels is a sensitive and specific index of myocardial injury in 95% of cases, leading some authors to conclude that prolonged strenuous exercise leads to silent myocardial ischemia or infarction. Levels of CK-MB in runners may exceed those used by some authors as the reference point for diagnosis of recurrence of myocardial infarction (MI) (so-called extension) or the standard for initial injury.

Biochemical estimates of infarct size have been extrapolated from time-activity curves for CK-MB release. A quantitative relationship has been reported between the cumulative release of CK-MB and infarct size, as estimated by myocardial emission-CT with thallium-201. This suggests the usefulness of radionuclide scintigraphy in marathon runners for evaluating the clinical significance of elevations in serum CK-MB levels. Acute myocardial perfusion imaging with thallium-201 is sensitive enough to detect silent myocardial ischemia or injury. However, infarct-avid myocardial scintigraphy using technetium-99m pyrophosphate may fail to detect non-Q-wave myocardial damage. Masking of perfusion defects by overlying normal myocardium in athletes with left ventricular hypertrophy must also be considered with thallium scanning.

Data on serum CK-MB concentrations in asymptomatic runners should modify the estimate of specificity of CK-MB measurements for myocardial injury from 95% to less than 50%. If one assumes that the probability of MI in an asymptomatic marathon runner is 1%, then the posttest probability of MI based on elevated CK-MB levels would increase to a range of 15%. If one also assumes that a thallium scan has a sensitivity and specificity of 90% for myocardial ischemia, the posttest probability of MI after a normal thallium scan with elevated cardiac enzyme levels drops from 15% to less than 1%. These changes, reflected by line A in Figure 1–2, are relatively minor, but they may be highly relevant in clinical assessment. The posttest risk for myocardial injury rises sharply in middle-aged or elderly marathon runners, particularly in those with risk factors

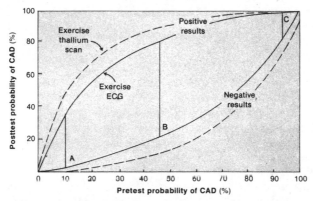

Fig 1–2.—The posttest probability of myocardial infarction after exercise. Vertical line B shows the difference in posttest probabilities for positive and negative results on exercise thallium scanning in a male runner aged 45 years with atypical chest pain [pretest probability of coronary artery disease (CAD) when risk factors equal .46]. Posttest probability of CAD is 80% for an elevated serum creatine kinase (CK)-MB level and rises to more than 90% with positive findings on the exercise thallium scan. A normal result of exercise thallium scanning with an elevated serum CK-MB level reduces the posttest probability of CAD to less than 10%. Lines A and C show that there is less difference for asymptomatic men aged 55 years and those with typical angina (pretest probabilities of .10 and .92, respectively). Exercise ECG: sensitivity, 75%, specificity, 85%; exercise thallium scan: sensitivity, 85%, specificity, 90%. From Epstein, S.E.: Am. J. Cardiol. 46:491–499, 1980. (Courtesy of Siegel, A.J.: J. Cardiopulmonary Rehabil. 5:415–420, September 1985.)

for coronary disease. Clinical judgment is more severely tested when the runner has symptoms of gastrointestinal tract upset or atypical chest pain.

An alternative diagnostic approach uses cardiac radionuclide testing to define cardiac status. Myocardial perfusion imaging with thallium-201 and concurrent, sequential, cardiac enzyme determinations were performed in marathon runners immediately after completion of a race. That normal radionuclide perfusion imaging correlated with cumulative CK-MB release similar to that in patients with transmural MI strongly suggests that the cardiac isozymes originate from a noncardiac source. This is illustrated in line B in the figure. Here the difference between posttest probabilities for discordant test results is greatest near the middle of the pretest range. A marathon runner with symptoms compatible with myocardial ischemia and positive findings for an elevated serum CK-MB level may have an 80% chance of having an MI. Normal findings on exercise thallium scanning would reduce this probability to less than 10%, whereas abnormal findings would increase it to more than 95%. This clinical setting emphasizes sequential noninvasive testing in athletes or other patients with suspected acute myocardial ischemia. In a runner with classic signs of MI, positive findings in the thallium scan would add little to the probability of AMI.

▶ Editorial comments in prior years (1985 YEAR BOOK OF SPORTS MEDICINE, pp. 64–67; 1984 YEAR BOOK OF SPORTS MEDICINE, pp. 72–75, and 1982 YEAR BOOK OF SPORTS MEDICINE, pp. 20–21) have commented on the lack of specificity and the unreliability of the CPK enzyme, even when broken down into its MB component. The further step of thallium radionuclide scanning is of significant value when results are negative. If results are positive, one must go to an additional step, coronary arteriography. The unreliability of exercise testing or EKG treadmill testing in this situation is accepted as a given. A negative finding from thallium scanning is therefore of considerable value in ruling out acute myocardial infarction. A positive test is of little clinical value.—Lewis J. Krakauer, M.D., F.A.C.P.

**Elevated Cardiac Enzymes After Contact Sport**
J. H. N. Eisenberg, N. A. Moore, and A. Wilcockson (Northern Gen. Hosp., Sheffield, England)
J. Sports Cardiol. 1:76–79, 1984                                    1–3

Serial measurements of creatine kinase and its MB isoenzyme have been widely held as the most specific and sensitive test of acute myocardial infarction. The purpose of this study was to document the rise of these enzyme levels after more common forms of exercise. Serial enzyme levels were measured before, 16 hours after, and 40 hours after a soccer match (6 subjects), a rugby match (6 subjects), and a rigorous rugby training (6 subjects). All were well-trained men, aged 19 to 26 years.

No subjects developed any cardiac symptoms before or after exercise. In 7 of the 18, the level of total creatine kinase before exercise was elevated.

The level of total creatine kinase was elevated at 16 hours and at 40 hours. Serum creatine kinase MB isoenzyme level ws elevated at 16 hours in 9 of 18 subjects. In no case was creatine kinase MB fraction greater than 5% of total creatine kinase. Some subjects (4 of 18) had a modest elevation of lactate dehydrogenase and asparate aminotransferase. Enzyme levels after rugby tended to be higher than after soccer.

This study confirms previous work demonstrating a rise in total creatine kinase after exercise. The observation that the rise may peak to 5 times the upper limit of normal after a game of rugby emphasizes that it is not just in marathon runners that the total creatine kinase needs to be interpreted with caution. The authors feel that measurement of creatine kinase MB isoenzyme after contact sport is still important. It should, however, be taken into consideration with other enzymes and with electrocardiographic and clinical evidence to obtain maximum sensitivity and specificity in the diagnosis of myocardial infarction.

► It has been recognized that a rise of MB isoenzymes needs to be interpreted cautiously after marathon running (Ohman et al., *Br. Med. J.* 285:1523, 1982; Siegel et al., *JAMA* 246:2049, 1981), but this difficulty seems to extend to many sports. Nevertheless, a diagnosis of myocardial infarction can still be drawn with reasonable accuracy if the MB isozyme is considered in relation to total enzyme levels and if this information is considered in conjunction with clinical symptoms and ECG changes.—Roy J. Shephard, M.D., Ph.D.

---

**Left Ventricular Systolic and Diastolic Function in Coronary Artery Disease: Effects of Revascularization of Exercise-Induced Ischemia**
John D. Carroll, Otto M. Hess, Heinz O. Hirzel, Marko Turina, and Hans Peter Krayenbuehl (Univ. of Chicago and Univ. of Zurich, Switzerland)
Circulation 72:119–129, July 1985                                                1–4

The extent to which surgery alters the left ventricular dysfunction often associated with exercise in patients with coronary artery disease is uncertain. Twenty-four such patients, with a mean age of 56 years, were evaluated before and after uncomplicated bypass grafting for exercise-induced ischemia. All major stenotic lesions were bypassed, and the patients were symptomatically improved after surgery. Cycle ergometer exercise tests were carried out at identical work rates before and after revascularization.

Ejection fraction fell from 57% to 49% on exercise before operation, as new asynergy developed and the end-systolic and end-diastolic volumes increased. After operation the ejection fraction increased from 59% to 61% because of an increased end-diastolic volume (table). Peak left ventricular systolic pressure during exercise rose significantly after but not before surgery. Diastolic pressure elevations on exercise were less marked after revascularization. The left ventricular pressure decay on exercise was greatly improved and the early diastolic peak filling rate was greater after surgery. Late diastolic filling was restricted compared with control data.

Patients who have good symptomatic results from myocardial revas-

| | Before surgery (n = 24) | | After surgery (n = 24) | | Before vs after | |
|---|---|---|---|---|---|---|
| | Rest | Exercise | Rest | Exercise | Rest | Exercise |
| HR (beats/min) | $67 \pm 12$ | $115 \pm 11^C$ | $75 \pm 16$ | $129 \pm 19^C$ | p<.05 | p<.001 |
| EF (%) | $57 \pm 9$ | $49 \pm 9^C$ | $59 \pm 11$ | $61 \pm 11^A$ | NS | p<.001 |
| ESVI (ml/m²) | $49 \pm 14$ | $64 \pm 19^C$ | $44 \pm 18$ | $46 \pm 21$ | NS | p<.001 |
| EDVI (ml/m²) | $114 \pm 24$ | $125 \pm 23^B$ | $108 \pm 25$ | $115 \pm 27^B$ | NS | p<.05 |
| LVEDP (mm Hg) | $23 \pm 6$ | $37 \pm 8^C$ | $17 \pm 4$ | $25 \pm 10^B$ | p<.001 | p<.001 |
| $P_L$ (mm Hg) | $9 \pm 4$ | $21 \pm 8^C$ | $5 \pm 3$ | $6 \pm 3$ | p<.001 | p<.001 |
| Peak LVP (mm Hg) | $149 \pm 23$ | $156 \pm 19$ | $144 \pm 21$ | $177 \pm 20^C$ | NS | p<.001 |
| Max +dP/dt (mm Hg/sec) | $1530 \pm 274$ | $2210 \pm 512^C$ | $1637 \pm 370$ | $3314 \pm 113^C$ | NS | p<.001 |
| Max −dP/dt (mm Hg/sec) | $1546 \pm 284$ | $1873 \pm 419^C$ | $1589 \pm 297$ | $2653 \pm 555^C$ | NS | p<.001 |
| T (msec) | $54 \pm 9$ | $37 \pm 9^C$ | $52 \pm 11$ | $30 \pm 9^C$ | NS | p<.01 |
| $P_B$ (mm Hg) | $-9 \pm 8$ | $10 \pm 9^C$ | $-10 \pm 10$ | $-7 \pm 12$ | NS | p<.001 |

*HR, heart rate; EF, ejection fraction; ESVI, end-systolic volume index; EDVI, end-diastolic volume index; LVEDP, left ventricular end-diastolic pressure; Max + dP/dt, maximum rate of left ventricular pressure rise; Max − dP/dt, maximum rate of left ventricular pressure decline; T, negative reciprocal of slope; $P_B$, pressure axis intercept; NS, not significant.
$^A P < .05$, rest vs. exercise.
$^B P < .01$, rest vs. exercise.
$^C P < .001$, rest vs. exercise.
(Courtesy of Carroll, J.D., et al.: Circulation 72:119–129, July 1985; by permission of the American Heart Association, Inc.)

cularization exhibit improved left ventricular systolic and diastolic function. Persistent abnormalities of diastolic function are sometimes seen and may reflect chronic structural changes. Revascularization may prevent or minimize acute exercise-induced ischemia with acute stiffening of the left ventricular chamber, but chronic alterations in chamber compliance would not be expected to change.

▶ Clinicians have attached increasing importance to the role of myocardial ischemia in causing delayed ventricular relaxation and an increase of diastolic pressures for a given filling volume (Barry et al.: *Circulation* 49:255, 1974; Mann et al.: *Circulation* 49:255, 1974). The above paper by Carroll et al. provides a nice demonstration of this; once ischemia was corrected through bypass surgery, the ejection fraction rose rather then fell during exercise, and there were parallel improvements in the elevation of diastolic pressure and delays in left ventricular relaxation. However, benefit cannot be anticipated from surgery if an initial poor ejection fraction is due to an asynergic sector of ventricular wall, rather than an acute ischemic disturbance of myocardial function.—Roy J. Shephard, M.D., Ph.D.

## On Physiological Edema in Man's Lower Extremity
C. Stick, P. Stöfen, and E. Witzleb (Christian-Albrechts-Universität Kiel, Kiel, Federal Republic of Germany)
Eur. J. Appl. Physiol. 54:442–449, October 1985                    1–5

Many studies have shown that the increased venous pressure in the lower extremities on standing is countered by activation of the muscle pump,

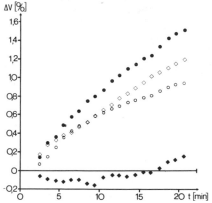

Fig 1–3.—Calf volume changes during muscular exercise *(solid symbols)* and increase in calf volumes during quiet standing *(open symbols)*. Whereas in one subject *(squares)*, volume of calf during muscular exercise is nearly unchanged, in other subject *(circles)*, calf volume during rhythmic heel raising increases faster and more markedly than during motionless standing, where increase in calf volume is similar in both subjects. (Courtesy of Stick, C., et al.: Eur. J. Appl. Physiol. 54:442–449, October 1985; Berlin-Heidelberg-New York: Springer.)

but standard plethysmographic methods are not ideally suited to measuring filtration-induced volume changes during muscle contraction and throughout the day. Impedance plethysmography was used to measure volume changes in the lower extremity during 20 minutes of relaxed standing and 20 minutes of standing with rhythmic muscle contraction and during regular daily activities. Twenty-three healthy subjects of both sexes, aged 20 to 35 years, with no evident venous valve incompetence were studied.

About half the subjects exhibited an edema-protective effect of musculovenous pumping. In the other subjects, muscle exercise led to increases in calf volume that exceeded what was observed in the normal upright position (Fig 1–3). Daytime studies showed that in nearly all subjects, calf volume was greater in the evening than in the morning. Volume elevations in the evening were due to increased extravascular fluid.

The calf muscle pump does not consistently have an edema-protective effect. Muscle contractions also activate mechanisms that stimulate fluid extravasation. Accumulation of extravascular fluid during the day is fairly low compared with the volume increase seen in a short period of standing. Increased lymph flow begins at a certain level of interstitial volume and acts to prevent edema. The muscle pump that contributes to lymph drainage apparently is maximally effective only when a certain volume is exceeded.

▶ An accumulation of fluid in the legs was well recognized by the editor during his period with the Royal Air Force High Altitude Unit, when the use of pressure breathing equipment caused a sufficient exudation of fluid to produce a loss of consciousness in resting subjects in a matter of 5 minutes.

The main role of the muscle pump is probably to return fluid in the veins rather than to avoid an accumulation of fluid in the tissues and lymphatics. The escape of fluid into the muscles depends largely on the balance of intracapillary hydrostatic and osmotic pressures. In some cases, escape of protein into the tissues is increased by exercise, raising the extravascular osmotic pressure and exaggerating the likelihood of exudation of fluid. If systemic blood pressure rises, there may also be some increase of pressure at the arterial end of the capillaries. Local hypoxia may increase the permeability of the capillary membrane. It is hardly surprising that the relatively small reduction of venous pressure achieved by muscle pumping is not enough to outweigh these effects. Indeed, a progressive escape of fluid from the circulation is one reason for the upward drift of heart rates during sustained exercise.—Roy J. Shephard, M.D., Ph.D.

---

**Reliability of the Heart Rate Response to Submaximal Upper and Lower Body Exercise**
Richard A. Washburn and Henry J. Montoye (Univ. of Pittsburgh and Univ. of Wisconsin–Madison)
Res. Q. Exerc. Sport 56:166–169, 1985                                        1–6

Heart rate responses to submaximal exercise commonly are used in exercise science and in documentation of cardiovascular training effects. The reliability of responses to several submaximal intensities of arm cranking and leg cycling exercise was examined in a study of 20 men, with a mean age of 32 years, who were laboratory-naive. Heart rate was monitored during 5-minute exercise periods. Arm cranking was performed on a cycle ergometer at 5, 10, 30, and 50 W, and leg exercise was performed at no load and at 25, 50, and 100 W.

Significant differences were found during the three test sessions. Resting heart rate exhibited high reliability. Exercise rates did not differ significantly over time. Reliability increased as power output rose with arm exercise. Heart rate was highly reliable during leg cycling at all power outputs. Differences in mean heart rate with varying power output were very small. There were no significant differences in oxygen uptake at rest or during arm or leg exercise.

The heart rate response to arm cranking exercise may be less reliable than the response to leg cycling. Responses to submaximal leg cycling are quite reliable and are relatively constant over work rates from no load to 100 W. Heart rate responses to submaximal arm cranking exercise are reliable at higher power outputs.

▶ This paper provides straightforward documentation that at rest, or during submaximal leg cycling at low to moderate power outputs, heart rate response and measurement is highly reliable. This reliability suffers when one switches to submaximal arm cranking, although heart rate responses are still reliable at the higher power output levels. Leg cycling is preferable. It is not always an option in the impaired.—Lewis J. Krakauer, M.D., F.A.C.P.

---

**Increased Morning Heart Rate In Runners: A Valid Sign of Overtraining?**
Rudolph H. Dressendorfer, Charles E. Wade, and Jack H. Scaff, Jr. (William Beaumont Hosp., Royal Oak, Mich.)
Physician Sportsmed. 13:77–86, August 1985                                        1–7

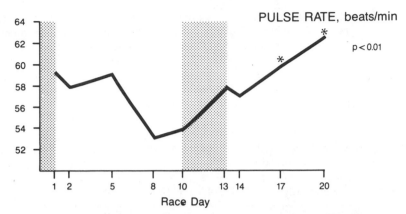

Fig 1–4.—Average morning heart rate in 12 male marathon runners during a 500-km road race over 20 days. Rest periods *(shaded areas)* of 36 and 70 hours preceded m measurements on days 1 and 13, respectively. Asterisks indicate that heart rate values on days 17 and 20 are significantly higher ($P < .01$) than day 8 ($P < .01$). (Courtesy of Dressendorfer, R.H., et al.: Physician Sportsmed. 13:77–86, August 1985. Reprinted by permission. A McGraw-Hill publication.)

An elevated resting pulse rate is generally considered to be a marker of overtraining in endurance athletes who greatly increase their workout distance. This prospective study examined changes in the morning heart rates of 12 experienced marathon runners competing in a 500-km road race held over 20 days. Daily race distances averaged 28 km, twice the runner's usual mileage. Subjects were men aged 23 to 60 years who entered the 1979 Great Hawaiian Footrace.

Eleven subjects completed the full 500-km distance in 18 days. Running speeds averaged 188 meters/minute, about 15% slower than their best marathon speed. Compared with day 8, pulse rates were significantly elevated by 7 beats/minute on day 17, and by 10 beats/minute on day 20 (Fig 1–4). All subjects showed increases from day 8 to day 20. Subjects with an initial heart rate over 60 beats/minute showed a reduction from day 1 to day 8 and an increase from day 8 to day 20. There were no significant changes in oral temperature, body weight, or blood chemistries.

This study demonstrates that a sudden increase in long-distance running mileage above the regular training level can elevate the morning heart rate. Monitoring the morning pulse rate may therefore be useful in the early diagnosis and prevention of the overtrained state. The authors speculate that increased basal heart rate in overtrained endurance runners possibly reflects, in part, intrinsic myocardial fatigue. Further studies are needed in this area.

▶ Industrial physiologists have long recognized a rising heart rate as a sign of excessive effort. In the industrial situation, the usual explanation of the tachycardia is a progressive depletion of blood volume, due to either sweating or to an exudation of fluid into the muscles. In the present study, body mass did not change, so sweat loss could not be responsible. However, a peripheral sequestration of fluid takes several hours to reverse even after a much shorter run, and a peripheral fluid shift may have been a contributory factor as the race continued. The other possibility is that local muscle injury caused an inflammatory reaction, with both edema and increased blood flow to the affected tissue.

Before accepting a high testing heart rate as an adverse sign, it would be nice to have some clearer association between the tachycardia and other manifestations of overtraining.—Roy J. Shephard, M.D., Ph.D.

---

**Training-Induced Bradycardia in Rats on Cardioselective and Non-Selective Beta Receptor Blockade**
Eva Nylander (Univ. of Linköping, Sweden)
Acta Physiol. Scand. 123:147–149, February 1985                                    1–8

---

· For reasons that remain uncertain, endurance training produces bradycardia at rest and on submaximal exercise. Previous studies suggest that the increased heart rate during training sessions is not the chief factor. The development of bradycardia with training was examined in rats treated with either the cardioselective β-blocker metoprolol or the nonselective β-blocker propranolol. Training was performed on a treadmill for 1 hour a day, 3 days a week, for 12 weeks, at a treadmill speed of 25–30 m/minute, producing a heart rate increase to 500–550 beats/minute in untreated rats and 400–450 beats/minute in metoprolol-treated animals.

Plasma propranolol levels were 380–1,340 nmole/L during treatment, whereas metoprolol levels were 500–1,040 nmole/L. Trained, untreated rats had significantly lower heart rates than sedentary rats had at all work loads. The exercise heart rate in both treated groups did not differ significantly from that of the trained control animals at any work load. No major differences in body weight were noted at the end of the study.

Cardioselective β-blockade during training does not attenuate the development of bradycardia on submaximal exercise. Adrenergic stimulation of the heart or a heart rate rise above a certain level would not seem to be the chief stimulus for the development of training-induced bradycardia. More data are needed on training effects in human beings treated with β-blockers.

▶ In the *rat,* bradycardia following submaximal exercise is not only independent of any β-blockade, but one cannot distinguish in a physiologic sense between those rats treated with nonspecific and cardioselective β-receptor blockade.— Lewis J. Krakauer, M.D., F.A.C.P.

---

**Effect of Beta₁ Selective Adrenoceptor Blockade on Physiological Response to Exercise**
N. F. Gordon, J. P. van Rensburg, H. M. S. Russell, D. L. Kawalsky, C. P. Celliers, J. F. Cilliers, and D. P. Myburgh (Inst. for Aviation Medicine, Pretoria, South Africa, and Chamber of Mines of South Africa, Johannesburg)
Br. Heart J. 54:96–99, July 1985                                                    1–9

Exercise training commonly is prescribed for patients with hypertension or angina who receive β-blockers. The effects of the $\beta_1$-selective blocker atenolol on exercise physiology were studied in 12 healthy men whose mean age was 21 years. A double-blind, crossover design was used. An oral dose of 100 mg of atenolol or placebo was given 90 minutes before upright cycle exercise was performed in a controlled environment.

Maximal oxygen consumption, pulmonary ventilation, $CO_2$ output, and the respiratory exchange ratio all were unaffected by β-blockade with atenolol. The maximal heart rate was reduced by 23%, and cycle ergometer performance time was decreased by 4%, after β-blockade. The relationship between percent maximal oxygen consumption and percent maximal heart rate was not altered by β-blockade. Both the relative and the absolute oxygen consumption for 70% and 85% of the maximal heart rate were unchanged.

It seems feasible to recommend exercise intensity on the basis of a calculated percentage of the predetermined maximal heart rate in persons without symptomatic coronary heart disease who are receiving a $\beta_1$-adrenoceptor blocker. Different training responses in persons given $\beta_1$-selective and nonselective β-blockers, and with differing cardiac status, may result in part from the differential effects of these variables on the absolute exercise intensity corresponding to a specific percentage of maximal heart rate.

▶ In this South African study, 12 healthy, fit young males were studied in double-blind crossover fashion, using oral atenolol and placebo. Maximal effort oxygen consumption, pulmonary ventilation, carbon dioxide output, and respiratory exchange ratio were not influenced by atenolol. In contrast, the maximal heart rate and performance time were significantly reduced in the atenolol-treated group.—Lewis J. Krakauer, M.D., F.A.C.P.

## β-Adrenoceptors and the Regulation of Blood Pressue and Plasma Renin During Exercise

P. Hespel, P. Lijnen, L. Vanhees, R. Fagard, and A. Amery (Univ. of Louvain)
J. Appl. Physiol. 60:108–113, January 1986                                 1–10

β-Receptors are important in blood pressure regulation and renin secretion, but whether $\beta_1$- or $\beta_2$-type receptors are involved is uncertain. The effects of atenolol, a predominantly $\beta_1$-blocking agent and ICI 118551, a reportedly selective $\beta_2$-antagonist, on blood pressure and the renin-aldosterone system were compared in 17 normal men with an average age of 23 years. Graded cycle ergometer exercise tests were performed to exhaustion, in conjunction with administration of 50 mg of atenolol daily, 20 mg of ICI 118551 three times daily, or matched placebos.

Both drugs reduced heart rate, but no further decline occurred on exercise with ICI 118551. Only atenolol reduced the systolic blood pressure at rest, and it suppressed the exercise-induced rise in pressure. Renin activity at rest and on exercise was lowered by atenolol and was unaffected by ICI 118551 (Fig 1–5). Atenolol did not affect the exercise-related rise

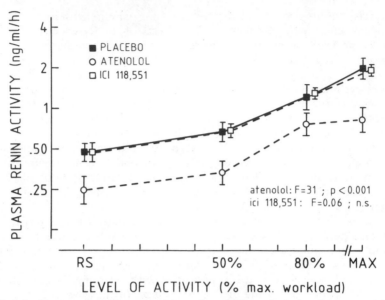

Fig 1–5.—Plasma renin activity at rest sitting and at graded exercise during placebo, atenolol, and ICI 118551. Means ± SE of logarithmically transformed data are given; $n = 17$. (Courtesy of Hespel, P., et al.: J. Appl. Physiol. 60:108–113, January 1986.)

in plasma renin activity. Urinary aldosterone excretion was reduced after atenolol, but the plasma aldosterone concentration was unchanged. Exercise capacity was reduced by 5% with atenolol and by 3% with ICI 118551.

Adrenoceptors mediating renin release at rest and on exercise are partially of the $\beta_1$ subtype. $\beta_2$-Receptors probably have only a minor role, especially on exercise. Differential effects on blood pressure are observed with predominantly $\beta_1$- and $\beta_2$-blockade.

▶ General β-blockers are increasingly being replaced by selective $\beta_1$- and $\beta_2$-blockers. This paper demonstrates fairly conclusively that the $\beta_1$ mechanism is involved in the exercise-induced secretion of renin, and that consequently the exercise blood pressure is lower after $\beta_1$- than after $\beta_2$-blockade.—Roy J. Shephard, M.D., Ph.D.

---

**Beta-Blockade and Response To Exercise: Influence of Training**
Jack H. Wilmore, Michael J. Joyner, Beau J. Freund, Gordon A. Ewy, and Alan R. Morton (Univ. of Arizona)
Physician Sportsmed. 13:60–69, July 1985                                    1–11

Both β-blockers and exercise training frequently are prescribed for patients with hypertension and coronary artery disease. β-Blockade reduces heart rate and systolic blood pressure during submaximal exercises, but maximal exercise data are equivocal. Review was made of the findings in

93 individuals based on four laboratory studies. The participants, aged 18 to 35 years, ranged from relatively sedentary to highly trained. The drugs used included 320 mg of sotalol, 160 mg of propranolol, and 100 mg of atenolol daily. Drug or placebo was given in a double-blind manner for 7 days before testing.

The maximal oxygen consumption was significantly attenuated by β-blockade in individuals having values of 50 ml/kg/minute and higher. The decrement in maximal heart rate was substantially greater than that in maximal oxygen uptake. In persons having a higher maximal oxygen uptake, the decrement was much more closely related to that in maximal heart rate in the blocked state.

These findings suggest that untrained individuals can maintain maximal oxygen uptake in the β-blocked state through a compensatory increase in stroke volume and/or arteriovenous oxygen difference. Trained individuals have maximized their ability to increase stroke volume and oxygen extraction and are less able to compensate for the effects of acute β-blockade. This may help explain conflicting data in previous reports when populations differing in fitness level were studied.

▶ Ninety-three subjects were studied in four different groups. The study was both randomized and double-blind. These authors, in contrast to the previous group, make a distinction between the trained and the untrained group. The case is made well that β-blockers will increase exercise capacity in angina, decrease exercise capacity in the highly trained and fit individuals, and will have little or no effect on the exercise capacity of healthy *untrained* individuals.—Lewis J. Krakauer, M.D., F.A.C.P.

---

**Effect of Beta-Adrenergic Blockade on the Results of Exercise Testing Related to the Extent of Coronary Artery Disease**
Stephen W.-C. Ho, Michael J. McComish, and Roger R. Taylor (Royal Perth Hosp., Perth, Australia)
Am. J. Cardiol. 55:258–262, Feb. 1, 1985                                                    1–12

---

Exercise testing is being used increasingly to select for angiography those patients most likely to have extensive coronary artery disease and those with a worse prognosis who may benefit from surgery. The effect of β-blockade on patient selection was examined in individuals with angina referred for coronary angiography. All had 50% stenosis of at least one major coronary vessel. The study group included 50 patients whose mean age was 54 years. Metoprolol was used by 32 patients, propranolol by 12, atenolol by 5, and pindolol by 1. Symptom-limited treadmill exercise was performed according to the Bruce protocol.

The average duration of exercise was 1.3 minutes longer during β-blockade, regardless of coronary anatomy, and the maximum heart rate and systolic blood pressure were significantly lower. Eight of 20 patients with 3-vessel or left main coronary disease completed three stages of exercise during β-blockade, as did 4 without treatment. β-Blockade suppressed ST depression or delayed its occurrence. The grade of ST segment change was decreased by β-blockade in 19 patients and increased in 7.

These findings indicate that β-blockade obscures the diagnostic interpretation of exercise testing to a significant extent and decreases the ability to select patients likely to have extensive coronary artery disease. Angina was most often the limiting symptom in patients with severe coronary disease, and this association was abolished by β-blockade.

▶ As a further extrapolation of the prior studies, this work from Australia underscores the point that β-blockade will obscure the diagnostic value of exercise testing cardiograms and impair the ability of that particular screening device to select subjects who have extensive coronary artery disease. Turning that around, any patient in whom exercise testing is planned as a diagnostic procedure should either be taken off β-blockade or the test should be considered as much less reliable in that circumstance.—Lewis J. Krakauer, M.D., F.A.C.P.

---

**Oxygen Uptake and Plasma Catecholamines During Submaximal and Maximal Exercise After Long-Term β-Receptor Blockade**
I.-W. Franz, F. W. Lohmann, and G. Koch (Free Univ. of Berlin and Neuköln Hosp., Berlin, Federal Republic of Germany)
Int. J. Sports Med. 6:202–206, August 1985                                                        1–13

Beta-receptor antagonists lower exercise heart rate and cardiac output. These agents can thus be expected to interfere with oxygen transport, and hence physical performance, particularly at higher levels of activity. The effects of 4-week and 15-month treatment periods with the $\beta_1$-selective receptor blocker acebutolol (500 mg daily) on oxygen uptake and plasma catecholamines during submaximal steady-state, maximal exercise, and on maximal work load were studied in 8 hypertensive men (mean age, 36.4 years) classified as stage 1 by the World Health Organization.

Oxygen uptake, ventilation, and plasma norepinephrine (NE), epinephrine (E), and dopamine levels during steady-state exercise did not differ from control conditions either after 4 weeks or after 15 months of receptor blockade, although heart rates were significantly reduced (27% and 25% respectively) (Fig 1–6). After the 4-week treatment period, maximal oxygen uptake (3.9% reduction) and maximal work load (2.4% reduction) tended to be slightly lower after acebutolol compared with control values; maximal oxygen pulse was significantly increased. However, after long-term treatment of 15 months, maximal oxygen uptake was virtually identical compared with pretreatment values. Maximal work load tended to be higher (5.2%); plasma NE and E levels were significantly elevated.

These results confirm previous findings demonstrating that β-adrenoceptor blockades do not affect oxygen uptake under conditions of steady-state submaximal exercise despite substantial reductions of heart rate. This indicates that aerobic capacity during submaximal exercise is not reduced. After 15 months of treatment with acebutolol, maximal oxygen uptake

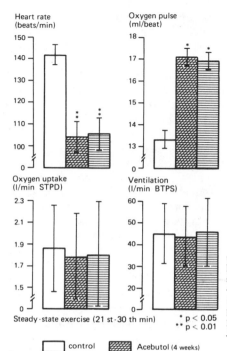

Heart rate (beats/min)

Oxygen pulse (ml/beat)

Oxygen uptake (l/min STPD)

Ventilation (l/min BTPS)

Steady-state exercise (21 st-30 th min)

\* p < 0.05
\*\* p < 0.01

☐ control    ▨ Acebutol (4 weeks)    ▤ Acebutol (15 months)

Fig 1–6.—Heart rate, oxygen pulse, oxygen uptake, and ventilation (means ± SD) in 8 hypertensive patients during steady-state submaximal exercise before (control) and after a 4-week and 15-month treatment with acebutolol (500 mg daily). BTPS = body temperature pressure saturated, STPD = standard temperature pressure dry. (Courtesy of Franz, I.-W., et al.: Int. J. Sports Med. 6:202–206, August 1985.)

and maximal physical work capacity remained unchanged under chronic β₁-adrenoceptor blockade. Previous reports concerning maximal oxygen uptake during β-receptor blockade are conflicting.

Only marginal differences exist among different types of β-receptor antagonists regarding the degree of reduction of cardiac output and rise in peripheral vascular resistances, under conditions of submaximal exercise. The nonselective blocking agent pindolol, presumably because of its intrinsic sympathetic activity, causes a less pronounced reduction of cardiac output and basically no rise in total systemic vascular resistance. It is possible that a blockade of vascular β₂-receptors by a nonselective antagonist could play a role under conditions of maximal exercise. This may restrict maximal vasodilation and perfusion, and thus interfere with the compensatory increase in oxygen extraction under these conditions.

Previous studies have shown distinct differences in the effects on carbohydrate metabolism exerted during prolonged exercise by cardioselective and nonselective antagonists, respectively. β₁-Selective receptor blockers, as opposed to nonselective β-receptor antagonists, lack an inhibitory effect of glycogen breakdown and affect the exercise performance less with respect to individual muscle fiber composition. Thus, β₁-selective antagonists appear preferable for patients in preventive and rehabilitative training programs.

With respect to the NE and E responses to exercise during β-blockade, the present results obtained after 15 months of treatment confirm the authors' previous findings. These revealed that significant reductions of exercise heart rate and blood pressure do not necessarily imply a compensatory increase of sympathetic activity. The significant increases of plasma NE and E levels at maximal work compared with pretreatment values and after a 4-week treatment period can be explained by the higher maximal work loads achieved by the patients after 15 months. However, a desensitivity process of β-receptors cannot be excluded.

▶ Apparently there is a difference between treatment for 4-weeks and treatment for 15 months in terms of maximal oxygen uptake and maximal work load after β-blockade. In the long-term situation, maximal oxygen uptake was virtually identical compared with the pretreatment value, and the maximal work load tended to be higher. In clinical terms, the $β_1$-selective receptor blockers may be preferable for long-term treatment, as well as for patients involved in rehabilitation training programs. If confirmed by others, this is an argument for the long-term use of these selective agents without physiologic penalty of diminished cardiac output or diminished maximal $O_2$ uptake.—Lewis J. Krakauer, M.D., F.A.C.P.

---

**Skeletal Muscle Glycolysis During Submaximal Exercise Following Acute β-Adrenergic Blockade in Man**
P. Kaiser, P. A. Tesch, A. Thorsson, J. Karlsson, and L. Kaijser (Karolinska Inst., Stockholm)
Acta Physiol. Scand. 123:285–291, March 1985                                      1–14

---

This study describes the influence of β-adrenergic blockade on glycogen use and lactate accumulation in skeletal muscle of exercising human beings. Twelve physically active men were examined during 25 minutes of continuous cycle exercise equivalent to 65% of their maximal oxygen uptake both with and without oral administration of 80 mg of propranolol (Inderal). Heart rate, oxygen uptake, rate of perceived exertion (RPE), and blood lactate concentration were measured during exercise. Muscle biopsy specimens were obtained from M. vastus lateralis after 5 and 25 minutes of exercise.

Plasma propranolol concentration averaged 42 ng/ml. Heart rate after 25 minutes of exercise was 35 beats per minute lower ($P < .001$) with than without β-blockade. Oxygen uptake (STPD) decreased ($P < .01$) as a result of β-blockade. Pulmonary ventilation (BTPS) was unaltered and R increased slightly with β-blockade. Blood lactate concentrations after 15–25 minutes of exercise were lower with than without the drug ($P < .05$, Figure 1–7). Muscle lactate concentration was significantly higher ($P < .01$) with than without β-blockade after 5 minutes and insignificantly lower ($P < .1$) after 25 minutes of exercises. Lactate was significantly lower after 25 minutes than after 5 minutes of exercise ($P < .05$) (Figure 1–7). Muscle glycogen concentration decreased equally from 5–25 minutes with and without β-blockade (both $P < .001$). Individual differences in

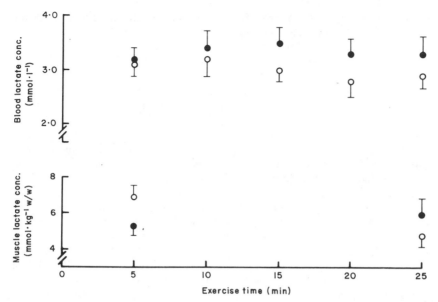

**Fig 1–7.**—Blood and muscle lactate concentration in control *(black dot)* and β-blockade *(white dot)* experiments. Values are mean ±SE. (Courtesy of Kaiser, P., et al.: Acta Physiol. Scand. 123:285–291, March 1985.)

glycogen use and muscle lactate concentration with and without β-blockade were not correlated with individual differences in the muscle histochemical variables examined.

Beta-blockade is suggested to cause an increased muscle lactate accumulation at the onset of exercise by increased production or possible reduced release of lactate. In a later phase of exercise, the rate of lactate production is reduced by the blockade. This latter effect may be caused either by a direct inhibition of glycogenolysis or by a more complete oxidation of the available carbohydrates to compensate for a reduced fat combustion or by both.

▶ Muscle fatigue is a common complaint of patients who are receiving treatment with β-blocking agents. This paper looks at some possible metabolic explanations of the phenomenon. The dose of propranolol used was sufficient to cause increases in the rating of perceived exertion for local muscular effort throughout a 25 minute stress test, and central (cardio-respiratory) effort was also significantly greater for the first 10 minutes of exercise. Arnold and Seberis (*Experimentia* 24:1010, 1968) had earlier argued that blockade of β-receptors in the muscles depressed glycolysis, but in the present experiments, the rate of glycogen utilization was unchanged by propranolol. The most likely explanation of the present results is that because of a slower heart rate, the perfusion of the muscles was reduced, leading to delay in transfer of lactate from the muscular to the vascular compartment, and that this gave rise to the sensation of fatigue.—Roy J. Shephard, M.D., Ph.D.

### Effects of Chronic β-Adrenergic Blockade on Hemodynamic and Metabolic Responses to Endurance Training

Michael R. Lawlor, D. Paul Thomas, John J. Michele, Rita A. Carey, Albert M. Paolone, and Alfred A. Bove (Temple Univ. and Mayo Clinic and Found.)
Med. Sci. Sports Exerc. 17:393–400, 1985                                1–15

To study the influence of chronic propranolol therapy on hemodynamic and metabolic adaptations associated with endurance training, 5 dogs given 250 mg/day of propranolol therapy (P) and 5 control dogs (NP) were endurance trained for 7 weeks using a continuously increasing tread-mill work load. The P group was also evaluated before and after training off the drug (P-OD) to separate drug and training effects.

Training lowered mean heart rate score (HR) to a standardized multi-stage dog treadmill test in the NP and P-OD ($P < .05$) and had no effect on the HR of the P group while on propranolol. At a fixed submaximal work load there were also slight reductions in cardiac output in the P group that were more pronounced ($P < .10$) following training and there was a corresponding increase in a-vDO$_2$. Metabolic studies before and after training were performed at rest, during a fixed submaximal work load, and following 30 minutes of recovery. During exercise, blood glucose levels were significantly lower in the P group both before and after training. Though NP showed no significant change in high-density lipoprotein bound cholesterol after training (table), the P-OD group demonstrated a significant fall in high-density lipoprotein bound cholesterol after training ($P < .05$).

These data indicate that endurance exercise training done in the presence of chronic β-adrenergic blockade produces training-induced hemodynamic adaptations to exercise, but β-blockade inhibits the changes in serum lipids and lipoprotein fractions normally seen in response to an exercise conditioning program. These findings suggest that subjects who train while under the influence of this drug can benefit hemodynamically from an

EFFECTS OF TRAINING AND PROPRANOLOL ON RESTING
PLASMA TRIGLYCERIDES, CHOLESTEROL, AND HIGH-
DENSITY LIPOPROTEIN BOUND CHOLESTEROL

| | Pre-training | | Post-training | | |
| | | | | Propranolol | |
| | Control | Propranolol | Control | On Drug | Off Drug |
| --- | --- | --- | --- | --- | --- |
| TG† (mg·dl⁻¹) | 33 ± 8 | 40 ± 3 | 32 ± 11 | 37 ± 3 | 35 ± 12 |
| CHL (mg·dl⁻¹) | 203 ± 50 | 187 ± 55 | 184 ± 19 | 187 ± 54 | 168 ± 37 |
| HDL (mg·dl⁻¹) | 88 ± 17 | 85 ± 18 | 93 ± 13 | 73 ± 28 | 59 ± 23* |
| CHL/HDL | 2.3 ± 0.4 | 2.2 ± 0.5 | 2.5 ± 0.9 | 2.7 ± 0.4 | 3.1 ± 0.2* |

Data are mean ± SE.
*Significant difference from NP group ($P < .05$).
†TG = triglycerides; CHL = cholesterol; HDL = high-density lipoprotein-bound cholesterol.

aerobic conditioning program. Chronic propranolol therapy may alter both central and peripheral adaptations known to occur with endurance training.

▶ The fact that a cardiac training response can develop during propranolol administration has been well documented over the past 2 years. However, the suggestion that β-blockade may inhibit the normal favorable effect of training upon the lipid profile merits further study. Certainly, propranolol causes some interference with fat metabolism, particularly the mobilization of free fatty acids from adipocytes. However, one must be a little cautious about accepting the present results, because the control dogs failed to increase their high-density lipoprotein significantly in response to training, a finding that the authors blame upon a relatively short training period (7 weeks).—Roy J. Shephard, M.D., Ph.D.

---

**Beta Receptors in Peripheral Mononuclear Cells Increase Acutely During Exercise**
Kenneth D. Burman, Earl W. Ferguson, Yin-Ying Djuh, Leonard Wartofsky, and Keith Latham (Walter Reed Army Med. Center, Washington, D.C., and Uniformed Services Univ. of the Health Sciences, Bethesda, Md.)
Acta Endocrinol. (Copenh.) 109:563–568, August 1985                     1–16

Five healthy well-trained men (averaging 49 miles running per week) were exercised to exhaustion on a treadmill to investigate whether endogenous elevations in plasma catecholamines would also be associated with short-term increases in β-receptor density.

β-RECEPTOR DENSITIES (MBC) AND EQUILIBRIUM
DISSOCIATION CONSTANTS (Kd) DURING ACUTE
EXERCISE IN HIGHLY CONDITIONED SUBJECTS

| Patient | Pre-exercise MBC* | Kd† | Post-exercise MBC | Kd | 1 h post-exercise MBC | Kd |
|---|---|---|---|---|---|---|
| 1 | 54 | 1.6 | 93 | 1.8 | 153 | 1.5 |
| 2 | 32 | 1.0 | 85 | 1.4 | 11 | 1.0 |
| 3 | 7 | 1.3 | 246 | 1.0 | 50 | 2.6 |
| 4 | 118 | 1.7 | 268 | 1.5 | 60 | 2.1 |
| 5 | 56 | 1.9 | 424 | 2.0 | 141 | 1.7 |
| Mean | 53 | 1.5 | 223‡ | 1.5 | 83§ | 1.8 |
| SE | 18 | 0.2 | 63 | 0.2 | 27 | 0.3 |

*MBC expressed as fmol/mg protein.
†Kd expressed as $\times 10^{-11}$M.
‡: $P < .05$ compared to pre-exercise.
§: $P < .05$ compared to postexercise.
(Courtesy of Burman, K.D., et al.: Acta Endocrinol. (Copenh.) 109:563–568, August 1985.)

Plasma epinephrine levels increased significantly prior to exercise ($P <$ .025) immediately after the exercise epinephrine, then gradually decreased 1 hour after the exercise was stopped ($P < .025$). Plasma norepinephrine levels showed a similar pattern. Preliminary studies showed that specific binding was optimal at 28 or 37 C incubation for 60–120 minutes for β-receptors (table), whereas it was markedly decreased at 0 C. Maximal binding capacity (MBC) increased immediately after exercise ($P < .025$) and then decreased 1 hour later ($P < .025$) compared to postexercise. Following correction for hemodilution, serum total and free $T_4$ and $T_3$ concentrations were unchanged during exercise.

These findings suggest that plasma epinephrine, norepinephrine, and β-receptor density, but not Kd, increase acutely during exercise. When corrected for hemodilution, total and free $T_4$ and $T_3$ do not change during acute short term maximal exercise. These data indicate that acute exercise represents an unusual condition during which "down regulation" is not observed, but, rather, there appear to be parallel alterations in β-receptor density and plasma catecholamine levels.

▶ The "normal" response to catecholamine infusion is a decrease in β-receptor activity (Motulsky and Insel, *N. Engl. J. Med.* 307:18, 1982). It is not completely clear from the report of Burman et al. whether the exercise-induced increase of β-receptor density that they describe is a general phenomenon or whether it is limited to a change in the type, number, or characteristics of the peripheral mononuclear cells. Other reports have suggested unchanged lymphocyte β-receptors after a marathon run (Williams et al., *J. Appl. Physiol.,* 51:1232, 1981), but a decrease of β-receptors in lymphocytes after 30 minutes of treadmill exercise (Fitzgerald et al., *J. Appl. Physiol.* 51:1232, 1981). If the increase of β-receptor sensitivity is indeed a general phenomenon, it might help to explain why a combination of cold exposure and exercise is helpful in reducing body fat (O'Hara et al., *J. Appl. Physiol.* 46:872, 1979).—Roy J. Shephard, M.D., Ph.D.

---

**Catecholamine Modulation of Rapid Potassium Shifts During Exercise**
Mark E. Williams, Ernest V. Gervino, Robert M. Rosa, Lewis Landsberg, James B. Young, Patricio Silva, and Franklin H. Epstein (Harvard Univ. and Beth Israel Hosp., Boston)
N: Engl. J. Med. 312:823–827, March 28, 1985                    1–17

---

The plasma potassium level rises during muscular exercise and falls rapidly when exercise is stopped. Because the sympathoadrenal system is stimulated with exertion and both α- and β-adrenergic agonists affect internal potassium homeostasis, the influence of catecholamines on potassium shifts was examined during and after exercise. Six healthy men aged 20 to 41 years performed maximal exercise stress tests under three conditions: unmedicated (control), during β-blockade with propranolol, and during α-blockade with phentolamine.

Compared with a mean peak rise in the plasma potassium level of 1.23 mmole/L during the control study, propranolol treatment caused a rise of 1.89 mmole/L and a sustained elevation during recovery (Fig 1–8). Phentolamine administration diminished the potassium level rise and lowered the potassium level throughout recovery (Fig 1–9). These effects were independent of venous pH, plasma bicarbonate, and serum glucose levels, and urinary potassium excretion and did not appear to be caused by insulin secretion. High norepinephrine and epinephrine levels confirmed the release of catecholamines capable of stimulating α- and β-receptors. The exercise work level did not differ among the groups.

Plasma potassium levels rise during vigorous exercise, presumably because contracting muscles release potassium to the extracellular fluid, and then fall abruptly. The α-adrenergic receptors and β-adrenergic receptors have important but opposite roles in modulating the resulting potassium shifts. These results confirm earlier reports of the effect of β-adrenergic blockade in exaggerating the increase in plasma potassum levels during exertion. The β-adrenergic blockade with propranolol significantly increased the rise in the plasma potassum concentration at the peak of exercise and resulted in a modest but significant elevation throughout recovery. The changes during β-adrenergic blockade occurred despite performance of identical amounts of work by the skeletal muscle and in the presence of diminished cardiac work. Impairment of potassium disposal did not depend on other factors known to regulate the plasma potassium

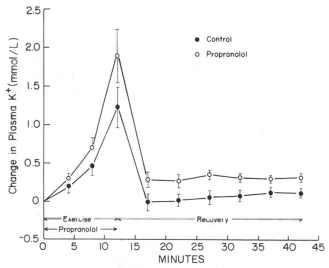

**Fig 1–8.**—Effect of propranolol administration on the rise and fall of the plasma potassium (K⁺) level during and after exercise. Changes in the plasma potassium level are indicated by *solid circles* in the absence of propranolol and by *open circles* when the drug is present. Values shown represent the mean values ± SEM in 6 patients. The probability of the difference at peak exercise was <.01 by Student's *t* test. The overall probability of the difference between treatments was <.01 by analysis of variance. (Courtesy of Williams, M.E., et al.: N. Engl. J. Med. 312:823–827, March 28, 1985. Reprinted by permission of The New England Journal of Medicine.)

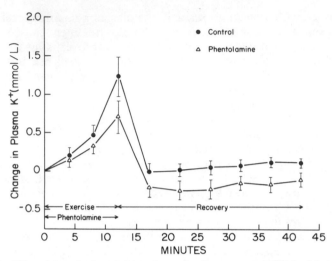

**Fig 1–9.**—Effect of phentolamine administration on the plasma potassium ($K^+$) level during and after exercise. Changes in the plasma potassium level are indicated by *solid circles* in the absence of phentolamine and by *open triangles* when the drug is present. Data points represent the means ± SEM in 6 patients. The probability of the difference at peak exercise was <.01 by Student's $t$ test. The probability of the difference between treatments was <.02 by analysis of variance. Phentolamine lowered the overall potassium curve. (Courtesy of Williams, M.E., et al.: N. Engl. J. Med. 312:823–827, March 28, 1985. Reprinted by permission of The New England Journal of Medicine.)

concentrations. The results illustrate the role of β-adrenergic receptors in enhancing cellular potassium uptake.

Thus, α-adrenergic receptors and β-adrenergic receptors have opposing roles in modulating the cellular uptake of potassium. Released by vigorous exercise, β-adrenergic hormones protect against hyperkalemia by stimulating β-mediated cellular potassium uptake. Through an opposite mechanism, α-receptor stimulation contributes to hyperkalemia and may protect against hypokalemia after exercise ceases.

▶ There are always some dangers in interfering with body systems, because a dose of drug that is appropriate and helpful under resting conditions may have adverse consequences during the stress of prolonged and intensive exercise

Although β-blocking agents are commonly given to counter myocardial irritability, this paper demonstrates the important role of the β-receptors in protecting against hyperkalemia during exercise, a function that is seriously impaired after administration of propranolol. Figure 1–8 illustrates clearly the rapid development of up to a tenfold increase of plasma potassium, probably resulting from leakage of this ion from the working muscle. This reinforces the point made earlier (Kavanagh T. and Shephard R. J.: Fluid and mineral needs of post-coronary distance runners, in Landry F. and Orban W. A. R. (eds.): *Sports Medicine.* Miami: Symposia Specialists, 1978, pp 143–151), that it is a very unwise practice to offer fluids containing potassium to patients during a period of exercise. After exercise, there is a period of hypokalemia, regulated by the α-receptors; at this stage, there may be some logic in providing potassium for replenishment of muscle stores, although this can normally be accomplished by the salting of food (because table "salt" contains potassium ions).—Roy J. Shephard, M.D., Ph.D.

---

**Physical Performance and Serum Potassium Under Chronic Beta-Blockade**
T. Kullmer and W. Kindermann (Univ. of Saarland, Saarbrücken, Federal Republic of Germany)
Eur. J. Appl. Physiol. 54:350–354, October 1985                              1–18

---

There is evidence for a β-receptor-regulated transmembrane potassium transport system in skeletal muscle, but little attention has been given to the possible effect of altered ionic equilibrium on physical performance capacity under β-blockade. Serum potassium concentrations were related to type of β-blockade in 63 healthy, untrained males who received, double blind, 100 mg of metoprolol, a $\beta_1$-selective agent, 80 mg of the nonselective drug propranolol, or placebo daily over 3 months. Cycle ergometer exercise tests were performed in the morning by subjects who had fasted.

Serum potassium concentrations were reduced during and for 30 minutes after exercise without medication. Recovery-phase potassium concentrations were significantly higher under β-blockade (Fig 1–10). No differences were apparent 3 days after the end of treatment. Physical performance was reduced 6% with both types of blockade. Individual anaerobic thresholds were reduced more with propranolol than with metoprolol. No change in maximum performance or endurance was apparent with placebo administration.

$\beta_1$-Selective blockers are preferable to nonselective agents in physically

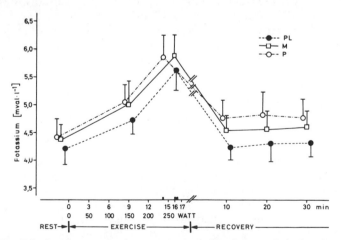

Fig 1–10.—Behavior of serum potassium concentration before, during, and after bicycle exercise after 3-month medication period. Means ± SD are shown. *PL*, placebo; *M*, metoprolol; and *P*, propranolol. (Courtesy of Kullmer, T., and Kindermann, W.: Eur. J. Appl. Physiol. 54:350–354, October 1985; Berlin-Heidelberg-New York: Springer.)

active persons, because of their lesser effects on metabolism and on serum potassium concentrations. A higher serum potassium concentration should be expected during and after physical stress, however, even with $\beta_1$-selective blockade. Transmembrane potassium transport in human skeletal muscle is regulated chiefly via $\beta_2$-receptors.

▶ The paper of H. Joborn (Digest 1–48) has already discussed the role of catecholamines in regulating tissue magnesium levels. The above paper points out that serum potassium is also influenced by β-blockade, particularly $\beta_2$ blockade. The authors suggest that an adverse effect of potassium exudation upon membrane excitability may contribute to the fatigue that is observed during β-blockade (Carlsson et al.: *Lancet* II:424, 1978). However, it is also possible that the increase of plasma potassium during β-blockade may be linked to an inhibition of lipolysis (Frisk-Holmberg et al.: *Clin. Pharmacol. Ther.* 30:611, 1981), with an increased depletion of glycogen reserves (Gorski and Pietrzyk: *Eur. J. Appl. Physiol.* 48:201, 1982).—Roy J. Shephard, M.D., Ph.D.

---

**Effects of Nifedipine on Systemic and Regional Oxygen Transport and Metabolism at Rest and During Exercise**
Christopher Y. P. Choong, Gary S. Roubin, Wei-Feng Shen, Phillip J. Harris, and David T. Kelly (Royal Prince Alfred Hosp., Sydney, Australia)
Circulation 71:787–796, April 1985                                        1–19

---

Nifedipine produces systemic vasodilatation during exercise beyond that occurring physiologically, and it might reduce the normal redistribution of cardiac output to exercising muscles. The effects of a sublingual dose of 20 mg of nifedipine on central hemodynamics and on systemic and regional leg oxygen extraction and metabolism examined during rest and symptom-limited bicycle exercise in 12 men (mean age, 55 years) with stable New York Heart Association class II or III exertional angina of at least 3 months' duration. Six patients had had myocardial infarction, but none had heart failure. All patients had positive exercise test results. The study was done with a placebo control in a double-blind manner.

Mean exercise capacity was unchanged by nifedipine. Systemic vascular resistance fell by 38% at rest and by 28% on exercise after nifedipine. Exercise cardiac output increased from 10.6 to 11.8 L/minute. The arterial-mixed venous oxygen content difference on exercise decreased from 10.5 to 8.8 ml/100 ml after nifedipine. Oxygen consumption did not change significantly, but the mixed venous $P_{CO_2}$ was reduced by nifedipine. Arterial lactate concentration increased more on exercise after nifedipine. Changes in leg blood flow are shown in Figure 1–11.

Generalized vasodilatation by nifedipine can produce opposite changes in regional and systemic oxygen extraction and metabolism during exercise. Redistribution of cardiac output to the legs during dynamic leg exercise is reduced by nifedipine, probably through shunting of blood flow away from exercising muscles by generalized vasodilatation. Worsening

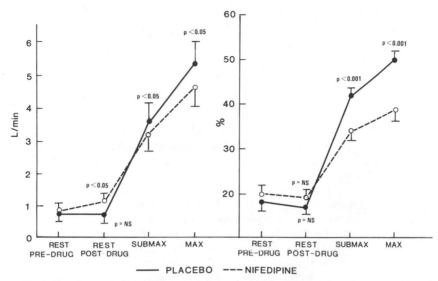

PLACEBO --- NIFEDIPINE

**Fig 1–11.**—Changes in blood flow to both legs at rest before and after drug therapy, at identical intermediate work loads (SUBMAX) and at the common maximal work loads (MAX) on the placebo and nifedipine days (values are expressed as mean ± 1 SEM). **Left panel,** data expressed as calculated blood flow. **Right panel,** same data expressed as a percent distribution of cardiac output. (Courtesy of Choong, C.Y.P., et al.: Circulation 71:787–796, April 1985; Berlin-Heidelberg-New York: Springer.)

of leg fatigue or peripheral vascular disease may be clinically relevant in some patients with exercise-induced angina.

▶ Constriction of the vascular bed in nonexercising muscle is normally an important part of the circulatory adjustment to vigorous exercise (Clausen: *Prog. Cardiovasc. Dis.* 18:459, 1976). The calcium-blocking agent nifedipine is beneficial in angina in part because it causes arteriolar dilatation and thus reduces cardiac after-load. However, this same arteriolar dilatation could "steal" blood flow from active to inactive muscles, with a greater potential for peripheral muscular fatigue during exercise.

The present controlled trial showed no change of exercise tolerance after nifedipine, probably because the limiting symptom remained chest pain. Cardiac output was increased about 12%, so it may be that the reduction of after-loading also allowed some compensation for the "steal" by an increase of total blood flow. However, there was a lesser blood flow to the legs, with a greater acumulation of lactate, so that in those patients who are not limited by anginal symptoms, a greater leg fatigue might be anticipated after administration of nifedipine.—Roy J. Shephard, M.D., Ph.D.

**Some Limitations of Exercise Testing**
Roy J. Shephard (Univ. of Toronto and Toronto Rehabilitation Ctr.)
J. Sports Med. 25:40–48, March–June 1985

1–20

Most family physicians and cardiologists in the United States now have equipment for stress ECG, and the test sometimes is used in routine work-up of older adults. Defibrillators may have reduced the mortality risk, but life-threatening complications continue to occur with exercise testing, especially at maximum exercise. Less risk is present when normal and post-coronary subjects perform voluntary recreational exercise; the presence of symptoms and anxiety in the laboratory may increase the risks. Safety might be enhanced by preliminary questioning of patients and by an awareness of contraindications to exercise. Submaximal testing will be safer. The informal, relaxed nature of the Canadian Home Fitness Test may help explain its safety relative to medically supervised tests. A "warm-up" phase should be incorporated into all exercise tests.

Exercise ECG testing is, at best, 80% sensitive and 90% specific in diagnosing coronary artery disease. An accuracy rate of 33% is the best that can be expected in a typical population with a 5% prevalence of significant coronary disease. The ECG response to exercise is not prognostically very helpful in the individual case. Testing also is of limited value when used to prescribe an exercise program. One approach might be to supplement the exercise protocol with other tests such as scintigraphy, and another is to seek alternative evidence of poor fitness and significant coronary disease. In prescribing exercise, it might be best to simply give general guidance on appropriate patterns of exercise and rely on the subject to limit activity to the bounds set by simple symptoms.

▶ A sophisticated overview of the complex question of exercise testing from an experienced source. I share Dr. Shephard's view that the patient must be relied upon to do most of his own exercise prescribing within broad limits, rather than make an attempt to adhere to a precise and detailed prescription.—Lewis J. Krakauer, M.D., F.A.C.P.

**Influence of R-Wave Amplitude on Exercise-Induced ST Depression: Need for a "Gain Factor" Correction When Interpreting Stress Electrocardiograms**
Milton Hollenberg, Mateo Go, Jr., Barry M. Massie, Judith A. Wisneski, and Edward W. Gertz (VA Med. Ctr., San Francisco, and Univ. of California, San Francisco)
Am. J. Cardiol. 56:13–17, July 1, 1985                    1–21

The authors investigated if 2 mm of ST depression induced by exercise have the same clinical significance in a patient with a 30-mm R wave as a patient with a 10-mm R wave in the same monitored lead. The exercise responses of 85 patients were compared by two quantitative methods of assessing myocardial ischemia. A computer-derived treadmill exercise score, based largely on the characteristics of exercise-induced ST-segment depression, was compared with a thallium exercise score.

Both scores correlated well over a wide range of values ($P < .001$). Then the treadmill exercise score was corrected by adjusting the magnitude of

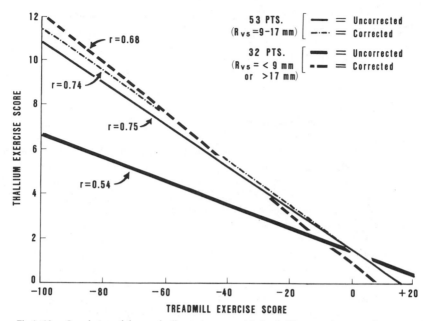

Fig 1–12.—Correlation of the treadmill exercise score with the thallium exercise score. Correction of the treadmill exercise score for R-wave amplitude does not change the slope and intercepts for patients with an $R_{V5}$ of 9 to 17 mm *(thin solid and dashed lines)*, but does for those with $R_{V5} < 9$ or >17 mm *(thick solid and dashed lines)* (P < .01). In this latter group, R-wave correction increases the correlation coefficient from .54 to .68 and the linear regression equation becomes similar (difference not significant) to that of patients with less extreme voltages. (Courtesy of Hollenberg, M., et al.: Am. J. Cardiol. 56:13–17, July 1, 1985.)

ST depression to a standardized R-wave amplitude of 12 mm in $V_5$ and 8 mm in aVF to determine if this would improve its correlation with the thallium exercise score. Patients were separated into two groups by R-wave amplitude: 53 had an $R_{V5}$ of 9–17 mm and 32 had an $R_{V5}$ <9 or >17 mm. Correction of the treadmill exercise score for R-wave amplitude did not change the slope and intercepts of the regression line for patients with an $R_{V5}$ amplitude of 9–17 mm, but did for those with an $R_{V5}$ amplitude <9 or >17 mm. In this latter group, R-wave correction changed the regression line from one that differed significantly from that of patients with less extreme $R_{V5}$ voltage to one that was indistinguishable from it. Correction of the treadmill exercise score also increased the correlation coefficient from 0.54 to 0.68 in this group (Fig 1–12). In several patients an abnormal score became normal when it was corrected for R-wave voltage. This corrected score was consistent with the coronary arteriographic findings, lack of symptoms, and the good exercise tolerance.

Thus, as judged independenly by a thallium exercise score, the degree of exercise-induced ST depression is influenced by R-wave amplitude, and if not normalized to a standard voltage, may either exaggerate or underestimate the degree of exercise-induced myocardial ischemia.

▶ I have long been bothered by the interpretation of marginal ST depression in a patient with a low voltage ECG. It is useful to have this study that shows that in order to obtain a good correlation with thallium data, corrections must be applied to patients whose R-wave magnitude falls outside the range 9–17 mm.—Roy J. Shephard, M.D., Ph.D.

---

**Comparison of a Quantitative Treadmill Exercise Score With Standard Electrocardiographic Criteria in Screening Asymptomatic Young Men for Coronary Artery Disease**
Milton Hollenberg, Jerel M. Zoltick, Mateo Go, Sandra F. Yaney, William Daniels, Richard C. Davis, Jr., and Julius L. Bedynek (VA Med. Ctr., San Francisco, Univ. of California, San Francisco, Walter Reed Army Med. Ctr., Washington, D.C., Fitzsimmons Army Med. Ctr., Denver, and U.S. Army Research Inst. of Environmental Medicine, Natick, Mass.)
N. Engl. J. Med. 313:600–606, Sept. 5, 1985                                    1–22

---

A quantitative treadmill test score that minimizes false positive responses in detecting coronary artery disease has been developed. The computerized score measures the cumulative area of ST depression during exercise and recovery, which then is normalized for R-wave height and work load. The score was compared with conventional interpretation of the treadmill test in a cardiovascular risk screening program conducted by the United States Army on 950 military officers. Secondary screening was completed on 400 subjects designated as being at high risk and controls.

Forty-five of 377 evaluable subjects had positive tests on conventional criteria, compared with only 3 evaluated by the treadmill exercise score. Two of the latter subjects had left ventricular hypertrophy and did not meet criteria for coronary artery disease. The remaining subject had single-vessel disease on coronary angiography. Nine other subjects with the positive scores on standard testing and the highest risk factor scores had negative angiographic findings.

These findings support use of the treadmill exercise score in asymptomatic populations with a low prevalence of disease. It may be feasible to apply treadmill testing to a broader group of asymptomatic subjects to identify those who may have silent myocardial ischemia. The treadmill exercise score improves the diagnostic specificity of exercise ECG recording compared with conventional interpretation.

▶ The accuracy of this computer-derived treadmill scoring technique would be impressive if confirmed by multiple studies. In this one study, which involved 377 healthy individuals, the accuracy was very precise. This is not a sufficient number to provide the data base to warrant complete acceptance at this point. The theoretical approach has appeal: use coronary arteriography only in those at highest risk, and not ubiquitously in the entire study group. The procedure of angiography still has some small risk. It would be of interest to add thallium scintiscan studies to a similar group.—Lewis J. Krakauer, M.D., F.A.C.P.

**Different Recovery Process of ST Depression on Postexercise Electrocardiograms in Women in Standing and Supine Positions**

Masahiro Murayama, Kiyoshi Kawakubo, Toshiaki Nakajima, Shizuo Sakamoto, Shoichi Ono, Tsutomu Itai, and Norihisa Kato (Kanto-Teishin Hosp., Tokyo)

Am. J. Cardiol. 55:1474–1477, June 1, 1985                    1–23

False positive exercise test responses are frequently observed in women. To differentiate a false positive from a true positive test response, the effect of postures for recording a postexercise electrocardiogram to the recovery process of ST depression was investigated in 26 women with nonischemic ST depression and in 14 patients with typical angina pectoris. Exercise tests were performed twice, and the postexercise electrocardiogram was recorded while the patient was standing during the first test and in the supine position during the second test. Group 1 (n = 26) had a mean age of 45 years and group 2 (n = 14) had a mean age of 50 years.

The ST segment was isoelectric or depressed in a minor degree at the control state in leads II, III, aVF, and $V_5$ to $V_6$ in group 1. Fourteen of the 26 completed up to stage III of the exercise test. Maximal ST depression was observed in lead aVF in all subjects. There was a significant difference in the magnitudes of ST depression at the two postures, from 3–9 minutes of recovery phase (Fig 1–13). Exercise was discontinued because of angina development in association with ST depression up to stage II or III in all group 2 subjects. Maximal ST depression developed in leads $V_4$ to $V_5$ but was less prominent in lead aVF in this group. Recovery of ST depression was gradual in the time that elapsed while patients were standing and in the supine positions.

This discrepant pattern in recovery process of ST depression by changing postures was not observed in the true positive test results. Changing postures for recording postexercise electrocardiograms could be helpful in differentiating a false positive response from a true ischemic response.

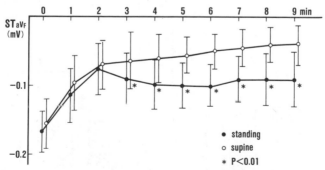

**Fig 1–13.**—ST depression of the recovery phase in abnormal exercise test response in group 1 patients. There was no significant difference in ST depression in the immediate postexercise period to 2 minutes of the recovery phase between standing and supine positions. The magnitude of ST depression was greater in the standing than in the supine position ($P < .01$) from 3 to 9 minutes of the recovery phase. (Courtesy of Murayama, M., et al.: Am. J. Cardiol. 55:1474–1477, June 1, 1985.)

Although sensitivity of this procedure for diagnosing a false positive response is not high (47% for 7 minutes) and the precise mechanism of this phenomenon is not clear, it can be easily performed and is helpful in differentiating a false positive from a true positive response.

▶ The problem of false positive ECGs in older women has been recognized for some time (Cumming et al.: *Br. Heart J.* 35:1055, 1973; Sidney and Shephard: *Brit. Heart J.* 39:1114, 1977). The approach suggested may provide one simple way of eliminating some of the false positive responses; because the person is already in the exercise laboratory, a second exercise ECG stress test is more economical than requesting some alternative form of examination.—Roy J. Shephard, M.D., Ph.D.

---

**Value of Arm Exercise Testing in Detecting Coronary Artery Disease**
Gary J. Balady, Donald A. Weiner, Carolyn H. McCabe, and Thomas J. Ryan (Boston Univ.)
Am. J. Cardiol. 55:37–39, Jan. 1, 1985                                             1–24

---

Dynamic arm exercise testing could be a useful alternative to leg exercise in patients with suspected coronary disease who have disease of the lower extremities. The sensitivity of arm exercise testing was examined in 30 patients with angiographically documented coronary artery disease. Two maximal, symptom-limited, graded exercise tests were done using an arm ergometer and treadmill, in random order, in the morning and afternoon. The 29 men and 1 woman tested had a mean age of 59 years. All had a history of exertional angina, and 12 patients had had myocardial infarction. Twenty-two patients had more than single-vessel coronary artery disease.

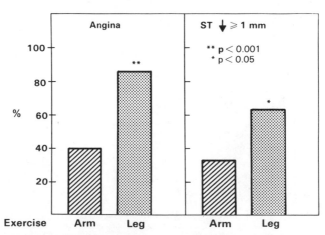

Fig 1–14.—Ischemic responses to exercise. (Courtesy of Balady, G.J., et al.: Am. J. Cardiol. 55:37–39, Jan. 1, 1985.)

The exercise endpoint was more often moderate angina during leg exercise, and more often fatigue during arm exercise. Ischemic responses occurred in 86% of cases during leg exercise and in 40% during arm exercise, despite similar peak rate-pressure products during the tests (Fig 1–14). Peak oxygen consumption was significantly less during arm exercise. Oxygen consumption was higher on leg exercise both at the onset of angina and at the onset of ST-segment depression.

Arm exercise testing is less sensitive than leg exercise testing in detecting coronary artery disease, and it is not an equivalent alternative. Peak oxygen consumption is less during arm exercise, but peak rate-pressure products do not differ significantly.

▶ There are patients in significant number who have sufficient vascular, orthopedic, or neurologic disease for whom standard treadmill testing is impossible. For such patients, arm exercise can be of appreciable value. It is not as precise as leg-exercise testing. Some is better than none. It could be an option available for this clinical subgroup.—Lewis J. Krakauer, M.D., F.A.C.P.

---

**Use of Transcutaneous Electrical Nerve Stimulation for a Patient With a Cardiac Pacemaker: A Case Report**
Sandra K. Shade (Cook County Hosp., Chicago)
Phys. Ther. 65:206–208, February 1985                                    1–25

---

Transcutaneous electrical nerve stimulation (TENS) characteristically has been contraindicated in patients with cardiac pacemakers because it is a source of external interference. A TENS stimulator was, however, used in a patient with a temporary demand pacemaker in whom no interference occurred.

Man, 74, with metastatic cancer primary in the prostate, had a history of traumatic right above-knee amputation, bronchitis and asthma, chronic heart failure, and questionable myocardial infarction. Severe pain the left lateral chest area was resistant to moist heat and electrogalvanic stimulation, but relatively responsive to TENS. The TENS unit was used 24 hours a day until admission with *Legionella* pneumonia and cardiopulmonary arrest. Transcutaneous electrical nerve stimulation was discontinued, but the patient requested its reinstitution because of severe pain after responding to intensive care.

A dual-channel four-electrode TENS unit was applied in the intensive care unit, at the fifth and tenth thoracic levels, as far as possible from the cardiac area. Pacemaker interference did not appear despite relief of pain, and the patient was able to wear the TENS unit continuously without difficulty. Static relief occurred only when the patient moved, with and without the TENS unit in operation.

The TENS unit and cardiac pacing can be used simultaneously with safety in some cases, and not all patients with pacemakers should be precluded from access to this treatment. Patients can be simply monitored by ECG. Newer pacemaker models are more resistant to external stimuli, and TENS units are being modified to accommodate patients with pacemakers. Further work is needed to prevent misuse of TENS and to define guidelines for its use.

▶ If a TENS unit is clinically indicated for the relief of pain, the author makes the valid point that careful empirical testing should be carried out. The probability is that it will not interfere with a cardiac pacemaker. There are important safety guideines involved and this requires skilled therapists and careful monitoring. The newer pacemaker models are more resistant to external stimuli, and at the same time, some of the new TENS units have been modified to accommodate the patients who require cardiac pacemakers. The two are not mutually exclusive if skilled judgment is used.—Lewis J. Krakauer, M.D., F.A.C.P.

---

**High Blood Pressure in the Competitive Athlete: Guidelines and Recommendations**
Raymond J. Walther and Charles P. Tifft (Harvard Univ. and Boston Univ.)
Physician Sportsmed. 13:93–114, May 1985                                    1–26

---

The management of abnormal arterial blood pressure in athletes remains a problem. The use of a cuff with markings that match cuff size to arm circumference is helpful. Young persons with elevated blood pressure are at increased risk of hypertension with advancing age and possibly of cardiovascular disease later in life. In addition, elevated blood pressure can increase the risk in athletes who have Marfan's syndrome or berry aneurysm. Athletes should be observed at rest before a workout. A diastolic pressure of 90 mm Hg or above on three separate occasions is significant. Unless moderate or severe hypertension is present or the findings suggest a secondary form of hypertension, routine evaluation should be limited to assessing cardiovascular risk factors and target organ damage.

Athletes with elevated blood pressure but no target organ damage generally should be allowed to compete. Ideally, treatment should reduce the systolic and diastolic pressures at rest and on exercise while allowing maximal performance and producing no adverse side effects. Static trinin need not be routinely prohibited. Higher arterial pressures or significant risk factors may require treatment with a sympathetic inhibiting agent. Diuretics are used only when this treatment is ineffective and probably require potassium supplement or a potassium-conserving agent as well as close monitoring of the serum potassium. Calcium channel antagonists may prove useful in treating the exercising hypertensive patient. A goal of 90 mm Hg or less diastolic is suitable.

▶ This paper deserves to be read in its entirety because of the highly complex nature of hypertension and its therapy. The authors recommend a specific gradation of response with persisting levels of hypertension. Many would disagree with these specific recommendations. Hypertensive therapy is constantly changing as new agents appear and calcium channel blockers become more widely used. Diuretics must be used with caution in the exercising person because of the sweat loss involved and the thermal factors that are influenced by diuretic therapy. Note is made that potassium should not be taken close to a practice session or event per se, because of exercise-induced hyperkalemia and the cardiac risk associated therewith if unduly elevated.

The point is seconded that mild to moderate hypertension itself is not a reason for excluding individuals from athletic competition or athletic training. On the other hand, it seems prudent to test such people with treadmill cardiography and interval blood pressure readings at rest, during, and after treadmill exercise, because there is such great individual variation to such testing. Significant and sustained blood pressure elevations during treadmill testing are a contraindication to exercise.—Lewis J. Krakauer, M.D., F.A.C.P.

**Influence of Calcium Antagonists on Physical Capacity and Metabolism**
W. Kindermann, W. Schmitt, and E. Stengele (Univ. of Saarland, Saarbrücken, Federal Republic of Germany)
Dtsch. Med. Wochenschr. 110:1657–1661, 1985                    1–27

Calcium antagonists are being used increasingly in hypertension therapy. Since many patients are young and active, it was asked whether calcium antagonists influence physical activity.

In a crossover double-blind trial on 15 healthy male volunteers (age 25.7 ± 2.6 years; height 177.5 ± 6.4 cm; weight 71.2 ± 7.8 kg; maximal oxygen intake 57.0 ± 7.7 ml/minute/kg body weight), the effects on physical exercise capacity and metabolism of single oral doses of 90 mg diltiazem or 20 mg nifedipine were compared. Both maximal physical exercise capacity and sustained exercise capacity remained unchanged after administration of each calcium antagonist. Heart rate was higher after nifedipine administration, but lower after diltiazem administration than after administration of placebo, although the differences at the individual exercise steps were small and significant in only some. Plasma norepinephrine levels on submaximal exercise rose more significantly after nifedipine administration than after diltiazem or placebo administration. Somatotropin, cortisol, and insulin levels as well as levels of carbohydrate and fat metabolic substrates were similar. The same holds true for triglyceride levels.

The literature includes reports of studies of physical exercise capacity among hypertensive patients without cardiovascular complications under diltiazem treatment. Here, too, an impairment of physical exercise capacity could not be established. Due to the response mechanism of the calcium antagonists, a decrease of physical exercise capacity is not expected. Depending on muscle type, the inhibition of the transmembranous flow of calcium leads to various results. While the activation of the contractile systems of cardiac muscle and smooth muscle is essentially dependent on extracellular calcium concentration and transmembranous calcium transport, respectively, this mechanism has only minor significance for skeletal muscle. The sarcoplasmatic reticulum in skeletal muscle is better developed than in smooth muscle or cardiac muscle, and enough calcium can be liberated intracellularly to activate the contractile protein. The unchanged behavior of STH and cortisol under the influence of diltiazem and nifedipine corresponds to the unaffected metabolism. In healthy subjects, the ACTH-stimulated cortisol release under verapamil also remained unchanged. For insulin levels, contradictory findings are reported. Some studies show an unchanged and others an influenced glucose-induced insulin secretion through calcium antagonists whereby in vitro and in vivo examinations show different results.

It is concluded that short-term administration of diltiazem and nifedipine does not influence physical exercise capacity and metabolism and therefore offers a sensible alternative treatment for physically active patients with hypertension.

▶ Many of the drugs that have been proposed for the treatment of hypertension have undesirable side effects, including a decrease of physical working capacity through depression of myocardial contractility, a reduction of maximum heart rate, or a reduction of stroke volume, postural hypotension after exercise, and inhibition of enzyme activation in the skeletal muscles. Because calcium transport is an integral part of the contraction process in both cardiac and skeletal muscle, in theory, calcium blockers might have adverse effects on both myocardial contractility and skeletal muscle function. It is encouraging to find from this report that if given in appropriate doses, the physical work capacity of young and healthy volunteers was unaffected. It might be argued that in patients where myocardial function is impaired by ischemic heart disease, the reserve of myocardial function would be smaller, and an adverse response would be observed. However, this does not seem to be the case (see Digest 1–19).—Roy J. Shephard, M.D., Ph.D.

---

**Effects of Oral Prajmaline Bitartrate on Exercise Test Responses in Patients With Coronary Artery Disease**
C. E. Handler, A. Kritikos, I. D. Sullivan, A. Charalambakis, and E. Sowton (Guy's Hosp., London)
Eur. J. Clin. Pharmacol. 28:371–374, June 1985                                    1–28

Prajmaline bitartrate is a derivative of a *Rauwolfia* alkaloid with class 1 antiarrhythmia properties, and it is suitable for both oral and intravenous administration. The safety and tolerance of oral prajmaline therapy were examined in 22 men, aged 43 to 66 years, with proved coronary disease and stable angina. None had had myocardial infarction. Prajmaline was given in a dosage of 20 mg three times daily, in a crossover design with placebo tablets for 1-week periods. Symptom-limited multistage treadmill exercise tests were carried out.

The results in 21 evaluable patients are given in the table. There were no significant changes in resting heart rate or systolic blood pressure, work capacity, or hemodynamics at maximal exercise with prajmaline. No new arrhythmias or conduction abnormalities were observed. The occurrence of ectopic beats did not change significantly with prajmaline administration. Prajmaline did not influence the occurrence of ST-segment depression on exercise testing. No side effects were observed.

RESULTS EXPRESSED AS MEAN (±SD)

|  | Control | Placebo | Prajmaline |
|---|---|---|---|
| Number of anginal attacks |  | 4.6 (5.5) | 4.6 (6.1) |
| GTN consumption* |  | 4.2 (7.1) | 4.1 (4.1) |
| Resting heart rate [beats/min] | 74.4 (9.8) | 74.8 (9.1) | 80.0 (9.7) |
| Resting systolic BP [mmHg] | 128.3 (13.3) | 130.9 (13.3) | 127.1 (16.2) |
| Time to onset of angina [min] | 8.4 (5.1) | 9.3 (6.8) | 9.3 (4.7) |
| Heart rate at onset of angina [beats/min] | 128.2 (17.5) | 120.0 (17.0) | 125.0 (18.3) |
| ST segment depression at onset of angina [mm] | 0.8 (0.9) | 0.8 (0.9) | 0.6 (0.8) |
| Total exercise time [min] | 12.1 ( (4.0) | 13.2 (4.6) | 13.3 (4.3) |
| ST segment depression at maximum exercise [mm] | 0.7 (1.1) | 0.7 (1.1) | 0.6 (1.1) |
| Heart rate at end exercise [beats/min] | 134.4 (24.6) | 135.4 (22.4) | 138.8 (19.0) |
| Systolic BP at maximum exercise [mmHg] | 154.0 (21.8) | 160.7 (27.6) | 159.7 (22.1) |
| (Heart rate × systolic BP) × 1000 at maximum exercise | 20.6 (4.2) | 21.2 (6.3) | 22.0 (6.3) |
| Number of ectopics during 5 min before exercise | 11.7 (31.2) | 7.3 (13.4) | 10.5 (29.7) |
| Numbers of ectopics during 5 min before the end of exercise | 21.8 (83.1) | 2.3 (4.7) | 3.2 (7.8) |
| Number of ectopics during 5-min recovery period | 17.8 (38.9) | 9.2 (16.9) | 10.4 (25.5) |
| Mean heart rate 5 min after exercise [beats/min] | 86.2 (14.2) | 88.1 (16.2) | 90.8 (12.2) |

*GTN, nitroglycerin.
(Courtesy of Handler, C.E., et al.: Eur. J. Clin. Pharmacol. 28:371–374, June 1985, Berlin-Heidelberg-New York: Springer.)

Oral prajmaline therapy for 1 week in a dosage of 20 mg three times daily was well tolerated by the patients in this study with coronary artery disease. Exercise capacity was not impaired. The safety of oral prajmaline therapy is of clinical interest for the management of patients with coronary disease and cardiac arrhythmia.

▶ One disadvantage of this type of agent is that it frequently has a negative inotropic effect upon the heart (L. H. Opie: *Lancet* I:861, 1980). The present report confirms the observations of E. Sowton (*Eur. J. Clin. Pharmacol.* 26:147, 1984) in showing that moderate doses of prajmaline bitartrate do not have a negative effect on either hemodynamics or working capacity. The one disturbing feature of the report is that the frequency of ventricular ectopic beats was not decreased relative to control; this raises the question as to how far the dose used would have been effective in the clinical control of arrhythmias.—Roy J. Shephard, M.D., Ph.D.

---

**Evaluation of Acute Cardiorespiratory Responses to Hydraulic Resistance Exercise**
Frank I. Katch, Patty S. Freedson, and Carole A. Jones (Univ. of Massachusetts–Amherst)
Med. Sci. Sports Exerc. 17:168–173, February 1985                              1–29

---

Accurate evaluation of the acute responses to resistance exercise training depends on the stability of the criterion measures. This is particularly true for maximal effort exercise in which continuous, "all-out" effort for each repetition is encouraged. The authors evaluated the reliability of repetition number (repN), respiratory gas parameters and heart rate (HR) for shoulder (SE), chest (CE), and leg (LE) exercises performed maximally on a single-unit, three-station, hydraulic resistance exercise machine. On 2 separate days, 20 college men completed three 20-second bouts of SE, CE, and LE with a 20-second rest between bouts and 5 minutes between exercise modes.

There were no significant differences between bouts or test days for repN, gas measures, or HR. Subjects performed 17, 19, and 21 repetitions during SE, LE, and CE, respectively. Oxygen consumption ($\dot{V}_{O_2}$) was 1.7 L per minute for SE, 1.87 for CE, and 2.1 for LE. These values, averaged, represented 52.8% of the maximum $\dot{V}_{O_2}$ determined on a continuous cycle ergometer test. The corresponding HRs during hydraulic exercise averaged 84.6% of maximum HR. Test-retest reliability coefficients ranged from .67 to .87 for repN, .41 to .83 for gas measures, and .72 to .89 for HR. The MET level averaged 7.5 (heavy) and caloric expenditure per minute averaged 35% higher, compared with literature values for free weights, and 29.4% and 11.5% greater than circuit exercise on Nautilus or Universal Gym equipment, respectively (table).

The caloric expenditure for the three hydraulic exercises averaged 37.7 kilojoules. The energy expenditure values averaged 8.9% less than slow and fast isokinetic circuit exercise. It seems reasonable that differences in kilocalories (and associated physiologic measurements) between the present results and those of other studies of circuit exercise are due in part to methodological differences. The authors have reported values associated with each bout of exericse (and the average) in contrast with an average value determined throughout circuit exercise.

Although the reliability of individual differences in work performance was only moderate, it was high enough to provide for consistency across

COMPARISON OF MAXIMAL PHYSIOLOGIC
RESPONSES TO RESISTIVE EXERCISE*

| Study | Mode | Sex | % MaxVO₂* | % Max HR | kJ | kcal |
|-------|------|-----|-----------|----------|----|----|
| Hempel | Nautilus, Circuit | M | 35.9 | 71.7 | 29.7 | 7.1 |
|  |  | F | 38.3 | 76.1 | 24.3 | 5.8 |
| Liverman | Nautilus, Circuit | M | — | — | 22.6 | 5.4 |
| Wilmore | Universal, Circuit | M | 41.4 | 78.2 | 33.1 | 7.9 |
|  |  | F | 46.8 | 87.6 | 28.5 | 6.8 |
| Gettman | Isokinetic, slow | M | 49.0 | 69.0 | 40.2 | 9.6 |
|  | Isokinetic, fast |  |  |  | 41.4 | 9.9 |
| McArdle | Isometric, free weights | M | — | 69.0† | 25.1 | 6.0 |
| Present Study | Hydraulic | M | 52.8 | 84.6 | 37.7 | 9.0 |

*Based on body weight of 68.03 kg (150 lb).
†Estimated from age-predicted maximum HR of 195 beats per minute.
(Courtesy of Katch, F.I., et al.: Med. Sci. Sports Exerc. 17:168–173, February 1985. Copyright 1985, the American College of Sports Medicine. Reprinted by permission.)

days in the physiologic response to maximal effort exercise. The use of on-line analog to digital devices interfaced with a microcomputer would provide two important advances in this type of equipment: (1) feedback to the user regarding effort, e.g., time to peak effort, average work and power, total work and power, and work and power expressed relative to range of motion, and (2) quantification for precise evaluation and comparison with other modalities of resistance exercise.

Exercise performed on a three-station hydraulic resistance apparatus produces reliable personal differences in repN, heart rate, and associated respiratory gas measurements. The magnitude of the average heart rate and metabolic response patterns with maximal effort hydraulic exercise is in the range recommended by the American College of Sports Medicine to promote improvements in cardiorespiratory fitness. When energy expenditure is expressed in the MET classification scheme for defining exercise intensity, the MET level averages about 7.5, which would be considered heavy-intensity exercise.

▶ Will circuit training improve cardiorespiratory fitness? Many studies have indicated that it will. It appears that using hydraulic restive exercises with a maximal effort in a circuit training fashion will improve cardiorespiratory fitness. If the ACSM guidelines are followed for aerobic type exercises, then any aerobic exercise, if it is sustained for a long enough period, should produce favorable results.—Frank George, A.T.C., P.T.

**Learned Control of Heart Rate During Exercise in Patients With Borderline Hypertension**
Mats Fredrikson and Bernard T. Engel (Natl. Inst. on Aging, Bethesda, Md., and Baltimore City Hosp.)
Eur. J. Appl. Physiol. 54:315–320, September 1985                    1–30

Heart rate responses to dynamic or static exercise or cold exposure can

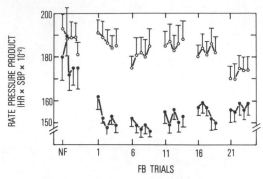

**Fig 1–15.**—Rate-pressure product ($\pm$ SEM) for experimental *(closed circles)* and control *(open circles)* groups during a nonfeedback (NF) day and 5 experimental days when the experimental group received heart rate (HR) feedback; SBP indicates systolic blood pressure. (Courtesy of Fredrikson, M., and Engel, B.T.: Eur. J. Appl. Physiol. 54:315–320, September 1985.)

be attenuated by feedback in normal subjects. The ability of patients with borderline hypertension to learn heart rate control was assessed in 12 outpatients, most of whom had diastolic blood pressures of 90–95 mm Hg and all of whom had systolic pressures of 140–160 mm Hg. Experimental subjects were given continuous beat-to-beat information and were instructed to keep the heart rate low while exercising on a cycle ergometer. The 6 experimental subjects had a mean age of 39 years; the 6 control subjects, 43.5 years.

Experimental subjects had an exercise heart rate of 98 beats per minute, averaged over 5 days with 25 training trials, compared with 107 beats per minute for control subjects. Systolic blood pressure was unchanged by feedback training. Changes in rate-pressure product generally reflected those in heart rate (Fig 1–15). Oxygen consumption was lower in experimental subjects later in the course of training.

In this study, patients with borderline hypertension were trained to attenuate their heart rate response to dynamic muscular exercise. Physical work appears to have been maintained while left ventricular work was reduced. After-load may have been reduced, but it would be helpful to measure cardiac output and total peripheral resistance in hypertensive patients before and after behavioral conditioning. The clinical significance of these findings remains to be ascertained.

▶ The wisdom of drug therapy in the treatment of borderline hypertension in the elderly has had vigorous debate over the past few years; problems include poor compliance, complications such as hypotensive attacks and falls, and adverse interactions with other drugs the patient is taking.

There is thus much interest in nonpharmaceutic interventions. If the patient has the required physique, exercise itself can lower blood pressure by 5–10 mm Hg. Biofeedback has also been viewed as a possible method of controlling blood pressure. The present report confirms earlier work by the same laboratory (Perski and Engel: *Biofeedback Self Regul.* 5:91, 1980) in showing that feedback can reduce the exercise heart rate but not the systolic blood pressure. The reduction in rate-pressure product may nevertheless be of value for patients with angina or a tendency to heart failure.—Roy J. Shephard, M.D., Ph.D.

## Respiratory Physiology

### Maximal Ventilation After Exhausting Exercise

Paul R. Bender and Bruce J. Martin (Indiana Univ. at Bloomington)
Med. Sci. Sports Exerc. 17:164–167, February 1985                    1–31

It remains unclear whether the hyperapnea of exercise severely stresses the ventilatory musculature. The authors hypothesized that the ability to ventilate maximally is decreased during and immediatelly following exhausting exercise. Subjects performed isocapnic maximal voluntary ventilations (60-s MVV) before, during the final minute, and after exhausting treadmill exercise lasting either 3–10 minutes or 60 minutes. Subjects included 14 male and 3 female volunteers.

A 3–10 minute run to exhaustion did not change the 60-s MVV. During initial long-term exercise experiments, runners showed constant 60-s MVV throughout, whereas 60-s MVV declined in the final minutes of exercise in nonrunners. Nonrunners had significantly lower ($P < .01$) exercise and recovery 60-s MVV compared with control valves, and, further, the final recovery 60-s MVV differed from the exercise value (Fig 1–16; $P < .05$). In runners, the second recovery 60-s MVV was lower than the control and exercise values ($P < .05$) but no other changes were seen (Fig 1–16).

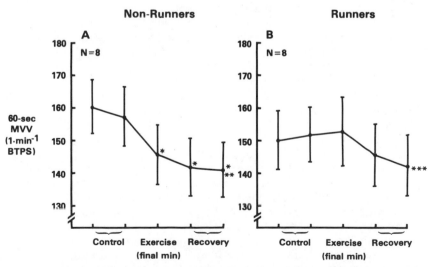

Fig 1–16.—Control, exercise, and recovery 60-s MVV performed while running in a 60-minute run to exhaustion. Values are means ± SE. Bracketed "control" measures were made 5 and 10 minutes before exercise. "Recovery" measures took place 5 and 10 minutes after exercise. *Significantly different ($P < .01$) from control, **significantly different ($P < .05$) from exercise, ***significantly different ($P < .05$) from control and exercise. (Courtesy of Bender, P.R., and Martin, B.J.: Med. Sci. Sports Exerc. 17:164–167, February 1985. Copyright 1985, the American College of Sports Medicine. Reprinted by permission.)

During long-term exercise the nonrunners and runners displayed similar exercise minute ventilation ($\dot{V}_E$), as well as $\dot{V}_E$ expressed as a percentage of control 60-s MVV. The flow rate for nonrunners in the final minute of the 60-minute run declined from the first 15 seconds to the final 15 seconds ($P < .05$).

These data suggest that the capacity to ventilate maximally declines only in long-term exhausting exercise and that this decrement is most pronounced in nonrunners. Thus, ventilatory endurance may be one of several factors limiting prolonged, heavy exercise.

▶ Early experiments in our laboratory (Shephard: *Clin. Sci.* 32:167, 1967) suggested that the power of the ventilatory muscles did not limit endurance exercise; even after 15 minutes of running, subjects were still able to develop 75%–80% of their maximum voluntary ventilation (MVV), and indeed with vigorous encouragement could realize almost 100% of MVV, a volume far larger than that used in vigorous exercise. Against this evidence, Fregosi et al. (*Fed. Proc.* 42:3, 1983) observed end-exercise levels of lactate as high in the diaphragm as in the leg muscles of a rat, while various studies of electromyographic patterns also suggested that the chest muscles were becoming fatigued.

Bender and Martin, in the above digest, attempted to resolve this question by measuring the MVV over a longer period than some authors (60 seconds), and comparing 3–10 minutes with 60 minutes of exercise. They found fatigue only after the very long periods of exercise. Most patients do not attempt 60-minute bouts of exhausting exercise, but the data may nevertheless have clinical relevance, because the fatigue could be of much earlier onset if the work of breathing is increased by chronic obstructive lung disease and the muscles have been weakened by a prolonged period of inactivity.—Roy J. Shephard, M.D., Ph.D.

---

**Ventilatory Changes During Exercise and Arterial $P_{CO_2}$ Oscillations in Chronic Airway Obstruction Patients**
J. G. Prior, M. Powlson, G. M. Cochrane, and C. B. Wolff (Guy's Hosp. and Med. School, London)
J. Appl. Physiol. 58:1942–1948, June 1985                                   1–32

---

Respiratory $P_{CO_2}$ oscillations may be attenuated or even absent in chronic airway obstruction. Ventilatory kinetics during exercise at 30 W over 6 minutes were monitored in 14 patients with chronic obstructive airway disease, including 11 with bronchial and 3 with emphysematous changes, and in 3 asthmatic patients. Five age-matched normal subjects were also studied. Oscillations in $Pa_{CO_2}$ were monitored indirectly, as in vivo pH at rest, with a fast-response pH electrode. Exercise studies were carried out separately.

Ventilatory increase in early exercise was normal in the asthmatics, whose respiratory oscillations showed the least attenuation, and in patients with emphysematous airway obstruction, whose oscillations as a group were most attenuated. In patients with bronchial airway obstruction, the reduction in ventilatory increase on early exercise correlated with attenuation of the upslope of respiratory $Pa_{CO_2}$ oscillations. The latter did not correlate with the change in in vitro $Pa_{CO_2}$ from rest to the immediate postexercise period.

The findings suggest that attenuation of the upslope slows ventilatory kinetics during exercise in patients with bronchial-type airway obstruction, but not in emphysematous patients. It is concluded that intact respiratory oscillations are not necessary for carbon dioxide homeostasis after the first few minutes of exercise. Further studies are needed to determine the role of the carotid bodies and respiratory $P_{CO_2}$ oscillations in the control of breathing during exercise.

▶ English respiratory physiologists have long been fascinated by the hypothesis of W. S. Yamomoto (*J. Appl. Physiol.* 15:215, 1960) that respiratory $P_{CO_2}$ oscillations may provide an important clue to the respiratory centers during exercise.

The extent of such oscillations is plainly reduced by various types of lung disease, particularly emphysema, and it seems somewhat at variance with the oscillation hypothesis that in such patients the speed of ventilatory kinetics cannot be linked to the suppression of oscillations.

Nevertheless, there are many other abnormalities in a patient with emphysema, and it could be that an early drop in arterial oxygen pressure is replacing the signal normally obtained from $CO_2$ oscillations.—Roy J. Shephard, M.D., Ph.D.

**Airway Responses to Low Concentrations of Adrenaline and Noradrenaline in Normal Subjects**
K. E. Berkin, G. C. Inglis, S. G. Ball, and N. C. Thomson (Western Infirmary, Glasgow, Scotland)
Q. J. Exp. Physiol. 70:203–209, 1985                                      1–33

Airway, cardiovascular, and metabolic responses were measured in 6 normal subjects during separate infusions of adrenaline (epinephrine) and noradrenaline (norepinephrine). The subjects (mean age, 29 years) were nonsmokers. A 30-minute reference infusion of sodium chloride was followed by the catecholamine infusion at four incremental rates per minute of 4, 10, 25, and 62.5 ng/kg, each infusion lasting 20 minutes. This was followed by a second reference saline infusion after which 200 μg of salbutamol was inhaled from a metered dose inhaler.

Infusion of epinephrine at four different rates increased circulating epinephrine levels sequentially. Statistically significant increases occurred during the two highest infusion rates ($P < .05$). Epinephrine concentration fell during the second saline infusion. Norepinephrine concentration remained constant during epinephrine infusion. Norepinephrine infusion increased circulating norepinephrine levels, during the two highest infusion rates reaching statistical significance ($P < .05$). Maximal expiratory flow rates at 25% of vital capacity measured from partial flow-volume curves increased sequentially with increasing epinephrine concentration. Increases in maximal expiratory flow rates at 25% and 50% of vital capacity measured from complete flow-volume curves were not statistically significant, nor were the changes in specific conductance. Small but insignificant changes were observed in heart rate and blood pressure during adrenaline infusion. Plasma glucose level increased and serum potassium level fell during epinephrine infusion. No significant airway, cardiovascular, or metabolic responses were seen during noradrenaline infusion.

Circulating epinephrine, at concentrations within the physiologic range, has a bronchodilator effect predominantly in small airways in normal subjects. The lack of responsiveness of airway caliber to norepinephrine suggests that α-adrenoceptors are not important in the regulation of bronchomotor tone in normal subjects.

▶ Dose/response curves for adrenaline and noradrenaline show that the plasma levels of adrenaline encountered in vigorous exercise are sufficient to increase airflow. In contrast to a previous report (Warren and Dalton: *Clin. Sci.* 64:475, 1983), the main effect is on the peripheral rather than the central airways, since the $\dot{V}_{25}$ is affected more than the specific conductance. This may reflect either a greater number of adrenaline receptors in the peripheral airways or a difference in the vascular distribution of the drug.—Roy J. Shephard, M.D., Ph.D.

---

**A Simple, Valid Step Test for Estimating Maximal Oxygen Uptake in Epidemiologic Studies**
Steven F. Siconolfi, Carol Ewing Garber, Thomas M. Lasater, and Richard A. Carleton (Brown Univ.)
Am. J. Epidemiol. 121:382–390, March 1985                    1–34

---

Measurement issues have made it difficult to include physical fitness in epidemiologic studies. A simple, safe, valid test administered at home was sought, and a step test was developed that was validated against directly measured maximal oxygen uptake. Forty-eight subjects aged 19 to 70 years who participated in a community fitness program were studied. Maximal oxygen uptake was determined using a bicycle protocol at a submaximal exercise level. Subjects stepped on a portable 10-inch-high braced box for 3 minutes per stage up to three stages, at rates of 17, 26, and 34 steps per minute. These rates approximate the MET levels required for the first three stages of the Bruce treadmill protocol. The goal was a heart rate 65% of the age-predicted maximum.

All subjects completed both submaximal exercise tests. Directly measured maximal oxygen uptake was similar to that of the general population. Correlation between the maximal oxygen uptake as measured directly and

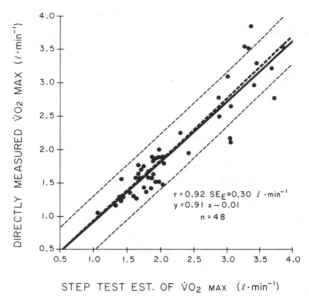

STEP TEST EST. OF $\dot{V}O_2$ MAX $(\ell \cdot min^{-1})$

**Fig 1–17.**—Directly measured (bicycle protocol) maximal oxygen uptake ($VO_{2max}$) vs. estimated $VO_{2max}$ from the step test protocol in 48 men and women, aged 19–70 years, who took part in a community fitness program in Pawtucket, Rhode Island in January–February, 1983. The *solid line* is the line of identity with a 10% adjustment for the expected difference between exercise modalities. The *thick broken line* is the regression line. The *thin broken line* represents ± standard error of estimate. (Courtesy of Siconolfi, S.F., et al.: Am. J. Epidemiol. 121:382–390, March 1985.)

that estimated from the step protocol (Fig 1–17) was 0.98. The standard error in predicting bicycle estimates from step estimates was 0.17 L/minute. Step test estimates were about 12% higher than directly measured values for peak oxygen uptake.

This step test protocol provides valid estimates of cardiorespiratory fitness over a wide age range. Inexpensive digital tachometers are used, and a low level of exercise is required to complete the step test protocol. The test can be used to assess cardiorespiratory fitness in the home and elsewhere, and it should be well-suited for use in epidemiologic studies of apparently healthy adults, as well as in community fitness programs conducted outside the laboratory.

▶ The measurement of $VO_2$ is a classic physiologic concept. The inconvenience and expense of carrying out such a study in a laboratory or medical center is clear. This technique bypasses that problem, providing a test that can be performed in the home. It cancels, as well, the negative response problem of the 50%–75% factor of patient compliance. The step test estimate of $VO_2$ max was 12% higher than directly measured $VO_2$ max—this anticipated with the difference between stepping and cycling. When this factor is corrected for, there is a very high correlation, in the order of 0.98. In sum, a safe and simple test for the home.—Lewis J. Krakauer, M.D., F.A.C.P.

**Absence of Refractoriness in Asthmatic Subjects After Exercise With Warm, Humid Inspirate**
Allan G. Hahn, Stephen G. Nogrady, Grahame R. Burton, and Alan R. Morton (Australian Natl. Univ., Sports Science Labs., Australian Inst. of Sport, and Univ. of Western Australia, Perth, Australia)
Thorax 40:4180–421, June 1985                                                    1–35

Exercise-induced asthma often is followed by a refractory period during which the bronchospastic response to further exercise is much reduced. The effect generally is ascribed to depletion of mediators released by airway mast cells. Inspiration of warm, humid air was used to examine the mechanisms of exercise-induced asthma in 12 adult patients, none of whom used steroids. All had a history of exercise-induced asthma and had a greater than 15% reduction in $FEV_1$ on exercise testing. Two treadmill runs were carried out with a 20-minute interval, with warm, humid air replacing cool, dry air for the first run in experimental sessions.

The mean peak reduction in $FEV_1$ from baseline was 39% for the first of the paired runs with cool air and 11.5% for the second, despite a lower baseline $FEV_1$ for the second trial. Total ventilation and total respiratory heat loss were similar between trials. On exercise with warm, humid air, the peak fall in $FEV_1$ averaged 3%, and no subject had a reduction greater than 15%. On subsequent testing with cool, dry air, the average peak fall in $FEV_1$ was 37%.

These findings are in accord with refractoriness following exercise-induced asthma as a result of depletion of mediators associated with airway mast cells, but other mechanisms may be operative. Experimental manipulation of air temperature and humidity during recovery periods between exercise challenges may aid the understanding of exercise-induced asthma.

▶ This study provides support for the theory that depletion of the mediators released by airway mast cells is the reason for the refractory period in exercise-induced asthma, when the bronchoconstrictive response is much diminished. This mediator depletion occurs during the initial exercise-induced asthmatic attack, apparently, and warm humid inspirate is not a critical factor in the equation.—Lewis J. Krakauer, M.D., F.A.C.P.

---

**Oxygen Cost of Running at Submaximal Speeds While Wearing Shoe Inserts**
Kris Berg and Stan Sady (Univ. of Nebraska at Omaha and Miriam Hosp., Providence, R.I.)
Res. Q. Exerc. Sport 56:86–89, March 1985                                         1–36

The authors studied 15 healthy men, aged 19 to 35 years, lean and highly trained runners, who had run a minimum of 25 miles per week in the previous 6 months. Submaximal oxygen uptake was determined for running speeds of 241 and 268 m per minute at zero grade with and without inserts. Submaximal testing was done on two nonconsecutive days at least 48 hours after a maximum oxygen consumption $\dot{V}O_{2max}$ test. The inserts of Sorbothane, a viscoelastic polymer, were full length and placed directly into the shoe. Twelve subjects wore 100-gm inserts and 3 wore 75-gm inserts, depending on shoe size. No standardization of manufacturer of running shoe, shoe weight, or sole characteristics was attempted. Subjects were allowed to train during the study but were asked to limit the intensity and duration the day before a test by not doing speed work or running longer than 30 minutes. Subjects were also instructed not to run on the day of a treadmill test before the actual test.

At the submaximal running speeds selected, 241 and 268 m per minute, no significant increase in absolute $\dot{V}O_2$ was found. This was true whether $\dot{V}O_2$ was compared as an average over the 6 minutes or as the sum of the 6 minutes (table). The differences were slight. The increased oxygen uptake (1 minute) was 0.4% greater while the inserts were worn at 241 m per minute and 1.1% greater at 268 m per minute. This yielded increases in kilojoules expended of only .25 and .80 per minute at the two speeds, respectively. During 1 hour, this would amount to increased energy expenditures of only 15.12 kilojoules at 241 m per minute and 47.0 at 268 m per minute. Expressed relative to body weight, the increases in $\dot{V}O_2$ were 0.9% at 241 m per minute and 1.5% at 268 m per minute.

The use of Sorbothane shoe inserts did not significantly alter the oxygen cost of running, although the cost increased at both 241 and 268 m per

OXYGEN COST OF 6 MINUTES OF TREADMILL RUNNING AT 241 AND 268 METERS PER MINUTE WITH AND WITHOUT SHOE INSERTS ($n = 15$)

| Speed ($m \cdot min^{-1}$) | Variable | No Insert | Insert |
|---|---|---|---|
| 241 | Mean of 6 min | | |
| | $\dot{V}O_2$ ($l \cdot min^{-1}$) | 3.16 ± .24 | 3.17 ± .28 |
| | $\dot{V}O_2$ ($ml \cdot kg^{-1} min^{-1}$) | 47.77 ± 2.50 | 48.29 ± 1.85 |
| | 6 min total | | |
| | $VO_2$ (l) | 18.96 ± 1.42 | 19.02 ± 1.50 |
| | $VO_2$ (ml) | 286.62 ± 14.99 | 289.62 ± 11.09 |
| 268 | Mean of 6 min | | |
| | $\dot{V}O_2$ ($l \cdot min^{-1}$) | 3.53 ± .31 | 3.53 ± .32 |
| | $\dot{V}O_2$ ($ml \cdot kg^{-1} min^{-1}$) | 53.10 ± 2.81 | 53.58 ± 2.76 |
| | 6 min total | | |
| | $\dot{V}O_2$ (l) | 21.19 ± 1.88 | 21.18 ± 1.89 |
| | $VO_2$ (ml) | 318.58 ± 16.84 | 321.48 ± 16.51 |

(Courtesy of Berg, K., and Sady, S.: Res. Q. Exerc. Sport 56:86–89, March 1985. Reprinted by permission of the American Alliance for Health, Physical Education, Recreation and Dance, 1900 Association Drive, Reston, Virginia 22901.)

minute. Frederick et al. found that heavier, air-cushioned running shoes lowered the oxygen cost 5.7 ml/kg/km, compared with standard running shoes each weighing 16.5 gm less each. Reduced effort was not observed when the Sorbothane inserts were used. Frederick et al. compared the physiologic differences with differences calculated by use of equations for potential and kinetic energy. The calculated added oxygen cost of running at 268 m per minute with 100 gm added to each shoe was 44 ml per minute, a 1.3% increase. The actual increase in $Vo_2$ in their study was 33 ml per minute (1.9%). Thus agreement was good between the calculated value and the actual data. At the same speed, an increased oxygen cost of 37 ml per minute, a 1.5% increase, was found in the present study.

▶ If inserts are needed to improve biomechanics or for increased shock absorption, it appears that if they weigh 100 gm or less, they should not significantly interfere with cardiorespiratory responses. The athlete may reject them because they feel "too heavy." However, if the inserts are tested in a fashion similar to this study and the runners responses are similar, runners may accept the inserts more readily. Our feeling has been if they work (i.e., if they alleviate the problem), wear them.—Frank George, A.T.C., P.T.

---

**The Effects of Passive Inhalation of Cigarette Smoke on Exercise Performance**
Robert G. McMurray, Lindsay L. Hicks, and Dixie L. Thompson (Univ. of North Carolina at Chapel Hill)
Eur. J. Appl. Physiol. 54:196–200, August 1985                                    1–37

This study evaluated the effect of passive smoke inhalation on submaximal and maximal exercise performance. Eight women (average age, 21.8 years) ran on a motor drive treadmill for 20 minutes at 70% $Vo_{2max}$ followed by an incremental change in grade until maximal work capacity was obtained. Each subject completed the exercise trial with and without the presence of residual cigarette smoke.

Passive inhalation of smoke significantly reduced the $Vo_{2max}$ ($P < .05$). It also reduced the duration of exercise ($P < .05$). The presence of smoke increased the maximal R value indicating a greater $CO_2$ output at a given $VO_2$. The rating of perceived exertion at the end of the control trials was significantly increased during the smoke trials (Fig 1–18). Maximal heart rate responses were similar for both conditions. Postexercise venous blood lactates averaged 6.8 mM during the smoke trials, significantly greater than the controls (5.5 mM). The presence of smoke increased the $VE/VO_2$ ratio ($P < .05$). Inhalation of smoke did not significantly affect the submaximal $VO_2$ but increased the relative intensity to 76% of the smoking trial $Vo_{2max}$. Inhalation of smoke significantly elevated the $CO_2$ output ($P < .05$). Consequently, R values were also increased with passive smoking. Resting oxygen uptake was unaffected by the smoke.

Although the number of subjects in the study was relatively small, the results imply that passive inhalation of cigarette smoke has a significant

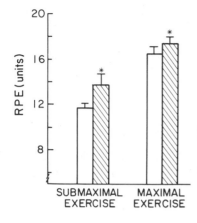

Fig 1–18.—Rating of perceived exertion during submaximal and maximal exercise with *(hash marks)* and without *(open)* smoke inhalation (mean ± SEM). *Significant difference (P < .05) no smoke versus smoke. (Courtesy of McMurray, R.G., et al.: Eur. J. Appl. Physiol. 54:196–200, August 1985.)

detrimental effect on exercise performance, specifically, by reducing maximal aerobic power and endurance capacity and increasing the need for anaerobiosis. The results suggest that people participating in activities that demand high intensity for a prolonged period should avoid smoke-filled areas.

▶ The question of health effects from the passive accumulation of cigarette smoke in enclosed spaces is of increasing public concern. The main arguments in favor of clean air are the avoidance of chronic diseases, particularly lung carcinoma (Hirayama: *Br. Med. J.* 282:183, 1981), annoyance, visual problems, and impaired psychomotor performance (Shephard: *The Risks of Passive Smoking.* London, Croom Helm, 1982). There have also been reports that smoke exposure has minor effects upon the performance of submaximal exercise. However, this is the first paper to attempt a measurement of maximum oxygen intake in a smoke-laden atmosphere.

No details are given of either the smoking machine or the room concentrations of smoke that were developed, both important points for the generalization of the information presented. The authors speculate that carbon monoxide accumulation was responsible, but this could hardly explain the 12% decrement of oxygen transport that they observed. Carboxyhemoglobin does not normally rise by more than about 0.5% over a couple of hours of smoke exposure. The authors themselves query how far maximum effort was realized, and some decrease of motivation in the smoke seems a more probable explanation.—Roy J. Shephard, M.D., Ph.D.

---

**Ozone Inhalation Effects Consequent to Continuous Exercise in Females: Comparison to Males**
Susan K. Lauritzen and William C. Adams (Univ. of California, Davis)
J. Appl. Physiol. 59:1601–1606, November 1985                    1–38

---

Exercise appears to enhance the resting effects of $O_3$ exposure in metropolitan areas, and an exercise-induced increase in minute ventilation has been implicated. Few data are available on $O_3$ effects in female subjects. The effects of $O_3$ inhalation on lung function and exercise respiratory metabolism were studied in 6 women, aged 22 to 29 years, who exercised for 1 hour on a cycle ergometer while exposed to $O_3$ concentrations of 0.2, 0.3, and 0.4 ppm. Exercise intensities were set to induce minute ventilations of about 23, 35, and 46 L/minute at each $O_3$ concentration.

Pulmonary responses to $O_3$ inhalation in male and female subjects were compared. Dose-dependent reductions in FVC, $FEV_1$, and forced expiratory flow rate in the middle half of FVC were observed, with an increase in RV during $O_3$ exposure. Effects on FVC, $FEV_1$, and respiratory frequency were more marked in female subjects. Differences persisted but were less marked when minute ventilation was reduced for female subjects as a function of exercise intensity at the same percent of maximal $Vo_2$ ($Vo_{2\ max}$).

Enhanced responses of female subjects to $O_3$ inhalation appear to be due in part to differences in lung size between the sexes. Other studies have failed to show a difference in $O_3$-induced effects when female and male subjects exercised at a similar percent of $Vo_{2\ max}$ (hence, a substantially reduced minute ventilation for the female subjects).

▶ Ozone accumulation is becoming a concern in many large cities, particularly Los Angeles, where it is one of the active constituents of photochemical smog. This type of air pollution is of interest to the sports physician, in that there have been suggestions of impaired track performances on days when pollutant levels are high; mechanisms for the degradation of performance are not known, but could include acute respiratory discomfort and ventilatory changes of the type described in this report.

Whether women are more sensitive to such pollution than men depends on the nature of the question that is asked. If women attempt to carry out the same relative amount of work, the sensitivity seems about equal to that of men, but if they attempt to match the absolute work performance of a man, they fare worse. This is probably because women breathe about the same quantity of ozone into smaller lungs.—Roy J. Shephard, M.D., Ph.D.

## Metabolism and Nutrition

### The Effects of Exercise and Weight Loss on Plasma Lipids in Young Obese Men

George Sopko, Arthur S. Leon, David R. Jacobs, Jr., Nedra Foster, James Moy, Kanta Kuba, Joseph T. Anderson, David Casal, Carl McNally, and Ivan Frantz (Univ. of Minnesota)
Metabolism 34:227–236, March 1985                                    1–39

Cross-sectional data have shown higher levels of HDL-C (high-density lipoprotein cholesterol) in physically active persons, but experimental studies have given conflicting results. The effects of exercise conditioning and weight loss on lipid levels and lipoprotein profiles were examined in 24 overweight men aged 19 to 44 years who were at least 110% of standard weight but in good general health, and were not physically active for more than 30 minutes a day. One group of subjects walked on a treadmill 5 days a week to use about 3,500 kcal weekly as caloric intake was increased; another had caloric intake reduced by 3,500 kcal weekly to promote weight loss of 1 pound per week; and a third group exercised with no increase in caloric intake. Two 18-week observation periods with a crossover were separated by an 8-week "washout" interval.

Both groups on a weight-loss regimen lost 13–14 pounds during the study. Maximal oxygen uptake increased 6% in exercising subjects, and the percentage of body fat decreased only in these subjects. Significant increases in HDL-C were associated with both exercise and weight loss, and an additive effect was evident. Plasma triglycerides and very-low-density lipoprotein (VLDL) cholesterol increased with exercise at constant weight and decreased with exercise associated with weight loss.

Exercise and weight loss independently increase HDL-C levels in an additive manner in overweight young and middle-aged men. The increases in triglycerides and VLDL-cholesterol associated with exercise at stable weight could result from increased caloric intake.

▶ The most important and modifiable environmentally related variables that can effect HDL-cholesterol are total body weight, smoking, physical activity, diet, alcohol, and drugs. This study examines the variables of body weight and physical activity, holding all others constant.

Exercise training and weight loss in men will increase HDL-cholesterol, independently of each other. The two levels are roughly equal. They are additive and complement one another. This is further support for the concept that exercise itself is desirable, as is an elevation of HDL-cholesterol. Less clear in the literature to date has been the effect of weight loss as an independent factor.—Lewis J. Krakauer, M.D., F.A.C.P.

**Effects of Interval and Continuous Running on HDL-Cholesterol, Apoproteins A-1 and B, and LCAT**

T. R. Thomas, S. B. Adeniran, P. W. Iltis, C. A. Aquiar, and J. J. Albers (Univ. of Kansas)

Can. J. Appl. Sports Sci. 10:52–59, March 1985                1–40

The effects of interval and continuous exercise programs on the levels of plasma lipoproteins, apoproteins, and lecithin:cholesterol acyltransferase (LCAT) were compared in 36 males aged 18 to 25 years. All were active students but had not participated in systematic aerobic exercise for 6 months. The students were assigned to a program of 5-mile continuous running at up to 8 minutes a mile; or to intervals for 4 or 2 minutes at a work:rest ratio of 1:1 and 1:1½, respectively; or to a control group. All exercise groups used about 500–550 kcal per session, 3 times a week. Dietary fat did not change significantly during the study.

Maximal aerobic capacity increased significantly in the continuous and longer-interval groups compared with results in controls. No significant group differences were seen in the levels of cholesterol, high-density lipoprotein (HDL)-cholesterol, or apoproteins A-1 and B, and there were no significant changes over time. Changes in LCAT activity could not be related to exercise.

Both continuous and longer-interval exercise programs led to increased aerobic capacity in these normal young adults, but no significant changes in the levels of plasma lipoproteins or apoproteins were observed. Short-term continuous running or long-interval training does not alter plasma HDL-cholesterol or LCAT activity in active young men.

▶ An opposing philosophical position to the editorial comments following Digest 1–39 is held by these authors in Digest 1–40. In their study, activity did not correlate with changes in HDL-cholesterol nor in the cholesterol-related enzyme LCAT. It is possible, as this paper suggests, that the adaptation of plasma HDL-cholesterol induced by exercise training may require an extended time period. The issue remains to be resolved definitively. It is an open-ended question.—Lewis J. Krakauer, M.D., F.A.C.P.

---

**Effect of Exercise Training on Glucose Tolerance, In Vivo Insulin Sensitivity, Lipid and Lipoprotein Concentrations in Middle-Aged Men With Mild Hypertriglyceridemia**
R. M. Lampman, J. T. Santinga, P. J. Savage, D. R. Bassett, C. R. Hydrick, J. D. Flora, Jr., and W. D. Block (Univ. of Michigan)
Metabolism 34:205–211, March 1985                                    1–41

---

Physical conditioning has important effects on the metabolism of glucose and other metabolic fuels. The effects of moderate dynamic exercise training on glucose tolerance and insulin responses, as well as lipid and lipoprotein levels, were studied in 10 sedentary men aged 34 to 58 years as weight was held constant. The men had mild endogenous hypertriglyceridemia, with fasting serum triglyceride levels of more than 150 mg/dl and plasma cholesterol levels of less than 260 mg/dl. A weight-maintenance diet was prescribed. Training was carried out for 9 weeks by jogging to reach 85% of the maximal heart rate.

Aerobic capacity improved from 33.5 ml/kg/minute to 39 ml/kg/minute after training. Body weight remained stable. Little change in the plasma glucose level was noted, but plasma insulin levels fell significantly as determined by oral glucose tolerance testing (Fig 1–19). The fasting plasma glucose value did not change during exercise training; there was some decrease in the fasting level of insulin. Total cholesterol and triglyceride levels declined during training, with a decrease in very-low-density lipoprotein (VLDL)-cholesterol. The high-density lipoprotein (HDL)-cholesterol level increased insignificantly with training, but the HDL-cholesterol/total cholesterol ratio rose to near significance. Insulin-mediated glucose uptake improved after training, with no significant change in the steady-state plasma insulin value.

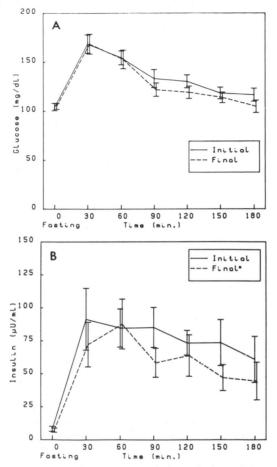

**Fig 1–19.**—*A*, Concentrations of glucose and *B*, insulin during the first oral glucose tolerance test and the final one. (Mean ± SEM). *Significant (P < 0.01) reduction following exercise training by one way repeated measures ANOVA.) (Courtesy of Lampman, R.M., et al.: Metabolism 34:205–211, March 1985.)

Exercise training is a potent means of reducing the plasma triglyceride levels in sedentary, mildly hyperlipidemic middle-aged men. Insulin-mediated glucose disposal is enhanced at the same time. The insulin response to orally administered glucose is reduced with no change in glucose tolerance. The level of VLDL-triglyceride is decreased, and the ratio of HDL-cholesterol to total cholesterol is favorably altered.

▶ HDL-cholesterol ratio was favorably improved in the direction of elevated HDL-C following exercise. Note the difference in the study group, however. These are middle-aged men with known hypertriglyceridemia. The VLDL-triglycerides were favorably altered in a downward direction, at a level of statistical significance. I think this is the consensus in the literature that has assessed lipid elevations in subjects exposed to exercise training. This present group may be the more valid, correlating as it does with the general population.

The obvious question is, is exercise beneficial for mild elevations of lipids? (This is a common circumstance in the American population, particularly with regard to the male at risk.) The paper confirms earlier work that indicated an inverse association between high-density lipoprotein cholesterol and total triglyceride concentrations.

Note that a threshold of approximately 8 to 10 miles of running per week for an extended training period, is necessary to bring about such beneficial numbers in the low- and high-density lipoprotein concentrations. This raises the problem of compliance for a significant portion of society. The relevance is clear for middle-aged men with hyperlipidemia.—Lewis J. Krakauer, M.D., F.A.C.P.

---

### Oxidation and Metabolic Effects of Fructose or Glucose Ingested Before Exercise

J. Décombaz, D. Sartori, M.-J. Arnaud, A.-L. Thélin, P. Schürch, and H. Howald (Nestec Ltd., Vevey, Switzerland, and Research Inst. of the Swiss School for Physical Education and Sports, Magglingen, Switzerland)
Int. J. Sports Med. 6:282–286, October 1985                    1–42

---

The extent to which hypoglycemia can affect performance is uncertain, but D-fructose has been recommended as an alternative to glucose as an energy substrate because it is rapidly metabolized and does not induce insulin release. The oxidation of ingested fructose and that of glucose were compared in 10 trained cyclists with a mean age of 25 years who exercised twice after ingesting each sugar at an interval of at least 1 week. Mean peak oxygen uptake was 62 ml per minute per kg. Test solutions were ingested in a dose of 1 gm/kg after overnight fasting, and subjects exercised 1 hour later for 60 minutes on a cycle ergometer, at 61% of maximal oxygen uptake for 45 minutes and then at the maximum level for 15 minutes.

No subject had a fall in blood glucose concentration to less than 3.4 mmole/L after glucose intake. Glucose and insulin concentrations were more stable after fructose ingestion; glucose values rose only during exercise. There were no treatment-related effects on uric acid, glucagon, or lactate values. Respiratory quotients did not differ significantly. Ninety percent of muscle glycogen was utilized in both groups. Work production varied widely, but it was unrelated to treatment. As much ingested fructose as glucose was utilized in the 2 hours after intake.

Fructose was utilized at least as well as glucose during cycle ergometer exercise in this study, when ingested 1 hour before exercise. More-stable glycemia resulted, and performance was unaffected. Moderate amounts of fructose may be useful in insulin-dependent diabetics who perform endurance exercise.

▶ While some authors have pointed with alarm to the insulin production stimulated by a pre-competitive ingestion of glucose, others have argued that the working muscle is still able to utilize glucose because the insulin not only causes hypoglycemia but is also having a permissive effect with respect to glucose uptake and oxidation (Berger M., et al.: *Diabete Metabol.* 6:59, 1980). The present results show that there is no difference in the rate of muscle glycogen utilization between fructose and glucose experiments, supporting the second viewpoint. On the other hand, the blood glucose level is more stable with fructose ingestion. This may be an advantage not only for the insulin-dependent diabetic, but also for the athlete who must make difficult judgments during exercise (for example, the dinghy sailor; see Niinimaa V., et al.: *J. Sports Med. Phys. Fitness* 17:83, 1977).—Roy J. Shephard, M.D., Ph.D.

---

**Serum Hormones During Prolonged Training of Neuromuscular Performance**
Keijo Häkkinen, Arto Pakarinen, Markku Alén, and Paavo V. Komi (Univ. of Jyväskylä and Univ. of Oulu, Finland)
Eur. J. Appl. Physiol. 53:287–293, 1985                                   1–43

---

The effects of 24 weeks of progressive training of neuromuscular performance capacity on maximal strength and on hormone balance were studied periodically in 21 male subjects (mean age, 26.3 years) during the course of training and during a subsequent detraining period of 12 weeks. Group A (11 subjects) participated in heavy resistance strength training and group B (10 subjects) participated three times a week in controlled strength training, which included various jumping exercises performed without extra load and with light extra weights.

Experimental group A gained significantly $(P < .05)$ in body mass during the 24-week strength training, whereas there were no changes in this parameter in group B or in controls (8 healthy volunteers). Percentage of body fat decreased during the experimental training both in group A *(P*

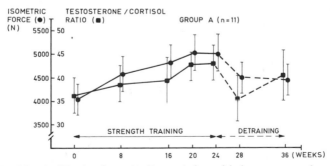

**Fig 1–20.**—Mean (± SE) values for maximal isometric force of the leg extensor muscles and for serum testosterone/cortisol ratio of the experimental group A during the course of the 24-week strength training and the 12-week detraining periods. (Courtesy of Häkkinen, K., et al.: Eur. J. Appl. Physiol. 53:287–293, 1985.)

< .05) and group B (*P* < .01), and there was no change in this variable for controls. Maximal isometric leg extension force increased during the 24-week strength training in group A (*P* < .001) and in group B (*P* < .05). In group A, a mean serum cortisol level decrease (*P* < .01) was observed after the 24-week training period. Mean serum testosterone level did not change after 24-weeks of training. Figure 1–20 shows the serum testosterone/cortisol ratio, which increased during training and decreased during detraining. In group B mean serum cortisol level decreased, but not significantly, after training, and there was a significant increase in serum testosterone level after 8 and 16 weeks of training. During the last 4 weeks of training for group A, significant correlations were observed betv een the changes in testosterone/cortisol ratio and the change in maximal isometric force (*P* < .01). This was also observed for group B (*P* < .01).

The present findings suggest the importance of the balance between androgenic-anabolic activity and the catabolizing effects of glucocorticoids during the course of hard strength training.

▶ A few years ago, Sidney and Shephard (*Can. J. Appl. Sport Sci.* 2:189, 1977) noted that in elderly subjects the exercise-stimulated increase of growth hormone secretion was enhanced by training; they speculated that in this age group a lessening of androgen secretion weakened anabolic processes, creating a greater need for growth hormone during exercise. Certainly, it is well recognized that vigorous exercise stimulates not only a strengthening of the active muscles, but a loss of lean tissue in inactive regions of the body.

The above digest takes up this theme, demonstrating the importance of the ratio of the anabolic hormone (testosterone) to the catabolic (cortisol), and showing also the importance that testosterone be in the free form (because the development of strength is influenced by the concentration ratio of testosterone relative to its binding protein). It is worth commenting that, at least during the first 16 weeks of strength training, the body produces its own increment of testosterone. However, this increase is not apparent when pretest and posttest comparisons are made over a longer period; this may account for some earlier negative reports concerning the influence of strength training on testosterone levels (i.e., Young et al., *Br. J. Sports Med.* 10:230, 1976, and Hetrick and Wilmore: *Med. Sci. Sports* 11:102, 1979).—Roy J. Shephard, M.D., Ph.D.

---

**Energy Metabolism During the Postexercise Recovery in Man**
R. Bielinski, Y. Schutz, and E. Jéquier (Univ. of Lausanne, Switzerland)
Am. J. Clin. Nutr. 42:69–82, July 1985                                    1–44

---

To study the magnitude and duration of the long-term residual effect of physical exercise, a mixed meal (55% carbohydrate (CHO), 27% fat, and 18% protein) was given to 10 young male volunteers (mean age, 21.8 years) on two occasions: after a 4-hour resting period and on the next day, 30 minutes after completion of a 3-hour exercise at 50% $Vo_{2max}$.

Energy expenditure and substrate utilization were determined by indirect calorimetry for 17 hours after meal ingestion.

During the control period (day 1), baseline (premeal) energy expenditure was 1.35 kcal/minute. Consumption of the test meal induced an increase in energy expenditure. When net increase in energy expenditure during the 5-hour postprandial phase on day 1 was related to energy content of the meal, postprandial thermogenesis was found to be 10.5%, or an increase averaging 32.8% over the premeal baseline. On day 2, during the exercise, energy expenditure increased progressively. In the postexercise postmeal period, significantly greater energy expenditure values were obtained than in the control period. There was a progressive decrease to 1.81 kcal/minute, 4.5 hours after consumption of the test meal. Cumulated energy expenditure was 9% greater ($P < .05$) on the exercise day than on the control day. Time course of energy expenditure during the late recovery period showed no significant difference in energy expenditure during the evening and during the sleep period between the two days. During the exercise itself (day 2), heart rate increased after onset of exercise. During the afternoon the postexercise heart rate decreased continuously. During the entire 4.5 hours postprandial period, all the values were significantly more elevated during day 2 than during day 1 ($P < .005$). Ingestion of the meal (day 1) increased the respiratory quotient (RQ). Mean RQ during the exercise period rose but had a sharp decrease 90 minutes after onset of exercise ($P < .05$). Eighteen hours after cessation of exercise, RQ during postabsorptive state was still lower ($P < .001$) as compared without exercise. Figure 1–21 shows, during premeal baseline period, 16% of energy expenditure was from CHO oxidation, 62% from fat, and 22% from

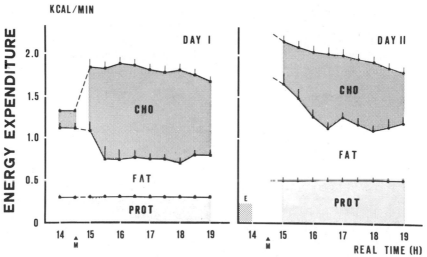

Fig 1–21.—Proportion of substrates oxidized before and after the test meal (M) (Mean ± SEM). *Black square,* day 1 = control day. *Black circle,* day 2 = exercise day. Prot = protein, CHO = carbohydrate. (Courtesy of Bielinski, R., et al.: Am. J. Clin. Nutr. 42:69–82, July 1985.)

protein. The meal induced a large increase in CHO oxidation. There was a significantly greater CHO storage ($P < .001$) after exercise and a lower fat storage ($P < .005$) as compared with the control day. On day 2 (exercise) postprandial plasma glucose had a higher peak and a delayed return to baseline values. The significantly elevated glucagonemia found at the end of the exercise showed a rapid return to control values. On day 2 there was a significant increase in nitrogen excretion only during postexercise.

The main implication of the present study is that the postexercise energy expenditure was moderately stimulated over 4 to 5 hours, as well as during resting metabolic rate on the following day. This rise in energy expenditure was accompanied by a marked and continuous stimulation of lipid oxidation for at least 18 hours. These results emphasize the long-lasting metabolic effect of an acute bout of exercise.

▶ This paper provides evidence supporting the suggestion of Pavlou et al. (Digest 1–51) that exercise has a prolonged stimulatory effect upon metabolism that can be exploited in the control of obesity. Possible explanations of the increased metabolism include the costs of refilling glycogen stores and synthesizing protein, increased cycling of body constituents, hormonal changes, and a persistent elevation of body temperature.—Roy J. Shephard, M.D., Ph.D.

### Responses of Endurance-Trained Subjects to Caloric Deficits Induced by Diet or Exercise
Robert G. McMurray, Victor Ben-Ezra, William A. Forsythe, and Ann T. Smith (Univ. of North Carolina at Chapel Hill)
Med. Sci. Sports Exerc. 17:574–579, October 1985                    1–45

Dieting alone results in substantial protein loss, but exercise stimulates protein synthesis and may forestall protein wasting and maintain lean body mass while fat stores decline. The effects of an exercise-induced caloric deficit on weight loss and physiologic responses to exercise were compared with those of diet alone in 6 healthy, endurance-trained subjects, aged 20 to 31 years, with an average body fat content of 11%. All were involved in vigorous training, but were not actively competing in sports. A daily diet of 35 kcal/kg was given in the control week. The next week, subjects exercised enough to use 15 kcal/kg daily. Exercise was about 80% running but also included bicycling, swimming, and racquetball. A daily diet of 20 kcal/kg subsequently was given, and exercise was discontinued.

Nitrogen balance at different phases of the study is shown in the table. Weight loss during exercise was significantly less than with dietary restriction alone. Resting Hc and plasma levels of protein and albumin were significantly reduced during the exercise period. Maximal exercise capacity did not change significantly. Plasma lactate levels were significantly lower during the exercise and diet weeks than during the control week.

The use by trained persons of extensive exercise to lose weight can result in less weight loss than would be expected with dietary restriction. The

RESULTS OF 24-HOUR URINALYSIS IN THREE PHASES
OF STUDY*

| | Control | Exercise | Diet |
|---|---|---|---|
| Urine output † (l·d⁻¹) | 1.22 ± 0.15 | 1.05 ± 0.22 | 2.02 ± 0.37 |
| Ketones | 0 | Trace | Trace |
| Urea nitrogen † (mg·100 ml⁻¹) | 5.43 ± 0.49 | 5.78 ± 0.37 | 6.77 ± 0.40 |
| Nitrogen balance † (g·wk⁻¹) | −8.46 ± 1.90 ‡ | −11.10 ± 3.00 § | −24.50 ± 2.10 |

*Values are expressed as mean ± SE.
†Difference between diet and control or exercise weeks was significant ($P < .05$).
‡Difference between exercise and diet or control weeks was significant ($P < .05$).
§Nitrogen balance was negative on days 1–5 but neutral by day 7.
(Courtesy of McMurray, R.G., et al.: Med. Sci. Sports Exerc. 17:574–579, October 1985. Copyright 1985, the American College of Sports Medicine. Reprinted by permission.)

latter, however, may lead to a greater loss of lean body mass, which, if sustained, will ultimately reduce work capacity. A combination of diet and exercise seems optimal, reducing weight while maintaining lean body mass. Dieting for 1 week without exercise does not impair short-term exercise performance or reduce maximal aerobic capacity.

▶ This article further reinforces the point made by Pavlou et al. (Digest 1–51) that a 1,000 kcal (4.2 MJ) daily energy deficit brought about by exercise induces less loss of lean tissue than an equal energy deficit produced by dieting alone. The period of observation is very short (7 days), and much of the observed change in body mass could reflect fluid shifts rather than permanent weight loss. Nevertheless, a significant difference in nitrogen balance is demonstrated between the two types of treatment.

One interesting finding is that the exercised group showed a substantial decrease of plasma protein relative to both controls and dieted subjects; the authors link this finding to an early suggestion that the plasma provides a labile reserve of protein during protein deficiency (Yamaji, J.: *Physiol. Soc. Japan* 13:483, 1951), although it is a little surprising to see a "deficiency response" with a daily protein intake of 1 g/kg. Possibly, those who argue that active subjects need a larger protein intake than 1 g/kg are right!—Roy J. Shephard, M.D., Ph.D.

---

**Oxygen Uptake in Exercising Subjects With Minimal Renal Disease**
Alvin E. Parrish, Mary Zikria, and Richard A. Kenney (George Washington Univ.)
Nephron 40:455–457, August 1985                                    1–46

---

Patients with varying degrees of renal failure were studied for their blood lactate response to exercise on either a treadmill or a cycle ergometer. The

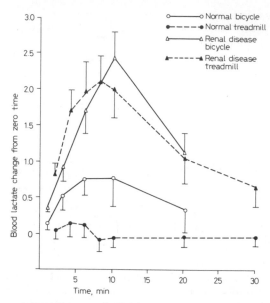

Fig 1–22.—Change in blood lactate (μmol/dl) during exercise for normal subjects and subjects with renal disease. The plots are for both bicycle and treadmill exercise. (Courtesy of Parrish, A.E., et al.: Nephron 40:455–457, August 1985. Reproduced with permission of S. Karger AG, Basel.)

cycle study was undertaken to obtain a more uniform exercise to study oxygen uptake. Eleven subjects with renal disease and 4 normal individuals were studied in the treadmill studies. Subjects with renal disease were undergoing regular hemodialysis for 4 hours three times a week. In the cycle studies, 7 normal and 5 renal disease subjects were observed. The subjects with renal disease included 3 with functioning renal allografts and 2 with chronic graft rejection.

Initial and all subsequent blood alanine levels in the experimental subjects were lower than in the control normal subjects ($P < .01$). Blood lactate, however, rose (Fig 1–22) as has been previously reported. In the cycle study, at an increase in pulse rate of 25% over resting levels, subjects with renal disease had an oxygen uptake that was not significantly different from nonrenal disease subjects. This degree of exercise was accompanied by an increase in blood lactate in renal disease subjects (Fig 1–22) but not in normal control subjects ($P < .01$) and was similar to previous findings. The increase in serum lactate occurred in these patients even though they were asymptomatic and had normal to low serum creatinine levels.

These findings suggest that the increased blood lactate observed in the patients with kidney disease during exercise is not due to muscle anoxia. It could be interpreted that, in renal disease of even a minimal degree, there is a decreased metabolism of pyruvate by the citric acid cycle with a resulting increase in lactate formation, but that this is unaccompanied by an increase in serum alanine levels at this level of exercise.

► In renal disease, even minimal exercise causes a rise of blood lactate, and this has been attributed to muscle anoxia (Parrish: *Clin. Nephrol.* 16:135, 1981). In this report, both normal subjects and those with renal disease were exercised to about the same level of oxygen intake (15–16 ml/kg/min). The authors hypothesized that if hypoxia were responsible for the high lactate readings in the patients, they should have seen an oxygen deficit and an accumulation of alanine, neither of which occurred. Since the normal subjects were students and hospital staff, it is likely that they were much fitter than the renal patients, and I think this is the most probable explanation of the greater lactate accumulation observed in the clinical material. The curves for the patients are essentially what would be seen in a normal person at a higher fraction of maximum oxygen intake (about 60%). They reflect an initial inadequate perfusion of the muscle, but later balance between oxygen demand and supply as the vessels dilate and blood pressure rises. Blood pressures were not reported, but it is conceivable that the renal disease could also have modified the cardiovascular response to exercise, and thus muscle perfusion.—Roy J. Shephard, M.D., Ph.D.

---

**Urinary Excretion of Electrolytes During Prolonged Physical Activity in Normal Man**
P. Lijnen, P. Hespel, E. Vanden Eynde, and A. Amery (Univ. of Louvain, Belgium)
Eur. J. Appl. Physiol. 53:317–321, February 1985                                    1–47

---

   Conflicting reports concerning the effects of physical exercise on urinary electrolyte excretion have appeared. Electrolyte excretion was examined in 9 normal men, average age 23 years, during 2 days of relative rest, 2 days of physical training, and another 2 days of relative rest. No dietary changes were made. They participated in 3 daily exercise sessions of bicycling, outdoor circuit training, and jogging. A 50-km bicycle ride was completed in about 90 minutes at an average speed of 33 km/hour. The running distance of the last 12-minute run averaged 2,633 m.

   Sodium and potassium excretion was lower during exercise days, whereas urinary aldosterone excretion was increased. The excretion rate of creatinine, calcium, and magnesium was similar on exercise days and rest days. The hemoglobin and hematocrit values and red blood cell count were decreased within 14 hours and 42 hours after exercise. The serum level of bilirubin was increased. Plasma renin activity and levels of angiotensin II and aldosterone were increased within 14 hours after exercise, but baseline values were present at 42 hours.

   The effect of recent exercise must be taken into account when interpreting the results of certain laboratory tests. In the present study, sodium and potassium excretion, the hemoglobin value, plasma renin activity, and levels of angiotensin II and aldosterone all were altered in normal persons in relation to exercise.

▶ The literature contains conflicting reports with regard to electrolyte variability after exercise. This is important in terms of inappropriate use of electrolyte supplementation, pointed out in the 1983 YEAR BOOK OF SPORTS MEDICINE, pp. 37–38 with reference to a benchmark article by Costill, et al. To quote from the comment appended to that article: "From the practical point of view, the main lesson seems to be that the body is equipped with a good potassium regulator in the kidneys." The same comment, I think, would pertain to the renin-angiotensin system. We must have reservations about establishing a true steady state before conclusions can be drawn regarding the impact of exercise on any aspect of urinary electrolytes.—Lewis J. Krakauer, M.D., F.A.C.P.

### Effects of Exogenous Catecholamines and Exercise on Plasma Magnesium Concentrations
H. Joborn, G. Åkerström, and S. Ljunghall (Univ. of Uppsala, Sweden)
Clin. Endocrinol. (Oxf.) 23:219–226, September 1985                    1–48

The effects of infused catecholamines, with and without β-blockade, on plasma magnesium concentrations were examined in healthy men with a mean age of 30 years. Six subjects received epinephrine infusions, 5 in conjunction with β-blockade with propranolol. Six subjects received norepinephrine at infusion rates of 1 to 3 μg per minute for 20-minute periods. The effects of exercise were studied in 10 subjects, 4 of whom performed maximal bicycle exercise with and without β-blockade. Isokinetic testing was used to assess the effects of maximal muscular work.

The plasma magnesium concentration declined with the highest infusion rate of epinephrine of 10 μg per minute, with no significant change in urinary magnesium excretion. No significant change occurred with norepinephrine infusion. β-Blockade prevented the fall in plasma magensium concentration induced by epinephrine infusion. The plasma magnesium concentration increased with short-term exercise at a near-maximal level (Fig 1–23), as did plasma sodium and albumin concentrations. No significant change in the magnesium value occurred during an hour of bicycle exercise, but the concentration fell during recovery. Plasma magnesium concentration was increased on short-term, intensive exercise; plasma volume was reduced.

β-Adrenergic stimulation appears to reduce the plasma magnesium concentration, as does long-term exercise, whereas maximal exercise increases the concentration. Magnesium homeostasis is influenced by both the β-adrenergic system and muscular activity. The rise in plasma magnesium concentration that accompanies short-term exercise may reflect a decreased plasma volume and an influx of magnesium into the vascular pool.

▶ Hypomagnesemia has attracted increasing attention as a possible precipitating cause of cardiac arrhythmias and myocardial infarction (Dyckner T.: *Acta Med. Scand.* 207:59, 1980). Exercise can influence the situation in several fashions. In a hot climate, there can be an appreciable loss of magnesium ions in the sweat. A decrease of plasma volume and an efflux of magnesium from the working muscle tends to increase plasma magnesium levels, at least acutely. If exercise is sufficiently stressful to increase circulating adrenaline,

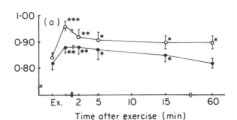

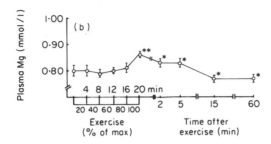

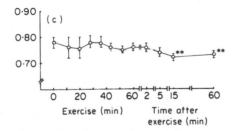

Fig 1–23.—**a,** Effects of maximal exercise *(Ex.),* with *(solid circles)* and without *(open circles)* propranolol, on plasma magnesium concentrations (*n* = 4). **b,** Effects of stepwise increases in exercise loads on plasma magnesium concentrations (*n* = 7). **c,** Effects of 1-hour exercise (at about 65% of maximum capacity) on plasma magnesium concentrations (*n* = 4). Means ± SEM are given. Single asterisks indicate $P < .05$, double asterisks $P < .01$, and triple asterisks $P < .001$, compared with zero values. (Courtesy of Joborn, H., et al.: Clin. Endocrinol. [Oxf.] 23:219–226, September 1985.)

this may reduce plasma magnesium levels, particularly during the recovery period.

Normally, reserves of magnesium are quite large. Thus, a clinically significant hypomagnesemia would not be anticipated, except with repeated bouts of exercise in a very hot climate, possibly coupled with a magnesium-deficient water supply.—Roy J. Shephard, M.D., Ph.D.

## Plasma Adrenaline and Noradrenaline During Mental Stress and Isometric Exercise in Man: The Role of Arterial Sampling

Lars Stig Jörgensen, Lars Bönlökke, and N. J. Christensen (Aarhus Kommunehospital, Orthopedic Hosp., Aarhus, and Herlev Hosp., Denmark)

Scand. J. Clin. Lab. Invest. 45:447–452, September 1985 1–49

Tissue extraction of catecholamines may complicate the interpretation of studies of their concentrations in forearm venous blood samples as reflecting sympathoadrenal activity. Arterial and venous plasma catecholamine concentrations were measured at rest and during isometric exercise and mental stress in 5 men and 3 women whose median age was 29 years and who had orthopedic disorders or slight dyspepsia. Isometric work was done by using a hand exercise, and an arithmetic test was administered.

Arterial epinephrine concentration increased significantly during isometric exercise. Extraction of epinephrine from arterial blood rose from 42% at rest to 61% on exercise in the resting arm, but it was nearly constant in the exercising arm. Venous epinephrine concentration also rose more on exercise in the exercising forearm than in the resting extremity. Venous and arterial norepinephrine concentrations were nearly unchanged in both arms during exercise, but the venous value was significantly increased in the resting arm 5 minutes after exercise. The epinephrine concentration increased significantly during mental stress in both arterial and

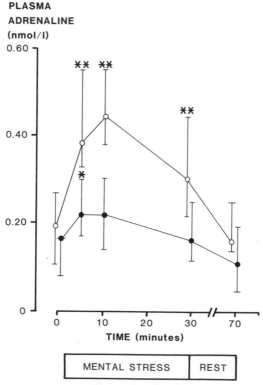

Fig 1–24.—Plasma epinephrine *(adrenaline)* concentrations in arterial *(open circles)* and venous *(solid circles)* blood during mental stress test. Median values and first and third quartiles are indicated. Plasma epinephrine concentrations increased significantly in both arterial $(P < .01)$ and venous $(P < .05)$ blood. Single asterisk indicates significant increment at $P < .05$ from pretest value, and double asterisks indicate significant increments at $P < .01$ from pretest value. (Courtesy of Jörgensen, L.S., et al.: Scand. J. Clin. Lab. Invest. 45:447–452, September 1985.)

venous blood (Fig 1–24). Venous norepinephrine values tended to decrease during mental stress, whereas arterial concentrations were unchanged.

A substantial increase in plasma epinephrine concentration is observed during both isometric exercise and mental stress, whereas arterial plasma norepinephrine concentration is unchanged. It seems best to measure arterial epinephrine concentration as an indicator of sympathoadrenal activity. A selective increase in the arterial epinephrine value may indicate a preferential increase in sympathoadrenal activity in visceral organs. Sympathetic activity to the heart and splanchnic region may be increased during exercise and mental stress, but these areas contribute little to the circulating norepinephrine concentration.

▶ It is easier to collect venous than arterial blood specimens, and in consequence many responses to physical activity have been examined in venous blood. However, this can give rise to misleading information, because time is required for the blood to pass through the peripheral capillary bed, and the substance to be assayed may be added to or removed from the blood as the capillaries are traversed.

This paper stresses not only a considerable extraction of catecholamines in the peripheral tissues (Hilsted J., et al.: *J. Clin. Invest.* 71:500, 1983), but that such extraction is modified during exercise, leading to differences of venous concentrations between an exercising and a resting arm.

The catecholamine response to isometric exercise differs from that seen during dynamic exercise, when both adrenaline and noradrenaline concentrations are increased. Jörgensen et al. suggest that this may reflect an increase in sympathetic discharge to the viscera as opposed to the skeletal muscles.— Roy J. Shephard, M.D., Ph.D.

---

**Age-Related Augmentation of Plasma Catecholamines During Dynamic Exercise in Healthy Males**
Jerome L. Fleg, Stephen P. Tzankoff, and Edward G. Lakatta (Natl. Inst. on Aging, Baltimore, Md.)
J. Appl. Physiol. 59:1033–1039, October 1985                    1–50

---

Enhanced norepinephrine (NE) responses to various stimuli in older persons may represent true augmentation of sympathetic nervous activity or merely exposure to greater stresses. Relations among age, circulating catecholamine levels, and $Vo_2$ during aerobic stress were examined in 24 healthy men, aged 22 to 77 years, who had no evidence of cardiovascular disease on careful assessment and had normal ECG responses to maximal treadmill exercise. Most subjects walked on a treadmill at 3.5 mph at an increasing incline to the point of exhaustion. Seven of the subjects were aged 65 years or older.

Systolic blood pressure at rest increased with advancing age, but remained within the normotensive range. Plasma epinephrine (E) concentrations at rest were increased in the oldest subjects. Heart rate increased linearly as exercise progressed, and plasma NE and E levels increased

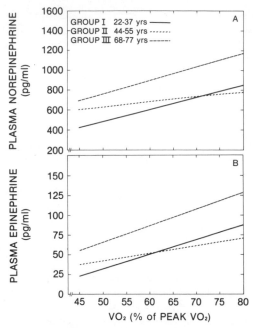

**Fig 1–25.**—Plasma norepinephrine (NE) and epinephrine (E) concentrations plotted as a function of relative effort (% of maximal $\dot{V}O_2$) at submaximal work loads between 45% and 80% of peak $\dot{V}O_2$ for 3 age groups. **Panel A,** by analysis of covariance, plasma NE concentration was seen to be augmented with age for given relative effort ($F = 5.41, P < .014$). **Panel B,** plasma E level also tended to be higher in older male subjects, although this difference did not reach statistical significance ($F = 2.77, P = .09$). (Courtesy of Fleg, J.L., et al.: J. Appl. Physiol. 59:1033–1039, October 1985.)

exponentially. Concentrations of both catecholamines were higher in the oldest subjects, but only the difference in NE was significant. Catecholamine levels were higher in the oldest subjects when effects were compared at submaximal work loads (Fig 1–25). Catecholamine levels rose above peak exercise levels during recovery in all age groups.

The exercise-mediated rise in plasma catecholamine levels appears to be exaggerated in elderly men during both submaximal and maximal treadmill exercise, even after normalization for relative effort. Age-related differences in exercise cardiovascular performance seem related, at least in part, to decreased target organ responsiveness to adrenergic stimulation.

▶ Although the sample size is fairly small, the results show that at any given percentage of maximum effort, the plasma levels of epinephrine and norepinephrine are about one third higher in the elderly. While the authors incline to the belief that a diminished sensitivity to catecholamines is responsible for this reaction, they are careful to point out that a slower plasma clearance of the type described by Esler (*Clin. Sci.* 60:217, 1981) could also be involved.

Although the heart rate response to a given catecholamine level drops with aging, it is less clear that the heart is protected against arrhythmias; more research is needed on the relationship of rhythm disturbances to plasma catecholamine levels.—Roy J. Shephard, M.D., Ph.D.

## Effects of Dieting and Exercise on Lean Body Mass, Oxygen Uptake, and Strength

Konstantin N. Pavlou, William P. Steffee, Robert H. Lerman, and Belton A. Burrows (Boston Univ.)

Med. Sci. Sports Exerc. 17:466–471, August 1985          1–51

Safe and effective programs for weight reduction still are needed. Most present programs emphasize weight loss rather than the nature of the tissue lost. The effects of dieting and exercise on lean body mass, oxygen uptake, and strength were studied in 72 mildly obese men, aged 26 to 52 years, who had an average of 38% body fat (21% above ideal body weight). Subjects were randomly assigned to four restricted dietary regimens and to exercised and nonexercised groups. Aerobic exercise was performed at 70%–85% of maximal heart rate, 3 days a week for 8 weeks, along with calisthenics. Overall dietary intake averaged about 800 kcal daily.

Lean body mass, determined by the $^{40}K$ method, decreased in the non-exercised group but did not change significantly in exercising subjects. Total body fat decreased significantly in both groups, but the reduction was much greater in the exercised group. Total energy loss was nearly twice as great in the exercised subjects. Posttreatment mean maximal $Vo_2$ increased 20% in the exercised group and did not change significantly in the nonexercised group. Quadriceps strength increased by 22% in the exercised group, and declined by 3% in the nonexercised group.

Addition of a progressive exercise program to a weight-reducing dietary regimen helps preserve lean body mass and increase $Vo_2$ and muscle strength. Fat utilization for energy production is increased, and fat stores are reduced more effectively than with diet alone. Further work is needed to determine the factors responsible for maintaining an elevated thermogenic effect after activity ceases.

▶ Clinical conferences still speak more of weight loss than of fat loss, and the authors are right to stress the importance of considering the nature of the tissue to be removed by a dietary regimen.

This experiment had a good sample size and was nicely designed, but the period of treatment was rather short. Exercise is essentially a long-term method of achieving fat loss, and a much greater benefit might have been seen over a longer period. Moreover, there would have then been a chance to assess the relative adherence to the several regimens.

Nevertheless, the 8-week fat loss for the exercised group (as estimated from a potassium 40 determination of lean mass) is impressive (11.2 kg), particularly when it is noted that the exercised group did not lose lean tissue at the same time. The benefit was larger than would have been anticipated merely from the immediate exercise performed (this would have added a loss of only about 1.5 kg to the effect of diet alone) and the authors postulated that there may have been a more prolonged stimulation of resting metabolism by exercise. It is not easy to estimate fat from lean body mass data, particularly when drastic dieting may have altered tissue potassium levels, and it would be interesting to repeat these experiments with an alternative method of estimating body fat.—Roy J. Shephard, M.D., Ph.D.

### Per Cent Body Fat Alone Is a Poor Predictor of Physical Fitness

Michael C. Slack, Earl W. Ferguson, and Guy Banta (Uniformed Services Univ. of the Health Sciences, Bethesda, Md.)
Military Med. 150:211–214, April 1985                                1–52

An inverse relationship between percent body fat and maximal oxygen consumption has been described. This correlation was examined in a controlled prospective study of 62 healthy adult males, age 19–59 years, none of whom smoked. Twenty subjects ran more than 50 miles a week, 22 were joggers who ran 5–15 miles a week, and 20 took no regular exercise. Percent body fat was calculated from seven skinfold thickness measurements, and maximal oxygen uptake was measured directly during a multistaged treadmill test to maximal effort.

Percent body fat was significantly lower in the marathoners than in either joggers or sedentary subjects; comparable values were obtained in the latter groups. Considerable scatter was found when percent body fat was plotted against maximal oxygen uptake, and there was greater scatter when oxygen uptake was expressed in terms of lean body weight. Correlation between percent body fat and maximal oxygen consumption was poorest for the joggers.

Percent body fat should not be considered a primary factor in assessing physical fitness, although body fat standards may be important for maintaining a "military image." Some subjects may be fat and fit, and others lean and unfit. The former subjects can become much fitter by losing weight. However, there is wide variability in individual aerobic capacities, and this parameter depends on many factors.

▶ The prediction of the percentage of body fat is in vogue at this time. This also has been used by some, and inappropriately, as a predictor of physical fitness. The sense of this paper is summed up best by a direct quote of one sentence from the authors' summary: "There is no substitute for direct aerobic performance testing in the evaluation of physical fitness."—Lewis J. Krakauer, M.D., F.A.C.P.

### Accuracy of Anthropometric Equations for Estimating Body Composition in Female Athletes

J. L. Mayhew, B. A. Clark, B. C. McKeown, and D. H. Montaldi (Northeast Missouri State Univ., Univ. of Missouri at St. Louis, and South Dakota State Univ., and Kirksville Osteopathic Hosp., Kirksville, Mo.)
J. Sports Med. 25:120–126, September 1985                                1–53

Participation by women in high-caliber competition makes it important to delineate relevant performance and health variables. With increasing concern over optimal playing weight, large errors in estimates of body fatness could endanger the athlete's career and health. Data from 111 college women athletes representing seven sports were used to assess the accuracy of existing anthropometric prediction equations for estimating body composition. Twenty-four anthropometric measures were recorded, and hydrostatic weighing was carried out.

Validity coefficients ranging from .61 to .75 were obtained. The most satisfactory equations were the Jackson-Pollock generalized formula and three population-specific athletic formulas. Fat weight and lean body mass prediction equations were less accurate than density prediction equations in estimating percent fat. A curvilinear relationship was found between sum of skin fold thicknesses and body density.

Existing equations, though possessing validity, may underestimate density in lean women athletes. This, combined with attempts to reach minimal fat levels established in samples of elite athletes, could lead to inappropriate dietary and exercise prescriptions. Caution is in order when using predictive equations to establish optimal playing weight for women athletes.

▶ Anyone who uses percent body fat measurements must know that they are merely estimates and not exact. Therefore, it would be inappropriate to set fat levels at the low end of the scale and expect athletes to reach those levels merely because some elite athletes are reported to have done so. Although the investigation used 13 equations and hydrostatic weighing in this study, one method they did not use is visual observation and estimation. Sterner from West Point showed that visual estimation is as accurate as some prediction formulas. For athletes, coaches can be taught to visually estimate off times easier than some of the other methods. The requirement for accuracy for athletes is not the same as for laboratory or clinical measurements. It is doubtful that more than visual estimation is needed.—Col. James L. Anderson, PE.D.

**Effect of Physical Exercise and Sleep Deprivation on Plasma Androgen Levels: Modifying Effect on Physical Fitness**
K. Remes, K. Kuoppasalmi, and H. Adlercreutz (Univ. of Helsinki)
Int. J. Sports Med. 6:131–135, June 1985                                    1–54

Intense physical exercise is associated with a fall in plasma androgen. The possible modifying effects of fitness and sleep deprivation on plasma androgen responses to long-term exercise were studied in 22 recruits who had trained for a month in military service. A 21-km march was undertaken, with participants carrying a 20-kg pack. The march was repeated after a 4-month training period. Subgroups of subjects had initial mean maximal oxygen uptakes of 68 and 50 ml/kg/minute. About half of the subjects had an increase in maximal oxygen uptake after further training. Fourteen subjects had minimal sleep on two consecutive nights during military terrain activities.

Fit subjects had lesser decreases in plasma testosterone (T) at baseline and after marching (Fig 1–26). Relatively fit subjects tended to have lesser decreases in the T/SHBG (sex hormone binding globulin) ratio during both control and exercise days. After conditioning, the plasma testosterone and T/SHBG ratio decreased less on control and exercise days, especially in well-conditioned subjects. Exercise led to a fall in plasma luteinizing hormone (LH), especially in less fit subjects. Morning levels of testosterone

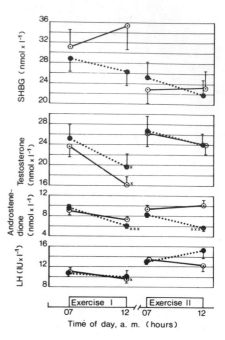

**Fig 1–26.**—Effect of submaximal 21-km marching exercise on plasma SHBG binding capacity, testosterone, androstenedione, and LH levels before (exercise I) and after 4 months of military training (exercise II) in the 11 army recruits participating in both exercises. *Solid line* = exercise; *dotted line* = respective normal day variation; [X]$P < .05$; [XXX]$P < .001$. (Courtesy of Remes, K., et al.: Int. J. Sports Med. 6:131–135, June 1985.)

and LH were depressed after sleep deprivation, abolishing the normal diurnal variation.

Unbalanced hormonal regulation in stress situations may be a significant finding in relation to exhaustion. In athletic training, chronic hormonal dysrhythmia may indicate lessened conditioning, a frequent problem in athletes participating in progressive high-intensity training.

▶ The trained organism or individual will maintain a more optimal hormonal balance, in this instance an unchanged or increased plasma testosterone level. However, if exercise is carried to excess, there will be prolonged depression of biologically active testosterone, coupled with a catabolic cortisol elevation. This combination is undesirable, and may be what is termed the overtrained state.

Plasma testosterone is very sensitive to sleep deprivation, particularly if in association with prolonged exercise of several days' duration. Whether sleep deprivation influences this depressed testosterone level via FSH mechanisms, or stress related impact on pituitary and adrenal axis, or via relationships to plasma prolactin, is not known. Overtraining has a physiologic and hormonal penalty. These data may be just the tip of the iceberg.—Lewis J. Krakauer, M.D., F.A.C.P.

---

**Fat Utilization Enhanced by Exercise in a Cold Environment**
Barbara A. Timmons, John Araujo, and Tom R. Thomas (Univ. of Kansas, Lawrence)
Med. Sci. Sports Exerc. 17:673–678, December 1985                    1–55

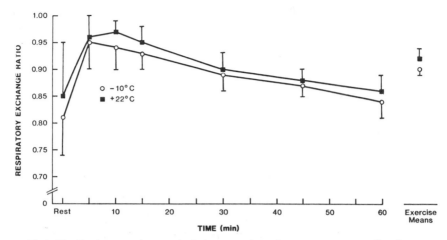

**Fig 1–27.**—Respiratory exchange ratio during rest and exercise at two temperatures. Exercise means were different between temperatures (F [1,6] = 5.51; $P < .05$); average ratio for both groups differed during exercise bout (F [5,30] = 33.59; $P < .05$), with average for both groups over last 30 minutes being significantly different from those at 5, 10, or 15 minutes ($P < .05$). Vertical bars indicate SD. (Courtesy of Timmons, B.A., et al.: Med. Sci. Sports Exerc. 17:673–678, December 1985. Copyright 1985, the American College of Sports Medicine. Reprinted by permission.)

Environmental temperature can influence the utilization of foodstuffs, and a lipolytic effect of exercise in cold temperatures has been indirectly documented. The effects of acute endurance exercise in the cold on fat utilization were studied in 7 male college students who were physically active and nonobese. Mean age was 28 years, and the mean body fat was 13.7%. Submaximal cycle exercise was performed at 22 C and in a climatic chamber at −10 C, in random order at an interval of 8 days or less. Subjects fasted for 12 hours before testing. Exercise was performed at 66% of maximum heart rate in both environmental conditions.

Average oxygen consumption was 56% greater at rest in the cold, and the exercise mean was 10% greater than under temperate conditions. The average respiratory exchange ratio was 2% lower during exercise in the cold (Fig 1–27), indicating increased use of fat as an energy source. The average rate of total energy expenditure was 10% greater during exercise in the cold, and the average rate of fat energy expenditure was 41% greater. In both environments, fat energy utilization increased significantly after 30 minutes of exercise. Total cumulative energy expenditure during 1 hour of exercise was 13% greater in the cold, and cumulative fat expenditure was 35% higher.

A cold environment can significantly enhance fat utilization during endurance exercise. The risks of frostbite and angina increase in the cold, however, and systemic blood pressure and myocardial oxygen consumption increase. It would be of interest to learn whether an enhanced caloric effect is obtained at lesser temperature reductions.

▶ The possibility that a combination of exercise plus cold exposure would enhance body fat loss was previously raised by W. O'Hara, et al. (*J. Appl. Physiol.*

46:872, 1979), and one sign of enhanced fat usage (a decrease of respiratory gas exchange ratio) has been demonstrated relative to exercise in a temperate-climate (Romet T., et al., *Med. Sci. Sports Exerc.* 15:156, 1983).

When considering the possible application of exercise in the cold to the clinical treatment of obesity, a critical question becomes the degree of cold exposure that is required. The subjects of O'Hara et al. wore arctic clothing, and were thus reasonably well protected against the climate, but in the present experiments subjects wore shorts, a T-shirt, and gym shoes at a temperature of -10 C. Though Timmons et al. demonstrated an increase of metabolism during the period of exercise, relative to temperate conditions, this was probably shivering in an attempt to restore core temperature. Unfortunately, no figures are given for the amount of cooling that developed over the 1-hour exposure period.—Roy J. Shephard, M.D., Ph.D.

---

### Muscle Metabolism During Exercise in the Heat in Unacclimatized and Acclimatized Humans
Douglas S. King, David L. Costill, William J. Fink, Mark Hargreaves, and Roger A. Fielding (Ball State Univ.)
J. Appl. Physiol. 59:1350–1354, November 1985                                1–56

---

Exercise in the heat has been found to lead to increased utilization of muscle glycogen, compared with exercise in the cold. The effects of heat acclimatization on utilization of muscle glycogen during prolonged submaximal exercise in the heat were studied in 10 healthy, untrained males, 2 of whom were engaged in heavy resistance training at the time of the study. Trials were conducted in the winter, when environmental temperatures were less than 7 C. Sprint exercise tests were performed on a cycle ergometer before and just after exposure to a temperature of 39.7 C at 31% relative humidity. Subjects exercised intermittently at 50% of maximal oxygen uptake for 6 hours and were reevaluated after 8 days of

MUSCLE GLYCOGEN (MEANS ± SE) AND pH BEFORE AND
AFTER 45-SECOND SPRINT EXERCISE TESTS*

| Sample | Sprint 1 | | Sprint 2 | |
|---|---|---|---|---|
| | Pre | Post | Pre | Post |
| Glycogen | | | | |
| UN | 131.7 ± 9.1 | 103.7 ± 9.2 | 46.6 ± 6.9 | 31.8 ± 5.8 |
| ACC | 131.1 ± 9.2 | 113.1 ± 4.5 | 80.1 ± 4.4† | 60.2 ± 4.7† |
| pH | | | | |
| UN | 7.15 | 6.67 | 7.12 | 6.86‡ |
| ACC | 7.14 | 6.73 | 7.17 | 6.77 |

*UN and ACC, unacclimatized and acclimatized trials, respectively. Sprints 1 and 2 refer to before and after 6-hour heat exercise test, respectively. Glycogen is expressed as mmole/kg wet weight; *n* = 9.
†Significantly different (*P* < .05) from UN trial.
‡Significantly different (*P* < .05) from sprint 1 UN trial.
(Courtesy of King, D.S., et al.: J. Appl. Physiol. 59:1350–1354, November 1985.)

acclimatization. Glycogen utilization was assessed by vastus lateralis muscle biopsy.

Mean resting plasma volume increased 9% during acclimatization. Maximal oxygen uptake was not altered. Mean muscle glycogen utilization during the heat-exercise test was lower after than before acclimatization (table). There were no significant changes in blood glucose, lactate, or respiratory exchange ratio values after heat acclimatization.

Heat acclimatization shifts fuel utilization during submaximal exercise in the heat so that muscle glycogen is spared. This effect may be related to an enhanced ability to exercise intensively after prolonged exertion in the heat. Acclimatization for about a week markedly reduced muscle glycogen utilization during prolonged exercise in the heat in normal males in this study. The subjects were better able to exercise vigorously after heat-exercise stress.

▶ This paper provides a nice foil to those on fat loss in the cold (Digest 1–55). The present authors earlier noted (Fink W.J., et al.: *Eur. J. Appl. Physiol.* 34:183, 1975) that people exercising in the heat used more glycogen than they would have done if they had been exercising in the cold. Evidence is given that acclimatization to heat reduces this effect.

The hot environment reduces blood flow to muscle (Rowell L.B.: *Physiol. Rev.* 54:75, 1974), and it might thus be thought that more of the work would be performed anaerobically. However, lactate levels were not very high even before heat acclimatization (3.64 mmole/L). Another possibility is that the reduced perfusion restricts delivery of metabolites to the working muscle, either glucose from the liver, or fat from the fat depots. After acclimatization to heat, there was no evidence of a shift in the relative usage of fat and carbohydrate. King et al. thus propose that the hepatic release of glucose was enhanced by the process of acclimatization, sparing glycogen reserves.—Roy J. Shephard, M.D., Ph.D.

---

**Exercise, Performance and Temperature Control: Temperature Regulation During Exercise and Implications for Sports Performance and Training**
Suzanne M. Fortney and Neil B. Vroman (Johns Hopkins Univ. and Univ. of New Hampshire)
Sports Med. 2:8–20, 1985                                                    1–57

---

Evolution of man in a tropical environment may account for his well-developed system of heat loss. Most naturally occurring ambient temperatures are tolerated, while the chief threat to thermoregulatory balance comes from exercise. A rising body temperature leads to inhibition of cutaneous vasomotor tone and increased sweat output. Blood flow is redistributed in several vascular beds during exercise, especially in a hot environment. Vasodilation in response to increased body temperature is an active process not reliant only on release of tonic sympathetic vasoconstrictor tone. The dependence of cutaneous blood flow on core temperature is attenuated on severe or prolonged exercise. Pre-existing hypovolemia significantly alters the skin blood flow response.

Respiratory water loss increased markedly during exercise. Evaporative loss accounts for about 20%–25% of total heat loss at rest under comfortable conditions. Sweat output is influenced by neural, hormonal, and mechanical factors. The chief efferent signal stimulating sweat production is sympathetic cholinergic output from the anterior hypothalamus. Specific ions and changes in blood or cerebrospinal fluid osmolality may affect sweat production. Mechanical block of sweat ducts by epidermal cell swelling may reduce the rate of sweating despite persistently elevated core and skin temperatures.

Physical training is thought to improve heat tolerance, but it may be difficult to distinguish the effects of training from heat acclimatization. Training improves thermoregulatory balance through both improved sweating and improved cutaneous perfusion. If exercise must be performed under adverse conditions, fluid intake should be encouraged and participants closely supervised to detect heat-related changes at an early stage.

▶ Thermoregulation is of considerable importance, not only in terms of athletic performance, but in terms of athlete safety. This article presents an excellent overview of the mechanisms by which body heat is dissipated in a given exercising individual placed in a hot environment. Important factors of nonthermal nature, such as changing blood volume and blood flow distribution, are discussed.

The authors' point is reiterated that *irrespective of training, only acclimatization programs are effective in preventing heat stress during prolonged exercise in hot environments.*—Lewis J. Krakauer, M.D., F.A.C.P.

---

**The Effect of Water Intake on Body Temperature During Rugby Matches**
C. Goodman, I. Cohen, and J. Walton (Univ. of the Witwatersrand, Johannesburg, South Africa)
S. Afr. Med. J. 67:542–544, April 6, 1985                                    1–58

---

The effect of drinking up to 1 liter of fluid on water deficit, sweat loss, and rectal temperature was determined during three separate rugby matches played in thermoneutral environments. Each player was allotted a liter of fluid and encouraged to drink 500 ml before the start of the game and an additional 500 ml at halftime. The players were weighed and rectal temperatures were determined before and after the matches. The players were aged between 20 and 36 years.

In Figure 1–28, the final rectal temperatures are plotted against water deficits developed by the players. It shows that, with the exception of one player, rectal temperatures are higher in rugby players than in the marathon runners at all levels of dehydration. There were large differences in mean mass between players in this study and in a 1966 study (Wyndham et al.). It appears that a large proportion of subjects, under the environmental conditions of this study, had sweat rate/rectal temperature relationships similar to those of heat-acclimatized subjects.

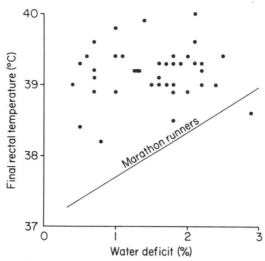

**Fig 1–28.**—Relationships between water deficit and final rectal temperature for marathon runners and for the rugby players (black dots) studied. (Courtesy of Goodman, C., et al.: S. Afr. Med. J. 67:542–544, April 6, 1985.)

These findings suggest that the role of clothing worn during rugby may have a greater influence on thermoregulation than was previously thought. Some researchers have suggested that the length of rugby jerseys should be restricted to waist level and the length of the sleeves to the elbow. The thermoregulatory advantages that could be obtained from wearing ankle-length socks probably outweigh the disadvantage of a potential increase in superficial abrasions of the lower leg.

▶ It is unlikely that the energy expenditure over an 80-minute rugby match is greater than in a marathon race. The higher rectal temperatures of rugby players cannot be attributed to greater dehydration, or, in the present experiments, to a lack of heat acclimatization, and the authors thus argue that inappropriate clothing is the culprit. Possible factors amenable to change are the extent of the body surface covered by clothing, the tightness of the clothing, and its permeability to sweat (see Digest 1–59).

The water deficit developed (about 1½% of body mass on average) is not enough to have an appreciable influence on sweat rate—indeed, much of this water would have been bound to glycogen prior to the game. It is thus not surprising that little benefit was obtained from drinking a liter of water.—Roy J. Shephard, M.D., Ph.D.

---

**Evaluation of Vapor Permeation Through Garments During Exercise**
Richard R. Gonzalez and K. Cena (Yale Univ.)
J. Appl. Physiol. 58:928–935, March 1985                    1–59

---

Five men (mean age, 28 years) exercised on a cycle ergometer, placed on a Potter scale, at 31% $VO_{2\,max}$ for up to 2 hours at an ambient temperature ($T_a$) of 25 C and a dew-point temperature of 15 C. Air movement was varied from still air to 0.4 to 2 meter per second. Each subject, in separate runs, wore a track suit (TS ensemble) of 60% polyester-40% cotton (effective clo = 0.5); a Gortex parka (GOR ensemble), covering a sweatshirt and bottom of TS (effective clo = 1.4); or the TS ensemble covered by polyethylene overgarment (POG ensemble). Esophageal temperature, skin temperature ($T_{sk}$) at 8 sites, and heart rate were continuously recorded. Dew-point sensors recorded temperatures under the garments at ambient and chest and midscapular sites. Local skin wettedness (loc w) and ratio of evaporative heat loss ($E_{sk}$) to maximum evaporative capacity were determined. An observed average effective permeation ($\bar{P}_e$, $W.m^{-2}.Torr^{-1}$) was calculated as $E_{sk}$/loc w, where w is the average of chest and back loc w and ($P_s,sk-P_w$) is the gradient of skin saturation vapor pressure at $T_{sk}$ and $T_a$.

Results show the GOR ensemble produced an almost as high $P_e$ as the TS ensemble (82%–86% of $P_e$ with TS in still air (Fig 1–29) and 0.4 – and 2-meter per second conditions). The metabolic heat productions obtained during exercise at steady state were not significantly different among the three garments. There were no significant differences in heart rate at the end of exercise with TS and GOR ensembles. In contrast, the final 1-hour runs with the vapor-impermeable overgarment caused heat strain, as evident by the increase in heart rate ($P < .001$) compared with experiments using the other two garments. At all levels of air movement, significantly ($P < .05$) cooler chest and back skin temperatures underneath the GOR ensemble at 25 C were observed compared with the POG ensemble.

These data show that the laminated garment used in this study allowed less sensible heat loss than the air-and water-permeable ensemble used by

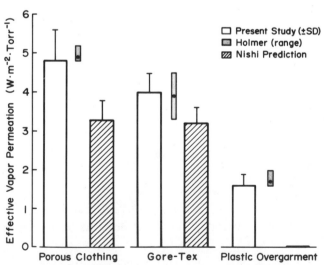

Fig 1–29.—Comparison of effective permeation ($P_e$) of water vapor through 3 garment types for still air conditions, (3-4 met), obtained by present method, using a $P_e$, Holmer and Elnas and Nishi and Gagge prediction. (Courtesy of Gonzalez, R.R., and Cena, K.: J. Appl. Physiol. 58:928–935, March 1985.)

itself during exercise up to wind speeds of $\leq 2$ m/second, primarily because of the higher clo value and air impermeability. There was an almost equal insensible heat loss when the GOR ensemble was compared with a lower clothing insulation garment, confirming suitable porocity to water vapor as measured by this dew-point technique.

▶ Evaporative heat loss plays an important role in homeostasis even under temperate conditions. In the present experiments, a combination of 2 hours of exercise and a relatively vapor-impermeable polyethylene overgarment increased the heart rate of a subject exercising at 31% of maximum oxygen intake by more than 20 beats per minute, relative to subjects wearing a more appropriate type of clothing. Each gram of sweat that is successfully evaporated dissipates 2.43 kilojoules of heat; thus the entire heat production associated with a 31% maximum effort (about 15 kilojoules per minute) could be accommodated by the evaporation of about 6 ml of sweat per minute.

Runners usually wear permeable clothes when exercising under warm conditions, but there have been fatal problems in football players when their clothing has been relatively impermeable to sweat. This is an early point to check when purchasing new uniforms!—Roy J. Shephard, M.D., Ph.D.

---

**Influence of Diuretic-Induced Dehydration on Competitive Running Performance**
Lawrence E. Armstrong, David L. Costill, and William J. Fink (Ball State Univ.)
Med. Sci. Sports Exerc. 17:456–461, August 1985                    1–60

---

A diuretic drug (40 mg of furosemide) was used to study the effects of dehydration (D) on competitive running performance, without prior thermal or exercise stress. The 8 subjects were healthy men, ages 22 to 27 years, who had competed in at least four prior road or track races and who had previously run on the treadmill. Maximal oxygen consumption, maximal ventilation, and maximal heart rate values were collected under standardized laboratory conditions on a motor-driven treadmill. Six competitive performance trials were run by these subjects on an outdoor 400-meter synthetic track. One hydrated (H) control trial and one dehydrated (D) trial were run at distances of 1,500m (n = 7), 5,000m (n = 6), and 10,000m (n = 8).

Oral ingestion of 40 mg furosemide induced the mean pretrial conditions. Body weight changes equaled the following percent changes in initial body weight: $-1.9\%$ for the 1,500m run, $-1.6\%$ for the 5,000m run, and $-2.1\%$ for the 10,000m run. None of the H versus D comparisons exhibited statistically significant differences. A statistically significant difference ($P < .05$) in H and D trials was seen in treadmill time to volitional exhaustion (Fig 1–30). Running trials on the track resulted in significantly different H versus D final performance times at the 5,000m and 10,000m distances only (Fig 1–30). Linear regression analysis indicated that a $-1\%$ change in body weight following diuretic use corresponded to running time increases of $+0.17$, $+0.39$, and $+1.57$, respectively, for the 1,500 m, 5,000m, and 10,000m trials.

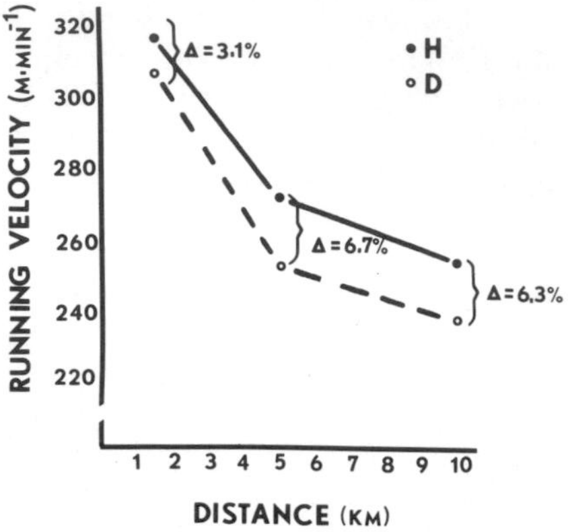

Fig 1–30.—Group mean running velocities of hydrated *(H)* and dehydrated *(D)* outdoor track trials. (Courtesy of Armstrong, L.E., et al.: Med. Sci. Sports Exerc. 17:456–461, August 1985. Copyright 1985, the American College of Sports Medicine. Reprinted by permission.)

Rapid body water loss prior to long-distance running is detrimental to performance, irrespective of thermal, dietary, or metabolic stress. Competitive performance in trials of long duration (5,000m and 10,000m) can be expected to degrade to a greater extent than shorter events (1,500m). Performance decrements observed during the competitive running trials of this investigation are most logically explained by altered anaerobic function, impaired thermoregulation, increased perception of effort, or combinations thereof.

▶ Previous studies have used heat exposure, fluid deprivation, or exercise to look at the effects of dehydration upon performance. By giving a diuretic, the authors were able to change plasma volume and body water suddenly, with little impact upon either plasma substances or resting muscle water. A 1% change in body mass was enough in these circumstances to impair performance, particularly over longer distances. This does not imply the same would be true of exercise-induced dehydration; if activity is of sufficient vigor to mobilize body glycogen, about 3% of body water can be lost before there is any significant dehydration.

The cause of the poor performance after dehydration remains obscure, since subjects were well aware that they had been treated with a powerful diuretic. To the extent that the response was physiologic rather than psychological, the most likely influences seem a reduction of both skin blood flow and sweating, with augmentation of the normal rise in body temperature.—Roy J. Shephard, M.D., Ph.D.

**Thermoregulatory Responses to Weight Training**
N. F. Gordon, H. M. S. Russell, P. E. Krüger, and J. F. Cilliers (Cardiac Rehabilitation Ctr., Voortrekkerhoogte, South Africa)
Int. J. Sports Med. 6:145–150, June 1985                    1–61

Previous studies of the effects of acute physical activity on thermoregulation have been limited chiefly to lower-power-output dynamic work. The effects of weight training, which includes both static and dynamic

PERCENTAGE CHANGES IN TOTAL CIRCULATING
SERUM ELECTROLYTES IMMEDIATELY AFTER AND 24
HOURS POST-WEIGHT TRAINING

|  | After | 24 h after |
|---|---|---|
| Sodium | - 11.0** | 4.1 |
|  | ± 4.4 | ± 2.6 |
| Potassium | - 13.1* | 2.9 |
|  | ± 9.6 | ± 10.0 |
| Chloride | - 11.2** | 4.3 |
|  | ± 4.7 | ± 3.1 |
| Calcium | - 5.5* | 1.5 |
|  | ± 4.7 | ± 3.8 |
| Magnesium | - 5.7* | 6.5 |
|  | ± 6.0 | ± 9.8 |

Values are means ± SD; n = 8; *$P < .05$; **$P < .001$. Values reflect percentage changes in total circulating electrolytes as compared to pre-exercise levels.

(Courtesy of Gordon, N.F., et al.: Int. J. Sports Med. 6:145–150, June 1985.)

components, were examined in 8 healthy men with a mean age of 25.5 years. The mean body fat was 14.7%. No subjects were using anabolic steroids or other drugs. Three sets of 15 repetitions of 9 exercises were performed at a rate of 15 repetitions/minute with 1-minute recovery intervals. The load was raised from 50% of the 15-repetition maximum for the first set to 5% and 100% for the second and third sets, respectively. Tests were done at an ambient temperature of 27.5 C dry-bulb and 21 C wet-bulb.

Rectal temperature rose from 37.1 C to 38.4 C after weight training. A water deficit of 0.8% was incurred, with sweat loss of 0.6 L. Minor elevations in serum creatine kinase, aspartate aminotransferase, and lactate dehydrogenase were observed, despite a rise in blood lactate from 1.2 to 7.0 mmole/L immediately after weight training. The calculated plasma volume fell by 12%, but the 24-hour plasma volume was normal. All serum electrolytes were significantly reduced after weight training, but baseline levels were present at 24 hours (table).

Weight training did not appear to impose a clinically significant demand on thermoregulatory control mechanisms in this study, but further work on different weight training programs is needed, in subjects of varying capability and under different environmental conditions.

► Weight training under reasonable limits of intensity and environment is unlikely to be complicated by a significant core temperature elevation or need for electrolyte supplementation. This is in contrast to intensive endurance activity of a cardiotonic nature. It does not stand as an absolute rule if one is engaged in patterns of mixed exercise.—Lewis J. Krakauer, M.D., F.A.C.P.

### Iced Gastric Lavage for Treatment of Heatstroke: Efficacy in a Canine Model

Scott A. Syverud, William J. Barker, James T. Amsterdam, Gordon L. Bills, David D. Goltra, Joseph C. Armao, and Jerris R. Hedges (Univ. of Cincinnati)
Ann. Emerg. Med. 14:424–432, May 1985                    1–62

About 4,000 deaths from heatstroke occur each year in the United States. Mortality rates as high as 70% have been reported. The effectiveness and safety of iced gastric lavage were studied in an anesthetized dog model of heatstroke produced by external heating to a core temperature of 43 C (109.4 F). Control animals were cooled passively in room air, whereas study animals had gastric lavage with iced tap water, using a large-bore orogastric tube. Temperatures were monitored by thermocouples in the brain, pulmonary artery, subcutaneous chest wall tissue, and rectum. The animals were killed 12 hours after induction of heatstroke.

Cooling occurred 5–6 times faster in the lavaged animals than in control dogs (Figs 1–31 and 1–32). Differences were significant at all temperature monitoring sites. Platelet counts at 12 hours were higher in the group treated by lavage. Prothrombin times lengthened more in control animals,

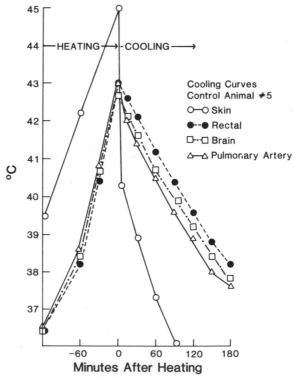

Fig 1–31.—Typical cooling curves in control animals. (Courtesy of Syverud, S.A., et al.: Ann. Emerg. Med. 14:424–432, May 1985.)

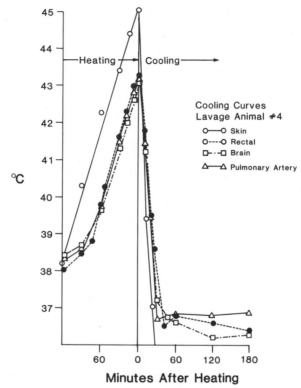

**Fig 1–32.**—Typical cooling curves in lavaged animals. (Courtesy of Syverud, S.A., et al.: Ann. Emerg. Med. 14:424–432, May 1985).

but not significantly so. Blood gas values did not differ significantly during the study. Serum creatinine levels were significantly lower in lavaged animals, as were potassium levels; the serum calcium levels were higher. Levels of lactate dehydrogenase were higher in control dogs. Heart rates were lower in lavaged animals, but differences in arterial pressure and cardiac output were not significant. Pathologic changes of heatstroke were only slightly less prominent in the lavaged animals.

Iced gastric lavage promoted cooling in this canine model of heatstroke, and improved hemodynamic and laboratory parameters were noted. Iced gastric lavage may be an effective and safe means of cooling after the development of heatstroke.

▶ It is hard to believe that 4,000 deaths occur yearly in the United States from heatstroke with mortality rates as high as 70%, but this appears to be the data that have been established. This study sacrificed 12 animals and did prove that iced gastric lavage was effective in promoting cooling in the canine model. This method has not been a standard therapy in the human model. See the following digests.—Lewis J. Krakauer, M.D., F.A.C.P.

### Aspirin in Exercise-Induced Hyperthermia: Evidence for and Against Its Role
Stephen C. Johnson and Robert O. Ruhling (Univ. of Utah)
Sports Med. 2:1–7, 1985                                        1–63

It might seem logical that aspirin would reduce the elevated core temperature associated with exercise. However, pyrogen-induced fever and exercise hyperthermia, though quantitatively similar, differ qualitatively. Fever is mediated by an actual elevation in the thermoregulatory set point about which the body core temperature is regulated, while exercise-associated hyperthermia is not. Exercise hyperthermia is independent of ambient temperatures in the range of 10–30 C, but it is not truly defended. Exercise hyperthermia represents increased heat storage resulting from a marked increase in the rate of heat production and subsequent storage as a byproduct of an increased metabolic rate.

Aspirin acts by blocking prostaglandin-induced modification of the set point, and initial studies confirmed a lack of effect of aspirin on exercise hyperthermia. At least part of the normal hyperthermic response to exercise, however, can be mediated by factors that alter the set point through prostaglandin-dependent processes. Recent work suggests that postexercise hyperthermia has no components that are affected by aspirin treatment. Core temperature is not, however, a direct measure of set point activity, and it is possible that a study of cutaneous blood flow or sweat threshold effector responses relative to experimental changes in body core temperature after exercise would show subtle set point modifications.

From a practical viewpoint, aspirin has no effect on the body core temperature elevation following exercise. Postexercise hyperthermia is probably the product of metabolic or ionic effects, or both.

▶ Aspirin was the old standby for use against fever, and it was not unreasonable for endurance athletes to assume that it would be effective for exercise-induced hyperthermia. In quantity, the thermal elevation may be similar in both, but in quality they are quite different. One would predict that aspirin should have little effect upon exercise-related hyperthermia, because that is not basically mediated by a prostaglandin related set point, in terms of hypothalamic function. This has been verified experimentally, by the work of Downey and Darling in the early 1960s. The present study supports that contention, at least for 60 minutes of observation. It is likely that postexercise hyperthermia is the product of metabolic and ionic factors.—Lewis J. Krakauer, M.D., F.A.C.P.

### Be Serious About Siriasis: Guidelines for Avoiding Heat Injury During "Dog Days"
Robert E. Sinclair (Univ. of Alabama)
Postgrad. Med. 5:261–276, April 1985                              1–64

Heat injury may occur abruptly or insidiously whenever the humidity and temperature are high. Heat cramps, precipitated by excessive loss of electrolytes through sweating, are the most common sign of heat stress. They are relieved by rest in a cool environment and replacement of fluids and electrolytes. Heat exhaustion occurs when blood is shunted from the viscera to a dilated venous surface pool, reducing the circulating blood volume. Orthostatic hypotension, irritability, nausea, and extreme fatigue are noted in the presence of mental alertness. Cooling by sponging with ice water or cold water is indicated, followed by prompt hospitalization. Heat stroke is a life-threatening state. A marked change in mentation is noted, as well as tremors and, possibly, decerebrate posture before unconsciousness and coma occur. Immersion in ice water can be lifesaving. Too rapid fluid replacement should be avoided.

Acclimatization is important in athletes who are to participate in strenuous work in high heat and humidity. Heavier athletes must make a greater effort to minimize body fat and guard against heat injury, because they generate more metabolic calories than others do and require more cooling. Cardiac conditioning and good circulatory tone promote temperature regulation. Athletes with febrile illness should not participate during high heat and humidity. The use of certain drugs (e.g., diuretics and β-blockers) may increase the risk of heat injury. Overly competitive athletes may fail to report early signs of heat injury. Fat produces more body heat than protein or carbohydrate does. Careful measurement of ambient conditions can help in developing safe exercise programs. Wearing proper clothing is important, as is the reflective nature of the playing surface.

---

**Treating Thermal Injury: Disagreement Heats Up**
Heyward L. Nash
Physician Sportsmed. 13:134–144, July 1985                                    1–65

---

Many physicians support Castelli's opinion that avoiding thermal injury in endurance athletes is merely a matter of providing adequate fluid, while others emphasize the complexity of thermoregulation. The body can gain heat during exercise despite the processes of convection, conduction, evaporation, and radiation, and the body temperature rises as a result. High humidity promotes this trend, because sweat will not evaporate. Both the time of day and the degree of acclimatization are important factors. Faster runners have a higher risk of hyperthermia, while slower ones are more at risk of hypothermia, especially if the weather cools. Chills and cold skin may be noted despite a high core temperature. Impaired consciousness impedes the recognition of hyperthermia. An immediate body core temperature reading with a rectal thermometer or probe is critically important.

Castelli treats hyperthermic and hypothermic patients the same, giving them fluids and allowing the body to equilibrate itself. Nequin, in contrast, is of the opinion that each should be evaluated individually. An intravenous line is recommended to keep a vein open. Hypothermic patients must be carefully monitored, as it is not clear whether low blood pressure is a result of peripheral vasoconstriction or hypovolemia. Massage may help promote cutaneous blood flow. Some recommend packing ice on the axillae, groin, and neck. A vapor spray or mist may be more effective and also safer than an ice bath. Intravenous treatment takes up less space than vapor spray units and fans in crowded circumstances.

▶ It is not commonly appreciated that slow runners in prolonged races, such as the marathon, are quite prone to hypothermia. Most of the emphasis has been on the opposite phenomenon, hyperthermia. Hyperthermia relates more to faster runners or to an adverse environment of heat plus humidity acting in concert. Dr. Castelli's experience with the Boston marathon population is most impressive. Hydration seems to be the critical therapy. Given hydration (oral usually being sufficient), an athlete will equilibrate, recover, and suffer no ill effects. Fluid appears to be the critical preventive and therapeutic measure.

Others, like Dr. John Sutton of McMaster University, feel that the chance of missing an elevated core temperature is present if everybody is not given the benefit of a core temperature reading and that this could be lethal in the isolated instance. There is further argument about the beneficial effect of ice bath for hyperthermia. Most would agree that if an individual is carefully monitored after a race and appropriate attention is paid to core temperature and cardiovascular status, little harm can be done starting with the simplest measures of fluid replacement, and then moving on to ice and/or heat as appropriate in a given individual. The lack of observation in an afflicted runner is a major sin.

It has been pointed out in prior Year Books that runners' symptoms can be deceptive: they may include a relative bradycardia and still have significant core elevation of temperature because of the phenomenon of training adaptation of pulse rate. It is also possible that β-blockers and diuretic therapy predispose to heat injury. This is something that those who indulge in extended exercise in the heat should make note of.—Lewis J. Krakauer, M.D., F.A.C.P.

**Metabolic and Vasomotor Insulative Responses Occurring on Immersion in Cold Water**
Louis H. Strong, Gin K. Gee, and Ralph F. Goldman (U.S. Army Research Inst. of Environmental Medicine, Natick, Mass.)
J. Appl. Physiol. 58:964–977, March 1985                          1–66

Twenty male volunteers (aged 17 to 28 years) with a range of body weights and body fat underwent total immersion while at rest in water between 36 and 20 C. Metabolic heat production measured as a function of time and water temperature was converted to explicit linear functions of core ($T_{re}$) and mean skin ($T_{sk}$) temperature for each individual immersion.

Mean weighted skin temperature falls exponentially for all nude subjects, approaching in the asymptotic limit a temperature only slightly higher than the bath temperature. The relationship between area-weighted mean heat flow and water temperature appeared to be linear below the thermal neutral zone. Individual skin temperatures showed a small variability between subjects. The surface heat transfer coefficient increased with metabolic rate. In general, metabolic rates increased as the water temperature decreased, until shivering exhaustion saturated the response. The variation of metabolic heat production was plotted against skin and rectal temperature for five typical subjects whose body types included (1) heavy and fat, (2) average, and (3) small and lean. For the 10 subjects studied for cardiovascular responses, the heart rate of all but one dropped from the control rate upon immersion in water at temperatures ranging between 32 and 28 C.

For any morphological group, the intensity of the cold compensation increased with the subject's heat debt. However, compared with large subjects, small subjects exhibited a greater increase in both metabolic heat production and in percent change of body insulation per decrement of surface temperature, as well as a greater increase in metabolic heat production per decrement of core temperature. This finding implies that the intensity of metabolic or insulative compensation does not scale with the magnitude of the heat debt when comparing different morphological groups.

▶ The classical studies of Scholander et al. (*J. Appl. Physiol.* 12:1, 1958) suggested that humans could respond to the stress of sudden cold-water immersion in two ways. Some people reacted by shivering violently to sustain their core temperature, while others reacted mainly by cutting off the blood flow to the extremities, thereby reducing heat loss. With acclimatization to cold, there was usually a tendency to switch from the shivering to the insulative type of response.

Much of the early knowledge of body cooling was obtained in the notorious "experiments" of the Dachau concentration camp, where rates of cooling were determined on emaciated subjects. It has since been appreciated that these figures have little relevance to the well-nourished and often overnourished North American. The present experiments illustrate clearly the influence of subcutaneous fat thickness on the potential for an insulative type of response; the thinnest and smallest subjects quickly reach the limits of possible adaptation by an insulative response, and thus show a much larger increase of metabolism than those who are obese.

The subjects of Strong et al. were all resting before the experiment. However, the insulative type of reaction becomes yet more difficult to develop if the person has been very active before falling into cold water. Recent studies by Dr. R. C. Goode in our laboratory have shown a substantial increase in the rate of cooling when the subject was engaged in vigorous exercise prior to immersion.—Roy J. Shephard, M.D., Ph.D.

---

**Comparison of Thermal Responses Between Rest and Leg Exercise in Water**

Michael M. Toner, Michael N. Sawka, William L. Holden, and Kent B. Pandolf (U.S. Army Research Inst. of Environmental Medicine, Natick, Mass.)
J. Appl. Physiol. 59:248–253, July 1985                                    1–67

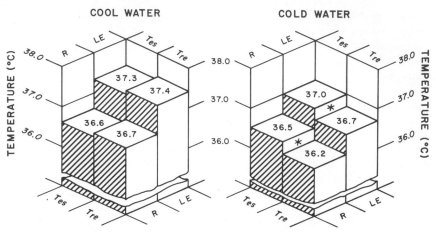

Fig 1–33.—Comparison of esophageal ($T_{es}$) and rectal ($T_{re}$) temperatures (60 minutes) during rest (R) and leg exercise (LE) in cool (left) and cold (right) water. (Courtesy of Toner, M.M., et al.: J. Appl. Physiol. 59:248–253, July 1985.)

This study examined both the thermal and metabolic responses of individuals in cool (30 C, n = 9) and cold (18 C, n = 7; 20 C, n = 2) water. Male volunteers were immersed up to the neck for 1 hour during both seated rest (R) and leg exercise (LE).

In cool water, metabolic rate (M) was significantly higher ($P < .01$) during LE compared with R, and M did not change with R and LE across time. During the R exposure, M was significantly greater at 30 and 60 minutes compared with 5 minutes, whereas there were no changes across time during LE. During cool-water exposures, esophageal temperatures ($T_{es}$) increased ($P < .05$) during the first 30 minutes of LE and remained unchanged for the final 30 minutes. The R exposure showed no change during the first 30 minutes, whereas $T_{es}$ dropped ($P < .05$) during minutes 30 to 60. In cold water, $T_{es}$ increased ($P < .05$) with time during LE, whereas there was a significant decline ($P < .05$) during R. Rectal temperatures ($T_{re}$) were similar to those of $T_{es}$. Figure 1–33 illustrates a comparison between final $T_{re}$ and $T_{es}$ during R and LE in cool and cold water. In cool water, there were no differences between $T_{re}$ and $T_{es}$ during R or LE. After 60 minutes of cold water exposure the average $T_{re}$ was significantly lower than $T_{es}$ during both R and LE. In cool water, each regional heat flow was generally greater ($P < .05$) during LE than R. In cold water, both chest and leg heat flows were generally greater ($P < .05$) during LE than R.

These data indicate that LE is more effective than R in maintaining core temperatures in both cool and cold water. Immersion in cold water elicits differing core temperatures, indicating that chest cavity temperature is maintained at a higher level than other core areas.

▶ This paper challenges the conventional wisdom (Hayward and Keatinge: *J. Physiol.* 320:229, 1981) that it is dangerous to swim when immersed in cold water (e.g., after a sailing vessel has capsized). However, a great deal depends on what one means by "cold." Hayward did much of his research around Victoria, British Columbia, where the water is very cold for much of the year. Depending on the amount of body fat, there is a critical water temperature, probably around 20 C, above which it is better to swim, and below which it is better to await rescue. Exercise of the legs alone may be tolerated to a somewhat lower temperature limit, because the mass/surface area ratio is more favorable than for the arms; however, it would be difficult to swim using the legs alone, avoiding displacement of water over the rest of the body. Thus, unless the water is warmer than about 20 C, or the shore is very near, the best advice for the sailor seems to huddle in the fetal position and await rescue.—Roy J. Shephard, M.D., Ph.D.

---

**Heat Exchanges in Wet Suits**
A. H. Wolff, S. R. K. Coleshaw, C. G. Newstead, and W. R. Keatinge (London Hosp. Med. College)
J. Appl. Physiol. 58:770–777, March 1985                                     1–68

---

Models designed to predict changes in body temperatures require values for metabolic heat production and internal and external insulations. It is not known whether in practice flow of water under some regions of wet suits substantially reduces the insulation that they could otherwise provide. The present experiments were designed to assess this and to see whether such flow has important effects on the level and pattern of skin temperature. Five male and 1 female volunteer subjects, aged 21 to 35 years, took part in the study. These volunteers were immersed in cold and warm water wearing wet suits of different thicknesses and configurations.

During the experiment summarized in the table, the subject was under only moderate cold stress, as indicated by little fall in core temperature and by internal conductances that were similar in rest and exercise and only slightly lower in the extremities than in the trunk, indicating only moderate vasoconstriction. The lower water-flow conductance on the extremities accordingly allowed higher skin temperatures there than on the trunk. With subjects at rest, skin temperatures on the extremities were generally lower than on the trunk. Surface skin temperatures of the hands and feet were lower than those of the trunk. Exercise usually caused increases in skin temperatures on muscular parts of the extremities, which are attributable to increased internal conductance due to blood flow in muscle during exercise. During vasoconstriction in the cold, skin temperatures on distal parts of extremities were lower than were those of the trunk, allowing adequate metabolic responses. In warm water, minor postural changes and movement made flow under suits much higher, both at rest and at work. These changes in flow allowed for a wide range of water temperatures at which people could stabilize body temperature in any given suit, neither overheating when exercising nor cooling below 35 C when still. Even thin people with 4- to 7-mm suits covering the whole body

REGIONAL HEAT LOSSES FROM SUBJECT 1 WEARING
FITTED 4-MM-THICK FULL-LENGTH WET SUIT*

| | Mid-trunk | Upper Arm | Lower Leg |
|---|---|---|---|
| *Still in Water at 10.4°C ($T_{re}$ = 37.2°C)* | | | |
| Skin heat loss, $W \cdot m^{-2}$ | 198 | 166 | 129 |
| Suit heat loss, $W \cdot m^{-2}$ | 109 | 115 | 82 |
| Water flow heat loss, $W \cdot m^{-2}$ | 89 | 51 | 47 |
| Temperature under suit, °C | 23.8 | 24.7 | 25.2 |
| Conductance of suit, $W \cdot m^{-2} \cdot °C^{-1}$ | 8.1 | 8.0 | 5.5 |
| Conductance due to water flow, $W \cdot m^{-2} \cdot °C^{-1}$ | 6.6 | 3.6 | 3.2 |
| Internal conductance, $W \cdot m^{-2} \cdot °C^{-1}$ | 14.8 | 13.3 | 10.8 |
| *Exercising in Water at 10.0°C ($T_{re}$ = 36.8°C)* | | | |
| Skin heat loss, $W \cdot m^{-2}$ | 225 | 162 | 159 |
| Suit heat loss, $W \cdot m^{-2}$ | 91 | 92 | 68 |
| Water flow heat loss, $W \cdot m^{-2}$ | 134 | 70 | 91 |
| Temperature under suit, °C | 21.8 | 24.1 | 24.1 |
| Conductance of suit, $W \cdot m^{-2} \cdot °C^{-1}$ | 7.7 | 6.5 | 4.8 |
| Conductance due to water flow, $W \cdot m^{-2} \cdot °C^{-1}$ | 11.4 | 5.0 | 6.5 |
| Internal conductance, $W \cdot m^{-2} \cdot °C^{-1}$ | 15.0 | 12.8 | 12.5 |

*Measurements were made at end of each experiment. $T_{re}$ = rectal temperature.
(Courtesy of Wolff, A.H., et al.: J. Appl. Physiol. 58:770–777, March 1985.)

could stabilize their body temperatures in water near 10 C in spite of cold vasodilatation.

Most of the water exchange in these suits seems to have taken place through the neck seal and the zipper. In theory, either a tighter neck seal or a closer fit on the trunk could improve the effective insulation of suits in cold water, but the second alternative is impractical even in a suit of distensible material such as foam neoprene, because suits that provide a close fit on the trunk during expiration hamper breathing. A tight seal at the neck and zipper is practicable, but would have to be capable of being easily loosened if flexibility in effective insulation is to be retained.

▶ The insulation provided by clothing depends in substantial measure on the film of still air (or in the case of a wet suit, a film of still water) trapped beneath the garment. The efficiency of insulation thus depends greatly on the sealing of the clothing, in some instances around the wrists and ankles, and in the present instance around the neck and the zip fastener. The extent of heat loss occurring in this fashion is enough to limit the effectiveness of an increase in suit thickness; the lesson is drawn that however good the suit, thin people cannot stabilize their core temperature in water at 0 C. One interesting feature of the present report is a demonstration that subjects can modify the movement of water under the suit. Heat flow was much greater in hot than in cold water, and only a very small part of this change could be attributed to a change in the viscosity of the water. The main factor was that the users found ways of changing posture that increased water flow through the garment.

Further variables influencing the heat loss in a wet suit are how the body distributes cooling between the trunk and the extremities, and the way in which peripheral insulative responses are modified by physical activity. It is important that some cooling of the extremities occur in order to stimulate an adequate metabolic response to cold (Van Someren et al., *J. Appl. Physiol.* 53:1228, 1982).—Roy J. Shephard, M.D., Ph.D.

**Muscular Exercise and Fatigue**
H. Gibson and R. H. T. Edwards (Univ. of Liverpool)
Sports Med. 2:120–132, 1985                                                    1–69

Muscular fatigue during exercise is a common phenomenon, and several forms arise from a particular type of exercise. The causes are still not clearly established, although electrical and metabolic factors have been shown to be involved. There are several techniques that allow for the analysis of muscle function as electrical activation and energy metabolism: (1) a needle biopsy of muscle for histochemical and metabolic studies; (2) magnetic resonance spectroscopy for the noninvasive study of muscle energy metabolism and pH; (3) electromyographic analysis of the electrical characteristics of muscle; and (4) percutaneous electrical stimulation of muscle for the force-frequency and relaxation characteristics of muscle. Endurance training increases the capacity to sustain exercise, possibly by altering muscle energy metabolism and contractile properties.

Fatigue is a self-protective mechanism against the damage of contractile machinery of muscle—as, for example, in rigor, which occurs if the energy stores are depleted. Recovery of fatigued muscles depends on the type of fatigue that develops and on the form of the exercise. The long-term effects of exercise depend on the type of exercise carried out and on the activity history of the muscle. With endurance exercise, there is an increase in the activity of mitochondrial enzymes in muscle. The capacity to sustain endurance-dynamic exercise is increased through endurance training, through cardiovascular, respiratory, and metabolic adaptations. The "catastrophe theory" model from engineering and mathematics maintains that fatigue might result from energy loss, excitation or activation failure, or a combination of both.

There appear to be different kinds of fatigue, and each may occur with a particular form of muscular activity. The catastrophe theory of fatigue may be a valid description for the final common pathway in cellular function that leads to impaired performance.

▶ An excellent review of the subject matter. The interested reader is referred to the original article.—Joseph S. Torg, M.D.

## Physiology of Specific Sports

**Applied Physiology of Marathon Running**
Bertil Sjödin and Jan Svedenhag (Karolinska Inst., Stockholm)
Sports Med. 2:83–99, 1985                                                    1–70

Performance in marathon running is influenced by a variety of factors, most of which are physiologic in nature. The marathon runner must rely on a high aerobic capacity. But great variations in maximal oxygen uptake ($VO_{2max}$) have been observed among runners with a similar performance capacity, indicating that complementary factors are important to performance.

The oxygen cost of running, or the running economy (expressed as $VO_{215}$ at 15 km/hour), as well as the functional utilization of $VO_{2max}$ at marathon-race pace ($\%VO_{2\,Ma} \times VO_{2max}^{-1}$, where Ma indicates mean marathon velocity) are additional factors that are known to affect performance capacity. Together $VO_{2max}$, $VO_{2\,15}$, and $\%VO_{2max}$ can almost entirely explain the variation in marathon performance. These variables have also been found to explain the variations in the so-called aerobic threshold. This factor, which is closely related to the metabolic response to increasing exercise intensities, has the single highest predictive power for marathon performance. But a major limiting factor in marathon performance is probably the choice of fuels for the exercising muscles, which is related to the $\%VO_{2\,Ma} \times VO_{2max}^{-1}$.

Current research shows that marathon runners, when compared with normal individuals, have a higher fat metabolism at given high exercise intensities, expressed both in absolute (meters per second) and relative ($\%VO_{2max}$) terms. The selection of fat for oxidation by the muscles is important, since carbohydrates, the stores of the most efficient fuel, are limited. The large amount of endurance training done by marathon runners is probably responsible for similar metabolic adaptations, which contribute to a delayed onset of fatigue and raise the $VO_{2\,Ma} \times VO_{2max}$. There is probably an upper limit in training kilometrage above which there are no improvements in the fractional utilization of $VO_{2max}$ at the marathon race pace. However, the influence of training on $VO_{2max}$—and, to some extent, on the running economy—appears to be limited by genetic factors.

▶ An elegant paper that speaks concisely to the multiple factors involved in the running of and training for the masochistic sport of the marathon. It supports the position held by some, that the marathon is an extreme activity, for which the influence of training and the general function of performance is limited primarily by genetic factors at the upper level of competition. For those not so lucky in their endowment, it may be a less than reasonable pursuit. Compared with the normal rate marathon runners have a higher turnover rate in fat metabolism expressed both in meters per second and $VO_{2max}$ terminology. Carbohydrate stores are very finite, and after they are used the efficiency of fat oxidation becomes the key to muscle function. The marathon elite can train in addition, enhancing metabolic adaptation, which permits an increased efficiency of fat utilization. The pioneering work of Costill and Saltin and others has built a large foundation for the present writings and insights into this topic of muscle function.—Lewis J. Krakauer, M.D., F.A.C.P.

**Sleep Disruption Following a Marathon**
Iain Montgomery, John Trinder, Susan Paxton, Geoff Fraser, Max Meaney,

and Garry Lloyd Koerbin (Univ. of Tasmania, Hobart, Australia, and Tasmanian College of Advanced Education, Tasmania, Australia)
J. Sports Med. 25:69–74, March–June 1985                                1–71

The present study examined the effects of intense physical exercise on the sleep of a group of subjects whose average age was 40 years. Eight runners slept in the sleep laboratory on eight occasions: an adaptation night, two consecutive nights each following a 90-minute hard training run between 4 and 6 p.m., two consecutive nights on nontraining days, and the three nights following a standard 42.4 km marathon.

Sleep was dramatically disturbed on marathon night 1 compared with training and nontraining nights and marathon nights 2 and 3. Total sleep time was significantly decreased on marathon night 1 relative to each condition. In 7 subjects slow wave sleep (SWS) was decreased and total time awake was increased. Subjects reported being significantly more physically tired and physically stressed on marathon night 1. Cortisol secretion rates were significantly higher in the premarathon, the marathon, and the postmarathon periods and the first postmarathon night when compared with postmarathon days 2 and 3.

The results show that a marathon disturbs sleep in an older population. The results do not support the view that exercise facilitates SWS level, and therefore do not support the hypothesis that SWS has a restorative function.

▶ Montgomery and associates provide a useful review of the conflicting literature concerning the effects of exercise on sleep patterns. Their own data show, perhaps not surprisingly, that the sleep of 40-year-old marathoners is disturbed the night after competition. More importantly, the usual 90-minute training run taken between 4 p.m. and 6 p.m. had no effect upon sleep. The conflicting results previously reported reflect differences in the age of the subjects, the intensity of the activity undertaken, the fitness of the participants, and above all the time of the day when the exercise is performed. If a patient is complaining of sleep disturbance, exercise should be moderate rather than stressful, and it should not be undertaken immediately before retiring.—Roy J. Shephard, M.D., Ph.D.

---

**Thermoregulation in Marathon Competition at Low Ambient Temperature**
R. J. Maughan (Univ. of Aberdeen, Scotland)
Int. J. Sports Med. 6:15–19, February 1985                                1–72

The 1982 Aberdeen marathon race (42.2 km) was held on a cool (12 C) day on a flat, fast course. Fifty-nine of the 750 runners volunteered to take part in this study. Rectal temperature of these competitors was measured within 5 minutes of completing the race. Venous blood samples were obtained before and immediately after the race; body weight of these subjects was also recorded before and after the race. During the race, 200 ml of fluid, either water or a glucose-electrolyte drink, was consumed at each of the seven feeding stations. A major aim of the study was to examine the effects of glucose and electrolytes on the biochemical response to marathon running.

All subjects successfully completed the marathon race in mean finishing time of 3 hours 41 minutes. Mean rectal temperature recorded immediately after completing the race was 38.3 C. There was a tendency for the faster runners to record the highest values for rectal temperature. The postrace rectal temperatures were significantly ($P < .01$) negatively correlated with the time taken to complete the second half of the course. A significant correlation ($P < .01$) was observed between the difference in time between the two halves of the race and the postrace rectal temperature. Assuming that all subjects drank the entire contents of the bottle handed to them at each feeding station, total fluid intake would have been 1.4 kg. Total weight loss due to substrate oxidation was fairly constant between individuals and amounted to less than 100 gm. Body weight decreased and this weight loss was not related to finishing time. A highly significant correlation ($P < .001$) was observed between sweat rate and finishing time. The increase in hemoglobin concentration was statistically significant ($P < .05$).

The results of this study show that hyperthermia was not a problem among this group of runners. Rather, the results suggest that hypothermia may be a problem for marathon runners competing under these conditions.

▶ Much has been written about hyperthermia in marathon racing, but it is salutary to remember that if a runner who is lightly clad in sweat-soaked garments slows down under cool conditions, hypothermia can also develop. Earlier reports of hypothermia were sometimes dismissed as erroneous, because the temperatures were recorded orally, and it was thought that local cooling of the tongue had given a misleading impression of low core temperatures. However, there is much less possibility of an artifact with rectal temperatures, some of which were as low as 35.6 C following a race at an environmental temperature of 12 C and a wind speed of 14 knots.—Roy J. Shephard, M.D., Ph.D.

---

**Water Intoxication: A Possible Complication During Endurance Exercise**
Timothy D. Noakes, Neil Goodwin, Brian L. Rayner, Trevor Branken, and Robert K. N. Taylor (Univ. of Cape Town and Univ. of Natal, South Africa)
Med. Sci. Sports Exerc. 17:370–375, 1985                                    1–73

---

Most authorities have advised that only hypotonic solutions with low or no sodium chloride be ingested during prolonged exercise. The authors report four cases of hyponatremia, 2 severe, in athletes competing in prolonged endurance events. Their condition was almost certainly aggravated by the ingestion of excessive amounts of hypotonic fluids with low sodium chloride content during and after exercise.

Woman, 46, had been running for 3½ years and trained a total of 1,700 km in 5 months before the 1981 88 km Comrades Marathon. After she had run about 30 km of the race, she developed watery diarrhea that persisted in the next 40 km. During the race she drank an estimated 250 ml of fluid at every aid station, which were situated about every 3 km. The fluid she drank consisted of a mixture of Coca-Cola and water in equal volumes (estimated total sodium chloride intake during the race was 20 mmole). After 70 km, the athlete was removed from the race by her husband, whom she did not recognize. During the drive to the hotel, she had a grand mal seizure and was rushed to the hospital. On admission, she was comatose and showed marked neck stiffness and generalized muscular hypertonia. Figure 1–34 shows bilateral perihilar shadowing with numerous septal lines, changes associated with acute pulmonary edema. Blood analysis revealed hyponatremia and hypochloremia, both of which normalized after 3 days. An intravenously given infusion of 0.9% saline was begun and after 48 hours, the patient's mental state was normal.

On the basis of this case and other cases, the authors suggest that the advice to restrict sodium chloride intake during marathon and ultra-marathon races is basically sound, but it should be tempered with the proviso that intake of hypotonic fluids in excess of that required to balance sweat

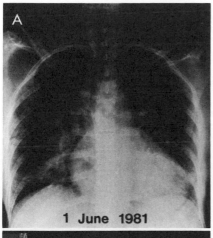
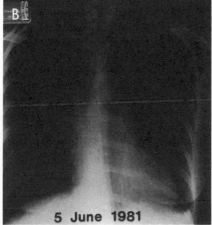

Fig 1–34.—**A**, the chest radiograph taken on June 1, 1981, shows cardiomegaly (cardiothoracic ratio, 60%) and bilateral perihilar shadowing with numerous septal lines, changes that are in keeping with acute pulmonary edema. **B**, with the exception of the increased heart size, which had nevertheless reduced somewhat (cardiothoracic ratio, 53%), all of these features had cleared in the chest radiograph taken 5 days later. (Courtesy of Noakes, T.D., et al.: Med. Sci. Sports Exerc. 17:370–375, 1985. Copyright 1985, the American College of Sports Medicine. Reprinted by permission.)

and urine losses may be hazardous in some individuals. Advice on the fluid and sodium chloride requirements of endurance athletes should probably be specific to the event and to the different classes of athletes. It should stress the importance of weight, not speed, as the determinant of fluid losses during the race.

▶ Is it possible to have too much of a good thing? We have previously advocated ad-libitum water for marathon runners (Shephard and Kavanagh, *Phys. Sportsmedicine* 6(5): 90, 1978), although in one of the races that we monitored in Hawaii, runners were sufficiently hyperhydrated to feel a need to urinate during the course of the race.

The experiments described by Noakes and his colleagues are somewhat specialized, because the races covered distances of up to 160 km, almost four times the normal marathon distance. The less well trained participants inevitably took this course quite slowly, so that there was less sweating and less inhibition of gastric emptying, plus a total exhaustion of glycogen depots with a resultant release of the water of hydration. When these special circumstances were combined with a cool day, serious overhydration developed. This problem is unlikely in a normal marathon race, run at normal speeds and normal North American temperatures. However, if there is any doubt, it is a simple matter to ensure that subjects allow their body mass to drop by the 1.0 to 1.5 kg anticipated with liberation of the glycogen-linked water reserve.—Roy J. Shephard, M.D., Ph.D.

---

**Alterations in Pulmonary Function Consequent to a 5-Mile Run**
Daniel S. Miles and Richard J. Durbin (Wright State Univ.)
J. Sports Med. 25:90–97, September 1985                                    1–74

---

Marathon running and other strenuous long-term exercise have been associated with significant transient changes in lung function, and even moderate exercise may have such effects, possibly representing early closure of the small airways by constriction or subclinical interstitial edema. Pulmonary function was monitored in 8 healthy men with a mean age of 28 years who were capable of completing a 5-mile run without difficulty. None smoked or had a history of asthma or lung disease. Pulmonary function was recorded just before and after a 5-mile run.

Prerun and postrun spirometric and lung volume data were compared. Forced vital capacity (FVC) was significantly reduced and residual volume (RV) was increased, with no apparent change in total lung capacity (TLC). Peak flow (PF) rate and 1-second forced expiratory volume ($FEV_1$) were unchanged after the 5-mile run. The volume at closing was significantly reduced, and closing capacity was increased after the run. Conductance tended to decline, whereas resistance to diffusion increased. The ratio of diffusion to cardiac output was significantly reduced after the run.

Decreased vital capacity and increased residual volume after running reflect an expiratory limitation. Early closure of small airways is observed in conjunction with running. The findings are consistent with a transient increase in pulmonary extravascular fluid volume, leading to subclinical edema. Increased pulmonary interstitial fluid volume and decreased elastic recoil have been implicated in the altered lung function observed after running.

▶ Another paper in this volume (Digest 1–73) has drawn attention to the possible risk of developing hyperhydration during a distance run. The respiratory findings observed by Miles and Durbin, although less-direct evidence, are compatible with some accumulation of fluid in the lungs over a 5-mile run. Unfortunately, no details of fluid intake or of sweat losses are provided for this run.—Roy J. Shephard, M.D., Ph.D.

**Physiological Responses to a 20-Mile Run Under Three Fluid Replacement Treatments**
Christine L. Wells, Teresa A. Schrader, Joel R. Stern, and Gary S. Krahenbuhl (Arizona State Univ.)
Med. Sci. Sports Exerc. 17:364–369, 1985                                    1–75

Ten experienced male marathon runners (mean age, 44 years) ran 20 miles on an outdoor course in a warm climate to measure responses in selected physiologic variables as a result of drinking water, an electrolyte-glucose solution (ERG), or a caffeine solution (5 mg/kg body weight) before and during the run. The caffeine solution and water were colored and flavored to resemble the electrolyte-glucose solution so that a double-blind condition could be maintained. Subjects ingested a different fluid in each of the three trials in a counterbalanced design. The only variable that indicated statistical significance by trial day was rating of perceived exertion.

No significant differences among the three fluid replacement treatments were found for changes in heart rate, changes in rectal temperature, or body weight losses. No statistical differences among the fluid replacement treatments were seen in the venous blood constituents measured (table). Average postrun serum free fatty acids (FFA) were elevated 7- to 8-fold but there were no differences among the three treatments in prerun, postrun, or change in FFA values. No differences in blood volume, plasma volume, or red blood cell volume changes were found among the three treatments. There was a significant difference ($P < .05$) between respiratory exchange ratio obtained during the water trial and the caffeine trial. Fractional utilization of $V_{O2max}$ was significantly lower during the water trial than during the caffeine trial.

Consumption of ERG$_{TM}$ did not result in higher values for either blood glucose or serum electrolyte levels in runners in this study. Caffeine consumption failed to elicit results, indicating either a glucose sparing effect or a significant increase in FFA mobilization as seen in laboratory studies using cycling. An increase in oxygen consumption during the caffeine trial gave some evidence to suggest an increase in lipid metabolism. The authors believe these data indicate that the consumption of either ERG$_{TM}$ or caf-

Changes in Heart Rate, Rectal Temperature, Body Weight, and Selected Blood Constituents Under Three Fluid Replacement Trials*

| Variable | WAT Trial | | | ERG Trial | | | CAF Trial | | |
|---|---|---|---|---|---|---|---|---|---|
| | Pre | Post | Δ | Pre | Post | Δ | Pre | Post | Δ |
| HR (bpm) | 56.3 ± 8.3 | 149.5 ± 13.8 | 93.2 ± 9.9 | 56.6 ± 8.0 | 148.0 ± 13.2 | 93.0 ± 12.9 | 53.7 ± 7.6 | 147.4 ± 14.2 | 93.2 ± 11.4 |
| $T_{re}$ (°C) | 36.62 ± 0.40 | 38.68 ± 0.38 | +2.06 ± 0.58 | 36.68 ± 0.52 | 38.60 ± 0.41 | +1.92 ± 0.62 | 36.62 ± 0.52 | 38.60 ± 0.42 | ±1.98 ± 0.65 |
| Nude wt. (kg) | 70.73 ± 5.75 | 67.33 ± 5.26 | -5.03 ± 0.63† | 70.39 ± 5.57 | 66.67 ± 5.22 | -4.81 ± 0.88† | 70.47 ± 4.50 | 66.70 ± 5.43 | -4.93 ± 0.96† |
| Clothed wt. (kg) | 71.64 ± 5.73 | 68.33 ± 5.25 | -4.94 ± 0.60† | 71.28 ± 5.56 | 67.65 ± 5.16 | -4.73 ± 0.81† | 71.42 ± 5.51 | 67.70 ± 5.39 | -4.94 ± 0.90† |
| Glucose ($mmol \cdot l^{-1}$) | 4.46 ± 0.77 | 4.75 ± 0.58 | 0.28 ± 1.19 | 4.33 ± 0.98 | 5.17 ± 1.02 | 0.85 ± 1.12 | 4.88 ± 0.36 | 4.77 ± 0.82 | -0.10 ± 0.94 |
| Free fatty acids ($mmol \cdot l^{-1}$) | 0.243 ± 0.133 | 2.041 ± 0.817 | 1.798 ± 0.752 | 0.172 ± 0.103 | 1.376 ± 0.954 | 1.204 ± 0.710 | 0.309 ± 0.211 | 2.186 ± 1.831 | 1.877 ± 0.875 |
| Sodium ($mmol \cdot l^{-1}$) | 135.2 ± 2.5 | 141.5 ± 3.3 | 6.3 ± 2.4 | 136.3 ± 4.0 | 140.8 ± 4.7 | 4.5 ± 3.1 | 135.8 ± 2.0 | 141.0 ± 3.8 | 5.2 ± 2.7 |
| Potassium ($mmol \cdot l^{-1}$) | 4.45 ± 0.28 | 5.00 ± 0.43 | 0.44 ± 0.31 | 4.50 ± 0.50 | 4.88 ± 0.26 | 0.40 ± 0.53 | 4.36 ± 0.41 | 4.82 ± 0.59 | 0.46 ± 0.38 |
| Chloride ($mmol \cdot l^{-1}$) | 96.9 ± 2.56 | 100.4 ± 3.69 | 3.5 ± 2.76 | 98.1 ± 2.8 | 104.8 ± 4.12 | 6.7 ± 3.20 | 97.6 ± 4.07 | 101.5 ± 4.41 | 3.9 ± 3.02 |

*Values are mean ± SD.
†Weights have been corrected for fluid ingested and urine excreted.
(Courtesy of Wells, C. et al.: Med. Sci. Sports Exerc. 17:364–369, 1985. Copyright 1985, the American College of Sports Medicine. Reprinted by permission.)

feine does not offer a greater advantage to the long-distance road racer than does the consumption of water.

▶ The manufacturers of proprietary drinks for runners have been quite aggressive not only in advertising their wares at meetings for sports physicians, but also in financing research that "proves" the value of their products. However, there is now increasing support for the view expressed by Kavanagh and myself nearly 10 years ago (*Brit. J. Sports Med.* 11: 26, 1977) that such solutions offer no real advantage relative to unadulterated tap water.—Roy J. Shephard, M.D., Ph.D.

**Effect of Fructose Ingestion on Muscle Glycogen Usage During Exercise**
M. Hargreaves, David L. Costill, A. Katz, and W. J. Fink (Ball State Univ.)
Med. Sci. Sports Exerc. 17:360–363, 1985                                      1–76

Eight healthy male subjects (mean age, 23 years) were studied to compare the effects of preexercise fructose and glucose ingestion on muscle glycogen usage during exercise. Subjects performed three randomly assigned trials, each involving 30 minutes of cycling exercise at 75% $V_{O2max}$. Forty-five minutes prior to commencing each trial, subjects ingested either 50 gm of glucose (G), 50 gm of fructose (F), or sweet placebo (C).

No significant differences were observed between trials for oxygen uptake, respiratory exchange ratio, total energy expenditure, or heart rate. Forty-five minutes after ingestion of the drink, mean blood glucose was elevated ($P < .05$) in trial G. This value was higher ($P < .05$) than after trials F and C. Fructose feeding also resulted in an elevation ($P < .05$) of blood glucose, but at 45 minutes postdrink this was not different from trial C value. No significant differences between trials F and C were observed in the blood glucose response during exercise (Fig 1–35). Plasma insulin was elevated ($P < .05$) as a result of both the fructose and glucose feedings. Muscle glycogen levels were similar in all three trials. Muscle glycogen utilization was greater ($P < .05$) during trial G than trial C.

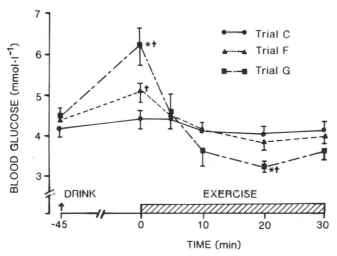

**Fig 1–35.**—Blood glucose during exercise preceded by the ingestion of either glucose (G), fructose (F), or sweet placebo (C). Data are reported as mean ± SE (N = 8). *denotes different from F and C ($P < .05$). †denotes different from predrink value ($P < .05$). (Courtesy of Hargreaves, M., et al.: Med. Sci. Sports Exerc. 17:360–363, 1985. Copyright 1985, the American College of Sports Medicine. Reprinted by permission.)

Fructose is absorbed more slowly from the gut than glucose and is primarily metabolized by the liver. During recovery from exhaustive exercise, fructose is preferentially retained as liver glycogen compared with glucose, which contributes more to muscle glycogen resynthesis. The major benefit of fructose feeding may be the maintenance and/or supplementation of liver carbohydrate stores. Fructose may be of benefit prior to prolonged exercise by providing a source of carbohydrate for later use, without stimulating muscle glycogenolysis during the early stages of the exercise.

▶ Koivisto et al. (*J. Appl. Physiol.* 51: 783, 1981) have previously pointed out the disadvantages of drinking a glucose solution shortly before a race. Because of a rise of serum insulin and a decrease of glucagon, blood glucose falls rapidly, muscle glycogen usage is accelerated, and the time to exhaustion is decreased. The insulin response to fructose is blunter (Bohannon et al.: *J. Am. Diet. Assoc.* 76: 555, 1980), and accordingly this provides a better method of getting carbohydrate into the body before a race. Hargreaves and associates further suggest that fructose accumulates specifically in the liver, offering a chance of supercharge hepatic reserves of carbohydrate.—Roy J. Shephard, M.D., Ph.D.

---

### Plasma Volume and Protein Content in Progressive Exercise: Influence of Cyclooxygenase Inhibitors

James Pivarnik, Thomas Kayrouz, and Leo C. Senay, Jr. (St. Louis Univ.)
Med. Sci. Sports Exerc. 17:153–157, February 1985                           1–77

---

Nonsteroidal anti-inflammatory compounds such as ibuprofen and naproxen reduce plasma volume loss in sheep following injection of endotoxin. It was investigated whether these drugs would change the course of plasma volume reduction during progressive exercise on a cycle ergometer. Fifteen male subjects with a mean age of 26 years exercised for 5 minutes at 20, 30, 40, 50, 60, and 70% of peak $Vo_2$ with and without a 24-hour pretreatment with either ibuprofen or naproxen. The two tests for each subject were done a week apart and blood samples were drawn before and after each exercise level.

Resting plasma osmolalities for ibuprofen and naproxen were not significantly different from control values. The influence of the relative exercise level upon plasma volume loss was identical for controls and for experimental subjects. For control experiments, the actual changes in protein concentration agreed quite well with those theoretically based on complete protein retention with concomitant reduction in plasma volume. For the experimental group, this was not true. At all degrees of plasma volume loss, actual increase in protein concentration is less than that calculated solely on the basis of plasma volume loss. This difference in response proved significant ($P < .05$).

Use of cyclooxygenase inhibitors probably increased the permeability of vascular endothelium to large molecules, which was only evident when hydrostatic and osmotic events in muscle capillaries caused an increase in bulk flow across the capillary walls.

▶ Marathon runners commonly take aspirin and other anti-inflammatory drugs in an attempt to relieve discomfort in the later stages of the race. There are significant increases of prostaglandins $E_2$ and $F_2$ at this stage, and it is thus tempting to administer cyclooxygenase inhibitors such as ibuprofen.

Though there are situations where such agents reduce plasma efflux, this does not appear to be the case during sustained exercise; indeed, by allowing the escape of protein, the potential for sustaining plasma volume is probably somewhat reduced after administration of ibuprofen.—Roy J. Shephard, M.D., Ph.D.

---

**Jogging in Middle Age**
Michael J. Lichtenstein (Vanderbilt Univ.)
J. R. Coll. Gen. Practitioners 35:341–345, July 1985                    1–78

---

Those who participate in regular exercise note an improvement in work performance, increased stamina, a feeling of being more healthy, decreased stress, and an increased ability to sleep and rest. Another possible benefit of regular exercise is based on the hypothesis that exercise protects against the development of ischemic heart disease. Surveys in the United States during the past 10 years indicate that about 50% of the population engage in some form of regular exercise, including walking (14%), jogging (13%), and calisthenics (9%). In general, younger persons exercise more than older persons do, and men exercise more than women. A striking feature is the inverse relationship between education levels and attitudes toward health. Individuals with less than a high school education were more likely to smoke cigarettes, be overweight, be dissatisfied with their physical condition, and to undertake half the rate of exercise of those who completed high school.

Regular aerobic exercise has a cardiovascular training effect and improves physical fitness (the ability to perform more work at a given heart rate). Persons who are more physically fit have higher levels of high-density lipoprotein cholesterol and lower blood pressure, and smoke cigarettes less often compared with less fit individuals of the same age. A prospective study of 6,000 exercisers found that in a median time of 4 years, those with the lowest level of fitness were 1.5 times more likely to have high blood pressure than were those whose level of fitness was high. In a prospective study of Los Angeles policemen it was found that asymptomatic individuals with a below-median capacity for exercise were more than twice as likely to sustain a myocardial infarction in the ensuing 5 years than were those having an above-median capacity for exercise. These findings support an association between level of fitness and risk of ischemic heart disease.

Thus, advice that physicians might give to middle-aged men concerning jogging and its potential cardiac benefits should include a number of points. A lifelong habit of vigorous physical exercise results in a lower incidence of ischemic heart disease. However, whether incidence rates are lowered when sedentary middle-aged individuals decide to become exercisers remains unclear. The changes brought about by exercise (e.g., improvement in physical fitness, reduction in blood pressure and weight, and the possibility of giving up cigarette smoking) make this an attractive procedure for risk factor modification in motivated individuals. There may be other coronary risk factors (e.g., socioeconomic factors or a family history of ischemic heart disease) that jogging cannot alter. There is a small risk of death from ischemic heart disease associated with jogging: About 12 sudden deaths per 100,000 male joggers occur yearly in the United States. Performance of screening treadmill tests to detect asymptomatic ischemic heart disease is unnecessary prior to initiating jogging. If the level of exercise is increased gradually and any prodromal symptoms heeded, the number of unexpected deaths from ischemic heart disease associated with jogging may be minimized. Musculoskeletal injuries in joggers are not uncommon.

A survey of 1,423 joggers capable of running a 10-km road race revealed that 35% had experienced a musculoskeletal injury associated with running in the preceding year. The most commonly affected sites were the knees (25%), Achilles tendon (18%), forefoot (10%), shin (10%), ankles (9%), arch (8%), heel (8%), and hamstring muscles (5%). Of those running 50 miles weekly, 70% of men and 58% of women reported a musculoskeletal injury in the preceding year.

▶ There is a small but definite risk of cardiac disease, including sudden death, when jogging is instituted in middle age. A significant percentage of this population, roughly ⅓, will have musculoskeletal injury of consequence within a 12-month interval. For all of this, most physicians have accepted the philosophic position that this study supports, that exercise will result in improved work performance, stamina, sense of well-being, ability to handle stress, and increased ability to sleep and rest. Whether the start-up of significant exercise levels in middle age will impact on the development of cardiovascular disease remains to be answered, and will interrelate with multiple factors of race, weight, socioeconomic class, and family genetics. It is not a simple equation.—Lewis J. Krakauer, M.D., F.A.C.P.

### The Effect of Running on the Pathogenesis of Osteoarthritis of the Hips and Knees

Roger S. Sohn and Lyle J. Micheli (Children's Hosp. Med. Ctr., Boston)
Clin. Orthop. 198:106–109, September 1985                                    1–79

Former college varsity athletes were surveyed by questionnaire to determine if long-distance running can be implicated as a factor in the future development of osteoarthritis of the hips and knees. Subjects were divided into two groups. One group consisted of 504 former varsity cross-country runners. A control group consisted of 287 college swimmers. Follow-up periods ranged from 2 to 55 years, with a mean of 25 years.

Overall there was a 2% incidence of severe hip or knee pain among former runners. Among former swimmers, there was an incidence of severe hip or knee pain of 2.4%. When mild and moderate pain were included, runners had an incidence of 15.5% and swimmers had 19.5%. There were 7 surgical procedures for osteoarthritis for relief of pain in 6 swimmers. There were 4 such surgical procedures in 4 runners. The number of runners reporting severe pain was so proportionally small that no meaningful conclusions could be drawn. There was no difference in the number of years run between the group of runners reporting painful joints and those reporting no pain.

The authors conclude that there is no association between running at moderate levels (about 25 miles per week) and the development of osteoarthritis. Heavy mileage (50–140 miles per week) appears not to be associated with osteoarthritis. And, there is no association between the number of years of running and the development of osteoarthritis.

▶ The findings and conclusion of this study are similar to that of Panesh et al. (*Am. Med. Assoc. J.* 255: 9, 152–154, March 7, 1986), who compared the problem of degenerative joint disease among 17 male runners with 18 male nonrunners. The running subjects ran a mean of 28 miles per week for 12 years. That study demonstrated no increase in prevalence of osteoarthritis among the runners and the authors concluded that long-distance, high-mileage runners need not be associated with premature degenerative disease in the lower extremity.—Joseph S. Torg, M.D.

---

**Ski Injuries in 1976–1982: Ybrig Region, Switzerland**
A. Blankstein, M. Salai, A. Israeli, A. Ganel, H. Horoszowski, and I. Farine (Chaim Sheba Med. Ctr., Tel Hashomer, Israel)
Int. J. Sports Med. 6:298–300, October 1985                    1–80

---

Ski injuries are increasing with the widening interest in the sport. A review was made of 1,763 consecutive injuries occurring at a popular middle-sized ski resort at Ybrig, Switzerland in the 1976–1982 ski seasons. Injuries increased with the crowd size and were most frequent on weekends. The estimated rate of injury was 3.7 per 1,000 skiers' days. The mean age of injured skiers was 19 years.

One third of all injuries were fractures. Total injuries decreased over the review period. Nearly all skiers used higher, stiffer boots. Tibia and fibula fractures declined in frequency over the years. Knee injuries were the next most common in downhill skiing. Shoulder injuries, especially dislocations, increased, whereas rates of ankle and foot injuries remained the same. Most of the dislocations involved the shoulder.

Ski injuries have declined at Ybrig, in accordance with those occurring at other ski resorts. More tibia and fibula fractures and fewer ankle fractures generally are seen with the use of higher, stiffer ski boots. Refinement of ski slopes may contribute to the decrease in injuries. More attention should be given to the preparation (e.g., training and teaching) of skiers. Knowledge of the slopes to be skied will help reduce the occurrence of ski injuries.

▶ The observed change in skiing injury patterns, a decrease in ankle fractures while tibia fracture and knee injuries increased, is related to the use of the higher, stiffer boot. The decrease in incidence with a concomitant increase in severity of injuries is disconcerting. The suggestion for improvement of slope design and maintenance as well as skier preparation deserves evaluation.—Joseph S. Torg, M.D.

---

**Serious Ski Jumping Injuries in Norway**
Knut Wester (Rikshospitalet, Oslo)
Am. J. Sports Med. 13:124–127, March–April 1985                    1–81

Serious injuries caused by ski jumping were classified and the possible etiologic factors causing them were analyzed. Data were collected from three sources: the files of insurance company covering all licensed jumpers in Norway, ski clubs, and all Norwegian hospitals.

At least 12 persons were seriously injured while ski jumping in Norway in the period 1977–1981. Seven injuries were very serious (4 CNS lesions, 2 leg amputations, and blindness in one eye), and 5 were slightly to moderately disabling (all sequelae associated with leg fractures). In the 1981–1982 season, Norway had 2,238 licensed jumpers aged at least 12 years. An estimated national total of 5 million ski jumps were made during the 5 years studied, resulting in a risk of sustaining a serious injury in one ski jump of only 0.003%. Serious injuries were not recorded in jumpers younger than age 12 years. The risk of injury was more than doubled for children aged 15 to 17 years and was decreased in adults.

Serious injuries seemed to occur in the beginning and at the end of the season. Four jumpers fell before they reached the takeoff point, sustaining very serious injuries (3 complete spinal cord transections and 1 leg amputation). All 4 blamed uneven snow conditions. Also, all 4 used higher heel blocks than the other injured jumpers used. Four jumpers blamed personal errors for the accident.

The following precautions should be taken to prevent serious injuries in ski jumping: The jumper and coach should examine the jump thoroughly before the first jump of the day; trainers should be careful not to allow young jumpers to attempt longer jumps than they are qualified for; the jump should be thoroughly prepared all the way to the takeoff point; more than one standard heel block should not be used; and special care should be taken at the beginning and end of the season.

▶ A more meaningful way to view this data is to compare the seasonal quadriplegic rate for Norwegian ski jumpers to that of scholastic and intercollegiate football players in this country. Over a 5-year period, three accidents resulted in quadriplegia, with 2,238 licensed jumpers participating annually. Thus, the yearly quadriplegic rate is 27.3 per 100,000 jumpers. This compares to a quadriplegic rate in American football of 0.8 per 100,000 participants per season.—Joseph S. Torg, M.D.

---

**Snow, Cold and Energy Expenditure: A Basis for Fatigue and Skiing Accidents**
John R. Brotherhood (Univ. of Sydney, Australia)
Aust. J. Sci. Med. Sports 17:3–7, March 1985                                     1–82

---

Muscle fatigue from the energetic demands of skiing may be a factor in ski injuries. Walking in snow and skiing require considerable muscular effort. In cross-country skiing, a linear relation exists between speed and energy expenditure. Bulky clothing may be worn in cold conditions, increasing energy expenditure substantially. There is little doubt that muscle performance deteriorates during continued skiing, and a level of fatigue that increases the risk of injury may occur in as short a time as 2 hours. Fatigue occurs much more rapidly whenever physical demands exceed the muscle oxygen supply, as in extended downhill runs. Increased demand for heat production in a cold environment hastens the onset of fatigue. If heat output is inadequate to prevent cooling, more clothing must be put on, or shelter sought. Spare clothes and emergency shelter always should be taken by the ski tourer.

Good physical fitness is the best protection against fatigue during skiing. Endurance and strength training for the legs and arms is especially important. An awareness of the inevitability of fatigue and its possible effects may dispose skiers to avoid the "one last run." Adequate recovery times and appropriate food are important aspects of a ski holiday. At least 12 hours may be necessary to recover from 3–4 hours of energetic skiing. Parties of ski tourers should include persons of comparable ability, and the pace should be set by the slowest members. Route planning should take the weather into account. Adequate water replacement should be assured, and the food should be predominantly carbohydrate.

▶ The author states that "the aim of this paper is to examine the possibility that, for many, the energetic demands of skiing lead to muscular fatigue, which in turn may be a predisposing factor for some accidents." However, he relies on others (Eriksson A., et al.: *International Series on Sports Sciences,* Baltimore, University Park Press, pp. 279–286, 1978, and Korbel C. J. and Zelcer J., *Proceedings of International Society for Ski Safety,* Munich, TUV Publications, 1982) to substantiate this thesis. However, the paper does present a good review of relevant literature on the physiology of traveling in snow, downhill skiing, and responses to low temperatures. —Joseph S. Torg, M.D.

### Outcome of Sports Injuries Treated in a Casualty Department

J. Sandelin, O. Kiviluoto, S. Santavirta, and R. Honkanen (Univ. Central Hosp., Helsinki)
Br. J. Sports Med. 19:103–106, June 1985                    1–83

Data on 2,493 patients with a sports injury treated in a casualty department during 1978 were reviewed. Of the patients, 73% were men. The average age was 26 years and mean follow-up time was 24 months. Soccer and indoor ball games caused 24% and 23% of the injuries, respectively; these were followed by injuries in ice hockey in 14%. Track and field injuries occurred in only 2% of all injuries. Injuries of the lower extremity predominated.

At follow-up, 1,813 (73%) patients were free of any discomfort, whereas 680 (27%) were still bothered by their injury. Pain during exercise was reported by 54% of those still suffering from the sequelae of their injury. This symptom was significantly ($P < .001$) the most common form of late discomfort, followed by limited motion of a joint (19%). Distortions proved to be the type of injury causing most of the discomfort at follow-up (41%) ($P < .001$), followed by fractures and dislocations (36%), contusions (13%), and wounds (10%). Most injuries causing discomfort at the time of follow-up were located in the lower extremities (56%) ($P < .001$). Patients who had had an injury in the upper extremities comprised 36% of this group. Dislocations and fractures caused significantly more long-term discomfort than other injuries ($P < .001$). Upper extremity injuries caused long-term discomfort significantly more often than injuries at other locations ($P < .001$). Individuals between ages 35 and 44 years had the longest period of absence from sports after injury, with an average of 4 weeks. In the age group 25 to 34 years, this absence averaged 3 weeks, and in the rest of the age groups it was 1–2 weeks.

The authors conclude that the sports injuries they recorded were modest. The significance of adequate primary diagnosis is emphasized, especially in knee injuries, which can account for 30% of all injuries.

▶ The authors establish that the 211,000 athletic injuries that occur in Finland annually are a considerable national health and economic problem, because 60% of the injured are permanently employed. The injury patterns reported in a population of 2,493 patients are somewhat unique. Only 5% of the injuries involved the knee. Perhaps this is a reflection of a lack of American football, basketball, field hockey, and lacrosse. At follow-up, it was noted "rather unexpectedly" that injuries involving the upper extremities "cause more discomfort." The authors conclude that acute athletic injuries can be effectively and correctly treated in a general traumatologic unit. A death knell for the "Helsinki Sports Medicine Center." Anyway, so much for socialized medicine.—Joseph S. Torg, M.D.

### Physiological and Biochemical Measurements During a 4-Day Surf-Ski Marathon

T. D. Noakes, M. Nathan, R. A. Irving, R. Van Zyl Smit, P. Meissner, G. Kotzenberg, and T. Victor (Univ. of Cape Town, South Africa)
S. Afr. Med. J. 67:212–216, Feb. 9, 1985                    1–84

The authors studied competitors in the 1983 Texan Challenge surf-ski paddle marathon to determine the effects of 4 days' prolonged paddling on sweat rates, rectal temperatures, renal function, serum glucose, free fatty acid, porphyrin and C-reactive protein levels, and serum creatine kinase activity. A total of 30 subjects participated: group 1 (n = 6) were weighed each morning and studied for fluid balance, group 2 (n = 6) were studied for rectal temperatures, group 3 (n = 5) were studied for renal function, and group 4 (n = 13) participated in the serum creatine kinase (CK) activity determination.

There was a significant fall in early-morning body weight on the second and third days of the competition, but by the fourth day the early-morning weight had returned to control levels. Rectal temperatures at the end of the last stage in group 2 subjects had a mean of 37.7 C. These 6 subjects

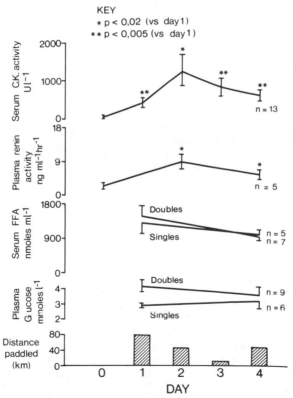

**Fig 1–36.**—Changes in serum CK and plasma renin activities and in serum FFA and blood glucose levels during the 4 days of the competition. Note the marked elevation in serum CK and plasma renin activities. (Courtesy of Noakes, T.D., et al.: S. Afr. Med. J. 67:212–216, Feb. 9, 1985.)

paddled considerably faster than group 1 subjects and were considerably more dehydrated. Biochemical values showed urine flow and creatinine clearance rates and electrolyte excretion remained within normal limits. Urine osmolality did not diminish. Figure 1–36 shows that serum CK activity rose markedly after the first day's paddling and fell progressively but was still significantly elevated after the fourth day.

These data emphasize that the avoidance of hyperthermia is not a factor in surf-ski paddling, at least under the mild environmental conditions in this study. The avoidance of hypoglycemia during paddling would seem to be far more important. Ski-paddlers must be encouraged to eat a high-carbohydrate diet for the duration of the race and to ingest carbohydrate-containing drinks and foods while paddling.

▶ This is probably the first detailed scientific report concerning very long distance paddling; owing to weather conditions, 186 km of the intended 244 km was covered over 4 days.

As in running over a comparable period, C-reactive protein increased, and the serum creatine kinase activity rose to over 1,000 units per liter.

One important factor limiting performance was the drop in serum glucose. Even after the first day, more than 70% of race participants had levels of less than 3.9 mmole/L, and 27% had figures of less than 3 mmole/L (54 mg/dl). The authors stress that these levels are low enough to have effects upon the judgment of the competitor—an important safety consideration when paddling in rough water or in isolated territory. One competitor even needed intravenous glucose on the beach.—Roy J. Shephard, M.D., Ph.D.

---

**Fresh Water Swimming as a Risk Factor for Otitis Externa: A Case-Control Study**
Gerald L. Springer and Eugene D. Shapiro (Yale Univ.)
Arch. Environ. Health 40:202–206, July–August 1985                                    1–85

---

Otitis externa (OE), an inflammatory condition of the skin of the external ear canal, is associated with swimming, thus giving rise to its common name of "swimmer's ear." Repeated exposure to water is thought to remove the protective waxy coating of the external ear canal, allowing it to become macerated and predisposing it to infection by gram-negative bacteria, particularly *Pseudomonas aeruginosa. Pseudomonas,* ubiquitous in inanimate moist environments, has been incriminated in many outbreaks of OE among swimmers in pools with poorly functioning chlorination systems.

A case-control study, comprising emergency department patients, was conducted in which the amount and site (a freshwater lake or river, a chlorinated pool, or the ocean) of recent swimming by 105 patients with OE were compared with those of 239 controls. Swimming during the week before the visit was strongly associated with OE. When the 80 cases and 127 controls with a history of recent swimming were compared, OE was positively associated with the amount of swimming during the preceding week. Otitis externa was also positively associated with swimming in fresh water compared with ocean or pool swimming; the magnitude of this association was more pronounced at higher levels of exposure.

Socioeconomic status was considered to be a potentially important variable since the poor, who tend to use the emergency department as their main source of primary care, might be expected to have different patterns of swimming than the economically advantaged. However, no significant differences were found between the groups with respect either to the mode of payment or the place of residence, both indicators of socioeconomic status that were readily available. Additionally, multivariate analysis did not suggest that means of payment played a confounding role in this study.

Several forms of bias may have occurred. Because of the well-known association between swimming and OE, case subjects might have recalled past swimming more readily than those in the control group. However, since subjects were asked only about swimming during the week before enrollment, any such recall bias should have been minimized. Similarly, physicians may have been more likely to diagnose OE in those with a recent history of swimming than in those without such a history. Two tactics were employed to minimize this potential bias. First, the data for the study were collected by someone other than the physician who assessed the patient and were not shared with him. Second, before the study was begun, the diagnostic criteria for OE were reviewed with all physicians who worked in the emergency department, with stress being placed on physical rather than historical findings.

Swimmers with OE were more likely to have swum longer, more frequently, and with more frequent submersion of their heads than swimmers without OE. These relationships were independent of the type of water in which the individuals had swum. Swimmers with high exposure scores who had OE were much more likely to have swum in fresh water than were swimmers with high exposure scores who did not have this condition. Extensive swimming, therefore, seems to be a risk factor for development of OE regardless of the type of water to which one is exposed. However, swimming in fresh water (as opposed to pool or ocean water) seems to substantially increase the risk of OE only in those who swim frequently. Frequent or prolonged swimming appears to be a precondition for the adverse effects of freshwater exposure to manifest themselves.

▶ There is no question that the duration of exposure to water correlates with the expression of otitis externa. This is further enhanced by swimming in fresh waters compared with swimming in the ocean or in a chlorinated swimming pool. The common denominator remains the duration of exposure and the amount of immersion. The common villain is the *Pseudomonas*. The risks of swimming in inadequately chlorinated pools are not confined to otitis externa. They may also put one at risk of pharyngoconjunctival fever due to adenovirus, hepatitis virus, poliovirus, ECHO virus, Coxsackie virus, and parainfluenza viruses; all of which have been isolated from swimming pools without 2 ppm or higher of chlorine (1982 YEAR BOOK OF SPORTS MEDICINE, pp. 313–314).—Lewis J. Krakauer, M.D., F.A.C.P.

## Influence of Transdermal Scopolamine on Motion Sickness During 7 Days' Exposure to Heavy Seas

W. F. van Marion, M. C. M. Bongaerts, J. C. Christiaanse, H. G. Hofkamp, and W. van Ouwerkerk (Marine Hospitaal, Overveen, The Netherlands)
Clin. Pharmacol. Ther. 38:301–305, September 1985                    1–86

A double-blind, placebo-controlled study was conducted to evaluate the utility of transdermal scopolamine in the prevention of motion sickness (MS) aboard a frigate during 7 days of continuously moderate or heavy seas. Forty-nine healthy sailors with a previous history of MS were randomly assigned to receive a transdermal therapeutic system for delivery of scopolamine (TTS-S) or transdermal placebo (TD-P). Patches were 2.5 sq cm in area and contained either scopolamine, 0.5 mg, or placebo. Patches were placed behind the ears at least 4 hours before departure and were removed 72 hours later. Subjects were observed on days 1–4 and 6.

During the first two days, the overall feeling of MS in the TTS-S group was reduced, the difference being maximal on the second day. This is confirmed by the parallel course of the diminished frequency of nausea, an objective endpoint of MS. The increased ability to perform daily work on the second day reflects the decline of MS. The efficacy of TTS-S was also demonstrated by the decrease in subjective feelings of MS and the reduced need for additional cyclizine tablets. The reduced protection represented by the overall feeling of MS on the first day compared with that on the second day can be explained by the time of application of TTS-S before departure (4 hours). Since signs of MS, nausea, and subjective feelings of MS did not diminish in the TD-P group, adaptation did not contribute to the greater protection in the TTS-S group during the second day. During the 48–72 hours after application, the four principal symptoms of MS occurred less frequently in the TTS-S group than in the TD-P group. However, the differences were not significant because of a substantial reduction in symptoms due to adaptation in the TD-P group. On day 6, 3 days after removal of the TTS-S patch, vomiting occurred in 6 (23%) subjects in the TTS-S group; these subjects had an increased subjective feeling of MS, were nauseated, and were pale. This phenomenon was probably due to a delay in adaptation because of the use of TTS-S.

A withdrawal effect of scopolamine is unlikely, because vomiting on the sixth day was not reported under light sea conditions. The absence of signs and symptoms of MS on the fourth day, 1 day after removal of the TTS-S patch, can be ascribed to the lasting effect of scopolamine. The latter also caused the persistence of dry mouth reported by 33% of the subjects in the TTS-S group 1 day after removal of the TTS-S patch. The lasting presence of scopolamine after removal of the TTS-S may have implications for the repeated use of TTS-S. A new patch applied within 24 hours after removal of the previous one may increase unwanted side effects. The most frequently reported unwanted effect was dry mouth. The persistence of dry mouth 1 day after removal of the TTS-S patch can also be ascribed to continuing effects of scopolamine. Five of the 88 patches used, all from the TTS-S group, became dislodged. Skin irritation was noted in 17% of all applications, a finding comparable with that of Homick et al. However, skin irritation did not increase after 72 hours of continuous patch use.

It appears that TTS-S applied at least 4 hours, but preferably longer, before exposure to moderate or heavy seas offers effective protection against MS for at least 48 hours and probably longer. This allows improved ability to function during exposure. Dry mouth, the only side effect associated with TTS-S, was mild. Visual disturbances were reported infrequently and never influenced the ability to perform daily work aboard a frigate. Because of the lasting presence of scopolamine, a new TTS-S patch should not be applied within 24 hours after removal of an earlier patch.

---

**Transdermally Administered Scopolamine vs. Dimenhydrinate: I. Effect on Nausea and Vertigo in Experimentally Induced Motion Sickness**
I. Pyykkö, L. Schalén, and V. Jäntti (Univ. of Lund)
Acta Otolaryngol. (Stockh.) 99:588–596, June 1985                    1–87

---

The transdermal therapeutic system (TTS) for delivery of scopolamine has been shown to protect against motion sickness in laboratory studies and at sea. The benefits and adverse effects of TTS-scopolamine were compared with those of dimenhydrinate in 8 healthy subjects of each sex aged 21 to 38 years. One TTS-scopolamine programmed to deliver about 5 μg of scopolamine base per hour was compared with 2 TTS-scopolamine and with 100 mg of dimenhydrinate in capsule form with 50 mg of caffeine. The TTS-scopolamine was applied retroaurally 12 hours before testing by the Coriolis maneuver. Dimenhydrinate was given 12 hours and 1 hour before testing. A double-blind, crossover, dummy-blind design was used. Vertigo was induced by caloric stimulation of the ear.

Scopolamine was adequately absorbed consistently. All treatments significantly reduced nausea compared with placebo, but dimenhydrinate was somewhat more effective than 1 TTS-scopolamine. Vertigo was significantly reduced by 2 TTS-scopolamine and by dimenhydrinate. Side effects were negligible, although gait disorder sometimes followed 2 TTS-scopolamine. Visual disorder was not observed with active treatments.

Both TTS-scopolamine and dimenhydrinate are effective against motion sickness, but the former must be administered 6 to 8 hours before exposure. Subjects with established symptoms should be given scopolamine in conventional form. Otherwise, good protection is provided for several days. Transdermal administration may be the only safe route in subjects with esophageal dysfunction.

---

**Seasickness: A Look at the Remedies**
Lynda Morris
Cruising World 30–36, August 1985                    1–88

---

Seasickness is not a psychological disorder. The sensory conflict theory based on confusion between what the eye sees and the information transmitted to the brain is currently popular. Overstimulation of nerve fibers in the inner ear also is a possibility. Early symptoms include drowsiness, lethargy, and abnormal fatigue. Pallor, queasiness, and nausea-vomiting ensue, and dehydration and electrolyte imbalance can result. Victims may have impaired judgment and loss of physical coordination.

Scopolamine now is available in patch form and probably is one of the most effective available agents, although side effects have been reported. Ocular difficulties can occur when medication enters the eyes via the hands. It may be difficult to distinguish side effects from scopolamine from symptoms of motion sickness. The antihistamines act by reducing the sensitivity of nerve endings in the inner ear. Cyclizine and meclizine have caused birth defects in laboratory animals. Buclizine has allegedly caused birth defects in humans.

Seasickness may occur in association with excessive alcohol or inadequate sleep before boating. A position amidships is best. Those with early symptoms should remain in the open air and avoid reading or preparing food. Some have obtained relief from acupuncture. Biofeedback is under evaluation for use by astronauts to alleviate space sickness, and appears to be effective.

▶ Double-blind studies have shown with little argument that the TTS-scopolamine disks are effective in dealing with motion sickness, and more so if used prophylactically. However, the effect of scopolamine may be long lasting. The patch should not be repeated within 24 hours of the first usage, or significant side effects will occur. Dry mouth is common. Blurred vision is not a rarity despite the comments in Digest 1–86. Perhaps dealing with young Navy people makes the blurred vision less likely than with an older population group.

Digest 1–87 reiterates the point that scopolamine will be most effective in the patch form if given 6 to 8 hours before exposure. After symptoms develop, the use of *regular* scopolamine is more effective, and is probably equaled by Dramamine or Bonamine.

Standard use in many oceanography programs is that of antihistamine, promethazine, and ephedrine (25 mgs each) 2 hours prior to departure and every 6 hours thereafter. This has been widely tested in the Coast Guard and Navy, and is quite effective.

The only remedy more effective still is that which has been used by NASA, a combination of scopolamine and low-dose dexedrine taken at the same time. This is not available to the general population because of the tight restrictions on dexamphetamine use, even though it is the most effective treatment. The amphetamine counters the drowsiness induced by most of the other agents. This combination was omitted from the table published in the original abstract, presumably because of the legal implications of suggesting the use of an amphetamine.

It is difficult to distinguish sometimes between the side effects of scopolamine and the actual symptoms of motion sickness. The simplicity of the attachable scopolamine disk has much appeal. Most people are inappropriately afraid of motion sickness. It is usually milder than anticipated and is responsive to fresh air and other simple measures, such as avoiding the extreme fore and aft of a vessel. Motion sickness is uncommon in the age of jet travel, considering air travel alone. My own preference would be to recommend the promethazine and ephedrine regimen as the simplest and least expensive, with the scopolamine disks only for those with a recurrent history of severe motion sickness, and with an awareness of the anticipated side effects.—Lewis J. Krakauer, M.D., F.A.C.P.

**Neurologic Presentation of Decompression Sickness and Air Embolism in Sport Divers**
Arthur P. K. Dick and E. Wayne Massey (Duke Univ.)
Neurology 35:667–671, May 1985                                    1–89

Decompression sickness and air embolism have been characterized in industrial, navy, and experimental studies but not in modern sport divers. During 1981 and 1982 there were 117 cases of sport diving accidents with neurologic injury who received treatment with help from the National Diving Accident Network (D.A.N.). The authors reviewed the course of illness in recreational divers by reviewing D.A.N. injury and incident reports for the years 1981 and 1982.

Of the 117 cases studied, 70 had neurologic decompression sickness and 39 had cerebral air embolism. In 8 cases, etiology was not established. Decompression sickness most commonly caused a progressive sensory or motor loss of extremities. Symptoms began with a warm or prickly paresthesia, often followed by regional numbness and occasionally with weakness or paralysis of the affected extremities. Only 19% of these cases started within 10 minutes of surfacing. Almost half occurred 1 hour or more after the dive, and 28% started 6 hours after the dive. In 41% of the incidents, patients with cerebral air embolism were unconscious; unconsciousness almost always occurred within minutes of surfacing. Cognitive dysfunction was prominent. Sixty-nine percent of those with cerebral air embolism had symptoms upon surfacing from the dive and 91% had symptoms within 10 minutes. Four divers in this study were adolescents, but most were between the ages 20 and 40 years. In decompression sickness, 22 patients gave histories of dives that exceeded accepted safety standards, but 42 met these standards. In air embolism, 6 cases occurred in training; 10 other cases had determinable causes, but 18 cases (53%) occurred after apparently acceptable and reasonable dives. The primary treatment of decompression sickness and air embolism is recompression therapy. The outcome of mild decompression sickness, rated as less than 3/10 on their severity scale, was generally excellent, whether divers were treated or not. With scores of 7–10, therapy was seldom successful and residual symptoms were commonly present at 6 months. Of the 39 patients with cerebral air embolism, 8 lost consciousness immediately and required CPR. Five of these 8 died and one has persistent cognitive impairment. Of 8 who lost consciousness but did not require CPR, none died. Twenty-three remaining patients did not lose consciousness and resolved all symptoms.

Although no controlled studies have been done to examine the benefit of early breathing of 100% oxygen in these injuries, the authors observed prompt improvement in the few cases when injured divers breathed oxygen immediately after onset of neurologic symptoms from either decompression sickness or air embolism.

▶ This is a useful paper, setting in some perspective the risks of sport diving. As in most problems of this type, the incidence of the various disorders cannot be calculated precisely, because the numbers diving within and beyond the accepted safety limits are not known. Nevertheless, it seems clear that an appreciable number of enthusiasts are developing neurologic forms of decompression sickness and cerebral air embolism following dives well within accepted tables; some of those with decompression sickness are permanently paralyzed, and about one in seven patients with cerebral air embolism die. Possibly, there is a need to revise the diving tables, or to provide the recreational diver with an analog computer of the type used by naval divers. The physician must also be vigilant for cases of late onset, given that 28% of the incidents of decompression sickness began as late as 6 hours after the dive. The outcome is strongly influenced by prompt recognition of the condition and the early initiation of recompression.—Roy J. Shephard, M.D., Ph.D.

---

## Decompression Syndrome of the Spinal Cord: Results of Early and Late Treatment

A. A. Bühlmann (University of Zurich)
Schweiz. Med. Wochenschr. 115:796–800, 1985                    1–90

---

Decompression syndrome of the spinal cord consists of multiple gas bubbles in the capillaries of the spinal cord, resulting in focal blockage of the microcirculation. Development of a perifocal edema enlarges the ischemic areas; sensorimotor deficits are thus more severe as a rule than would seem justified by the initial capillary obstruction. In general, neurologic findings due to multilocular damage in decompression sickness of the spinal cord are clearly distinguishable from symptoms associated with a transverse lesion. In scuba diving, the central pulmonary rupture with infiltration of alveolar gas into the blood stream is a relatively frequent cause of gas embolism.

Between 1969 and 1984 a total of 20 scuba divers with decompression syndrome of the spinal cord were treated at the University of Zurich; reanimation and maintenance of thermal status should be the first consideration. In the absence of spontaneous breathing, intubation precedes recompression with artificial respiration. In 12 of the divers recompression was initiated with a latency of several hours; this early treatment was successful in 11 patients. Remission of neurologic symptoms was noted already during recompression even in 7 paraplegic patients of this group. Most of the gas bubbles in the spinal cord will largely resorb within 2–3 days; restitution of the injured spinal cord is now the focus of attention. In 9 patients late treatment (48 to 192 hours after diving) consisted of repeated hyperbaric oxygen exposures. Three patients with mild neurologic disturbances responded with total remission. In 5 of 6 paraplegic patients treatment remained without success, albeit in 3 of these there had been a 15 to 24 hour delay of therapy. Still, all 6 paraplegics clearly improved during late treatment. Of the 9 patients exposed to hyperbaric oxygen, 8 were transported by air with slightly reduced cabin pressure without deterioration of neurologic symptoms.

▶ As in the U.S. survey (Digest 1–89), this report from Switzerland shows a substantial number of very serious problems arising in recreational divers. In general, the depths involved were 30–60 meters, but one was as little as 12 meters. The message of early recompression is again stressed; where there was a 15–24 hour delay, there was a likelihood of permanent paraplegia, despite the use of hyperbaric oxygen 4 hours per day.— Roy J. Shephard, M.D. Ph.D.

---

**Central Nervous Dysfunction Associated With Deep-Sea Diving**
Johan A. Aarli, Ragnar Vaernes, Alf O. Brubakk, Harald Nyland, Haavard Skeidsvoll, and Stein Tønjum (Univ. of Bergen, Norway)
Acta Neurol. Scand. 71:2–10, January 1985                                      1–91

---

The increasing importance of the deep-sea industry makes the possible neurologic consequences of deep-sea diving significant. Twenty-three professional divers aged 26 to 37 years, with 6 to 20 years of experience in diving, were evaluated. All were in good health and without significant medical disorders. Twelve divers were evaluated after onshore (chamber) trial dives to 350 m sea water (msw) and 13 after an open sea dive to 300 msw. All dives were done using helium/oxygen as the breathing gas, at a partial pressure of oxygen of 0.4–0.6 barometric pressure. Compression was staged, with stops for acclimatization. Decompression from 350 msw required about 10 days.

All of the divers had neurologic symptoms and signs during compression. The high-pressure nervous syndrome (HPNS) includes ataxia, intention tremor, motor weakness, sensory symptoms, vertigo, nausea, and impaired memory. Mental symptoms developed first. Behavioral disturbances and euphoria were not infrequent. Motor symptoms included unsteadiness and clumsiness. Five of the 12 divers had marked EEG disturbances, with impaired alpha rhythm and increased 2–7 Hz activity. Considerable differences were noted among the divers with regard to clinical and EEG abnormalities. Changes were most evident in divers who made 2 dives 3 months apart. Four divers had transient signs of focal cerebral dysfunction immediately after diving. Neuropsychological testing showed impairment persisting for a month after diving.

Pressure-induced cerebral dysfunction can persist for some time after a deep-sea dive. Loss of short-term memory is a prominent finding. Minimal subclinical CNS lesions may be unmasked by a deep-sea dive. Some time may be required for neurologic recovery to take place between deep dives. Further studies are needed to determine the mechanisms involved in diving-related neurologic changes.

▶ This study is concerned with deep-sea diving at a depth appreciably greater than the maximal 100–200 foot depth of scuba diving, and is not a syndrome that relates to sport diving except in the extreme exception. The difference is that scuba diving uses compressed air and deep-sea diving uses mixtures of helium and oxygen as the breathing gas.

This paper describes a pressure-induced dysfunction of the cerebral cortex. It is interesting that the most prominent symptom will be the loss of short-term memory. It would be unusual for dysfunction to last longer than 30 days without underlying neurologic disease. It would seem to me that this order of cerebral dysfunction could present in scuba diving if there were a predisposing clinical neurologic deficit such as hydrocephalus or occult vascular disease. Such symptoms presenting in a scuba diver would have implications of underlying neurologic disease warranting appropriate referral and work-up.—Lewis J. Krakauer, M.D., F.A.C.P.

---

**Loss of Consciousness While Diving**
C. Bares (Brest, France)
Med. Sport. 59:153–157, 1985                                                    1–92

---

The various causes for loss of consciousness while diving are considered with emphasis on the particular aspects of professional diving. Just as all diving accidents accompanied by loss of consciousness may result in drowning, all cases of drowning while diving can become complicated by a decompression problem. Loss of consciousness in the context of this review is understood both in its literal sense, a state of unconsciousness with amnesia, as well as syncopal episodes where a death-like state with cardiocirculatory arrest results in cerebral ischemia. Three types of syncope are distinguished: (1) thermo-differential shock or cryogenic syncope linked to vasomotor disequilibrium, (2) allergic syncope, described in carriers of cold cryoglobulins, with liberation of histamine and serotonin, accompanied by massive loss of arterial tonus, and (3) nasopharyngeal ictus due to irritation of internal mucous membranes of upper respiratory pathways. Loss of consciousness may be caused by previously unrecognized pathology made manifest by stress; total exhaustion, or even toxic influences (alcohol, psychostimulants) may also be responsible. Among specific causes are those of mechanical, biochemical, and biophysical origin, as well as those involving environmental elements (temperature, submarine fauna).

Whatever the cause of the loss of consciousness, these subjects must be considered as drowning victims, hypercapnic anoxics in acute respiratory distress, dehydrated and in a state of metabolic acidosis; therapeutic efforts must be oriented accordingly. Diagnosis is largely determined by the clinical context: status of major functions, neurologic signs suggesting a decompression accident, evidence of disturbed thermal regulation, nystagmus suggesting an accident to the inner ear. Differential diagnosis is frequently possible by careful interrogation of attending others, analysis of the time course of the dive, and the physical status of the diver.

▶ This brief review provides a useful entrée to some of the recent French literature on diving medicine. Emphasis is given to the frequency of cochleo-vestibular problems associated with asymmetric thermal stimulation of the semi-circular canals.—Roy J. Shephard, M.D., Ph.D.

## A Comparison of Depth Estimation Between Novice and Experienced Sport Divers

N. Gassman (Univ. of Stirling, England)
J. Sports Sci. 3:27–31, Spring 1985                          1–93

Many depth gauges are dangerously inaccurate. The authors studied how accurately divers can estimate depth, and whether this varies with diving experience. Six novice and 6 experienced divers followed a rope along the shelving bottom of a quarry and estimated their depth at 9 marked points.

There was a tendency for all divers to estimate their depths as shallower than they actually were, except for novices at shallow depths. Experienced divers made shallower estimates than novices, with novices tending to estimate closer to the true depth than experienced divers. An analysis of variance showed that there was a significant difference between the groups ($P < .05$) but not between depths ($P > .05$). The depth effect was nearly significantly ($P = .059$), and appeared to be related to true depth. The table shows the standard deviations of the depth estimates for each group. A Wilcoxon test showed the differences between them was insignificant.

It is difficult to explain why novices tended to give more accurate depth

| STANDARD DEVIATIONS OF ERROR OF DEPTH ESTIMATES (M) | | |
|---|---|---|
| Depth (m) | Experienced | Novices |
| 3 | 1.5 | 1.9 |
| 6 | 1.9 | 1.8 |
| 7 | 1.8 | 1.4 |
| 8 | 1.6 | 3.4 |
| 9 | 2.1 | 3.1 |
| 12 | 3.0 | 1.9 |
| 13 | 3.0 | 2.4 |
| 14 | 2.6 | 4.7 |
| 15 | 1.6 | 4.9 |
| Mean | 2.12 | 2.86 |

(Courtesy of Gassman, N: J. Sports Sci. 3:27–31, Spring 1985.)

estimates. A post-dive questionnaire indicated that experienced divers may have had a greater awareness of possible depth cues, but seemingly were unable to use them to advantage. Divers generally rely on depth gauges as their sole source of depth information and so rarely learn to make independent depth judgments. The individual results in the present study were so variable that divers would be ill-advised to rely on their own depth estimates when accuracy is necessary. A tested depth gauge of known accuracy is possibly the only safe means for a diver to obtain knowledge of his depth.

▶ Other papers in this chapter indicate the serious risks associated with underwater exploration. One reason for trouble seems that the divers cannot estimate their depth accurately; a carefully checked gauge is thus vital.—Roy J. Shephard, M.D., Ph.D.

---

**Barodontalgia—Dental Pain Related to Ambient Pressure Change**
Joseph W. Rauch
Gen. Dent. 33:313–315, July–August 1985                                    1–94

---

Aerodontalgia or flier's toothache attracted great interest during World War II, the first time large numbers of men were subjected to swift changes in ambient pressures. Today, the preferred term is barodontalgia, because it describes dental pain resulting from any change in barometric pressure. As there are many air travelers, sport and commerical divers, balloonists, and skydivers and an increasing number of patients undergoing hyperbaric oxygenation treatment, barodontalgia should be considered in the differential diagnosis of dental pain.

Changes in barometric pressure do not cause dental disease, but some pathologic conditions that are quiescent at ambient pressures may become exaggerated and painful. The idea that gas bubbles under restorations cause pain has long been known to be without merit. Almost every case of confirmed barodontalgia, however, occurs only in association with previously restored teeth or teeth demonstrating some pathosis. There may be a definite correlation between the character of the symptoms of barodontalgia and the underlying pulp disease. A system of classification has been proposed to aid the dentist in establishing diagnosis and treatment. The etiology of barodontalgia may be related to air embolism of the pulp, pulp hyperemia, gases trapped during root canal therapy, or a combination of these and other factors. However, what may be most important are circumstances leading to the dental pain. The diagnosing dentist can use the symptom to help locate previously undetected caries, leaking restorations, periodontal problems, or other oral cavity abnormalities. It has been reported that aerodontalgia can be distinguished from the pain of barosinusitis because aerodontalgia invariably begins during ascent. Barosinusitis occurs during descent; a person with this condition will have the pain on every flight and at the same altitude.

A questionnaire that asks about jobs or hobbies may be helpful in treatment planning. For example, if it is known that a patient is a scuba diver or a balloonist, the dentist may wish to complete root canal therapy so that intracanal medicaments or unfilled canals do not cause problems when the patient experiences changes in pressure. Even for routine procedures such as amalgam restorations, the dentist may wish to advise patients to allow at least 24 hours between treatment and any air travel or baromedical therapy. When patients report severe pain while in flight or diving, barodontalgia should be considered in the differential diagnosis.

▶ Dental pain as a consequence of changing ambient pressure is not confined to the sport diver alone. It is a potential symptom for anyone traveling by air, for both sport and deep-sea divers, and for those who are involved in hyperbaric therapy. There are nice subtle points in this paper; one is that aerodontalgia will commence during ascent in a flight or equivalence in diving, whereas barosinusitis occurs during descent. Of more practical importance, dental therapy should be completed 24 hours before air travel, or any baromedical therapy, or diving. The original article contains a table that has a classification of barodontalgia and is very helpful for a subject not commonly considered in the medical literature.—Lewis J. Krakauer, M.D., F.A.C.P.

**Conservative Management of Inner Ear Barotrauma Resulting From Scuba Diving**
G. Joseph Parell and Gary D. Becker (Bay Mem. Med. Ctr., Panama City, Fla., and Kaiser-Permanente Med. Ctr., Los Angeles)
Otolaryngol. Head Neck Surg. 93:393–397, June 1985            1–95

Middle ear barotrauma usually is self-limiting and resolves without treatment, but inner ear barotrauma, while much less common, is potentially more serious because it may cause permanent injury to the cochleovestibular system. Rupture can occur in water as shallow as 7 ft. In a 3-year period, 14 divers were seen with inner ear barotrauma. Eight had inner ear hemorrhage, two had a tear of the intracochlear membrane, and four had a perilymph fistula. These changes usually result from forceful autoinflation of the middle ear and often coexist with middle ear barotrauma. The differential diagnosis of cochleovestibular symptoms in diving includes decompression sickness, nitrogen narcosis, high-pressure nervous syndrome, alternobaric vertigo, and sensory deprivation.

Patients with inner ear hemorrhage are placed at bed rest with the head elevated and are cautioned against sneezing or straining. Mild activities can be resumed in 10 days if symptoms do not progress. Excellent recovery from sensorineural hearing loss is the rule. Patients who have a tear in Reissner's membrane are treated like those with inner ear hemorrhage. When an inner ear fistula is present, a period of bed rest with avoidance of strain is necessary for spontaneous healing to occur. Deterioration of hearing or persistent significant vestibular symptoms in the first 10 days after injury indicate the need for surgical exploration. If significant middle ear hemorrhage and edema are present, however, exploration probably should be delayed.

▶ For those of us not in the subspecialty or common practice of ear, nose, and throat disease, it is important to learn the distinction between inner ear barotrauma (IEBT) and middle ear barotrauma. The latter is much more common, often self-limiting, and self-resolving. The inner ear trauma may cause the permanent injury to the systems that result in both deafness and balance disorders. Three types of IEBT that can result from the forceful autoinflation of the middle ear are hypothesized: (1) hemorrhage within the inner ear, (2) labyrinthine membrane tear, or (3) perilymph fistula through the round or oval window.

Conservative therapy may suffice, but both the diagnostic distinction and the therapy should be in the hands of ear, nose, and throat specialists, if undue risk is to be avoided. It is nice to note that surgery is not obligatory.—Lewis J. Krakauer, M.D., F.A.C.P.

---

**Primary Prevention of Aquatic Morbidity**
Ronald V. Marino (Univ. of Medicine and Dentistry of New Jersey)
J. Am. Osteopath. Assoc. 85:367–369, June 1985          1–96

Aquatic accidents are becoming more frequent with the increased number of residential pools and the continued popularity of shore activities. Drowning causes more than 8,000 deaths in the United States each year and is the second-leading cause of accidental death at ages 1 to 34 years. Cases of near drowning are much more common. Most drownings occur in pools and bathtubs; 14% occur during boating activities.

Teenagers should be informed of risk factors that include drinking alcoholic beverages and long-distance underwater swimming, which can produce "shallow-water black-out." Infants enrolled in "water baby" programs must be watched constantly even after they acquire some skill and comfort in the water. Water intoxication may occur after repeated submersions. Other risks are dental enamel erosion from water with a low pH and transmission of the intestinal parasite *Giardia*.

Epileptics must weigh the benefits of aquatic activities against the risk of submersion injury. Drowning is three to four times more frequent among epileptics than among the rest of the population, but much of the risk is associated with bathing. Swimmers should not remain in the water longer than 20 minutes. Chilling should be avoided. Swimming in open water should be avoided except for the shallow water along the shore.

Scuba diving requires proper training and certification. Both sound judgment and physical strength are necessary for safe scuba diving. Most authorities discourage participation for those younger than 16 years of age.

▶ Our society remains callous to the number of deaths and to the morbidity from water-related activities, just as we remain callous to highway carnage.

This paper provides a good overview of the water-related risk question. Interesting to me was the point that drowning is three to four times more frequent among epileptics than among the rest of the population and is often associated with simple bathing. Common sense, but not in my area of common knowledge.—Lewis J. Krakauer, M.D., F.A.C.P.

---

**Break Dancer's Wrist**
Samuel D. Gerber, Paul P. Griffin, and Barry P. Simmons (Children's Hosp. Med. Ctr. and Brigham and Women's Hosp., Boston)
J. Pediatr. Orthop. 6:98–99, January–February 1986                    1–97

Break dancing is a part of current popular culture, and it has been associated with a variety of skeletal disorders. An adolescent boy developed a distal ulnar growth plate disorder in conjunction with break dancing.

Boy, 14, was seen after crush injury to the distal phalanx of the right index fiber and also reported persistent right wrist pain, present for 6 months. He was an avid break dancer and customarily rotated with all weight supported on the maximally dorsiflexed wrists. The wrist pain had begun in relation to break dancing. Right distal ulnar tenderness was noted, with limited dorsiflexion and ulnar deviation of the wrist. Radiography showed widening of the distal ulnar physis and metaphyseal irregularity. Treatment by immobilization in a short arm cast for 6 weeks was followed by resolution of the symptoms and radiographic evidence of healing.

The course of this patient's symptoms suggests a causal relation between repetitive trauma from break dancing and development of a distal ulnar physis disorder. The lesion probably represented a chronic slip of the distal ulnar epiphysis through the physis. The relationship with break dancing is supported by the occurrence of clinical and radiographic healing on immobilization.

▶ This is the first case reported of a distal ulnar growth plate disorder in conjunction with this activity. This strikes some as an extreme physical activity, surprisingly not associated with more physical havoc.—Lewis J. Krakauer, M.D., F.A.C.P.

---

**Eye Injuries in Canadian Amateur Hockey**
Tom Pashby (Don Mills, Ontario)
Can. J. Ophthalmol. 20:2–4, February 1985                    1–98

More than a decade has passed since national concern over eye injuries in Canadian amateur hockey, and the incidence of injuries has declined sharply since certified face protectors and helmets were adopted. Certified face protectors attached to helmets were made mandatory for all minor hockey players in 1981. A total of 257 eye injuries were reported in the 1974–1975 season, and 124 in the 1983–1984 season. None of the latter injuries were in players wearing certified equipment. The average age of injured players increased from 14 to 24 years. Hockey sticks and pucks were the most frequent causes of eye injuries at both times, but hyphema surpassed soft tissue damage in 1983–1984. The frequency of legal blindness has declined from 19% to 11% of eye-injured patients.

The use of certified face protectors has decreased serious eye injuries in young Canadian hockey players. A suitable face protector now must be developed for older players. Casual ice hockey players also require protection against eye injury. Patients with hyphema usually require 5 or 6 days' bed rest, preferably in a hospital, if secondary glaucoma, recurrent bleeding, and blood staining of the cornea are to be avoided.

▶ This describes a point of medical concern for many years that resulted in certified face protectors being made mandatory for all minor hockey players in Canada in 1981 and after. Injuries have declined sharply, and no injuries were reported in players using the appropriate equipment during 1983 and 1984. The next logical step of preventive care is to make such protective gear mandatory for older players (which it is not at this time) and mandatory for the casual amateur.—Lewis J. Krakauer, M.D., F.A.C.P.

---

**Rhabdomyolysis of the Upper Extremities Associated With Weight Lifting: Report of a Case**
James C. Bartlett, Theodore W. Rooney, and Janet C. Hunter (University of Osteopathic Medicine and Health Sciences, Des Moines, Iowa)
JAOA 85:646–648, October 1985                                              1–99

---

Most cases of exercise-induced rhabdomyolysis are seen in marathon

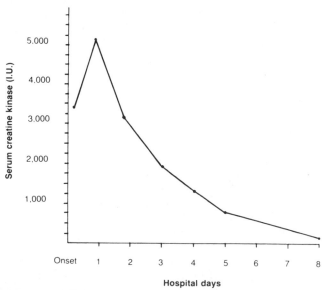

Fig 1–37.—Serum creatine kinase levels of patient in reported case. (Courtesy of Bartlett, J.C., et al.: JAOA 85:646–648, October 1985.)

runners and involve the lower extremities. A patient with swollen upper extremities was encountered after strenuous weight-lifting.

Man, 22, presented with swollen elbows 3 weeks after having begun an intensive weight-lifting routine lasting 1 hour on alternate days. Nontender swelling of both elbow joints was present, with normal range of motion. Naproxen was prescribed, but joint swelling increased and pitting edema developed. Extension became somewhat limited. The serum creatine kinase (CK) was 3150 IU. Electrolytes were within normal limits. The CK rose to a peak of 4790 IU, 99% of it from skeletal muscle. Intravenous and oral fluids and bicarbonate were administered, and the arms were elevated and packed in ice. The CK declined (Fig 1–37). The aldolase level was 46.5 IU/ml, indicating cell destruction. The CK had fallen to 89 IU 8 days after presentation.

The laboratory features of acute, nontraumatic rhabdomyolysis are quite variable. The syndrome usually is self-limiting, but acute renal failure occurs in 5%–7% of cases. Vascular compromise by increased fluid within a vascular compartment also is a possibility. Replenishment of extracellular fluid loss is of primary importance. Mannitol will improve volume expansion and renal hemodynamics. The usefulness of furosemide or bicarbonate is uncertain.

▶ This single case illustrates a clinical syndrome that can result from injury to skeletal muscle, with the subsequent release of cellular components into the plasma. It is probably common in both traumatic and nontraumatic events. This particular case was basically nontraumatic and involved elbow joints alone. The significance of nontraumatic rhabdomyolysis is that it can lead to acute renal failure in 5%–7% of patients. When patients present with fever, malaise, pain, and swelling, the syndrome may be more apparent. Fifty percent of patients can appear *without* muscle pain and fewer still without swelling of the affected extremities. Even myoglobinuria is not always clinically apparent. The CPK level, with or without isoenzymes, is the laboratory key. If this syndrome is present, the elevation will be massive. If associated with urinopathy, specifically proteinuria, myoglobinuria, or hematuria, the diagnosis should be apparent. Elevated potassium levels are present in 50% of such patients. This level correlates with renal function and is important as it relates to cardiac arrhythmias.—Lewis J. Krakauer, M.D., F.A.C.P.

---

**Knee Joint in Soccer Players: Osteoarthritis and Axis Deviation**
Alex Chantraine (Hôpital Cantonal Universitaire, Geneva)
Med. Sci. Sports Exerc. 17:434 439, August 1985                    1–100

---

The knee joints of 81 veteran soccer players between ages 40 and 74 years were examined. An analysis of and relationships between soccer practice at a top level, osteoarthritis, meniscectomy, and leg axes were evaluated. Some 162 knees were assessed through clinical examination and x-ray examination using a large table in order to observe the entire lower extremity's axis in weight bearing.

All of the 42 knees operated on showed radiographic signs of osteoar-

138 / Sports Medicine

thritis at follow-up, whereas of the 120 knees not operated on, only 40 (41%) demonstrated radiologic changes. In the decade between 40 and 49 years, 32% had roentgenographic signs of osteoarthritis in the knees not operated on. All of the joints that underwent meniscectomy had roentgenographic signs of osteoarthritis. In those aged between 50 and 59 years, only 1 knee had a meniscectomy. During the fifth decade, 43% of the 37 knees not operated on had signs roentgenographically of osteoarthritis. From the sixth and seventh decades, 7 of 12 (60%) and 5 of 6 (83%) had signs roentgenographically of osteoarthritis, respectively, of the joints not operated on. From a total of 91 knees (56%) having radiologic signs of osteoarthritis, 70% (63 knees) of those had no clinical symptoms. Evaluation of axial deviation revealed that 59 subjects (118 knees or 73%) displayed a varus angulation of both knees, whereas 131 knees or 81% of all knees showed a varus deviation. In 13 veteran players (16%) there was a varus knee associated with a physiologic axis (4 cases) or with a valgus deviation (9 cases) in the opposite knee. Among the 25 who had a medial meniscectomy, 23 had varus deviation and 2 had valgus deviation.

The author concludes that this study shows in long-term follow-up of national caliber soccer players, radiologic signs of osteoarthritis were present much earlier than would be expected for a comparable population. In those who had a previous meniscectomy, radiologic signs of degenerative changes were present in all patients. The presence of significant varus axial knee alignment was also found to be much higher than expected. Clinical symptoms of osteoarthritis were quite small and did not correlate with the overall incidence of radiologic changes in the knee not operated on (41%) and the knee that had operation (100%).

▶ An excellent long-term retrospective study of roentgenograms and clinical symptoms following meniscectomy in the anterior cruciate ligament intact knee. It is interesting to note the finding of a "high incidence" of very early roentgenographic osteoarthritis in the knees that were not operated on, as well as lack of correlation between minimal clinical symptoms of osteoarthritis and evidence of radiographic changes in knees that were operated on and knees that did not undergo operation.—Joseph S. Torg, M.D.

---

**Effects of Reduced Training on Muscular Power in Swimmers**
David L. Costill, Douglas S. King, Robert Thomas, and Mark Hargreaves
Physician Sportsmed. 13:94–101, February 1985                    1–101

---

Seventeen male collegiate swimmers were studied before, during, and after 14 days of reduced training (tapering). Maximal arm power was measured on a biokinetic swim bench and during a tethered (power) swim test, and each swimmer also swam 200 yd (182.9 m) at an evenly paced velocity corresponding with 90% of his best performance of the season. On average, the subjects were swimming 9,500 yd (8,687 m) a day during the 4 weeks before testing. The more intense portion of the training consisted of intermittent interval swims, which constituted about 75% of each training session. During the 14-day tapering period, the total distance swum each day declined progressively from 7,500 yd (day 1) to 3,500 yd (day 13). The swimmers did not train on the fifth and seventh days of the tapering period.

All swimmers improved their season's best performances at the conference championship meet (table). Regardless of length of the swim (50 to 1,650 yd) or the stroke used, the improvements were all from 2.2% to 4.6% of the swimmers' season best times, and the overall mean improvement was 3.1%. Due to reduced training, the swimmers showed an increase in power on both the biokinetic swim bench and the power swim apparatus. On average, power measured on the swim bench improved 17.7%, and power measured in the water increased 24.6% above the pretapering value. However, correlation was low between the improvements in these two measurements of power. Performance changes as a result of the reduced training correlated significantly with the percentage of improvements during the power swim test.

The improvements in performance with reduced training seem to be at least in part due to significant gains in muscular power but to be unrelated to changes in the metabolic demands of swimming. The swimmers said they felt easily fatigued and unable to swim fast throughout the tapering period, but they experienced a noticeable increase in strength and stamina during the final competition.

Recent tests with national- and world-class swimmers revealed that biokinetic power measurements do not discriminate between individual swimming abilities in men and women who have power values of more than 300 W. That does not mean that arm power is unimportant for success in these swimmers; it suggests that other factors, e.g., biomechanics, may

SWIMMING PERFORMANCES (MINUTES:SECONDS) BEFORE AND AFTER 2 WEEKS OF REDUCED TRAINING

| Stroke | Distance (Yards) | n | Pretaper | Posttaper | Change* (%) |
|---|---|---|---|---|---|
| Freestyle | 50 | 2 | 22.90 | 22.34 | − 2.5 |
|  | 100 | 2 | 49.83 | 48.76 | − 2.2 |
|  | 200 | 3 | 1:48.38 | 1:44.33 | − 3.7 |
|  | 500 | 6 | 4:55.06 | 4:45.46 | − 3.3 |
|  | 1,650 | 4 | 17:06.42 | 16:28.24 | − 3.7 |
| Breaststroke | 100 | 3 | 1:03.28 | 1:01.29 | − 3.1 |
|  | 200 | 3 | 2:20.84 | 2:15.49 | − 3.8 |
| Backstroke | 100 | 2 | 59.30 | 56.57 | − 3.0 |
|  | 200 | 2 | 2:06.26 | 2:01.89 | − 3.5 |
| Butterfly | 100 | 3 | 53.44 | 52.16 | − 2.4 |
|  | 200 | 3 | 2:00.16 | 1:57.56 | − 2.2 |
| Individual medley | 200 | 5 | 2:10.86 | 2:04.80 | − 4.6 |
|  | 400 | 3 | 4:31.37 | 4:23.85 | − 2.8 |

*Average improvement: −3.1%.

(Courtesy of Costill, D.L., et al.: Physician Sportsmed. 13:94–101, February 1985. Reprinted by permission. A McGraw-Hill publication.)

contribute more to the performance differences in swimmers who have a high level of arm strength and power.

Although the precise mechanisms underlying the improvements in muscular power and swimming performance cannot be explained, the causes may be linked to peripheral or central factors, or both, that might influence force development. The period of reduced training may have allowed for an increase in maximal tension development through changes in the contractile mechanisms, neural controls on fiber recruitment, or both. Repeated days of hard training may prevent swimmers from performing at or near their full potential, which can only be achieved by reducing the physical stress associated with training.

▶ "Tapering" or reducing training prior to competition may benefit swimmers, runners, and other athletes. Many athletes make dietary adjustments, especially by increasing carbohydrate intake, along with reducing training to further improve their performance. There are still many questions to be answered regarding these practices (e.g., "How often can this be done in one season and still provide significant results?" "Do all athletes respond the same to tapering and dietary changes?" "Can a modified version of this be used on a weekly basis for sports such as football?").

Reducing training toward the end of the season may prevent some of the overuse injuries and "staleness" that often occurs. Many athletes may benefit both physically and psychologically if their practice schedules are reduced toward the end of a long season.—Frank George, A.T.C., P.T.

## Physiology of Drugs

### Enhanced Metabolic Response to Caffeine in Exercise-Trained Human Subjects

Jacques LeBlanc, Michel Jobin, Jacques Côté, Pierre Samson, and Antoine Labrie (Lavral Univ., Quebec City)
J. Appl. Physiol. 59:832–837, September 1985                    1–102

Caffeine is a central stimulant possessing peripheral action. It exerts a postreceptor effect by blocking phosphodiesterase, the enzyme that inactivates adenosine $3',5'$-cyclic monophosphate (cAMP). Thus, caffeine is generally considered a potentiator of catecholamine action on β-receptors. The effect of caffeine on the resting metabolic rate was investigated in eight trained and eight nontrained young men aged 26 to 36 years whose coffee consumption was one to three cups daily.

The ingestion of caffeine, 4 mg/kg produced a greater increase in the resting metabolic rate of the trained group (Fig 1–38). This effect was associated with a greater increase in plasma free fatty acids (FFAs) and a greater fall in the respiratory quotient. An initial fall in the plasma glucose level occurred in the trained men. Caffeine did not affect the plasma insulin concentration in either group. It caused a significant decline in the plasma norepinephrine level and an increase in the plasma epinephrine level in both groups, with these effects being significantly greater in the trained men.

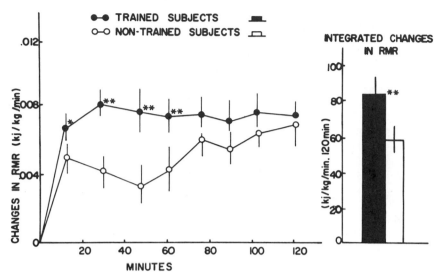

Fig 1–38.—Effect of caffeine, 4 mg/kg ingested orally, on the resting metabolic rate (RMR) in trained and nontrained men. *Bars* indicate SEM; *columns* represent total area under curves for a 120-minute period. **P < .01, differences between groups. (Courtesy of LeBlanc, J., et al.: J. Appl. Physiol. 59:832–837, September 1985.)

The previously reported increase in the metabolic rate caused by caffeine ingestion was confirmed in this study. During the first 20 minutes after drinking coffee, the greater increase in the resting metabolic rate in trained individuals may be related to a greater rise in the plasma epinephrine level; subsequently, FFAs would become the preferred substrate. Elevation of plasma FFAs produces increased lipid metabolism. Thus, these results indicate enhanced lipid utilization in trained compared with nontrained men. This conclusion is consistent with the changes observed in respiratory quotient measurements that indicated greater lipid oxidation in the trained group. However, the exact relationship between the respiratory quotient and plasma FFAs was not established. The respiratory quotient declined at 25 minutes, but no data for the plasma FFAs were obtained at that time. If overall responses are considered, however, the changes in the respiratory quotient fit with those for plasma FFAs. The greater increase in the resting metabolic rate in trained individuals may be related to greater lipid mobilization and utilization.

Whether the greater increase in plasma epinephrine caused by caffeine in trained persons can explain their greater metabolic response is unknown. Possibly, increased epinephrine secretion combined with the sparing effect of caffeine on cAMP, by blocking phosphodiesterase, and the increased lipolytic activity associated with exercise training could explain the greater effect of caffeine on the resting metabolic rate. Similar reasoning may be used to explain the beneficial action of caffeine on performance in prolonged high-level muscular activity. In this study significant differences were found in plasma FFAs and the respiratory quotient between trained and sedentary individuals. These differences, noted between 20 and 40 minutes, were preceded by a significantly greater increase in the plasma epinephrine level in the trained group. The larger increment in oxygen consumption caused by caffeine in exercise-trained persons may be related to enhanced lipid mobilization produced by increased epinephrine secretion.

▶ Caffeine may be the most prevalent drug used by the American public, followed closely by ethanol. A potent stimulant of catechol activity on the sympathetic nervous system, it is deleterious in such situations as cardiac arrhythmias, anxiety, and hypertensive syndromes. (Isolated papers have even linked caffeine with cancer of the pancreas and malignancy of the breast.)

On the positive side, it has been shown that caffeine can enhance athletic performance and that it exerts a sparing effect on muscle glycogen (Essig, et al.). This paper suggests that caffeine, causing an increase in plasma epinephrine and a simultaneous fall in norepinephrine, results in an increased metabolic rate. This probably relates to enhanced lipid mobilization and increased lipid oxidation. Training potentiates this pharmacologic action of caffeine.

Should caffeine be on a list of proscribed drugs for athletic competition? If caffeine use becomes widespread among athletes, will there be long-range cardiovascular risk factors as a consequence?—Lewis J. Krakauer, M.D., F.A.C.P.

---

**Effect of Coffee on Exercise-Induced Angina Pectoris due to Coronary Artery Disease in Habitual Coffee Drinkers**
Kenneth M. Piters, Antonio Colombo, Harold G. Olson, and Samuel M. Butman (Long Beach VA Med. Ctr. and Univ. of California, Irvine)
Am. J. Cardiol. 55:277–280, Feb. 1, 1985                                          1–103

---

A large majority of adults in the United States consume an estimated average of 186 mg daily of caffeine from all sources. A double-blind treadmill protocol was designed to assess the acute effects of caffeinated and decaffeinated coffees on exercise-induced angina in 17 men with chronic stable angina and an angina-limited exercise test. The mean patient age was 59 years. All patients had established coronary disease with 75% narrowing of at least one major artery. The mean left ventricular ejection fraction was 65%. All patients were coffee drinkers; the average consumption was 3½ cups a day. Seven patients were using propranolol, and 1, nifedipine; the rest were on nitrates alone. Bruce treadmill tests were performed 30 minutes after patients drank 2 cups of either caffeinated or decaffeinated coffee or 1 cup of each type.

Baseline cardiovascular findings were unchanged after coffee consumption, but 1 or 2 cups of caffeinated coffee significantly prolonged the duration of exercise until angina developed. Decaffeinated coffee had no such effect. The extent of ST-segment depression and the heart rate-blood pressure product at angina were similar after the two types of coffee, as was exercise duration to 0.1 mV of ST depression. Mean serum caffeine levels after 1 and 2 cups of coffee were 1.97 and 3.89 µg/ml, respectively.

Similar results were obtained in the patients on propranolol and the others.

Ingestion of 2 cups of caffeinated coffee had no adverse effects on patients with exercise-induced angina in this study. Possible explanations include tolerance to caffeine and a different response to coffee by patients with coronary artery disease compared with normal subjects.

▶ For the short term at least, the use of 1 to 2 cups of caffeinated coffee did not affect angina pectoris adversely in a double-blind study of exercise-induced angina. This does not speak to possible long-term adverse effects on the cardiovascular system, ischemic heart disease, or hypertension.—Lewis J. Krakauer, M.D., F.A.C.P.

---

**Methylprednisolone Acts at the Endothelial Cell Level Reducing Inflammatory Responses**
J. Björk, T. Goldschmidt, G. Smedegård, and K.-E. Arfors (Univ. of Uppsala)
Acta Physiol. Scand. 123:221–224, February 1985                    1–104

---

Glucocorticoids maintain vascular integrity at sites of inflammation, but the exact mechanisms involved are unknown. Administration of steroids counters vascular leakage in an immune complex-induced inflammatory reaction in the hamster cheek pouch. Increased vascular leakage in this model is mediated in part by histamine. Methylprednisolone does not reduce histamine release despite marked attenuation of the microvascular response. Vascular leakage induced by exogenous histamine, leukotriene $C_4$, or platelet-activating factor was inhibited by methylprednisolone treatment.

Ovalbumin-immunized hamsters received methylprednisolone, 15 mg/kg intramuscularly 16–18 hours before study and 10 mg/kg intravenously 45 minutes before the start of experiments. Macromolecular permeability was assessed by leakage of fluorescein-labeled dextran. Microvascular leakage in immunized animals exposed to antigen occurred only on the venular side of the microcirculation and was largely inhibited by treatment with methylprednisolone. Mast cells in antigen-exposed preparations appeared degranulated. Methylprednisolone treatment did not reduce histamine release from cheek pouches of antigen-exposed animals, but leakage was inhibited in preparations of treated animals exposed topically to histamine. Methylprednisolone also countered the increase in vascular permeability induced by leukotriene $C_4$ and platelet-activating factor. Accumulation of polymorphs in small venules, produced by antigen exposure, was inhibited by pretreatment with methylprednisolone.

The effect of methylprednisolone in this model would seem to be central in nature. General suppression of agonist receptor function might be responsible, or treatment with methylprednisolone could modulate a final common effector mechanism of the endothelial cell after interaction with an agonist receptor.

▶ Corticosteroids of various types have been prescribed by physicians and have been self-prescribed by many people, including athletes. Steroids reduce pain and swelling before and after vigorous activity. For example, the infiltration of an acute bursitis with corticosteroids may be both valid medical usage and commonly effective. The study cited throws more light on the precise mechanism of action. The authors suggest that corticosteroids, for which methylprednisolone is a model, act at the endothelial cell level, probably by agonist receptor suppression.—Lewis J. Krakauer, M.D., F.A.C.P.

**Controlling Performance Anxiety**
Patricia Normand (Massachusetts General Hosp., Boston)
Drug Therapy 33–40, May 1985                                            1–105

Performance anxiety, or stage fright, can be defined as a social phobia in which variable anticipation and subjective anxiety is experienced, followed by acute arousal and somatic symptoms. There may be tachycardia, tremor, palpitations, weakness, and gastrointestinal distress. Many subjects treat themselves with tranquilizers or alcohol. Athletes, musicians, actors, speakers, and students taking exams all may be affected. The cause is uncertain, but the disorder can be considered a variant of the fight-or-flight reaction. Anxiety has been shown to adversely affect performance when cognitive and motor skills are required, especially if more complex tasks are involved. The differential diagnosis includes other primary anxiety disorders, thyrotoxicosis, drug or alcohol withdrawal, and hypoglycemic reaction.

Beta-blockers (i.e., propranolol) reduce autonomic symptoms of performance anxiety such as tachycardia and tremor, and may limit CNS-directed general arousal. They are especially useful for musicians. The usual dose of propranolol is 40 mg, taken 1–2 hours before performance; alternately, dosage may be titrated to the symptoms. Benzodiazepines reduce general arousal via a direct CNS action, but their effects on motor skills may limit their use in musicians. Behavioral techniques may be used alone or with drugs to treat performance anxiety. Systematic densensitization, forced immersion, and modeling methods all have been used. Traditional psychotherapy may be helpful when performance anxiety is present along with other psychiatric disorder, or if a strong component of secondary gain is suspected. Psychotherapy alone probably is not adequate for the management of social phobia.

▶ An argument for the acceptance of β-blockers for performance anxiety, particularly in musicians, in whom tremor is of consequence. I should agree with this from observations of various patients and note that the long-term problems of fatigue, depression, and sexual dysfunction are not present when β-blockade is used short term, nor is there risk of habituation. Beta-blockers appear to be preferable to benzodiazepines, having less negative effect on manual dexterity and psychoreactive patterns. They seem to be superior to modification of behavioral techniques alone or formal psychotherapy. Such pharmacotherapy is not intended as a replacement for psychotherapy when there is severe disruptive performance anxiety or major personality problems of psychologic nature.—Lewis J. Krakauer, M.D., F.A.C.P.

---

**Anabolic Steroids: A Review of the Literature**
Herbert A. Haupt and George D. Rovere (Wake Forest Univ.)
Am. J. Sports Med. 12:469–484, November–December 1984          1–106

---

The use of anabolic steroids by athletes remains controversial, and questions concern both the effects on athletic performance and side effects. Findings were reviewed as reported in 25 well-documented studies of anabolic steroid effects on athletic performance. An attempt was made to determine whether conflicting findings may result from the use of different protocols.

A significant association was evident between studies of athletes trained in weight lifting before starting to take anabolic steroids and significant improvement in strength. Insignificant strength gains were reported in studies of previously untrained athletes. Neither weight training during steroid intake as a single variable nor a high-protein diet correlated with results. All but one of the studies that failed to show a significant increase in strength was a double-blind investigation. The type of strength-measuring technique used correlated with the results of a given study to a significant degree. Methandrostenolone had been used predominantly in studies reporting significant increases in strength. Strength changes were unrelated to changes in cardiorespiratory function or aerobic performance after steroid administration. Increases in body size and weight were associated with significant strength gains.

Athletes previously trained in weight lifting before receiving anabolic steroids who continue training during treatment consistently increase their muscle strength, whereas untrained individuals do not. Both subjective side effects and liver dysfunction have been associated with anabolic steroid use. Peliosis hepatis has been described, as well as rare liver tumors. Hepatic toxicity seems related to the duration of treatment and to the use of orally active C-17 alpha alkyl testosterone derivatives.

► This is an excellent and comprehensive review of the anabolic steroid question; the most thorough and objective to date. This is a careful analysis of 25 former studies evaluating anabolic steroids and performance; 14 of these assess human strength.

The authors conclude that these agents consistently result in significant strength increases if three conditions are satisfied: (1) intensive weight training is instituted immediately before the steroid regimen and continued throughout; (2) a high-protein diet is used; (3) measurement of strength is done by the single repetition-maximal weight technique for those exercises for the given athlete.

The section on the side effects of anabolic steroids is detailed and well documented. See the editorial comments following the next paper, by Kantor et al., and the leading article to this Year Book by Lombardo.—Lewis J. Krakauer, M.D., F.A.C.P.

---

### Androgens Reduce HDL$_2$-Cholesterol and Increase Hepatic Triglyceride Lipase Activity

Mark A. Kantor, Adam Bianchini, David Bernier, Stanley P. Sady, and Paul D. Thompson (Brown Univ.)
Med. Sci. Sports Exerc. 17:462–465, August 1985                1–107

---

Exogenous anabolic-androgenic steroids cause a profound, acute reduction in high-density lipoprotein (HDL)-cholesterol levels in both athletes and sedentary subjects. This effect has potential health implications because of the strong inverse relationship between plasma HDL-cholesterol levels and the risk of coronary heart disease. Despite the possible health risks of steroid use, androgens are widely used by both amateur and professional athletes, especially weight lifters, seeking to gain a competitive advantage in strength or endurance.

The authors quantified serum lipid levels and postheparin plasma lipolytic activities in 5 weight lifters who were self-administering androgenic steroids (users) and an equal number not currently using these drugs (nonusers). Mean age (23 vs. 25 years), body weight (102.7 vs. 86.8 kg), and percent body fat (8.6% vs. 7.8%) were not significantly different in users and nonusers, respectively. There were also no significant differences in total cholesterol (183 vs. 176 mg/dl), low-density lipoprotein (LDL)-cholesterol (138 vs. 108 mg/dl), or triglyceride (93 vs. 93 mg/dl) levels in the two groups. However, HDL-cholesterol levels were significantly lower in the users (26 vs. 50 mg/dl), with most of the difference being due to lower HDL$_2$-cholesterol levels (6 vs. 22 mg/dl). Postheparin plasma lipoprotein lipase (LPLA) activity was only slightly lower in the users (3.49 vs. 5.36 $\mu$mole of free fatty acid [FFA] per milliliter-hour). Hepatic triglyceride lipase (HTGLA) activity was significantly higher in this group (27.99 vs. 11.5 $\mu$mole of FFA per milliliter-hour), and correlated inversely with HDL$_2$-cholesterol concentrations ($r = -.81$).

These results demonstrate that weight lifters who self-administer anabolic-androgenic steroids have significantly lower HDL-cholesterol levels and higher postheparin plasma HTGLA activities than weight lifters not currently using these drugs. The steroid users had 47% less HDL-cholesterol, owing primarily to a 73% reduction in HDL$_2$ subfraction, although HDL$_3$-cholesterol levels were decreased as well. Total cholesterol and LDL-cholesterol levels were elevated by 4% and 28%, respectively, in the steroid users, but neither of these differences was statistically significant. The data provide further evidence that a reciprocal relationship exists between HDL concentration and postheparin plasma HTGLA activity. This observation strengthens the argument that HTGLA has an important role in HDL metabolism, possibly by removing circulating HDL particles, particularly those in the HDL$_2$ subfraction. In this small group of subjects, HTGLA was strongly and negatively correlated with $HDL_2$ levels in all subjects and in the subgroup using anabolic steroids. These drugs appeared to have little effect on LPLA activity, which suggests that anabolic steroids selectively augment HTGLA. The time required for anabolic steroids to affect lipase activity is not clear from the present results, but a 15 mg/dl decrease in HDL level has been observed in a subject within 2 days of drug administration.

In contrast to the reciprocal relationship of HTGLA and HDL levels, LPLA activity appears to be positively correlated with HDL- and $HDL_2$-cholesterol levels. Endurance athletes not receiving exogenous anabolic steroids have elevated tissue and postheparin plasma levels of LPLA. This augmentation of LPLA activity appears to be both an acute and a chronic exercise effect. It may facilitate the more efficient utilization of circulating triglycerides during exercise and the more rapid replacement of muscle triglyceride stores in the postexercise period. Elevated LPLA levels may also mediate the increase in plasma levels of HDL- and $HDL_2$-cholesterol seen in endurance-trained individuals. During the catabolism of triglyceride-rich lipoproteins by LPLA, part of the surface material containing apoproteins, unesterified cholesterol, and phospholipids is thought to be transferred to the HDL class of lipoproteins, increasing the total mass of HDL particles and transforming $HDL_3$ to $HDL_2$. Thus, LPLA and HTGLA appear to work in opposite directions in regulating plasma levels of HDL- and $HDL_2$-cholesterol.

▶ This paper is one of several that have documented an adverse effect upon HDL-cholesterol levels in athletes and sedentary individuals after the use of anabolic-androgenic steroids. The use of these agents, often to vast excess, is prevalent in the weight lifting and power lifting underground. It may well have been prevalent, as claimed, at Olympic levels for some 20 years. Its use is common in many sports where strength is a factor, such as long-distance swimming. The problem with the use of androgens in any form is that there are multiple dangerous side effects, that cited in this study being just one. These range from disordered liver function to frank hepatic tumor formation. Hypertension and altered glucose metabolism (diabetes) are potentiated by androgen use. Impact on sexual function and fertility is a further risk. The masculinization of the female subject is a very clear risk and not always reversible.

The problems of androgen use have been caused in part by the medical profession, slow to grant that there was a valid correlation between androgen use and increased strength and muscle mass. That effect is unequivocal. When a danger flag is raised now by the same profession, there are many who are reluctant to heed any warnings. This is most unfortunate because the risks are great.

Excessive use pre-competition at national and international levels will probably be curtailed by fears of testing, even though testing is not all that reliable for the more pure testosterone derivatives. The problem really lies at the local health club level, persuading the average user that the risks far outweigh the ergogenic benefits.

This topic is also covered in Dr. Lombardo's excellent lead paper.—Lewis J. Krakauer, M.D., F.A.C.P.

## Anabolic Steroid Use and Perceived Effects in Ten Weight-Trained Women Athletes

Richard H. Strauss, Mariah T. Liggett, and Richard R. Lanese (Ohio State Univ.)
JAMA 253:2871–2873, May 17, 1985                                              1–108

Women have been reluctant for social reasons to acknowledge using steroids in conjunction with athletic competition. Ten weight-trained female athletes who consistently used anabolic steroids were interviewed. All competed at the national level in strength sports, and trained several times a week with heavy weights. Five women were married, and 3 had children. The mean age was 33 years, and their mean height and weight were 163 cm and 69 kg, respectively. They had trained with weights for 5 years on average, and had used anabolic steroids for about 2 years.

Anabolic steroids were used in cycles, often before a particular event. The mean length of the last complete cycle was 9 weeks. An average of

PERCEIVED SIDE EFFECTS OF ANABOLIC STEROIDS (TEN WOMEN)

| Effect | No. Reporting Effect | Perceived as : | | |
|---|---|---|---|---|
| | | Desirable | Undesirable | Not Significant |
| Lower voice | 10 | | 7 | 3 |
| Facial hair | | | | |
|   Increased | 9 | | 8 | 1 |
|   No change | 1 | | | |
| Clitoris | | | | |
|   Enlarged | 8 | 2 | 2 | 4 |
|   No change | 2 | | | |
| Libido | | | | |
|   Increased | 6 | 5 | 1 | |
|   Decreased | 1 | | 1 | |
|   No change | 3 | | | |
| Breast size | | | | |
|   Decreased | 5 | 1 | | 4 |
|   No change | 5 | | | |
| Menstruation | | | | |
|   Diminished or stopped | 7 | 3 | 2 | 2 |
|   Regular | 1 | | | |
|   Hysterectomized | 2 | | | |
| Aggressiveness | | | | |
|   Increased | 8 | 6 | 2 | |
|   No change | 2 | | | |
| Acne | | | | |
|   Increased | 6 | | 6 | |
|   No change | 4 | | | |
| Body Hair | | | | |
|   Increased | 5 | | 5 | |
|   No change | 5 | | | |
| Scalp Hair | | | | |
|   Increased loss | 2 | | 1 | 1 |
|   No change | 8 | | | |
| Appetite | | | | |
|   Increased | 8 | 2 | 5 | 1 |
|   No change | 2 | | | |
| Body fat | | | | |
|   Decreased | 8 | 8 | | |
|   No change | 2 | | | |

three types of anabolic steroids was used during this time. Both oral and injectable preparations were used. Subjects averaged three cycles a year, and 40% of them used smaller amounts of anabolic steroids between cycles. A wide range of steroids was used, in addition to various analgesic/anti-inflammatory agents and growth hormone. All subjects reported significantly increased muscle strength and size and better sports performance. Other perceived effects are shown in the table.

These athletes felt that anabolic steroid use was necessary to compete effectively, and that the side effects were acceptable, although occasionally undesirable. Masculinizing effects were noted, and the subjects advised caution for others considering the use of these drugs.

▶ The side effects of anabolic steroids on women that are reported in this study are not necessarily the most significant or dangerous effects. The possible effects on the liver and other internal organs cannot be seen by the athlete, and the full effects may not be felt in the short run. The true sport person should not require the use of steroids in order to compete. More and more sports organizations are using steroid testing for the purpose of abolishing the use of these drugs. The National Collegiate Athletic Association (NCAA) will be using steroid testing at its major championship events beginning this year.— Col. James L. Anderson, PE.D.

---

**Response of Serum Hormones to Androgen Administration in Power Athletes**
Markku Alén, Matti Reinilä, and Reijo Vihko (Univ. of Jyväskylä, Finland)
Med. Sci. Sports Exerc. 17:354–359, 1985                                         1–109

---

Endocrine effects of self-administration of high doses of anabolic steroids and testosterone were investigated in 5 power athletes during 26 weeks of training, and for the following 12–16 weeks after drug withdrawal. The control group consisted of 6 athletes who had decided not to take any steroid drugs during the next 9 months of training and follow-up. All 5 men in the drug group were experienced in use of androgenic steroids.

Serum concentrations of testosterone and estradiol in the drug group are shown in Figure 1–39. No significant differences were noticed between the study and control groups at the study's beginning. Concentrations of circulating FSH, LH, and PRl decreased significantly in the study group during the first 8 weeks of steroid administration. Concentrations of FSH and LII remained at or below the lowest level of detection during the entire period of anabolic steroid administration and returned slowly to pretreatment level following drug withdrawal. Serum PRL level decreased rapidly after drug withdrawal. There were no changes in serum FSH level in controls, in which a gradual increase in LH did occur. Serum testosterone level tended to increase throughout the period of anabolic steroid-testosterone administration, and the mean concentration reached at 26 weeks was significantly ($P < .05$) higher than at the beginning of the study. The

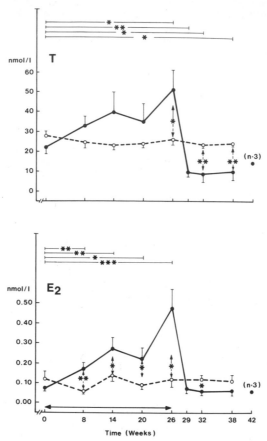

**Fig 1–39.**—The serum concentrations of testosterone (T) *(upper panel)* and estradiol (E2) *(lower panel)* in the study group *(closed circles)* and in the control group *(open circles).* (Courtesy of Alén, M., et al.: Med. Sci. Sports Exerc. 17:354–359, 1985. Copyright 1985, the American College of Sports Medicine. Reprinted by permission.)

pattern of serum estradiol levels followed closely those of testosterone. During drug administration, serum ACTH levels were lower than at the beginning and end of the study.

These data suggest that steroid formulation self-administered by the athletes led to a decrease in serum ACTH levels, which returned to initial levels in 12 weeks after drug withdrawal. Despite this effect, only an initial and transient decrease in serum cortisol level was observed. It is suggested that testosterone turnover was increased at 26 weeks and the decreasing tendency of serum testosterone level was compensated for by augmented LH secretion.

▶ This report concerns the sustained self-administration of large doses of anabolic compounds. One particularly interesting feature is that there was a sevenfold increase of circulating estradiol, to the levels anticipated in a female.

This explains the gynecomastia found in many of those who abuse anabolic compounds. It is likely that testosterone and nandrolone serve as precursors for the formation of estradiol (Caminos-Torres, et al., *J. Clin. Endocrinol. Metab.* 44:1142, 1977).

Though the depression of FSH and LH secretion recovered when drug administration was stopped, it is disturbing that the endogenous production of testosterone was still depressed 12 weeks after cessation of treatment.—Roy J. Shephard, M.D., Ph.D.

---

**Physical Health and Fitness of an Elite Bodybuilder During 1 Year of Self-Administration of Testosterone and Anabolic Steroids: A Case Study**
M. Alén and K. Häkkinen (Univ. of Jyväskylä, Finland)
Int. J. Sports Med. 6:24–29, February 1985                     1 110

---

An adult male bodybuilder at an international level, who had decided to complement his training by self-administration of androgenic hormones (53 mg/day), volunteered as a subject for investigation of his physical health and fitness over a training period of 1 year including only a 4-week abstinence from drugs in the middle of the year.

The subject was able to gain greatly in fat-free weight (from 83 to 90 kg), in mean fiber area of the vastus lateralis (VL) muscle (enlargement of 11.4% after a half year's training) and in maximal strength (from 5,145 to 5,948 N). Figure 1–40 shows the subject's success to increase in muscle strength during the phase training together with higher daily caloric intake (15,000 kilojoules/day) including greater drug usage. The high serum testosterone and low level of serum sex hormone binding globulin (SHBG) observed tend to strengthen suggestions of the anabolic effects of androgenic steroids during training. The subjects's health status was affected by this combination. A high serum estradiol ($E_2$) level during use of androgens, atrophic testicles, and low LH, FSH, and testosterone levels after drug withdrawal indicate that sustained testosterone-anabolic steroid administration affects the function of the pituitary and leads to long-lasting

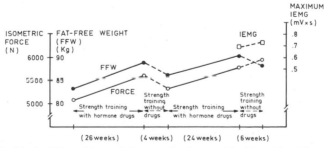

**Fig 1–40.**—Maximal bilateral isometric leg extension force and fat-free weight of the subject during the study period. The values of integrated electromyographic activity (IEMG averaged for the vasti lateralis and medialis muscles) of maximal isometric contraction are also shown before and after the last 6-week training period. (Courtesy of Alén, M., and Häkkinen, K.: Int. J. Sports Med. 6:24–29, February 1985.)

impairment of testicular endocrine function and consequently to azoospermia and gynecomastia.

The authors conclude that the observed decrease in serum HDL-cholesterol and in $HDL_2$-cholesterol may indicate a higher risk for atherogenesis. The man described in this study also experienced a substantial increase in sebaceous secretion. At the end of the study he was treated with lymecycline because of the inflammatory papulopustules on the upper back and face. In addition to psychological reasons for use of androgens, it is possible that some degree of physiologic addiction might have developed because of the partial chemical castration.

▶ Many body-builders are narcissistic, and the suggestion that large doses of anabolic steroids cause a blotchy face may have more effect upon steroid abuse than threats of hepatic carcinoma at some future date. The adverse effect upon HDL cholesterol is one further expression of liver dysfunction.—Roy J. Shephard, M.D., Ph.D.

---

**Androgenic Steroid Effects on Liver and Red Cells**
M. Alén (Univ. of Jyväskylä, Finland)
Br. J. Sports Med. 19:15–20, March 1985                      1–111

Hematologic and hepatic effects of testosterone-anabolic steroid self-administration were investigated in 5 power athletes during 26 weeks of training. The purpose of this study was to assess the effects of sustained high-dose use of testosterone and anabolic steroids in association with strength training on red blood cell values and liver function indicators. A control group consisted of 6 athletes who had declined to take any steroid drugs during the next 9 months.

The study and control groups were similar for various laboratory parameters at the beginning of the study. In the study group, there was an initial decrease in blood hemoglobin (Hb) concentration at 8 and 14 weeks, which returned to pretreatment levels at 20 and 26 weeks. Hematocrit (PVC) values increased throughout testosterone-anabolic steroid administration and, at 26 weeks, was significantly ($P < .05$) higher than at the beginning of the study. Mean corpuscular hemoglobin concentration decreased significantly ($P < .001$) in the study group during the first 14 weeks of steroid administration. The table presents mean values of red blood cells (RBC), mean corpuscular volume, platelet and leukocyte count. Mean RBC value during phase I increased significantly ($P < .05$) in the study group, but did not change in controls. At 26 weeks, the difference between groups in RBC mean values was significant ($P < .001$). A significant increase in mean platelet count ($P < .05$) and in mean leukocyte count ($P < .05$) occurred at 26 weeks in the study group. Activities of serum alanine aminotransferase and alkaline phosphatase occurred in the study group but not in controls.

The author concludes that erythropoiesis was stimulated and liver function was mildly impaired due to sustained high-dose testosterone-anabolic steroid administration.

PLATELET, LEUKOCYTE, AND ERYTHROCYTE (RBC) COUNTS
AND MEAN CORPUSCULAR VOLUME (MCV) IN THE
GROUPS STUDIED BEFORE AND AFTER PHASE 1. THE
VALUES INDICATE MEAN ± SEM. THE INTERGROUP
VALUES FOR SIGNIFICANCE LEVELS ARE ALSO GIVEN.*

| Variable | Study group (n = 5) | Control group (n = 6) | t-test |
|---|---|---|---|
| Platelets ($\times 10^9$/l) | | | |
| Before | 316 ± 33 | 281 ± 23 | N.S. |
| After | 357 ± 39 | 244 ± 17 | p < 0.05 |
| Leucocytes ($\times 10^9$/l) | | | |
| Before | 6.3 ± 0.3 | 6.4 ± 0.7 | N.S. |
| After | 7.4 ± 0.4 | 6.1 ± 0.5 | p < 0.05 |
| RBC ($\times 10^{12}$/l) | | | |
| Before | 5.3 ± 0.2 | 5.1 ± 0.2 | N.S. |
| After | 5.8 ± 0.3 | 5.2 ± 0.1 | p < 0.001 |
| MCV (fl) | | | |
| Before | 88.8 ± 2.2 | 89.6 ± 0.6 | N.S. |
| After | 84.7 ± 2.5 | 89.8 ± 0.7 | N.S. |
| MCH (pg) | | | |
| Before | 30.5 ± 0.9 | 30.6 ± 0.3 | N.S. |
| After | 28.1 ± 1.0 | 30.5 ± 0.3 | p < 0.05 |

*In serum γ-GT activities in the study group, there was an initial significant
($P < .05$) decrease at 14 weeks, which also remained at this lower level during the
use of steroids. The return to pretreatment level took 12 weeks.
(Courtesy of Alén, M.: Br. J. Sports Med. 19:15–20, March 1985.)

▶ There are ethical difficulties in carrying out human research on anabolic steroids, and in general the doses permitted by university committees on human experimentation are miniscule relative to those chosen by athletes for self-administration. In the present paper, higher doses were achieved by allowing the athlete to choose the dose, but drug administration was monitored with modern gas chromatographic techniques. The average quantity used was 65 mg/day. As in an earlier report from our laboratory (Shephard, et al., *Brit. J. Sports Med.* 11:170, 1977), there was an increase of hemoglobin level and mild impairment of liver function over the 38 weeks of observation.—Roy J. Shephard, M.D., Ph.D.

## Testosterone and Muscle Hypertrophy in Female Rats
Frederick E. Kuhn and Stephen R. Max (Univ. of Maryland)
J. Appl. Physiol. 59:24–27, July 1985                                    1–112

Anabolic steroids are widely used with weight-bearing exercise to enhance muscle bulk and strength, but such effects have not generally been found in studies of humans or animals. The effects of chronic testosterone propionate therapy on compensatory muscle hypertrophy secondary to synergist removal were examined in female CD rats. "Overload" was produced by bilateral removal of the soleus and gastrocnemius muscles. Testosterone was given subcutaneously at the time of synergist removal in a dose of 2.5 mg daily.

Neither synergist removal nor testosterone administration altered body weight, but overload caused a significant increase in the wet weight of plantaris muscle. Muscle noncollagen protein concentration was not significantly altered by overload. Muscle weight and noncollagen protein content generally were unchanged by chronic testosterone administration. Synergist removal led to a marked decrease in pyruvate oxidation by plantaris muscle. Malate dehydrogenase and lactate dehydrogenase activities also were reduced, but not when expressed on a noncollagen protein basis.

These findings fail to support the assertion that androgens, in conjunction with weight-bearing exercise, effectively increase muscle mass or function in female subjects. This conclusion probably also applies to those anabolic-androgenic steroids that bind to the same muscle androgen receptor as testosterone.

▶ Anecdotal reports suggest that the abuse of anabolic steroids by females is increasing (Lamb, *Am. J. Sports Med.* 12: 31, 1984), and in theory females might be more responsive to such treatment than males, because they have lower testosterone levels but more cytosolic androgen receptors (Dahlberg, et al., *Endocrinology* 108: 1431, 1981).

The rat model used here provides a good test of this hypothesis. There is no question that high drug levels were achieved (a 20-fold increase of testosterone), and training by removal of the synergists was also highly effective (a doubling of muscle bulk). However, as in many experiments on males, testosterone did not change the response to rigorous training. The only possible area of discussion is whether an anabolic androgen would have had the same effect as testosterone. However, current evidence is that such compounds bind to the same receptors as testosterone (Saartok, et al., *Endocrinology* 114: 2100, 1984).—Roy J. Shephard, M.D., Ph.D.

---

**Laboratory Detection of Marijuana Use**
Richard H. Schwartz and Richard L. Hawks (Children's Hosp. Natl. Med. Ctr., Washington, D.C., and Natl. Inst. on Drug Abuse, Rockville, Md.)
JAMA 254:788–792, Aug. 9, 1985                                   1–113

---

Evidence that marijuana use in adolescence may be associated with behavioral, social, and academic deficiencies has raised interest in chemical methods for detecting its use. In addition, intoxication by marijuana at any age can lead to impaired driving skills. Urine tests for marijuana are effective, highly specific, and relatively inexpensive. Many commercial and governmental laboratories have begun screening urine specimens for cannabinoids. The homogenous enzyme immunoassay technique (EMIT) is a semiquantitative immunochemical test for 9-carboxy-THC and other cannabinoid metabolites. Addition of adulterants to the urine can produce false negative results. Both the EMIT and radioimmunoassays are less specific than gas chromatography, high-pressure liquid chromatography, or mass spectrometry. Thin-layer chromatography also is more specific than immunoassay methods, but less specific than gas chromatography/mass spectrometry.

Urine screening for cannabinoids is not cost effective in an unselected middle-class adolescent population. Where maladaptive behavior of some type is independent of drug use, the drug use can be used as an excuse by an individual to evade direct responsibility for such behavior. A reluctant patient might be helped to seek counseling if marijuana use is confirmed by urine analysis. A first-voided weekend or Monday morning specimen should be obtained. If possible, the sample should be voided under direct observation by a concerned adult. Dilute urine should not be tested. Analysis within a few days is desirable. A sample volume of 20 ml is adequate for detecting marijuana metabolites as well as other drugs such as stimulants or opiates.

▶ There are several methods of testing for the metabolites of marijuana, the most convenient being a urine test. More complex and expensive blood tests are available. The important question of a 5% false positive pattern is noted. I should raise the larger question of how far do we test whom, and for what, in our Orwellian society. The reader is well aware of the local headlines on testing with reference to cocaine use, marijuana derivatives, and the like, often in sports figures. We should bear in mind, before there is a weekly screening at every junior high school for THC derivatives, that there is a cost factor of consequence. Furthermore, there is a major civil liberties question involved in any testing at any time. A greater drug problem of our country, in my view, possibly more dangerous than cannabis, is ethanol—in a recreational sense, in work-time loss, in person-abuse, and as it interrelates with automobile morbidity and mortality.—Lewis J. Krakauer, M.D., F.A.C.P.

---

**Effects of Endurance Training on the Androgenic Response to Exercise in Man**

N. Fellmann, J. Coudert, J.-F. Jarrige, M. Bedu, C. Denis, D. Boucher, and J.-R. Lacous (Faculté de Médecine, Clermont-Ferrand, France, and UER Médicine, Saint-Etienne, France)
Int. J. Sports Med. 6:215–219, August 1985                    1–114

---

Six healthy subjects, with a mean age of 35.8 years, volunteered to participate in a 40-week training program on a cycle ergometer (three 60-minute sessions per week at 80%–85% of maximal oxygen uptake [$VO_{2max}$]). Before training and at the 10th, 20th, 30th, and 40th weeks of the training program, plasma testosterone, cortisol, and androstenedione concentrations were measured at rest and at the end of the 1-hour endurance exercise requiring 80%–85% $VO_{2max}$.

The training resulted in significant increases of $VO_{2max}$ ($P < .05$) and of the lactate anaerobic threshold as expressed in % of $VO_{2max}$ ($P < .02$). Training did not significantly change the initial time level of plasma testosterone. At the end of the endurance run, the plasma testosterone was significantly increased ($P < .001$). Before, during, and after training, exercise induced significant increases in plasma androstenedione and cortisol ($P < .001$) (Fig 1–41). Relative individual training resulted in a significant

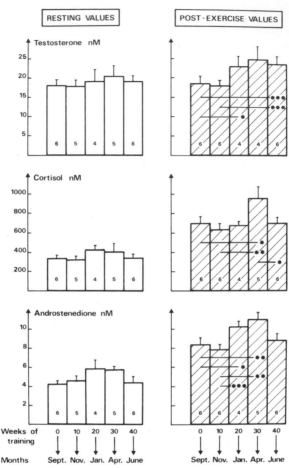

Fig 1–41.—Plasma concentrations in testosterone, cortisol, and androstenedione before training ($W_0$) and at the tenth week ($W_{10}$), twentieth week ($W_{20}$), thirtieth week ($W_{30}$), and fortieth week ($W_{40}$) of the training program are compared at rest and after a 60-minute exercise. Values are means ± SE. The number of subjects is noted down on the histogram. All the resting values are not significantly different. Significantly different postexercise values: $*P < .05$; $**P < .02$; $***P < .005$. (Courtesy of Fellmann, N., et al.: Int. J. Sports Med. 6:215–219, August 1985.)

decrease in pre-exercise rectal temperatures. In contrast, the end exercise temperatures remained constant.

These results suggest that long-term training enhances both testicular and adrenal responses to endurance exercise. These findings raise two questions: What are the mechanisms involved in the increase of adrenal and androgenic response to exercise, and have these hormonal changes any effect on energy metabolism related to bioenergetic changes observed at the same time?

▶ Some reports have suggested that very prolonged endurance exercise

(Galbo H., et al.: *Eur. J. Appl. Physiol.* 36: 101, 1977), can depress serum testosterone. It is thus reassuring to learn that the more moderate levels of activity likely in a typical exercise enthusiast have no effect on resting testosterone levels, and actually enhance concentrations during exercise. Reasons for the enhanced exercise secretion remain a matter of speculation, but two interesting possibilities are that testosterone stimulates glycogen synthetase (Bergamini E., et al.: *Biochim. Biophys. Acta* 177: 220, 1969), which would conserve muscle glycogen, and that it stimulates protein synthesis (which would counter the catabolic action of cortisol in gluconeogenesis).—Roy J. Shephard, M.D., Ph.D.

## Hormonological Data in Competitive Walkers: Preliminary Study and Perspectives

J. C. Etienne, M. Gatfosse, J. Gougcon, C. Schwartz, T. Milcent, J. Caron, J. Talmud, and G. Deltour (Hôpital Sébastopol, Hôpital Robert-Debré, Hôpital Maison-Blanche, and Institut Jean-Godinot, Reims, France)
Med. Sport 59:196–199, 1985                                                                  1–115

Hormone levels were measured at the 250-km mark of the 1983 Paris-Colmar race in eight walkers (seven men and one woman) after 30–36 hours of nonstop walking. The data demonstrate a peculiar hormonal profile: while a hypercortisolism (two to three times normal) was expected, the more interesting results concerned the androgens.

The samples were immediately centrifuged at the site, and then the serums were transported in dry ice to the laboratory. It was not possible to measure urinary metabolites nor to carry out dynamic tests. Neither were anthropometric data obtained in this preliminary study.

The results are shown in Tables 1 and 2. The low level of testicular androgens observed during a prolonged and exhausting effort such as an athletic walk suggests the involvement of several factors, including peripheral factors (diminution of testicular secretion, consumption by extrahepatic target tissues, maintenance of a metabolic equilibrium through the action of a cortisol-testosterone balance) and hypothalamal-hypophyseal

TABLE 1.—Hormonal Measurements After 255 KM of Walking in Seven Men

| N° | T NI: $4,5 \to 10$ng/ml | DHT NI: $0,3 \to 1$ | $\Delta_4$ NI: $0,5 \to 2,2$ | DHA$_S$ NI: $2,2 \to 3,3$ | CORTISOL NI: $310 \to 500$ | PRL NI: $7 \to 18$ ng/ml | FSH NI: $1 \to 2$ | LH NI: $1 \to 3,5$ |
|---|---|---|---|---|---|---|---|---|
| 1 | 0,38 | $\sim 0,05$ | 1,7 | 4,3 | --- | $< 5$ | 0,5 | 1,4 |
| 2 | 0,81 | 0,11 | 0,8 | 3,2 | 688 | $<5$ | 2 | 2 |
| 3 | 0,5 | $< 0,05$ | 0,66 | 4,5 | 550 | $< 5$ | 0,6 | 1,1 |
| 4 | 0,31 | $< 0,05$ | 0,19 | 3 | 713 | $< 5$ | 0,7 | 1,8 |
| 5 | 0,45 | $< 0,05$ | 0,29 | 1,9 | 865 | 5 | 0,9 | 2,7 |
| 6 | 0,28 | 0,11 | 1,3 | 1,6 | 522 | $< 5$ | 0,9 | 2,1 |
| 7 | 0,42 | $< 0,05$ | 1 | 2,8 | --- | $< 5$ | 0,5 | 1,9 |

(Courtesy of Etienne, J.C., et al.: Med. Sport 59:196–199, 1985.)

TABLE 2.—HORMONAL MEASUREMENTS AFTER 255 KM
OF WALKING IN ONE WOMAN

| N° | T<br>n =<br>$0,1 \to 0,8$ | DHT<br>$0,06 \to 0,2$ | $\Delta_4$<br>$0,6 \to 1,8$ | DHA$_S$<br>$0,6 \to 3,6$ | E$_2$<br>NI:<br>F30→90Pg/mlFO, | Prog<br>NI:<br>$14 \to 1,6$ | Cortisol | PRL<br>NI:<br>$6 \to 24$ng/ml | FSH<br>NI:<br>$1 \to 2$ | LH<br>NI:<br>$1 \to 2$ |
|---|---|---|---|---|---|---|---|---|---|---|
| ♀<br>8 | 0,44 | 0,07 | 1,8 | 5,4 | 40 | 2,4 | 922 | 39 | 0,63 | 1 |

(Courtesy of Etienne, J.C., et al.: Med. Sport 59:196–199, 1985.)

factors revealed by the absence of elevated levels of luteinizing hormone and low levels of prolactin.

This preliminary study, despite its limited approach, opens the way to dynamic studies permitting a better pre- and postcompetition hormonal profile during very prolonged sporting events, such as athletic walking.

▶ This must be one of the longest sustained bouts of exercise which has been studied from a metabolic point of view. It provides an interesting foil to the study of Häkkinen et al. (Digest 1–43) in that testosterone dropped to about a tenth of normal values, while cortisol levels rose. Unfortunately, no details of nutrition are given, but it seems likely that the subjects ate very little during their prolonged effort, and presumably the testosterone/cortisol ratio was thus shifted drastically in the direction of catabolism, in order to sustain hepatic gluconeogenesis.

This is an unusual study mainly because of the duration of activity, 30–36 hours of continuous walking. As with a number of recent reports there are indications of low levels of testicular androgens. Though these are probably caused by the exertion, it is interesting that those training for endurance events also show other signs of lower "masculinity," including lesser beard growth and lower scores on the male/female scale of the Minnesota Multiphasic Personality Inventory. It is thus just possible that some fear about failing to conform to male stereotypes pushes the competitors to these extraordinary efforts.—Roy J. Shephard, M.D., Ph.D.

**Weight Loss in Amateur Wrestlers and Its Effect on Serum Testosterone Levels**
Richard H. Strauss, Richard R. Lanese, and William B. Malarkey (Ohio State Univ.)
JAMA 254:3337–3338, Dec. 20, 1985                                    1–116

Wrestlers who have lost weight through dietary restriction for competitive purposes have occasionally described a reduced sex drive and less strength and endurance. Since low body weight is associated with low testosterone concentrations in males with anorexia nervosa, hormonal studies were done in 19 wrestlers at the peak of the competitive season, when many were at their lowest weight, and again 2 months after the end of the season.

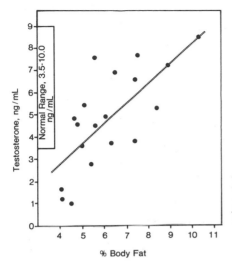

Fig 1–42.—Correlation of serum testosterone concentration and percent body fat at peak of competitive season in 19 amateur wrestlers ($r = .72$; $P < .001$). (Courtesy of Strauss, R.H., et al.: JAMA 254:3337–3338, Dec. 20, 1985. Copyright 1985, American Medical Association.)

Body weight and body fat were significantly lower during than after the wrestling season, as were testosterone and PRL concentrations. Low serum testosterone values correlated with low body fat (Fig 1–42). Large percentage changes in body fat or body weight were associated with low serum testosterone concentrations. There were no significant differences in gonadotropin, GH, cortisol, or thyroxine concentrations during the two measurement periods.

This study correlated low body fat and loss of body fat with decreased serum testosterone concentrations in collegiate wrestlers. The concomitant fall in serum PRL concentration and the lack of a compensatory increase in serum LH concentration suggest that a CNS defect is at least partly responsible for the testosterone decrease. A fall in sex hormone binding globulin is also a possibility. Whatever the mechanism, the effect is associated with loss of body fat and appears to reflect undernutrition.

▶ There is increasing recognition that the inhibition of the pituitary axis seen in women who develop a negative energy balance can also occur in men who restrict their nutritional intake relative to physical activity, either in distance running or in wrestling. In some of the present group of wrestlers, testosterone levels fell to less than 20% of normal during the competitive season. However, as in females with menstrual disturbances, there seems to have been a speedy recovery once energy balance was restored.—Roy J. Shephard, M.D., Ph.D.

---

**Vitamins and Endurance Training: Food for Running or Faddish Claims?**
E. J. van der Beek (Inst. of Civo-Toxicology and Nutrition, Zeist, The Netherlands)
Sports Med. 2:175–197, 1985                                              1–117

In the relationship between food and physical performance, food is regarded as a conglomerate of nutrients and human beings as a kind of organic pudding. This "machine" concept of human performance, together with the mystique surrounding vitamins, has led to the belief that a surplus of vitamins is necessary to improve physical performance. A marginal or subclinical vitamin deficiency is defined herein as falling somewhere between optimal vitamin status and frank clinical deficiency. A marginal deficiency is characterized by biochemical values deviating from statistically derived reference limits—but by the absence of clinical signs of deficiency.

A review of depletion studies, epidemiologic surveys, and supplementation studies shows that a restricted intake of some B-complex vitamins—consisting of less than 35% to 45% of the recommended dietary allowance—may lead to decreased endurance capacity within a few weeks. Studies on ascorbic acid (vitamin C) depletion and fat-soluble vitamin A deficiency have noted no decrease of endurance capacity. However, in a few recent epidemiologic surveys, biochemical vitamin C deficiency was actually shown to decrease aerobic power.

The general conclusion is that a reduced intake of water-soluble vitamins decreases endurance capacity. But further controlled experimentation is needed with B-complex vitamins and vitamin C individually to support this point. Available evidence shows that supplementation of the diet with either single or multivitamin preparations containing B-complex vitamins, vitamin C, or vitamin E does not improve physical performance in athletes who have a normal biochemical vitamin balance from a well-balanced diet. Another rationale for vitamin supplementation has been the belief that large vitamin losses occur during sweating. But body sweat has been shown to be almost completely devoid of vitamins. Although vitamin supplementation does not seem to produce any effect when the diet is adequate, it is possible that vitamin B-complex supplementation is useful in sports requiring a high energy expenditure, because of the unavoidable consumption of "empty calories"—i.e., food products with a low nutrient density.

▶ Vitamin supplementation has not been found to enhance performance. If athletes meet their increased energy requirements with a variety of nutrient-dense foods, vitamin requirements should be satisfied. Evaluation of daily nutrient intake is of primary importance. The saying "caveat emptor," let the buyer beware, should be heeded by all athletes.—Joseph S. Torg, M.D.

---

**Failure of Transdermal Nitroglycerin to Improve Exercise Capacity in Patients With Angina Pectoris**
Michael Sullivan, Marios Savvides, Sliman Abouantoun, E. Birk Madsen, and Victor Froelicher (VA Med. Ctr., Long Beach, Calif.)
J. Am. Coll. Cardiol. 4:1220–1223, May 1985          1–118

---

Sixteen patients with stable angina pectoris were studied in a double-blind crossover manner using treadmill exercise testing with the direct measurement of total body oxygen uptake, 1 and 24 hours after application of a 20 sq cm transdermal nitroglycerin system and identical placebo. The male volunteers ranged in age from 42 to 70 years. Points of analysis were peak angina and the submaximal work load occurring at 4 minutes of exercise.

No statistically significant differences in standing and supine rest heart rates and blood pressures at 1 and 24 hours were seen between application of transdermal nitroglycerin and placebo for any of the measured rest hemodynamic variables. At 1 hour after application, the rate-pressure product at the submaximal work load was significantly increased during transdermal nitroglycerin when compared with placebo application ($P < .05$). At 24 hours after application of either placebo or active drug, there were no statistically significant differences between the two treatments for any of the measured variables at a submaximal work load or peak angina. Separate analysis controlling for a β-receptor blocking effect revealed significantly more ST segment depression at peak angina during transdermal nitroglycerin than placebo application at 24 hours in the group of patients taking a β-receptor blocking agent. At 24 hours, this group also had greater rest supine systolic and diastolic blood pressures during nitroglycerin than during placebo application ($P < .05$).

The once daily application of a 20 sq cm transdermal nitroglycerin system was ineffective in altering the exercise capacity of patients with angina pectoris. The lack of efficacy at 1 hour appears to be due to inadequate nitroglycerin blood levels; at 24 hours it may be due to tolerance.

▶ Many patients with chronic angina would welcome the possibility of prophylactic relief of their symptoms by the transdermal application of 10 mg of nitroglycerin once per day. Thompson (*Angiology* 34:23, 1983) reported improved exercise tolerance at 2 and 26 hours after treatment, but others have been unable to substantiate such claims. The present report is one more piece of negative evidence, although proponents of transdermal therapy might object that the results from the patients were not titrated to find the maximum dose of nitroglycerine tolerated with this route of administration; moreover, some of the potential benefit could have been masked because half of the patients were also receiving β-blocking medication.—Roy J. Shephard, M.D., Ph.D.

## Miscellaneous Topics

**Exercise-Induced Anaphylaxis: A Serious Form of Physical Allergy Associated With Mast Cell Degranulation**
A. L. Sheffer, A. K. F. Tong, G. F. Murphy, R. A. Lewis, E. R. McFadden, Jr., and K. F. Austen (Harvard Univ. and Brigham and Women's Hosp., Boston)
J. Allergy Clin. Immunol. 75:479–484, April 1985                    1–119

Exercised-induced anaphylaxis (EIA) is a syndrome consisting of premonitory symptoms and signs of generalized body warmth, pruritus, and erythema, which progress on continued exertion to confluent urticaria, laryngeal edema with stridor or hoarseness, and gastrointestinal colic and frequently culminate in vascular collapse. In a previous study, 4 of 5 patients (4 women and 1 man, aged 21 to 47 years) with this condition had significant elevations of serum histamine concentration accompanying the early clinical manifestations after experimental exercise. To assess relevant morphologic alterations in the skin of these patients, cutaneous mast cells were examined by light and transmission electron microscopy before and during the initial appearance of erythema elicited by exertion.

The marked alterations seen in mast cells immediately after exercise consisted of loss of electron density and internal substructure of granules, fusion of granule membranes with those of adjacent granules and with mast cell membranes, creating conduits to the extracellular space, and an apparent decrease in the number of intact granules per cell (Fig 1–43). Biopsy specimens obtained before exercise from patients with EIA and from 2 normal individuals who served as control subjects were identical (Fig 1–44); the control subjects had normal mast cell morphologic features after exercise. Serum histamine levels were elevated in patients with EIA after exercise at the time of biopsy, whereas control subjects had normal levels.

This study demonstrates characteristic changes in skin mast cells in patients with EIA after exercise. The exercise-related alterations consisted of loss of granule substructure, fusion of perigranular membranes with each other and with the mast cell membranes, and apparent discharge of

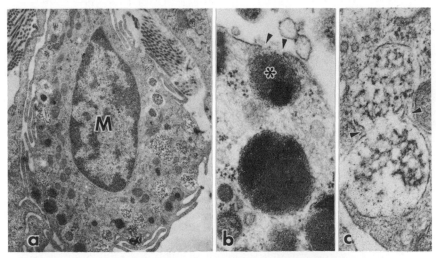

Fig 1–43.—Mast cells in patient with exercise-induced anaphylaxis immediately after exercise. a, mast cells (M) appear markedly depleted of normal complement of dense granules; X 14,400. b, at higher magnification, more dense granules exhibit some loss of electron density and substructure (asterisk) and appear to merge with focally disrupted plasma membrane (arrowheads); X 58,300. c, less dense granules contain only locally aggregated flocculent material, and membranes of adjacent granules have merged (arrowheads), creating a figure-eight contour; X 78,000. (Courtesy of Sheffer, A.L., et al.: J. Allergy Clin. Immunol. 75:479–484, April 1985.)

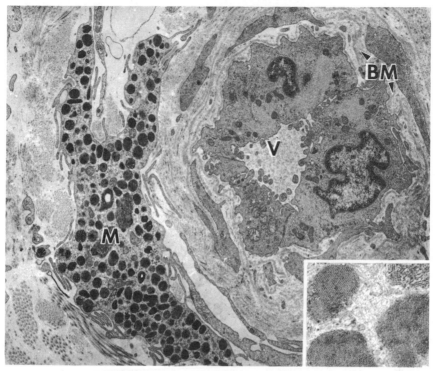

Fig 1–44.—Mast cells *(M)* in patient with exercise-induced anaphylaxis before exercise, which were indistinguishable from those of control subjects by cellular or subcellular criteria. Mast cells were principally located around superficial vessels *(V)* and surrounded by a well-developed basement membrane *(BM)*; X 10,000. *Inset,* granules; X 55,000. (Courtesy of Sheffer, A.L., et al.: J. Allergy Clin. Immunol 75:479–484, April 1985.)

granule contents. Association of intermediate filaments with discharging and solubilized granules and changes in the length of microvillus cell membrane projections were not observed. The findings are similar to those for cutaneous mast cell degranulation in vivo that was induced by intradermal injection of ragweed extract into allergic individuals. The solubilization of granule contents characterized by the appearance of amorphous material within the granule membrane and enlargement of granules probably occur early in the degranulation process of EIA. Subsequently, adjacent granule membranes merge, at times forming conduits where solubilized granule contents communicate with adjacent granules and ultimately with the extracellular space. Such merging of adjacent granules and formation of conduits to facilitate granule content discharge have been previously described with in vitro activation of human mast cells. Similar changes have also been noted in rat mast cells. However, the morphologic features of mast cells in the rat differ significantly from those in man, and comparisons should therefore be made with caution. The condition EIA was initially considered a distinct form of physical allergy distinguishable from other forms of physical allergy presenting as urticaria of conventional dimensions. The presence of elevated serum histamine levels after exercise had supported the presumption of mast cell participation in the genesis of these reactions. The morphologic alterations in the mast cell granules observed on light and electron microscopic assessments are consistent with alterations that occur in mast cells stimulated immunologically in vitro. The triggering mechanisms responsible for mast cell degranulation in EIA are unknown. The morphologic findings confirm the view that this syndrome represents an important and clinically distinct form of physical allergy.

▶ There is a growing body of literature on this syndrome. it is of rare frequency but obvious significance, culminating as it may in systemic collapse and death. The manifestations of this syndrome include a generalized pruritus with urticaria and upper respiratory obstruction and/or vascular collapse. It is clinically indistinguishable from anaphylactic reactions consequent to activation of IgE-sensitized mast cells by specific substances. It appears to be a mast cell degranulation phenomenon, and the study illustrates this well. This has been well defined morphologically, yet the triggering mechanisms remain unknown. Although the authors do not make the correlation, I think it is likely that the subset of patients that are prone to exercise-induced asthma may be more prone to this systemic allergic syndrome. At this point, they are considered distinct clinical entities.—Lewis J. Krakauer, M.D., F.A.C.P.

---

**Assessment of Circulating Immune Complexes by a Solid-Phase $C_{1q}$-Binding Assay During the First Hours and Days After Prolonged Exercise**
B. Dufaux, R. Müller, and W. Hollmann (Deutsche Sporthochschule Köln, Federal Republic of Germany)
Clin. Chim. Acta 145:313–317, Feb. 15, 1985                                              1–120

---

A sensitive and specific solid-phase $C_{1q}$-binding assay, using porcine $C_{1q}$ and microtiter plates as a solid phase, served to assess the immune complexes in serum during the first hours and days after a 3-hour running test. Fourteen moderately trained male subjects participated in the race and covered a mean of 36.3 km in 3 hours. Blood samples were drawn 1 day before, immediately before, immediately after, 1 and 3 hours after, and 1, 2, and 4 days after the race.

When compared with the changes of serum total protein, the apparent immune complex levels were 1 and 3 hours after the race clearly elevated and 1, 2, and 4 days postexercise slightly lowered (Fig 1–45). Correcting the postexercise immune complex values for the changes of serum total protein by dividing them by the quotient total protein after the race-total protein before the race (mean of the two preexercise values), significant elevations of the immune complexes were found 1 and 3 hours after the race ($P < .001$ and $P < .05$, respectively) and a significant decrease was observed 2 days later. Three out of 14 participants, who were in good health, demonstrated clearly higher resting immune complex values (mean: 21.6 mg/L) than the other participants (mean: 5.2 mg/L). The changes of

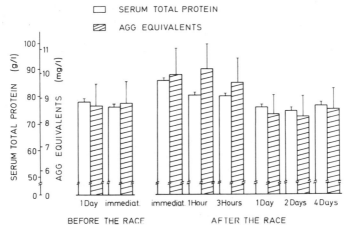

☐ SERUM TOTAL PROTEIN

▨ AGG EQUIVALENTS

**Fig 1–45.**—Serum concentrations (mean ± SEM) of immune complexes expressed as equivalents of aggregated gamma-globulins (AGG) and of serum total protein before and during the first hours and days after a 3-hour race in 14 subjects. (Courtesy of Dufaux, B., et al.: Clin. Chim. Acta 145:313–317, Feb. 15, 1985.)

serum apparent immune complexes induced by physical exercise, however, did not differ between the subjects with high and low preexercise values.

A rapid increase of immune complexes after prolonged exercise would be compatible with the concept that in the trained subject preformed antibodies against foreign components are present in the blood and can readily bind within minutes or hours to the liberated antigens. The present results agree with a previous study done by the authors, which revealed, during a 4-day footrace, an initial increase and a delayed decrease of circulating immune complexes.

▶ The acute and long-term effects of exercise upon immune function is a relatively recent area of inquiry, but has obvious practical application, particularly during seasons of major epidemics.

Dufaux and associates here demonstrate that 3 hours of exercise is sufficient to cause an acute inflammatory reaction, with the formation of immune complexes that presumably help to eliminate the products of nonspecific tissue destruction escaping from the overworked muscles.

The authors do not discuss the more long-term effects of rigorous endurance training, but there have been some suggestions that this can depress immune function if carried to the excess of a negative nitrogen balance.—Roy J. Shephard, M.D., Ph.D.

---

### Effect of Exercise on Plasma Interferon Levels

Antonio Viti, Michela Muscettola, Luana Paulesu, Velio Bocci, and Antonio Almi (Univ. of Siena, Italy)

J. Appl. Physiol. 59:426–428, August 1985                                    1–121

The effect of exercise on plasma interferon activity was studied in 8 male subjects before and after exercise on a cycle ergometer for 1 hour at 70% of their maximal $O_2$ consumption ($V_{O2max}$).

As shown in Figure 1–46, the average plasma glucose, protein, and lipid concentrations did not change significantly from preexercise values. The moderate elevation of lactate at the end of exercise is consonant with a submaximal physical exertion. Hemoconcentration did not occur. Interferon activity, $\alpha$-type and acid-labile, increased significantly at the end of exercise to 1 hour later. It decreased to the preexercise level 2 hours after the end of the exercise. Immediately after maximal exercise there was also a significant ($P < .01$) increase of plasma interferon level, which returned to preexercise level within 1 hour.

The transient increase of interferon levels in plasma can be tentatively

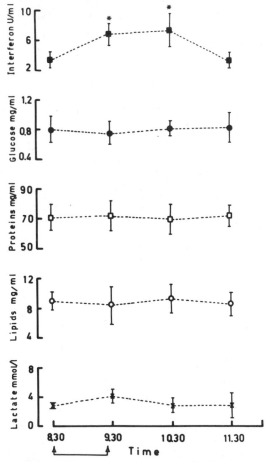

Fig 1–46.—Plasma interferon, glucose, protein, lipid and lactate levels before (8:30) and after exercise. Values are means ± SD; n = 8 subjects. Bracketed arrows, time of exercise. *Significantly different from resting value ($P < .01$). (Courtesy of Viti, A., et al.: J. Appl. Physiol. 59:426–428, August 1985.)

proposed as a convenient response to augment host defense, but its overall meaning requires follow-up studies in trained athletes.

▶ Interferons are not normally found in the plasma (Levin S. and Hahn T., *Clin. Exp. Immunol.* 46:475, 1981). Though it could be argued that the accumulation of interferon is due to a reduced plasma clearance (because of the effect of exercise on renal blood flow), it is more likely part of an immune reaction to traumatized tissue in the active muscle and/or the byproducts of renal ischemia.—Roy J. Shephard, M.D., Ph.D.

---

**Maximal Short Term Exercise Capacity in Healthy Subjects Aged 15–70 Years**
Lydia Makrides, George J. F. Heigenhauser, Neil McCartney, and Norman L. Jones (McMaster Univ)
Clin. Sci. 69:197–205, August 1985                                    1–122

---

Fifty male and 50 female subjects, aged 15 to 71 years, exercised maximally for 30 seconds on an isokinetic ergometer at a pedaling frequency of 60 rpm. Results were compared with maximal oxygen uptake ($Vo_{2max}$) obtained in a progressive incremental exercise test.

Total work in 30 seconds was higher in men than women, declined linearly by about 6% per decade of age ($r = -.65$), and was related closely to height ($r = .75$) and to lean thigh volume estimated anthropometrically ($r = .84$). A close association with vital capacity ($r = .86$) was also found that accounted statistically for the combined effects of age and height. The percentage of decline in power during 30 seconds (fatigue index) was lower in subjects reporting greater leisure activity. A close relationship was found between total work in 30 seconds and $Vo_{2max}$ ($r = .86$), with vital capacity and leisure activity exerting additional influences on $Vo_{2max}$ (multiple $r = .93$). The well-established reduction with age in $Vo_{2max}$ is associated with an apparent parallel reduction in the power output capacity of large muscle groups recruited in heavy dynamic leg exercise.

This study used a recently developed isokinetic cycle ergometer that enables power and fatigue to be measured precisely during dynamic cycling exercise. Although most studies that have investigated maximal exercise capacity have been concerned with aerobic power as reflected in $Vo_{2max}$, recently there has been increased interest in maximal short-term, or anaerobic, power, in which the duration of exercise is 30 seconds or less. At any given age, there were associations between the power variables and height and less significant correlations with weight. At any given size, age was significantly related to power variables; when thigh volume measurements were used in an analysis of covariance, age was not found to exert an independent effect. The estimate of lean thigh volume from anthropometry is potentially subject to error. However, this was the measurement to which power was most closely related. This finding is consistent with previously established relationships between maximal power during cycling and the size of muscles.

The finding of a decline with age in the peak power and total work in 30 seconds, without a significant change in the fatigue characteristics, may indicate a relative preservation of oxidative fatigue-resistant muscle fibers in older subjects. This hypothesis is consistent with the finding in several studies of a reduction in the size and number of fast-twitch type 2 fibers with age. Such age-related changes may be due to the motoneuron dysfunction shown by Campbell et al. to occur with age. Although $Vo_{2max}$ is conventionally used to assess aerobic power while the total work in 30 seconds mainly assesses anaerobic capacity, a close relationship was obtained between the two measurements. Both indices appeared to decline with age at similar rates. The high correlation between total work and $Vo_{2max}$ suggests that there are common factors contributing to both measures. Along with the relationship between thigh volume and $Vo_{2max}$, this finding suggests that, in the average population, the size of muscles and their capacity to generate power are important factors contributing to the maximal aerobic power in exercise.

It appears that subjects in active occupations will maintain muscle size and that the aerobic capacity of muscles will be maintained by regular leisure activity. It is possible that exercise at any age may help to improve aerobic capacity and thus help to maintain $Vo_{2max}$. Aniansson and Gustafsson trained 12 subjects aged 70 years and showed increases in the area of type 2 fibers associated with improvements in muscle function. Despite evidence of neurally mediated degeneration of muscle with age, training can improve muscular status.

▶ The value of this paper lies in part in that the authors used a recently developed isokinetic cycle ergometer, enabling them to measure power and fatigue fairly precisely during short-term dynamic cycling exercise. This permitted study of the factors that influence $Vo_{2max}$, as well as study of maximal short-term anaerobic power with a duration of exercise interval of 30 seconds or less.

Aging may be a series of measurable and unmeasurable losses of various functions. This study would suggest that muscle size, function, and aerobic power can be maintained by regular moderately vigorous leisure activity. Specifically, if you can show increase in type 2 fibers in 70-year-old individuals and improve muscle function, then this has to be optimistic against the known pattern of neurally mediated muscle degeneration that occurs inevitably with aging.—Lewis J. Krakauer, M.D., F.A.C.P.

---

**Does Fever or Myalgia Indicate Reduced Physical Performance Capacity in Viral Infections?**
Göran Friman, James E. Wright, Nils G. Ilbäck, William R. Beisel, John D. White, Dan S. Sharp, Edward L. Stephen, William L. Daniels, and James A. Vogel (U.S. Army Med. Research Inst. of Infectious Diseases, Fort Detrick,

Frederick, Md.; U.S. Army Research Inst. of Environmental Medicine, Natick, Mass.; and Univ. of Uppsala, Sweden)
Acta Med. Scand. 217:353–361, 1985                                    1–123

In a double-blind study, the authors assessed 9 healthy male volunteers, aged 19 to 29 years. After baseline measurements, 7 subjects were inoculated intravenously with 0.5 ml of diluted (1:10 in sterile physiologic saline) human plasma from a lot used to transmit sandfly fever in earlier studies, and 2 control subjects were given 0.5 ml of sterile isotonic sodium chloride. The subjects remained on the experimental ward from postinoculation day 2 through day 7. They were served regular mixed food in ordinary amounts and nonalcoholic beverages ad libitum. Subjects remained fully active on the ward during the entire study with the exception of about 1 day when 7 were febrile.

Fever began abruptly during a 14-hour period, 62–76 hours after inoculation in 7 cases, and lasted for 40–46 hours in all but 1, in whom the overall duration was 62 hours. Two subjects with no fever at any time proved to be the controls. All but 2 of the infected men experienced muscle aching or tenderness during fever, and all but 1 had chills and headache. However, there was no statistical correlation between subjectively perceived symptoms of illness and fever indices. All febrile subjects recovered quickly without complications or sequelae. Neither control reported any symptoms. In all but 1 of the virus-inoculated men detectable viremia developed; virus titers varied between $10^2$ and $10^5$ plaque-forming units/ ml of serum. Virus was recovered for 1–3 days, starting on day 2, 3, or 4 after inoculation. The highest titers and longest durations of viremia were observed in the subjects who experienced the highest total fever index. Neutralizing antibodies to sandfly fever virus developed in all virus-inoculated subjects, the titer rise being significant 11 days after inoculation and still more pronounced on day 28 (range, 1/160–1/320).

The viral infection, with 2 days of fever and prominent subjective symptoms including myalgia, caused no significant alterations in serum or muscle enzyme levels or muscle ultrastructure; decrements occurred in various muscle performance capabilities during but not after fever. Stroke volume decreased not only during fever but also in early convalescence in different body positions at rest. Febrile severity, which correlated positively with the virus titers in blood, also showed a significant correlation with the decrease in cardiac output recorded in early convalescence. Muscle performance decrements correlated with subjective symptoms during the illness rather than with the fever index.

No significant changes in serum total creatine kinase (CK), skeletal muscle CK isoenzyme, or myoglobin levels were found, nor could morphologic deviations from normal be found in muscle concentrations (with one exception). Thus, it appears unlikely that myalgia reported by 5 of the 7 men was caused by myositis. However, 1 of the infected subjects displayed prominent foci of myofibrillar disarray in his muscles during fever and in early convalescence but not in the preinfection biopsy specimen. High preinfection values of serum lactate dehydrogenase, CK, and myoglobin indicated a preexisting muscle abnormality in this man.

This brief infection did not cause any exaggerated heart rate reaction during tilt. This differs from previous recordings in infected patients confined to bed for 1 week, in whom infection plus bed rest, but not bed rest alone, caused significant orthostatic deterioration. Scheduled activity, including shift of the body angle (getting out of bed and walking 5–10 m once every half hour during waking hours), prevents orthostatic deterioration in febrile patients. Thus, the brevity of the infection and the amount of physical activity usually maintained by the subjects in this study were probably sufficiently preventive. However, a significant effect on cardiac output was noted. The cardiac output was lower after fever in both the supine and the upright positions, corresponding with a smaller stroke volume. The reduction in cardiac output after infection was correlated with the fever index. Repeated venous blood sampling showed that controls maintained their cardiac output throughout the study. Similar hematocrit decreases were noted in both infected and control subjects during the study.

▶ It is intriguing that there are not more changes in muscle enzymes in these subjects and that the biopsy results are relatively normal. Note further that there were only 7 subjects, and this is only one particular virus, which may or may not have a muscle phase. It is conceivable that a fever from another disease with more of a muscle phase could show alteration, or be completely different from this particular virus. The point I should make is that one cannot generalize to all viral infections from fever in 7 subjects from one known viral illness. The authors do note that in patients with severe myalgia resulting from influenza or echovirus infection a disturbance of the neuromuscular transmission has been recorded by single fiber electromyography.

See the closely related article in the 1985 YEAR BOOK OF SPORTS MEDICINE, pp. 64–65. "Muscle Soreness After Exercise: Implications of Morphological Changes," by Fridén. Exhaustive work in the human normal subject correlated with marked ultramicroscopic morphologic change but did not show correlative enzyme elevations in these biopsy results, all from nondiseased normal individuals.—Lewis J. Krakauer, M.D., F.A.C.P.

---

**Measurement of Exercise Tolerance in Patients With Rheumatoid Arthritis and Osteoarthritis**

Carol A. Beals, Richard M. Lampman, Barbara Figley Banwell, Ethan M. Braunstein, James W. Albers, and C. William Castor (Univ. of Michigan)
J. Rheumatol. 12:458–461, 1985                                                                    1–124

---

Paradoxically, in patients with rheumatoid arthritis (RA) or osteoarthritis (OA), feelings of fatigue are addressed with recommendations for reduced activity, even though physical exercise has been shown to increase stamina. Despite this clinical practice of advocating limited activity, little information is available to substantiate that vigorous exercise is detrimental or will exacerbate the inflammatory or degenerative processes in patients with either RA or OA.

The authors studied 14 patients, 6 women and 2 men with RA (mean age, 50.5 ± 8.6 years) and 4 women and 2 men with OA (mean age, 49.2 ± 6.3 years). The RA patients had definite RA, ARA Functional Class II; the OA patients had knee joint disease. All patients were on similar medical regimens, all of which included nonsteroidal anti-inflammatory drugs (NSAID). A third group (group 3), which served as controls, consisted of 6 very inactive, nonarthritic volunteers matched for age, sex, and weight.

The subjects with RA and OA were less physically fit than very inactive controls. Of the two disease groups, the RA patients were the least physically fit as demonstrated by lower accomplished indices of work load, exercise time, and aerobic capacity during exercise stress testing. Muscle strength showed significantly lower torque values in knee flexion for both RA and OA patients as compared with the controls. In addition, RA patients achieved significantly lower torque values in extension. These findings suggest atrophied muscle fibers, and exemplify the need for appropriate muscle strengthening therapy for arthritic patients. Adaptive changes in the metabolic characteristics of these muscles, concomitant with facilitation of oxygen transport, would be anticipated and higher oxygen uptakes might be attained following physical training. The lower grip strength in patients with RA further documents the greater muscle weakness in these patients as compared to those with OA.

The search for myopathic and neuropathic findings did not differentiate RA and OA patients from the controls, and these indices did not differ between the RA and OA groups. Assessment of disease activity by use of joint counts confirmed that the RA subjects had more joint involvement than the OA group and normal individuals. A single session of strenuous nonweight bearing exercise did not increase inflammation as measured by thermography in either the RA or OA groups, and these subjects did not report increased joint symptoms.

Specific measurements of maximum oxygen consumption and isotonic muscle activity appear to be sensitive indicators for evaluating impairments in physical work capacity in patients with RA and OA. Strenuous bouts of dynamic aerobic exercise did not exacerbate joint pain or cause inflammation of exercised joints in either patient group.

Exercise testing showed these patients to have weakened muscle strength and reduced physical fitness. Thus, it is conceivable that therapeutic programs of appropriate muscle strengthening exercises together with aerobic endurance training might enhance stamina and cardiovascular functional ability in patients with nonacute RA or OA.

▶ Exercise can be very important in patients with rheumatoid arthritis or osteoarthritis. Understandably, it is often interdicted or markedly reduced on recommendation from physicians, because of the concern of causing a flare of disease. Fatigue is often used as the judgmental point for decreasing exercise, yet is an integral part of the disease proper.

The important statement made by this paper is that vigorous exercise does not cause a flare of arthritis if the patient is in a nonacute stage, and should be recommended in that situation. This is of importance for aerobic training and cardiovascular disease prevention.

All subjects were characterized by a reduced functional capacity, as expected.—Lewis J. Krakauer, M.D., F.A.C.P.

---

**The Use of Strengthening Exercises in Post-Polio Sequelae: Methods and Results**
Rubin M. Feldman (Univ. of Alberta)
Orthopedics 8:889–890, July 1985                                                    1–125

---

An increasing number of post-polio patients are presenting after 20 to 30 years with altered muscle function, mainly muscle weakness and fatigue, and often muscle and joint pain as well. The pattern of weakness resembles that seen in the initial episode of poliomyelitis. Muscle atrophy occasionally is present, and ambulation deteriorates, along with compromise of function in activities of daily living. The added stress is especially evident in subjects aged 30 to 50 years, and ignorance as to the cause adds to the feelings of frustration. Motor nerve conduction velocity and repetitive stimulation studies are done as indicated, and orthotic management is reviewed. An attempt is made to strengthen all weakened muscles, using progressive resistive exercises. Lighter polypropylene braces sometimes are helpful.

When the same exercise was used for all muscle groups, muscles weakened by disuse improved, but those weakened by disease had reduced function. Better results were achieved by applying nonfatiguing exercise to muscles weakened by previous poliomyelitis. Occupational therapy and optimal orthotic management then enhanced improved ambulation and daily activities. Only muscles weakened by disease were electrophysiologically abnormal.

Muscles weakened by post-polio syndrome can be strengthened by nonfatiguing exercise over 3 to 6 months, when applied 2–3 times a week. Emotional support is very important. Occupational therapy can teach the patient how to improve function as muscle strength increases, and appropriate orthotic management also is used.

▶ In the post-polio syndrome, characterized by a recurrence of symptoms in the same muscle groups that were weakened in the initial onset of disease, physicians are now recognizing the appearance of a group of patients originally afflicted 20–30 years ago. This is a particularly insidious syndrome, presenting with muscle weakness, pain, fatigue, and insomnia; it is often progressive and depression is associated with the syndrome because of small hope for therapeutic improvement. Therapy is very different than for the standard muscle loss or joint weakness. Progressive exercise can have a weakening and deleterious effect rather than a beneficial effect in PPMS. Appropriate intervals must be provided for the weakened muscles to come back, and exercise must be prescribed with great delicacy. I am not sure that EMG testing and velocity studies are necessary to identify the weak muscles. They almost define themselves clinically. In any event, it requires a sophisticated therapist to deal with this syndrome. Often the initial poliomyelitis involved many muscles subtly that were not initially subject to atrophy, and the problem may be much more diffuse than was suspected. The author is optimistic that nonfatiguing exercise applied 2 to 3 times weekly for 3 to 6 months will usually bring about slow and steady strengthening of these muscle groups. The intensity of exercise is very gradually increased and concurrent emotional support is underlined as important. It has been suggested, but not documented to my knowledge, that the cholinergic drug group, which has been used in myasthenia (e.g., mestinon), may be of some benefit in dealing with the weakness.

In this situation, it seems to me that one is justified in using empirical therapy that is not absolutely proven, in the absence of any other alternative. This presumes side effects and risks are not unreasonable. Such empirical therapy might include anabolic steroids, caffeine, amphetamines, NSAID agents, and even possibly the judicious and careful trial of pituitary growth hormone. None of these are annotated in the present literature. I am aware of anecdotal beneficial reports of both caffeine and low dose (2.5–5 mgs per day) dextroamphetamine use. Because of the individual pathology of loss in each case, single-blind, double-blind, or even minimally controlled observations will be extremely difficult, more so perhaps than pharmacologic observations in pregnancy.—Lewis J. Krakauer, M.D., F.A.C.P.

**Gastrointestinal Symptoms During Exercise in Enduro Athletes: Prevalence and Speculations on the Aetiology**
L. J. Worobetz and D. F. Gerrard (Univ. of Otago, New Zealand)
N.Z. Med. J. 98:644–646, Aug. 14, 1985                    1–126

The prevalence of gastrointestinal (GI) symptoms was studied in athletes who participated in the Dunedin Enduro event in New Zealand in March 1984. The event consisted of an 800-m harbor swim, a 25-km cycle, a 5-km canoe paddle, and a 12-km run.

Of the 119 competitors, 70 (61 males), aged 14 to 46 years completed questionnaires. For 29 respondents, this represented their first Enduro-type event, whereas 20 were entering their second and 10 their third event, and 10 stated this was at least their fourth event. Seventy percent trained 6 to 10 hours per week. The duration of training varied considerably. Five subjects had trained less than 1 month, and 16 had been in constant training for at least 3 years.

Of the 70 respondents, 36 had GI symptoms just before competition; the symptoms were similar to those experienced during exercise. Twenty athletes described similar symptoms when emotionally stressed. Of those who denied precompetition symptoms, 72% at least occasionally experienced some symptoms during exercise.

Upper GI symptoms noticed during exercise including nausea, vomiting, belching, heartburn, regurgitation, and possibly chest pain were prevalent but rarely frequent or incapacitating. These symptoms were more commonly experienced with strenuous exercise, consumption of fluid during exercise, or eating or drinking just before strenuous exercise. Mild to moderate exercise has little effect on or may actually improve gastric emptying, but strenuous exercise delays emptying. This delay may contribute to nausea and gastroesophageal reflux, leading to regurgitation and heartburn. The delay after strenuous exercise may partly explain the anorexia experienced by many after such exercise. Ingestion of a meal, especially if fatty, immediately before exercise would aggravate this situation.

The effect of exercise on esophageal function and the lower esophageal sphincter is unknown. However, preliminary data suggest an increase in sphincter pressure with moderate exercise but no change in primary esophageal peristalsis. Whether athletes with prevalent esophageal symptoms during exercise have a lax or incompetent lower esophageal sphincter or lack the increase in sphincter pressure with exercise is unknown. Also unknown is whether the chest pain experienced by some athletes during exercise may represent gastroesophageal reflux or esophageal motor dysfunction.

▶ Gastrointestinal symptom distress is prevalent in endurance exercise such as extended running, or in what these authors studied, an equivalent of the triathlon. Fifty-eight percent of respondents spoke of notable upper GI symptoms, and 61% spoke of lower GI symptoms of still greater severity. The symptoms run the gamut from nausea and vomiting to chest pain, anorexia, cramps, and diarrhea. Not surprisingly, a fatty meal prior to activity aggravates symptoms. The basic physiology of the GI symptom complex remains to be elucidated and may interrelate with prostaglandin activity, and with cortisol activity involving the pituitary-adrenal axis. To persuade such a group to accept esophageal motility studies passively or to accept upper intestinal endoscopy will not be an easy task.—Lewis J. Krakauer, M.D., F.A.C.P.

---

**Exertional Headache**
William J. Perry (College of William and Mary)
Physician Sportsmed. 13:95–99, October 1985                              1–127

---

Some suggest that exertional headaches are caused by movements that increase intrathoracic pressure (as in lifting). However, the underlying pathophysiology has not been adequately demonstrated. Recently, it has been speculated that exertional headaches may be caused by vasodilatation of cerebral vessels from stress, suggesting the headaches are caused by prostaglandin release.

The author reports 4 cases among a college student population. Efforts were made to eliminate causes of the headache. Some headaches subsided promptly after cessation of activity, but 1 student had recurrent headaches for up to 3 days, and another had a headache that lasted 6 days.

Man, 22, was seen twice in 4 months. He initially described headaches that started at the back of the head and occasionally extended to the temporal area after he participated in karate exercises. Examination revealed no remarkable findings. Four months later he reported severe occipital headaches after performing arm presses and push-ups; the headaches diminished after several hours. He also noticed that stopping the push-ups eliminated the headaches. Blood pressure and basic neurologic screening tests were normal. There were no visual disturbances. The patient said that a close relative had similar headaches with exercise and had had a computed tomographic scan, which was apparently normal.

The term "exertional headache" was used by Rooke when he reported his studies that began in 1950. The designation at that time was meant to describe a process in which no abnormality could be detected and long-term symptoms subsided after several months. In Rooke's study, over a 2-year period, 93 of 103 patients had exertional headaches that were never associated with intracranial lesions. Later, however, 10 patients were found to have organic intracranial lesions, including parietal glioma, cerebellar hemangioendothelioma, unilateral subdural hematoma, and basilar impression. Hypertension was present but not severe in 16 of the 103 patients. Most of the patients in Rooke's sample were elderly.

Paulson discussed "weight lifter's" headache as an entity distinct from benign exertional headache. He believed the former was caused by pain referred specifically from the ligaments and muscles in the neck, and that the important distinguishing factor was that affected patients had a great deal of muscle tension across the neck and shoulders. The process may be similar to that in exertional headache.

It has been reported that the prostaglandin-inhibiting action of indomethacin provides temporary relief from exertional headaches. Aspirin and ibuprofen also block the cyclo-oxygenase cycle, in turn blocking the precursor fatty acids necessary for prostaglandin release. Goodwin discussed the role of nonsteroidal anti-inflammatory drugs as potent inhibitors of prostaglandin production, but other, less-expensive, and possibly better-tolerated drugs could be used. In college or high school students, the author recommends a simple drug with fewer side effects despite the use of indomethacin by some neurologists in headache clinics. The most important function physicians can perform is understanding this symptom and recommending a reduction or change of sports activity. Trainers, coaches, and team physicians should be alerted, however, to the possibility of underlying pathologic change.

▶ Exertional headache after vigorous exercise or after sexual function has been recognized for many years. This has been discussed previously in the Year Book (1983 YEAR BOOK OF SPORTS MEDICINE pp. 151–152). An initial report suggested the efficacy of indomethacin. This (or similar antiprostaglandin drugs) still seems to be the drug of first choice. Reduction of stress, more easily talked about than accomplished, would be helpful. If the exercise is the villain, one is reluctant to interdict something as valuable and ubiquitous as exercise itself (or sexual function). The basic problem is that if you are faced with a repetitive syndrome, there is an understandable unease while trying to avoid more costly or invasive studies such as neurologic consultation and CT scanning. Many would argue these should be mandatory in the setting of refractory symptoms. There is no way to exclude the more profound neurologic differential, including tumor or vascular disease, without such study.

A further point is that this population group not be started on analgesics of potency, whether it be Darvon or codeine-containing compounds, to avoid early patterns of habituation. The distinction from variants of true migraine must be made. The possibility of empirical trial with calcium channel blockers or tricyclic antidepressant medication should be considered in such individuals.—Lewis J. Krakauer, M.D., F.A.C.P.

---

**The Effect of Cold Exposure and Exercise Upon the Nasal Mucosal Responses in Nasal Allergy**
Akiyoshi Konno, Nobuhisa Terada, Yoshitaka Okamoto, and Kiyoshi Togawa (Akita Univ., Japan)
Ann. Allergy 54:50–59, January 1985                                        1–128

---

The hypersensitive airway mucosa is important in the onset of symptoms in both nasal allergy and bronchial asthma. Reactions of the nasal mucosa to cold air exposure and exercise were studied in subjects with nasal allergy and in control subjects. Twenty men (mean age 26 years) with perennial nasal allergy were studied along with 20 control subjects without airway disease. Changes in nasal resistance were estimated by anterior rhinomanometry during exposure to 1 C for 1 hour at rest and during 10 minutes of bicycle exercise. Responses to the same stimuli were studied during nasal reaction induced by an antigen disk containing house dust.

Exposure to cold led to nasal mucosal swelling that was similar in degree among subjects with nasal allergy and normal control subjects. Exercise increased the effective cross-sectional area of the nasal cavity in both groups to a similar extent. Neither stimulus enhanced nasal responses to antigen challenge, but rather they tended to suppress it both in subjects with nasal allergy and control subjects.

Neither exercise nor cold air exposure enhanced nasal reactions to antigen challenge in subjects with nasal allergy or normal control subjects in this study. The findings suggest that the direct effects of airway cooling or cold inspired air on mast cells and basophilic cells in the airway mucosa are not a significant factor aggravating allergic symptoms in nasal allergy, and this also may be true of bronchial asthma. Cold exposure swells the nasal airway and reduces the effective cross-sectional area of the nasal cavity, especially in subjects with nasal allergy, producing a greater relative increase in nasal airway resistance.

▶ There is a misconception that cold exposure and/or exercise will exaggerate the nasal responses after nasal antigen challenge in those with nasal allergy. That apparently is not the case, and those with nasal allergy do not differ from the normal controls with regard to cold exposure or exercise. An important distinction from the patient group with exercise-induced asthma.—Lewis J. Krakauer, M.D., F.A.C.P.

### Copper and Iron Complexes Catalytic for Oxygen Radical Reactions in Sweat From Human Athletes

J. M. C. Gutteridge, D. A. Rowley, B. Halliwell, D. F. Copper, and D. M. Heeley (Natl. Inst. for Biological Standards and Control, London; Univ. of London King's College; St. Mary's College of Education, Twickenham, England; and Alfred Chester Beatty Body Dynamics Lab., Kent, England)
Clin. Chim. Acta 145:267–273, February 1985                    1–129

There have been several reports that human athletes become anemic during training, possibly because of loss of iron in sweat. The authors tested human sweat samples for presence of iron and copper complexes potentially capable of catalyzing radical reactions.

All sweat samples from the trunk contained iron detectable by the bleomycin method. Analysis of the results by linear regression showed no significant correlations between bleomycin-detectable iron ($r \le .25$). Most of the trunk sweat samples stimulated the peroxidation of membrane lipids in the presence of ascorbic acid, a reaction known to be dependent on the pressure of traces of metal ions. Arm sweat contained much greater concentrations of total iron and phenanthroline-detectable copper than did trunk sweat, but bleomycin-detectable iron was not generally present in arm sweat. Most of the copper, but little of the iron, was ultrafilterable (table).

The authors conclude they have shown that sweat samples taken immediately postexercise from the arm or trunk of athletes contain copper detectable by the phenanthroline method, with the concentration of copper being much greater in the arm. Arm samples also contained much greater

PRESENCE OF CATALYTIC IRON AND COPPER COMPLEXES IN SWEAT SAMPLES
FROM THE ARMS OF ATHLETES

| Type of athlete* | Metal content of sweat ($\mu$mol/l) | | | Stimulation of lipid peroxidation $A_{532}$/h † |
|---|---|---|---|---|
| | Total iron | Bleomycin-detectable iron | Phenanthroline-detectable copper | |
| A | 95.5 | 0 | 20.0 | 0.265 |
| A | 43.7 | 0 | 18.8 | 0.274 |
| A | 34.2 | 8.6 | 10.6 | 0.431 |
| A | 31.5 | 0 | 12.9 | 0.348 |
| A | 33.8 | 0 | 20.8 | 0.274 |
| B | 16.2 | 0 | 17.3 | 0.286 |
| B | 18.0 | 0 | 20.4 | 0.265 |
| B | 48.2 | 0 | 21.5 | 0.316 |
| B | 26.1 | 0 | 19.6 | 0.262 |
| C | 12.2 | 0 | 18.5 | 0.299 |
| C | 100.4 | 0 | 23.8 | 0.124 |
| C | 69.4 | 0 | 13.5 | 0.135 |

*A, explosive athletes; B, endurance athletes; C, type of athlete not specified.
†The absorbances shown have been corrected for the rate of peroxidation in the absence of added sweat sample ($A_{532} = 0.187$). Each value shown is the mean of three separate determinations on each sample that differed by 5% or less.
(Courtesy of Gutteridge, J.M.C., et al.: Clin. Chim. Acta 145:267–273, February 1985.)

concentrations of iron as measured by the ferrozine method than did trunk samples. The authors do not yet know the physiologic significance of the presence of catalytic iron and copper complexes in human sweat.

▶ There have been persistent reports that iron loss in the sweat causes anemia in athletes (Paulev et al.: *Clin. Chim. Acta,* 127:19, 1983; Frederickson et al., *Med. Sci. Sports Exerc.* 15:271, 1983). Studies from our laboratory suggested an average sweat iron concentration of about 450 μg/l, giving a potential for 1.5–2.0 mg loss over a marathon race, perhaps enough to tip the balance towards anemia in a marginal situation (Shephard et al.: Fluid and mineral balance of post-coronary distance runners, in Ricci G. and Venerando A. (eds.): *Nutrition, Dietetics and Sports.* Turin, Minerva Med., 1978).

The present report used the bag method to collect sweat from the trunk and the arms. The figures for the trunk were similar to those we had found using small gauze pads, but those for the arms were substantially higher. One particularly interesting aspect, which is the main thrust of the present paper, is that a part of the iron was present in complexes that could cause a peroxidation of lipids and thus cellular disruption. The authors speculate that the compounds are having a beneficial effect in controlling skin bacteria, or are excreted in an attempt to reduce the tendency to peroxidation associated with an increase of body metabolism; there have been occasional reports that excessive activity can accelerate cellular aging through an enhanced production of free radicals, a process in which iron and copper complexes have been implicated.—Roy J. Shephard, M.D., Ph.D.

---

**Work Performance in Iron Deficiency of Increasing Severity**
Mikko V. Perkkiö, Lennart T. Jansson, George A. Brooks, Canio J. Refino, and Peter R. Dallman (Univ. of California, San Francisco, and Univ. of California, Berkeley)
J. Appl. Physiol. 58:1477–1480, May 1985                                              1–130

The effect of iron deficiency on work capacity was studied in groups of rats that had received diets with iron contents ranging between 9 and 50 mg/kg of diet from 3 to 6 weeks of age.

Blood hemoglobin (Hb) levels depended on the iron content of the diet. The Hb concentration started to decrease significantly when the iron content of the diet was < 30 mg/kg. In the 9-mg of iron/kg diet group cytochrome c was 40% of that of the control group, corresponding to an Hb percentage of 45%. The $V_{O2max}$ was linearly related to Hb concentration over the range between 8 and 14 gm/dl, but with a decline of only 16% over this broad Hb range (Fig 1–47). Below an Hb concentration of about 7 gm/dl, $V_{O2max}$ declined sharply and was significantly decreased only after the cytochrome c content of muscles was reduced to levels 40% below control values. Between an Hb value of 10 and 8 gm/dl, endurance capacity decreased drastically from 92% to 19% of the control value. Essentially the same relationship between Hb and endurance was observed when the treadmill speed was decreased so that the exercise work load

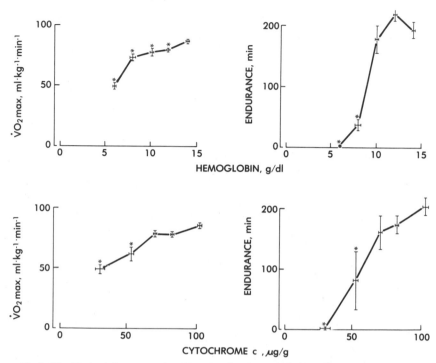

**Fig 1–47.**—Maximal $O_2$ consumption ($V_{O2max}$) and endurance capacity of rats plotted as a function of blood hemoglobin (Hb) and gastrocnemius muscle cytochrome c. Values are grouped by Hb increments of 2 g/dl and cytochrome c increments of 15 µg/g muscle. *With decreasing Hb or cytochrome c, values were significantly different ($P < .05$) from controls with Hb of 14 g/dl or cytochrome c of 104 µg/g. (Courtesy of Perkkiö, M.V., et al.: J. Appl. Physiol. 58:1477–1480, May 1985.)

was equivalent to the same percentage of the $V_{O2max}$ work load in control and iron-deficient rats (43%). There was a more pronounced deficit in endurance when the cytochrome c concentration was lower than about 60 µg/gm. After the endurance test and the standard 2-minute run, blood lactate concentrations were significantly elevated only in the most anemic groups compared with control rats.

Earlier experiments in iron-deficient rats had suggested that their severely impaired duration of performance in a submaximal exercise (endurance) was related primarily to a decreased muscle capacity for $O_2$ utilization rather than diminished $O_2$ delivery by the blood. The present study indicates that endurance becomes substantially impaired even under conditions of moderate iron deficiency that leave $V_{O2max}$ virtually intact. Endurance represents a type of exercise performance that in some respects resembles heavy manual labor in humans. These studies indicate that work performance in iron deficiency can become severely restricted by decreased skeletal muscle oxidative capacity while compensatory mechanisms to maintain $O_2$ delivery remain relatively effective.

▶ Although this work has been carried out on rats, it has a number of possible clinical implications. Some of the earlier studies of anemic humans suggested a rough parallel between hemoglobin level and work capacity, both in athletes who had donated blood (Ekblom et al.: *J. Appl. Physiol.* 33:175, 1972) and in workers on a rubber plantation (Edgerton et al.: *Br. Med. J.* 2:1546, 1979); the present work suggests that a rather slight fall of oxygen transport is greatly exaggerated at hemoglobin levels of less than 7 gm/dl. At this stage, cytochrome c formation is also greatly depressed, suggesting that tissue metabolism may have become the factor limiting performance. A correlation was found between endurance (the ability of the rats to run at a speed causing exhaustion in about 200 min) and cytochrome c levels; a parallel could also be drawn with the poor work tolerance of tea and rubber workers when faced by iron deprivation of this severity.—Roy J. Shephard, M.D., Ph.D.

---

**Work Performance in the Iron-Deficient Rat: Improved Endurance With Exercise Training**
Mikko V. Perkkiö, Lennart T. Jansson, Scott Henderson, Canio Refino, George A. Brooks, and Peter R. Dallman (Univ. of California, San Francisco, and Univ. of California, Berkeley)
Am. J. Physiol. 249:E306–E311, September 1985          1–131

---

Iron deficiency in humans impairs work performance during both brief, intense exercise and more prolonged endurance exercise. Studies in rats suggest that maximal Vo₂ is limited by the oxygen transport capacity, whereas endurance is related to the capacity of muscle mitochondria for oxidative metabolism. The effects of sustained endurance training on muscle oxidative enzymes and work performance were examined in iron-deficient rats given a diet with an iron content of 6 mg/kg, rather than 50

Fig 1–48.—Maximal oxygen consumption (V̇O₂ max) and endurance in iron-sufficient and iron-deficient rats. Values shown represent mean ± SE. Asterisk indicates a significant (P < .05) difference between untrained and trained rats within a diet group; +, between iron-deficient and iron-sufficient rats within a training group. (Courtesy of Perkkiö, M.V., et al.: Am. J. Physiol. 249:E306–E311, September 1985.)

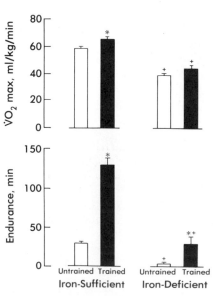

mg/kg for iron-sufficient rats. The goal was to produce a hemoglobin level of about 8–9 gm/dl in the former group. Treadmill training was begun after 2 weeks on the diet, and work capacity was estimated after 5 weeks of training.

Both sedentary and endurance-trained iron-deficient rats had significantly lower skeletal muscle cytochrome C, cytochrome oxidase, and succinic oxidase activities than iron-sufficient animals. Trained iron-deficient rats generally had a substantial increase in skeletal muscle oxidative enzyme concentrations when compared with iron-sufficient animals. Performance in endurance exercise improved more than 6-fold with training in iron-deficient rats, but peak $Vo_2$ during brief, intense exercise was not significantly altered (Fig 1–48).

Muscle oxidative capacity and endurance capacity both are improved in iron-deficient rats undergoing endurance training, but endurance capacity remains markedly limited. Prior training should be considered in studies of work performance as related to iron deficiency. Trained subjects may have milder anemia and a less marked reduction in skeletal muscle oxidative enzyme concentrations.

▶ North American sports physicians are unlikely to encounter an iron deficiency sufficient to impair tissue enzyme formation in normal practice, although there is at least a theoretical possibility that they might encounter such a condition in a competitor from an impoverished third world nation.

The present study is on rats, but has several points of interest. Apparently, vigorous training of iron-deficient animals increases the enzyme activity of exercised muscles to around the normal figure for untrained animals, presumably by robbing other tissues of their iron stores. Furthermore, as the tissue enzyme activity is restored, the endurance of the rats for treadmill running is extended from about 25 to 130 minutes, despite little change in their maximum oxygen intake. This indicates that at least in this species, under conditions of dietary deprivation, the endurance of prolonged running is determined more by tissue enzyme levels than by the circulatory transport of oxygen.— Roy J. Shephard, M.D., Ph.D.

---

**Distribution of Hemoglobin and Functional Consequences of Anemia in Adult Males at High Altitude**
Daigh A. Tufts, Jere D. Haas, John L. Beard, and Hilde Spielvogel (Cornell Univ., Pennsylvania State Univ., Instituto Bolivianode Biologia de Altura, and Universidad Mayor de San Andres, La Paz, Boliva)
Am. J. Clin. Nutr. 42:1–11, July 1985                                   1–132

---

Few valid data are available on what constitute normal hemoglobin levels at high altitude. A hematologic survey was undertaken in La Paz, Bolivia, at 3,700 m, to identify the anemic and polycythemic contributions to the hemoglobin distribution in 526 healthy men. The anemia cutoff level established statistically was validated against aerobic work capacity. Exercise testing was carried out in a subsample of 56 subjects.

---

AEROBIC CAPACITY OF ANEMIC AND NONANEMIC
SUBJECTS AS ESTIMATED BY INDIVIDUAL
REGRESSIONS OF HEART RATE AND $VO_2$*

| n | 10 | 46 |
|---|---|---|
| PWC150 ($VO_2$, l/min) | 1.54 ± .27 | 1.86 ± .34 † |
| Estimated $VO_{2\,max}$ (l/min) | 2.12 ± .36 | 2.69 ± .51† |

*Values are expressed as mean ± SD; PWC150 indicates heart rate of 150 beats per minute.
†Difference between anemic and nonanemic subjects was significant at the level of $P < .05$ (t test).
(Courtesy of Tufts, D.A., et al.: Am. J. Clin. Nutr. 42:1–11, July 1985.)

---

The hemoglobin levels had a Gaussian distribution, with a mean and SD of 18.8 ± 1.4 gm/dl. Cutoff levels of 15.8 and 22.0 gm/dl were chosen to identify anemic and polycythemic subjects. When exercise testing was carried out to validate the anemia cutoff level, subjects identified as anemic exhibited significantly reduced aerobic capacity, as measured by $VO_2$ at a heart rate of 150 beats per minute and maximal $VO_2$ (table). Reductions of 17% and 21%, respectively, were found in anemic subjects.

A reduction in aerobic capacity was observed in anemic subjects living at high altitude when anemia was defined by distribution analysis. Functional anemia is population-specific and dependent on the normal hemoglobin distribution of the population, rather than being a function of some absolute hemoglobin concentration. It may suffice in population work to estimate a hemoglobin level that identifies a group with a demonstrated functional abnormality.

▶ There have been a number of demonstrations that the working capacity at sea level is impaired by anemia, but this paper is an interesting attempt to define what constitutes anemia when living at very high altitude. The healthy athlete with a hemoglobin level of 15.6 g/100 ml is definitely anemic by this criterion, and from the plot of $PWC_{150}$ against hemoglobin, one might infer that hemoglobin levels could usefully be increased to 20 g/100 ml. This is somewhat at variance with theory, which has maintained that an excessive polycythemia would increase blood viscosity, limit cardiac output, and thus impair endurance performance.

One limitation of the research is its cross-sectional nature. Inevitably, those who were anemic tended to be the more poorly nourished members of the community, and this as much as the anemia may have limited their performance. There is no guarantee that dietary supplements would have raised hemoglobin, or that such a change would have improved work performance. Moreover, the authors did not measure maximum oxygen intake directly, but rather estimated it from sub-maximal data. There is a need to follow up this research with a longitudinal experiment, making more direct measurements of endurance performance.—Roy J. Shephard, M.D., Ph.D.

**The Clinical Assessment of Acute Mountain Sickness**
R. F. Fletcher, A. D. Wright, G. T. Jones, and A. R. Bradwell (Queen Elizabeth Hosp., Birmingham, England)
Q. J. Med. New Series 54:91–100, January 1985                    1–133

An attempt was made through three expeditions to high altitude to refine the methods of clinically assessing acute mountain sickness (AMS). Of all 33 persons involved, 16 participated in more than one expedition. All but one were males, and ages ranged from 22 to 55 years. A controlled study of the effect of slow-release acetazolamide was carried out in one expedition and, in another, participants took either 150 mg of methazolamide or 500 mg of acetazolamide daily.

Virtually all participants in all expeditions experienced some symptoms of AMS. Edema of the feet, hands, and face was unrelated to the severity of AMS, as assessed by interviews, self-assessments, and peer review. Physical examination was not helpful in assessing severity of AMS. Interviews allowed consideration of individual factors, e.g., fatigue. Self-assessments did not tend to indicate effects more or less consistently than the other methods did. All assessments of AMS correlated closely with the arterial oxygen pressure.

A combination of subjective methods of assessing AMS is recommended for use during expeditions to altitude. Peer review has merit because of the large number of observers. Daily interviews and examinations are obvious safety measures. Self-assessment is suspect, because the most severely affected individuals may have some loss of judgment concerning their status.

▶ All that can be said is that acute mountain sickness in its various presenting forms is common, if not ubiquitous. There are no simple tests for clarifying this other than the observations on symptom expression and the anticipation of same. Whether AMS is a face of the more severe clinical syndromes of high altitude pulmonary edema or cerebral edema is a moot point, if the risks of the more severe clinical syndromes are recognized and exposed individuals are aware that such symptoms exist, and how they present. The critical symptoms for concern are those of significant dyspnea *at rest* and the inability to sleep in other than the semi-recumbent or upright position. These are grave portents of pulmonary edema, and confusion is a portent of cerebral edema. These more severe expressions of mountain exposure warrant immediate evacuation. This is the real sense of the issue. The other point would be that prophylaxis can be employed at this time. See the following digest.—Lewis J. Krakauer, M.D., F.A.C.P.

**Acetazolamide and Exercise in Sojourners to 6,300 Meters: A Preliminary Study**
Peter H. Hackett, Robert B. Schoene, Robert M. Winslow, Richard M. Peters, Jr., and John B. West (Univ. of Washington and American Medical Research Expedition to Everest)
Med. Sci. Sports Exerc. 17:593–597, October 1985                    1–134

Acetazolamide is effective in preventing symptoms of acute mountain sickness (AMS), but past studies have dealt with lowland inhabitants who have been at moderate altitude for a relatively short time. Four members of an expedition to Mount Everest who had sojourned to and lived at 6,300 m, with a barometric pressure of about 350 mm Hg, were studied. They were healthy males aged 26 to 52 years. The subjects walked from an altitude of 730 m to 5,400 m in 3 weeks, and had been at 6,300 m for at least 2 weeks at initial evaluation.

All the subjects had a decrease in blood pH on acetazolamide. The mean reduction in base excess was 6.1 mEq/L. The DPG/Hb ratio was consistently lowered. Measurement of P50 showed no difference between drug and control conditions. Exercise ventilation was increased 10%–20% on acetazolamide at all work loads during exercise testing (Fig 1–49). Respiratory frequency was not significantly changed, but heart rates increased

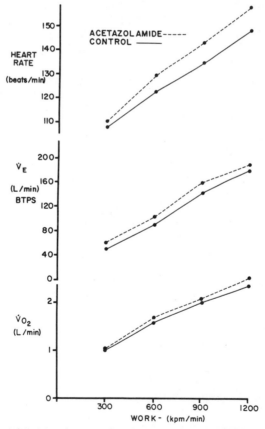

**Fig 1–49.**—Mean data points for acetazolamide and control trials. Acetazolamide *(broken line)* increases heart rate *(beats/min)*, minute ventilation *(V_E, L/min, BTPS)*, and oxygen consumption *(VO_2, L/min, STPD)* at each work load *(kpm/min)* compared to no drug *(solid line)*. (Courtesy of Hackett, P.H., et al.: Med. Sci. Sports Exerc. 17:593–597, October 1985. Copyright 1985, the American College of Sports Medicine. Reprinted by permission.)

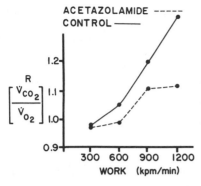

ACETAZOLAMIDE -----
CONTROL ———

Fig 1–50.—The respiratory exchange ratio $(R, VCO_2/VO_2)$ is lower at all work loads on acetazolamide *(broken line)* compared to no drug *(solid line)*. (Courtesy of Hackett, P.H., et al.: Med. Sci. Sports Exerc. 17:593–597, October 1985. Copyright 1985, the American College of Sports Medicine. Reprinted by permission.)

moderately. Arterial oxygen saturation increased slightly in 2 subjects on acetazolamide and decreased in 1. Oxygen pulse showed no consistent trend. The respiratory exchange ratio was markedly reduced on exercise testing following acetazolamide (Fig 1–50) in three 250 mg doses. Time at maximal work decreased in two instances because of breathlessness.

Acetazolamide produces the same degree of acidemia at 6,300 m as at low altitudes, despite preexisting respiratory alkalosis. Decreased plasma volume may affect exercise performance when acetazolamide is used. Exercise dyspnea is another possible limiting factor. However, dyspnea at near-maximal exercise may be acceptable in view of the benefits of improved resting ventilation, more rapid acclimatization, better sleep,and avoidance of acute mountain sickness.

▶ The use of this drug has been a breakthrough in dealing with the symptoms of AMS, but all prior studies have dealt with individuals who were short-term inhabitants of the high altitude arena, coming from lowland elevations. In this study, 4 members who were at 6,000 m or higher for at least 2 weeks were evaluated. The drug has the same benefits of improved resting ventilation, rapid acclimatization, positive effect on sleep, and the avoidance of the other symptoms of acute mountain sickness such as nausea and tachycardia. However, exercise dyspnea at near maximal exercise is increased, and exercise performance may be somewhat impaired. This would seem a reasonable trade-off, weighing these parameters against the severity of the symptoms in question. (Exception: extreme expedition mountaineering.) As the question relates to trekking or to similar activity in lowlanders anticipating high altitude exposure at a less vigorous level, acetazolamide remains the drug of choice for prophylaxis.—Lewis J. Krakauer, M.D., F.A.C.P.

**Headache at High Altitude Is Not Related to Internal Carotid Arterial Blood Velocity**
J. T. Reeves, L. G. Moore, R. E. McCullough, R. G. McCullough, G. Harrison, B. I. Tranmer, A. J. Micco, A. Tucker, and J. V. Weil (Univ. of Colorado Health Sciences Ctr., Denver, and Colorado State Univ.)
J. Appl. Physiol. 59:909–915, September 1985                1–135

The cause of headache in persons going to high altitude is unknown. Relatively severe hypoxemia in susceptible subjects could induce large increases in cerebral blood flow that then could initiate the headache. With the use of Doppler ultrasound, changes in internal carotid arterial blood velocity were measured in 12 subjects in Denver (altitude, 1,600 m) and repeatedly up to 7 hours at a simulated altitude of 4,800 m (barometric pressure, 430 torr). The subjects were healthy, nonsmoking men aged 24 to 50 years (mean, 31 years) who were permanent residents at elevations between 1,500 and 1,700 m.

Eight subjects were selected because of a prior history of high-altitude headache. Comparatively severe headache developed at 4,800 m in 6 of these subjects; moderate headache, in 2. Four subjects without such a history remained well. Velocity at 4,800 m did not correlate with symptom development, arterial $O_2$ saturation, or end-tidal $P_{CO_2}$. Neither velocity nor blood pressure was consistently elevated above low-altitude (Denver) baseline values. During measurements of hypercapnic ventilatory response at low altitude, velocity increased linearly with end-tidal $P_{CO_2}$, confirming that the Doppler method could demonstrate an increase. Also, 30 minutes of isocapnic or poikilocapnic hypoxia caused small increases in velocity ($+8\%$ and $+6\%$) during the baseline measurement at low altitude.

In this study, symptoms of headache occurring at high altitude could not be attributed to an increased internal carotid arterial blood velocity as measured by Doppler ultrasound. Headache occurred in some subjects in whom the internal carotid blood velocity decreased, while other subjects who remained free of headache showed modestly increased blood velocity. The headaches reported by the subjects occurred in those considered by the attending physician to have experienced altitude sickness, based on observations of lethargy, vomiting, cyanosis, and subjective data. Headaches tended to occur in the subjects with the most severe hypoxemia. Subjects reporting no headache had a history of few or no symptoms at high altitude. However, all 6 subjects with the most severe headaches had experienced headache on at least two previous visits to high altitude. Additionally, the time course of symptom development was that expected for susceptible subjects taken rapidly to high altitude.

One problem in interpreting blood flow velocities was the qualitative nature of the measurements, because neither the vessel diameter nor the Doppler angle were known. In a preliminary study during hypocapnia and hypercapnia, the Doppler velocity measurements showed changes similar to those found using the xenon-washout method.

The results confirm previous studies by more quantitative invasive methods: acute hypoxemia and acute hypercapnia were associated with increases in cerebral blood flow; and the increase with hypoxia appeared to be partly offset by the inhibitory effect of hypocapnia. The magnitude of increase with hypoxia, although small ($6\%-8\%$), was consistent with that reported by Shapiro et al. in 6 subjects during hypocapnic hypoxia. Given that arterial pressures were not different in ill and well subjects and that flow was not consistently high in ill subjects, decreased cerebrovascular resistance was not evident at high altitude and was not a likely primary cause of the reported headache symptoms. This is consistent with the finding that acute hypoxia caused only a small increase in cerebral arterial blood velocity. Although even a small increase in cerebral blood flow could contribute to symptoms, the data do not indicate a primary role for increased flow.

▶ There is little argument that sustained, large increases in cerebral blood flow velocity may cause headache. The authors demonstrate that it is not universal in the setting of high altitude headache. It would seem to me, apart from the fact that the precise cause of such headache is unknown, the headache syndrome when presenting in this setting must be considered part of acute mountain sickness and treated similarly in a preventive fashion. See Digest 1–134. Some day the precise physiology will be clarified.—Lewis J. Krakauer, M.D., F.A.C.P.

---

**Positive Airway Pressure for High-Altitude Pulmonary Oedema**
Eric B. Larson (Univ. of Washington)
Lancet 1:371–373, Feb. 16, 1985                                    1–136

---

High-altitude pulmonary edema (HAPE) is a potentially fatal form of noncardiogenic pulmonary edema that may occur more often as more persons travel to areas of high altitude. Only descent and oxygen administration have been effective therapeutic measures, but the application of positive airway pressure long has been used to improve oxygenation in patients with pulmonary edema and adult respiratory distress syndrome.

A lightweight, easily applied, positive pressure system incorporating a Down's mask and spring-loaded valves was used to administer positive airway pressure to climbers at 4,400 m. Three of 8 climbers whose findings were analyzed had HAPE. All 8 tolerated expiratory positive airway pressure without apparent difficulty. No effect was noted in controls, but the patients with HAPE had significant improvement in arterial oxygen saturation and a decline in respiratory rate. Two climbers with HAPE used the Down's mask with 10 cm water of expiratory positive airway pressure for 6 and 8 hours, respectively, before descending. Both climbers experienced dyspnea, cough, rales, and cyanosis when the mask was removed. The mean oxygen saturation increased from 53% to 72% with expiratory positive airway pressure of 10 cm water in the climbers with HAPE.

This procedure may be a useful first-aid measure in climbers with findings of HAPE. However, affected climbers must descend promptly. Barotrauma is unlikely because of the absence of serious cardiopulmonary disease in most climbers. The system exerts positive pressure only during expiration, permitting normal negative intrathoracic pressure during inspiration and, presumably, adequate venous return.

▶ It is impressive that the author was able to find 3 cases of pulmonary edema in an expedition of 8 members, accepting the severity of the Mount McKinley environs. A lightweight, easily applied positive pressure system for nonintubated individuals is described; it was tested and appears to be efficacious. An improvement in arterial oxygen saturation was confirmed and a return of symptoms of dyspnea, cough, and cyanosis with a presumptive fall in mean oxygen saturation on withdrawal served as clinical proof, of sorts, of efficacy. Double-blind studies in this circumstance are not reasonable. Granted this device is physiologically effective, it probably will be used routinely with high-altitude expeditions or in base hospitals. It is not intended for the ordinary tourist.—Lewis J. Krakauer, M.D., F.A.C.P.

---

**High Altitude Pulmonary Edema and Exercise at 4,400 Meters on Mount McKinley: Effect of Expiratory Positive Airway Pressure**
Robert B. Schoene, Robert C. Roach, Peter H. Hackett, Ginette Harrison, and W. J. Mills, Jr. (Univ. of Washington and Univ. of Alaska)
Chest 87:330–333, March 1985                                     1–137

---

Breathing against positive expiratory pressure has been used to improve gas exchange in many forms of pulmonary edema, and forced expiration against resistance during exercise has been advocated for climbing at high altitude as a method to optimize performance. To evaluate the effect of expiratory positive airway pressure (EPAP) on climbers with high-altitude pulmonary edema (HAPE) and on exercise at high altitude, 4 climbers with HAPE were studied at rest and 13 healthy climbers were studied during exercise on a cycle ergometer at 4,400 m. The authors measured minute ventilation ($\dot{V}I$, L/minute), arterial oxygen saturation ($Sa_{O_2}$ percent), end-tidal carbon dioxide ($PA_{CO_2}$, mm Hg) respiratory rate (RR), and heart rate (HR) during the last minute of a 5-minute interval at rest in the climbers with HAPE, and at rest, 300 and 600 kpm/minute workloads on a cycle ergometer in the healthy subjects (12 men, 1 woman, aged 23 to 41 years). The 4 HAPE volunteers included 4 men with a mean age of 33.4 years.

Resting $Sa_{O_2}$ percent was significantly lower in HAPE subjects than in normals at all levels of EPAP ($P < .005$). Climbers with HAPE increased their resting $Sa_{O_2}$ percent (Fig 1–51 A). The $Sa_{O_2}$ percent decreased significantly in normal subjects from rest to 600 kpm/minute at each level of EPAP ($P < .05$). The $PA_{CO_2}$ increased in HAPE subjects with each level of EPAP and was significantly higher in these individuals than normal subjects on EPAP 10 cm $H_2O$ ($P < .05$) (Fig 1–51 B). At rest, climbers with HAPE had lower $\dot{V}I$ than normal subjects on all levels of EPAP ($P < .05$) (Fig 1–51 C). In HAPE subjects, RR, breaths per minute decreased on 0, 5, and 10 cm $H_2O$ EPAP, respectively (Fig 1–51 D). The HR did not show a consistent trend in HAPE subjects with different levels of EPAP (Fig 1–51 E). The HR was significantly higher in normal subjects on EPAP 10 cm $H_2O$ than EPAP cm $H_2O$ at rest and 300 kmp/minute ($P < .05$)

The results of this study demonstrate that in a small number of climbers with HAPE at the same altitude at rest, increasing levels of EPAP increased oxygen saturation without increasing ventilation and changed the pattern

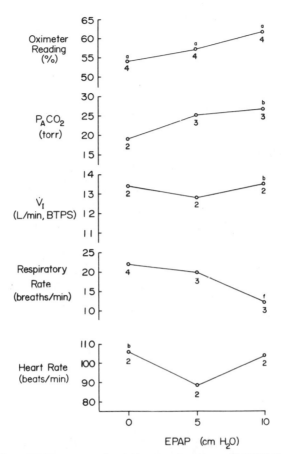

**Fig 1–51.**—Effect of EPAP on measured variables at rest in subjects with HAPE. Number under data points equal number of subjects. a < P = .05 from normals, b < P = .005 from normals, c < P = .05 from EPAP 0 cm $H_2O$. (Courtesy of Schoene, R.B., et al.: Chest 87:330–333, March 1985.)

of breathing to a higher tidal volume and lower frequency. The authors recommend that the climber would do better to hyperventilate consciously during exercise without pursed-lip breathing, and thereby, raise arterial oxygen saturation without significantly increasing the work of breathing.

► High-altitude pulmonary edema becomes a possibility in poorly acclimatized recreational climbers and skiers at altitudes in excess of 3,000 m. Where possible, the patient should be admitted immediately to hospital. Traditional treatment includes oxygen and antibiotics to minimize secondary infection. However, in some mountain expeditions immediate evacuation may not be possible, particularly under adverse weather conditions.

In such situations, positive expiratory pressure has been recommended as an emergency measure (Feldman and Herndon, *Lancet* 1:1036, 1977). The mask used to generate positive expiratory pressures in the present experiment had a useful effect on arterial oxygen saturation (Fig 1–51), and by not raising pressure over the entire respiratory cycle was less likely to have an adverse effect on cardiac output or to cause barotrauma.—Roy J. Shephard, M.D., Ph.D.

## Splenic Syndrome at Mountain Altitudes in Sickle Cell Trait: Its Occurrence in Nonblack Persons

Peter A. Lane and John H. Githens (Univ. of Colorado)
JAMA 253:2251–2254, April 19, 1985                                    1–138

Numerous anecdotal reports have appeared of splenic syndrome resulting from sequestration or infarction in persons with sickle cell trait exposed to high altitude, especially nonblacks. Since 1974, splenic syndrome at mountain altitudes developed in 6 males with sickle cell trait seen at the Colorado Sickle Cell Treatment and Research Center in Denver. All 6 experienced the acute onset of severe left upper quadrant pain within 48 hours of arrival from lower altitudes, and all were phenotypically nonblack. The age range was 18 to 37 years.

Three patients became symptomatic at moderate altitudes of 5,280 to 7,000 ft. above sea level. Three patients had nausea and vomiting, and 1 was febrile. Four patients reported having engaged in physical exercise before the onset of pain, and 3 had consumed alcoholic beverages. Splenomegaly was documented in 4 patients. Four of the 6 had similar symptoms during previous or subsequent exposure to mountain altitude. Two patients had mild anemia, which resolved. Reticulocyte counts were elevated initially. Three of 5 patients studied had pleural effusion or a left lower lobe infiltrate. Nuclide spleen scans yielded varying patterns.

The vast majority of individuals with sickle cell trait experience no medical complications directly attributable to their carrier state. Some, however, may experience acute splenic sequestration or infarction when exposed to moderate or high mountain altitudes. Left upper quadrant pain should suggest splenic syndrome, regardless of race. A positive sickling or solubility test should lead to quantitative hemoglobin electrophoresis. These findings do not justify travel or occupational restrictions for persons with sickle cell trait.

▶ Sickle cell trait can present in the nonblack individual. In the altitude environment higher than 7,000 ft., this can appear as a splenic syndrome. This usually means splenic infarction, sequestration, and pseudocyst formation. The patients in this study did not have a higher percentage of hemoglobin-S, typically found in black persons with the trait. It had been previously suggested that such individuals would have an increased susceptibility of the splenic syndrome.

Practically speaking, this means that physicians should consider the diagnosis of the splenic syndrome in any person, regardless of race, who develops significant left upper quadrant abdominal pain after exposure to any altitude greater than 5,000 ft., and sickling tests should then be carried out. The vast majority of persons who own the sickle cell trait will not experience symptoms, and such people should not be restricted from travel or occupation for that reason alone. None of the patients studied required splenectomy.—Lewis J. Krakauer, M.D., F.A.C.P.

---

**Moderate Altitude Exposure and the Cardiac Patient**
Ray W. Squires (Mayo Clinic and Found.)
J. Cardiopulmonary Rehabil. 5:421–426, September 1985                    1–139

---

Cardiac patients and cardiac rehabilitation staff are often concerned about travel to moderate altitude (3,000–10,000 feet) after a cardiac event. With increasing altitude, the barometric pressure decreases, resulting in a reduction in arterial oxygen partial pressure and content. This relative hypoxia could conceivably disrupt the balance between myocardial oxygen demand and supply, precipitating cardiac symptoms or a clinical event. Physiologic responses to moderate altitude exposure include increased pulmonary ventilation and heart rate (transient increase at rest and a more prolonged increase with submaximal exercise), hemoconcentration, a possible rightward shift in the oxyhemoglobin dissociation curve, and a modest reduction in physical work capacity. Clinical concerns include such altitude disorders as acute mountain sickness (AMS) and high-altitude pulmonary edema (HAPE), as well as congestive failure, and myocardial infarction.

Consider travel to a mountain resort at an altitude of 8,000 feet. Both patients and healthy individuals experience similar physiologic changes during the first several days at reduced barometric pressure. The reduction in partial pressure of oxygen ($P_1O_2$) at moderate altitudes may cause a reduction in the arterial oxygen partial pressure ($Pa_{O_2}$), together with a lowering of arterial oxygen saturation ($Sa_{O_2}$ [%]). Based on the sigmoidal shape of the oxyhemoglobin dissociation curve, the relative decrease in $Sa_{O_2}$ is much less than that of $Pa_{O_2}$ at moderate altitude. If $Pa_{O_2}$ decreases from 90 to 60 mm Hg, saturation decreases only from 96% to 88%. The decreased $Sa_{O_2}$ is mirrored by a reduction in arterial oxygen content ($Ca_{O_2}$). The most apparent response to physical activity at 8,000 feet is an increase in pulmonary ventilation, resulting in an increased feeling of breathlessness. Individual response is variable, and the maximum effect may not be achieved for several days. The relative hyperventilation, producing mild respiratory alkalosis, maintains $Pa_{O_2}$ at a higher level than it would be without this increased ventilation. Chemoreceptor activation due to decreased $Pa_{O_2}$ at altitude is probably involved because the $O_2$ breathing reduces ventilation.

The oxygen uptake ($V_{O_2}$) for constant-load submaximal exercise is independent of altitude. However, physical work capacity is decreased during exposure to moderate or high altitude. The critical factors involved in maximal oxygen transport are maximum cardiac output and maximum arteriovenous oxygen difference. Maximum cardiac output is variably affected by altitude. Determinants of arteriovenous oxygen difference include blood flow to the exercising muscles, tissue extraction of oxygen, and $Ca_{O_2}$. The limiting factor may be $Ca_{O_2}$ during physical work at altitude. Data demonstrate that a linear relationship exists between $V_{O_2}$ max and maximal oxygen transport (maximum cardiac output × $Ca_{O_2}$). With a reduction in $Ca_{O_2}$ less oxygen is supplied to the tissues, resulting in a decrease in arteriovenous oxygen difference and in $V_{O_2}$ max.

An overprotective attitude regarding travel to moderate altitude is unwarranted for most cardiac patients. However, several points may be noted. A gradual ascent, with time spent at intermediate altitude, may decrease the possibility of developing symptoms of AMS. A period of acclimation would be ideal. Acute mountain sickness symptoms include headache, insomnia, anorexia, and nausea. Symptoms will gradually disappear in a week. Prophylactic use of acetazolamide may decrease symptoms of AMS. Symptoms of HAPE, including severe shortness of breath, excessive fatigue, chest tightness, and cough, require immediate medical attention. A slight reduction in physical work capacity should be expected at moderate altitude. At moderate altitude, maximum heart rate will be unchanged from sea-level values. For a given walking, jogging, or cycle ergometer work load, heart rate will be higher.

▶ For most patients with cardiac disease, travel to an altitude of 10,000 feet, with moderate interval altitude exposure (3,000 to 10,000 ft.) seems reasonable, noting that for starters most airliners may be pressurized up to 8,000 ft. There are subgroups of patients with preexisting pulmonary hypertension, decompensated congestive heart failure, and unstable angina, or recent myocardial infarction, for whom this sort of exposure represents a higher risk than reasonable. This applies, as well, to patients with severe anemia and decreased arterial oxygen saturation. It presumes an educated patient population. The importance of gradual ascent is noted. Prophylactic use of acetazolamide (again) should be considered, attempting to avoid the symptoms of AMS. These people may be somewhat more vulnerable.

Awareness of the more severe altitude syndromes is imperative, and severe shortness of breath is an immediate indication for evacuation to lower altitude. I believe the risk may be exponentially higher if one goes to altitudes any higher than 10,000 ft. This can be done easily on the highways of the western U.S. or Canada, at some western resorts, and at some within taxi range of the Salt Lake City airport.—Lewis J. Krakauer, M.D., F.A.C.P.

**The Impact of Exercise Upon Medical Cost**
Roy J. Shephard (Univ. of Toronto)
Sports Med. 2:133–143, 1985                               1–140

Recent analyses of medical expenditures suggest that costs might be substantially reduced through improvements in life-style, including an increase in habitual physical activity. Improved immune function has been associated with physical activity; in contrast, the important risk factor of smoking is associated with a sedentary life-style. The concept of "perceived health" is very significant; one of the most common reasons given for exercising is to "feel better." Involvement in regular exercise may lead many to re-evaluate their overall life-style, with beneficial effects on both morbidity and mortality costs. Alcohol withdrawal may be promoted by an exercise program. There also are possibilities of reducing geriatric care costs through the judicious use of exercise programs.

Enhanced personal fitness might reduce the cost of both home and industrial injuries, although many sports activities themselves generate injuries. Participation in some vigorous competitive programs may involve an annual 50% risk of injury. It is likely that previous activity will promote more rapid rehabilitation from many illnesses, coronary disease being an example.

Involvement in exercise programs appears in general to reduce medical care costs. Savings from decreased acute medical and hospital costs and a decrease in premature death are most evident. Savings might be increased through more effective methods of recruitment of participants in exercise programs and better means of sustaining compliance with exercise.

▶ An excellent review of the interrelationship of fitness, exercise, and medical costs. Using a large data base from the literature, the author notes that training programs have reduced cardiac morbidity and mortality (for example, in a given police department or fire department). The dynamics of the medical costs are constantly changing and the dynamics of any population in terms of preexisting illness and medical state are constantly changing. Fixed numbers are difficult to come by. It is hard to argue that an investment in an exercise program can do anything but be positive in terms of economic values, as well as important sociologic values.—Lewis J. Krakauer, M.D., F.A.C.P.

---

**The Effect of Training on Responses of β-Endorphin and Other Pituitary Hormones to Insulin-Induced Hypoglycemia**
Kari J. Mikines, Michael Kjaer, Claus Hagen, Bente Sonne, Erik A. Richter, and Henrik Galbo (Univ. of Copenhagen and Herlev Hosp., Denmark)
Eur. J. Appl. Physiol. 54:476–479, November 1985                1–141

---

Concentrations of various pituitary hormones increase in response to both exercise and insulin-induced hypoglycemia, and the excercise response may be due in part to receptors sensing glucoprivation. A study was undertaken to determine whether hormonal responses to hypoglycemia are exaggerated in trained subjects. Seven healthy, sedentary men, aged 21 to 30 years, and 8 athletes of similar ages who competed in elite class endurance sports were studied. The mean maximal oxygen uptakes were 49 ml/kg per minute for untrained subjects and 65 for trained subjects. Insulin was infused to produce a blood glucose concentration of less than 2.5 mmole/L, after 2 or 3 days on a 250-gm carbohydrate diet.

Plasma glucose responses to insulin infusion were identical in the trained and untrained groups. Concentrations of β-endorphin and PRL increased similarly, but the GH nadir was higher in the trained subjects. Thyrotropin concentrations did not change in either group.

Training appears not to result in a general increase in anterior pituitary secretory capacity. Differences in β-endorphin responsiveness to exercise in trained and untrained subjects cannot be attributed to differences in responsiveness to hypoglycemia. β-Endorphin activity may not account for the chronic mood changes that may result from regular exercise.

▶ This is a cross-sectional comparison of athletes and sedentary subjects, and it would be nice to see the authors' conclusions tested by a longitudinal training experiment.

There has been considerable debate as to the importance of β-endorphin secretion in the mood changes associated with vigorous exercise (Markoff et al.: *Med. Sci. Sports Exerc.* 14:11, 1982). Mikines et al. do not dispute that exercise increases the output of β-endorphins; however, they argue that because trained people lack an enhanced endorphin response to hypoglycemia, and because hypoglycemia is one possible step in the secretion of endorphins during exercise, endorphins cannot therefore, be responsible for mood elevation in active subjects. It seems to me quite possible that mood could be elevated in active people not because the endorphin mechanism is more sensitive, but merely because it is used more frequently.—Roy J. Shephard, M.D., Ph.D.

---

**Motivation: The Key to Fitness Compliance**
Roy J. Shephard (Univ. of Toronto)
Physician Sportsmed. 13:88–101, July 1985                    1–142

It is difficult to sustain the motivation of participants in both individual and group exercise programs. Typically, only 20% of eligible workers will join a company-established program, and up to 50% of them will drop out during the initial 6–12 months. Recruitment and adherence are even worse in community programs. The author reviewed personal factors that influence participants' decisions to begin and continue exercise programs.

Fitness Canada conducted the Canada Fitness Survey in 1981. Teams of investigators visited 13,500 households across the nation to determine attitudes about exercise and to make field measurements of current fitness status; 88% of the households cooperated. Given some overestimation of personal activity, and a lesser participation rate among nonrespondents, one can assume that about 33% of Canadians currently exercise adequately, and that older individuals and blue-collar workers should be targeted for greater participation. Gender and income had more effect on sport than on exercise participation. Thus, attempts to increase activity will probably be more effective if they emphasize exercise rather than sports participation. The most frequently reported pursuits (walking, cycling, swimming, jogging, and gardening) require little organization or equipment. Apparently, for high participation rates, one should focus on simple programs, preferably performed at home as a family unit.

The Toronto Life Assurance Study provides matched control data for about 1,800 office workers. At one company an experimental employee fitness program was initiated, and at a closely matched control company three fitness tests were provided over a 9-month period. Almost twice as many managers and officers began the program than secretaries and clerks. This emphasizes the need to target not only blue-collar workers but also the lower levels of white-collar employees, particularly men. This might be done through a combination of incentives attractive to both sexes (possibly including childcare facilities) and a change of orientation (e.g., a less intellectual approach to fitness).

Earlier work had suggested a selective defection of obese, unfit cigarette smokers from exercise classes, but this was not noted in the Toronto Life Assurance Study. An additional factor is the goal set for a class; over several months, there will be a progressive loss of individuals who have either more or less ambitious goals than the class mean. The dropout rate for this study increased progressively to about 50% over 18 months. As in the Canada Fitness Survey, the prime reason cited was lack of time (46%). Other common explanations were loss of interest (20%), exercising on their own (10%), exercising elsewhere (8%), and other reasons (16%). The most urgent need is an alteration of the perception of free time.

The initial recruitment to an employee fitness program at the corporate headquarters of General Foods in White Plains, New York, was close to the anticipated 20% (535 to 2,400 workers), and almost 50% had been previously active. The men tended to be obese but also initially had higher aerobic power and muscle strength than average, and the women had about average fitness levels and were close to the ideal body mass. Reasons for exercise (health, fun, socializing, and making the body attractive) underscored the same elements of Kenyon's inventory, which uses a Likert-type scale to rate the value of physical activity on seven scales.

Participants can be encouraged to join if an exercise program has a wide range of activities and provides incentives to keep members active. Either community or industrial facilities will work, although community facilities often have a low initial recruitment rate. New facilities at the workplace or in a local neighborhood may overcome the perception that time is unavailable. Participation should be reinforced by a system of rewards and incentives until the intrinsic rewards of exercise arise.

▶ I want to be better physically fit. I want to have better health. I enjoy having fun. I enjoy socializing. I would like my body to be more attractive. Why don't I exercise more than I do? I know it will help me achieve all of the things I stated above. Why don't I exercise more than I do? I wish I knew.

More time would help. Participating in an activity I enjoy would help. Stronger motivation would help. I'm sure I would if I had to for serious health reasons. I always find the time when my weight gets above where I begin to get anxious about it. Motivation is the key to convincing myself and others that exercise will achieve the goals I've set.—Frank George, A.T.C., P.T.

### Lifetime Occupational Exercise and Colon Cancer
John E. Vena, Saxon Graham, Mariz Zielezny, Mya K. Swanson, Robert E. Barnes, and James Nolan (State Univ. of New York at Buffalo)
Am. J. Epidemiol. 122:357–365, September 1985                    1–143

The authors reviewed the data on white male patients aged 30 to 79 years who were admitted to the Roswell Park Memorial Institute in Buffalo in New York 1957–1965. The amount of lifetime occupational physical activity for 210 patients with cancer of the colon and 276 patients with cancer of the rectum was compared with the lifetime occupational physical exercise of 1,431 control patients with nonneoplastic, nondigestive diseases. Risk of cancer of the colon increased with increasing amount and proportion of time in jobs involving only sedentary or light work; this relationship was not found for rectal cancer. These findings corroborate those of Garabrant et al. There was an increasing risk of cancer of the colon with increasing work years, proportion of work years, and proportion of life in jobs with sedentary or light work. Findings are based on a lifetime occupational history that was filled out at home prior to first admission to the hospital. No attempt was made to validate the occupational histories. There is no reason to suspect that the patients with colon cancer would differentially recall sedentary occupations, nor is it probable that the cancer patients would underreport or overreport any specific occupations as compared with the controls.

The methods used to assign exercise or physical activity levels to each specific job title were developed by the Department of Labor. They were based on estimates of worker trait requirements for jobs in the 1950s and therefore should be fairly accurate ratings for the specific jobs held by the study subjects. This study considered only the physical activity involved in the job; no measures of avocational physical activity were available. Garabrant et al. found that the risk reduction associated with exercise increased with proximity to the descending colon. The current analysis by anatomical subsite of the colon suggests that risk associated with sedentary or light job work was increased for ascending colon and unspecified sites. However, the unusually small number of cases in the transverse and descending colon subsites makes the risk estimates for these subsites meaningless. This may be related to the fact that in 20% of the cases multiple or unspecified subsites were affected. Garabrant et al. suggested that the lower risk associated with physical activity could be related to the likelihood that peristalsis is stimulated by physical activity, while random, nonpropulsive segmentation activity is decreased. Also, peristalsis may be stimulated by prostaglandins engendered by exercise. Physical activity, therefore, could shorten the transit time of the stool and reduce the duration of contact of the lumen with a fecal carcinogen, perhaps a dietary fat-engendered steroid, or carcinogens ingested in occupational settings.

It is possible that the subjects with jobs involving heavy work required increased caloric intake compared with those with jobs involving sedentary or light work. Total caloric intake was not analyzed because the food frequency history used during the time period of this study grossly underestimates total calories consumed. Previous studies in which the diets of colon cancer patients and controls from Roswell Park were examined showed that the only significant high risks were associated with low vegetable consumption. Whether low vegetable consumption is associated with high caloric intake or occupational exercise is unknown. Caloric intake should be considered a potential confounding variable in future studies. Also, bowel movement frequency as a measure of motility should be studied in relation to levels of exercise.

The strength of the associations presented and the dose-response relationship indicate that physical activity on the job could be an important etiologic factor. It is possible that with increases in physical exercise there are decreases in risk for colon cancer. However, it is also possible that there may be a threshold in physical activity beyond which further reduction of risk is not gained. It may simply be the avoidance of a wholly sedentary existence that reduces the risk of colon cancer. The lack of relation between exercise and risk of cancer of the rectum may be paradoxical.

▶ This is a retrospective study, demonstrating a positive correlation between sedentary activity and malignancy of the colon but not of the rectum. To extrapolate beyond this, and attempt a correlation with physical exercise per se, is not justified on the basis of the present data. Such a statement would require prospective study. Tempting conjectures such as sedentary activity relating to bowel motility, and frequency of bowel evacuation are not attempted in this study.—Lewis J. Krakauer, M.D., F.A.C.P.

# 2 Biomechanics

**Muscle Imbalance and Extremity Injury: A Perplexing Relationship**
Thomas G. Grace (Albuquerque and Bernalillo County Med. Society, Albuquerque, N.M.)
Sports Med. 2:77–82, 1985                                                    2–1

It is evident that muscle imbalance and injury are related, because athletes with a history of joint injury often have muscle weakness and imbalance and also a high rate of reinjury. Correction of muscle imbalance theoretically can reduce serious athletic injuries. Although technological advances have been made in the quantification of limb muscle imbalance, there is relatively little clinical documentation relating actual imbalance with injury.

In muscle imbalance there is either asymmetry between the extremities or a differential with an anticipated normal value. The actual magnitude of what constitutes balance and imbalance never has been accurately defined, but a 10% to 20% discrepancy is used in practice as a guide to return to athletic participation following knee injury. What a significant discrepancy is may depend on the anatomic region involved, the sport, and the subject's age, size, and gender. The normalcy of a given isokinetic measurement or muscle imbalance is significant only as it relates to actual injury, or at least to decreased functional performance.

A better understanding of the relation between muscle imbalance and extremity injury will help justify physiological measurements and rehabilitative programs and will facilitate a shift in emphasis from the treatment to the prevention of injuries. Prospective, blind studies will be most informative.

▶ A valuable paper because it asks the right questions without presuming to have answers in a difficult and highly conjectural area of muscle physiology and pragmatic sports medicine. The question as to whether there is a relationship between imbalance and injury remains open. It is easy to hypothesize in this arena: For example, it would seem reasonable to me that if there is a lower extremity imbalance, particularly unilateral, that this could be reflected in diseases of the spine and premature arthritic change. We think we learned this from diseases such as poliomyclitis. But the data are lacking to support any conjecture, whether upper or lower extremity, whether unilateral or bilateral. This is best stated in the author's last paragraph: "The challenge of the future is for more detailed study of the relationship of isokinetic measurements and muscle imbalance with extremity injury. Is there a relationship? Is it sport-specific, age-sex-, or size-dependent? What is the effect of injury and previous surgery? A study which measures an imbalance, therapeutically corrects the imbalance and finally concludes that the injury rate seems to be lessened, cannot answer these questions. The design will have to be prospective, controlled and ideally avoiding bias by being judged blindly. The questions remain; the answers will, of necessity, await further study and analysis."—Lewis J. Krakauer, M.D., F.A.C.P.

---

**The Biomechanics of Running: Implications for the Prevention of Foot Injuries**
Steven I. Subotnick (California College of Podiatric Medicine and California State Univ., Hayward)
Sports Med. 2:144–153, 1985                                                    2–2

---

The sports medicine practitioner can help prevent foot injuries through an understanding of both functional and nonfunctional biomechanical factors in running. Natural differences remain despite the possibility of improving performance through training and practice. The gait cycle in running is similar to that in walking. The influence of various factors on loading of the lower extremities, such as the shoe or the surface, is important in the occurrence of pain and injury. Orthotic devices significantly affect selected parameters of running.

The perfect foot is rare; about one fifth of the population have relatively high-arch cavus feet that tend to absorb shock poorly with increasing inflexibility. Another fifth have excessive pronation associated with hypermobile flat feet. The latter foot has an apropulsive gait and, in maximal pronation, does not absorb shock well. With a higher-arch, cavus foot, the foot lands under the knee. A flat-footed person will land flat-footed rather than have most weight passing through the first and second metatarsal heads and the great toe. The cavus foot may have lateral instability, and absorption of excess force by the soft tissue and bone can produce injury. Biomechanical imbalances in the lower limb are an estimated three times more important to the runner than to the walker.

Most running injuries reflect overuse, occurring either gradually or as a result of accumulated microtrauma. Good lower limb biomechanics lead to efficient running and a low injury rate. Running injuries require reestablishment of optimal biomechanics in the lower extremity using appropriate shoes and orthoses as well as rehabilitative physical therapy. In this way the athlete can expend much more effort before incurring the same overuse injuries.

▶ Biomechanical considerations in running can now be broken down into the functional and nonfunctional categories, an important distinction. The functional biomechanical findings may be clinically more accurate predictors of injury and serve as diagnostic tools as well. The correlation between the two is important. Progress has been made in the instrumentation for the study of biomechanics such as the Kirstler stress plate, electronic goniometers, accelerometers, telemetry units for electromyographic study, and the digitalization of high-speed motion photography. In addition, there is now an Electrodynogram for qualifying and quantifying force and motion during walking and running. Many of these studies are primarily for research functions, but they do interact at this time with the available orthotics, prescribed by skilled hands in the multiprofessional sports medicine field.

Up to this point, therapists have been working on anecdotal and clinical experience. If biomechanics can be re-established in near-perfect fashion, then perhaps it follows that the mileage an athlete can accomplish could be tripled before the same overuse injury would recur. This remains for proof. It is an exciting concept.—Lewis J. Krakauer, M.D., F.A.C.P.

## A Comparison of Muscular Tightness in Runners and Nonrunners and the Relation of Muscular Tightness to Low Back Pain in Runners

Delanie Karen Bach, Diane Susan Green, Gail M. Jensen, and Emily Savinar (Stanford Univ.)

J. Orthop. Sports Phys. Ther. 6:315–323, May–June 1985          2–3

Back injuries are relatively frequent in runners, and muscle tightness is said to be a common sequela of running. A study was made of 91 subjects aged 18 to 43 years, including runners doing 18 miles or more a week on a regular basis and unselected subjects from the general population, to

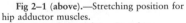

Fig 2–1 (above).—Stretching position for hip adductor muscles.

Fig 2–2 (above right).—Stretching position for hip flexor muscles.

Fig 2–3 (right).—Stretching position for hip extensor muscles.

(Courtesy of Bach, D.K., et al.: J. Orthop. Sports Phys. Ther. 6:315–323, May–June 1985.)

determine whether tightness of the hip adductor, flexor, and extensor muscles is more prevalent in runners, and whether it correlates with low back pain. Subjects were instructed in static stretches so that they would reach their maximum end range of motion (Figs 2–1, 2–2, and 2–3). Forty-five runners aged 18 to 43 years were compared with 46 nonrunners aged 18 to 40 years.

Runners had smaller measurements in straight leg raise tests than nonrunners. Scores for left abduction and right extension also were smaller in the runners. Men had lower hip motion scores than women in both the runner and nonrunner groups. Twenty runners reported having low back pain, 10 in relation to running. Pain could not be related to range of hip motion. Two thirds of the subjects spent at least 50%–75% of their day sitting. Subjects in both groups reported participating in various physical activities other than running.

Hip motion appears to be more limited in runners than in nonrunners. Runners appear to have more hamstring muscle tightness, and this may predispose to injury. Proper stretching can counter muscle tightness. Several runners in this study did not stretch regularly, and others may stretch improperly. Runners should learn to stretch properly in order to maintain or increase flexibility and lower the risk of injury.

▶ Over time, it has been my evaluation that runners tend to overemphasize the value of running as an overall conditioning exercise. It is true that running as an aerobic exercise may be one of the best exercises for conditioning the heart muscle, but it leaves much to be desired as an activity to strengthen and stretch the skeletal muscles. It should be generally understood that most low back pain is related to weakness in the antigravity muscles and tightness in the hip flexors, which limit hip extension, causing anteriorpelvic tilt. This causes increased lordosis at the low back and increased strain on the lumbar spine. The hamstrings are hip extensor muscles; tightness in the hamstring can cause posterior pelvic tilt and eventually level to low back pain. It is important for all of us to understand that we must maintain proper conditioning both of the heart muscle through aerobic exercises and of the skeletal muscles through the balanced muscular strength and endurance exercises for the agonists and antagonist muscles if we are to keep our bodies functioning efficiently and without pain.—Col. James L. Anderson, PE.D.

---

## Dynamic Stabilization of the Trunk

James A. Porterfield (Akron City Hosp., Akron, Ohio)
J. Orthop. Sports Phys. Ther. 6:271–277, March–Apr. 1985          2–4

---

Every human being who lives past the age of 20 and adopts a sedentary life-style is prone to develop a round-shouldered posture and a forward shift of the antigravity weightline, producing a countering force of backward bending and increased lumbar lordosis. The apophyseal joints are forced into an end range of extension and become vulnerable to injury.

Similar changes occur in those who gain weight in the third and subsequent decades of life. The lumbopelvic region, the hub of antigravity weight-bearing, is most vulnerable to spraining and straining tissues and also is the most difficult area to treat. The problems are compounded in persons with an asymmetrical skeleton from a structural or functional leg length difference. Stabilization of the skeleton requires maintenance of normal muscle strength. The abdominal wall, erector spinae, and gluteus maximus muscles are especially important in maintenance of an anatomically correct weightline.

Asymmetrical and abnormal forces acting on lumbopelvic tissues must be identified. Deep massage is most effective when it precedes prolonged passive stretching. Stretching produces the force needed to achieve physiologic and biochemical synthesis and lysis of collagen structures. The patient must avoid body positions that place excessive stress on injured areas. A weight-training program should increase the internal tension of the abdominal wall, erector spinae, gluteus maximus, and latissimus dorsi muscles. Maximal exercise on modern equipment in a pain-free range of motion, with emphasis on high repetitions, is a rewarding approach. Training at least three times a week will soon lead to positive musculoskeletal changes and an improved overall body image. A temporary lumbopelvic support may initially be helpful, especially in patients with mechanical lumbopelvic pain.

▶ Lumbopelvic pain is probably the most prevalent problem for people from their late 40s on. Most of these problems can be properly treated with proper exercise prescription and adherence, I mean for the rest of one's active life, not only until the pain goes away. Good educational programs that stress development of good posture or body balance in youth, a balanced exercise program to maintain the strength and endurance of the antigravity muscles—abdominals, erector spinae, and gluteus maximus—throughout life, and the importance of stretching to keep flexibility will prevent much of the lumbopelvic pain that we hear so much about today.—Col. James L. Anderson, PE.D.

---

**Alignment of the Human Body in Standing**
A. M. Woodhull, K. Maltrud, and B. L. Mello (Hampshire College, Amherst, Mass.)
Eur. J. Appl. Physiol. 54:109–115, May 1985                              2–5

---

The fact that the center of gravity of the whole body is not above the ankle joint, but is about midway in the base of support of the foot, makes it unlikely that the upper joint centers could be directly above the ankle, as is often depicted. The anteroposterior positions of body landmarks and center of gravity were ascertained in 15 normal subjects aged 18 to 29 years. Some were trained in various sports, but none were dancers or gymnasts. Dancers of similar age were also evaluated. The subjects were photographed in profile on a reaction board to determine the anteroposterior positions of the knee, hip, and shoulder joints and the ear compared with the ankle joint, and the positions of the partial centers of gravity above the knee and hip.

The knee, hip, shoulder, and ear were forward of the ankle in all subjects, but respective average amounts of 4, 6, 4, and 6 cm anterior to the ankle. The landmark positions correlated positively with one another, but not to a high degree. The position of the center of gravity was well predicted from the positions of landmarks in individual subjects, but not between subjects. The center of gravity above the knee was located 1.4 cm in front of the joint on average, and that of the hip, 1.0 cm behind the trochanter.

Perfect alignment of the weight-bearing segments of the body on top of one another is not a reality. Slight gravitational torques are present at both the knee and the hip in typical standing, which tend to extend the joints. None of the normal subjects in the present study were close to a linear alignment of joint centers.

▶ At West Point we do a great deal of work in assessing posture and when necessary use exercise to correct for excessive variations from what is considered either healthy or attractive. These investigators do explain that their data were taken from healthy young subjects and should be considered as typical rather than some kind of human "ideal" or "norm." We have found that most of our subjects at West Point present acceptable posture, but few can demonstrate the alignment that is generally accepted as ideal. However, that does not mean the ideal alignment should be discarded as the standard for perfection. Unfortunately, the normal posture for our population does have the head and hips carried too far forward. Much of the low back pain can be directly attributed to our "normal" posture. We need more education to teach people how to more nearly approach the mechanical "ideal."—Col. James L. Anderson, PE.D.

---

**Device for Stretching the Hamstring Muscles: Suggestion From the Field**
Wilfrid E. Dubuc and Richard W. Bohannon (Cape Fear Valley Med. Ctr., Fayetteville, N. C.)
Phys. Ther. 65:352–353, March 1985                                                     2–6

---

Hamstring muscles of inadequate length may impede the ability to perform various maneuvers. The most effective muscle stretching techniques probably are those incorporating prolonged lengthening loads. The method described by Gajdosik and Lusin for measuring hamstring muscle length was adapted for use in stretching the muscles. The muscles are stretched by extending the knee of the supine subject with the ipsilateral hip flexed to 90 degrees and the other hip extended. A plywood body, adjustable shelf, and quadriceps board are utilized. Patients with thighs of different lengths can be accommodated. The hamstrings of both legs can be stretched by simply placing the quadriceps board on either side of the shelf on which it rests.

This device has been used in a number of cases, with encouraging results.

A patient with cerebral palsy achieved a 40% increase in passive straight leg raising after 3 weeks of use of the hamstring stretching device.

▶ Although I have not tried this device, it is included here because tight hamstrings are the cause of many sports injuries and we need to continue to work on a solution. I would prefer to see a study done using this device to test the effects. For example, is it possible to actually stretch the hamstrings and improve function? How long will it take and what amount of improvement can we expect to see? Are there other ways to maintain the stretch improvement without continuing to use this device?—Col. James L. Anderson, PE.D.

**Changes in Leg Movements and Muscle Activity With Speed of Locomotion and Mode of Progression in Humans**
Johnny Nilsson, Alf Thorstensson, and Jünt Halbertsma (Karolinska Inst., Stockholm)
Acta Physiol. Scand. 123:457–475, April 1985                    2–7

A knowledge of body adaptations to altered speed and mode of progression is important in understanding the underlying neural control mechanisms and permits comparisons with animal studies. Man is capable of

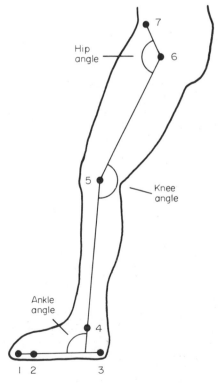

**Fig 2–4.**—Diode positions on the left leg: *(1)* most anterior part of the foot, *(2)* metatarsophalangeal joint of the small toe (V), *(3)* heel, *(4)* ankle joint (over the midpoint of the lateral malleolus), *(5)* knee joint (beneath the center of the lateral femoral epicondylis), *(6)* hip joint (on the superior part of trochanter major), *(7)* spina iliaca anterior superior. Joint angles were calculated from vectors drawn between adjacent diodes as shown in the figure. (Courtesy of Nilsson, J., et al.: Acta Physiol. Scand. 123:457–475, April 1985.)

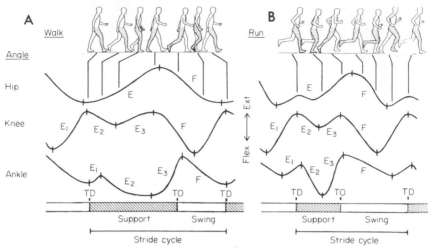

Fig 2–5.—Schematic description of the angular displacements in the hip, knee and ankle joints during a stride cycle in walking (**A**) and running (**B**). Corresponding body positions are depicted at the top of the figure. Movements are described for the right leg (shaded). The angular phases are defined according to Phillipson (1905), see general description in the original article ($F$ = flexion, $E$ = extension). The definitions of the stride cycle and the swing and support phases are given at the bottom of the figure. *TD* = touch down, *TO* = toe off. (Courtesy of Nilsson, J., et al.: Acta Physiol. Scand. 123:457–475, April 1985.)

locomotion over a wide range of velocity, and adaptation occurs with an increase in both the frequency and amplitude of leg movement. Leg movements and muscle activity patterns were examined in 10 healthy men aged 19 to 29 years, during level walking and running at velocities of 0.4–3 meters/second and 1–9 meters/second, respectively. Angular displacements were calculated as shown in Figures 2–4 and 2–5.

The duration of the entire stride cycle and that of the support phase decreased with velocity in a curvilinear manner. Duration of the swing and support phases were linearly related to cycle duration in walking, and curvilinearly related in running. A double support phase was evident in both walking and very slow running. Support length increased with velocity up to about 1.2 m in both walking and running, but was longer when walking at a given velocity. Increases in net angular displacement during the swing phase in running were greatest for hip movements and for knee flexion-extension. Rectus femoris activity shifted from knee extension to hip flexion with increasing velocity. The gastrocnemius lateralis was coactivated with the other leg extensors before foot contact in running, and later in the support phase in walking. The ankle flexor tibialis anterior was most active after touch-down in walking, and before touch-down in running.

The stride cycle in humans is basically like that in other animals, suggesting comparable underlying neural control. Speed adaptation in human beings is characterized by an increased frequency and amplitude of leg movements, and by the possibility of changing between a walking and a running type of movement pattern.

▶ Although there is nothing particularly new in this study, it is well done and contains considerable information that is of value to anyone who is prescribing either walking or running as an aerobic exercise for people. An understanding of the mechanics of these activities and the potential effects on the feet, legs, and hips is a must for proper and responsible exercise prescription. Another important mechanical factor in these locomotion activities that is too often overlooked is proper foot placement. That is one of the shortcomings of this study, because we only assume that the subjects demonstrated normal foot placement. We must always be careful that group data from a study such as this is not attributed to an individual who may exhibit totally different mechanical patterns.—Col. James L. Anderson, PE.D.

---

**Shoulder Motion and Muscle Strength of Normal Men and Women in Two Age Groups**
M. P. Murray, D. R. Gore, G. M. Gardner, and L. A. Mollinger (VA Med. Ctr., Wood, Wis., Med. College of Wisconsin, and Marquette Univ.)
Clin. Orthop. 192:268–273, Jan.–Feb. 1985                                2–8

---

Normal standards of shoulder joint range of motion and muscle strength were obtained in 40 healthy subjects of each sex, 20 of them aged 25 to 36 years, and the rest aged 56 to 66 years. Active ranges of shoulder flexion, extension, abduction, and inward and outward rotation were measured bilaterally using standard goniometric methods.

Men and women had similar ranges of motion, although women had

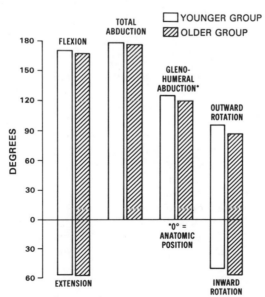

**Fig 2–6.**—Average ranges of shoulder joint motion for the younger (n = 20) as compared with the older (n = 20) group of subjects. Data for men and women are combined. (Courtesy of Murray, M.P., et al.: Clin. Orthop. 192:268–273, January–February 1985.)

greater total inward-outward rotation excursion than men. Younger men had more flexion and outward rotation than older men, but less inward rotation. Younger women had more glenohumeral abduction than older ones. Most range of motion values were similar on the dominant and nondominant sides. There generally was slightly more abduction than flexion, and more outward than inward rotation (Fig 2–6). The gleno-humeral joint contributed 124 degrees on average to total arm-trunk abduction. Muscle strength was consistently greater in younger subjects, and men were stronger than women of similar age when all muscle groups were tested. Inward rotators were stronger than outward rotators in the 0 degree shoulder joint position. In men, the flexor muscles were stronger than the extensors. With the shoulder in 45 degrees of abduction, the adductor muscles were stronger than the abductors. Shoulder flexion was stronger at 0 degrees than at 45 degrees. Strength on a second attempt at maximum contraction exceeded that on the first attempt for all muscle groups except the outward rotators.

Clear differences in shoulder joint range of motion were not found in relation to age or sex in this study. Muscle strength declined with advancing age and was less in women, as expected, but important differences between the two sides were not found. Subjects should be made familiar with test procedures before data are recorded, and several strength measurements should be made at a given session.

▶ I think all of us expect to see a reduction in range of motion as we get older. The data in this study are surprising because age-related reduction in shoulder flexibility was not found. Maybe the small sample size is the cause, or maybe our expectations are wrong. Only more studies and more data collection will answer the question.—Col. James L. Anderson, PE.D.

---

**Mechanical and Physiological Responses to Lower Extremity Loading During Running**
Philip E. Martin (Pennsylvania State Univ.)
Med. Sci. Sports Exerc. 17:427–433, August 1985                                    2–9

---

Little is known of the effects of loading on the mechanical characteristics of walking and running patterns, but relevant data could elucidate the variations in energy cost produced by added loading. The effects of lower extremity loading on seven temporal and kinematic parameters of running and mechanical work were studied in 15 highly trained men who ran on a treadmill at 12 km/hour. Studies were repeated under various loading conditions up to 1 kg, with loads added to the thighs and feet. The subjects had a mean age of 29 years and a mean body mass of 72 kg. Ten had completed a marathon run.

Oxygen uptake rose significantly with added loading of the thighs, and also on loading of the feet. Similar changes in heart rate occurred with lower extremity loading. Loading of the feet influenced temporal and kinematic variables more than loading of the thighs. Changes in mechanical work were limited to the thigh; it increased about 9.5% when the heaviest load state was compared with baseline.

Increased physiologic demand is directly related to increased mechanical work, which in turn is ascribed to increased inertia of the loaded segments in trained men, rather than to altered kinematics of lower extremity movements. Changes in the moment of inertia of the leg about the hip joint during the swing phase would seem to be especially important, as the hip serves as the primary axis of rotation for the leg in this phase.

▶ This is an excellent study that can be used to show what are the physiologic costs of wearing heavier shoes when running. At West Point we found that increased loading, wherever it is carried, produces an elevated oxygen uptake. It was also discovered that as the weight increased linearly the oxygen uptake increased curvilinearly and that the impact was more significant for women than for men.—Col. James L. Anderson, PE.D.

---

**Running Shoes, Orthotics, and Injuries**
D. C. McKenzie, D. B. Clement, and J. E. Taunton (Univ. of British Columbia, Vancouver)
Sports Med. 2:334–347, 1985                                                    2–10

---

Running is the most visible expression of continued interest in regular exercise. Some 60% of injuries related to running result from training errors. Other causes of running injuries include poor training surface, poor flexibility and strength, inappropriate stage of growth and development, poor footwear, and abnormal biomechanical features.

Clinically, the configuration of the longitudinal arch is a valuable method for classifying feet and has direct implications on the development and management of running problems. The runner with excessively pronated feet is predisposed to injuries at the medial aspect of the lower extremity: tibial stress syndrome, patellofemoral pain syndrome, and posterior tibialis tendinitis. These problems are caused by excessive motion at the subtalar joint and can be controlled by selecting appropriate footwear and using orthotic foot control. The runner with cavus feet often has a rigid foot that is unable to absorb most of the force of ground contact. These athletes have unique problems found most often on the lateral aspect of the lower extremity: iliotibial band syndrome; peroneus tendinitis; stress fractures; trochanteric bursitis; and plantar fasciitis. Appropriate foot wear advice and the use of energy-absorbing materials that will help dissipate shock will benefit these individuals.

Shoes for the pronating runner should be selected to control the excessive motion. The shoes should be board-lasted and straight-lasted, and have a stable heel counter, extra medial support, and a wider flare than shoes for the cavus foot. For athletes with cavus feet, a sliplasted, curve-lasted shoe with softer ethylene vinyl acetate and a narrow flare is appropriate. Orthotic devices are useful in those runners with demonstrated biomechanical abnormalities that contribute to the injury.

A review of injury data shows an alarming rise in the incidence of knee pain in runners—from 18% to 50% in 13 years. Errors in training judgment, with excessive loading (particularly in runners with compromised biomechanical features), represent the primary causative factors. These errors cannot be accommodated by running-shoe design nor by orthotic devices. The runner must participate in a comprehensive rehabilitation program that considers the other factors contributing to the injuries.

▶ A good review of shoes, orthotics, and running injuries. The interested reader is referred to the original article. To be noted, the authors have failed to specify the indications for the prescription of orthotic devices. Injuries caused by conditions such as leg length discrepancy, excess femoral retroversion, tight heel cords, and poor training techniques will not benefit from these devices, which cost approximately $275.00 a pair. This is a major shortcoming of the paper.—Joseph S. Torg, M.D.

---

**Foot Pressure Patterns During Gait**
R. W. Soames (King's College, London)
J. Biomed. Eng. 7:120–126, April 1985                    2–11

The behavior of the foot during the various phases of gait is incompletely understood. Peak pressure and temporal variables of foot function were assessed in 21 men and 11 women without foot problems or gait disorder. Measurements were taken from the left foot (Fig 2–7) during barefoot

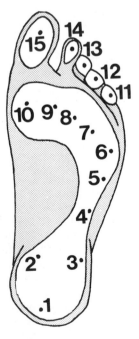

Fig 2–7.—Sites of transducer attachment. (Courtesy of Soames, R.W.: J. Biomed. Eng. 7:120–126, April 1985.)

walking and the wearing of normal shoes. Small semiconductor strain gauge transducers were used.

Few differences were found between men and women in any of the variables during barefoot walking or while they were wearing shoes. Shoes appeared to modify the behavior of the forefoot by altering pressure distribution across the metatarsal heads and increasing contact times for the toes. Pressure on the lateral side of the foot increased with body weight in both men and women. In men only the first metatarsal head had a significant increase in contact time while shoes were worn; in women the two lateral metatarsal heads both showed significant increases in duration of ground contact. Rise times to peak pressure generally declined beneath the metatarsal heads with the wearing of shoes and increased beneath the toes. Analysis of pressure-time integrals emphasized the importance of the first metatarsal and its phalanges.

Intersubject variability in the pattern of peak pressure distribution under the foot may be useful in providing a baseline from which change can be assessed. Pressure-time integrals could be a more useful single measure than either peak pressure or temporal variables. Improperly fitted orthopedic footwear may be as likely to cause secondary pathologic change as any other type of footwear.

► Although this study found relatively few differences between men and women in any measures, whether barefoot or wearing shoes of similar types, I wonder what the patterns would be like for women in flat shoes versus high-heeled shoes. If shoes influence the way we walk, as this study found, then certainly women's high-heeled shoes must have a significant effect.—Col. James L. Anderson, PE.D.

---

**A System to Measure the Forces and Moments at the Knee and Hip During Level Walking**
Jerome A. Gilbert, G. Maret Maxwell, James H. McElhaney, and Frank W. Clippinger (Duke Univ.)
J. Orthop. Res. 2:281–288, 1985                                               2–12

---

Maxwell's method of using accelerometers to measure leg accelerations and, later, knee force and moment, has now been extended to force/moment description of the hip in the sagittal plane. Studies were done in 12 normal subjects and 9 lower limb amputees, including below-knee, above-knee, and full hip disarticulation subjects. Accelerations were measured by accelerometers attached to the legs and the force reactions at the foot were measured using a force plate. The data were used to determine joint reactions through a Newtonian formulation, modeling the leg as articulated, rigid links.

Obvious differences were found when comparing data from the normal subjects and amputees, at both the knee and hip. The amputee curves lacked the steep slope associated with heel strike common in normal subjects. Weight was applied more slowly on the prosthetic side. The average amputee took 21% of the stance phase to reach 70% of body weight, compared with 11% for a typical normal subject. This was most apparent in vertical force curves for the full hip disarticulation amputee. The mean peak anterior/posterior force at the foot was 13% of body weight for 9 amputees, compared with 22% for normal subjects. The basic shape of knee moment was similar for the normal subjects and amputees. Hip moments of the amputees generally were of the same order of magnitude as the knee moments and lacked the higher-frequency components present in the curves of normal subjects.

Gait data obtained in this way can be used to form criteria for objective gait analysis, and for improved prosthesis design. Gait disorders may be usefully analyzed using an accelerometer/force plate system.

▶ A few years ago this study would not have been included in the YEAR BOOK OF SPORTS MEDICINE because the disabled, including amputees, were often overlooked as athletes. The disabled are now being encouraged to participate more and more in athletics, and the medical community must be prepared to advise and assist them. This study gives us data to help us understand the differences in gait patterns between amputees and normal subjects.—Col. James L. Anderson, PE.D.

**Biomechanics of the Shoulder**
Dennis L. Hart and Stephen W. Carmichael (West Virginia Univ.)
J. Orthop. Sports Phys. Ther. 6:229–234, Jan.–Feb. 1985          2–13

The obliquity of the osteologic structures of the shoulder girdle provides many bony borders and prominences for muscular attachments and improved limb control. Attachment of the entire upper limb proximally only at the sternoclavicular joint permits hand placement in various functional positions. The chief function of the clavicle is stability. The scapula increases the positions available for the hand in space and helps stabilize the upper extremity during functional activities of the hand. The humerus provides leverage for upper limb strength and a wide range of motion for hand placement. The glenohumeral joint is in a loose-packed position through most of its range, allowing the accessory movements of spin, slide, and roll.

The many muscular forces acting on the shoulder girdle provide a large range of movement. The deltoid muscle fibers are in a multipennate arrangement, providing for less change in fiber length while maximal force is obtained in contraction. Elevation of the deltoid origins during humeral elevation reduces the range over which the muscle must contract, in turn increasing muscle power. The weight of the extremity and action of the humeral head depressors contribute to smooth, coordinated elevation, whether forward or to the side. Intricate muscular force couples combine to move the clavicle, scapula, and humerus to provide the stability and mobility required by the arm.

A systematic approach based on forces, levers, axes, and planes of each movement will aid the development of an appropriate treatment plan, including the use of mobilization.

▶ The importance of understanding the biomechanics of the shoulder cannot be overstated for anyone who is working with an active athletic population. For reasons that we do not totally understand, injuries to the shoulders have become the most prevalent, producing the greatest amount of time lost, within our very active cadet population at West Point. Regardless of the activity that requires the use of the arms and shoulders as well as other body extremities, we see more shoulder injuries that take longer to rehabilitate than any other type of injury. It appears to me that the answer to the problem should be primarily prevention, by doing more to strengthen the musculature of the shoulders by starting at a very young age.—Col. James L. Anderson, PE.D.

**The Roentgenographic Evaluation of Anterior Shoulder Instability**
Helene Pavlov, Russell F. Warren, Carl B. Weiss, Jr., and David M. Dines (New York Hosp.-Cornell Univ. Med. College)
Clin. Orthop. 194:153–158, April 1985                          2–14

Various radiographic views were compared for evaluating the osseous pathology associated with shoulder instability in 83 patients who were operated on for unilateral anterior shoulder disability. The 64 men and 19 women had a mean age of 25 years. All lesions were posttraumatic. The mean interval from trauma to surgery was 5 years. Football, wrestling, and baseball injuries accounted for 66 cases, and a fall or throwing a punch for 15 cases. "Instability" exposures included the West Point, Stryker notch, and Didiee views. Standard radiographs included two frontal views, with the humerus in internal and external rotation, and an axillary view.

Eighteen percent of the patients had normal radiographic findings. A Hill-Sachs defect alone was present in 61% of patients, and an isolated Bankart defect in 5%. Thirteen patients had both defects. The Hill-Sachs defect was identified on 66 of 72 internal rotation views and on 35 of 38 Stryker notch views. The osseous Bankart defect was identified on 7 of 10 West Point views, 5 of 7 Didiee views, and 11 of 17 external rotation views.

A Hill-Sachs defect was demonstrated in about three fourths of the patients in this study with anterior shoulder instability. The osseous Bankart defect was most consistently seen on the West Point and Didiee views. A series including an internal rotation and a Stryker notch view, and either a West Point or a Didiee view, seems reasonable for evaluating patients with an unstable shoulder.

▶ At West Point it appears that the sports injury that is most prevalent and causes the greatest loss of time is to the shoulder. Most of the shoulder injuries are strains, sprains, or subluxations. Treatment of these injuries is often difficult, and surgical procedures often leave the patient unsatisfied with the results. Information from this study helps explain why prevention of the shoulder injury may be a better answer than trying to repair it surgically. As mentioned above, however, the prevention needs to start with arm and shoulder exercises at young ages and to continue as long as sports participation continues.—Col. James L. Anderson, PE.D.

---

**Three-Dimensional Cinematographic Analysis of Water Polo Throwing in Elite Performers**
William C. Whiting, James C. Puffer, Gerald A. Finerman, Robert J. Gregor, and Greg B. Maletis (Univ. of California, Los Angeles)
Am. J. Sports Med. 13:95–98, March–April 1985                    2–15

---

Past studies of water polo throwing have been limited to a qualitative assessment of wrist and shoulder motions and two-dimensional analysis of the overhand throw. Three-dimensional analysis now has been used to examine kinematic parameters of the water polo throw in 13 members of the United States national team. Two synchronized cameras were used to film the subjects as they shot at a goal. Three-dimensional coordinates of the shoulder, elbow, wrist, and ball were used to estimate elbow angle, elbow angular velocity, and ball velocity at release.

Ball release velocities ranged from 14.5 to 26 m/second, and peak elbow angular velocities averaged 1137 degrees/second. Peak elbow angular velocity typically was reached just before release, as the elbow approached full extension. Subjects who had had at least two episodes of rotator cuff tendinitis in the past year reached lesser angular velocities than uninjured subjects at the point of elbow extension. The injured subjects exhibited less flexion early in the cycle.

These findings compare fairly well with those obtained using dual-camera, two-dimensional analysis. Three-dimensional techniques can be useful in identifying characteristics of superior performers, and in studying differences in throwing technique between injured and uninjured subjects. Appropriate limb movements for strength testing of the upper extremity can be specified.

▶ Although in this study the investigator's use of three-dimensional analysis seems to confirm the results of other studies in which two-dimensional analyses were used, this is not always the case. As the practitioners of sports biomechanics continue to improve upon their investigative techniques and to develop new techniques, we will be better able to identify the injury mechanisms of various sporting activities. As with most studies such as this one, there are too many variables to be able to establish definite cause and effect relationships for rotator cuff injuries. For instance, the subjects with previous injuries were almost 5 years older than the noninjured subjects. We do not know whether the throwing patterns of the injured group were always different or whether they changed as a result of the injury. On the average, the injured subjects were also 6 cm shorter and 5 kg lighter than the noninjured. Much more controlled data will be necessary, probably from a longitudinal study, before we can fully understand the precise role that differences in throwing technique have in contributing to rotator cuff injuries.—James L. Anderson, PE.D.

### Shoulder Strength Following Acromioclavicular Injury
W. Michael Walsh, David A. Peterson, Guy Shelton, and Randall D. Neumann (Univ. of Nebraska)
Am. J. Sports Med. 13:153–158, May–June 1985                          2–16

Acromioclavicular (AC) joint dislocation routinely is managed by leaving the joint dislocated, but residual shoulder weakness has been cited as a reason for repairing the joint. The Cybex II was used to quantify residual shoulder weakness in 25 patients with AC injuries seen at 5 hospitals in a 2-year period. Eight patients had a diagnosis of grade II, and 17 had grade III injury. Nine of those with grade III injuries were operated on. In grade II cases the AC ligament and capsule were disrupted while the coracoclavicular ligaments remained attached. Grade III injuries included damage to both the AC and coracoclavicular ligaments.

Cybex testing of patients with grade II injuries, an average of 33 months after injury and simple immobilization, showed a significant deficit of 24% in horizontal abduction. Some patients with grade III injuries had treatment in a sling for 1–3 weeks, while others were not treated at all. Horizontal abduction was 11% stronger on the injured side on study an average of 30 months after injury. Patients who were operated on were studied an average of 25 months after injury. Most often coracoclavicular circlage was performed using Dacron grafts. An average 20% deficit in abduction was found.

Nonoperative management of grade III AC injuries seems to be as effective as repair from the standpoint of objective strength. Conservatively managed patients in the present study rated their outcome better than did operated patients. The proper management of grade II injuries remains uncertain. Significant deficits in muscle strength are found after conservative treatment. Patients' satisfaction after AC injury does not reflect objective deficits in muscle strength.

▶ This study supports our data at West Point concerning the increasing numbers of shoulder injuries and the problems present in treating those injuries. I have a strong feeling that prevention of the injuries by encouraging more arm and shoulder exercises to strengthen the shoulder muscles will pay great dividends. It appears that our increases in shoulder injuries began about 5 years after the running boom began. During that time, everyone looked at running and other aerobic exercises as all that was needed for health-related fitness and development of muscle strength and endurance was neglected.—Col. James L. Anderson, PE.D.

## Effects of Joint Load on the Stiffness and Laxity of Ligament-Deficient Knees: An In Vitro Study of the Anterior Cruciate and Medial Collateral Ligaments
Stephen C. Shoemaker and Keith L. Markolf (Univ. of California, Los Angeles)
J. Bone Joint Surg. [Am.] 67-A:136–146, January 1985                          2–17

Little attention has been given to the role of specific ligaments in stabilizing the loaded knee. The effects of sectioning the anterior cruciate and medial collateral ligaments on anteroposterior motion and tibial rotation were assessed, before and after the application of tibiofemoral contact force. Anterior-posterior force-versus-displacement and tibial torque-versus-rotation response curves were recorded for 7 fresh frozen cadaver knees at 0 degrees and 20 degrees of flexion, before and after application of up to 925 newtons of compressive load on the tibiofemoral joint. The effects of 5 degrees and 10 degrees of internal and external tibial rotation also were studied.

Sectioning the anterior cruciate ligament consistently increased anterior laxity in the unloaded specimen. Joint loading limited the increase more at 0 degrees than at 20 degrees of flexion. Loading limited anterior laxity more at low than at higher levels of applied anterior force. Sectioning the medial collateral ligament increased anterior laxity only if the anterior cruciate ligament had previously been sectioned. Joint loading eliminated the increase only at full extension. The medial collateral ligament was the more important of the ligaments in controlling torsional laxity. Increased torsional laxity after primary section of either ligament was not affected by joint loading, but loading reduced the rise in laxity after secondary sectioning of the medial collateral ligament.

Loss of the medial collateral ligament is better tolerated than loss of the anterior cruciate ligament. With loss of the anterior cruciate ligament or both ligaments, tibiofemoral motion is only minimally constrained. Similar effects are expected in vivo if muscle control cannot prevent large relative tibiofemoral motions. The findings emphasize the need for muscle stabilization in a knee with a ligament deficit.

▶ The investigators have done an excellent job in using cadavers to highlight the delicate balance between ligament function, tibiofemoral motion, and joint load. It is difficult to translate the result of cadaver studies to the treatment of sports injuries; however, I find this one to be an exception. The information provided from these experiments can be used to assist in making treatment decisions where the anterior cruciate ligaments and/or the medial collateral ligaments are affected. The investigators have once again underscored the need for muscular stabilization in a knee with a ligament deficit. We must impress upon the patients the necessity for complete rehabilitation after surgery and the need to continue an adequate muscular stability exercise program for the rest of their lives.—Col. James L. Anderson, PE.D.

### The Measurement of Anterior Knee Laxity After ACL Reconstructive Surgery

Lawrence L. Malcom, Dale M. Daniel, Mary Lou Stone, and Raymond Sachs (Kaiser-Permanente Med. Ctr., San Diego, Calif.)

Clin. Orthop. 196:35–41, June 1985                                    2–18

The knee ligament Arthrometer (Fig 2–8) can be used objectively to evaluate anterior and posterior knee laxity before and during operation and to document the maintenance of normal laxity after operation. Prereconstruction and immediate postreconstruction measurements were made with the patient on the operating table in 19 chronic and 24 acute cases. Four types of anterior cruciate ligament (ACL) reconstruction were studied, including the Mott semitendinosus anatomical reconstruction, the Insall iliotibial band over-the-top reconstruction, the Lambert patellar tendon bone-tendon-bone reconstruction, and the Marshall-MacIntosh patellar tendon over-the-top reconstruction. Displacement measurements were obtained by applying 20-lb anterior and posterior forces.

The mean difference in anterior displacement on stress testing between the ACL-deficient and the opposite knee was 6.8 mm in chronic cases. The load was applied at 30 degrees of flexion. In acutely injured patients the average difference was 4 mm. In chronic cases the average reconstructed knee was 1.4 mm tighter than the ACL-intact knee after repair. In acute cases the reconstructed knee averaged 0.8 mm tighter than the intact knee. All reconstructive procedures were equally effective in restoring normal laxity in ACL-deficient knees.

The knee ligament Arthrometer is useful in documenting ACL reconstruction in the operating room and in confirming that normal anteroposterior knee laxity has been reestablished. The device is expected to be useful as synthetic materials are increasingly used in knee ligament reconstruction.

▶ The clinical knee ligament arthrometer appears to be a very useful tool for the immediate preoperative and postoperative documentation of anterior cruciate ligament reconstructions.—Col. James L. Anderson, PE.D.

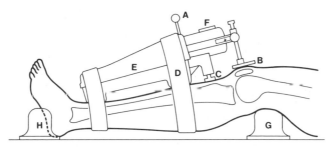

Fig 2–8.—Arthrometer used to measure anteroposterior knee laxity. *A*, force-sensing handle; *B*, patella sensor pad; *C*, tibial tubercle sensor pad; *D*, Velcro strap; *E*, Arthrometer case; *F*, displacement dial indicator; *G*, thigh support; and *H*, foot support. (Courtesy of Malcom, L.L., et al.: Clin. Orthop. 196:35–41, June 1985.)

### The Force-Velocity Relationship of Arm Flexion in Untrained Males and Females and Arm-Trained Athletes

F. L. de Koning, R. A. Binkhorst, J. A. Vos, and M. A. van't Hof (Univ. of Nijmegen)
Eur. J. Appl. Physiol. 54:89–94, May 1985                                        2–19

Force-velocity curves of arm flexion were recorded in 123 untrained men and 110 women aged 15 to 36 years, all of them healthy, and in 48 arm-trained, male athletes competing in various sports. The athletes, participated in the shot put, discus, decathlon, javelin throw, rowing, tug-of-war, karate, weight-lifting, body building, and handball. The force-velocity curve (FVC) was described by Hill's equation, and defined by maximal static moment ($M_o$), maximal angular velocity ($\omega_o$), maximal power ($P_o$), and the concavity of the FVC (H).

The level of the curve parameters in both untrained men and women was independent of age within the age limits of the sample. On average, H was the same in all groups. The athletes had a $M_o$ 33% higher than untrained men, and 38% higher than in untrained women. The respective differences for $P_o$ were 30% and 43%. Maximal angular velocity was the same for trained and untrained men, but women had a value 10% lower than men. The athletes generally had high lean body mass compared with the untrained men.

Most parameters of the FVC differ between untrained and muscle-trained subjects. At least part of the difference probably can be attributed to variations in arm and muscle dimensions.

▶ The measure for the concavity of the FVC is represented by the values of the parameter H, which is dimensionless and, for isolated muscle, has a magnitude that is dependent upon fiber type distribution. Slow-twitch fibers are represented by a smaller H than for fast-twitch fibers. The authors have stated that if this held true for in situ muscle, no difference would be expected in H between men and women, since no substantial differences have been found so far in the histochemically determined muscle fiber composition. Other studies have determined that we can expect differences in fiber composition between muscle of groups of elite athletes in various activities. When compared with untrained athletes, for example, we would expect the muscles of endurance-trained athletes to have a higher proportion of slow-twitch fibers and the muscles of sprinters to have a higher proportion of fast-twitch fibers. However, since the athletes in this study practiced what the authors called "normal muscle training," they did not expect that training to cause a significant degree of interconversion between fast- and slow-twitch fibers, which means that the differences shown in this study may be the result of genetic factors rather than training.—Col. James L. Anderson, PE.D.

---

### Biomechanics, Load Analysis and Sports Injuries in the Lower Extremities

Benno M. Nigg (Univ. of Calgary)
Sports Med. 2:367–379, 1985                                             2–20

The study of sports injuries has grown as sports become more important as a leisure-time activity. Some biomechanical considerations of the origin, reduction, and treatment of sport injuries are presented, with special emphasis on the lower limbs.

Sports injuries caused by overload are the result of forces or stress exceeding the critical limits. Overload can occur when one force is above the critical limit or a number of cyclic forces are below that limit, producing a combined fatigue effect. A biomechanical analysis of injury must take into account both the magnitude and the geometry of the acting forces. The most common measuring techniques are force-measure devices, accelerometers, and optical systems.

A study of the locomotor origins of pain and sports injuries can be carried out by assessing the critical limits of biomaterials and by reducing the load. The most effective strategies for reducing load and stress on the locomotor system involve changing the following: (1) the movement (e.g., running style); (2) the surface; (3) the shoe; and (4) the frequency of repetition. Athletes who plan an intensive activity in a sport or parents who plan a sports career for their children should be aware than an extensive analysis of the locomotor system will help identify any potential problems. Misalignment of the skeleton may be the origin of acute or—much worse—chronic injuries.

▶ An excellent review of several considerations in the mechanical aspects of the etiology, prevention, and treatment of sports injuries, with special emphasis on the lower extremity. Two possible approaches to load analysis are discussed. One deals with determining the critical limits of biomaterials. The second approach deals with ways of reducing load, assuming that it is usually too high in athletics. Playing surfaces and shoes are revealed as an important possibilities for load reduction. The interested reader is referred to the original article.—Joseph S. Torg, M.D.

---

**Biomechanics of Baseball Pitching: A Preliminary Report**
Arthur M. Pappas, Richard M. Zawacki, and Thomas J. Sullivan (Univ. of Massachusetts, Worcester)
Am. J. Sports Med. 13:216–222, July–August 1985                      2–21

---

Baseball pitching is a whole-body activity with sequential activation of body parts through a link system, proceeding from the left foot to the right hand in a right-handed pitcher. High-speed cinematography and computer analysis were used to examine the biomechanics of pitching in 15 major league players who were at spring training.

In the cocking phase, from the start of windup to maximal external rotation of the shoulder, a rhythm is established to correctly time subsequent movements, and the body is placed so that all segments can contribute to propelling the ball. The leg opposite the pitching arm pushes off and the arms flex forward initially. Weight shifts to the pivot leg, and the striding leg swings forward across the front of the body as the ball is taken from the glove. The throwing shoulder then is abducted, extended, and internally rotated, and the wrist is flexed. The pivot leg extends vigorously and the hips and pelvis start to rotate forward, with segmental rotation of the trunk. The striding leg is planted and the throwing arm starts to accelerate forward. The average acceleration phase lasted 50 msec, and was very explosive. The shoulder derotates, with release of the ball at 40 degrees to 60 degrees of external rotation. The average peak angular velocity of shoulder internal rotation was 6,180 deg/second. Wrist flexion starts just before ball release, as does radioulnar pronation. The follow-through phase involves comfortable deceleration of the throwing limb; it constitutes about one fifth of the entire sequence. Deceleration is generated by the posterior shoulder girdle muscles and the biceps. The body catches up with the arm through forward progression of the ipsilateral leg until the player is in proper fielding position.

Elbow stresses are incurred in both the acceleration and follow-through phases of pitching. The lower extremities and trunk contribute significantly to throwing. Further study is needed of the entire link system of the throwing mechanism. Cinematographic and electromyographic data can usefully be correlated.

▶ The art and science of baseball pitching calls for the generation of forces from various parts of the body and the sequential summation of those forces such that at time of ball release maximum velocity is imparted to the ball and the ball is accurately directed toward a target the size of a catcher's mitt. Studies done at Indiana University have shown that most of the basic components of the throwing patterns demonstrated by major league baseball pitchers are present in the throwing patterns of 5-year-old boys. The missing components appear to be the coordination necessary to cause the sequential summation of forces. Coaches should realize that many of the events that occur in sequence take only milliseconds and are too fast to be picked up by the naked eye. The use of cinematographic analysis of athletic activities may be a better way for coaches to determine what an athlete is really doing and what changes to suggest.—Col. James L. Anderson, PE.D.

---

**Measurement of the Motion Range in the Loaded Ankle**
Ulf Lindsjö, Göran Danckwardt-Lillieström, and Bo Sahlstedt (Univ. of Uppsala)
Clin. Orthop. 199:68–71, October 1985                                    2–22

---

To measure the motion range in the ankle under load, a patient is asked to put the foot on a stool 30 cm high and then lean forward as much as possible without lifting the heel from the stool. In this position the knee is flexed, and the greater part of the body weight is on the examined foot. Dorsal extension is measured with a protractor as the angle between the support line of the foot and the long axis of the leg. Loaded plantar flexion is measured in the same position but with the heel raised as much as possible. Among 317 healthy ankles in both sexes, this method gave greater and more reproducible values than measurements on unloaded ankles in the sitting or supine position. Loaded dosal extension was also measured on roentgenograms of 66 healthy ankles. The mean value was 32.5 degrees; the mean talar forward tilt was 5.0 degrees.

This simple clinical test of the motion range in the loaded ankle can be applied in nearly every patient. It provides information on maximum extension and flexion capacity in the ankle, which implies a high degree of iterative precision. Moderately restricted mobility of the knee or hip does not influence the result. During the test, the knee is flexed to a maximum, and the calf muscles are relaxed. Muscular obstacles to dorsal extensions are thereby largely eliminated. The method reveals factors in the ankle itself of significance for restriction of mobility.

Weseley et al. remarked on the problem of deciding whether the tibia is using all the available talar gliding surface during ankle movements. This information is useful in determining whether the cause of restricted motion lies in the soft parts or the skeletal parts of the joint. This tibiotalar motion potential can also be estimated from roentgenograms taken in the position the authors have described. Evaluation of the range of motion as the angle between the longitudinal axis of the tibia and the lateral margin of the foot means that the subtalar motions are included in the measurement. These subtalar motions can be estimated on x-ray films from the forward rotation of the talus during dorsal extension under loading. Using this method, the authors found that the subtalar movements are of minor importance to the total tibiopedal motility. The tibiotalar joint is responsible for about 85% to 90% of the whole range of dorsal extension in the method described.

Dorsal extension in the ankle is important for ankle function. During normal gait on flat ground, about 10 degrees of dorsal extension is used during the stance phase and toe-off. Dorsal extension of more than 10 degrees occurs in going down stairs, kneeling, and many athletic and sports activities. Patients who are not dependent on an ability to walk up and down stairs in their daily life can manage well with a dorsal extension of only 10 degrees. More-active patients involved in athletics and sports need a greater capacity for dorsal extension, at least 20 to 30 degrees.

▶ Aside from describing a simple and apparently effective way of measuring true ankle motion, the value of this paper is the emphasis it places on "dorsal extension" and athletic performance. It has been our experience that successful management of all lower extremity injuries requires a rehabilitation program that effectively re-establishes ankle dorsiflexion.—Joseph S. Torg, M.D.

---

**Reconstruction for Ankle Instability in Young Active Adults**
A. D. L. Green (Queen Elizabeth Military Hosp., London)
J. R. Coll. Surg. Edinb. 30:50–53, February 1985                                    2–23

---

Chronic inversion instability of the ankle following injury is a serious disability to persons with physically active jobs or sports activities. Twenty-four such patients had reconstruction of the lateral ligament by a modification of the Evans procedure. All had a significant, painful initial injury. Most patients were initially treated by strapping and physiotherapy; 4 were not treated. Participation in sports activities was impaired in 22 cases. Six patients were unable to continue their work. The average patient age was 23 years. The average time from injury to operation was 5 years, and patients were followed for 3½ years on average after operation. The upper end of the divided peroneus brevis tendon is passed through a fibular channel from below, doubled over the lateral aspect of the bone, and sutured to itself with the foot in neutral position. The rest of the muscle is sutured to the peroneus longus tendon.

The outcome was satisfactory in 83% of cases. Stress radiography 6 months postoperatively showed that only 1 ankle still had 5 degrees of varus tilt more than the normal side, in association with a poor functional result because of pain. Four ankles had a 3-mm or greater difference in anterior shift compared with the normal ankle, but the functional results were good. Inversion and eversion movements were restricted by 5 degrees on average. Of the 4 poor results, 3 were associated with 5–15 degrees of restriction of inversion.

The modified Evans tenodesis is a satisfactory method of restoring ankle stability in cases of chronic posttraumatic inversion instability. More than 80% of the present patients were able to return to strenuous work or normal sports activities.

▶ Kristiansen (*Br. J. Sports Med.* 16:40–45, March 1982) has recently reported a follow-up study of 18 athletes treated by the Evans technique. In this group, the results of repair were excellent in 28% of the patients and good in 39%. Thus, they conclude that two thirds of the ankles operated on in their series were functionally stable and that the level of athletic activity was lower in a third of the patients when compared to pre-injury status. These results may be compared with those in the report of Riegler (*J. Bone Joint Surg.* [*Am.*] 66A:336–339, March 1984), in which all but 1 of 11 patients with lateral instability of the ankle treated by a lateral reconstruction method of Chrisman and Snook returned to their previous primary sport.—Joseph S. Torg, M.D.

---

**Warming-up and Stretching for Improved Physical Performance and Prevention of Sports-Related Injuries**
Frank G. Shellock and William E. Prentice (Cedars-Sinai Med. Ctr., Los Angeles, and Univ. of North Carolina at Chapel Hill)
Sports Med. 2:267–278, 1985                                    2–24

---

Competitive and recreational athletes typically perform warm-up and stretching activities to prepare for more strenuous exercise. Their preliminary activities are used to enhance physical performance and to prevent sports-related injuries. Warm-up techniques work primarily by increasing body temperature and are classified as follows: (1) passive warm-up by external means; (2) general warm-up with nonspecific body movements; and (3) specific warm-up using body parts that will be used in the more strenuous activity. The best of these appears to be the specific warm-up exercise.

Most benefits of warm-up are related to temperature-dependent physiologic processes. An elevation in body temperature produces an increase in the dissociation of oxygen from hemoglobin and myoglobin; a lowering of the activation energy rates of metabolic chemical reactions; an increase in muscle blood flow; a reduction in muscle viscosity; an increase in the sensitivity of nerve receptors; and an increase in the speed of nervous impulses. Stretching to improve flexibility has been advocated for improved physical performance. The three stretching techniques (ballistic, static, and proprioceptive neuromuscular facilitation) are all based on the neurophysiologic phenomenon of the stretch reflex. Studies comparing the effectiveness of the various stretching techniques have been confusing and contradictory. However, most information on this subject tends to support the use of proprioceptive neuromuscular facilitation techniques for providing the best improvements in flexibility.

▶ The authors point out that there are a number of different proprioceptive neuromuscular facilitation techniques currently being used for stretching. These include the slow-reversal-hold, contract-relax, and hold-relax techniques. All involve some combination of alternating contraction and relaxation of both agonist and antagonist muscles, and usually involve a 10-second pushing phase followed by a 10-second relaxation phase.

"Using the hamstring stretching technique as an example, the slow-reversal-hold technique would be done as follows: with the individual lying on his/her back, with the knee extended and the ankle flexed to 90°, a partner passively flexes the leg at the hip joint to the point where slight discomfort is felt in the muscle. At this point, the individual pushes against the partner's resistance by contracting the hamstring muscle. After pushing for 10 seconds, the hamstring muscles are relaxed and the agonist quadriceps muscle is contracted while the partner applies passive pressure to further stretch the antagonist quadriceps. This should move the leg so that there is increased hip joint flexion. The relaxation phase lasts for 10 seconds, at which time the individual again pushes against the partner's resistance beginning at this new joint angle. This push-relax sequence is typically repeated at least 3 times.

The contract-relax and hold-relax techniques are variations on the slow-reversal hold method. In the contract-relax method, the hamstrings are isotonically contracted so that the leg moves toward the floor during the push phase. The hold-relax method involves an isometric hamstring contraction against immovable resistance during the push phase. During the relaxation phase, both techniques involve relaxation of hamstrings and quadriceps while the hamstrings are passively stretched. This same basic PNF technique can be used to stretch any muscle in the body."—Joseph S. Torg, M.D.

---

**Nontraumatic Injuries in Amateur Long Distance Bicyclists**
Barry D. Weiss (Univ. of Arizona)
Am. J. Sports Med. 13:187–192, May–June 1985                    2–25

All 132 participants in a 500-mile, 8-day bicycle tour were surveyed by questionnaire to analyze the demographics and bicycling experience of the riders and to determine the incidence of nontraumatic injuries. Riders who developed significant symptoms were interviewed, examined, or both. Eighty-six percent of riders responded to the survey. Mean age was 41.4 years. They rode an average of 95.8 miles per week on a routine basis, but the majority were new to long-distance touring. Most were healthy, but 5% had serious cardiovascular disease and bicycled as part of a rehabilitation program.

The most common nontraumatic injury was buttocks pain (32.8%); 4 riders had skin ulceration of the buttocks. Knee problems occurred in 20.7% of riders. Patellar pain syndromes and lateral knee symptoms were the most common. One cyclist withdrew from the tour because of knee pain. Neck-shoulder pain occurred in 20.4% of the riders. Groin numbness and palmar pain or paresthesias each occurred in about 10%. Other, less common problems were foot and ankle symptoms and sunburn.

It was difficult to identify factors that predisposed to or prevented buttocks symptoms. The use of padded bicycling pants was not related to the development of buttocks symptoms. Surprisingly, cyclists who used a padded seat were more likely to report buttocks symptoms. Although a history of bicycling-related buttocks problems increased the chance of having problems on this trip, cyclists with such a history were not more likely to use padded seats. Thus, the statistical association between padded seats and buttocks symptoms is unexplained.

Handlebar palsy (palm numbness) and pudendal neuropathy (groin numbness) have been well described. These problems occur to some degree in about 32% to 45% of riders and are of significant severity in 10%. No bicyclist discontinued riding because of palmar neuropathy, suggesting that although it is the most common nontraumatic bicycle-related problem described in the literature, it is a relatively unimportant cause of disability. Pudendal neuropathy, however, was more important; nearly 2% of riders had to discontinue riding temporarily because of this symptom. Possible causes of neck and shoulder pain include road vibration transmitted through the handlebars and arms to the shoulder girdle, hyperextension of the neck in normal riding position, and the wearing of a bicycling helmet that obscures part of the upper field of vision, forcing excessive neck hypertension.

Sunburn was felt to be significant by 5.4% of riders in this study. Protection against sunburn can be obtained by using a para-aminobenzoic acid (PABA) sunscreen. However, athletic performance may be diminished by the use of PABA sunscreens, especially in hot, dry climates. Sunscreens decrease the ability to evaporate sweat from the skin surface, resulting in increased body temperature and decreased performance. Body areas most affected by sunburn in bicyclists are the arms, thighs, and lips. If the sunscreen is applied only to these areas, athletic performance should not be significantly impaired.

**Stretching Exercise and Soccer: Effect of Stretching on Range of Motion in the Lower Extremity in Connection With Soccer Training**
M. H. L. Möller, B. E. Öberg, and J. Gillquist (Univ. of Linköping, Sweden)
Int. J. Sports Med. 6:50–52, February 1985                                    2–26

Soccer is the most popular game in the world, with more than 22 million participants. Muscle tightness predisposes to strain, and the question has been raised of whether soccer training itself can lead to muscle shortness. The effect of a single session of training on flexibility was studied in 48 soccer players aged 18 to 29 years from senior male teams. Range of joint motion was measured before, immediately after, and 24 hours after a regular training session. Sixteen subjects stretched for 10 minutes at the end of the session, and 9 others stretched in place of the usual warm-up. Contract-relax stretching was performed. The training session lasted 90 minutes.

Most ranges of motion were reduced after training without stretching, and all motions were reduced at 24 hours. After early stretching there were no reductions in range of motion. Subjects who stretched at the end of the training session had increased hip extension and flexion and increased knee flexion. Hip extension 24 hours after the session was better in subjects who stretched at the outset than when stretching ended the training session.

Stretching can counter the decrease in range of joint motions associated with regular soccer training. Contract-relax stretching may prevent certain types of injury such as muscle strains. For most ranges of motion, stretching is equally effective when done before or after the training session. The exercises are easy to teach and to perform.

▶ The significance of this study is that a single session of stretching exercises was shown to be effective in countering the decrease in range of joint motions, normally caused by a standard soccer workout. The stretching consisted of isometric contracting followed by relaxation and then passive lengthening of the muscle. All of us recognize the immediate benefits of a stretching session before beginning to play, but for a single session to produce benefits 24 hours later is surprising.—Col. James L. Anderson, PE.D.

# 3   Sports Injury

## Head, Neck, and Spine Injuries

### The Influence of Bandages on the Force of Impact of a Boxing Punch

B. Roy, M. Bernier-Cardou, A. Cardou, and A. Plamondon (University of Laval and University of Montreal)
J. Appl. Sports Sci. 9:181–187, December 1984
3–1

In boxing, a combat sport, a punch may be directed to the head as well as the torso of the opponent. Considering the severity of resulting injuries, the limit of tolerance of repeated impact is an important consideration. The purpose of the present study was to compare the force of impact attained with the bare fist as compared to that obtained with bandages of gauze and diachylon.

Twenty-two boxers were selected. The force of impact was measured on a Kistler plate covered by a synthetic mattress. A system of photoelectric cells was used to measure the velocity of the punch. Each boxer delivered 10 punches, barehanded as well as equipped with four types of bandages.

This study confirmed that not only was the force of impact influenced by bandaging, but that the type of bandage is clearly significant, allowing an augmentation of impact beyond 27%, the force increasing in relation to thickness of bandage. Diachylon was found to be of greater influence than gauze. It would seem that the bandaging increases the rigidity of the hand and facilitates the transfer of force.

▶ An interesting study that suggests a possible way to decrease the violence of boxing. It is interesting to note that the impact velocities in all four experimental situations ranged from 10.2 to 10.6 m/sec, whereas for the unbandaged fist it was 10.0 m/sec. The force, on the other hand, ranged from 2,722 to 3,063 N for the bandaged fists as compared with 2,400 N for the unbandaged fist. The next logical step is to determine the effect of different weight gloves.—Joseph S. Torg, M.D.

### The Damaging Punch

J. Atha, M. R. Yeadon, J. Sandover, and K. C. Parsons (Univ. of Technology, Leicestershire, England)
Br. Med. J. 291:1756–1757, Dec. 21/28, 1985
3–2

Brain damage from boxing results from both the cumulative effects of sustained exposure and from the acute effects of severe blows. The properties of the punch of a professional heavyweight boxer were investigated as the subject punched an instrumented padded target mass, suspended as a ballistic pendulum. The subject was the highest rated boxer of his weight class in Britain. Seven maximum punches were recorded following preliminary work.

Within one-tenth of a second the punch had traveled about 0.5 m and reached a velocity on impact of 8.9 m/sec. A peak force on impact of 0.4 ton was achieved within 14 msec of contact; it represented a blow of 0.63 ton to the human head. The impulse generated acceleration of 53 gm in the target head. An equivalent blow would be delivered by a padded wooden mallet with a 13-pound mass if swung at 20 miles per hour.

The chance of an opponent avoiding such a blow after seeing it coming are slim. Protection instead depends chiefly on the use of random evasion strategies or anticipation based on earlier clues. The peak delivered force exceeds that required to fracture facial bones. The characteristics of the punch as recorded in this study are consistent with the known medical consequences of boxing.

▶ The velocity of fist at impact was 8.9 m/sec. Unterhamscheidt (in Vinken P. J., Bruyn G. W. (eds.): *Hand Book of Clinical Neurology* 23. Amsterdam, North Holland, 1975, pp. 527–593) reported the effects of impacts on animals. A representative mass traveling with a velocity of 7 m/sec produced loss of consciousness, while those over 10.5 m/sec caused extended unconsciousness. Thus, it appears that the safety margin that separates sport from potential catastrophe is small.—Joseph S. Torg, M.D.

---

**Epidemiology, Pathomechanics, and Prevention of Athletic Injuries to the Cervical Spine**
Joseph S. Torg (Univ. of Pennsylvania)
Med. Sci. Sports Exerc. 17:295–303, 1985                                              3–3

---

Athletic injuries to the cervical spine associated with quadriplegia most often result from axial loading. Appropriate rule changes and education of the public can help minimize these injuries. The cervical spine is repeatedly exposed to potentially injurious energy levels in contact activities such as tackle football. Axial load injuries occur when the neck is slightly flexed and the normal cervical lordosis is straightened, converting the spine to a segmented column. Rule changes governing use of the helmet have been associated with a reduction in cervical spine fracture-dislocations and injuries causing permanent quadriplegia. The helmet itself likely is a secondary factor.

Cervical spine injuries also result from trampoline and minitrampoline activities, as well as from other sports. Public education is important to reduce the dangers of diving. Diving is best restricted to a properly maintained and supervised pool where the depth is measured and marked. Severe cervical spine injuries are emerging in ice hockey, most often resulting from a push or check where the player strikes the boards with the top of the head while the neck is slightly flexed. Player education and enforcement of rules prohibiting boarding and cross-checking may reduce these injuries.

### The National Football Head and Neck Injury Registry: 14-Year Report on Cervical Quadriplegia, 1971 Through 1984

Joseph S. Torg, Joseph J. Vegso, Brian Sennett, and Marianne Das (Univ. of Pennsylvania)

JAMA 254:3439–3443, Dec. 27, 1985                3–4

Experience with tackle football serves to illustrate how a knowledge of mechanisms of injury to the cervical spine can aid the development of effective preventive measures. Quadriplegia in 6 of 8 football players examined in Pennsylvania and New Jersey in 1975 was found to result from a defensive back using the head as a battering ram when tackling an opponent. A decrease in deaths accompanied the increase in quadriplegia, suggesting that improved protection from the helmet-face mask unit was responsible. Rule changes to prevent spearing were instituted as a result.

A marked reduction in cervical spine injuries and permanent cervical quadriplegia has occurred since the institution of rules banning both spearing and use of the top of the helmet as the initial contact point in tackling at both the high school and college levels. Changes over time are shown in Figure 3–1. The rule changes were effective starting in the 1976 season. Permanent quadriplegia declined from 34 at this time to 5 cases in 1984. Compression or axial loading continues to be the mechanism causing the highest proportion of quadriplegias and cervical fractures, dislocations, or subluxations.

Catastrophic head and neck injuries in football are related to axial loading of the cervical spine, and appropriate rules changes have significantly decreased such injuries. Continued research and education of

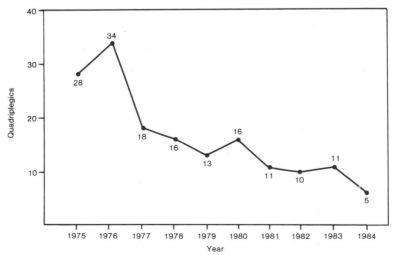

**Fig 3–1.**—Yearly incidence of permanent cervical quadriplegia for all levels of participation demonstrate significant decrease in 1977, the first year after the rule changes. Total quadriplegia has continued to decline to a low of five injuries in 1984. (Courtesy of Torg, J.S., et al.: JAMA 254:3439–3443, Dec. 27, 1985; copyright 1985, American Medical Association.)

coaches and players are essential. Axial loading of the spine probably also causes serious injuries in diving, rugby, ice hockey, and gymnastics. Appropriate alterations in equipment or playing techniques might also reduce the occurrence of cervical spine injuries in these sports.

▶ The theme of Digests 3–3 and 3–4 is basically "an ounce of prevention is worth a pound of cure." However, when dealing with cervical quadriplegics care must be measured in tons rather than pounds. The fact that an accurate description of the mechanism responsible for a particular injury transcends simple academic interest is emphasized. In order that appropriate measures be implemented to effect prevention, the manner in which injury occurs must be accurately defined. Similarly, erroneous concepts regarding injury causations as well as the willingness to accept "freak injury" as the cause of catastrophe only act to impede the implementation of effective preventive measures. Also, anecdotal examples and unusual case reports must be examined critically, lest inaccuracies become established or "fact."—Joseph S. Torg, M.D.

---

### Head and Neck Injuries in College Football: An Eight-Year Analysis

John P. Albright, Edward Mcauley, Robert K. Martin, Edward T. Crowley, and Danny T. Foster (Univ. of Iowa)
Am. J. Sports Med. 13:147–152, May–June 1985                    3–5

---

Head and neck injuries were analyzed in 342 college football players at a single institution between 1975 and 1982. All freshmen players were screened for a past history of head and neck injuries and for abnormalities of the cervical spine on physical examination and x-ray films. By recording all head injuries and those neck injuries with time loss, incidence rates and patterns of injury incurred in college competition were determined.

A total of 175 head and neck injuries were sustained by 100 players over the 8-year period. Players with abnormal findings on screening were twice as likely to have a head or neck injury at some point in their college careers as players with normal findings. The greater the degree of abnormality on freshman screening examination, the more severe the neck injury in college was likely to be. Of all players in the study, 29% sustained a head or neck injury during their college careers. The probability of a subsequent head or neck injury escalated sharply after a single incident. The overall incidence of injury was found to have been dramatically reduced over the 8 years.

The 29% incidence of collegiate head and neck injury study is expectedly higher than that reported by others. It was known that there was wide interinstitutional variation in the levels of sensitivity for reporting injuries. In most instances, the variation was probably due to underreporting reflected by lack of interest, insufficient manpower, or simply poor record keeping. This study was limited to a single team studied prospectively over several years by the same medical personnel who diligently reported all head and neck injuries according to an accepted and sensitive definition of injury.

Perhaps most important is that a considerable reduction of head and neck injuries over the 8 years of collegiate competition was documented. The decline in the national totals for catastrophic injuries to the head and neck has been associated with enforcement of National Operating Committee on Standards for Athletic Equipment safety standards for protective equipment and the rule changes that penalized the "spear-tackler." Unfortunately, though a similar decline in nonfatal head and neck injuries was also documented in this study group, establishment of the causal relations for the less severe injuries appears to be more complex.

The injury reduction in this study may be attributed to several important factors. The demonstrated reduction of pathologic findings in entering freshmen can be associated with lower injury risk in college. At least two of the three rule changes since 1975 may be temporally related to the decline in injuries to the blocker and tackler. Several factors under control of the coaching and medical staff may have affected the risk of injury to college football players.

▶ The "Iowa Study" has been quoted and used by many of us in sports medicine to bring about changes in rules and equipment as well as changes in blocking and tackling techniques. The original study really opened our eyes to the damaging effects upon the cervical spine that occur when the helmet and face mask are used as a "battering ram." It again gives me the opportunity to emphasize that hands and arms and chests and shoulders are used for blocking and tackling and that the helmet and face mask should never be the initial point of contact. If coaches will teach the proper method of blocking and tackling, injuries to the head and neck can be reduced.—Frank George, A.T.C., P.T.

---

**Sports Following Spinal Surgery in the Young Athlete**
Lyle J. Micheli (Harvard Univ.)
Clin. Orthop. 198:152–157, September 1985                    3–6

---

Decisions to allow young athletes to resume sports activity after injury or surgery always must be individualized. Both the level of spine involved and the extent of spinal fusion are relevant considerations, whether decompressive surgery or spinal fusion is undertaken. Catastrophic sequelae are possible with premature or inappropriate resumption of sports participation after spinal surgery or injury. Any associated neurologic injury must be taken into account. Computed tomography aids assessment of the residual neural canal and its capacity. The part of the spine on which arthrodesis has been performed can be evaluated for both stability and the residual capacity of the neural canal and foramina.

Heavy-contact sports usually are prohibited after disk surgery on the cervical spine. Fusion, however, is not a contraindication if the segments above and below the level of fusion are mechanically stable. Contact sports and gymnastics usually are not allowed after scoliosis fusion in the thoracolumbar spine. There may be an increased risk of spinal stress from either single-impact macrotrauma or repeated microtrauma at the segments adjoining the long segment of stiffened spine. Less limitation may be necessary after more confined fusion for vertebral compression or burst fracture or after resection of a benign neoplasm.

Most surgeons allow participation in sports after lumbar laminectomy if there is a full return of pain-free strength and flexibility of the spine. Spinal stability is not compromised by the procedure, but resumption of vigorous contact sports activity may entail a risk of accelerated degenerative change in the spine. Heavy activity usually is prohibited for a year after arthrodesis of spondylolysis or spondylolisthesis at the lumbosacral junction, until solid fusion is present.

► Should an athlete return to competition after a spinal injury or surgery? The author has given us some excellent guidelines to follow and has stressed that each case must be individualized and judged on its own. We must be careful in our rehabilitation and weight training programs that the spine is not jeopardized and that the healing that has occurred is not undone.—Frank George, A.T.C., P.T.

---

**Concussion in Contact Sports and Importance of Mouthguards in Protection**
Patrick J. Chapman (Univ. of Queensland)
Aust. J. Sci. Med. Sports 17:23–27, March 1985                                              3–7

---

The mandible occupies a prominent and exposed position in the facial skeleton and is therefore a common site for intentional and unintentional impact. Mandibular impacts usually result in concussion by causing linear or angular acceleration effects on the brain. Participation in many sports carries some risk of head injury, from mild concussion to intracerebral hemorrhage, but the risk is particularly high in contact sports.

Boxing is the contact sport mainly associated with a high incidence of concussion. In boxing, blows to the mandible produce most knockouts, and a knockout blow renders the boxer temporarily concussed for at least 10 seconds, often longer. A study of injuries occurring in 20,505 professional boxers showed that the incidence of concussion was 51% of all injuries, involving roughly 1 boxer out of 7. Oelman et al. reported that concussion comprised 62% of boxing injuries requiring hospital admission, with facial fractures comprising 28% and facial lacerations 15%. Sudden loss of consciousness in sport may also result from noncerebral causes (impact to the neck, precordium, and epigastric region) by interference with normal cardiac rhythm due to vagal stimulation.

Allowing an athlete to return to competition too soon can have serious consequences, and health may be permanently affected. For persons with mild concussion without amnesia and with immediate recovery, preferably assessed by a physician, it is generally agreed that continuation of play is permissible. An athlete sustaining any more serious type of concussion should not be allowed to resume activity. For patients who have mild concussion with amnesia, no training or playing is advised for 2 days and preferably not until after medical clearance is obtained. For those who have concussion with loss of consciousness for up to 1 minute, no training or playing is advised for a week, and then only after medical clearance is obtained. For losses of consciousness of up to 2 and 3 minutes, similar restrictions apply for 2 and 3 weeks, respectively. Patients who have concussion with loss of consciousness for over 3 minutes should be hospitalized as a precaution.

There are some deficiencies in the immediate management of cases of concussion in sport. The concussed athlete is usually given verbal instructions about precautions that should be followed over the ensuing period and instructions on when to seek an immediate medical opinion. Important instructions should not be given someone who has just been concussed and might still be confused. Wherever possible, an accompanying person

---

**HEAD INJURY CARD**
**Please read carefully**
**Give one to an accompanying person and one to the player.**

NAME . . . . . . . . . . . . . . . . . . . . . . . . . . . . . . . . . AGE . . . . . . . . . .

Sustained . . . . . . . . . . . . . . * concussion at (time) . . . . . . . . . . . . . .

on (date) . . . . . . . . . . . . . . . . . . . . . . . . . . . . . . . . . . . . . . . . . . . . . .

* Insert mild, medium or severe as appropriate.

**IMPORTANT WARNING**
He should be taken to a hospital or a doctor immediately if he:

- develops headache
- becomes restless, irritable or unsteady
- becomes drowsy or cannot easily be roused from sleep
- has a fit (convulsion)
- vomits or becomes nauseated
- or if anything else unusual occurs

For the rest of the day he should:

- rest quietly
- not consume alcohol
- not drive a vehicle.

He should not train or play again without medical clearance by a doctor.

Emergency phone numbers

- Doctor . . . . . . . . . . . . . . . . . . .
- Hospital . . . . . . . . . . . . . . . . . .
- Ambulance . . . . . . . . . . . . . . . .

Fig 3–2.—Head injury card. (Courtesy of Chapman, P.J.: Aust. J. Sci. Med. Sports 17:23–27, March 1985.)

is also given this advice. However, they may not fully understand the instructions either. For this reason the author devised a Head Injury Card (Fig 3–2).

In all amateur boxing (International Amateur Boxing Association rules), use of a mouth guard is mandatory. The custom-type mouth guard made by a dentist provides maximum protection and safety. In neither amateur nor professional boxing is there an international requirement for boxers to use such a type, and often the cheaper, but less protective types are worn. In the United States, since 1973, all high school and college football players have been required to wear mouth guards. Although it is not compulsory at the professional level of the sport, most professional players wear mouth guards because they have become accustomed to wearing them in high school and college competition. The use of mouth guards should be encouraged in all contact sports, as its most important value is its concussion-saving effect after an impact on the mandible. This advantage alone should make the wearing of mouth guards compulsory in all contact sports.

▶ After an athlete has suffered a concussion, he should never be sent home alone. If we do not admit him overnight to our Health Services, we insist that he remain with a roommate. This decision is based on the severity of the concussion and the recovery of the athlete. A similar card to the one used by the authors is issued to the athlete and his roommate. Concussions are a serious injury and should be treated as such.—Frank George, A.T.C., P.T.

**Pollex Valgus: Orthopaedic Management for Ulnar Instability of the Metacarpophalangeal Joint of the Thumb**
Kent E. Timm (St. Luke's Hosp., Saginaw, Mich.)
J. Orthop. Sports Phys. Ther. 6:334–342, May–June 1985          3–8

Pollex valgus (PV) includes phalangeal joint lesions that result from the hyperpositional forces of abduction and extension acting upon the thumb. The lesions may involve ligament sprain or rupture, avulsion fracture, joint locking, or the Kaplan or Stener injuries that disrupt thumb biomechanics. All lesions threaten joint integrity and become manifest as ulnar instability and decreased functional ability of normal index-pollex pinch activities.

Orthopedic management of PV involves clinical evaluation to distinguish between sprains, which require only conservative treatment by splinting or taping, and more serious lesions, which require operation for anatomical correction. Definitive distinction of lesions that need operation is achieved through resistive testing with signs of inability to stabilize the thumb against a hyperpositional stress and inability to maintain the position of index-pollex pinch. Arthrography and roentgenography are used to confirm these results.

Operation is recommended for all PV lesions, except ligament sprains, to assure anatomical alignment for proper tissue reparation. Improper healing results in ligament elongation that jeopardizes metacarpophalangeal (MP) joint stability and predisposes to recurrence of a Kaplan or Stener lesion. All of the following techniques, which are appropriate for any type of PV lesion, must be undertaken within 2 weeks of injury to assure surgical success. Classic operations include primary suture of a ruptured ligament, direct repair of the ulnar collateral ligament (UCL) for a Stenar lesion, Kirscher wire fixation of an avulsed bone fragment, and transfer of the extensor indicis tendon to the extensor expansion for a Kaplan lesion. More-contemporary approaches include suture of the UCL flap to the volar plate for a Stener lesion, transfer of a segment of the adductor aponeurosis to reconstruct a ruptured ligament, and distal advancement of the adductor pollicis insertion on the extensor expansion for a Kaplan lesion.

Operation is followed by cast immobilization for 4 weeks. The cast is applied from thumb tip to elbow, with the thumb positioned in 30 degrees of flexion, and is carefully molded about the web space and metacarpal to prevent any MP joint motion. The cast is followed by an orthoplast spica splint for another 2 to 4 weeks. Thumb spica taping may follow splinting for injury prophylaxis during functional activities and rehabilitation.

Active exercise is aimed at resumption of functional neuromuscular activity at the MP joint after operation and immobilization. The primary goals of rehabilitation are restoration of normal MP joint mobility and strength with specific application to the thenar actions of opposition and prehension. Opposition is restored through self-performed range-of-motion exercises involving approximation of the thumb to the tips and bases of the fingers. Active opposition is supplemented by cardinal plane range-of-motion exercises to counteract any deficits of MP joint flexion-extension or abduction-adduction and by resumption of normal prehensile activities. Hold-relax techniques may be added to increase mobility if MP joint motions are severely restricted.

Joint mobilization complements active exercise and is used if normal MP joint mobility does not return through range-of-motion, hold-relax, or functional activity exercises. Joint mobilization begins with mobility testing to assess the extent of joint restriction after immobilization. Treatment starts with distraction, progressing from slack to stretch grades, to remedy MP joint hypomobility. Distraction is followed by dorsal, ventral, radial, or ulnar glides, or a combination of these, depending on patient tolerance and the nature of accessory motion restriction. Abduction and extension are usually quite restricted and require radial and dorsal glides, respectively.

▶ All thumb injuries must be carefully evaluated by the athletic trainer and if there is any instability, the athlete must be referred to an orthopedist. The author describes a number of exercises including joint mobilization techniques to restore normal motion to the thumb that has undergone surgery and immobilization. The thumb should also be taped for protection when the athlete is allowed to return to activity.—Frank George, A.T.C., P.T.

### The Biomechanics of Helmets and Helmet Removal

Richard D. Meyer and William W. Daniel (Univ. of Alabama)
J. Trauma 25:329–332, April 1985
3–9

The American College of Surgeons has designed a method for helmet removal based on a two-person technique. The authors designed a study to visualize the cervical spine statically and dynamically in subjects wearing helmets and during helmet removal.

Seventeen volunteers were used for the static (nonfluoroscopic) examination, with the cervical spine x-rayed in helmet in three positions: supine-lateral without helmet; supine-lateral with helmet to determine changes in lordotic curve; and upright-lateral in forced hyperextension to determine posterior helmet contact points. Eight volunteers were examined with videotaped cross-table and lateral fluoroscopy of the cervical spine during actual helmet removal to compare the one-person and the two-person techniques (Fig 3–3). Five of these subjects were also studied with a folded sheet or a folded motorcycle jacket elevating the shoulders. Examinations were performed with open face of full coverage helmets.

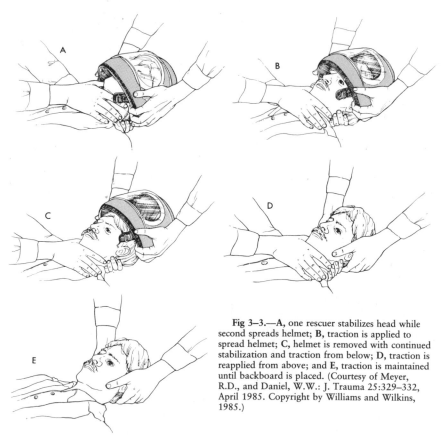

Fig 3–3.—A, one rescuer stabilizes head while second spreads helmet; B, traction is applied to spread helmet; C, helmet is removed with continued stabilization and traction from below; D, traction is reapplied from above; and E, traction is maintained until backboard is placed. (Courtesy of Meyer, R.D., and Daniel, W.W.: J. Trauma 25:329–332, April 1985. Copyright by Williams and Wilkins, 1985.)

The lateral spine films of helmeted and unhelmeted volunteers were compared. There was a tendency toward increased flexion, averaging 10 degrees between C4 and C5; however, 5 subjects were reexamined with slight traction on the helmets. When the forced-hyperextension films were reviewed, in no instance did the posterior lip of the helmet make contact with the neck above the spinous process of C6. Typically, the helmet touched the neck at the level of T1; the range was C6 to T2, with smaller sizes making contact higher, 1 at C6 and 2 at C7. Four others touched at T1 and 1 at T2. Videotaped fluoroscopy resulted in an image too "soft" for accurate measurements. However, there was no difference in cervical motion when the two techniques were compared. The most important observation was a mean flexion of 10 degrees for the occiput of the helmet to clear the skull occiput unless the shoulders were elevated.

Since in the forced-hyperextension study the larger helmets tended to impinge caudad to C6, the belief that cervical spine injuries are caused by a guillotine effect of the posterior helmet lip is not supported. The helmet is an excellent device through which to apply traction; its removal is not required in the field unless airway or fire problems are present. There appears to be no measurable difference between the American College of Surgeons two-person technique and the one-person technique regarding cervical spine motion in the normal subject. Cervical motion occurs with both modalities unless the shoulders are elevated, in which case there is virtually no motion.

▶ This study using motorcycle helmets substantiates the findings of Virgin (*Am. J. Sports Med.* 8:310–317, 1980) using football helmets that the "guillotine" theory of Schneider (*JAMA* 177:362, 1961) is in error. Specifically, Schneider postulated that in the helmeted football player extreme hyperextension resulted in impingement of the posterior rim of the helmet against the mid-cervical spine with fracture and dislocation resulting. This erroneous concept has been used by plaintiffs' attorneys in the early litigation against the various football helmet manufacturers. Fortunately, scientific evidence has prevailed over misconception. Today, it is recognized that cervical spine injuries from football associated with quadriplegia are due to the axial loading mechanism (Torg, et al.: *JAMA* 254:3439–3443, Dec. 27, 1985).—Joseph S. Torg, M.D.

---

**Alterations in Head Dynamics With the Addition of a Hockey Helmet and Face Shield Under Inertial Loading**
A. W. Smith, P. J. Bishop, and R. P. Wells (Univ. of Waterloo, Ontario)
Can. J. Appl. Sports Sci. 10:68–74, June 1985                                    3–10

---

At least 48 cases of spinal cord injury directly related to participation in ice hockey have occurred since 1976. Among these, 21 players sustained permanent paralysis below the level of the injury. Eighteen of the reported cases of cervical spine trauma followed a push or check, from the rear in 14.

The effect of a hockey helmet and face shield on the head and neck during inertial loading was studied. A Hybrid III Anthropometric Test Dummy (ATD) was struck from both the front and the rear by a spring-loaded, instrumented striker moving at 2.9 m per second (Fig 3–4). Data were collected from a triaxial force transducer mounted at the atlanto-occipital (a-o) junction of the ATD (Fig 3–5), by a load cell in the striker, and by cinematography (250 frames per second). Angular kinematics of the head and moments of force about the a-o junction were determined, besides impact force levels.

Compared with the barehead condition, addition of a helmet and face shield caused an increase in head angular displacement of 20% to 40% but did not affect head angular acceleration. Axial and shear forces at the a-o junction did not change significantly with addition of a helmet and shield. A triphasic pattern was evident for the neck moments. This included a small phase that represented a seating of the head form on the nodding blocks of the uppermost ATD neck sement, and two larger phases of opposite polarity that represented motion of the head relative to the trunk during the first 350 msec after impact. No substantial differences were apparent between the helmeted and the nonhelmeted trials. The magnitudes of forces and moments found were well within tolerance levels reported by others.

Addition of a helmet and face shield to the head of the ATD resulted in increased angular displacement, particularly in rear impacts. However, it did not appear that the magnitudes involved are the cause of increased cervical spine trauma. Angular accelerations were not substantially dif-

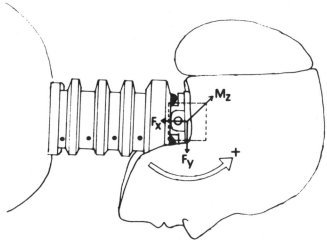

$+F_x$ : Compression

$+F_y$ : Dislocates Anteriorly

$+M_z$ : Resists Flexion

Fig 3–4.—Orientation of ATD reference frame. (Courtesy of Smith, A.W., et al.: Can. J. Appl. Sports Sci. 10:68–74, June 1985.)

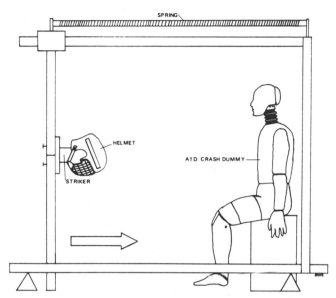

**Fig 3–5.**—Experimental setup. (Courtesy of Smith, A.W., et al.: Can. J. Appl. Sports Sci. 10:68–74, June 1985.)

ferent between trials, and the recorded forces were well below known tissue tolerances for injuries to the neck, supporting the findings of Bishop et al. Addition of a helmet and face shield does not predispose the player to risk of cervical injury. It appeared to increase sharply both peak axial and peak shear forces at the a-o junction in both chest and rear impact situations in this study. However, no obvious trends were evident for either head condition with respect to neck moments.

Further research is necessary to examine fully the hockey-related instances of cervical spine trauma. The most promising direction may lie in more complete simulations of reported injury conditions, beginning with initial impact and following through to subsequent collisions with boards, goal posts, and other players.

► The design of this particular study does not reproduce the injury mechanism responsible for hockey cervical spine injury. Tater (*Can. J. Neurol. Sci.* 11:34–41, 1984) reported six cases with cervical vertebral body burst fractures with associated quadriplegia in which the mechanism involved a collision of the helmet and head against the boards with axial loading of the cervical spine. A national survey of spinal injuries in hockey players by the Canadian Committee on Prevention of Spinal Injuries reported on 42 cervical spine injuries in which all injuries resulted from a collision between the player's head and the boards with the neck flexed (Tator and Edmonds: *Can. Med. Assoc. J.* 130:875–880, 1984). It appears that the mechanism is one of axial loading similar to that described for American football (Torg: *JAMA* 241:1477–1479, 1979). The testing apparatus in this study exerts a "whiplash" effect on the ATD crash dummy. Thus, on the basis of the data, a more reasonable conclusion would be that the helmet and face shield do not predispose to whiplash. The data do not relate to axial loading injuries or the role of the helmet and face shield in causation of these injuries.—Joseph S. Torg, M.D.

## Upper Extremity Injuries

### Osteoarticular Injuries of the Hand Caused by Punching
V. Mitz, F. Gasnier, C. Sokolow, and R. Vilain (Hôpital Boucicaut, Paris)
Ann. Chir. Plast. Esthet. 1:69–77, 1985                                    3–11

Although generally considered a relatively trivial gesture, punching an adversary exposes the aggressor to considerable risk of serious complications. Osteoarticular fractures and infections may have serious consequences, from loss of function of one or more fingers to amputation because of sepsis. During the past 2 years surgical treatment was chosen in 19 of 50 emergency cases, all men. The average age was 29½ years. There were 9 fractures, all involving the 5th metacarpal, associated in one instance with fracture of the shaft of the 4th metacarpal. Dislocations normally take the form of anterior displacement of the head with projection into the palm, leading to severe functional impairment if the angle exceeds 30 degrees. The radial rotational displacement prevents correct folding of the finger and reduces the prehensile strength of the hand. An overall setback of the 5th digit is noted. In the present series all patients with severe displacement underwent reduction under general anesthesia and immobilization.

In 8 of 10 cases open wounds led to severe arthritis, affecting the metacarpophalangeal joint in 6, and leading to permanent partial disability in 2. These wounds are caused by the impact of the closed fist on the victim's teeth and are often very small. They are ignored by the patient and even by the physician until they become purulent. If not treated within 24 hours, extensive cutaneous wound care may be required, including a flap to cover the joint, resection of the extensor muscle, as well as articular resection. The classification used as basis for the treatment distinguishes: (1) blunt wounds requiring wound care and suturing under local anesthesia, (2) open wounds requiring wound care, exploration and suturing under general anesthesia, (3) joint wounds treated within 24 hours by washing, joint preservation, and minimal immobilization, and (4) osteoarthritis, treated after 24 hours, requiring section of the joint, antibiotics, and immobilization.

### A Review of Scaphoid Fracture Healing in Competitive Athletes
John N. Riester, Bruce E. Baker, John F. Mosher, and Donald Lowe (Syracuse Univ.)
Am. J. Sports Med. 13:159–161, May–June 1985                              3–12

Since 1973 athletes with scaphoid fractures have been allowed to participate in contact sports with cast immobilization. Modified immobilization has been necessary where amateur sports rules prohibit unyielding immobilization below the elbow. Data on 13 patients with 14 scaphoid fractures were reviewed. All participated in contact sports, most often football. A short arm thumb spica cast was placed with the wrist in neutral position; it included the thumb to the level of the interphalangeal joint. Sports activities were resumed immediately and without restrictions. The casts were padded. A custom-made Silastic short arm thumb spica was applied before competition, and a new plaster made afterwards. In football players the procedure was repeated once a week.

All fractures of the middle third of the scaphoid that were treated early healed. The average time of immobilization was 6 months. Two of 3 fractures of the proximal third of the bone failed to heal. One patient healed after bone grafting but had refracture during football play. Most football injuries were in defensive players.

Undisplaced middle-third scaphoid fractures in athletes can be immobilized for competition in contact sports using a custom-made plaster or Silastic cast without compromising healing. Internal fixation of acute stable scaphoid fractures in athletes is not indicated. The outcome is impaired more by failure of internal fixation than by failure of nonoperative treatment.

▶ The authors have presented results of an interesting approach to what can be a vexing problem. In view of the failure to include such important data as Syracuse University's football won and lost record over this period, it does not appear that this may necessarily be the recommended mode of management for this problem.—Joseph S. Torg, M.D.

## Arthroscopy of the Elbow
James R. Andrews and William G. Carson (Hughston Orthopaedic Clinic, Columbus, Ga., and Tulane Univ.)
Arthroscopy 1:97–107, 1985                                           3–13

Diagnostic arthroscopy (DA) of the elbow was performed on 24 patients (21 males), aged 13 to 60 years; 16 were involved in athletics. Diagnostic arthroscopy was carried out in 7 patients, DA and open arthrotomy in 5, and DA and operative arthroscopy in 12. The last 12 patients comprise the basis of this study. Mean follow-up for these 12 patients was 10.6 months (range, 2 to 16).

TECHNIQUE.—General anesthesia is used. The patient lies supine with the forearm in a prefabricated wrist gauntlet connected to a overhead pulley and tied off at the end of the operating table. The entire arm is allowed to hang freely over the side of the operating table with the elbow flexed about 90 degrees. This allows excellent access to both the medial and the lateral aspects of the elbow, and the forearm may be freely pronated and supinated.

The anterolateral portal is used for the first entrance into the joint. Maximum capsular distention is achieved by injecting saline initially; after the first portal is established and the arthroscope is in place, injection of fluid directly through the arthroscope allows adequate distention. With the elbow flexed 90 degrees, an 18-

gauge needle is placed about 3 cm distal and 1 cm anterior to the lateral epicondyle. This point is just anterior to the radial head, which can be palpated by pronating and supinating the forearm. It is important that the larger instruments, such as the arthroscope and cannulas, be introduced with the joint maximally distended. This displaces the antecubital neurovascular structures anteriorly and allows more space above the bony epicondyles for placement of instruments.

Once the arthroscope is in place through the anterolateral portal, instruments may be placed in the anteromedial portal under direct visualization via the arthroscope. With the elbow flexed 90 degrees, this portal is initiated by placing an 18-gauge needle about 2 cm anterior and 2 cm distal to the medial epicondyle, aiming directly toward the center of the joint. A posterolateral portal may sometimes be necessary. The entry point is about 3 cm proximal to the olecranon tip just posterior and superior to the lateral epicondyle, near the lateral margin of the triceps. This portal is most easily established by extending the elbow to relax the triceps and inserting an 18-gauge needle at the appropriate landmarks and aiming for the olecranon fossa.

Among the 12 patients who underwent surgical arthroscopy of the elbow, removal of loose bodies produced the best objective and subjective results. Less acceptable outcomes were achieved by procedures such as capitellum and radial head chondroplasties. Before operation, 50% of patients objectively rated their elbows as satisfactory (excellent or good); after operation, 83% did so. Subjectively, before operation, 17% rated their elbows as acceptable; after operation, 58% did so. The only complication was a transient median nerve palsy caused by extracapsular extravasation of a local anesthetic.

---

**Arthroscopy and Arthroscopic Surgery of the Elbow**
James F. Guhl (Milwaukee)
Orthopedics 8:1290–1296, October 1985                                3–14

---

Arthroscopy and arthroscopic operation of the elbow were performed in 45 cases of 3,300 arthroscopic procedures between 1974 and 1984. Indications established included: loose body removal, treatment of osteochondritis dissecans, synovectomy for nonspecific and rheumatoid synovitis, treatment of some selected fractures, débridement of specific cases of degenerative arthritis, excision of osteophytes and evaluation and treatment of the undiagnosed painful elbow. The choice of two different methods is described; one with the arm on an arm table as for hand operation, and the other with the arm suspended overhead for easier access to the medial side.

There are eight distinct approaches to the elbow joint that are used when the need arises. Three of these (2 anterior approaches, medial and lateral, and the posterior lateral approach) are commonly used and are adequate for 80%–85% of arthroscopic elbow operation. The 2 anterolateral approaches are used for triangulation in the anterior joint. Triangulation to the posterior compartment of the elbow joint for loose bodies or synovitis can be done with two portals from the posterolateral side with the elbow extended. In the posterior elbow joint, a medial portal may be used for a drainage needle, provided the ulnar nerve is avoided. In all of these approaches, one is approximately 1 cm from a neurovascular structure.

Boy, 17, was a championship class swimmer who had a suspected loose body in a painful elbow. Complete arthroscopic examination showed no loose bodies, but there was a fairly marked chronic reactive synovitis and adhesions. A synovectomy and débridement was done and in a few weeks the patient returned to full activity.

Of the 45 cases reviewed, 20 required arthroscopic operation with excellent or good results in 15. There was only 1 complication: an area of numbness due to apparent damage of a sensory branch of the radial nerve. This gradually began to subside in part, although at the time of the report it was not completely improved.

▶ Digests 3–13 and 3–14 on arthroscopy and arthroscopic surgery of the elbow represent the first documentation of this technique. The indications for surgical arthroscopy are well delineated and the technique is most adequately described. The observations of Andrews and Carson that attention to detail is essential in performing a safe, reproducible arthroscopic examination of the elbow, that arthroscopy of the elbow is an effective diagnostic procedure, and that operative elbow arthroscopy is effective in certain elbow disorders appear valid. Surgeons who are considering using this technique should certainly read one or both of the above articles.—Joseph S. Torg, M.D.

---

**Percutaneous Extensor Tenotomy for Chronic Tennis Elbow: An Office Procedure**
Buford Yerger and Thomas Turner (Jackson Bone and Joint Clinic, Jackson, Miss.)
Orthopedics 8:1261–1263, October 1985                                          3–15

Percutaneous extensor tenotomy at the lateral humeral epicondyle is a safe, simple operation that can be performed as an office procedure under local anesthesia for chronic lateral epicondylitis that has failed to respond to adequate conservative treatment. Good or excellent results can be expected in at least 90% of patients.

TECHNIQUE.—Percutaneous extensor tenotomy is simple but attention to a few details is important. Position of the elbow should be 90 degrees with the patient supine. The posterior edge or ridge of the epicondyle should be palpated and a fingernail impression at a point 3/8 inch anterior to this ridge and midpoint of the width of the epicondyle should be made. At this exact point, insert the local anesthetic needle and infiltrate the entire extensor origin. Insert a #11 blade at the needle entrance site and cut through the entire thickness of the extensor origin from proximal to distal in a direction parallel to the axis of the humerus. A defect in the tendon about 1/2 inch wide can then be palpated. While digital pressure is maintained to control the bleeding, which can be brisk, have the patient extend the wrist vigorously to assure slight distal displacement of the tendon. No skin suture is needed.

The series reported here consists of 149 tenotomies on 144 patients with an age distribution of 29 to 67 years. Complications involved synovial fistula or cyst in 4 cases. Reasons for an unsuccessful result include, in 2 cases, suspected posterior interosseous nerve compression syndrome, but these patients did not want more surgical procedure. A total of 102 of the 144 patients had a good or excellent result after follow-up of 1 year or more.

▶ In offering a seemingly simple solution to what sometimes can be a vexing problem, the authors have failed to delineate the "conservative treatment" that results in relief of most cases of tennis elbow as well as the specific indications for operative intervention. Also not defined were the criteria for a "successful result." It is interesting to note that they state that gradual relief of pain can be expected within 3 months in 70% of patients, but 20% require 4 to 6 months and a few took 9 to 12 months for recovery.—Joseph S. Torg, M.D.

---

**Fracture Separation of the Olecranon Ossification Center in Adults**
John Kovach II, Bruce E. Baker, and John F. Mosher (State Univ. of New York Upstate Med. Ctr., Syracuse)
Am. J. Sports Med. 13:105–111, March–April 1985                                  3–16

---

Traumatic disruption of an incompletely fused olecranon physis in adults has been reported only once before. Three men with traumatic disruption of an incompletely fused olecranon physis were encountered. All were former throwing athletes and sustained a direct blow to the dominant elbow. Two patients were competing in football; 1 was injured in a fall.

Man, 32, sustained a direct blow to the dominant left elbow in a fall and noted immediate pain, swelling, and inability to actively extend the elbow. He had previously participated extensively in gymnastics, football, and baseball. A displaced fracture of the olecranon process was found. The fracture surfaces were smooth and sclerotic. Open reduction and tension band internal fixation were carried out. The fracture surfaces consisted of fibrous tissue and were relatively avascular; they were curetted to bleeding cancellous bone. Microscopy showed medullary bone and cartilage fragments and no callus. Full motion was present 6 months later, with no evidence of bone union. At 3 years the patient had an asymptomatic fibrous union with full range of motion. Bone grafting was refused.

Sclerotic fracture margins were found in these cases. The other 2 patients underwent bone grafting and returned to competitive athletics. Fibrous union can be expected after open reduction and internal fixation in these cases, making primary bone grafting advisable, especially in a competitive athlete. The lack of olecranon symptoms previously rules out stress fracture in these cases.

▶ The precursor to this fracture of the olecranon in adults has been previously described as a nonunion of a stress fracture through the olecranon epiphyseal plate as observed in adolescent baseball pitchers (Torg, et al.: *J. Bone Joint*

*Surg.* 59A:264–265, 1977). It is interesting to note that roentgenograms of two of the patients taken 4 and 5 years prior to the fracture separation demonstrate the sclerotic "fracture" line similar to those described as having a nonunion.—Joseph S. Torg, M.D.

**Rupture of the Distal Tendon of the Biceps Brachii: A Biomechanical Study**
Bernard F. Morrey, Linda J. Askew, Kai Nan An, and James H. Dobyns (Mayo Clinic and Found.)
J. Bone Joint Surg. [Am.] 67-A:418–421, March 1985                    3–17

Excellent function has been reported in patients with rupture of the distal tendon of the biceps after attachment of the tendon to the brachialis muscle. Ten patients with rupture of the distal biceps tendon were evaluated. All had lifted a heavy object with the elbow flexed about 90 degrees, and had palpable and visible retraction of the distal end of the biceps, and weakness of elbow flexion and forearm supination. Three patients im-

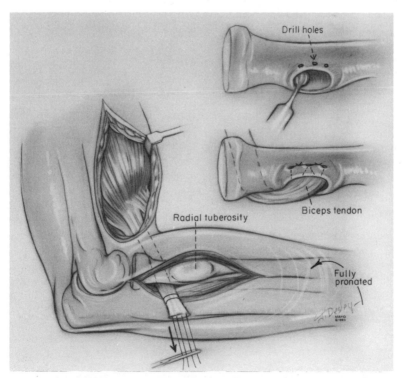

**Fig 3–6.**—A simple modification of the two-incision technique for reinsertion of the biceps tendon into the radial tuberosity uses a burr to excavate the tuberosity. Three holes are placed on the radial side of the tuberosity. The tendon is drawn into the defect and the sutures are tied with the forearm in neutral or supination. (By permission, Mayo Foundation.) (Courtesy of Morrey, B.F., et al.: J. Bone Joint Surg. [Am.] 67-A:418–421, March 1985.)

mediately had the tendon reinserted into the biceps tuberosity by a two-incision technique, and 1 was reinserted via an anterior approach. One patient had excision of a synostosis after initial treatment elsewhere, and 1 had the biceps tendon inserted into the brachialis muscle. Another patient had delayed insertion of the tendon into the tuberosity. Three patients were managed by immobilization and then isometric strengthening exercises.

Most patients had normal strength 1 year after surgery, especially those having immediate reattachment of the ruptured tendon. Three unoperated patients lost significant strength in forearm supination. The only complication was heterotopic ossification at the proximal radioulnar joint in a referred patient who had had the two-incision procedure.

Anatomic reattachment of the ruptured distal biceps tendon seems to be the best approach. A two-incision technique is preferred. The authors use a burr to create a defect in the tuberosity for insertion of the tendon (Fig 3–6), rather than raising a bone flap from the tuberosity. Use of a fascia lata graft has been recommended when surgery is delayed and the tendon retracts into the arm, making direct reattachment difficult.

---

**Rupture of the Distal Tendon of the Biceps Brachii: Operative Versus Non-Operative Treatment**
Bruce E. Baker and David Bierwagen (State Univ. of New York Upstate Med. Ctr., Syracuse)
J. Bone Joint Surg. [Am.] 67-A:414–417, March 1985                          3–18

---

Various results have been reported with the nonoperative management of ruptures of the distal bicipital tendon. Cybex testing was carried out on 13 patients with rupture of the distal tendon of the biceps brachii, 15 months to 6 years after injury. Ten patients had surgical repair by the two-incision technique, followed by 4 weeks of immobilization and then active and passive range of motion exercises for 4 weeks longer, followed by progressive resistance exercises. Three patients had sling immobilization for 3 weeks and then active range of motion movements with minimal resistance for 5 weeks before progressive resistance exercises. Both groups were allowed to return to normal activities after 4 months. All the patients were men; 10 normal men also were evaluated.

The repaired extremity was 13% stronger than the opposite extremity on supination strength testing. The unoperated patients had 27% weakness in the unrepaired dominant upper extremity, representing 40% less strength than in operated patients. Supination endurance was increased 32% in the operated extremity and decreased 47% in conservatively treated patients. Elbow-flexion strength was increased 9% in the operated limb and decreased 21% in unoperated patients. Elbow flexion endurance showed similar trends.

Weakened flexion and supination and diminished endurance can be expected after following conservative management of rupture of the distal tendon of the biceps brachii. The double-incison technique of Boyd and

Anderson appears to be an effective and safe means of restoring function in these cases.

▶ There is a remarkable similarity in the patient groups, operative techniques, complications, and results presented by these two groups of independent observers (Digests 3–17 and 3–18). Also, each study has the same problems with regard to reproducibility of their respective testing methods. Baker and Bierwagen do not report reproducibility determinations and Morrey et al. rely on the reproducibility of the test procedure as documented by McGarvey (*Clin. Orthop.* 185:301–305, 1984). Morrey et al. note that "Rupture of the attachment of the distal tendon of the biceps, even if treated conservatively, does not usually result in an incapacitating loss of strength of flexion of the elbow or supination of the forearm. However, there routinely is a decrease in both those functions and supination strength was only about 60 per cent of normal in our patients who were treated non-operatively. While this may be adequate for many activities, patients with that weakness do complain of fatigue if repeated and forceful supination is necessary. If normal supination is required by a patient, it can be attained only by anatomical reattachment of the ruptured tendon to the tuberosity of the radius."—Joseph S. Torg, M.D.

---

**US of the Biceps Tendon Apparatus**
William D. Middleton, William R. Reinus, William G. Totty, G. Leland Melson, and William A. Murphy (Washington Univ.)
Radiology 157:211–215, October 1985                                          3–19

---

High-resolution real-time sonography of the biceps tendon was performed on 55 male and 25 female patients aged 15 to 82 years (mean age, 50 years) who were referred for shoulder arthrography. Findings on arthrograms and sonograms were compared at the levels of the groove of the biceps tendon and distal tendon.

Sonography and arthrography were both successful in facilitating the evaluation of the bony configuration of the groove of the biceps tendon, but sonography gave a superior image of the biceps tendon within the groove. In 16 patients effusions or swelling of the sheath of the biceps tendon was detected by using sonography; 15 of these patients had associated pathologic conditions elsewhere in the joint. Arthrograms did not disclose an abnormality of a biceps tendon or sheath in any of these patients.

As expected, arthrography was more often superior than sonography for evaluating the bony configuration of the groove of the biceps tendon. In imaging the biceps tendon at this level, sonography was superior more often than arthrography. In a number of cases the two methods were equally successful. In 3 patients, sonography enabled the detection of abnormalities of the biceps tendon or sheath other than effusions of the tendon sheath.

Despite the reported findings at arthrography, in this patient population arthrography was generally unsuccessful for detecting abnormalities of the biceps tendon. On prospective interpretation and retrospective review of all 80 arthrograms, no specific lesions of the biceps tendon or tendon sheath could be diagnosed. A correlation existed between the amount the sheath of the biceps tendon was filled and the presence of shoulder conditions in general, with an increased number of associated lesions occurring in patients with poorer filling. However, there was enough overlap between the groups that grading the filling of the sheath of the biceps tendon was not clinically useful in an individual patient.

Sonograms, however, often provided useful information. Effusion of a tendon sheath was detected in 20% of patients and was associated with rotator cuff tears in 11%. The association with rotator cuff tears is particularly important, given the recent reports that describe the use of ultrasound (US) in detecting these tears. In the first 39 patients tested there was a 93% sensitivity of sonography in detecting rotator cuff tears that were documented by arthrography.

It is likely that US will be used with increasing frequency to evaluate patients with suspected rotator cuff tears. The finding of effusions in the sheaths of biceps tendons in such patients increases the likelihood of a tear and indicates the need for a careful sonographic inspection of the rotator cuff. If no abnormality is seen at sonography, then arthrography should be performed. If arthrography and sonography both fail to reveal an associated lesion, further radiologic evaluation with subacromial bursography or computed tomography should be considered.

It is believed that US is better than arthrography in evaluating the biceps tendon. The slight advantage that arthrography has in determining the bony configuration of the groove of the biceps tendon is outweighed by the superiority of US in imaging the tendon itself. Because US is noninvasive, less expensive, and quicker, it could be the imaging method of choice in patients suspected of having lesions of the biceps tendons. In patients who are undergoing scanning for abnormalities of the rotator cuff routine views of the biceps tendon should be obtained. An effusion of the sheath of the biceps tendon can be expected in many of these patients and indicates an increased probability of rotator cuff tears and other internal derangements.

---

### US Evaluation of the Rotator Cuff
Laurence A. Mack, Frederick A. Matsen III, Ray F. Kilcoyne, Peter K. Davies, and Mary Elizabeth Sickler (Univ. of Washington)
Radiology 157:205–209, October 1985                                          3–20

---

Data were studied on 79 patients aged 29 to 84 years with symptoms referable to the rotator cuff. The sonographic findings were correlated with those at surgery or double-contrast arthrography. Eleven patients had had previous operations on the shoulder in question. Forty patients had all three examinations (sonography, arthrography, and surgery), 32 had sonography and arthrography, and 7 had sonography and evaluation of the rotator cuff at surgery.

In 47 patients the findings at sonography could be correlated with those at surgery. There were 31 true positive, 13 true negative, and 3 false negative results. The false negative results were in shoulders with small, complete cuff tears less than 14 mm wide. Compared with operative findings, ultrasound (US) demonstrated a sensitivity of .91, a specificity of 1.00, and an overall accuracy of .94.

In 72 patients findings at sonography could be compared with those of arthrography. There were 37 true positive, 31 true negative, and 1 false positive result. Three examinations disclosed abnormal findings on the arthrogram and normal findings on the sonogram. At surgery these 3 shoulders were found to have cuff tears. Compared with arthrography, US demonstrated a sensitivity of .93, a specificity of .97, and an overall accuracy of .94.

In 41 patients, the findings at arthrographic study could be correlated with operative findings, which resulted in 31 true positive and 9 true negative findings. Results of 1 arthrogram were false positive. In this case, air was seen in the subdeltoid bursa at double-contrast arthrography. However, at surgery, a rotator cuff lesion could not be found. This resulted in a sensitivity of 1.00, a specificity of .90, and an accuracy of .98.

Plain films are unreliable in the diagnosis of cuff lesions. Although arthrography of the shoulder provides an accurate technique for determining the presence of a complete-thickness cuff tear, this procedure has a number of disadvantages. Initial attempts to visualize the rotator cuff with US were compromised by problems of technique and equipment. The accuracy of sonographic evaluations has increased with the experience of the ultrasonographer, and improvements in sonographic instrumentation have also increased the accuracy of the examination. This is especially true when high-resolution, linear-array devices are used.

Sonography of the rotator cuff is clinically useful in the treatment of patients with shoulder problems. Because US is rapid, safe, noninvasive, painless, and inexpensive, the authors now use it instead of arthrography as the routine test of the integrity of the rotator cuff. At the university shoulder clinic an arthrogram is now obtained only if the sonographic findings are normal in a patient whose shoulder symptoms demonstrate strong clinical evidence of a cuff lesion.

If this approach had been used in the present series, arthrography would have been unnecessary in 68 of 72 studies. Two false positive findings would have resulted (1 in a patient who had surgery for impingement symptoms), and 3 patients would have had arthrography to resolve the clinical suspicion of a cuff lesion with a normal sonogram.

▶ Maximum preoperative information is beneficial to both the patient and the operating surgeon (see Digests 3–19 and 3–20). Ultrasound and arthrography are complementary studies, not competitive. Lesions of the rotator cuff and biceps tendon occur in combination with each other as well as with other osseous and cartiliginous lesions that will not be seen on ultrasound. If the equipment and expertise for both ultrasound and arthrography are available, both examinations are recommended.—Joseph S. Torg, M.D.

### Shoulder Impingement Syndrome in Athletes Treated by an Anterior Acromioplasty

James E. Tibone, Frank W. Jobe, Robert K. Kerlan, Vincent S. Carter, Clarence L. Shields, Stephen J. Lombardo, and Lewis A. Yocum (Southwestern Orthopaedic Med. Group, Inc., Inglewood, Calif.)

Clin. Orthop. 198:134–140, September 1985

3–21

Shoulder pain caused by an impingement syndrome commonly affects an athlete's performance. Between 1977 and 1980, 35 shoulders in 30 males and 3 females aged 16 to 40 years underwent anterior acromioplasty after failure of conservative treatment for impingement syndrome. After a minimum follow-up period of 18 months (mean, 27 months), 31 of 35 shoulders (89%) were subjectively judged improved by the patients compared with the preoperative status. Moderate and severe pain was reduced from 97% of the shoulders preoperatively to 20% postoperatively. Pain at rest and with activities of daily living was reduced from 71% preoperatively to 9% postoperatively. However, results in only 15 of the 35 shoulders (43%) allowed return to the same preinjury level of competition, and only 4 of 18 athletes involved in pitching and throwing returned to their former preinjury status.

TECHNIQUE.—A 10-cm saber incision, rather than Neer's anterior oblique incision, is made at the superior aspect of the shoulder between the lateral margin of the acromion and the acromioclavicular joint. The subcutaneous tissue is undermined laterally to expose the deltoid. The fascial raphe between the anterior and middle third of the deltoid is identified and split distally about 5 cm. With sharp dissection, the deltoid is reflected from the anterolateral aspect of the acromion. The acromioclavicular joint is not disturbed. The subacromial bursa is resected, and the undersurface of the anterior and lateral aspect of the acromion is removed as described by Neer. The coracoacromial ligament is resected, if it is not removed with the undersurface of the acromion. The rotator cuff is then inspected. The deltoid is repaired with no. 1 nonabsorbable sutures directly into the bone of the anterolateral acromion. The patient is placed in a sling for 1 week. On the first day postoperatively, Codman's pendulum exercises, passive abduction, and external rotation exercises are begun. No active abduction and forward flexion are allowed for 6 weeks after surgery to protect the deltoid muscle repair. At 6 weeks, the patient can start to perform active shoulder exercises to restore full shoulder motion, and at 3 months a strengthening program is begun. This should progress slowly, and the athlete should not return to competition until 6 months postoperatively.

The findings at surgery, consisting of an inflamed subacromial bursa or biceps tendon, showed the decreased space in the subacromial arch in these patients. Whether this was the score of pain cannot be proved, but substantial relief was obtained in most patients with surgical decompression of the subacromial arch. The athlete must be cognizant of the long rehabilitation period. Surgical decompression of the coracoacromial arch results in pain relief, but it usually does not allow an athlete to return to his former competitive status.

▶ The authors conclude that this operation is satisfactory for pain relief: 89% of the shoulders were subjectively improved. However, 76% had persistent difficulty with throwing or overhead sport activities. Although tennis players all had good results, this was true for only 22% of pitchers and throwers. No swimmer was competitive following surgery.

There is a major problem with the design of the study. Actually, the operation consists of three different procedures: (1) resection of subdeltoid bursa; (2) resection of the coracoacromial ligament; and (3) anterior-lateral acromioplasty. On the basis of the data one cannot determine if one, a combination of two, or all three procedures were responsible for the subjective improvement. More importantly, did any part of the operations, namely reflections of the deltoid from the acromium, contribute to persistent disability.—Joseph S. Torg, M.D.

---

**Recurrent Posterior Dislocation of the Shoulder: Treatment Using a Bone Block**
Carol A. Mowery, Steven R. Garfin, Robert E. Booth, and Richard H. Rothman (Univ. of California, San Diego, and Pennsylvania Hosp., Philadelphia)
J. Bone Joint Surg. [Am.] 67-A: 777–781, June 1985          3–22

---

Soft tissue procedures alone often have proved inadequate in treating posterior shoulder dislocation, while rotational procedures on the humerus are technically demanding. A bone block procedure was used to treat recurrent posterior dislocation of the shoulder in 5 patients between 1975 and 1982. The 3 men and 2 women were aged 17 to 44 years. Nonoperative

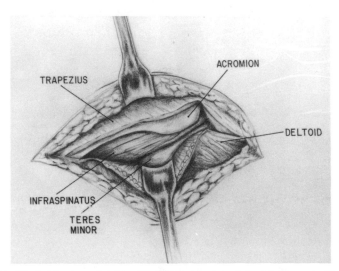

Fig 3–7.—The incision is carried down through the insertion of the deltoid muscle. The deltoid is retracted caudally and the infraspinatus and teres minor muscles are visualized. (Courtesy of Mowery, C.A., et al.: J. Bone Joint Surg. [Am.] 67-A:777–781, June 1985.)

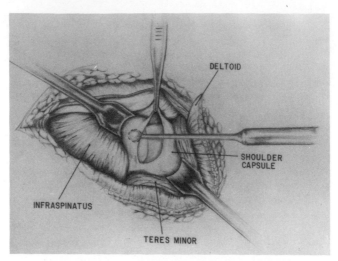

**Fig 3–8.**—The interval between the infraspinatus and teres minor muscles is identified and is widened by blunt dissection. The infraspinatus muscle is retracted superiorly and the teres minor is retracted distally. The posterior aspect of the shoulder joint can then be entered, and a periosteal elevator is used to free the capsule from the neck of the glenoid. (Courtesy of Mowery, C., et al.: J. Bone Joint Surg. [Am.] 67-A:777–781, June 1985.)

management had failed to prevent recurrent dislocation in all cases. Follow-up ranged from 2½ to 8 years. The operative approach is shown in Figures 3–7 and 3–8. A 2 × 3-cm bone block graft is taken from the posterior superior iliac spine and shaped to fit over the posterior aspect of the glenoid (Fig 3–9), and positioned after removing the cortex of the posterior aspect of the glenoid neck, using the lag-screw principle.

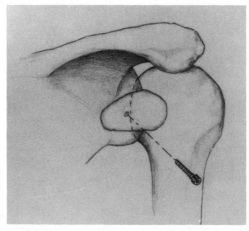

**Fig 3–9.**—The bone graft is depicted in a position extending 1.5 to 2.0 cm lateral to the glenoid, over the medial aspect of the humeral head. The capsule is closed over this internally fixed bone graft. (Courtesy of Mowery, C., et al.: J. Bone Joint Surg. [Am.] 67-A:777–781, June 1985.)

Four patients had excellent results, and 1 had a good result. The latter patient had a subsequent anterior dislocation that produced slightly decreased range of motion but no pain. All patients returned to their previous levels of activity, and none reported pain. Two patients required revision of a widened, irregular operative scar.

The posterior bone block technique is a safe and relatively secure means of treating recurrent posterior shoulder dislocation. It is less demanding technically than glenoplasty or humeral osteotomy. The operation may be applicable to patients with ligament insufficiency and those in whom other measures have failed. An encouraging result has been obtained in a patient with recurrent posterior dislocation and Ehlers-Danlos syndrome.

▶ Management of recurrent posterior dislocation of the glenohumeral joint is a difficult problem. As the authors have pointed out, both soft tissue and bony procedures are associated with technical difficulties, complications, and marginal results. On the basis of our own experience with the posterior bone block operation as well as the data presented in this paper, this operation has not been established as the definitive procedure for the competitive athlete. In this small series of five cases, four (80%) of the patients were determined to have excellent results; however, none were athletes—two were laborers, one a manager, and the other a homemaker. Also, three of the five had complications requiring subsequent surgery.—Joseph S. Torg, M.D.

---

**CT Findings in Normal and Dislocating Shoulders**
Steven E. Seltzer and Barbara N. Weissman (Harvard Univ. and Brigham and Women's Hosp., Boston)
J. Can. Assoc. Radiol. 36:41–46, March 1985                    3–23

---

Conventional radiography may fail to demonstrate the severity of shoulder dislocation and detect subtle malalignments. Computed tomography (CT) could be useful in this area because images are in the axial plane and there are no overlapping structures. Computed tomography of the shoulder was carried out in 6 patients with recent or recurrent shoulder dislocation, men aged 20 to 62 years, and in 10 normal subjects of both sexes aged 24 to 69 years. Contiguous 8- or 10-mm thick sections were obtained with a third or fourth generation CT unit. Intra-articular contrast was not used.

Detection of subtle subluxation by CT is illustrated in Figure 3–10. Glenoid surfaces were found to be fragmented in two cases. The ventral surface of the glenoid made an abrupt anterior turn as a result, producing augmented glenoid-spine and glenoid-body angles (Fig 3–11). One patient had an irregular inferior glenoid but normal angles. A coracoid fracture was seen in 1 patient. Two patients had several loose joint bodies visualized. Two Hill-Sachs deformities and 1 Bankart deformity were not seen on CT.

Computed tomography can demonstrate subtle subluxation of the shoulder and various lesions such as bony abnormalities of the glenoid, loose

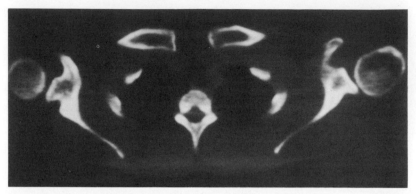

Fig 3–10.—Posterior subluxation. Scan at the upper one third of the shoulder joint on the left and slightly more cephalad on the right shows posterior subluxation of the left humeral head. The center of the left humerus projects posterior to the middle one third of the glenoid fossa. On the right, the head is normally located. (Courtesy of Seltzer, S.E., and Weissman, B.N.: J. Can. Assoc. Radiol. 36:41–46, March 1985.)

bodies, and coracoid fracture, but not capsular or labral abnormalities. Computed tomography without intra-articular contrast has a secondary role in demonstrating intra-articular cartilage or labral abnormalities, behind conventional arthrography or CT arthrography.

▶ As a "work in progress" this is a worthwhile paper with many potential ap-

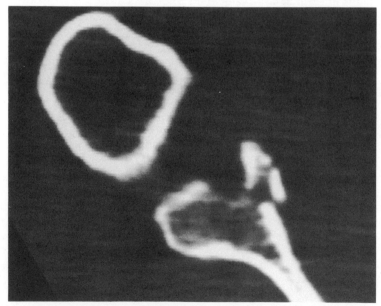

Fig 3–11.—Several centimeters lower, an oblique, displaced fracture of the glenoid is seen. The fracture has produced an abnormal angulation of the glenoid surface. (Courtesy of Seltzer, S.E., and Weissman, B.N.: J. Can. Assoc. Radiol. 36:41–46, March 1985.)

plications. However, a more extensive study with more normal and abnormal participants is necessary before serious conclusions can be drawn.—Joseph S. Torg, M.D.

---

**Shoulder Dislocation in Skiing: Choice of Surgical Method Depending on the Degree of Humeral Retrotorsion**
H.-G. Pieper (Univ. of Marburg)
Int. J. Sports Med. 6:155–160, June 1985                                3–24

---

Dislocation of the shoulder is a typical upper extremity injury in alpine and cross-country skiing. Dislocations constitute nearly 50% of all shoulder injuries in skiing and 3.5% to 6% of all skiing injuries. In competitive sports, shoulder dislocations occur much more frequently. Among the German National Alpine Skiing Team, consisting of some 30 active top athletes, at least 5 shoulder dislocations are registered yearly. A fall forward or sideward onto the slope at relatively high speed leads to the typical trauma, consisting of a forced retroversion and external rotation of the abducted arm. Due to the disproportion between the size of the humeral head and the glenoid cavity, the head is turned out of the articular surface anteriorly and forced against the anterior part of the glenoid labrum and the ventral joint capsule. The resulting axial pressure produces an anterior dislocation.

With respect to the axis of the elbow, the humeral head is directed backward (retrotorsion of the humerus). If the angle of retrotorsion is smaller than normal, the humeral head is directed more ventrally in the shoulder. It can already be forced anteriorly out of the osseous fossa articularis by only a small amount of external rotation of the arm (Fig 3–12). This consideration leads to the hypothesis that a reduced humeral retrotorsion might be a supporting factor in the occurrence of a first dislocation or might represent a triggering element in the recurrence of a shoulder dislocation.

The angle of humeral retrotorsion was determined in 40 patients with recurrent anterior shoulder dislocation and 5 with posterior dislocation. The values were compared with those of 130 shoulders with no known

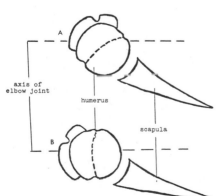

Fig 3–12.—Position of humeral head in relation to glenoid cavity at normal (A) and at pathologically reduced (B) angle of humeral retrotorsion. (Courtesy of Pieper, H.-G.: Int. J. Sports Med. 6:155–160, June 1985.)

previous dislocation. In patients with anterior dislocations, the average angle of retrotorsion was pathologically reduced to 24.3 degrees, compared with 40.1 degrees in controls, a highly significant difference. The patients with posterior dislocations had an average angle of retrotorsion of 55.7 degrees. Most retrotorsion angles in recurrent anterior shoulder dislocations were clearly below the average, although some shoulders with a history of recurrent dislocations had standard retrotorsional angles. The two distribution curves cross at a value of about 30 degrees.

This study suggests that pathologic retrotorsion of the humerus is an important element in the development of recurrent dislocation of the shoulder. This factor should be considered in operative planning.

In the author's department, surgical treatment of recurrent shoulder dislocation is based on the retrotorsional angle of the patient's humerus measured preoperatively. If the angle is pathologically less than 30 degrees, the subcapital derotation osteotomy of Weber is performed. The amount of derotation is determined by the patient's deviance from the average. It does not generally amount to 20 to 25 degrees, as stated by Weber. If shoulder dislocation recurs at a normal humeral retrotorsion angle, other causes must be considered, such as defects in the glenoid labrum and capsular laxity. In these instances the Eden-Hybbinette operation as modified by Lange is employed. In both methods, capsulorrhaphy or transposition of the subscapularis tendon is important to eliminate the capsular laxity caused by previous recurrent dislocations. Choice of a surgical method guided by individual torsional angles could lead to a considerable improvement of therapy at small expense: one extra x-ray film and determination of the respective torsional angle.

▶ An interesting paper from the standpoint of dealing with the concept of humeral retroversion as a factor in anterior glenohumeral instability. However, it should be noted that no data are presented with regard to the clinical effectiveness of the operation. In the original paper (*J. Bone Joint Surg.* [*Am.*] 66-A:1443–1450, December 1984), Weber reported 207 rotational humeral osteotomies done in 205 patients, in which there was a incidence of postsurgical recurrence of 5.7%. Certainly, this is no better than numerous other less complicated soft tissue procedures available to the surgeon. Considering that extensive surgery is necessary to externally rotate the humeral shaft so that the humeral head defect is shifted more posteriorly, and that a second surgical procedure may be necessary to remove fixating devices, it would appear that a less complicated surgical approach would be preferable.—Joseph S. Torg, M.D.

---

**A Modification of the Bristow Procedure for Recurrent Anterior Shoulder Dislocation and Subluxation**
W. Grant Braly and Hugh S. Tullos (Baylor College of Medicine)
Am. J. Sports Med. 13:81–86, March–April 1985          3–25

---

A modified form of the Bristow procedure for recurrent anterior shoulder dislocation and subluxation is based on intracapsular visualization and accurate, firm repair of the Bankart lesion. A standard anterior deltopectoral approach is used. The capsule is incised in a "T" manner to expose the joint and the anterior glenoid rim is decorticated and drilled before securing the coracoid to the rim with a malleolar screw. The avulsed labrum is excised and the capsule sutured to the lateral edge of the conjoined tendon as close as possible to the base of the coracoid. The longitudinally split part of the capsule is then repaired.

Twenty-eight patients had this operation, and 19 patients with dislocation and 1 with subluxation were followed up after an average of 42.5 months. The average age was 25 years. Football injuries were most frequent. Nineteen patients had perfect or good subjective results, and 1 had an acceptable result. Wound healing was uneventful in all instances. One patient required screw removal but nevertheless had an excellent subjective outcome. The average loss of external rotation was 10 degrees, or 7 degrees, excluding 1 patient who lost 65 degrees. Fourteen of 16 patients with injuries on the dominant side were able to return to throwing sports at about the preoperative level of activity.

This modified Bristow procedure provides excellent results in cases of recurrent anterior shoulder dislocation and subluxation. Limitation of external rotation is not necessary for shoulder repair. Secure fixation allows range of motion exercises to be initiated earlier and shortens the course of rehabilitation.

▶ It is interesting that the authors refer to their procedure as a modification of the Bristow procedure. Actually, the matter in which the subscapularis tendon is handled, being divided transversely and then imbricated over the transpositioned coracoid, is similar to the method of Latarjet (Latarjet, M.: *Lyon Chir.:* 49:994–997, 1954). That is, the Latarjet procedure, described in 1954, is one in which he completely transected the subscapularis tendon, fixed the coracoid to the scapular neck, then reefed the entire subscapularis tendon anterior to the transplanted coracoid and tendon. The fact that the authors found no recurrent dislocation or subluxations in this group of 28 patients followed up for an average of 42.5 months is impressive. They state that 14 of 16 patients with operated dominant arms were able to return to throwing sports postoperatively. However, it is important to note that none of these patients were "high level athletes." It is doubtful what significance can be placed on the ability of an individual to resume recreational throwing or overhead sports "roughly commensurate" with preoperative levels of activity.—Joseph S. Torg, M.D.

**Latarjet's Operation for Recurrent Anterior-Internal Dislocation of Shoulder**
B. Kerboul, J. Le Saout, C. Lefevre, E. Malingue, L. Fabre, L. Roblin, and B. Courtois (CHU A. Morvan, Brest, France)
J. Chir. (Paris) 122:371–374, June–July 1985                                    3–26

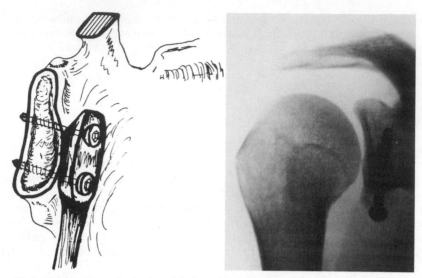

Fig 3–13 (left).—Two-point fixation of the bony ridge in laterally recumbent position.
Fig 3–14 (right).
(Courtesy of Kerboul, B., et al.: J. Chir. (Paris) 122:371–374, June–July 1985.)

Accidents related to instability of the shoulder may result in serious impairment, with recurrences often triggered by minimal trauma. Treatment is surgical. The authors of this study have practiced Latarjet's technique since 1976 on 51 patients, mostly men whose average age was 24 years. In 28% an accident had occurred during athletic activity; the right shoulder was affected in 70%.

Radiologic examination revealed a "worn-down" aspect in 23 cases, fracture of the anterior rim in 9, and a dysplasia in 3. The surgical technique is relatively simple: after delto-pectoral access, the coracoid process is sectioned at the level of its angle, encroaching on its vertical position, while preserving the insertion of the coraco-biceps. The subscapular is sectioned in its two upper thirds, the authors preferring fixation of the coracoid in laterally recumbent position by way of two screws (Figs 3–13 and 3–14). This bony ridge must be placed at the edge of the glenoid without capsular interposition.

Results could be evaluated in 49 cases after an average of 3½ years. No recurrences were reported. Results were excellent in 46 cases, and only 3 patients complained of residual instability. All athletes had resumed their previous activity. In all, Latarjet's operation is considered a reliable procedure, with consistently good results achieved with accurate technical execution. Most importantly, the bony ridge, playing both an active and passive role, must be level with the anterointernal border of the glenoid.

▶ The authors describe this procedure as "Latarjet's operation." However, from their description of the procedure it appears to be more in keeping with Collins' *(Orthopaedic Clinics of North America* 4:759–774, 1973) description of his modification of the Bristow procedure. Specifically, subscapularis is sectioned in its superior two thirds. The transposed coracoid and conjoined tendon are placed over the inferior segment of the tendon. The fact that there were no redislocations in the 49 patients at 3½ years follow-up is noteworthy.—Joseph S. Torg, M.D.

---

**Failed Anterior Reconstruction for Shoulder Instability**
Robert H. Hawkins and Richard J. Hawkins (Shaughnessy Hosp., Vancouver, and St. Joseph's Hosp., London, Ontario)
J. Bone Joint Surg. [Br.] 67-B:709–714, November 1985                 3–27

---

Glenohumeral instability is well known as a major cause of disability, especially among athletes. Successful operation for anterior instability should restore stability while maintaining a painless functional range of movement. Failure may be caused by recurrence of instability, significant postoperative pain, or marked loss of movement. Forty-six patients with one or more of these problems were referred for assessment and treatment. In 31 patients instability was present; in 12 of them, posterior or multi-directional instability had not been recognized and another 11 had uncorrected anatomical defects. In 20 patients with significant pain there was often more than one cause, including impingement syndrome in 9, osteoarthritis in 7, implant irritation in 4, and instability alone in 2. A disabling medial rotation contracture was found in 10 patients, 4 of whom had painful osteoarthritis.

Eight patients had recurrence of instability after an injury severe enough to break down a satisfactory repair, whereas uncorrected pathology was thought to be responsible in 11. Lesions found at reoperation included capsular detachments from the anterior glenoid rim, redundant anterior capsule, and deficiency of the bony glenoid. The development of painful osteoarthritis after a stabilizing procedure is especially disturbing. Of the 7 instances described, 1 was related to a staple in the joint. In the other 6 patients osteoarthritis occurred an average of 13 years after the primary operation, and the only associated factor was a tight anterior repair. These patients could all remember vain attempts to regain movement, particularly lateral rotation. Apparently, excessively tight repair may provoke significant glenohumeral arthritis, especially in a joint already been damaged by recurrent instability. Any repair may restrict mobility to some extent, but in this series significant loss of movement was the principal complaint of 10 patients; the Putti-Platt reconstruction accounted for 9 of these, and 6 of the 9 patients had osteoarthritis.

Management of glenohumeral instability depends on understanding the causes of failure. The authors' patients all start exercises to strengthen the medial and lateral rotators and the supraspinatus muscle. Occasionally, use of a harness to limit abduction may be appropriate. If these measures fail to control instability, surgical repair is considered. A preoperative assessment is made to identify the directions of instability and to determine any associated pathology, e.g., generalized laxity, bony defects, rotator cuff tears, and neuromuscular disorders.

If an operation is performed, under anesthesia both shoulders are carefully tested for stability, with particular attention paid to direction(s) of displacement and to crepitus. The joint is exposed through a standard anterior approach and again examined fully, both to confirm the direction(s) of instability and to identify any anatomical deficiencies. The methods used for repair or reconstruction depend on the pathology. Bankart lesions longer than 1 cm require reattachment. Capsuloligamentous laxity, especially if it is the only abnormality, is treated by advancing the medial flap laterally to restrict lateral rotation; at least 25 degrees of lateral rotation, as tested with the elbow at the side, should be retained. If significant anteroinferior instability is noted, an inferior capsular shift is performed.

▶ The authors have clearly defined four criteria for failure of anterior shoulder reconstruction: (1) recurrent instability; (2) significant postoperative pain; (3) degenerative arthritis; and (4) marked loss of motion. Because patients were referred by other physicians, it was not possible to report these complications on a "rate" basis. A review of other large series recently reported in the literature is enlightening. Hill et al. (*Am. J. Sports Med.* 9:283–287, 1981) have reported a redislocation rate of 2% and a resubluxation rate of 21% for the Bristow procedure. Hovelius et al. (*J. Bone Joint Surg.* [*Am.*] 65-A:926–934, 1983) reported a 6% redislocation rate and a 7% resubluxation rate for the Bristow procedure. With regard to complications following the Putti-Platt procedure, Hovelius et al. (*J. Bone Joint Surg.* [*Am.*] 61-A:566–570, 1979) reported a 19% redislocation rate and Morrey et al. (*J. Bone Joint Surg.* [*Am.*] 58-A:252–260, 1976) reported a 13.6% redislocation rate for this procedure. Morrey et al. also reported a 4.1% redislocation rate for the Bankart procedure. On the basis of this report of Hawkins and Hawkins and the cited references, it would appear that surgery for anterior shoulder instability is certainly not without significant failure rates.—Joseph S. Torg, M.D.

---

**Arthroscopy of The Shoulder in the Management of Partial Tears of the Rotation Cuff: A Preliminary Report**
James R. Andrews, Thad S. Broussard, and William G. Carson (Hughston Orthopaedic Clinic, Columbus, Ga., and Tulane Univ.)
Arthroscopy 1:117–122, 1985                                          3–28

---

Thirty-six patients with partial tears of the supraspinatus portion of the rotator cuff underwent arthroscopic examination and debridement of the lesion. All patients, whose average age was 22 years, were involved in competitive athletics; 64% were baseball pitchers. Average duration of symptoms prior to arthroscopy was 12 months. The most common presenting complaint was pain in the shoulder during overhead activities. Associated pathology included tears of the glenoid labrum and partial tearing or tendinitis of the long head of the biceps tendon.

Average length of follow-up was 13.1 months. Evaluation consisted of telephone interviews for 20 patients (60%), and personal interviews and physical examinations in 14 (40%). Of the 34 patients available for follow-up, 26 (76%) were rated as having had an excellent result, with no spontaneous pain and with the ability to return to their competitive athletic activities. Three (9%) had good results, with subjective improvement and with the ability to return to their previous athletic activities at a somewhat reduced level. The remaining 5 (15%) had poor results, with symptoms subjectively unchanged or worse postoperatively. Presence of biceps tendinitis or frank partial tearing of the long head of the biceps tendon did not appear to affect overall results. There were no complications. The average length of time until return to full activity was 5 months.

The authors believe that this preliminary study demonstrates the effectiveness of arthroscopy of the shoulder in establishing a definitive diagnosis of partial rotator cuff tears. It also suggests the usefulness of debridement of the lesion to provide a stimulus to healing.

▶ In addition to partial tears of the supraspinatus portion of the rotator cuff, all 36 patients had associated tearing of some portion of the glenoid labrum and were unable to participate maximally in their sport. Also, 81% had, on physical examination, a palpable catching in the shoulder when the arm was completely forward flexed and abducted and the humerus internally and externally rotated.—Joseph S. Torg, M.D.

---

**Glenoid Labrum Tears Related to the Long Head of the Biceps**
James R. Andrews, William G. Carson, Jr., and William D. McLeod (Hughston Orthopaedic Clinic, Columbus, Ga., and Tulane Univ.)
Am. J. Sports Med. 13:337–341, September–October 1985          3–29

---

This report describes a mechanism that might be responsible for tearing the glenoid labrum during the throwing act. This hypothesis is based on observations made during arthroscopy of the shoulder, three-dimensional high-speed cinematography, computer-assisted analysis of the pitching mechanism, and biomechanical analysis of the biceps tendon as it relates to the elbow and shoulder in the pitching mechanism. Of 120 patients who underwent diagnostic or operative arthroscopy of the shoulder between 1979 and 1983, 73 were throwing athletes with 51 of these 73 involved in baseball (35 were pitchers, 22 playing at the professional level). Average duration of symptoms before arthroscopy was 12 months. Physical examination revealed a demonstrable popping or catching in 79%.

Only the observations made at arthroscopy regarding the biceps-labrum complex relationship and the biomechanical observations will be reported. At arthroscopy, the tendon of the long head of the biceps appeared to originate through and be continuous with the superior portion of the glenoid labrum. In many cases it appeared to have pulled the anterosuperior portion of the labrum off the glenoid. This observation was verified at arthroscopy by viewing the origin of the biceps tendon into the glenoid labrum as the muscle was electrically stimulated. With stimulation of the muscle, the tendinous portion became quite taut, particularly near its attachment to the glenoid labrum and actually lifted the labrum off the glenoid.

Three-dimensional high-speed cinematography with computer analysis revealed that the moment acting about the elbow joint to extend the joint through an arc of about 50 degrees was in excess of 600 inch-pounds. The extremely high velocity of elbow extension that is generated must be decelerated through the final 30 degrees of elbow extension. Of the muscles of the arm that provide the large deceleration forces in the follow-through phase of throwing, only the biceps brachii traverses both the elbow joint and the shoulder joint. Additional forces are generated in the biceps tendon in its function as a "shunt" muscle to stabilize the glenohumeral joint during the throwing act.

The authors conclude that there is a high frequency of tearing of the anterosuperior aspect of the glenoid labrum in the throwing athlete. They believe this results from the forces imparted by the biceps tendon, particularly during the follow-through phase of throwing.

▶ The authors have presented a well documented and interesting observation regarding one probable cause of shoulder pain in the throwing athlete. They have emphasized that their explanation for the observed disruption of the superior labrum from the glenoid resulting from the biceps pull is hypothetical. Of significance is the further observation that tearing of the labrum in this area can give the throwing athlete a subjective sensation of instability without the presence of the Bankart lesion associated with structural instability of the shoulder.

They further point out that DePalma's anatomical dissection of the shoulder demonstrated that 40% of the 40- to 50-year-old and 100% of the 80-year-old population have some form of anterior labrum degeneration (*A.A.O.S. Instructional Course Lecture* 7:168–180, 1950).—Joseph S. Torg, M.D.

---

**Stress Fracture of the Ipsilateral First Rib in a Pitcher**
Robert Gurtler, Helene Pavlov, and Joseph S. Torg (Univ. of Pennsylvania and Cornell Univ.)
Am. J. Sports Med. 13:277–279, July–August 1985                              3–30

---

Fracture of the first rib resulting from trauma has been well documented. The first rib may be fractured in an isolated manner or in association with multiple rib fractures. In such cases the history is clear-cut, complications involving the contiguous neurovascular structures can occur, and management is well delineated. Fatigue fractures of the first rib have previously been reported in laborers involved in heavy lifting. The course is insidious, and the lesion is usually identified incidentally on a radiograph.

Boy, aged 17, a left-handed high school pitcher, who had pitched no more than one game per week throughout the spring, heard a snap in his shoulder followed by severe pain while pitching a game in late May. Initial radiography demonstrated a vertical radiolucency in the anterior axillary line within an area of rib hypertrophy. Ten days after injury, the patient had pain associated with deep breathing but was otherwise asymptomatic. He had tenderness at the root of the neck on the same side as his pitching arm. A bone scan confirmed fracture, with an area of augmented radionuclide uptake in the left first rib.

Four months after injury, without return to pitching, the radiograph indicated delayed union, including a widened radiolucent line with trumpeting and sclerosis at the fracture line. Because of concern about nonunion, the patient was restricted from throwing. During the subsequent off-season, there was total healing of this first rib fracture, with complete bridging and marrow continuity across the fracture site by 9 months after injury.

Stress fracture of the first rib is infrequent. In a review of 62,782 chest radiographs of young male draftees, 17 cases of first rib defect were found, 16 with no specific history of trauma. All subjects were asymptomatic. Male predominance is universally reported. All reported stress fractures of the first rib have been nondisplaced. No acute neurovascular complications have been described. Chronic complications have been few. Horner's syndrome and thoracic outlet syndrome have been reported as late complications. Pseudarthrosis or nonunion has been described repeatedly and has been consistently reported as nonpainful.

The first rib is broad and flat, with grooves in the superior margin for the subclavian artery (posterior) and the subclavian vein (anterior). The groove for the artery is deeper than that for the vein, forming the weakest point in the first rib. This groove also lies between forces pulling up (scalenus) and forces pulling down (intercostals and serratus anterior). The groove for the subclavian artery, therefore, is the most common location for stress fractures.

Stress fracture of the first rib caused by pitching can occur as an acute injury or with an insidious onset. The fracture may initially look incomplete or indefinite. Cortical disruption can be documented by a history of repetitive throwing and corroborated by bone scan. These fractures are slow to heal. During healing the fracture margins are likely to appear sclerotic, with a widened radiolucent fracture line. This evidence of delayed union may persist for some time. However, with continued absence of throwing, these fractures will heal.

**Stress Fracture of the First Rib: A Case Report**
Peter A. Lankenner, Jr., and Lyle J. Micheli (Children's Hosp., Boston)
J. Bone Joint Surg. [Am.] 67-A:159–160, January 1985          3–31

Stress fractures are becoming more prominent as the cause of pain in the musculoskeletal system of recreational and more serious athletes. The lower extremity in runners and the spine in gymnasts are frequent sites of such fractures.

Boy, 15, who was right-handed, had been active in Little League baseball for the past 7 years and at the time he was seen was left fielder on the varsity high school baseball team. Twenty-four hours before he was seen, he had a dull, aching pain in the posterior aspect of the right shoulder. When he subsequently tried to swing a bat, there was a "snap" in the right shoulder, with excruciating pain and a decreased range of motion. He was given a sling by the trainer. On physical examination, the patient had full but painful range of motion of the right shoulder. There was no evidence of subluxation, dislocation, or rotator cuff tear, but there was a tender area in the axilla and on the inferior border of the scapula. Scapular pain increased with shoulder elevation and depression against resistance. Antero-posterior radiographs of the right shoulder showed an apparent fracture of the right first rib, which was later confirmed by a $^{99m}$Tc bone scan.

The patient was advised not to play baseball for 4 weeks and was instructed in gentle isometric shoulder exercises. After 4 weeks, he was allowed to begin active shoulder exercises against resistance and to return to playing baseball. He was asymptomatic, with full sports participation. Radiographs 1 year after injury showed complete healing.

Factors that predispose to overuse syndromes, including stress fractures, have been previously reported. This boy had undergone a rapid increase in training over a 4-week period before onset of symptoms, implicating a training error as the most likely predisposing factor. Stress fracture of the first rib should be included in the differential diagnosis of shoulder pain in the young, throwing athlete.

---

**Surfer's Rib: Isolated First Rib Fracture Secondary to Indirect Trauma**
Patricia Bailey (Kaiser Permanente Med. Care Program, Harbor City, Calif.)
Ann. Emerg. Med. 14:346–349, April 1985                                3–32

First rib fracture has been described as a "harbinger of serious potential injury" since the association between first rib fracture and injury to the subclavian artery was reported in 1869. The number of patients with first rib fracture described in the literature is increasing; the most common cause is direct trauma from motor vehicle accidents. It is being recognized that stress-induced first rib fractures can be managed conservatively with outpatient observation. As the more benign nature of stress-induced fractures is recognized, the automatic use of invasive procedures for all first rib fractures may decrease.

Boy, 17, felt sharp left shoulder pain while performing a lay-back maneuver, crouched on a surfboard with his left arm extended behind him and his hand in the water. Onset of pain coincided with a sudden pull on the extended arm by the force of the wave in which his hand was immersed. At the time, he was aware of a brief period of shortness of breath. He was able to finish the surfing run without difficulty but he felt pain localized to the left shoulder throughout the range of motion of the left arm.

The chest was symmetric and breath sounds were equal bilaterally. The only area of chest tenderness was deep in the left axilla. No node was palpated, and the point tenderness was believed to be on palpation of the chest wall through the axillary tissue. The left shoulder was nontender to palpation, but there was pain in the proximal part of the upper arm along the course of the triceps on range of motion, especially with posterior extension of the arm. No tenderness was palpable along the humerus or biceps. Posteroanterior and lateral views of the chest showed a clearly visible fracture through the anterolateral aspect of the left first rib. There was a 3-mm separation of the fracture fragments, but no displacement. The mediastinum did not appear to be widened, and no other abnormality was seen.

The patient was treated with a sling and analgesia and was discharged. Chest radiograph and an ECG next day showed no change, and there were no complications during the ensuing weeks. One month after injury there was no discomfort when the patient reproduced the movements that provoked the injury. He had resumed surfing against medical advice. There have been no delayed complications.

The importance of diagnosis and proper treatment of first rib fracture lies in its potential severity because of the proximity to major vessels, nerves, and the lung. Those who have primarily considered first rib fractures caused by direct trauma have listed various criteria for invasive diagnostic procedures: presentation with other rib injuries; marked displacement of the fragments; altered serial chest films with increased pleural cap or hemothorax; changes in blood pressure or pulse in the affected extremity; brachial plexus injury; and subclavian groove fracture. Sacchetti et al., who reported a case of stress fracture, however, stated that generally if no immediate complications are present on examination and chest radiography shows no vascular injury, angiography is probably unnecessary and the patient can be discharged but observed. Periodic rechecks with serial radiographs would seem to be prudent for up to 6 months after stress fracture of the first rib, with emphasis on any changes occurring in the first 2 weeks.

▶ It appears that fractures of the first rib should be divided into those resulting from direct trauma and those resulting from indirect trauma or repetitive cyclic loading. The association of fractures of the first rib resulting from direct trauma and such complications as hemothorax, pneumothorax, brachial plexopathy, or great muscle injury is well recognized. On the basis of the review of these three cases (Digests 3–30, 3–31, and 3–32) as well as Sacchetti's description of rebound rib, a stress-induced first rib fracture (*Ann. Emerg. Med.* 12:177–179, March 1983), it appears that stress fractures of the first rib can occur with acute symptomatic onset, but their course is benign and uncomplicated. It is interesting to note that Alderson (*Br. J. Radiol.* 20:345–359, 1947), on the basis of a review of a large number of chest roentgenograms of military recruits, only pointed out that the lesion of incidental findings on chest films taken from unrelated complaints was a part of physical screening examination. It appears that a stress fracture of the first rib should be included in the differential diagnosis of shoulder pain in the young athlete.—Joseph S. Torg, M.D.

## Lower Extremity Injuries

### Acute Tears of the Medial Head of the Gastrocnemius
Clarence L. Shields, Jr., Louis Redix, and Clive E. Brewster (Southwestern Orthopaedic Med. Group, Inglewood, Calif.)
Foot Ankle 5:186–190, January–February 1985                     3–33

Twenty-five patients with acute tears of the medial head of the gastrocnemius were evaluated 1 to 3 years after injury. Patients were treated with a heel lift, calf sleeve, and physical therapy. Most patients were men who injured their dominant lower extremity in one explosive episode. The purpose of this study was to institute a standard treatment protocol and to measure the plantarflexion strength of the damaged extremity with the Cybex II dynamometer.

Ten of the patients were injured playing tennis; 8, jogging; 4, playing basketball; and 3, playing racquetball. Age range was 23–57 years; men predominated with a ratio of 2 to 1. The period of convalescence ranged from 3 to 9 weeks with a mean of 4.5 weeks. Mean for resumption of athletics was 6.7 weeks. The Cybex evaluation of the control group of athletes revealed a significant difference in strength between legs at only one speed of plantarflexion. The dominant leg produced 32.9 ft-lb/second compared to 28.4 ft-lb/second in the minor leg, at speed of 90 degrees per second ($P < .05$). There were no significant differences in dorsiflexion strength at any test speed. At full recovery, there were no statistically significant differences in the patient group between involved and noninvolved limb strength measurement at the $P < .05$ level. The plantarflexion values were nearly identical in both legs, as were dorsiflexion values, at all test speeds.

▶ A clear documentation of the efficacy of management of this problem with a neoprene rubber calf sleeve, a one-half-inch felt heel pad, ice packs 20 minutes twice a day, oral nonsteroidal anti-inflammatory medication, and passive calf stretching.—Joseph S. Torg, M.D.

---

**Demonstration of Achilles Tendon on CT: Normal and Pathological Changes**
M. Reiser, N. Rupp, K. Lehner, O. Paar, R. Gradinger, and P. M. Karpf (Technical Univ. of Munich)
Fortschr. Geb. Röntgenstr. Nuklearmed. Erganzungsband 143:173–177, August 1985                                                    3–34

---

Ligaments and tendons, including the Achilles tendon, show the highest density among normal soft tissue structures in the body. Traumatic and degenerative changes of the Achilles tendon are often associated with marked thickening and reduction in density associated with increased opacity of the space in front of the Achilles tendon. These changes are easily demonstrated by CT, whereas conventional radiologic techniques only show nonspecific changes. Twenty-five patients were examined, including 9 with pain, 7 following rupture of the Achilles tendon and 9 postoperative controls; 5 of the latter complained of painful movements and limited function, whereas 4 patients experienced satisfactory results. In all cases the changes extended over the total length of the tendon. Besides morphological changes and circumscribed reduction in density, complete hypodensity of the tendon was observed.

After rupture the Achilles tendon shows an increase of the sagittal diameter averaging twice the norm and an increase in the section area av-

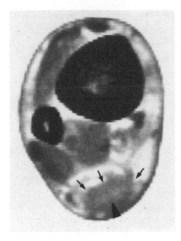

Fig 3–15.—Examination of a man, aged 42 years, 2 months after left tendon suture. Thickening and density reduction of the left Achilles tendon *(arrow)* with central hypodensity *(arrowhead)*, striped density in the space in front of the Achilles tendon. (Courtesy of Reiser, M., et al.: Fortschr. Geb. Röntgenstr. Nuklearmed. Erganzungsband 143:173–177, August 1985.)

eraging three times the norm, as well as a reduction of the inner density of about 40%. A striped density in the space in front of the tendon was observed in all cases. With the so-called tennis-leg, an avulsion of the medial gastrocnemius muscle from the common tendon plate, only a slight thickening and density reduction of the tendon could be found. In such cases a substance deficiency appeared at the muscle-tendon-transition of the triceps surae muscle.

The operated Achilles tendons also show an increase in the section area averaging three times the norm; the reduction of the inner density was about 50%. A normal density could not be proved in any case, and the density observed was mostly similar to that of the muscle tissue. The space in front of the tendon also showed a striped density and therefore a poorly defined ventral tendon contour. In one case the circumscribed central hypodensity of the tendon was demonstrated (Fig 3–15).

In patients with achillodynia the pathology of the tendon was slight; however, a significant increase of the sagittal diameter (average 2 mm) could be determined. In all cases of rupture and postoperative conditions, a hypodensity of the whole tendon was evident. In 6 cases circumscribed, almost cystic hypodensities were found. In 2 cases a striped density in the space in front of the tendon was observed.

In cases of premature burdening a rerupture may occur; this is difficult to repair. Achillodynia is first treated conservatively; if degenerative foci cause the continuance of complaints, operation is indicated. It was found that CT can add information important for the diagnosis and treatment planning of abnormalities of the Achilles tendon.

## MR Imaging of a Ruptured Achilles Tendon

James W. Reinig, Robert H. Dorwart, and William C. Roden (Natl. Inst. of Health, Bethesda, Md., and Walter Reed Army Med. Ctr., Washington, D.C.)
J. Comput. Assist. Tomogr. 9:1131–1134, November–December 1985    3–35

Rupture of the Achilles tendon is an urgent, but usually clinically apparent, orthopedic problem. Repair must be made promptly for full recovery. A number of methods of radiographic evaluation have been proposed to confirm the diagnosis of Achilles rupture. In the described patient, resonance (MR) imaging provided exquisite definition of the injury to the Achilles tendon.

Man, 35, sustained an injury to his lower leg while playing basketball. Cramping pain of sudden onset occurred in the calf as the player pivoted from backpedaling to forward movement. The lowermost calf was swollen posteriorly just above the dorsal surface of the calcaneus. A soft tissue defect could be palpated at the site of the Achilles tendon. Results of the Thompson test (lack of reflex plantar flexion of the foot induced by manual compression of the gastrocnemius muscle) were positive. A lateral radiograph of the ankle was nondiagnostic. Computed tomography and MR imaging were performed 18 hours after injury. Noncontrast-enhanced CT, performed at 10-mm intervals, revealed asymmetry in the appearance of the Achilles tendons. On the normal right side the tendon could be traced throughout, whereas on the left the tendon sheath was irregular and swollen. The ends of the torn tendon could not be identified. The maximum diameter of the tendon sheath was at the site of the palpable soft tissue defect.

Sagittal contiguous 1-cm images of the ankles were obtained on a superconducting MR imager at 0.50 T. The Achilles tendon appeared as a structure with little signal on both spin echo (SE) and inversion recovery (IR) sequences. On the injured side a high signal intensity zone was present between the ends of the ruptured Achilles tendon on the SE images. On IR images the signal strength of this area was intermediate between fat and muscle. The retracted ends of the tendon were thicker than the normal Achilles tendon. On the normal side the tendon could be traced easily in its normal position to the point of insertion on the calcaneous. The SE images provided better anatomical depiction of the injury than the IR scans did. A percutaneous approximation of the tendon segments was performed 45 hours after the injury. The tendon was torn at a point about 3 cm above its insertion, which correlated well with the MR findings. A repeat SE examination was obtained 4 weeks after surgical repair. The ends of the torn tendon were much more closely approximated. The high signal stength zone at the site of the injury was smaller and displayed a less intense signal, suggesting resolution of some of the edema and hemorrhage. A follow-up SE study 4 months after the injury revealed an intact tendon with complete resolution of edema and hemorrhage.

Compared with CT scanning, MR can provide several significant advantages. Definition of the soft tissue planes and muscular bundles is much better with MR than with any other imaging modality. Also, sagittal imaging can easily be obtained to show the margins of the injured tendon in one image. On SE imaging the weak signal of the tendon contrasts sharply with the greater signal intensity of the tissue that occupies the gap between the injured tendon segments.

▶ Imaging methods available to demonstrate Achilles tendon integrity are several (Digests 3–34 and 3–35). Plain radiology is not diagnostic per se. Xeroradiography, although providing a better definition of soft tissue planes, is limited to reviewing secondary evidence of injury. Although ultrasonography is capable of demonstrating Achilles ruptures, limited clinical experience to date has hindered its widespread application. Computed tomography provides better definition of tendon, adjacent soft tissue, and muscle. However, it is limited by lack of contrast between the tendon and the hemorrhage and edema that fill the injury site. Also, CT is limited by the lack of direct sagittal imaging. On the other hand, magnetic resonance imaging can provide several advantages. Soft tissue and muscular bundle definition is much better than with any other imaging modality. Possibly, magnetic resonance imaging will be capable of providing definition of partial Achilles tears, something that is most difficult to image with any other modality.—Joseph S. Torg, M.D.

## A Review of Ruptures of the Achilles Tendon

Steven J. Hattrup and Kenneth A. Johnson (Mayo Clinic and Found., Rochester, Minn.)

Foot Ankle 6:34–38, August 1985                                           3–36

The diagnosis of Achilles tendon rupture is often indicated by the history. The classic history of an acute rupture involves a middle-aged man in a white-collar profession, who is engaged in a sports activity. He feels a sudden pain in the calf, perhaps associated with an audible snap, followed by difficulty in stepping off on the foot. Patients who have chronic ruptures have weakness, inability to ascend stairs or stand on tiptoe, and a "lame" gait. Many report that pain immediately after injury was minimal or absent, leading the patient to dismiss the injury as trivial. Physical examination of a fresh rupture can reveal swelling of the calf and a palpable defect in the tendon. Active plantar flexion is often present and can be forceful.

Ruptures in the Achilles tendon are usually limited to a definite segment 2 to 6 cm proximal to its insertion onto the calcaneus. In a cadaver study, the proximal muscle and the distal insertion were well supplied with vessels, which decreased in number toward the tendon segment that was more prone to rupture. The poor blood supply in this segment may contribute to rupture. Many patients with complete rupture have had symptoms for a variable period, suggesting a role for inflammation.

Numerous methods of repair or reconstruction have included: direct suture, fascial or Achilles tendon turn-down techniques, fascia lata grafts, reinforcement with plantaris or peroneus brevis tendon, end-to-end suture with local anesthesia, and percutaneous repair of closed ruptures. Recent reports describe the use of carbon fiber scaffolds for both acute repair and delayed reconstruction. The strength and stability of the repair allow shorter immobilization and more rapid rehabilitation.

Nonoperative treatment of acute Achilles tendon rupture is preferred. Properly conducted, it provides for return of adequate plantar flexion strength but avoids the complications inherent in operation. Reruptures occur with significant frequency and may be minimized by longer immobilization. However, there is usually some decrease in plantar flexion strength after conservative treatment relevant to operation. Therefore, surgical repair should be considered for younger patients who are more likely to demand more from their legs for strenuous athletic activities and who desire to maximize their chances of achieving normal or near-normal strength in the injured extremity.

▶ The authors present a good review of current thinking regarding management of acute Achilles tendon ruptures. Noteworthy data include that of Nistor (*J. Bone Joint Surg. [Am.]* 63-A:394–399, 1981), who reviewed 2,647 reported surgical cases in which there was a major complication rate of 8%, including 2% rerupture. This must be compared with the reported rerupture rate of conservative treatment of 22% by Jacobs et al. (*Am. J. Sports Med.* 107–111, 1978), 29% by Inglis (*J. Bone Joint Surg. [Am.]* 58-A:990–993, October 1976) and 35% by Persson and Wredmark (*Int. Orthop.* 3:149–152, 1971).—Joseph S. Torg, M.D.

---

**Chronic Compartment Syndrome: Diagnosis, Management, and Outcomes**
Don E. Detmer, Kim Sharpe, Robert L. Sufit, and Forrest M. Girdley (Univ. of Wisconsin–Madison)
Am. J. Sports Med. 13:162–170, May–June 1985                    3–37

---

Chronic compartment syndrome (CCS) is typically an exercise-induced condition with a relatively inadequate musculofascial compartment size, resulting in chronic or recurrent pain, disability or both. It is seen chiefly in active persons; the history is very important. A reduction or cessation of exercise generally leads to symptomatic improvement. The physical findings are unimpressive in nearly all cases. Compartment pressure measurements can confirm the diagnosis. A number of techniques of fasciotomy have been described.

A total of 233 compartments were released in 100 consecutive operated patients with CCS. Most patients were athletes, especially runners. The mean duration of symptoms was 22 months. A large majority of patients had bilateral involvement. The posterior compartment was involved in about half of the cases. Eleven patients had operative and postoperative complications. More than 90% of the patients were cured or significantly improved symptomatically and/or functionally on follow-up, a median of 4½ months after operation. The median time to the resumption of conditioned running was 3 weeks. A complete functional cure was obtained in 73 cases, and no patient was functionally worse after operation. Recurrences were observed in 5 patients. Overall patient satisfaction with the outcome was high.

Fasciotomy is an effective and safe means of managing patients with CCS. The best results are obtained when surgery is done before severe symptoms have developed or serious functional impairment is present. Fasciectomy is favored in patients who developed new symptoms after a good initial response to fasciotomy. Both procedures can be done under local anesthesia on an outpatient basis.

► This series is a report of 233 fasciotomies for chronic compartment syndrome in 100 patients who received surgical treatment between 1976 and 1984. However, the range of follow-up is 8 to 1,425 days, with a mean of 304.8 days. Thus, although surgery was performed as long as 10 years ago, the mean follow-up period was 10 months. This certainly speaks for itself. Also to be noted is the complication rate of 18%. On the positive side, however, this paper indicates that identification and fasciotomy of the involved compartment will effect the desired therapeutic response. This certainly rejects the concept of routine four compartment fasciotomies. The performance of fasciotomies on the superficial compartment on an outpatient basis is also noteworthy.—Joseph S. Torg, M.D.

---

**Shin Splints: A Literature Review**
P. Bates (Sydney, Australia)
Br. J. Sports Med. 19:132–137, September 1985                    3–38

---

Shin splints account for about 10% to 15% of all running injuries and up to 60% of lesions producing pain in athletes' legs. Some recommend limiting the term to musculotendinous inflammation, excluding the stress fracture or ischemic disorder. There is no "usual" site of involvement, but many studies have focused on chronic medial shin pain. Pain is present on or about the tibia on exertion, initially toward the end of a run. Markedly affected subjects can have pain on walking or even at rest. Few physical signs are present, though most patients have tenderness at the site of pain.

Pain from shin splints may be due to a bony reaction to the stress of overuse. Increased muscle compartment pressures have been demonstrated in athletes with shin pain. Biomechanical factors are often implicated, as in cases of forefoot varus, tibia vara, or internal femoral torsion. Overused, fatigued muscle can cause or exacerbate the disorder. Both radiography and bone scanning can diagnose stress fracture. The use of ultrasound in diagnosis of chronic tibial pain is still experimental.

Avoidance of training errors can prevent shin splints. The use of proper shoes and a gradual increase in mileage are important measures. All treatment regimens include rest. Ice and nonsteroidal anti-inflammatory drugs are widely recommended. Muscle strengthening can help prevent the effects of fatigue on bone and muscle. Correction of biomechanical defects is important where these are a factor. Injection of corticosteroids into the medial tibial border has had limited success.

► The author correctly states that shin splints is not a specific diagnosis and has many different causes. When evaluating an athlete with shin pain, all of the different causes must be considered and explored. The obvious weak or tight muscle problems, as well as biomechanical problems, must be corrected. Footwear and running surfaces must be looked at closely. We have found that changes in training regimens and running techniques must accompany the usual treatment of these injuries to prevent recurrence.—Frank George, A.T.C., P.T.

### Radiographic and Histologic Analyses of Stress Fracture in Rabbit Tibias

Guoping Li, Shudong Zhang, Gang Chen, Hui Chen, and Anming Wang (Natl. Research Inst. of Sports Science and Academy of Traditional Chinese Medicine, Peking)
Am. J. Sports Med. 13:285–293, September–October 1985          3–39

Sequential changes in remodeling of the internal structure of the tibia caused by controlled, excessive jumping and running were studied in 20 rabbits. An electric cage with high pulsive voltage was used to induce animal jumping and running activities under a controlled frequency and period. Radiographic and histologic methods of analysis allowed description of the developing pathologic signs of stress fracture formation throughout a 60-day period.

Progressive periosteal reaction was found radiographically in 20 tibias of 18 rabbits (55%) as the training progressed, whereas the remaining tibias showed only soft tissue swelling or no radiographic change. At the seventh day (after about 2,160 jumps) only soft tissue around the tibia was swollen. At day 14 (after about 4,320 jumps), some periosteal reaction was noted. At day 21 (after about 6,480 jumps) increased periosteal new bone formation was present. After 30 days (about 8,640 jumps) the periosteal new bone formation was markedly increased, and the cortex was thickened and had an irregular edge. Osseous changes included, on the second day, an increase in erythrocytes in the vessels of the haversian canals. By the seventh day, generation of osteoclast and resorption cavities were observed in the tibia's cortex. Incomplete fracture of the tibial cortex was found in 2 rabbits at the 21st day of exercise. On the fourth day, collagen fibers of the periosteum had a loose appearance. By the 12th day subperiosteal osteoblastic activity had increased. Bone remodeling occurred in both the newly formed bone and original bone of the tibial cortex. Osteoclasts accompanied the large amount of new bone. An increase of capillaries was accompanied by the osteoclastic process and was followed by some haversian canal-like structures, which appeared gradually as new bone changed to mature bone.

The authors conclude that stress fracture of the tibia caused by excessive stress is not periostitis or a single event but a sequential pathologic process of impairment and repair of bone, including the periosteum. Accelerated resorption of bone is the initial stage of stress fracture of the tibia. Periosteal proliferation and new bone formation are compensatory responses. Fracture may appear if excessive stress continues in a tibia weakened by osteoclastic resorption. However, such fractures do not occur in most tibias because the bone adapts to changes in stress requirement through proper bone remodeling.

### Periosteal Stress-Induced Reactions Resembling Stress Fractures: A Radiologic and Histologic Study in Dogs

Hans K. Uhthoff and Z. F. George Jaworski (Univ. of Ottawa)
Clin. Orthop. 199:284–291, October 1985          3–40

An external callus is always associated with so-called stress fractures, but a fracture line cannot always be shown radiologically. In such cases it is assumed that an undisplaced fracture or microfracture must exist for an external callus to form. Eighteen beagles were immobilized in a shoulder spica for 6–32 weeks and then remobilized. At the time of sacrifice 4–28 weeks after remobilization was begun, an external fusiform bone formation on the distal metacarpal metaphysis was seen radiographically in eight dogs without evidence of a fracture line. Serial histologic examination in seven metacarpi also failed to reveal the presence of any break in the bone's continuity.

In the absence of inflammation, neoplasia, or infection, the elaboration of periosteal callus is attributed to a fracture. Mechanical factors alone, however, can lead to new bone formation, e.g., hypertrophy of the radius after resection of the ulnar diaphysis, and periosteal new bone formation after removal of rigid plates used for internal fixation of fractures. Similarly, following remobilization after prolonged immobilization of young adult beagles, a lamellar periosteal bone apposition was noted. It is postulated that, because of reduced bone mass secondary to prolonged immobilization, bones are subjected to increased strain during remobilization, which in turn leads to new bone formation.

Diaphyseal bone loss during immobilization is not uniform. It affects the anterior and posterior diaphyseal cortices more than it affects the lateral ones. Also, smaller bones, especially their distal metaphyses, showed the greatest loss radiologically. This was also the site of a fusiform periosteal reaction without radiologic or histologic evidence of a fracture. This reaction, observed mostly at the palmar aspect, was interpreted as a periosteal stress reaction. It was composed of both lamellar and woven bone.

Stress fractures observed in clinical practice may occasionally occur after remobilization following prolonged immobilization. More often, however, they occur in individuals having a normal bone structure and strength when bones are exposed to unusual amounts of repetitive stress, as reported in army recruits. Adaptive changes occur in response. Often, the first clinical sign is local tenderness followed by a radiologically visible callus formation. A break in continuity is not always seen radiologically. However, should it occur, the break is usually preceded by a callus formation.

A periosteal fusiform bone formation seen at the distal metacarpal metaphysis seems to be caused by a discrepancy between fatigue endurance of bone and applied stresses. The resulting periosteal reaction can thus be considered a protective mechanism, allowing bone to adapt to higher levels of stress.

▶ These two well-designed laboratory studies (Digests 3–39 and 3–40) clearly demonstrate that reaction of bone to the stress of repetitive cyclic loading is a continuum that begins on a cellular level and may or may not progress to radiographically demonstrable fracture. The clinical implications are obvious. The liberal designation of a positive $^{99m}$Tc bone scan as representing a stress fracture is unwarranted. The terms asymptomatic stress reaction of bone or symptomatic stress reaction of bone are more appropriate when results of roentgenograms are negative. The term stress fracture of bone should be reserved for those incidences when cortical infraction or cancellous sclerosis is demonstrated roentgenographically.—Joseph S. Torg, M.D.

**Nonunions of Stress Fractures of the Tibia**
Neil E. Green, Richard A. Rogers, and A. Brant Lipscomb (Vanderbilt Univ.)
Am. J. Sports Med. 13:171–176, May–June 1985                              3–41

Tibial stress fractures are relatively infrequent in the middle part of the bone. Six such cases with nonunion were encountered in a 5-year period, all in young males. None of the fractures healed on simple immobilization. Five became complete fractures, and 3 of these patients had no symptoms before completion of the fracture. The patients with complete fractures were immobilized for 6½ months on average. Three patients had excision of the nonunion with iliac bone grafting an average of 11 months after diagnosis. One patient each had electromagnetic stimulation, simple biopsy, and open reduction and internal fixation of a second complete fracture.

Man, 20, a college football player, was in early conditioning when he developed aching pain in the middle of the left tibia, especially on long runs. A stress fracture involved the anterolateral cortex. Symptoms resolved with rest, but the fracture persisted at 5 weeks, and the leg gave way when the subject ran an obstacle course. Radiographs then showed completion of the fracture, and the limb was casted. Partial weight-bearing was allowed after 6 weeks. The fracture remained present 4½ months after completion when the patient resumed jogging. The bone later refractured during wrestling. Open reduction and internal fixation were carried out, with a bone graft from the iliac crest. The tibia was healed clinically and radiologically 7 months later, and the patient returned to full participation. He is presently a professional running back.

None of the stress portions of these fractures healed with immobilization only. Fractures in the tibial midshaft probably result from tensile forces rather than compressive forces, and they seem to be prone to nonunion. Initial immobilization is reasonable, but iliac bone grafting should be seriously considered if there is no radiologic evidence of healing after 4–6 months. Athletic activity should be avoided until there is definite and complete union of the stress fracture.

▶ Although this is a small series, the authors certainly make the point that stress fractures of the midshaft of the tibia behave differently than most other stress fractures. It is interesting to note that although they have not encountered a stress fracture of the mid-tibia that has healed without bone grafting, they hesitate to recommend primary grafting for these lesions. This paper has clearly defined a clinical problem and the need for a controlled perspective study. In view of the variety of the lesions, it is apparent that a multicentered effort is in order.—Joseph S. Torg, M.D.

**A Prospective Study of the Effect of a Shock-Absorbing Orthotic Device on the Incidence of Stress Fractures in Military Recruits**

C. Milgrom, M. Giladi, H. Kashtan, A. Simkin, R. Chisin, J. Margulies, R. Steinberg, Z. Aharonson, and M. Stein (Hadassah Univ., Jerusalem, Tel-Aviv Med. Ctr., and Osteoporosis Inst., Jerusalem)

Foot Ankle 6:101–104, October 1985                                    3–42

Stress fracture is a major problem in both military trainees and athletes. An orthotic device designed to provide shock absorption when worn in military boots was evaluated in 312 male recruits from infantry units of the Israeli army entered into a prospective study of stress fractures. Orthotics sized according to shoe size were given to 143 of 295 recruits entering basic training. A shell of polyolefin plastic extended to the metatarsal necks and was prefabricated for an "average" arch height. A styrene butadiene rubber hindfoot post was added to the shell at three degrees varus, and a 1/8-in. PPT pad of open cell urethane foam was placed beneath the heel post. The shell was covered with a layer of PPT laminated with moisture-resistant expanded vinyl. The men were followed for 14 weeks of training.

Scintigraphy demonstrated stress fractures in 31% of the recruits in training. A total of 184 such fractures occurred in 91 recruits, more than half in the tibia and a third in the femur. The orthotic device was used throughout training by 113 recruits. Femoral stress fractures were significantly less frequent in these men. Tibial and metatarsal stress fractures also were less frequent in orthotic users, but not significantly so. Overall, 74% of the recruits were considered to have average arches. None had severe pes planus.

Orthotic prophylaxis against stress fracture deserves further study in persons at risk, e.g., military recruits. The effects of orthotics on metatarsal and calcaneal stress fractures are of particular importance in a military setting. Femoral stress fractures are potentially the most dangerous type because of their tendency to be "silent" for long periods and because of the risk of displacement.

▶ The conclusion to be drawn from the data presented is that orthotic devices can reduce the occurrence of increased femoral uptake of $^{99}$Tc MDP in military recruits. However, this is certainly a "step" in the right direction.—Joseph S. Torg, M.D.

---

**Stress Fractures in Military Recruits: A Prospective Study Showing an Unusually High Incidence**

C. Milgrom, M. Giladi, M. Stein, H. Kashtan, J. Y. Margulies, R. Chisin, R. Steinberg, and Z. Aharonson (Hadassah Univ. Hosp. and the Osteoporosis Inst., Jerusalem)

J. Bone Joint Surg. [Br.] 67-A:732–735, November 1985              3–43

Beginning in February 1983, a group of 295 male military recruits from selected combat units underwent a 14-week evaluation as part of a prospective study of stress fractures. During 14 weeks of basic training, 171 of the 295 men had symptoms suggesting possible stress fractures. Based on radiographic and scintigraphic findings, 184 stress fractures were diagnosed in 91 of the 295 soldiers (31%). In 20% the radiographic findings were positive. The number of fractures at each site was as follows: tibia (not including the tibial plateau), 51.2%; femur (not including the femoral condyles), 29.8%; and the feet (tarsus and metatarsus), 8.7%. Of tibial diaphysial fractures, 80% were in the midshaft. There were no stress fractures in the femoral neck or in the calcaneus.

For 12 fractures, the time of onset could not be determined precisely; of the remaining 172 fractures, 61 (35%) were asymptomatic and time of onset could not be determined. Of the 111 symptomatic fractures, onset in 11 (10%) was before basic training; in 59 (53%) onset occurred during weeks 1–4 of training; in 24 (22%), during weeks 5–8; and in 17 (15%), after 8 weeks. Only 8% of tibial diaphysial stress fractures caused no symptoms, but 69% of femoral stress fractures were asymptomatic.

According to studies of American servicemen, the incidence of stress fractures among recruits is less than 2%. The 31% incidence of stress fractures in this study far exceeds this figure or that reported from any previous study. One possible explanation is that the study was prospective and included detailed follow-up examinations of all soldiers. Most other military studies have been retrospective, calculating the incidence by dividing the number of soldiers found to have stress fractures at morning sick call by the total basic training population for the period studied. Thus, there was no assessment of the group not present at sick call. Further, the soldiers and medical staff were all made acutely aware of the existence of stress fractures. The medical staff interviewed and examined all soldiers every 3 weeks, and thus discovered those who otherwise might not have attended a clinic. Therefore, a far larger number of fractures was detected than in previous basic training periods at the same military base.

Even if a stress fracture was seen on the radiographs, scintigraphy also was performed, leading to the detection of stress fractures at other sites. The authors agree with Greaney et al. that "in the appropriate clinical setting, a scintigraphic abnormality is diagnostic of a stress fracture even if radiographs are normal." In a population subjected to strenuous physical training, the incidence of stress fractures apparently can reach very high proportions.

---

**Stress Fractures and Bone Pain: Are They Closely Associated?**
David Groshar, Menahem Lam, Einat Even-Sapir, Ora Israel, and Dov Front (Rambam Med. Ctr. and Technicon-Israel Inst. of Technology, Haifa)
Injury 16:526–528, September 1985                                           3–44

---

The relationship between bone pain and stress fractures diagnosed by bone scintigraphy was investigated in 64 military recruits during active training. In three males aged 18 years, pain developed in the site of abnormal uptake of $^{99m}$Tc-methylene diphosphonate within 7–14 days after the bone scan in a previously asymptomatic site. Overall, 124 sites of stress fractures were found in the 64 patients; 32 (26%) sites were asymptomatic. Thirty-eight patients (59%) had multiple stress fractures, 32 of which (33%) were asymptomatic. Also, 53% of the femoral regions with abnormal uptake were painless, as were 17% in the tibia.

Male military recruit, 18 years, was seen after 4 weeks of training because of pain in both feet during exercise. Bone scintigraphy showed increased uptake of radioisotope in the middle thirds of both tibias. No abnormal uptake was seen in his feet, but the patient was instructed to avoid exercise. One week later pain and tenderness developed in the middle third of the left tibia where bone scan findings were positive.

Radiography is much less sensitive than bone scanning is in the diagnosis of stress fracture. Only 28% of the fractures are identified in the early stages, and up to 50% are missed by radiography even several weeks after the development of symptoms or after bone scan results are positive. Many studies demonstrate the usefulness of bone scanning in the early diagnosis of stress fractures, with a reported sensitivity of 100%. Bone scintigraphy thus definitively makes the diagnosis in patients complaining of bone pain.

Findings in the three patients reported suggest the possibility that an abnormality noted on bone scintigraphy may appear earlier than pain does. Even when certain areas of abnormal uptake may be associated with pain, others may temporarily be painless. Asymptomatic stress fractures are more common in the femur than in the tibia. These results stress the necessity for scintigraphy of all susceptible bones in a population prone to the development of stress fractures. The data do not indicate the percentage of patients having stress fractures without pain in such a population, but they do show that there may be a delay between confirmation of the diagnosis by scintigraphy and onset of pain.

Bone scintigraphy should not be done routinely in all military recruits or in persons who jog. However, abnormal uptake indicating stress fracture may be observed in the absence of pain, which may occur only later. The appearance of asymptomatic scintigraphic lesions is not confined to stress fractures; this phenomenon has also been described in bone metastases.

▶ Digests 3–43 and 3–44 raise the question: What is a stress fracture? It is recognized that repetitive cyclic loading, the application of alternating compressive and tensile forces to bone, can result in fatigue fracture. Commonly, a fracture is a defect in the continuity of at least one cortex that can be demonstrated roentgenographically. It is also generally recognized that increased uptake of injected $^{99m}$Tc methylene Diphosphonate at the fracture site occurs prior to roentgenographic demonstration of the defect. In both of these papers, the authors have confused the entity of stress reaction of bone, as manifested by positive results from bone scintigraphy, as a stress fracture. The validity of this assumption is to be questioned. The fact that a third of the subjects in each group had, on examination, positive results from bone scintigraphy in the absence of symptomatology further questions the justification of making a diagnosis of stress fracture solely on the basis of a positive scan.

We believe that there are three criteria involved in the diagnosis of stress fracture: (1) bone tenderness at the involved sites; (2) positive results from scintigraphy; and (3) eventual roentgenographic demonstration of a cortical defect.—Joseph S. Torg, M.D.

## Iliotibial Band Syndrome in Distance Runners

Allan N. Sutker, F. Alan Barber, Douglas W. Jackson, and John W. Pagliano (Plano Orthopedic and Sports Med. Ctr., Plano, Tex.; Southern California Ctr. for Sports Med., Long Beach, Calif.; and St. Vincent Med. Ctr., Los Angeles)
Sports Med. 2:447–451, 1985                                            3–45

Iliotibial band syndrome is an overuse syndrome seen primarily in distance runners. The iliotibial band is a thickened strip of fascia lata that extends from the iliac crest to the lateral tibial tubercle and receives part of the insertion of the tensor fascia lata and gluteus maximus. At the knee, the band acts as a stabilizing ligament between the lateral femoral condyle and the tibia. In cadaver dissections of the region, Orava noticed a reddish brown bursal thickening under the iliotibial band. He concluded that it developed because of friction of the iliotibial band over the lateral femoral epicondyle (a prominent ridge just above the condyle). Walking stiff-legged keeps the iliotibial band anterior to the epicondyle. Activities in which the knee is repeatedly flexed caused the band to pass posteriorly over the lateral femoral condyle and may lead to irritation.

Among 1,030 runners seen for lower extremity musculoskeletal problems during 1 year, the authors diagnosed iliotibial band syndrome in 48 (39 males). Average age was 31 years. Thirteen runners had bilateral involvement, the right knee was involved in 20, and the left knee was involved in 15. Before onset of lateral knee symptoms, 11 patients had been running less than 1 year, but most had been running 20 to 40 miles a week for at least 3 years. Eleven runners had competed in at least one marathon, and only 1 patient had never run farther than 5 miles at one time. Symptoms often persisted for 2 to 6 months, but in 2 runners, symptoms were unrelieved for 2 years. Once gone, pain usually did not return if the runner avoided certain offending factors.

Pain was aggravated by repetitive movement of the knee during running and usually became limiting at a constant distance for each person. The runners could generally walk long distances without symptoms, but stairs aggravated the pain. No runner reported any direct trauma or twisting injury to the knee before onset of symptoms. Diagnosis was made primarily by history and by localizing the tenderness by palpation to the area of the lateral femoral epicondyle and occasionally Gerdy's tubercle. The lateral joint line, popliteal tendon, lateral collateral ligament, and anterior lateral fat pad were not tender. There were no cystic masses on the lateral side of the knee. The runners could jog in place, hop, squat, and arise without significant discomfort. There was no intra-articular effusion and no ligamentous laxity. Conservative treatment consisted of reducing the distance run by the patient. Other nonsurgical measures included iliotibial band stretching, local heat or ice applications, use of anti-inflammatory medication, local corticosteroid injections, or use of orthoses. No single treatment appeared to be better than the others, and not all were acceptable to every runner. Only two runners in this series did not respond to this conservative program, but they refused operation.

Recent experience has indicated a tendency for runners with normal-appearing feet to develop the iliotibial band syndrome after switching to shoes with a so-called varus wedge. These shoes may be excellent for a runner with pronated feet, but the increased lateral knee stress can initiate the syndrome. Return to a normally configured sole eliminates the symptoms. The long-term prognosis for iliotibial band syndrome appears to be good, although some runners have recurrent symptoms if they increase mileage rapidly.

▶ This article presents an excellent delineation of the so-called iliotibial band syndrome. To be noted, the authors observed that a variety of foot structures were seen in these patients and they could not implicate any particular arch structure as the responsible etiological factor. Also, surgery was not used as treatment.—Joseph S. Torg, M.D.

## Hamstring Injuries: Proposed Aetiological Factors, Prevention, and Treatment
James C. Agre (Univ. of Wisconsin–Madison)
Sports Med. 2:21–33, 1985                                          3 46

Injuries to the hamstring muscles can be devastating to the athlete because these injuries frequently heal slowly and have a tendency to recur. It is thought that many of recurrent injuries to the hamstring musculotendinous unit are the result of inadequate rehabilitation after the initial injury. The severity of hamstring injuries is usually of first or second degree, but occasionally third-degree injuries involving complete rupture of the musculotendinous unit do occur.

Most hamstring strain injuries occur while running or sprinting. Several causes have been proposed: poor flexibility, inadequate muscle strength or endurance or both, dyssynergic muscle contraction during running, insufficient warm-up and stretching prior to exercise, awkward running style, and a return to activity before rehabilitation is complete. Treatment for such injuries includes immediate rest and immobilization, and then a gradual increase in movement, strengthening, and activity. Athletic competition should be avoided until full rehabilitation is achieved. Failure to achieve full rehabilitation will only predispose the athlete to recurrent injury. The best treatment for hamstring injuries is prevention, which includes training to maintain or improve strength, flexibility, endurance, coordination, and agility.

More research is needed on muscle strain injuries. To date, no prospective studies have been performed to identify the factors most strongly associated with hamstring strain injuries. As for prevention, a gradually progressive warm-up and stretching program prior to training sessions and competition is highly recommended, as is stretching during the cool-down period.

▶ An excellent review article dealing with the etiology, prevention, and treatment of hamstring strains. Emphasized is the point that return to competition after treatment and rehabilitation of these injuries requires complete return of muscle strength, endurance, and flexibility in addition to coordination and agility.—Joseph S. Torg, M.D.

---

**Pelvic Stress Fractures in Long Distance Runners**
Timothy D. Noakes, James A. Smith, Graeme Lindenberg, and Clive E. Wills (Cape Town, South Africa, and Groote Schuur Hosp., South Africa)
Am. J. Sports Med. 13:120–123, March–April 1985                    3–47

---

Five cases of radiographically diagnosed pelvic stress fracture were encountered with 2 other cases in which scintigraphy showed stress fractures that were not apparent radiographically. Five runners had identical clinical findings but did not have bone scanning. The 12 patients were seen in 1 year among about 1,000 runners visiting a sports injury clinic. The 8 men and 4 women were aged 21 to 54 years. Ten of the runners ran 100 km or more per week, and had done so for at least 1 year.

Most runners reported the onset of symptoms during a race or fast training run. A dull groin ache progressed to the point that running was not possible. Patients consistently had discomfort or frank pain in the groin when standing on the affected leg. Marked tenderness was well localized to the affected inferior pubic ramus. No clinical features, including recovery time, could be related to the presence or absence of radiographic abnormality. One patient developed symptoms on the opposite side 6 months after initial injury without radiographic evidence of a new fracture. The only treatment was avoidance of running. One patient elected to use crutches, but the recovery period was not shortened as a result.

A minority of pelvic stress fractures in this series were evident radiographically, despite the consistent presence of marked tenderness and a positive "standing sign." All the patients were competitive distance runners; women are often affected disproportionately. Injury is especially likely to occur during competitive racing or interval training, and it may result from excessive repetition of muscle contraction, not from a change in force.

▶ This paper documents three features: (1) groin pain of sufficient severity to prevent running; (2) localized tenderness; and (3) a positive "standing test" as diagnostic of pelvic stress fracture despite negative radiographic results. The authors' contention that this injury may be under-diagnosed if bone scans are not routinely obtained is valid. Other than observing the predilection of marathon runners, especially women, to develop pelvic stress fractures, the article does not deal with possible etiologic factors of such fractures. Pavlov et al. (*J. Bone Joint Surg.* [*Am.*] 64-A:1020–1025, 1982) observe that the occurrence of this injury during intense training indicates that the fracture results from the excessive repetition of muscle contractures and not from a change in their force.—Joseph S. Torg, M.D.

## Avulsion Fractures of the Pelvis
Jeffrey N. Metzmaker and Arthur M. Pappas (Univ. of Massachusetts)
Am. J. Sports Med. 13:349–358, September–October 1985          3–48

Avulsion fractures of the pelvic apophyses occur infrequently, but they show a consistent pattern with regard to mechanism, patient's age, symptoms, physical findings, and radiographic appearance. Some disagreement exists in the literature concerning the treatment of these fractures. Findings were reviewed in 27 consecutive children aged 13 to 17 years with avulsion fracture of the pelvis. None had complete skeletal maturation at the time of injury. A single pathologic specimen was available for review.

Boy, 14 years, noted a snapping pain in the left groin and buttock when he suddenly accelerated out of the batter's box. Bed rest relieved the symptoms, but severe pain recurred 2 weeks after injury when he attempted to run again. Radiographic examination confirmed a minimally displaced avulsion fracture of the left ischium at the origin of the hamstring muscles. After 7 weeks of minimal activity the boy was allowed to begin ice skating, but at a slow pace. After another 6½ weeks he progressed to playing competitive hockey.

A patient with avulsion injury of an anterior iliac spine or specifically near the iliopsoas may complain of right lower quadrant abdominal pain and ileus. Treatment of the patients described in the present article involved five levels of progression: (1) rest and protection; (2) gradual increase in excursion of the injured musculotendinous unit; (3) start of a comprehensive progressive resistance program; (4) use of the injured musculotendinous unit integrated with use of other muscles of the pelvis and lower extremity; and (5) preparation for return to competitive status. Of the 27 patients, 24 had an excellent result, i.e., return to preinjury status within 4 months. Two patients had delayed excellent results, i.e., return to preinjury status after more than 4 months. One result was good; this patient returned to preinjury status but continued to report an intermittent local aching sensation 1 year afterward.

The incremental course of rehabilitation described is recommended for patients with uncomplicated fractures of the pelvis. Excision or surgical reattachment of the fragment might be considered if the physician is concerned that weakness and pain will persist after nonoperative management. However, results in this series of patients provide evidence that surgical intervention should not be considered as a primary treatment course.

▶ The conclusion that early diagnosis and a carefully supervised nonoperative rehabilitation course will result in satisfactory union of avulsion fractures of the pelvis apophyses is in keeping with my own experience. To be noted is that in rare patients with suggestive radiographs who lack a clear history of injury, the differential diagnosis must include osteomyelitis, Ewing's sarcoma, chondroblastoma, and other unexpected lesions.—Joseph S. Torg, M.D.

---

**Herniography in Athletes With Groin Pain**
Sam G. G. Smedberg, Albert E. A. Broome, Åke Gullmo, and Harald Roos
(Central Hosp., Helsinborg, Sweden)
Am. J. Surg. 149:378–382, March 1985                                           3–49

---

Of more than 1,000 consecutive patients examined by herniography between 1974 and 1981, 78 were male athletes, 47 of whom were soccer players. Four were previously operated on for hernia, 2 in childhood. Twenty-three of the 78 had bilateral groin pain; thus there were 101 symptomatic cases, 60 on the right side and 41 on the left, and 55 groin sides without pain. Duration of symptoms before herniography ranged from 1 month to 5 years. Four patients reported sudden onset of the pain caused by a special strain; the others had gradual onset. Groin pain was provoked by lifting, running, and kicking the ball in soccer in most of the patients.

At physical examination before herniography, a hernia was found in 8 groin sides with symptoms (7.9%) and in none of the 55 asymptomatic groin sides. Herniography was performed with intraperitoneal injection of positive contrast medium after puncture of the abdominal wall in the lower left quadrant. The findings were classified as hernia (Fig 3–16), weakness and bulging of the posterior inguinal wall without true herniation, so-called deep fossae, or normal. After herniography, the patients were reexamined, and exploration was planned when hernia was the most

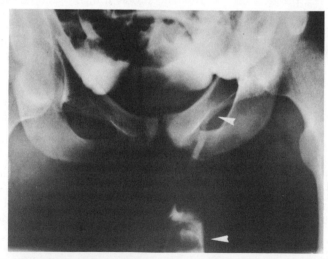

Fig 3–16.—Soccer player, aged 22, with obscure groin pain on left side. Congenital hernia (*arrows*) was found at herniography, and he underwent successful operation. (Courtesy of Smedberg, S.G.G., et al.: Am. J. Surg. 149:378–382, March 1985.)

probable explanation of groin pain. Mean follow-up after treatment was 41 months (range, 11 to 100 months). Two patients were lost to follow-up after herniography. There was no difference in follow-ups between patients who were and those who were not operated on. The 78 patients received a questionnaire, which was answered by 73.

Significantly more hernias were found in the groin sides with symptoms in both sides, compared with the contralaterally asymptomatic groin sides (84.2% and 49.1%, respectively); significantly more asymptomatic groin sides were normal (43.6% vs. 8.9%). A direct hernia alone or with another hernia was the most frequent herniographic finding, seen in 57 (56.4%) of the groin sides that produced pain and in 18 (32.7%) of the asymptomatic groin sides. Incompetence of the posterior wall (deep fossae) was the only finding in 11 groin sides, but it was seen in combination with hernias in another 18 symptomatic and 4 asymptomatic groin sides. Indirect hernias were seen in 6 sympatomatic groin sides in patients who were not operated on.

Fifty-three athletes were operated on for hernia. Seventeen had bilateral symptoms, and 10 had operations on both sides. Forty operations were performed on the right side and 23 on the left. In 44 of 63 groin sides that were operated on the pain was cured, in 13 sides pain was improved, and in 6 sides pain was unchanged. In 25 athletes, no hernia operation was performed. Two were lost to follow-up, and the other 23 had 29 groin sides with pain. Ten groin sides were cured, 16 were improved, and 3 had unchanged or increased pain. Sixteen of 19 without diminution of pain had chronic tenoperiostitis.

Some of the patients with symptoms of tenoperiostitis postoperatively were initially pain free for some time after the operation. When they returned to sports activities, pain recurred. Whether there was any hidden case of chronic tenoperiostitis among the 43 cured patients who were operated on is unknown. No patient with chronic tenoperiostitis who was not operated on, however, was fully recovered during follow-up. The changes in the pubis and symphysis appearing as osteochondritis found in many of these patients are well known in soccer players. The changes require long periods of rest to heal or, in advanced cases, operation.

▶ The authors note that "when using an excellent diagnostic tool like herniography, there is an obvious risk of relying too much on its illustrative diagnostic capacity while overlooking other conditions that parallel the not infrequently asymptomatic hernias. The importance of a thorough clinical investigation before herniography must therefore be strongly emphasized."—Josph S. Torg, M.D.

## Knee Injuries

### Instrumented Measurement of Anterior Laxity of the Knee

Dale M. Daniel, Lawrence L. Malcom, Gary Losse, Mary Lou Stone, Raymond Sachs, and Robert Burks (Kaiser Hosp., San Diego; Univ. of California, San Diego; and Donald Sharp Rehabilitation Ctr., San Diego)
J. Bone Joint Surg. [Am.] 67-A:720–726, June 1985                    3–50

Anteroposterior laxity of the knee was measured using the Medmetric knee arthrometer in both limbs of 33 cadaver specimens, 338 normal subjects, and 89 patients with unilateral disruption of the anterior cruciate ligament (ACL). Testing of cadaver specimens is illustrated in Figure 3–17. Total anteroposterior laxity produced by anterior and posterior loads of 20 pounds was measured, as was the anterior compliance index, defined as anterior displacement between anterior loads of 67 and 89 newtons. All measurements were made with the knee flexed 20 degrees.

Total anteroposterior displacement at a load of 89 newtons (20 pounds) in cadaver studies was 8.7 mm, with a range of 5–15 mm. Displacement anteriorly was 12.1 mm after section of the ACL. Force-displacement curves in normal and ACL-deficient knees are compared in Figure 3–18. Mean anterior displacement at 89 newtons was 5.7 mm in normal subjects and 13 mm in patients with a disrupted ACL. Only 8% of normal subjects had a difference of more than 2 mm between the two knees, compared with 96% of patients with disruption of the ACL. The difference in left-right compliance indices exceeded 0.5 mm in 7% of the normal group and 85% of the patient group.

This portable test system leaves the knee joint minimally constrained and measures relative motion in the anteroposterior plane. A consistent increase in anterior laxity is associated with disruption of the ACL, and a difference in anterior laxity between the two knees is a sensitive measure of the integrity of the anterior cruciate ligament.

---

**Instrumented Measurement of Anterior Knee Laxity in Patients With Acute Anterior Cruciate Ligament Disruption**
Dale M. Daniel, Mary Lou Stone, Raymond Sachs, and Lawrence Malcolm (Kaiser Hosp., San Diego, and Univ. of California, San Diego)
Am. J. Sports Med. 13:401–406, Winter 1984                                      3–51

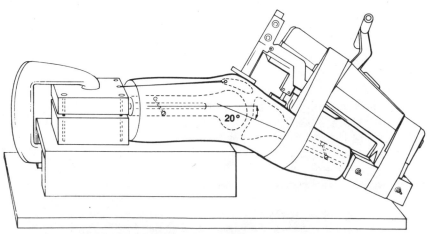

Fig 3–17.—Testing a cadaver specimen with the arthrometer. (Courtesy of Daniel, D.M., et al.: J. Bone Joint Surg. [Am.] 67-A:720–726, June 1985.)

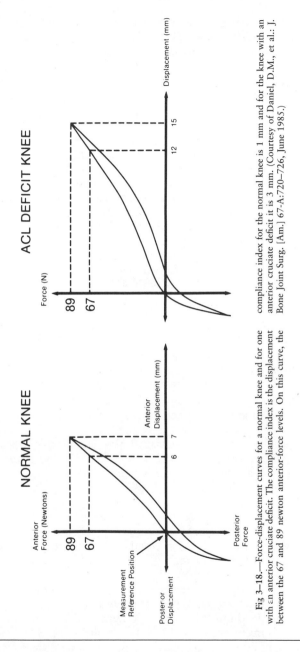

**NORMAL KNEE**

Anterior Force (Newtons)

89

67

Measurement Reference Position

Posterior Displacement

Anterior Displacement (mm)

6    7

Posterior Force

**ACL DEFICIT KNEE**

Force (N)

89

67

12    15

Displacement (mm)

Fig 3–18.—Force-displacement curves for a normal knee and for one with an anterior cruciate deficit. The compliance index is the displacement between the 67 and 89 newton anterior-force levels. On this curve, the compliance index for the normal knee is 1 mm and for the knee with an anterior cruciate deficit it is 3 mm. (Courtesy of Daniel, D.M., et al.: J. Bone Joint Surg. [Am.] 67-A:720–726, June 1985.)

Disruption of the anterior cruciate ligament (ACL) permits increased anterior excursion of the tibia in relation to the femur. Anteroposterior laxity was measured instrumentally in 138 patients seen within 2 weeks of injury, with their initial traumatic knee hemarthrosis. The MEDmetric Arthrometer model KT-1000 was used. Thirty-three patients had arthrometer laxity testing under anesthesia. Seventy-five patients had knee arthroscopy; 87% were found to have ACL tears, and 41% had meniscal tears. The mean time from injury to clinical evaluation was 3 days. Normal values for anterior laxity were obtained from 120 subjects.

A wide range of normal laxity was found on anterior displacement with 15- and 20-pound forces and with high manually applied force. Right-left differences were less than 2 mm in 88% of normal subjects. Anterior laxity measurements suggested or established pathologic laxity in 50 of 53 patients who were found on arthroscopy to have complete ACL tears. No patient had evidence of pathologic posterior laxity. Mean excursion with a 20-pound anterior displacement was 11.4 mm in ACL-injured knees and 7.3 mm in the normal knees of the same patients. Greater displacement was observed under anesthesia in some instances. Abnormal anterior laxity persisted in patients with complete ACL tears who were not operated on.

The ACL disruption results in a measurable increase in anterior laxity of the acutely injured knee. The wide range of anteroposterior displacement in normal knees suggests that the two knees be compared in injured patients. Measurements of acute displacement may be indicative of longer-term ligamentous laxity in patients with ACL disruption who elect not to have ligament operation.

▶ The development of the MEDmetric knee arthrometer model KT-1000 represents the first device capable of quantitating knee laxity in the clinical setting. The above two papers (Digests 3–50 and 3–51) clearly document the efficacy and clinical relevance of this device in quantitating normal laxity as well as that resulting from anterior cruciate ligament disruption in both the laboratory and clinical setting. One major problem with the report is the failure of the authors to document the reproducibility of the device. Although they state the test was repeated a total of 32 times on two specimens, the results and reproducibility of these determinations are not mentioned. We use the device extensively in our clinic and our observation is that results are reproducible in the hands of a single tester. However, there can be problems when two or more testers are involved.—Joseph S. Torg, M.D.

---

**Complications of Arthrography**
Arthur H. Newberg, Charles S. Munn, and Alan H. Robbins (Tufts Univ. and New England Baptist Hosp., Boston)
Radiology 155:605–606, June 1985                                              3–52

Arthrography is considered to be extremely safe, since reactions to intra-articular contrast mediums are rare. The authors have seen only 1 severe complication among more than 2,000 arthrographies. To determine the incidence of complications, a questionnaire was sent to 84 radiologists experienced in arthrography. The 57 respondents had performed more than 126,000 arthrographic procedures.

There were no deaths, 3 cases of infection, and 61 cases of hives in the survey. Other acute reactions included hypotension, seizures, air embolism, and laryngeal edema. Related complications included sterile chemical synovitis, severe pain after the procedure, and vasovagal reactions.

In a retrospective evaluation such as this, the most severe reactions are probably more vivid in the respondent's memory so that mild reactions may be more difficult to document. Also, the questionnaires were sent to a skewed group of radiologists, i.e., those who had a primary interest in skeletal radiology. Further, it is difficult to assess the frequency of reactions that occur after the patient has left the radiology department.

Adverse reactions to intravascular administration of contrast material occur at a rate of about 5%. Death rates vary from 1/10,000 to1/30,000, with as many as 500 deaths per year in the United States from reaction to contrast material. Complications resulting from arthrography are rare. Allergic reactions to local anesthesia, contrast medium, and epinephrine are possible. Sepsis is unusual, and mild allergic reactions are seldom seen. Urticaria is rare and almost always occurs 15 to 20 minutes after injection. Many respondents in this survey reported vasovagal syncope (sweating, bradycardia, hypotension) in young athletic men. The pathophysiology is unclear, but the finding has been reported previously.

Various explanations have been offered for the pain that follows arthrography. Injection of room air appears to cause less pain than does injection of carbon dioxide. Reaspiration of the joint after the study is not recommended, unless a large sterile effusion develops, because it does not decrease pain but may increase the risk of infection. The use of epinephrine decreases absorption of contrast from the joint and influx of fluid through the synovium into the joint, which may sustain the reaction.

After intra-articular contrast injection the synovium becomes edematous and hemorrhagic within 2 hours. At 24 hours there is tissue eosinophilia and vascular congestion. The use of sodium-containing contrast agents may lead to a more severe reaction that includes contraction and adhesions of the synovium, greater tissue eosinophilia, and mast cell proliferation. Sodium-containing agents may cause more pain, especially if they are injected inadvertently into the soft tissues, and should therefore be avoided. Eosinophilia of the synovial fluid has also been found after arthrography.

▶ It is important to recognize that a properly performed arthrogram is a short, painless procedure that yields accurate diagnostic information with minimal risk of complications.—Joseph S. Torg, M.D.

## Meniscal Lesions of the Knee Joint: CT Diagnosis

Roberto Passariello, Fausto Trecco, Fosco de Paulis, Carlo Masciocchi, Giuseppe Bonanni, and Bruno Beomonte Zobel (Cattedra di Radiologie della Universita and the Civil Hosp., L'Aquila, Italy)
Radiology 157:29–34, October 1985                                        3–53

Computed tomography resulted in a diagnostic accuracy of 89.2% and 96.1% for medial and lateral meniscal lesions, respectively, in 109 patients who underwent surgery after direct CT study of the knee for a clinically suspected meniscal lesion. The meniscal lesions were the only pathologic condition found in 59 patients. In 35 others they were associated with various lesions of the cruciate ligaments (31), collateral ligaments (15), and cystic bursitis (6). In the remaining 15 patients the menisci were normal, but 8 had lesions of other knee structures.

The best visualization of meniscal structures on CT scans is obtained on the planes of the intercondylar eminence and intercondylar spines. They appear as a characteristic C shape for the medial meniscus and as an incomplete O for the lateral meniscus. Both have homogeneous fibrocartilaginous density (70–90 Hounsfield units) (Fig 3–19). They are easily distinguishable from the adjacent structures and visible at the site of capsular ligament connections and bone insertion. Connections to the medial meniscus most relevant to radiologic examination are, at its middle part, the medial collateral ligament and, more posteriorly, the Hughston ligament and posterior joint capsule. The relevant connections for the lateral meniscus are the popliteus muscle tendon and the fibular collateral ligament at its middle and posterior parts, and the meniscofemoral ligaments at the posterior horn.

Meniscal tears appeared as alterations in normal morphology and ho-

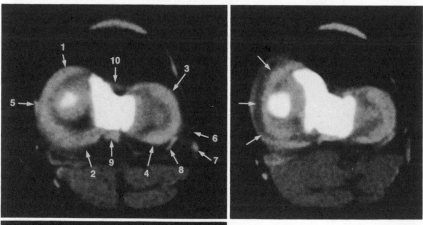

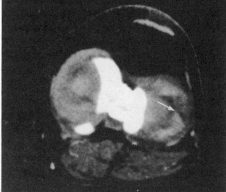

Fig 3–19 (top left).—Normal anatomy of the menisci as seen on CT scanning at the level of the intercondylar eminence plane: the regular and homogeneous appearance of the C-shaped medial meniscus with its anterior *(1)* and posterior *(2)* ends, and of the O-shaped lateral meniscus with its anterior *(3)* and posterior *(4)* ends; 5, the tibial collateral ligament; 6, the fibular collateral ligament; 7, the tendon of the biceps femoris muscle; 8, the popliteus muscle tendon; 9, the posterior cruciate ligament; 10, the anterior cruciate ligament.

Fig 3–20 (top right).—A complete longitudinal lesion of the medial meniscus is apparent as a convex hypodense tear *(arrows)* along the external part of the meniscal structure.

Fig 3–21 (bottom).—A transverse rupture of the lateral meniscus *(arrow)* is seen on CT scanning.

(Courtesy of Passariello, R., et al.: Radiology 157:29–34, October 1985. Reproduced with permission of the Radiological Society of North America.)

mogeneous density. They were characterized by hypodense streaks or gaps in a longitudinal direction (Fig 3–20) or, less frequently, in a transverse or oblique direction. The hypodense streaks may be single or multiple and vary in size and irregularity, according to the type of tear. If they are to have value for diagnosis, such alterations should be checked on two or more scanning planes. Complex lesions are most frequently identified with meniscal fragment displacements. The clear morphological alteration and presence of meniscal fragments that appear as hyperdense formations permit diagnosis easily, as well as definition of the extent of the tear.

The meniscal detachments may or may not be associated with lesions of the capsular ligament structures of the internal compartment. The appearance on CT is characterized by a hypodense longitudinal area. This produces a plane separating the meniscal structures from the capsular ligament formations, which normally adhere closely to the posterior horn.

Lateral meniscal tears had the same CT characteristics as medial meniscal tears. The most common clinical findings were complete longitudinal tears, complete transverse tears, and multiple fragmentations (we have never seen the latter in the medial meniscus) (Fig 3–21). The lateral meniscus could also be affected by cystic degeneration on its outer edges or spread throughout the structures, subjecting it to a complete morphological change. There were lateral diskoid menisci in five patients, three of whom had complete transverse tears. The clear morphological alteration and disappearance of the characteristic O shape allow, with only axial images, formulation of an accurate diagnosis.

Three false negative diagnoses resulted, two of which were capsular displacements (medial meniscus and lateral meniscus) that were not demonstrated by CT. The third was a tear limited to the anterior horn of the medial meniscus that had been neglected in the first evaluation but was clearly visible on subsequent review.

▶ Computed tomography may be useful as a complementary procedure to an arthrogram but not as an independent study. The CT image of the meniscus is suboptimal because of the following factors: (1) it is dependent on exact positioning of the CT gantry with the tibial plateau and the ability of the patient to maintain this position; (2) it has inherent limited resolution of fine detail and (3) it gives summation of information for each image. Additionally, the majority of meniscal lesions do not occur in isolation but are associated with articular cartilage and ligament injuries, intra-articular loose bodies, and popliteal cysts. The concurrent sources of knee pain and effusion are evident by arthrography. An arthrogram provides much more information and at a much less expense than CT.—Joseph S. Torg, M.D.

**Meniscal Tears of the Knee: Evaluation by High-Resolution CT Combined With Arthrography**
Bernard Ghelman (Hosp. for Special Surgery, New York)
Radiology 157:23–27, October 1985                                    3–54

The knees of 27 patients with evidence of meniscal tears were examined with high-resolution computed tomography (HRCT) immediately after double-contrast arthrography. Then anatomical and pathologic details that were displayed by each technique were compared.

Eight of 27 patients had normal menisci, 16 had a torn medial meniscus, 1 had a torn lateral meniscus, 1 had a discoid lateral meniscus, and 1 had a cystic medial meniscus. Three patients also had popliteal cysts. Four cases were confirmed with subsequent arthroscopy and 1 was confirmed with arthrotomy.

The anatomy of the semilunar cartilage and surrounding structures was more clearly outlined on the HRCT scans, which also made possible the differentiation of menisci from surrounding anatomical parts (popliteal tendon sleeve and popliteal cyst) and good visualization of the relationship of torn meniscal fragments.

The HRCT scans showed a gap between the base of the meniscus and surrounding capsular structures. Large recesses appear as air gaps at the base of the meniscus; however, in one or more scans, these gaps should be absent. The peripheral recesses at the base of meniscus should not be confused with the peripheral detachment. In these cases the HRCT scans should be correlated with the arthrograms to avoid confusion. On the HRCT scan the data about peripheral detachments and condition of the meniscus help the arthroscopist decide whether to remove the torn fragment or reattach the separated meniscus to its base.

Technically, HRCT scans are best when a large amount of air is injected into the knee. At least 40 to 60 ml of air should be introduced into the joint, and in most cases not more than 5 ml of positive contrast agent should be used. Epinephrine is helpful in delaying absorption of contrast agent.

Good HRCT scans also depend on the position of the knee at the time of the examination. The scout anteroposterior film of the knee must be examined to make sure that the leg is not rotated and that the joint compartment is sufficiently distracted. Delay between the scout image and the actual study must be avoided to prevent movement by the patient. Because the study is carried out with a spacing of 1 mm between 9 to 12 images, a total section of only 0.9 to 1.2 cm is imaged. Even minimal motion of the knee can prevent visualization of the meniscus.

After arthrography HRCT scans should be used as a complement to demonstrate meniscal tears. Although double-contrast arthrography remains a sensitive test for diagnosing such tears, it cannot compare with the HRCT scan after arthrography if alignment of the torn fragments is to be analyzed. The greatest advantage of the HRCT scan is that the depiction of the meniscus closely simulates the anatomy of the semilunar cartilage as it is seen via arthrotomy or arthroscopy.

By combining HRCT with arthrography, arthroscopists can plan appropriate surgery for torn menisci (removal of fragments vs. reattachment of the meniscus), because the torn cartilage is better seen on the HRCT scans after arthrography.

▶ The adjunct of CT to the arthrographic study is not unexpected. This report, however, fails to demonstrate that the CT study adds significantly important information about the menisci to justify the expense or the patient's time. In addition, this study lacks sufficient surgical correlation (only 5 out of 27 patients) to determine the accuracy of the CT examination.—Joseph S. Torg, M.D.

## Acute Injury of the Ligaments of the Knee: Magnetic Resonance Evaluation

David A. Turner, Chadwick C. Prodromos, Jerry P. Petasnick, and John W. Clark (Rush Med. College and Rush-Presbyterian-St. Luke's Hosp., Chicago)
Radiology 154:717–722, March 1985                                          3–55

The cruciate ligaments of the knee can be visualized on magnetic resonance imaging (MRI). A preliminary study of MRI was undertaken in 11 patients with acute knee injuries and 11 normal subjects below age 30 years. Ten patients had arthroscopy or arthrotomy or both; 1 had no significant ligament injury. A single-section technique was utilized except in 2 cases in which multislice imaging was available. Most patients were examined within 72 hours of injury. A spin-echo imaging technique was used.

All ligaments emitted a signal of relatively low intensity. The cruciate ligaments were best demonstrated on sagittal images (Fig 3–22); the collateral ligaments, on coronal images through and adjacent to the anterior aspect of the fibula. The menisci and articular cartilages also were visualized, with signals of very low intensity. Eleven of 15 torn ligaments were correctly identified by MRI. Only 1 of 81 normal ligaments was erro-

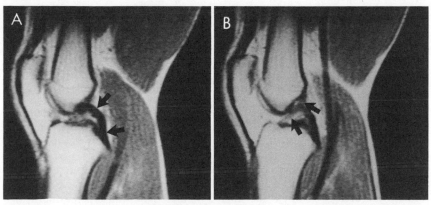

Fig 3–22.—Sagittal images of extended normal knee, obtained using head coil and multisection technique (section thickness, 1 cm; time of excitation, 30 msec; time of relaxation, 2,030 msec). **A,** normal curvilinear posterior cruciate ligament *(arrows)* is seen on section through medial aspect of intercondylar notch. **B,** anterior cruciate ligament *(arrows)* is seen on section through lateral aspect of intercondylar notch. (Courtesy of Turner, D.A., et al.: *Radiology* 154:717–722, March 1985. Reproduced with permission of the Radiological Society of North America.)

neously considered abnormal. All complete cruciate tears of the midsubstance were readily identified. Only 1 of 39 normal cruciate ligaments was thought to be abnormal on MRI. All 5 torn tibial collateral ligaments were correctly identified as such, but a torn fibular collateral ligament was not diagnosed by MRI. Hemarthrosis was evident on images in all knees with 1 or more torn cruciate ligaments.

In this series, complete midsubstance tears of the cruciate ligaments of the knee were reliably diagnosed by MRI, but an incomplete tear or avulsion of the ligament without substantial displacement or fragmentation of the ligaments was difficult to detect. Useful information was obtained in several cases. Improved image quality may make MRI more useful in evaluating acutely injured knees.

▶ The results are misleading because the authors base their accuracy on the sum total of all four ligaments examined instead of reporting the individual MRI accuracy to diagnose tears of the anterior cruciate, posterior cruciate, tibial collateral, and fibular collateral ligaments. This study is premature and, as stated by the authors, biased. At present, arthrography is more accessible and less expensive, and it has proven accuracy for the diagnosis of knee ligament injuries.—Joseph S. Torg, M.D.

---

## The Course of Partial Anterior Cruciate Ligament Ruptures
Magnus Odensten, Jack Lysholm, and Jan Gillquist (Univ. of Linköping)
Am. J. Sports Med. 13:183–186, May–June 1985                                    3–56

---

Twenty-one consecutive patients (17 males), aged 13 to 53 years, were followed for an average of 6 years after partial tear of the anterior cruciate ligament (ACL). This was the only lesion in 6 patients. Nine also had a tear of the medial collateral ligament, and 2 had a tear of the lateral collateral ligament. Nine patients had a rupture of the posterior oblique ligament, and 3 had a meniscus tear (medial, 2; lateral, 1). Most patients were injured in sports activities, 48% in contact and 14% in noncontact sports. Thirty-eight percent had work- or traffic-related injuries. Eleven patients were treated within the first week of injury and the rest within 2 weeks.

The partial tear of the ACL was left untreated. Associated ligament injuries were repaired anatomically in 12 patients, and the knee was immobilized in a long-leg cast for about 6 weeks. In the other 9 patients an intensive rehabilitation program was begun immediately.

Follow-up included physical examination and evaluation by a knee function score. The maximum score was 100 points; a score of more than 82 points was rated good or excellent. At a mean of 70 months after operation (range, 42 to 143) the mean score was 93. All patients achieved more than 82 points. Three patients had an unstable knee with a positive pivot shift test, but the score was high. Four patients later treated by medial meniscectomy also achieved good scores. There was no difference in mean score between patients surgically treated and those managed with immediate physiotherapy, nor was there a difference between patients treated within 1 week and those treated within 2 weeks after injury. Eleven patients were also examined a mean of 21 months after operation; the mean score was unchanged at the later follow-up. All knees were stable and rated over 82 points at the early follow-up.

The overall results were encouraging at the 2-year follow-up. There was no exacerbation of the knee symptoms 6 years after injury, even in patients treated by an immediate rehabilitation program. No patient had swelling or symptoms of instability, and only 1 had pain during activities of daily living. However, 3 patients showed clinical signs of knee instability at the late follow-up. They had probably sustained almost total rupture of the ACL, followed by atrophy leading to instability. With a partial tear of the ACL the course is benign, and the long-term result good, in contrast to total ruptures of the ACL. It is therefore important to make an accurate diagnosis and to choose the proper treatment.

▶ The conclusion of this paper that partial or incomplete disruption of the anterior cruciate ligament follows a benign course and has good long-term results is in keeping with our own observations and experience. Credit should be given to Marshall (*Clin. Orthop.* 106:216–231, 1975) for having described the anterior cruciate ligament consisting of two bands, the posterior lateral mass and the anterolateral band. Generally, in incomplete ruptures, it is the anterior medial band that remains intact, with the posterolateral mass being avulsed from the medial aspect of the lateral femoral condyle. The question arises as to whether or not the intact anteromedial band acts as stent and enables partial healing to occur at the site of posterolateral mass avulsion. With regard to this report, it should be mentioned that the scoring system used to evaluate results is rather arbitrary. Also, four patients subsequently required medial meniscectomy. This cannot be considered a good or excellent result from the standpoint of cruciate function.—Joseph S. Torg, M.D.

---

**A Perspective of Lesions Associated With ACL Insufficiency of the Knee: A Review of 100 Cases**
Peter A. Indelicato and Edward S. Bittar (Univ. of Florida)
Clin. Orthop. 198:77–80, September 1985                                    3–57

---

A retrospective study covering 1979–1983 was conducted to determine the extent of intracapsular damage associated with anterior cruciate ligament (ACL)-insufficient knees in both the acute and chronic situation. Knees previously not operated on were examined to assess the effect that reinjury had on the joint. The 78 males and 22 females (aged 15–53 years) with confirmed ACL damage were examined arthroscopically both clinically and under general anesthesia and the findings recorded on videotape. Both anterolateral and posteromedial approaches were used to visualize the intra-articular structures of the knee.

Ninety-eight patients had complete disruption of the ACL and two had attenuated nonfunctional ACL (lax during anterior drawer and probing).

Associated injuries were numerous, with meniscal tears predominating. Of those with "acute" injuries (44 patients), 26 (60%) had medial meniscus tears and 14 (32%) had lateral meniscus tears. Ten patients (23%) had combined medial and lateral meniscal tears. Of those with "chronic" lesions, (56 patients), 45 (80%) had medial meniscus tears and 20 (36%) had lateral meniscus tears. Fourteen patients (24%) had combined medial and lateral meniscal tears. Chondral fractures involving the femoral condyles and resulting in free fragments of articular cartilage were seen in 10 of the 44 acute patients (23%) (Fig 3–23). Thirty of the 56 chronic patients (54%) had significant articular changes (chondromalacia of the femoral condyles) frequently juxtaposed to the meniscal lesion if one were present.

Relative to meniscal pathology, the incidence of tears increases from 77% in the acute group to 91% in the chronic reinjured group. Only 10 of 44 patients with acute injuries and 5 of the 56 with chronic conditions had normal menisci. Although some of the meniscal tears were not considered to be significant (acute, 7%; chronic, 12%), most were thought to be so. Repeat episodes of anterior tibial subluxation on the femur may account for the increased incidence of both meniscal pathology and articular disease in patients with associated chronic ACL insufficiency of the knee. The integrity of the meniscus is jeopardized in patients who experience repeated episodes of "buckling" or "giving out." Careful counseling to avoid activities that involve sudden stopping and cutting should be provided to an individual with a functionless ACL and no proven evidence of meniscal tears or significant articular disease.

Regardless of initial treatment goals for significant ACL tears in young, active persons, one should not underestimate the likelihood of coexisting lesions of the menisci and articular cartilage. A significant percentage of associated meniscal tears are located in the peripheral rim of the posterior horn and are amenable to repair rather than removal. This review provides further evidence that "isolated" tears of the ACL are unlikely in the acute case, and even more so in the chronic reinjured knee. Despite how one treats the ACL damage itself, maintenance of the articular cartilage is

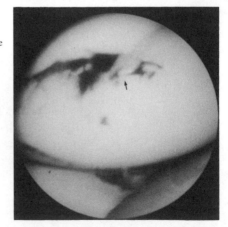

Fig 3–23.—Medial femoral condyle with acute articular fracture. (Courtesy of Indelicato, P.A., and Bittar, E.S.: Clin. Orthop. 198:77–80, September 1985.)

directly related to the preservation of as much meniscal function as possible. Thus, one should not ignore the likelihood of finding associated, and frequently reparable, damage to these structures. Once the spectrum of intracapsular pathology is appreciated, management to achieve long-term good results may be planned.

▶ With regard to historical perspective, it should be noted that Torg (*Am. J. Sports Med.,* 1:84–93, March–April 1976) first reported the extraordinarily high incidence of both anterior cruciate ligament repairs as well as the association of concomitant meniscal lesions. Specifically, of 250 consecutive knees that came to arthrotomy for internal derangement, 62 (25%) had tears of the lateral meniscus; 200 (80%) had tears of the medial meniscus; and 172 (69%) had tears of the anterior cruciate ligament. This observation has been subsequently substantiated by Noyes (*J. Bone Joint Surg.* [*Am.*] 62-A:687, 1980), DeHaven (*Am. J. Sports Med.* 8:9, 1980), and Warren (*Clin. Orthop.* 172:32, 1983).—Joseph S. Torg, M.D.

---

**Polypropylene Braid Augmented and Nonaugmented Intra-articular Anterior Cruciate Ligament Reconstruction**
James H. Roth, John C. Kennedy, Harry Lockstadt, Catherine L. McCallum, and Leonard A. Cunning (Univ. of Western Ontario)
Am. J. Sports Med. 13:321–336, September–October 1985          3–58

---

This retrospective clinical study attempted to determine whether a polypropylene braid (PB) used to augment an intra-articular autograft to reconstruct the anterior cruciate ligament (ACL) is safe and to determine whether the PB improves the efficacy of the procedure. A simultaneous review was performed of patients who had undergone an intra-articular ACL reconstruction using an autograft composed of the central quadriceps tendon, prepatellar periosteum, and patellar tendon left attached distally to the tibial tubercle and of patients who had undergone the same procedure with PB augmentation of the autograft. Preoperatively, all patients had chronic ACL insufficiency and were experiencing symptomatic giving way. A subjective questionnaire and a physician examination were completed on each patient. Objective laxity and functional testing KT 1000 arthrometer measurement, Cybex isokinetic strength analysis, and one leg horizontal hop for distance were performed. Six radiographs of each operated knee were obtained.

TECHNIQUE.—In the PB augmented surgical technique, the appropriate length PB was sutured to the autograft using interrupted 2–0 nonabsorbable sutures in the proximal and distal third of the autograft and interrupted 2–0 absorbable sutures in the middle third of the composite graft. Routing and tensioning of the composite graft was identical to that performed in nonaugmented operation.

Data on 38 of 43 (88%) nonaugmented procedures were reviewed, with a mean follow-up of 64 months. Also, data on 45 of 48 (94%) PB augmented reconstructions with a minimum follow-up of 42 months were reviewed. On objective laxity and function testing, the PB augmented patients had better results than the nonaugmented patients. On subjective questioning, physician's examination, and radiographic analysis, the PB augmented results were significantly better. There were 12 (32%) knees with recurrent symptomatic giving way in the nonaugmented group and 5 (11%) in the PB augmented group. Chondromalacia patellae and arthrofibrosis were seen in both groups. No adverse reaction to the PB was seen.

The authors conclude that the PB is safe and that PB augmentation improves the efficacy of the intra-articular autograft to reconstruct the ACL.

---

**A Partially Biodegradable Material Device for Repair and Reconstruction of Injured Tendons: Experimental Studies**
William G. Rodkey, H. Edward Cabaud, John A. Feagin, and Paul C. Perlik (Letterman Army Inst. of Research, San Francisco)
Am. J. Sports Med. 13:242–246, July–August 1985                    3–59

---

The authors assessed the applicability of a partially biodegradable synthetic material composed of polyglycolic acid (PGA) and dacron to repair or replace severely injured tendons. Adult rabbits underwent complete laceration and repair of one Achilles tendon. Group 1 (N = B) had end to end tenorrhaphy with size 0 braided polyester suture; group 2 (N = 16) tendons were similarly repaired with the bicomposite designed PGA-dacron device; and group 3 (N = 16) received laceration and removal of 1 cm of tissue and the defect was bridged with the same PGA-dacron material. No postoperative immobilization was used. Biomechanical testing or histologic inspection was done at 4 and 8 weeks after tenorrhaphy.

All severed and repaired Achilles tendons in this study healed. Clinically, all rabbits had some functional use of the operated leg by 4 weeks and most ambulated normally by 8 weeks. Six animals had a marked deficit in gait at the time of sacrifice (3 from group 1, 1 from group 2, and 2 from group 3). Superficial infection was observed in 3 in group 1 and in 2 in each of groups 2 and 3. Gross appearance of the repair sites ranged from that of a near normal tendon to that of a markedly elongated, thin fibrous scar. Group 1 tendons lengthened 22.0 mm. Groups 2 and 3 tendons also lengthened but at 12.4 mm and 12.6 mm, respectively. This increased length was significantly less than group 1. In every instance, the polyester suture material or biomaterial device was intact and present in the drill hole through the calcaneus. All repaired tendons at 8 weeks were significantly weaker than the unoperated control tendon. There was a trend for the group 2 repairs to be stronger than those in groups 1 and 3. Histologic inspection revealed that the elongated scar at the tenorrhaphy site in group 1 specimens was poorly vascularized hypocellular fibrous tissue. No adverse reaction to the braided polyester suture was apparent. Histologic appearance of the groups 2 and 3 tendons was similar. There was a thin envelope of fibrous tissue surrounding the PGA-dacron device, but ingrowth of fibrous tissue into the remaining dacron scaffold was inconsistent and unpredictable.

The authors conclude that the PGA-dacron material had adequate strength and physical properties to use both for primary tenorrhaphy and to bridge the tendon defect. However, this material lacks significant advantage over materials available or known to be under evaluation to support neotendon formation when an actual soft tissue defect exists.

---

**Carbon Reconstruction in the Anterior Cruciate Deficient Knee**
David G. Mendes, Michael Soudry, David Angel, Anatoli Grishkan, and Moshe Roffman (Haifa Med. Ctr., Israel)
Orthopedics 8:1244–1248, October 1985                                    3–60

---

Ten patients (7 men), aged 22 to 60 years, underwent carbon fiber reconstruction of the anterior cruciate ligament (ACL) for knee instability between July 1981 and November 1982. There were 7 chronic and 3 acute instabilities. Six patients had an accompanying medial instability, 1 an anterolateral instability, and 1 a posterior instability. No patient was a professional athlete.

TECHNIQUE.—Plastafil carbon fibers 8 μ in diameter were used. Each tow was 40,000 fibers bonded with gelatin. The tow was anchored to bone with expanding rivets (bollards) and toggles made of carbon polysulfone. The surgical technique of Strover and Hunt was employed. The goal was to restore the anatomical anchorage of each ligament, tighten the tow, and cover the intra-articular portion of the carbon by a broad-base, pedicled synovioma.

A long-leg cast was used for 4–14 days at 45 degrees of flexion. Mobilization of the knee was begun 2 weeks after operation. Ambulation with partial to full weight-bearing using two crutches progressed according to recovery of motion and power, followed by use of a cane. Patients with rotatory instability were given a Lenox Hill brace for 6–12 months.

Patients were scored by a knee-rating system that covered stability, range of motion, muscular power, and overall function. Patients were evaluated at 6 month intervals, and all but 1 at late follow-up after 2–3.5 years. Six of the 7 chronic cases improved by one grade and 1 by two grades. Of the 3 knees with acute injury, 2 were rated as good and 1 as excellent with regard to stability. The Lachman test, measured clinically, exceeded 10 mm in 1 case, and in 4 cases the anterior excursion was up to 5 mm. Of the 6 patients in whom the medial collateral ligament was also reconstructed, 2 were radiographically measured to have 12 and 13 degrees of instability, respectively (1 acute and 1 chronic); 4 had 5–7 degrees of instability with valgus stress. A patient who underwent repair for chronic anterolateral rotation instability had a 10-degree instability with varus stress. Muscle power was excellent in all but the acute repairs and improved in all but 1 of the chronic repairs. Range of motion was good to excellent in 7 patients and fair in 3. Overall function was good to excellent in 4 patients and fair in 6.

Five patients had knee effusion at late follow-up. Two were tapped 3 months after operation, and a few carbon particles were found in the synovial fluid. After this, carbon particles were absent from the fluid. Two patients showed a resorptive reaction around the expanding rivet in the femur and tibia. The holes that were predrilled for the rivets enlarged with a sclerotic wall resembling a cyst, "carbon polysulfone pseudocyst." There were no infections; however, a warm joint was common for 3–6 months.

Carbon fiber as a synthetic substitute for reconstruction of an augmented ligament is promising, although the technique is still being developed. Treatment of knees with acute cases was more successful than that of knees with chronic cases, except in a patient who had extensive combined damage after dislocation of the knee. In patients in whom function was suboptimal, recurrent synovitis and effusion were found; in 2, instability was due to loosening of the fixation rivets. Synovitis was found in 50% of the patients, compared with the 30% reported by Jenkins. Pollution of the joint cavity with carbon must be avoided to prevent synovitis and possible long-term ill effects. The carbon tow should be sealed extrasynovially by an envelope of tissue, which concurrently should also invade and interlace with the carbon fibers.

---

### Strength of Carbon and Polyester Fibre Tendon Replacements: Variation After Operation in Rabbits

A. A. Amis, J. R. Campbell, and J. H. Miller (Imperial College of Science and Technology, London)
J. Bone Joint Surg. [Br.] 67-B:829–834, November 1985                    3–61

The development of artificial finger flexor tendons has involved the study of tissue ingrowth into multifilamentous implants to form tendon anchorages. Polyester fibers have been used, which had already gained acceptance for implants requiring tissue ingrowth, such as arterial grafts. This work involved tissue ingrowth in small anchorage areas, rather than along the entire length of the implant. The properties of polyester fibers used in the manner described by Jenkins et al. were compared. The relatively inert polyester fibers should function as a scaffold on which fibrous tissue can be laid down, in a fashion similar to that demonstrated for carbon fibers. Polyester fibers are less brittle than carbon and thus easier to handle at operation; they do not fragment and could therefore be removed in case of infection; and they could be designed to be elastically compatible with the natural structure (carbon fibers are too stiff for this).

The calcaneal tendons of rabbits were excised and replaced with a carbon or polyester fiber implant or left as controls. The strength of the neotendons and their mode of failure under tension were examined at intervals up to 6 months after operation. Return to near-normal strength took 6 months, suggesting that patients undergoing ligament or tendon reconstructions should not resume normal activity for several months. Carbon fiber-based neotendons showed progressive elongation, which, unless prevented by a sufficient period of immobilization, would affect the functional result.

Previous workers have suggested that repair based on carbon fiber would reach normal strength in 6 weeks. The calcaneal tendon is conveniently placed for experimental tendon surgery, but its choice could be questioned because it has an inherent capacity for repair, which might overshadow any deficiency of an implant and produce overencouraging results. If these implants are used at sites where there is less-pronounced tissue generation, e.g., within a knee, full strength probably would not be attained for considerably more than 24 weeks.

Although carbon-based reconstructions are subject to progressive elongation in use, the experiences of other workers suggest that this might be avoided by prolonging immobilization beyond 4 weeks. Since carbon fibers fracture at extremely low elongations, fracture must have occurred before 6 weeks in the present study, subsequent strength deriving from the soft tissues alone. Two failures at 9 and 10 weeks suggest that 4 weeks in plaster was barely adequate, and that patients should avoid strenuous activities after tendon implants for at least 3 months.

Filamentous implants of different but relatively inert materials can be the basis of a tendon repair that will attain normal strength, but this may take more than 6 months. Perhaps 8 weeks' immobilization is required to allow sufficient tissue augmentation; protection from excess loading is needed for even longer. This period could probably be shortened after ligament reconstructions by combining a bone anchorage system, which gives immediate high strength, with an implant material that is less vulnerable to damage.

**Histological Response to Carbon Fibre**
David G. Mendes, David Angel, Anatoli Grishkan, and Jochanan Boss (Haifa Med. Ctr. and Technion-Israel Inst. of Technology)
J. Bone Joint Surg. [Br.] 67-B:645–649, August 1985       3–62

In a 4-year period, 45 patients underwent carbon fiber reconstruction of ligaments or tendons in various joints for both acute and chronic injuries. In two patients the lateral collateral ligaments of the knee were completely excised 12 and 18 months, respectively, after augmentation by carbon fiber. This was done during further attempts to improve knee stability. These two ligaments formed the basis for the histologic study.

The carbon fiber strands, the collagenous and reticulin fibers, and the fibroblasts and fibrocytes were always accompanied by inflammatory cells. On cross section, the individual carbon fibers were seen surrounded by two to four concentric layers of cells, most of which were fibroblasts and macrophages, with a minor admixture of lymphocytes. In contrast to the abundance of collagen and reticulin fibers, no elastic fibers were found except in the wall of blood vessels. In the longitudinal sections, the fibroblasts and the connective tissue fibers produced by them were consistently oriented in the direction of the carbon fibers with which they were associated. This organization of fibroblasts and other cells resulted in formation of "units of composite ligament." Each unit comprised a centrally located carbon fiber surrounded by cells. These units were separated from each other by small amounts of loosely textured connective tissue, which was also infiltrated by a small number of leukocytes. There were a few small foci of necrosis less than 2 mm in diameter and sharply demarcated. No vascular or inflammatory changes were seen that could have caused the evolving necrosis. In a few sections irregular, fusiform spaces were seen. These spaces appeared to be empty, but were lined by cells of synovial appearance. The synovial-like spaces appeared between bundles of the carbon fiber tow, which ran in different directions.

Previous work showed that implanted carbon fiber tow does not fragment in vitro. Its satisfactory function probably depends on preservation of the entire tow. However, fragments of carbon fiber were present in sections cut parallel to the direction of the fibers. These may have been artifacts caused by fracture of carbon fibers during sectioning of the paraffin blocks. Carbon fiber has inherent elastic energy and may therefore displace when cut. However, genuine breakage of carbon fiber also occurred in vivo, though rarely. Carbon debris resulting from this was observed in mononuclear and polynuclear macrophages.

Although functionally adequate augmented ligaments and tendons can be induced by the implantation of tows of carbon fiber, the morphology of these is far from identical to that of natural tissue. The association of carbon fiber with abundantly synthesized collagen and reticulin fibers that can function as replacement of the original ligament may be the important factor, rather than failure to simulate its histology. Biomechanical analysis of the results of animal experiments showed that the tensile strength of a composite tendon 1 year after insertion was about 85% of that of the neutral one.

▶ To date, none of the synthetic ligament devices have been cleared for general use by the Federal Drug Administration (see Digests 3–58 to 3–62). Each of the devices has shortcomings in biomechanical characteristics, with excessive stiffness and bone interface posing significant problems. Clinical experience, although extensive, is still lacking adequate follow-up, making a critical assessment difficult and early favorable reports suspect.—Joseph S. Torg, M.D.

---

**Surgical Treatment of Anterolateral Rotatory Instability: A Follow-up Study**
James R. Andrews, Richard A. Sanders, and Benoit Morin (Hughston Orthopaedic Clinic, Columbus, Ga.)
Am. J. Sports Med. 13:112–119, March–April 1985                    3–63

---

A new method of iliotibial band tenodesis was used to treat anterolateral rotatory instability in 31 acutely injured knees and 31 chronically unstable knees, all with a stretched, torn, or absent anterior cruciate ligament. Meniscal injury was present in a large majority of cases in both groups.

The anterior cruciate ligament was repaired in 16 of 20 patients with acute injury who were followed up. The iliotibial tract was attached to the distal femur by parallel rows of Bunnell sutures, tied to one another on the medial side of the femur to create a "ligament" extending from the linea aspera to Gerdy's tubercle. The repair must be isometric through a full range of motion.

Twenty acutely injured patients and 11 with chronic instability were followed up 2 years or longer after surgery. Repair of the anterior cruciate ligament did not influence the outcome. All but 7% of patients had returned to competitive or recreational athletic activities involving cutting or pivoting movements. The subjective and objective results were excellent or good in 94% of the cases. There was only 1 poor result.

The iliotibial band transfer tenodesis has given consistently good results in patients with acute and chronic anterolateral rotatory instability of the knee, on long-term follow-up. Careful technique is very important. Good functional results are obtained when surgery prevents anterior subluxation of the lateral tibial plateau. The menisci should be repaired or at least only partially resected where possible to preserve their stabilizing effect.

▶ The authors note that this procedure should not be used as an isolated procedure on knees with severe, chronic, "complex" instability, because the stretching of capsular structures places excessive stress on the iliotibial tract tenodesis. For more complex instabilities they suggest a more extensive reconstructive procedure that combines an interarticular anterior cruciate reconstruction with capsular or extracapsular reconstruction as required. They suggest that these instabilities be managed by reconstruction of anterior cruciate ligament using the middle third of the patella tendon or a prosthetic ligament combined with capsular and extracapsular reconstruction and iliotibial tract tenodesis.—Joseph S. Torg, M.D.

---

**Intra-Articular Transfer of the Iliotibial Tract: Two to Seven-Year Follow-up Results**
W. Norman Scott, Pierce Ferriter, and Michael Marino (Lenox Hill Hosp., New York)
J. Bone Joint Surg. [ Am.] 67-A:532–538, April 1985          3–64

---

An intra-articular reconstruction using various parts of the iliotibial band has been used to substitute for the anterior cruciate ligament (ACL) in 111 consecutive ACL-deficient knees that were followed up for 2 years or longer. A proximally based transfer of the iliotibial tract, its osseous insertion, the lateral retinaculum, and part of the vastus lateralis is carried out as shown in Figure 3–24. Use of a trough from the interspinous area to the front of the tibia eliminates the problem of screw loosening. The mean patient age was 25 years. Fifty-two patients had undergone previous surgery on the affected side.

Thirty patients had decreased extension at follow-up. In 81% of knees

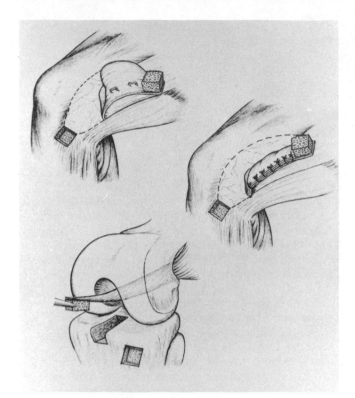

Fig 3–24.—The composite structure is tubed to enhance its strength. A trough from the interspinous area to the front of the tibia eliminates the problem of screw-loosening. (Courtesy of Scott, W.N., et al.: J. Bone Joint Surg. [Am.] 67-A:532–538, April 1985.)

results were negative for Lachman test; 27%, for drawer sign, and 94%, for pivot-shift sign. Most knees had no more than 1 + valgus or varus on stress testing. Five of 6 patients with poor results had had previous surgery. The objective results were unacceptable in 16% of patients. Few complications occurred.

Enduring stability has been observed after this intra-articular iliotibial tract transfer procedure in the ACL-deficient knee. Immediate fixation of bone allows early motion of the knee and promotes rehabilitation. In patients with chronic multiplanar instabilities, the reconstruction should be used in conjunction with both conventional and newer extra-articular procedures.

▶ This is certainly a unique approach to the anterior cruciate ligament deficient knee. It is my understanding that although Nicholas and Minkoff described the procedures in 1978 (*Am. J. Sports Med.* 6:341–353, 1978), actually Insall devised and was the first to perform the operation (*J. Bone Joint Surg.* [Am.] 63-A:560–569, April 1980). The duration to, and the completeness of, follow-up is impressive. Although I have not performed the procedure, others have found that the technical aspects can be a challenge. Twelve (10%) of the patients required additional surgery; of these two were because the bone block crumbled and six because of screw removal. The authors note that the only statistically significant factors that adversely affected the results were previous operations and a long interval between the injury and surgery. If the patient was operated on within 6 months following injury, the results were always satisfactory.—Joseph S. Torg, M.D.

---

**Anterior Cruciate Reconstruction Using the Jones-Ellison Procedure**
Jeffrey A. Fried, John A. Bergfeld, Garron Weiker, and Jack T. Andrish (Cleveland Clinic)
J. Bone Joint Surg. [Am.] 67-A:1029–1033, September 1985          3–65

---

Evaluation was made of 40 consecutive combined Jones-Ellison anterior-cruciate reconstructions in a young, athletic population. Mean interval from injury to operation was 2.7 years. Preoperatively, all patients had a 3+ or 4+ pivot shift and instability. All but 5 patients had a meniscal tear and 30 patients had arthritic changes in the knee at time of operation.

Thirty-one patients were satisfied with the knee at follow-up. Thirty-four said they would have the reconstruction performed again if they had the same kind of trouble. Eight patients said they had regained full athletic function after the procedure and 18 had resumed their previous athletic activities but not their prior level of expertise. Eleven returned to less vigorous sports than before injury and 3 chose not to return to athletic activities but were able to perform normal daily activities despite some instability of the knee. At follow-up 30 did not have to wear a brace, 8 wore a brace only during sports activities, and 2 always wore a brace during walking hours. Thirteen patients had no pain, 15 had only occasional pain, 9 had pain only after exercise, and 3 had pain with exercise and stair-climbing. Thirty-eight could run in place and hop on one lower limb. Mean loss of extension compared with the opposite knee was 4.1 degrees. Mean amount of atrophy of the thigh was 1 cm. Radiographs showed 9 patients had no arthritis, 16 had mild arthritis, 11 had moderate arthritis, and 2 had severe arthritis. Cybex evaluation showed mean percent torque compared with the normal knee averaged 87% for the extensors and 91% for the flexors. Overall, there were 15 excellent, 9 good, 10 fair, and 6 poor subjective results. Complications were minor.

The authors recommend that, before performing a surgical reconstruction of the anterior cruciate deficient knee, it may be prudent to warn the patient that the odds are that he or she will not return to full preinjury athletic function. At present, they are not performing the described reconstruction, but are using a laterally based, vascularized-pedicle patellar-tendon graft.

▶ There are several striking features regarding this series of 40 patients with anterior cruciate ligament deficient knees who underwent the described procedures. First, 75% had significant arthritic changes observed at surgery. Second, of the 80 menisci, only 27 were not torn. Also, 33 patients had a 4 + pivot shift preoperatively. Certainly, as far as selection for reconstructive surgery, this series represents worst-case situations. In that four different types of procedures were performed (Jones-Ellison alone, or with medial reconstruction, or Jones-Ellison and pes anserinus transfer alone, or with medial reconstruction), no meaningful conclusion can be drawn from this material with regard to the efficacy of the Jones procedure in properly selected anterior cruciate ligament deficient knees.—Joseph S. Torg, M.D.

## The Lower-Extremity Musculature in Chronic Symptomatic Instability of the Anterior Cruciate Ligament
Christian Gerber, Hans Hoppeler, Helgard Claassen, Guido Robotti, Rolf Zehnder, and Roland P. Jakob (Univ. of Berne Inselspital, Switzerland)
J. Bone Joint Surg. [Am.] 67-A:1034–1043, September 1985         3–66

The musculature of the lower extremity in 41 patients with chronic symptomatic instability of the anterior cruciate ligament was studied. Computed tomographic and clinical measurements of the limb were taken at levels 15 cm and 25 cm proximal to the medial joint line and 10 cm distal to it. Figure 3–25 showing cross-sectional views of both limbs, was obtained with a Somatom SF CT scanner with a 125-kv peak, 5 seconds and 230 mamp seconds. Biopsy specimens obtained from the vastus lateralis of both legs were analyzed by histochemistry and electron microscopy.

Computed tomography revealed a decrease in the muscle square area of the affected thigh of 8% as compared with the control leg. There was quadriceps atrophy of 10%, but hamstrings atrophy of only 4%. Atrophy of the vastus medialis was significantly greater than that of the entire quadriceps. Histochemistry revealed a similar decrease in fiber size for all fiber types, and hence no shift in fiber type. Electron microscopy showed an increase in intracellular fat, but no change in mitochondrial volume density or capillarization. Clinically, chronic instability of the anterior cruciate ligament was associated with atrophy of the thigh muscles that predominantly affected the quadriceps, and within the quadriceps, predominantly affected the vastus medialis. There was mild atrophy of the hamstrings corresponding to the degree of muscular atrophy of the calf. Measurements of thigh circumference did not allow reliable estimation of the relative differences in muscle cross-sectional area. All muscular changes were still present 1 year after injury, but did not increase in severity thereafter.

These data suggest that there is no scientific rationale for selective rehabilitation of either type I (endurance training, electrostimulation) or type II (strength, high-speed isokinetic) muscle fibers in patients with chronic instability of the anterior cruciate ligament. To restore so-called normal muscle balance, vigorous training of the quadriceps would be mandatory. Although this might subjectively improve the stability of the knee with

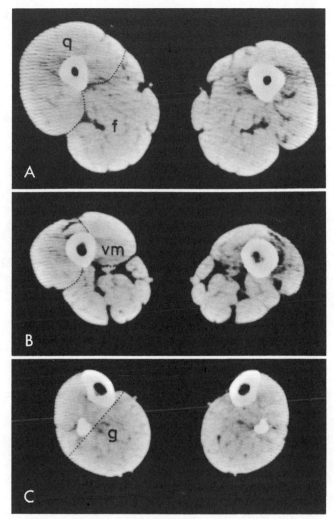

**Fig 3–25.**—Computed tomographic scans of the legs. **A,** the quadriceps *(q)* and flexors *(f)* are identified on a scan of a point 25 cm proximal to the medial joint line. **B,** the vastus medialis *(vm)* is delineated within the quadriceps on a scan of a point 15 cm proximal to the medial joint line. **C,** the area of the gastrocnemius-soleus complex *(g)* was estimated on a scan at a point 10 cm distal to the medial joint line. (Courtesy of Gerber, C., et al.: J. Bone Joint Surg. [Am.] 67-A:1034–1043, September 1985.)

dysfunction of the anterior cruciate ligament, such rehabilitation could actually be detrimental.

▶ The authors demonstrated that the quadriceps muscle atrophied to a greater extent than the hamstring group (10% vs. 4%, respectively). Vegso et al. also observed this finding (*Medical Science in Sports and Exercise,* Vol. 17, No. 5). The significance of the finding relates to rehabilitation and the emphasis that must be placed on the quadriceps group.—Joseph S. Torg, M.D.

### Hamstring Control and the Unstable Anterior Cruciate Ligament-Deficient Knee

Donald J. Walla, John P. Albright, Edward McAuley, Robert K. Martin, Vincent Eldridge, and George El-Khoury (Univ. of Iowa)
Am. J. Sports Med. 13:34–39, January–February 1985          3–67

The diagnosis of an anterior cruciate ligament (ACL) injury to the knee can lead to a difficult decision regarding proper treatment. The accepted prognosis for the knee with an ACL rupture has been summarized by Allman as "the beginning of the end for the knee" in terms of progressive deterioration, subsequent reinjuries, ever-increasing instability, meniscal tears, and posttraumatic arthritis. However, the long-term sequelae of this injury are not well documented. The ACL "pop" has been an indication to repair or reconstruct the cruciate ligament.

Data were reviewed on 38 former athletes (25 men, 13 women, aged 18 to 45 years; mean, 24 years) who met the following criteria: (1) history of an ACL injury with a positive Lachman's test result, positive anterior drawer sign, and documented pivot shift; (2) initial injury sustained at least 24 months prior to the study; (3) no prior attempts at reconstruction of the ligamentous laxity; and (4) no sign of medial or lateral laxity of more than 5 mm when tested at 30 degrees of flexion.

The original injury occurred between 2 years and 27 years prior to the study (mean, 5.6 years). Seven patients (19%) had never had a major reinjury, whereas 31 (81%) sustained significant reinjuries after the initial injury (mean follow-up period 6.1 years in both groups). A total of 38 reinjuries occurred in these 31 patients, with 28 of them sustaining reinjury within the first year. Twenty of the latter group continued to experience reinjuries during the second year after initial injury. Twenty-three patients (61%) underwent meniscectomy, including three who had excision of both menisci in the injured knee. Twenty-two of the menisci removed were medial and four were lateral. Thirty-three patients (87%) reported that they could walk without difficulty. Twenty-eight (73%) were able to run straight ahead with no complaint of pain, swelling, or instability, but seven others experienced symptoms while running. Twenty-eight (61%) reported minimal symptoms when engaged in light recreational activities. Twelve individuals participated in vigorous athletic activities without pain, swelling, or instability.

Chief complaints at the follow-up examination were pain (39%), instability (37%), limitation of motion (13%), and swelling (10%). Five patients (13%) had a grade 1 (mild) anterolateral rotary instability (ALRI), 20 (53%) had a grade 2 (moderate) ALRI, 12 (31%) had a grade 3 (severe) ALRI, and 1 (3%) had a grade 4 (gross) rotator instability. The grade of instability was not related to the length of time between injury and follow-up study. Active hamstring control that reduced the pivot shift was present in 36 patients (95%). This control was considered partial in 12 patients (33%) in whom anterior subluxation of the lateral tibial plateau was lessened but not eliminated. The functional rating score for the entire group ranged from 32 to 92 (mean score, 70.6). Ten patients (26%) had normal radiographic findings. Moderate or severe radiographic changes were present in five patients (23%) injured less than 5 years prior to the study and in ten (66%) injured more than 5 years prior to the study. Thirteen of 35 athletes (37%) had a lateral rim sign after a mean follow-up period of 7 years.

It appears that these patients have recovered well without surgical treatment. Although they were relatively young and the presence of radiographic changes and a rim sign may be indicative of future problems, no deterioration was noted in those examined 5 years after injury.

▶ The title of this paper implies that the hamstring muscle group can dynamically control the unstable anterior cruciate deficient knee. The authors do not support this thesis with any data. Their statement, "Active hamstring control that reduced the pivot shift was present in 36 patients (95%)" simply affirms that the pivot shift maneuver must be performed while the patient is totally relaxed. One cannot assume that there is any correlation between a static, clinical test of instability and dynamic function of the knee.—Joseph S. Torg, M.D.

**Chronic Posterolateral Rotatory Instability of the Knee**
Jack C. Hughston and Kurt E. Jacobson (Hughston Orthopaedic Clinic, Columbus, Ga., and Tulane Univ.)
J. Bone Joint Surg. [Am.] 67-A:351–359, March 1985                    3–68

Posterolateral rotatory instability of the knee, usually accompanied by other instabilities, is easily missed, misdiagnosed, or mistreated. The correct diagnosis requires complete examination of the knee, including both the external rotation-recurvatum and posterolateral drawer tests. The most effective operative approach when the lesion is interstitial or at the site of the femoral attachment consists of advancing the arcuate ligament complex with its osseous attachment anteriorly and distally on the femur to support the arcuate ligament repair. When the lesion is distal and the arcuate ligament attachment to the tibia and fibula is loose, this area must be stabilized.

Between 1970 and 1982, 140 consecutive patients (141 knees) underwent reconstruction with this procedure. Ninety-five patients (96 knees), with a follow-up of 2 to 13 years, form the basis for this report. Seventy-one had undergone a combined total of 112 prior operations on the knee without functional recovery. After operation directed at the arcuate ligament complex, 82 knees (85%) were objectively rated as good, 13 (14%) as fair, and 1 as poor. Subjectively, 75 (78%) of the patients considered the result to be good, 21 (22%) fair, and none poor. Functionally, 77 (80%) knees were rated by the patient as good, 16 (16%) as fair, and 3 (4%), as poor.

When the true nature of a prolonged disability of the knee continues to be unrecognized, the patient may be subjected to repeated operations. This continually occurred among these patients with posterolateral rotatory disability and sometimes disabled them for 4 to 5 years. The initial injury that results in instability may cause only slight discomfort and no immediate disability, even in continued competitive athletics. Over the next several weeks, however, the injury can become a severe and disabling chronic instability. Tears of the arcuate ligament complex result in an almost continuous distraction force on the posterolateral corner of the knee, even when the patient is standing still. Simultaneously, the medial compartment of the knee is compressed, causing medial joint line pain that is frequently misdiagnosed and results in a so-called simple meniscectomy.

Initially, the authors dissected the individual components of the arcuate complex and reconstructed each individually, producing undue surgical trauma to these tissues and further compromising their blood supply. In an acute injury, the arcuate ligament may be seen dissected from its surrounding tissues as a result of the trauma. However, a similar distinction of tissue planes is almost impossible to duplicate by attempted surgical dissection. In old, chronic injuries, the tears in the arcuate complex structures are healed with scar tissue. By 1972, the authors had devised an operative approach for chronic injuries that consisted of advancing the scarred arcuate ligament complex en masse. The bone attachment was moved anteriorly and distally on the femur, effectively restoring function of the structures. This approach is designed to interrupt a minimum number of afferent nerves. The importance of pathologic change in the fibular collateral ligament should not be underestimated. Many surgeons think that if the fibular collateral ligament is intact and appears to be normal, complete lateral stability will result.

The diagnosis of chronic posterolateral rotatory instability is subtle and challenging, as evidenced by the 112 unsuccessful prior operations that had been performed in this series. Clinical examination will not demonstrate instability unless the examiner performs both the external rotation-recurvatum test and the posterolateral drawer test. That some knees have a positive external rotation-recurvatum test and no posterolateral drawer sign, whereas others demonstrate just the opposite, probably relates to the type of tear in the arcuate complex.

▶ The authors state that "the correct diagnosis requires a complete examination of the knee. . ." However, in not one of the 140 cases reported do they mention the status of the anterior cruciate ligament. For that matter, the term anterior cruciate ligament does not appear once in this paper. Rather, their representation of a "correct diagnosis" is predicated upon the performance of two mechanical-gymnastic tests. In addition to the described operation, more than half of the patients had concomitant meniscectomies. The effect of meniscectomies as well as the fact that a number of knees required subsequent cruciate reconstructions are ignored. It appears that this operation will go the way of the Nicholas 5–1 procedure, the Slocum pes plasty, and the Ellison procedure. We hope it will not experience a degree of clinical application as these other "fad" operations.—Joseph S. Torg, M.D.

---

**Recurrent Dislocation of the Patella Treated by the Modified Roux-Goldthwait Procedure: A Prospective Study of Forty-Seven Knees**
F. B. Fondren, J. Leonard Goldner, and Frank H. Bassett, III (Duke Univ.)
J. Bone Joint Surg. [Am.] 67-A:993–1005, September 1985                    3–69

---

Results in 47 knees in 10 male and 27 female patients who had recurrent dislocation of the patella were studied. These patients were treated by a modified Roux-Goldthwait procedure (lateral retinacular release, medial transfer of the lateral patellar tendon without advancement, plication of the medial retinaculum, and advancement of the vastus medialis). Results were analyzed after follow-ups ranging from 3.0 to 16.3 years.

TECHNIQUE.—To begin the procedure, a pneumatic tourniquet is applied to the proximal part of the thigh. A 9-cm straight transverse incision, midway between the inferior pole of the patella and the prominence of the tibial tubercle, is usually used. A lateral retinacular release is performed by incising the retinaculum beginning at the level of the tibial tubercle and extending the incision proximally under direct vision. A second incision is made in the medial retinaculum and anterior and posterior retinacular flaps are mobilized proximally as far as the insertion of the vastus medialis obliquus on the quadriceps tendon. This tendon is then incised obliquely. The muscle is then mobilized for advancement to the superomedial margin of the patella. The anterior flap of the retinaculum is pulled medially and sutured to the undersurface of the posterior retinacular flap. The lateral half of the patellar tendon is passed under the medial half and secured beneath a periosteal flap on the medial side of the intact half of the patellar tendon.

Results were excellent in 12 knees, good in 31, fair in 1, and poor in 3. Fair and poor ratings were due to pain caused by severe chondromalacia patellae. There was one serious complication which was a large subcutaneous hematoma with necrosis of a skin flap. Patients with mild chondromalacia improved and showed no progressive patellofemoral arthritis after simple realignment, whereas those with severe chondromalacia were not improved by shaving, drilling, and realignment.

This study shows that the modified Roux-Goldthwait procedure, without advancement of the tibial attachment of the patellar ligament, can stabilize the patella without increasing patellofemoral compression.

▶ This paper, a prospective evaluation with an average of 5.8 years follow-up of 37 modified Roux-Goldthwait procedures, is certainly an impressive endeavor. Although an abundance of data relating to the numerous parameters of patella subluxation/dislocation are presented, the results are disappointingly subjective in nature. That is, 66% of the cases were determined to have had a good result, which by definition meant that the knee lacked 5–10 degrees of flexion, occasionally ached mildly or caused a momentary feeling of giving way, or at times prevented strenuous physical activity. The authors also stated that with severe chondromalacia patellae a modified Maquet procedure is also performed. However, no data are given as to how many required this supplementary procedure or the results to support the conclusion that the modified Maquet procedure had diminished pain and improved function. Also, the data do not deal with or support the conclusion that acute traumatic dislocation may be best treated by immediate, early surgical repair.—Joseph S. Torg, M.D.

---

**Anterolateral Dislocation of the Head of the Fibula in Sports**
Vincent J. Turco and Anthony J. Spinella (St. Francis Hosp., Hartford, Conn.)
Am. J. Sports Med. 13:209–215, July–August 1985                                3–70

---

Traumatic anterolateral dislocation of the fibular head is an uncommon sports injury, which is easily overlooked. Seventeen cases (10 chronic and 7 acute) were collected during private practice. The typical mechanism of injury is a fall on the affected flexed knee with the leg adducted under the body and the ankle inverted. Physical examination shows an obvious lateral bony prominence of the fibular head and varying disability with activities. There is no significant effusion or sign of internal knee derangement or instability. Comparison of identical radiographic views is necessary to confirm the diagnosis. On the anteroposterior view the fibular head is displaced laterally, and the proximal interosseous space is widened; on the lateral view there is a greater overlap of the fibula on the tibia on the affected side. Peroneal nerve and ankle injuries can occur concomitantly with anterolateral proximal tibiofibular dislocation.

If the dislocation is seen immediately, closed reduction can be easily accomplished by direct pressure on the fibular head with the knee flexed and is frequently associated with an audible pop, immediate relief, full knee function, and slight lateral discomfort. Acute dislocations so treated have been stable and supported with an elastic bandage and crutches for comfort. One case seen 7 days after injury was reduced closed with general anesthesia, and 1 case spontaneously reduced 3 days after injury. Operation was required in 3 chronic cases, in 2 because of chronic disabling symptoms and in 1 because of peroneal palsy. All 3 patients were treated successfully with resection of head and neck of the fibula, reconstruction of periosteal soft tissue sleeve, and immobilization. These 3 patients had good results with no functional disability and were unrestricted and asymptomatic after operation.

Arthrodesis of superior tibiofibular joint should be avoided because of the possibility of ankle symptoms due to loss of fibular mobility. In the authors' experience, open reduction of dislocations has been unnecessary. If indicated due to instability of reduction or irreducibility, temporary screw transfixion of the tibia and fibula and repair of injured ligaments similar to the repair of syndesmosis ruptures at the ankle appear to be the treatment of choice. Patients with chronic dislocation and instability have also been successfully treated with local strapping, similar to tennis elbow strapping, and symptomatic care.

Boy, 17, a soccer player, fell and landed sitting on his adducted left leg, with resulting pain in the left knee and ankle. The next day he had findings of a sprained ankle syndesmosis. After ankle pain subsided, knee pain prohibited sports. Three months later a typical lateral displacement of fibula was evident. The patient had lateral knee pain with intermittent tingling but no peroneal palsy. Closed reduction was unsuccessful, and the family refused operation. After 1.5 years, there was persistent lateral dislocation, and operation became mandatory because of peroneal palsy with footdrop. Resection of the fibular head relieved nerve compression, and peroneal function began to return in 4 months. Two years later, function had fully returned, except for weakness of the extensor hallucis longus, and the patient was able to play all sports.

Anterolateral dislocation is uncommon, but it probably occurs more often than has been reported.

▶ This is a relatively rare lesion, and a high index of suspicion is required to make the diagnosis. Subtle radiographic changes require comparison with comparable lateral projections of the contralateral uninvolved knee. The practice of resecting the fibular head in instances of chronic dislocation must be questioned. The arcuate ligament, lateral collateral ligament, capital ligaments, as well as the biceps insert into this structure. The authors have failed to mention the effect of fibular head resection on lateral stability of the knee joint.—Joseph S. Torg, M.D.

---

## Frequency, Associated Factors, and Treatment of Breaststroker's Knee in Competitive Swimmers

George D. Rovere and Andrew W. Nichols (Bowman Gray School of Medicine)
Am. J. Sports Med. 13:99–104, March–April 1985                                                3–71

---

Thirty-six competitive breaststroke swimmers were interviewed and examined for knee pain specifically related to the breaststroke kick. Of the subjects studied, 86% had a history of at least one episode of breaststroke knee pain, and 47.2% had breaststroke knee pain that occurred at least once a week. There was a significant relation between more frequent knee pain and increased swimmer's age, years of competitive swimming, breaststroke training distance, stretching exercises, and decreased warm-up distance. The subjects with frequent knee pain were found to have less internal rotation at the hip.

The most common site of breaststroke knee pain was the medial portion, with specific sites differing among subjects. The medial synovial plica syndrome may be a cause of breaststroke knee pain, because 47% of subjects with weekly knee pain had tender, thickened medial plicae. Palpation of plicae produced pain similar to that experienced with the breaststroke kick.

This study revealed a surprisingly high incidence of knee pain in breaststroke swimmers; 75% of the 36 subjects had had three or more episodes of knee pain per season. Findings suggest that both a short-term "overuse syndrome" and a long-term, progressive process may be significant in the frequency of breaststroke knee pain.

Internal rotation of the hip is a crucial component of the proper breast-stroke kick technique, and limited hip flexibility may contribute to improper technique. By increasing internal hip rotation flexibility, changes in technique necessary to avoid knee pain may be made. The absence of knee instability in the subjects surveyed is consistent with earlier findings of others. Apparently, the non-weight-bearing nature of swimming protects against internal knee derangement.

The medial patellar plica is a remnant of an embryonic membrane. Inflammation, thickening, and fibrosis of the plica lead to medial synovial plica syndrome. The pain is thought to be secondary to friction produced as the plica snaps across the medial femoral condyle during repeated flexion and extension of the knee. Medial synovial plica syndrome apparently has never been suggested as a potential cause of breaststroke knee pain.

Diagnosis of medial synovial plica syndrome is important, because if it is present, it is a potentially curable form of breaststroker's knee. Therapeutic possibilities include arthrotomy with partial synovectomy, arthroscopic resection of the plica, or the more recently attempted injection of anti-inflammatory corticosteroids and long-acting anesthetic agents into the plica. However, tender plicae may occur in the presence of other intra-articular or periarticular lesions that can cause synovitis.

The medial knee joint was the most common site of knee pain in this and earlier studies. The medial collateral ligament has been proposed as the primary cause of breaststroker's knee pain. Pain localized in the region of the medial collateral ligament may represent ligament strain, general synovitis, or medial synovial shelf syndrome.

▶ Breaststrokers often complain of medial knee pain. We agree with the treatment outlined by the authors when they recommend eliminating or reducing breaststroke training distances, changing the kick technique, resting, and using ice and nonsteroidal anti-inflammatory agents. After reading this article we will also incorporate stretching exercises to increase internal rotation of the hips.—Frank George, A.T.C., P.T.

---

**An Unusual Lesion in the Knee of a Breaststroke Swimmer**
J.-O. Wethelund and A. de Carvalho (Aarhus Kommunehospital, Aarhus, Denmark)
Int. J. Sports Med. 6:174–175, June 1985                     3–72

---

Idiopathic knee pain seems to be common among breaststroke swimmers. The authors describe a breaststroke swimmer with a type of lesion not previously reported in this setting.

Man, 21, had participated in competitive breaststroke swimming from age 10 to age 15, swimming at least 2 hours a day. After 3½ years, medial pain in the right knee increased progressively, and for 1½ years he was so disabled that he could not swim. Pain was related to the medial patellar facet and the anteromedial aspect of the joint. The knee was often swollen, and sometimes a 3 × 3-cm tender intumescence was felt medially in the popliteal fossa. The patient resumed breast-stroke swimming, and 2½ months later, all symptoms recurred and were related to the intensity of the training.

There was a small joint effusion and tenderness in the anteromedial aspect of the knee but no obvious signs of a ligamentous or meniscal tear. Rheumatologic studies yielded normal results. Double-contrast arthrography clearly demonstrated a tear of the joint capsule. There was illustrated leakage of positive contrast medium into the extracapsular soft tissue along the periphery of the meniscus and the proximal 5 cm of the medial tibial condyle. The synovial membrane must have been deficient or herniated. The lesion could not be visualized at arthroscopy. Transarthroscopic synovial membrane biopsy revealed chronic synovitis at the medial aspect of the joint.

It must be assumed that the whip kick caused the capsular tear, because no other trauma to the knee could explain the lesion. The synovial reaction and pain were likely caused by the whip kick, because the symptoms recurred when the patient resumed swimming. Chondromalacia, one cause of knee pain in breaststroke swimming, was absent.

According to Stoker, the synovial lining of the knee can seal within a few days after injury. The arthrographic finding of a contrast leakage indicates that the lesion could be a synovial hernia or a defect in the capsule, with or without synovial hernia, possibly dependent on recurrent capsular ruptures. It cannot be determined from this case whether this lesion is caused directly by the whip kick or simply by overuse.

## Knee Arthroscopy

### Videoarthroscopy: Present and Future Developments

Douglas W. Jackson and Daniel N. Ovadia (Southern California Center for Sports Medicine, Long Beach, and Oregon Health Sciences Univ., Portland)
Arthroscopy 1:108–115, 1985                                                3–73

The benefits of videoarthroscopy are recognized by most orthopedic surgeons who perform a significant volume of arthroscopic surgery. The technique offers a more comfortable position for the surgeon, maintains the sterility desired for a surgical field, and enhances the freedom to perform operative procedures. Continuing advances in video technology, and their application to arthroscopic surgery, have resulted in some confusion about decisions concerning the purchase of specific equipment. Good reproducible visualization is the key factor in selecting this equipment.

The videoarthroscopic system has six components: the arthroscope, the fiber cable light guide, the light source, the camera/optics, the monitor/television, and the recorder/video cassette. There is also the human element, i.e., the physician and other staff members who care for this equipment. When purchasing the arthroscope it is important to recognize these differences: Light transmission may differ from one manufacturer's arthroscope to another's; resolution of the image may differ; and the field of view may vary, as may the color in the optics of the arthroscope. Two kinds of cameras are preferred and both are widely used. One, a subminiature camera, uses various types of vacuum chamber pickup tubes. The other is the solid state camera; one model weighs only 2 oz. All monitors and television sets interface with any camera. However, for best compatibility, they should be matched in terms of numbers of lines of resolution. The future in cameras will be the solid state system.

The future of videoarthroscopy lies in more simplified systems. The neutral-density wheel will markedly improve the light source, allowing for consistency in intra-articular lighting. Solid state cameras will allow interface between videoarthroscopy and computers. Reducing the camera size still more eventually will enable both the camera and the light source to be placed inside the arthroscope. Wireless cameras await development.

▶ An excellent review article on the components of the videoarthroscopic system. The authors emphasize that the quality of the video image is no better than the compatibility of the entire videoarthroscopic system. Certainly, the surgeons who perform arthroscopic surgery should have a grasp on the basic concepts dealt with in this article.—Joseph S. Torg, M.D.

---

### Complications of Arthroscopy and Arthroscopic Surgery: Results of a National Survey

Committee on Complications of Arthroscopy Association of North America
Arthroscopy 1:214–220, 1985                                                    3–74

---

Data on complications of arthroscopic procedures were obtained from 10 geographic regions of the United States in a total of 118,590 procedures. The 930 complications represented a rate of 0.8%. Use of a leg holder did not appear to influence the incidence of complications.

Hemarthrosis accounted for nearly one fourth of all complications. Three quarters of the cases were in patients having lateral retinacular release. Equipment failure such as broken instruments accounted for 17% of complications. Sixty-three patients required arthrotomy for removal of a broken instrument. Thrombophlebitis constituted 15% of complications. Thirty-two patients had clinical pulmonary embolism, and 4 of them died. Ninety-five patients required drainage and antibiotic therapy because of intra-articular infection. In only 3 cases was a septic focus identified distant to the knee that could have caused the infection. In 18 cases the final range of knee flexion was less than 90 degrees. Neurologic injury occurred in 63 cases; the popliteal and saphenous nerves were most often involved. Knee ligament injury constituted 4% of complications; the medial collateral ligament was involved in all cases. Forty-four patients had reflex sympathetic dystrophy, often in association with procedures directed to the patellofemoral joint. Thirty synovial fistulas required excision or immobilization. Nine penetrating vascular injuries occurred.

The complication rate of 0.8% in this series is artificially low. The risk of serious complications should be kept in mind when recommending "bandaid" operation.

▶ The authors emphasize the problems associated with a retrospective questionnaire survey that is dependent on the memories of the participants. Because of the low incidence of reported complications combined with a higher number of procedures claimed than actually were performed, the rate of complications of 0.8% represents an absolute minimum. However, the paper does delineate the numerous potential complications. Certainly, awareness of the possibility of a particular complication is the first step in prevention. Here lies the value of this study. Reading of the original article is recommended for all surgeons doing arthroscopy.—Joseph S. Torg, M.D.

**Local Anesthesia With Sedation for Arthroscopic Surgery of the Knee: A Report of 100 Consecutive Cases**
Ignacia U. Ngo, William G. Hamilton, W. Adam Wichern III, and Ronald A. Andree (St. Luke's Roosevelt Hosp. Ctr., New York)
Arthroscopy 1:237 241, 1985                                                    3–75

An attempt was made to avoid complications of general anesthesia by performing arthroscopic operation under local anesthesia in 100 consecutive patients operated on by a single surgeon. A tourniquet was placed on the thigh, and an amnestic or sleep dose of thiamylal or methohexital was given intravenously. Three portals were injected with 10–15 cc of 1% lidocaine with 1:100,000 epinephrine. The joint then was insufflated with 50–60 cc of a local anesthetic mixture including 30 cc of 0.5% bupivacaine and 50 cc of 0.5% lidocaine with 1:200,000 epinephrine, via a 14-gauge Jelco needle catheter or a Profex cannula. Surgical procedure was begun after 10 minutes, and patients received small doses of diazepam or fentanyl as indicated.

Most patients were aged 20 to 25 years. Fifty-seven patients were sedated preoperatively. There were 2 American Society of Anesthesiologists type II patients in the series. A wide range of anesthetic adjuvants was used. Only 2 patients required supplementation with a general inhalational anesthetic. Operation lasted 90 minutes or less in 88% of cases. Nearly 80% of patients were very pleased with their anesthetic experience, and required no anesthetic supplementation after the initial sleep dose of thiobarbiturate. Two patients rated the experience as fair, and 4 rated it poor. Shorter procedures were rated higher by patients.

Operative arthroscopy of the knee can be performed under local anesthesia with intravenously given sedation in a safe and acceptable manner. The same approach now is used for operative arthroscopy of the ankle.

▶ This paper describes the technique for, and feasibility of, performing surgical arthroscopy of the knee under sedation and local anesthesia. This experience parallels that described by Clancy (Snowmass Orthopaedic Conference, March 17, 1986) as well as ourselves. The day has arrived when both diagnostic and surgical arthroscopic procedures will be routinely performed under local anesthesia on an outpatient basis.—Joseph S. Torg, M.D.

**Meniscus Repair—Open vs. Arthroscopic**
Kenneth E. DeHaven (Univ. of Rochester)
Arthroscopy 1:173–174, 1985                                             3–76

The author has repaired 155 menisci by an open technique since 1976. Eight menisci are known to have retorn (5%); the remainder exhibited no symptoms or findings on examination, despite strenuous activities. No neurovascular complications or deep infections were observed. The main shortcoming has been that only a relatively small percentage of torn menisci treated (15% to 20% in the author's practice) are peripheral lesions suitable for open repair.

It seems logical to extend arthroscopic techniques to meniscus repair as has been done with partial meniscectomy, lateral retinacular release, removal of loose bodies, and intra-articular débridement. Performance of these procedures by arthroscopic rather than by open techniques has significantly reduced postoperative morbidity, permitted earlier return to function, and improved cosmesis. However, there is a fundamental difference with meniscus repair in that the time required for maturation of collagen healing sufficient to allow return to strenuous activities is the same in both open and arthroscopic procedures. The degree of postoperative protection and time necessary before return to strenuous activity tend to offset the low morbidity advantage of arthroscopic treatment. Also, since posterior exposure is advised to protect the neurovascular structures during arthroscopic repair, the cosmetic results are similar by both techniques. However, arthroscopic methods may allow repair of more meniscus lesions than can be repaired by open methods.

The two major concerns surrounding arthroscopic repair are safety and efficacy. To minimize the possibility of neurovascular damage, most advise posteromedial or posterolateral skin incisions to isolate and protect the neurovascular structures before the repair sutures are passed, making the procedure a combined arthroscopic and open technique as initially advocated by Henning. To minimize infection, repair sutures should be tied beneath the skin over the capsule or deep fascia, and antibiotic prophylaxis should be considered. Routine use of posterior incisions with arthroscopic meniscus repair can help prevent both neurovascular damage and deep infection.

There are suspicions that arthroscopic repair may not be as effective as open repair for peripheral lesions suitable for either method. Whether preparation of the capsular bed and rim of the meniscus can be as meticulous and accurate arthroscopically as at open repair is debatable. Henning now makes a posterior capsular incision to insure proper rim and capsular preparation before passage of the repair sutures under arthroscopic control.

For peripheral lesions that can be repaired by either arthroscopic or open procedures, the author recommends open repair. Future experience may show arthroscopic repair to be just as effective, however, and it may be easier for the surgeon. At such time, the open technique should be abandoned. Nonperipheral tears in the avascular zone of the meniscus are generally held to be irreparable and are managed by partial meniscectomy. In the future it may be feasible to use methods such as vascular access channels requiring arthroscopy.

**Arthroscopic Meniscus Repair**
Russell F. Warren (Hosp. for Special Surgery, New York)
Arthroscopy 1:170–172, 1985                                                   3–77

Certain tears of the meniscus lend themselves to an arthroscopic approach, including those of the avascular portion of the meniscus in which open operation is difficult because of the location of the tear. Generally these are posterior horn lesions, but they may extend anteriorly. Extensive tears involving the midportion or anterior portion of the meniscus, if managed with an open technique, require both posterior and anterior approaches. Arthroscopy allows relatively easy access to the anterior portion and midportion, and the posterior region can be dealt with as in an extensive bucket-handle tear. Initial experience with open repair has basically involved tears of the posterior horn of the medial meniscus, to which access is relatively easy. The anatomy of the posterior lateral corner of the knee, however, makes open repairs of the lateral meniscus more difficult.

The two most significant complications of arthroscopic meniscus repair involve the peroneal nerve and popliteal artery injury. Other significant complications include saphenous nerve injury, infections, and flexion contractures. Injury to the peroneal nerve is a potential hazard when any tear of the lateral meniscus is dealt with. Injury can be minimized by several steps. (1) In dealing with the lateral meniscus, if a suture is passed anterior to the popliteus tendon the peroneal nerve should not be at risk. (2) If the knee is flexed to 90 degrees, the peroneal nerve drops posteriorly and allows passage of instruments at the joint line. (3) If sutures are passed from outside the knee into the joint, rather than the converse, the peroneal nerve can be avoided. (4) Some prefer to perform combined procedures to avoid potential complications. Presently, this is reasonable, particularly in certain tears involving the posterior portion of the lateral, more than the medial, meniscus. It allows the capsule to be exposed and curved retractors to be inserted that will receive the needles passed from within the joint. Whether absorbable or nonabsorbable sutures are used, it is best to tie them under the skin.

In treatment of chronic tears of the meniscus or tears within the avascular zone, an attempt to create a healing response must be made. Henning advocates roughening of the synovial fringe above and below the meniscus to encourage a cellular response. For peripheral tears, simply freshening the outer portion with a basket or bur is sufficient to create a bleeding bed. For tears involving the white area of the meniscus, it appears that repair can be obtained by creating vascular access channels. A basket or bur is used to make an opening in the central portion of the meniscus, establishing contact between the tear and the peripheral circulation.

### Meniscal Repair: An Arthroscopic Technique

F. Alan Barber and Robert G. Stone (Univ. of Texas Health Science Ctr. at Dallas)

J. Bone Joint Surg. [Br.] 67-B:39–41, January 1985                    3–78

Repair of a longitudinal peripheral meniscal tear allows salvage of this structure in many patients. Whereas others have reported using arthrotomy to perform this repair, here an arthroscopic technique was used. However, the potential risks are significant, including damage to the peroneal nerve and popliteal vasculature, failure of meniscal healing, and the usual complications of arthroscopy.

TECHNIQUE.—The standard video arthroscopy setup is used. After the longitudinal tear is identified, its length and distance from the periphery are noted; reduction of the bucket handle is performed if necessary. Once the inner rim portion is properly positioned, the following technique for suturing is used: A hollow inflow cannula is inserted through the anterolateral or midpatellar lateral portal, positioned in the medial compartment, and aligned toward the meniscal tear. The best access is obtained if the knee is held in 10 degrees of flexion and a valgus stress is applied. A 3-mm basket forceps is inserted through the cannula and used to debride the outer rim of the meniscus until bleeding occurs from the perimeniscal capillary plexus. A 7.6-cm Keith needle is bent to a 30-degree angle at 1 cm from its tip and threaded with a 3–0 Mersilene suture. The threaded Keith needle is placed in a Henning needle holder and advanced through the cannula with the curve directed anteriorly. The needle is passed through the superior surface of the meniscal bucket handle about 2 mm in from the tear and advanced through the tear and into the medial capsule (Fig 3–26).

The needle should emerge from the skin anterior to the semitendinosus tendon. The index finger, protected by a thimble, can be placed behind the tendon to protect the popliteal artery. As the Keith needle is advanced, it tents the skin; a knife is then used to make a portal at this point. The needle is pulled through with needle holders and the suture unthreaded. Sufficient suture should remain outside the cannula to permit rethreading of the Keith needle. The standing end of the suture is then threaded, the needle is placed in the Henning needle holder, and the needle is again passed in the same fashion through the bucket handle, outer rim, and capsule, and out through the previously made portal. A Z retractor placed in the posteromedial portal acts as a neurovascular shield and needle guide, and facilitates the exit of this and subsequent sutures through a single portal. The second pass of this suture should be 2 mm lateral to the first, creating a horizontal mattress suture (Fig 3–27). A separate suture is needed for every 5 mm of tear above 1 cm, e.g., a 20-mm tear requires three sutures, a 25-mm tear needs four. Once all of the sutures have been placed, they are pulled tight to approximate the edges of the torn meniscus and capsule (Fig 3–28). If the repair is adequate, the matched sutures are tied snugly through the portal incision. A curved clamp is used to free the skin and subcutaneous tissues, preventing puckering. The portal is closed in the routine manner and the knee immobilized in 45 degrees of flexion for 6 weeks.

Even the experienced arthroscopic surgeon is advised to study the anatomical relationships by cadaver dissections when preparing for this technique. To be suitable for this method, the tear should be a single longi-

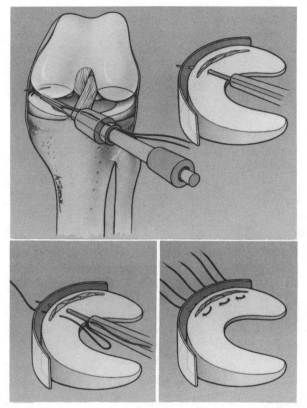

Fig 3–26 (top).—Using a Henning needle holder, the surgeon passes the threaded Keith needle through the torn meniscus and out through the capsule.

Fig 3–27 (bottom left).—After the proximal end of the suture is threaded onto the Keith needle, a horizontal mattress suture is created.

Fig 3–28 (bottom right).—After all of the sutures are in place, they are pulled tight and tied through the portal incision.

(Courtesy of Barber, F.A., and Stone, R.G.: J. Bone Joint Surg. [Br.] 67-B:39–41, January 1985.)

tudinal one extending completely through the meniscus and situated either at the synovial-meniscal junction or within 3 mm of it. Tears less than 1 cm long are treated in a brace without suture. Multiple longitudinal tears and single tears with a damaged inner rim are not suitable for repair.

▶ These three papers on arthroscopic repair of torn menisci (Digests 3–76, 3–77, and 3–78) have one thing in common—a complete lack of data to support any meaningful conclusion.—Joseph S. Torg, M.D.

---

**Resection of Painful Shelf (Plica Synovialis Mediopatellaris) Under Arthroscopy**

Tomihisa Koshino and Renzo Okamoto (Yokohama City Univ., Japan)

Arthroscopy 1:136–141, 1985                                                3–79

---

In a series of 3,250 patients with knee disorders, a painful shelf was diagnosed and resected in 39 knees of 32 patients. Thirty of them were done by arthroscopy and 9 by arthrotomy. There were 10 men and 22 women, with an average age of 19 years.

After resection of the plica, pain was relieved completely in 26 of 39 knees, and moderately in 13 knees. Medial patellar tenderness disappeared in 34 knees and was diminished in 1. Locking-like symptoms were noted in 5 knees; after surgery these symptoms disappeared in all of them. Clicks were audible in 11 knees and palpable in 23 knees. Postoperatively, they disappeared in 28 knees and were minimal in 6. Moderate joint effusion was noted in 6 knees and in none postoperatively. Preoperative limitation of range of motion in 7 knees was completely relieved in all after surgery. In two provocative tests, test 1 was a rotation valgus test and provocation test 2 was known as a "holding test" in which the examiner attempts to flex the knee against the patient's extension. In provocation test 1, the examiner attempts to flex the knee and force it into a valgus position with the lower leg internally or externally rotated. Provocation test 1 was performed on 28 knees and a positive test result was obtained in 23, all having had an enlarged plica. After surgery, results of provocation test 1 were negative in 21 knees and improved in 2. Provocation test 2 was performed on 23 knees, and resulted in positive scores in 14. After resection of the shelf, results of the test were negative in 12 and improved in 2.

In this study, relief of pain and other symptoms was obtained in 90% of the cases. The authors believe that the two provocation tests described were useful in making a correct preoperative diagnosis and postoperative evaluation.

▶ The incidence of a painful plica in this series of 3,250 patients with knee disorders is 1%. The authors hope "that this incidence will have an inhibitory effect on the enthusiasm that some surgeons have for diagnosing and treating these unusually benign anatomical structures." Their data regarding the specificity of provocation test 1 and provocation test 2 for painful plica is inconclusive.—Joseph S. Torg, M.D.

---

**Simple Arthroscopic Partial Meniscectomy Associated With Anterior Cruciate-Deficient Knees**
Stuart Marshall, Michael G. Levas, and Andrew Harrah (Girard Orthopedic Surgeon Med. Group, La Jolla, Calif.)
Arthroscopy 1:22–27, 1985                                          3–80

---

In 25 patients (18 men), aged 18 to 48 years, who had combined tears of the meniscus and anterior cruciate ligament (ACL) in the same knee, the functional results of a simple arthroscopic meniscectomy that preserved the meniscal rim were evaluated. The patients were recreational athletes. The average time from initial injury to arthroscopic surgery was 12 months (range, 1–24). Three patients had had arthrotomies before arthroscopic meniscectomy. Arthroscopic diagnosis revealed that all had significant meniscal tears and absence or marked laxity of the ACL. Twenty-two patients had complete, old ruptures of the ACL and 3 had incomplete ruptures with grade II Lachman test scores (5–10 mm of laxity). Each patient had a meniscal tear that was excised arthroscopically via two or three portals, leaving a stable peripheral rim. The types of tear were medial bucket handle (11 patients), posterior horn (4), degenerative flap or longitudinal (4), and lateral (6). All patients were advised before operation that simple meniscectomy might be only a preliminary step.

No complications followed operation. Hospitalization lasted 0.5–2 days. All patients had postoperative effusions that persisted 1–3 weeks. Splints and crutches were used for 2 days, after which quadriceps, hamstring, and gastrocnemius exercises were prescribed. Patients were evaluated by questionnaire and physical examination an average of 30 months after operation.

When the presence or absence of the pivot shift sign was used as the most important indicator of functional capability, partial meniscectomy was found to be effective in allowing patients to regain a high degree of normal functional activity and in permitting forward motion activities. However, all patients were left with an ACL deficient knee that caused laxity in the anterior plane and frequently in the rotatory plane. Rotatory laxity markedly limits activities, and patients unable to adjust to the instability are considering a further operation.

Patients with combined lesions of the meniscus and ACL have separate problems that together can exaggerate the symptoms of knee instability. These problems must be considered and treated separately, as the function of each structure and the response of each to operation are different. Intact menisci are important for load bearing and force transmission across the knee. Therefore, partial meniscectomy is indicated to preserve the load-bearing function of the meniscus and aid in protection of articular cartilage.

Simple meniscectomy can be effective in the recreational athlete whose demands are not extensive. Episodes of giving-way and instability decrease when more stability is obtained by restoring the meniscal rim, and the ACL deficiency can be overcome with proper rehabilitation. Still, patients who expect to return to sports requiring excessive pivoting, cutting, and moments of being airborne will not do well with simple meniscectomy, particularly if they have rotatory laxity characterized by a positive pivot shift test. Most persons do well with simple partial arthroscopic meniscectomy because they change their athletic requirements to activities that do not cause instability. Seventy-two percent of the patients studied did not consider or require reconstructive operations because either rotatory laxity was not significant or their activities were modified.

▶ This paper has attempted to answer a most important question: Can the anterior cruciate ligament deficient knee with associated meniscal injuries be treated by surgical arthroscopic techniques? Prior to the popularity of interarticular cruciate reconstructions, this problem was, for the most part, approached by meniscectomy via arthrotomy. Seventy-two percent of the 25 patients did not require reconstructive surgery. It is interesting to compare this group with that reported by McDaniel and Dameron (*J. Bone Joint Surg.* [*Am.*] 62-A:696–705, July 1980), who reported on 53 knees with untreated ruptures of the anterior cruciate ligament treated only by meniscectomy with an average follow-up of 10 years. None of the patients had surgery to attempt to deal with the completely torn cruciate ligament. Of this group, 72% were also able to return to strenuous athletic activity. The parallel between these groups, although criteria are certainly ill-defined, is most interesting. Perhaps Marshall et al. will report longer follow-up with emphasis on development, degenerative changes, and continued functional status.—Joseph S. Torg, M.D.

---

**Arthroscopic Partial Medial Meniscectomy: An Analysis of Unsatisfactory Results**
Richard D. Ferkel, J. Randall Davis, Marc J. Friedman, James M. Fox, Wilson Del Pizzo, Stephen J. Snyder, and Carl C. Berasi (Southern California Sports Medicine and Orthopedic Med. Group, Van Nuys, Calif.; Univ. of California, Los Angeles; and Doctors Hosp., Columbus, Ohio)
Arthroscopy 1:44–52, 1985                                    3–81

---

Results in 150 patients (110 men), aged 19 to 82 years, who underwent arthroscopic partial medial meniscectomy (APMM) were analyzed to identify the factors that lead to an unsatisfactory (fair or poor) outcome. Average follow-up was 36 months (range, 24 to 60). Overall results were 58% excellent-good, 28% fair, and 14% poor. Most tears involved the posterior horn (76%). Bucket handle, longitudinal, and flap tears were rated 88% excellent-good, whereas horizontal cleavage and degenerative and complex tears had only 45% excellent-good scores.

Mild chondromalacia in any of the five articular surfaces of the knee contributed to unsatisfactory results. With more severe degenerative changes, there were more unsatisfactory results. Degenerative changes in the lateral compartment were associated with a particularly high incidence of poor results. Injuries sustained at work were associated with prolonged disability and often necessitated a change in job. Patients with sports-related injuries had few unsatisfactory results and were rarely disabled. Though degenerative, regenerated, complex, and horizontal cleavage tears had more unsatisfactory results than did bucket handle, flap, and longitudinal tears, the difference was not statistically significant when matched for grade of chondromalacia. The delay between onset of symptoms and operation did not itself adversely affect the results of APMM. Age-related, preexisting degenerative arthritis, rather than age alone, appeared to affect meniscectomy results. Patients who had prior knee surgery had more unsatisfactory results but did not have more degenerative changes or tears associated with a poor result.

Significant laxity was associated with increased degenerative joint disease and more unsatisfactory results, but the number of cases was too small to be definitive. Lateral meniscal tears were associated with increased numbers of unsatisfactory results, probably secondary to the increased amount of chondromalacia. These results have not deteriorated over time, with follow-up of up to 5 years. Patients with degenerative posterior horn tears, severe chondromalacia, or prior knee surgery had a high percentage of unsatisfactory results. A standardized scoring system is needed to properly evaluate and to compare arthroscopic meniscectomy results.

## The Failures of Arthroscopic Partial Meniscectomy
D. M. Eastwood (General Hosp., Birmingham, England)
Injury 16:587–590, 1985                                                           3–82

A review was made of failures in a series of 291 consecutive arthroscopic partial meniscectomies done by a single surgeon in 1979–1983. All patients, aged 16 to 65 years, had evidence of a torn meniscus, and some also had concomitant damage to the knee ligaments. Meniscectomy was done under general anesthesia and a tourniquet, with a lateral parapatellar incision for the arthroscope and variable incisions for the instruments.

Arthroscopy was unsuccessful in 4 cases (1.3%), and arthrotomy was done instead. Of 217 patients with only meniscal damage, 84% were symptomatically cured by arthroscopic operation. Thirteen patients (6%) had no, or only short-term, relief. Three of the patients with no relief did well after further arthroscopic meniscectomy. Several patients with only short-term benefit reported further injury that could have damaged the meniscus. Five were cured by a second arthroscopic procedure. Of 62 patients with meniscal damage and damage to a cruciate ligament, 76% were improved or cured after arthroscopic partial meniscectomy alone, although 3 patients required two procedures. Physiotherapy led to improvement in some of the failures, and others had successful ligament reconstruction. None of 8 patients with meniscal damage and osteoarthritis improved significantly after arthroscopic operation. The overall true failure rate was 8%, excluding patients who were cured by a second arthroscopic procedure. No major complications occurred.

Arthroscopic partial meniscectomy is a useful approach to patients who are symptomatic from torn or damaged menisci, but failures do occur. Inaccurate assessment of the extent of meniscal damage and other lesions such as cruciate ligament damage or osteoarthritis explain some failures. Injury from further activity or from arthroscopy itself can result in recurrent symptoms.

## The Results of Arthroscopic Partial Meniscectomy
P. Aglietti, R. Buzzi, P. B. Bassi, and A. Pisaneschi (Univ. of Florence)
Arch. Orthop. Trauma Surg 104:42–48, June 1985                                   3–83

There are experimental and clinical reasons to preserve meniscal tissue where possible, and partial arthroscopic meniscectomy has given very satisfactory short-term results. A review was made of the first 100 closed partial arthroscopic meniscectomies performed in 1981–1982. The 82 male and 18 female patients had an average age of 29 years. Sports injuries accounted for nearly two thirds of the cases. The mean time from injury to operation was 23 months. Most patients had "mechanical" symptoms. Two patients had had previous operation. General anesthesia was used.

The average follow-up was 18 months. Satisfactory results were obtained in 85% of all cases. The meniscal lesion was considered the chief cause of symptoms in all stable knees. The medial meniscus was treated in 85 cases, and the lateral meniscus was treated in 15. The mean hospital stay after operation was 1½ days. Locking was relieved in all but 1 of 59 knees. Eighty percent of 63 stable knees were free of pain at follow-up at all levels of activity. Three patients had moderate to severe pain. The average time to return to work was 23 days, and to active sports activities, it was 49 days. Lower knee scores were obtained in knees with chondromalacia. The results of operation were not significantly influenced by age, sex, the site of meniscectomy, or the type of tear. The duration of symptoms also did not affect the outcome significantly.

Very satisfactory results are obtained 18 months after arthroscopic partial meniscectomy. Advantages of this approach include a short hospital stay, low morbidity, and relatively rapid recovery. Poorer results are obtained in patients with chondromalacia or chondritis and in those with thigh atrophy.

▶ These three reports (Digests 3–81, 3–82, and 3–83) on the results of arthroscopic partial meniscectomy have remarkably similar failure rates. Specifically, Eastwood reports that 84% of patients were symptomatically cured by arthroscopic operation (Digest 3–82). Aglietti et al. report satisfactory results obtained in 85% of their cases (Digest 3–83). Ferkel et al. report that 14% of patients had poor results (Digest 3–81). Although none of these reports establishes a significant correlation with unacceptable results and the presence of chondromalacia, arthritis, and cruciate ligament deficiency, these appear to be frequently associated with failure of arthroscopic partial meniscectomy.

The conclusion of Aglietti, et al. that partial arthroscopic meniscectomy is a new, promising addition to orthopaedic technology is well taken; however, we would also agree with the conclusion of Ferkel et al. that "a standardized scoring system is absolutely essential to enable investigators to communicate about the results of arthroscopic meniscectomy."—Joseph S. Torg, M.D.

---

**Prostaglandin Inhibition and the Rate of Recovery After Arthroscopic Meniscectomy: A Randomised Double-Blind Prospective Study**
D. J. Ogilvie-Harris, Mats Bauer, and Paul Corey (Toronto Western Hosp. and Univ. of Toronto)
J. Bone Joint Surg. [Br.] 67-B:567–571, August 1985                    3–84

---

Arthroscopic meniscectomy offers a substantial advantage in recovery, compared with open meniscectomy. However, not all patients do well in the early period after arthroscopic meniscectomy, and postoperative effusions that result from an inflammatory reaction mediated by prostaglandins are common. Prostaglandin inhibitors may therefore decrease the inflammatory component of the arthroscopic procedure, decrease the effusion, and speed recovery.

After arthroscopy 139 selected patients were randomly allocated to receive the prostaglandin inhibitor naproxen sodium, 550 mg twice a day for 6 weeks, or a placebo. Patients were given an analgestic (30 mg of paracetamol with codeine) to use if needed, and usage of this analgesic was assessed. Follow-up visits were at 7, 21, 42, and 84 days after operation.

Patients in the active treatment group had significantly less pain at rest up to 21 days after operation; both groups had little residual pain at rest by 84 days. The active treatment group also had significantly less pain during activity at all times. The use of analgesics was significantly less in the active treatment group.

The active treatment group had significantly less synovitis and effusion throughout the postoperative period. At 84 days about 15% of the active treatment group had residual synovitis or effusion, compared with 55% of the placebo group. The placebo group also had significantly greater magnitude of effusions.

Preoperative assessment showed there was significantly less movement in the active treatment group (mean, 111 vs. 121 degrees), but at 7 and 21 days after operation the range of movement of this group was significantly greater. By 42 days the groups were equal.

With respect to atrophy of the quadriceps, at 7 days after operation there were no significant differences between the groups, but atrophy started to diminish earlier in the active treatment group. By 84 days there was still a significant difference in the return of normal functions of the quadriceps, which had reached only 50% in the placebo group but had reached 72% in the active treatment group.

Median time for return to work was 14 days in the placebo group and 5 days in the active treatment group. Median time for return to athletic activities was 56 days in the placebo group and 22.5 days in the active treatment group. At 84 days there was still a significant difference in the return to sport in favor of the active treatment group.

After arthroscopic meniscectomy patients recover more rapidly than after open meniscectomy. This rapidity of recovery is, however, decreased by the presence of effusions, synovitis, and inflammation, as shown in the placebo group. This study demonstrates that significantly improved recovery after arthroscopic meniscectomy occurs when a prostaglandin inhibitor is used, and any risk to the patient is minimal. Patients who received the prostaglandin inhibitor had significantly more rapid recovery with less pain, less synovitis, less effusion, and more rapid return of movement and of quadriceps function. They took less time to return to work and to athletics.

The graphs of the results generally showed evidence of convergence, which indicates that at some time in the future recovery with or without the prostaglandin inhibitor would be equal. The effect of the prostaglandin inhibitor is probably to accelerate the rate of recovery rather than to increase its final degree.

▶ It appears that naproxen sodium suppresses the inflammatory reaction following arthroscopic meniscectomy of the knee. The fact that 15% of the active treatment group and 55% of the placebo group had residual synovitis or effusion 12 weeks after surgery is somewhat disconcerting. Although three subgroupings based on pathologic findings are mentioned (isolated meniscal pathology, associated chondral lesion, and associated osteoarthritis), these are not correlated with observations. Also, status of the anterior cruciate ligament and meniscus laterality are ignored. Unfortunately, in dealing with the traumatized knee, nothing is as simple as prescribing or not prescribing a drug.—Josph S. Torg, M.D.

## Arthroscopic Chondroplasty of the Patella
George J. Schonholtz and Benjamin Ling (George Washington Univ.)
Arthroscopy 1:92–96, 1985                                                3–85

Arthroscopic chondroplasty was performed on 41 knees in 40 patients with chondromalacia of the patella as the only lesion after unsuccessful conservative treatment. Average time of follow-up was 40 months. The 23 women and 17 men had a mean age of 40 years.

Results showed 4 excellent results (asymptomatic and no limitations) (10%), 16 good results (crepitus reduced, swelling absent, and activity slightly limited) (39%), 18 fair results (44%), and 3 poor results (7%). No patient's problems were worsened by the procedure. Thus, 93% of all knees studied showed some degree of improvement. Thirty-one (78%) of the 40 patients were sufficiently satisfied with the result of surgery to be able to recommend it. The 9 patients who would not recommend the procedure were previously categorized as having either a poor (n = 3) or fair (n = 6) result. Among this group, 4 patients had what were considered unrealistic expectations.

The authors believe that careful arthroscopic chondroplasty of the patella is effective in most patients because the procedure decreases the particulate and enzymatic load on the knee joint with minimal disturbance of the synovium, capsule, and other supporting structures. Improvement is also related to the decrease in crepitus in many instances and improvement in patella tracking with reduced sensations of instability.

▶ This article raises several interesting points. Like most other authors that discuss chondromalacia of the patella, they offer no explanation for the pain or why it is relieved following partial resection of tissue that is aneural. Of 1,083 arthroscopic procedures, only 63 or 5.8% of those patients were subjected to arthroscopic shaving. Emphasized is that there is no evidence that shaving itself will alter the ultimate prognosis of this condition. As has been our experience, there was no statistical correlation between the grade of chondromalacia and the end results.—Joseph S. Torg, M.D.

**Diagnostic Arthroscopy and Longitudinal Open Lateral Release: A Safe and Effective Treatment for "Chondromalacia Patella"**
Robert B. Dzioba, Andrew Strokon, and Leonard Mulbry (Univ. of Arizona)
Arthroscopy 1:131–135, 1985                                                    3–86

Sixty lateral release procedures in 45 patients (33 females), aged 13 to 63 years, were reviewed. Mean follow-up was 14.6 months. Most patients related onset of symptoms to a specific event, e.g., a sports exertion, a direct blow, or some other trauma. All patients were assessed with merchant views of the patella and routine radiographs of the knee. The indications for operation were acute or chronic dislocation of the patella and patellofemoral arthralgia with or without subluxation of more than 6 months' duration that failed to respond to conservative treatment. Diagnostic arthroscopy was performed in all cases.

TECHNIQUE.—A short, lateral parapatellar incision about 3 cm long is made in the skin about 1 cm posterior to the lateral margin of the patella. By precise undermining of surrounding subcutaneous tissues, the incision can be moved up and down to allow access to the entire lateral retinacular structure from the joint line inferiorly to a point almost 2 in. above the patella. The subtraction of laterally acting forces or tethers involves division of the lateral part of the capsule forming the transverse lateral patellofemoral ligament, the more superficial oblique fibers of the iliotibial tract that insert into the lateral side of the patella, the lowest fibers of the vastus lateralis tendon and its aponeurosis, and the lateral patellomeniscal ligament. This ligament may contribute to the lateral pull on the patella during lateral rotation of the tibia.

The division is carried proximally until, with flexion to 90 degrees, there is no palpable lateral tethering. The knee is flexed several times to demonstrate gaping in the retinaculum and to test the division of all fibrous bands. The synovial membrane is not divided. Great care is taken in identifying the superior lateral genicular artery that runs horizontally toward the middle of the patella and often adheres to the underside of the lateral retinaculum. Meticulous hemostasis is secured after release of the tourniquet. The patient is encouraged to perform straight-leg raising immediately after operation and is usually allowed home within 1 or 2 days, with full weight-bearing as tolerated.

The vast majority of patients examined were able to move their knees through a full range of motion by 3 weeks after operation. A postoperative rating of excellent denoted no postoperative symptoms and return to full activity; a rating of good denoted minimal symptoms, usually brought on by strenuous activity, but otherwise no restriction of activity; a rating of fair indicated diminished symptoms but persistent significant limitation of activity; and a rating of poor denoted no improvement. Overall, 87% of the patients had an excellent or good result, 10% were improved but still had problems, and 3% were unimproved. Follow-ups ranged from 6 to 29 months.

The good results in this series were due to a complete joint evaluation by arthroscopy as well as standard radiologic assessment, and clinical evaluation that allows the exclusion; open visualization to ensure the completeness of division of all lateral tethers that form the lateral retinaculum;

meticulous attention to hemostasis of the transected lateral superior genicular artery and its branches; and early mobilization that retarded quadriceps atrophy.

► This is an excellent paper, even though the data were not subjected to statistical analysis. In that the methods and observations are similar to my own, it is a paper that I wish I had written. The authors clearly indicate the necessity for complete division of lateral structures and adequate hemostasis of the superior lateral genicular artery and its branches if a good result is to be expected. The observation that neither the initial symptoms nor final results appeared to correlate with the degree of chondromalacia agrees with our own observations. Exception is taken to the statement that no particular parameters were found in the clinical features that affected the outcome of surgery. It has been our observation that patients with hypermobile patellae and significant extensors mechanism malalignment are not benefited by a lateral release. Perhaps the 80% rating of excellent and good results for all patients is a bit generous.—Joseph S. Torg, M.D.

## Foot and Ankle Injuries

### The Jones' Fracture in the Nonathlete
William H. Seitz, Jr., and S. Ashby Grantham (New York Orthopaedic Hosp. and Columbia Univ.)
Foot Ankle 6:97–100, October 1985                                    3–87

Fractures of the base of the fifth metatarsal were first described by Sir Robert Jones. All occurred about 0.75 in. from the base and were the result of "indirect violence," a forceful inversion injury. The fracture described by Jones occurs just distal to the intermetatarsal ligaments and 0.5 cm distal to the splayed insertion of the peroneus brevis tendon. It can have a less benign, more protracted clinical course than the avulsion injury or the epiphyseal plate injury that is seen in children. Recently there have been reports that chronic stress may be the causative factor in Jones' fractures.

Data were reviewed on 190 proximal fractures of the fifth metatarsal that were treated in 1976–1981; 147 were avulsion fractures of the tuberosity and 53 (19 men and 34 women aged 11 to 81 years; mean age, 39 years) were Jones' fractures. Thirty-nine (74%) of the 53 patients clearly described an inversion injury. Six of the remaining patients were injured in falls, 4 were injured in motor vehicle accidents, and 4 could not recall the circumstances. All injuries were described as acute; no patient had experienced antecedent foot pain or trauma.

Thirty-six of the 53 patients were followed up; all were treated nonoperatively. Sixteen were placed in short-leg walking casts and 20 were treated with bulky soft compressive dressings. All were allowed to bear weight to tolerance.

Those who received short-leg walking casts were left in plaster for 3 to 8 weeks; all were able to bear full weight by 2 weeks after injury. Duration of symptoms was 3–16 weeks (mean, 7.3 weeks). For those who received soft compressive dressings, treatment time varied from 1 to 8 weeks. Time to full weight-bearing averaged 4 weeks after injury; time to complete relief of symptoms ranged from 1 to 64 weeks (mean, 9.8 weeks). Two patients in this group had fractures that did not achieve union until 44 and 64 weeks, respectively.

The authors now treat all Jones' fractures in a short-leg walking cast for at least 4 weeks and see no need to limit weight-bearing. Surgical intervention has not been required in the care of this non-athletic population. They agree that the stress fracture reported by other groups, especially in young athletes, which occurs at the proximal diaphysis of the fifth metatarsal, carries a much less optimistic prognosis for conservative care. Although it develops at the same location, it is not the fracture or fracture mechanism described by Jones and should not be confused with it.

▶ It has been well established that fractures of the base of the fifth metatarsal distal to the tuberosity are difficult to manage in the athlete (Dameron: *J. Bone Joint Surg. [Am.]* 57-A:788–792, 1975; Kavanaugh et al.: *J. Bone Joint Surg. [Am.].* 60-A:776–782, 1978; and Torg et al.: *J. Bone Joint Surg. [Am.]* 66-A:209–214, 1984). A manifestation of repetitive cyclic loading with continued weight-bearing, these fractures follow a course of delayed union, refracture, and nonunion in the athlete. They are subsequently classified as (1) acute, sharp fracture line, with no evidence of intramedullary sclerosis; (2) delayed union, widened fracture line, with evidence of intramedullary sclerosis at the fracture site; and (3) delayed union, intramedullary sclerosis obliterating the fracture site. Guidelines for management of these fractures in the athlete are as follows: (1) acute, nonweight-bearing for 6 weeks; (2) nonunion and delayed union, surgery in the form of intramedullary curettage of sclerotic bone and inlaid graft or intramedullary screw fixation. The point made by the authors of this paper that in the sedentary patient there may be a different fracture that can be managed conservatively is extremely well taken.—Joseph S. Torg, M.D.

---

**Pressures on the Foot in Pointe Shoes**
Carol C. Teitz, Richard M. Harrington, and Hannah Wiley (Univ. of Washington, Seattle VA Hosp. and Med. Ctr., and Mt. Holyoke College, South Hadley, Mass.)
Foot Ankle 5:216–221, March–April 1985                                              3–88

---

Thirteen advanced ballet students were placed in three groups. Group 1 consisted of four dancers whose first three toes were of even length, group 2 of five dancers whose first three toes were of decreasing length, and group 3 consisted of four dancers with long second toes. New shoes of a single brand and style were fitted to each dancer's foot. Kulite pressure transducers were then applied to the tip of the first and second toes in the areas of anticipated maximal pressures and to the medial aspect of the first metatarsophalangeal (MTP) joint of one foot. Each dancer stood on a force plate and was asked to do five *relevés en pointe* in the way in which she was trained, and five *relevés* with her feet purposely elevated. *Relevé en pointe* is a movement in which the dancer rises from the foot-flat position to standing on her toes. The force plate and pressure transducers were connected to an eight-channel chart recorder.

Six dancers had clinically apparent bunions. The average absolute pressure on the toe box of each shoe was 220 psi (1.5 MPa). Relative pressures on the great toe did not vary significantly as a function of toe length. The first toe nearly always took more pressure, or at least as much pressure, as the second toe. Pressures on the second toe were significantly different from group 1 to group 2, and pressure ratios in these groups were also significantly different. In group 2, capping the second toe doubled the pressure on that toe, thereby changing the pressure ratio between the first and second toes from 14% without caps to 33% with caps and more nearly approximating the ratios in group 1 (52%). Despite the increased pressure on the second toe, there was no significant change in the pressure measured on the first toe or on the first MTP joint. When the foot was everted in the *relevé* position, the pressure on the first MTP joint increased by an average of 27%. In dancers with bunions, there was no significant difference noted in the MTP joint pressures compared to those without bunions.

The high pressures recorded on the first and second toes support the radiographic finding of cortical hypertrophy in the first and second metatarsals observed by others. It appears that the first ray bears most of the pressure to which the toes are exposed when the dancer is *en pointe*. This is true whether or not the first toe is of equal length to the second toe or shorter than the second toe. Increased pressure on the first MTP joint in eversion suggests that this positioning may contribute to MTP joint problems, e.g., arthritis or hallus rigidus. Normal (perpendicular) pressures rather than shear pressures, which theoretically would be increased by the everted position, were measured. Forced lateral deviation of the first toe in the toe box of the shoe or shear pressures may contribute more to bunion formation than do perpendicular pressures.

Thus, there is evidence of marked pressures on the toes when the dancer is *en pointe*. Properly designed padding may redistribute these pressures. There was no apparent correlation between axial pressure on the first ray and bunion formation. However, everted positioning, by increasing first MTP joint pressure, may contribute to the high incidence of first MTP joint arthritis in ballet dancers.

▶ Science has come to the ballet. The development of a method to measure the relative pressure on the first and second toes and first MTP joint when dancing *en pointe* is significant, considering the numerous foot problems experienced by ballet dancers. Documentation of the effect of modification of ballet pointe shoe design and fabrication, dancing technique, and capping may further delineate both etiology and preventive measures. It is also apparent that reproducibility studies of the test method and a larger number of subjects are necessary in further studies.—Joseph S. Torg, M.D.

**Foot and Ankle Injuries in Theatrical Dancers**
William T. Hardaker, Jr., Susan Margello, and J. Leonard Goldner (Duke Univ.)
Foot Ankle 6:59–69, October 1985                                          3–89

Although acute injuries do occur in the foot and ankle of theatrical dancers, most injuries are chronic. Unlike the runner who wears a specially designed shoe to absorb shock and stabilize the foot, the classical ballet dancer wears only a soft slipper or toe shoe; modern dancers wear no shoes at all. Thus most forces of the repetitive impact must be dissipated in the lower extremity, and failure to effectively dissipate these forces can lead to many of the injuries that are seen in the feet and ankles of dancers. Significant anatomical variation can block dissipation of the forces of cyclic loading. Excessive femoral anteversion, genu varum, genu valgum, internal rotation of the tibia, extreme pes valgus, and pes cavus can all lead to inability to absorb shock in the lower extremities.

Ankle sprains are the most common acute injury seen in both classical ballet and modern dancers. The injury occurs from incorrect landing from a jump while the foot is in plantar flexion. The usual mechanism is forced inversion of the ankle with injury to the lateral ligamentous structure.

Mild and moderate sprains involve a stretch or partial tear of the anterior talofibular ligament or combined injury to the anterior talofibular and calcaneofibular ligaments. If the ankle is stable, the injury is initially treated with ice, compression, and elevation. Severe sprains involve complete failure of the anterior talofibular ligament or combined anterior talofibular and calcaneofibular ligaments. With complete tearing of the lateral ligamentous structures, the ankle will be unstable. These instabilities can be shown clinically under Xylocaine block and radiographically with the anterior drawer or inversion talar-tilt signs. A structured rehabilitation program is essential in the aftercare of ankle sprains in dancers; swimming is an excellent technique for restoring range of motion to the ankle and contiguous joints.

The extreme dorsiflexion and plantar flexion required by certain ballet positions can lead to talar impingement syndromes that involve the anterior and posterior aspects of the ankle joint. One such position is the demi-plié, which can lead to impingement of the anterior lip of the tibia on the talar neck. The initial symptoms may be poorly localized, and the major complaint of the dancer is lack of adequate depth on plié; this complaint may be incorrectly interpreted as tight heel cords. On examination there is tenderness medially between the medial malleolus and the tibialis anterior tendon. Laterally, similar tenderness and sometimes mild swelling is located between the lateral malleolus and the extensor digitorum communis.

In advanced cases small exostoses on the anterior margins of the tibia and talar neck can be palpated. Lateral films of the ankle will reveal the tibiotalar contact present with the foot in extreme dorsiflexion. Exostoses may be present on the anterior talar neck and the anterior lip of the tibia. With repeated impact the exostoses become more prominent, and eventually the normal sulcus on the superior neck of the talus will be lost. Treatment consists of using a 0.5 inch heel lift when the dancer is not dancing and taking nonsteroidal anti-inflammatory agents. In advanced cases surgical excision of the exostoses may be necessary.

Tendinitis about the ankle is a common problem in dancers. Although inflammation can occur in any of the tendons locally, the Achilles and flexor hallucis longus are most often involved. Achilles tendinitis (actually, peritendinitis) involves inflammation of the peritenon. No tendon sheath is present in this area. Typically, symptoms occur 4 to 8 cm above the insertion of the Achilles tendon into the os calcis. Alternatively, the symptoms present more localized to the discrete area proximal to the calcaneal bursa.

Stress fractures can occur in any bone of the foot or ankle. Typically, they involve the second and third metatarsals, which are relatively immobile compared to the first, fourth, and fifth metatarsal rays. Stress fractures can occur in the beginning dancer who is gradually increasing activity in this discipline. Such fractures also occur in the experienced dancer who may be dancing on hard, unyielding surfaces while on tour.

▶ The point is made that the theatrical dancer is a combination of superior artist and high performance athlete. Sammarco has emphasized his belief that one "should never operate on a dancer" (personal communication). Presumably surgery and a protracted convalescence and rehabilitation period upsets the artist-athlete chemistry, a factor rarely, if ever, considered in the common athlete. With two exceptions, this article is nonsurgically oriented. With regard to chronic lateral ankle instability, the point is made that no dancer can perform well with peroneal weakness. Thus, reconstruction using the peroneus brevis tendon is contraindicated. Rather, late lateral ligamentous repair augmented with retinacular plication is recommended. When surgery is considered for removal of tibio-talar exostosis, it should be recognized that the exostosis will almost invariably recur after several years.—Joseph S. Torg, M.D.

---

**Stress Fractures of the Second Metatarsal Involving Lisfranc's Joint in Ballet Dancers: A New Overuse Injury of the Foot**
Lyle J. Micheli, Roger S. Sohn, and Ruth Solomon (Children's Hosp. Med. Ctr., Boston)
J. Bone Joint Surg. [Am.] 67-A:1372–1375, December 1985          3–90

---

Stress fractures of the metatarsal shafts, especially the second metatarsal, are frequent in ballet dancers. An oblique fracture of the proximal part of the second metatarsal involving Lisfranc's joint was encountered in four female ballet dancers. Lack of recognition of the injury delayed appropriate treatment in each instance.

Woman, 23, had begun dancing at age 4 years and had danced professionally since age 16. Dull aching had developed on the dorsum of the right foot about 5 years earlier. Intermittent pain on dancing had been managed by taping, massage, and physical therapy, with only transient relief. She occasionally had had to stop dancing for 4 to 6 weeks. Anteroposterior and lateral radiographs were difficult to interpret, but an oblique radiograph of the foot in supination showed a fracture

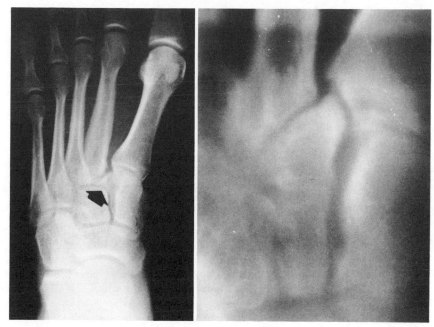

Fig 3–29 (left).—Anteroposterior roentgenogram of right foot. Arrow indicates oblique fracture at base of second metatarsal.
Fig 3–30 (right).—Tomogram of fracture.
(Courtesy of Micheli, L.J., et al.: J. Bone Joint Surg. [Am.] 67-A:1372–1375, December 1985.)

of the proximal part of the second metatarsal base (Fig 3–29). A tomogram confirmed the diagnosis (Fig 3–30). Exploration showed a sclerotic fragment at the site of nonunion on the medial plantar aspect of the second metatarsal. It included about one fourth of the articular surface of the joint. Necrotic bone was present in the resected fragment. Muscle strengthening and progressive dance training began after 2 weeks of immobilization. The patient returned to full-time dancing and had no recurrent symptoms in the next 3½ years.

These injuries, resulting from repeated minor trauma, appear to be specific to female ballet dancers. The full *en pointe* position, with the foot maximally plantar flexed and weight borne on the plantar aspect and tip of the first two distal phalanges, was most painful. Lisfranc's joint serves as the locking mechanism for the entire tarsometatarsal complex and is relatively immobile. Oblique radiographs and bone scans may be diagnostically helpful. All patients were able to resume professional dancing. The question of surgical resection vs. bone grafting in cases of nonunion remains open.

▶ With regard to delay in the diagnosis of this lesion, there is an interesting parallel with that seen with stress fractures of the tarsal navicular (Torg et al.: *J. Bone Joint Surg.* [*Am.*] 63-A:700–712, June 1982). Thus, it is important to have a high index of suspicion when dealing with predisposed individuals having ill-defined foot pain associated with "unremarkable" routine radiographs.

Similarly, the authors have indicated the role of special views, the oblique radiograph of the foot in supination, $^{99m}$Tc bone scan, and tomography.—Joseph S. Torg, M.D.

---

**Operative Arthroscopy of the Ankle: Three Years' Experience**
J. Serge Parisien and Thomas Vangsness (Hosp. for Joint Diseases Orthopaedic Inst., New York)
Clin. Orthop. 199:46–53, October 1985                                3–91

---

   This is a preliminary report on 15 cases of surgical arthroscopy of the ankle performed between 1979 and 1983. Age range of the patients was 14 to 35 years. Follow-up examinations were performed between 6 months and 2½ years after surgery, for an average of 14 months. Indications were pain or clicking sensations accompanied by painful limitation of motion for an average of 3 months.
   TECHNIQUE.—After general anesthesia, the patient was placed in the lateral decubitus position, with the body supported by kidney rests and tilted posteriorly, the lower leg elevated on a well-padded box. Anterior anatomic landmarks are outlined with a pen: the tibialis anticus tendon, and dorsalis pedis artery, the extensor hallucis longus, and the extensor digitorum communis. Three anterior portals during arthroscopic surgery are used for introduction of the fiberoptic instrument, the drainage needle, and operating instruments. The anterolateral approach is lateral to the peroneus tertius tendon, and the anterocentral approach is lateral to the extensor hallucis longus and anteromedial portal, medial to the tibialis anticus tendon. Small instruments such as knives, curettes, rasps, and motorized instruments with minishaver and abrader are used. A small pituitary rongeur is used to excise the body, followed by curettement and drilling of the bed. A compression dressing is applied as the final step of the procedure.
   Chondral and osteochondral fracture of the talar dome were observed in 9 cases; chondral and osteochondral lesions of the tibial plafond in 2 cases; osteochondral loose bodies in 2 cases and posttraumatic adhesions or arthritis were found in 3 cases. Treatment consisted of débridement of osteochondral lesions, removal of loose bodies, curettage, drilling, synovectomy, and abrasion of the subchondral bone. Satisfactory overall results were obtained in 85% of the cases. There were no major complications.
   This study suggests that arthroscopic surgery has a role in the management of intra-articular lesions of the ankle. Results are reproducible if the arthroscopic surgeon pays proper attention to the anatomy of the area and is familiar with the use of different arthroscopic portals.

---

**Arthroscopy of the Ankle: Technique and Normal Anatomy**
James R. Andrews, William J. Previte, and William G. Carson (Hughston Orthopaedic Clinic, Columbus, Ga., and Tulane Univ.)
Foot Ankle 6:29–33, August 1985                                3–92

A modified technique of ankle arthroscopy was developed and the intra-articular anatomy of the ankle described as it relates to the establishment of arthroscopic portals. Cadaveric dissection was used to demonstrate the relationship of the tendons and neurovascular structures to the placement of the arthroscope.

TECHNIQUE.—Arthroscopy of the ankle should be performed with the patient supine and the affected extremity secured in a leg holder with the knee flexed to about 70 degrees. Such positioning allows easy access to the anterior aspect of the ankle and provides gravity distraction of the tibiotalar joint. The anterolateral portal, which is the standard approach for arthroscopic evaluation of the ankle, is established at the level of the tibiotalar joint just lateral to the peroneus tertius and the common extensor tendons (Fig 3–31). Care must be taken to avoid the intermediate dorsal cutaneous branch of the superficial peroneal nerve, which courses just anterior to the lateral malleolus. An 18-gauge spinal needle is inserted into the tibiotalar joint and directed toward the center of the ankle; 20–30 ml of saline solution is then injected to distend the joint, with the presence of free backflow confirming correct placement of the needle. After the spinal needle is removed, a small skin incision is made and the cannula and the sharp trocar are inserted to the level of the joint capsule. A blunt trocar is then used to gain entrance

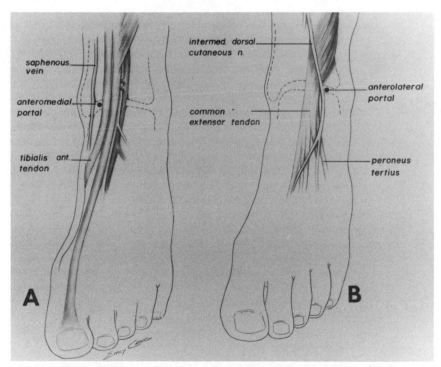

**Fig 3–31.**—*A,* anteromedial portal. The entrance point is medial to the tibialis anterior tendon and avoids the saphenous vein. *B,* anterolateral portal. The entrance point is lateral to the peroneus tertius and common extensor tendon at the level of the tibiotalar joint. (Courtesy of Andrews, J.R., et al.: Foot Ankle 6:29–33, August 1985. © by the American College of Foot Surgeons, Inc., 1985.)

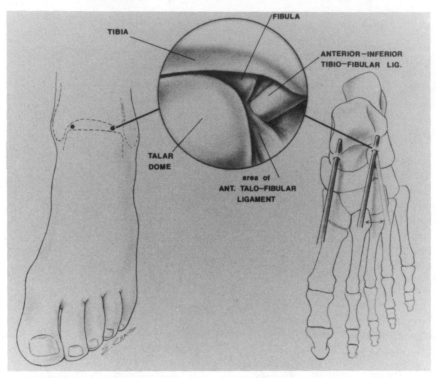

**Fig 3–32.**—Lateral arthroscopic anatomy. The anterior inferior tibiofibular ligament (the distal edge of the tibiofibular syndesmosis) runs from the anterior distal edge of the tibia to the tip of the lateral malleolus. The tibial plafond and the talar dome are seen over the center of the ankle. (Courtesy of Andrews, J.R., et al.: Foot Ankle 6:29–33, August 1985. © by the American College of Foot Surgeons, Inc., 1985.)

into the ankle. The arthroscope is inserted and diagnostic examination is begun.

Adequate distention of the joint is maintained by continuous inflow of saline solution through the arthroscopic sleeve. A second arthroscopic portal is usually not required for diagnostic arthroscopy of the ankle, but it may facilitate placement of a probe or operating instruments. In this case, an anteromedial portal can be established just medial to the tibialis anterior tendon at the level of the tibiotalar joint, thus avoiding the saphenous vein. As an alternative to the anteromedial portal, an anterocentral portal can be established at the joint line just lateral to the extensor hallucis longus tendon.

Both medial and lateral structures can usually be visualized from both the anteromedial and anterolateral portals when a 30-degree angled arthroscope is used. The choice of portal depends on the operative procedure performed. Over the medial aspect of the ankle, the distal tibia, talar dome, medial malleolus, and the tibiotalar or deep portion of deltoid ligament can be seen. Medial structures are more easily visualized by inverting the ankle to relax the soft tissues over the medial aspect. Over the lateral aspect of the ankle the distal anterior border of the tibia, the talus, and the lateral malleolus are noted (Fig 3–32). The lateral malleolus is situated well posterior to the talus. Ligamentous structures that may be identified occasionally include the anterior talofibular ligament and the anterior inferior tibiofibular ligament. Structures that are readily visualized over the center of the joint are the tibial plafond and the talar dome.

Certain technical factors must be observed to perform ankle arthroscopy successfully. Distention of the ankle, maintained by the continuous inflow of saline solution, is of paramount importance. Distraction of the tibiotalar joint is also important.

▶ Digests 3–91 and 3–92 are to be considered method papers describing diagnostic and surgical arthroscopy of the ankle. Although Parisien reports 15 cases of surgical arthroscopy, the average follow-up is 14 months and the criteria evaluating the results of the procedures are somewhat incomplete, lacking long-term roentgenographic evaluation. In Digest 3–92, of note is Andrew's observation that: "The instruments must pass through a thick capsule, unlike the knee, and must avoid the important neurovascular structures and tendons that lie in close proximity." Thus, in order to perform safe clinical arthroscopy a thorough knowledge of the extracapsular portal anatomy of the ankle is essential. This article provides an excellent description of these factors.—Joseph S. Torg, M.D.

---

**Malleolar Fractures: Nonoperative Versus Operative Treatment: A Controlled Study**
Mats Bauer, Björn Bergström, Anders Hemborg, and Jan Sandegård (Univ. of Lund, Malmö, and Östersund Hosp., Sweden)
Clin. Orthop. 199:17–27, October 1985                                    3–93

Ninety-two intra-articular ankle fractures diagnosed between 1968 and 1970 were randomly assigned to either open reduction and internal fixation, or closed reduction and casting. Surgery, based on AO principles, attempted to achieve stable fixation and anatomical reduction. Either general anesthesia or peripheral nerve block with a tourniquet was used. Ligament injuries were sutured. Weight-bearing was not allowed for 6 weeks in either treatment group. The average follow-up period was 7 years.

Surgically treated fractures healed in a better position than did those managed by closed reduction. All four infections occurred in patients operated on after failure of closed reduction. The median length of sick leave was 14 weeks in both groups. Fourteen conservatively treated and 11 surgically treated patients had significant symptoms at follow-up examination, usually pain and swelling. Clinical findings were similar in the two groups except for a greater malleolar circumference in the ankles that were operated on. Arthrosis was insignificantly less in patients having anatomical reduction, and was more frequent in patients with trimalleolar than with unimalleolar fractures.

Closed reduction of malleolar fractures yielded long-term clinical results comparable with those obtained by surgical treatment in this series, although surgery often produced more favorable early results. About a third of the patients in both groups had symptoms at follow-up study. Factors other than treatment may influence the development of arthrosis in these cases.

▶ This study presents a well designed, prospective, randomized study that unfortunately is also somewhat of a "Catch 22." With more than adequate long-term follow-up, the authors indicate that the initial course was more favorable for the surgically reduced fractures. However, follow-up examination showed little difference in results between the two forms of treatment. Thus, the reader is led to believe that in dealing with malleolar fractures the choice between nonoperative vs. operative treatment is a matter of six of one and a half dozen of another. This would be an oversimplification of the problem. To be noted is the fact that there were more trimalleolar fractures in the operative group and as well, a number of fractures that were initially treated nonoperatively required operative treatment because of unacceptable reductions. The authors state, "As expected, operative treatment resulted in a better reduction than nonoperative treatment." They also point out that the severity of the initial trauma is of great importance as far as development of arthritis which, of course, reflects directly on the end result. The article does indicate that, in properly selected cases, adequate reduction and satisfactory long-term results can be achieved with nonoperative treatment.—Joseph S. Torg, M.D.

### Reconstruction of the Lateral Ligaments of the Ankle Using the Plantaris Tendon

Martin E. Anderson (Denver)
J. Bone Joint Surg. [Am.] 67-A:930–934, July 1985                    3–94

Eight of 9 patients (5 females), aged 17 to 39 years, had an old injury of the lateral ligaments of the ankle, with subsequent instability limiting activity. The ninth was operated on the day after he sustained a severe ankle injury. All patients were active athletically or in occupations requiring much walking. Surgical reconstruction of the torn ligaments was advised on the basis of functional impairment and instability of the ankle as shown by a stress film.

TECHNIQUE.—A lateral skin incision about 9 cm long and curving under the lateral malleolus to midway across the front of the ankle is made. The retinaculum and capsule of the joint are incised along the same line. The joint is exposed by inverting the foot, and any intra-articular loose bodies are removed. The limb is externally rotated, the knee flexed, and the foot placed in plantar flexion. An incision about 5 cm long is made along the medial aspect of the Achilles tendon to expose the plantaris tendon at its insertion into the calcaneus. To expose the proximal portion of the plantaris tendon, a longitudinal incision 7 cm long is made on the posteromedial aspect of the leg. The plantaris tendon is severed proximally and is withdrawn from the distal incision. The insertion of the tendon must be left attached to the calcaneus. Small drill holes are made through the calcaneus, the lateral malleolus, and the neck of the talus; the holes are enlarged with a 4-mm drill bit. The initial hole is made in the calcaneus. The drill is directed downward, beginning at the posteromedial aspect of the calcaneus near the plantaris tendon insertion and exiting 1 cm posterior and 1 cm distal to the tip of the lateral malleolus. The leg is placed in internal rotation, with the knee flexed and the foot in plantar flexion. The lateral malleolus is exposed and a second drill hole 2 cm long is made in a distal and posterior direction from the anterior surface of the fibula to the tip of the lateral malleolus. With the foot in plantar flexion, the third hole is drilled vertically through the lateral aspect of the base of the neck of the talus to the sulcus tali.

The plantaris tendon is passed through the three drill holes in the order of their creation (Fig 3–33). A loop of 24-gauge copper wire facilitates pulling of the tendon through the holes in the bone. The wire is bent to form a loop that is passed through the hole and grasps the tendon near its end. The wire and the tendon are then pulled back through the drill hole. The plantaris tendon is first passed subcutaneously into the incision on the medial aspect of the heel and is pulled laterally through the drill hole in the calcaneus to exit about 1 cm posterior to the lateral malleolus tip. With a curved hemostat, it is then passed beneath the peroneal tendon sheaths forward into the sinus tarsi.

With the wire tendon-passer, the tendon is drawn proximally through the hole in the tip of the lateral malleolus, distally through the hole in the neck of the talus, back distally through the hole in the lateral malleolus, and under the peroneal tendon sheaths. The tendon is sutured to itself and to the remains of the origin of the torn calcaneofibular ligament. The rest of the plantaris tendon, about 8 cm long, is used to reinforce the repair by passing it back through the lateral malleolus and suturing it to itself. Thus, a double or triple strand of plantaris tendon replaces the calcaneofibular ligament.

After 2 to 18 years' follow-up, all patients had good outcomes. There were no infections, and no patient had permanent nerve damage. There was no significant loss of motion of the ankle or subtalar joint in any. All patients returned to their previous occupations and athletic activities. Use

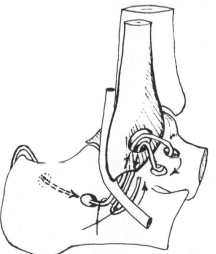

**Fig 3–33.**—Plantaris tendon is passed subcutaneously to drill hole on medial side of calcaneus and is pulled through all drill holes in direction of arrows, with fine wire loop used as tendon-passer. Calcaneofibular ligament repair is reinfored with the extra portion of plantaris tendon, as shown. (Courtesy of Anderson, M.E.: J. Bone Joint Surg. [Am.] 67-A:930–934, July 1985.)

of the plantaris tendon permits anatomical reconstruction of the lateral ligaments. Unlike previously described procedures, it avoids sacrifice of the dynamic effect of the peroneus brevis muscle in preventing inversion of the foot.

▶ The author's rationale for using the "rudimentary plantaris muscle" for reconstruction of the lateral ligaments of the ankle is that sacrifice of this structure does not lead to functional impairment. He suggests that this is preferable to using the peroneus brevis as described in the Evans procedure and in that of Chrisman and Snook (*J. Bone Joint Surg.* [*Am.*] 51-A:904–912, July 1969). This rationale has been contradicted by studies of St. Pierre et al. (*Am. J. Sports Med.* 12:52–56, January–February 1984), in which ankle eversion strength and power was evaluated objectively in 10 patients with Chrisman-Snook and 10 with the Evans lateral ligaments reconstruction by Cybex II Isokinetic Dynometry. These authors concluded that surgical transection of the peroneus brevis in the Evans procedure does not appear to cause significant loss of eversion strength and power when compared with findings in the contralateral normal ankle. They state that loss of peroneus brevis tendon should not be a factor in selecting an operative procedure for management of lateral ankle instability.—Joseph S. Torg, M.D.

---

### Nerve Injury and Grades II and III Ankle Sprains
Arthur J. Nitz, Joseph J. Dobner and Douglas Kersey (Univ. of Kentucky and Ireland Army Hosp., Fort Knox, Ky.)
Am. J. Sports Med. 13:177–182, May–June 1985                    3–95

Sixty-six consecutive patients with grade II (30) and grade III (36) ankle sprains were examined by electromyography (EMG) 2 weeks after injury to determine the presence and distribution of nerve injuries. Ankle active range of motion (AROM) and number of weeks after injury when the patient could heel-toe walk and return to full activity were also recorded.

Five patients with grade II sprains had mild peroneal nerve injury and 3 had tibial nerve injury. Clinical measurements were normal by the end of the second week. Thirty-one patients with grade III sprains had peroneal nerve injuries and 30 had posterior tibial nerve injuries. Ankle AROM was impaired, and heel-toe walking (5.1 weeks) and return to full activity (5.3) weeks were markedly prolonged.

The delayed onset of sensory and motor abnormalities and popliteal fossa tenderness suggested an epineurial hematoma at the level of the bifurcation of the sciatic nerve into the peroneal and tibial branches as a cause for the observed nerve injury. However, not all of the patients had pain over the nerve in the popliteal fossa or deep posterior part of the thigh, which seems to be a fairly consistent feature when an epineurial hematoma is present. Most of the patients had the pain typically associated with inversion sprains of the ankle, but none had the intractable neuritic pain reported by patients with an epineurial hematoma. Also, an epineurial hematoma sufficient to produce EMG evidence of denervation should have resulted in segmental nerve conduction slowing of the peroneal or posterior tibial nerve through the posterior part of the thigh. However, no patient had this finding, although a large majority of those with grade III sprains did have leg denervation.

Mild nerve traction sufficient to disrupt a limited number of axons, but not so severe as to rupture the nerve, is a plausible explanation for the findings. Peripheral nerve trunks are strong, deriving most of their strength from the resilient connective tissue sheaths. Myelin and axoplasm are much less elastic, behaving (with traction) as fluids; damage to the nerve occurs with as little as 6% elongation. Although the first structure to be ruptured during nerve stretch is the epineurium, nerve damage is likely to occur before epineurial rupture and results in a neurapraxia or axonotmesis. With a mild to moderate axonotmesis, one would expect to find EMG evidence of denervation and little or no nerve conduction abnormality. These were precisely the electric findings exhibited by most patients with grade III ankle injuries.

The data suggest that the presence of distal anterior tibiofibular ligament injury (grade III sprain) predicts with a high degree of confidence a significant injury to both nerves in the leg. It is an ominous prognostic sign, as indicated by the prolonged rehabilitation time. The possible presence of a nerve injury in patients with severe ankle sprains should be considered by clinicians.

▶ I was surprised by the high percentage of ankle injuries reported in this study that had significant neurologic problems. It strongly reaffirms the need for coordination and proprioceptive exercise in an ankle rehabilitation program. The balance boards have become and will remain a major part of our ankle rehabilitation program, along with all of the progressive functional exercises.—Frank George, A.T.C., P.T.

## Miscellaneous Topics

**Overuse Injuries in Sports: A Review**
Per Renström and Robert J. Johnson (Univ. of Göteborg, Sweden, and Univ. of Vermont)
Sports Med. 2:316–333, 1985                                              3–96

Knowledge of overuse syndromes is limited; hence the diagnosis and treatment of these conditions presents a challenge to sports-medicine physicians. Trial-and-error methods of treatment and too little attention to basic research have resulted in less-than-optimum solutions. Overuse maladies most frequently result from overload and repetitive microtrauma stemming from such extrinsic factors as training errors, poor performance, poor techniques, and inappropriate surfaces, or such intrinsic factors as malalignment and muscle imbalance. Overuse injuries involving the muscles include compartment syndromes and muscle soreness, while those involving the tendons result from stress fractures, apophysitis and periostitis.

General guidelines for establishing the appropriate diagnosis involve rest during the initial stages of therapy, which is often a modification or scaled-down version of the athlete's usual performance rather than complete abstinence. In acutely symptomatic cases, pain medications and various measures to control inflammation may be necessary. An exercise program should start early with range-of-motion exercises and isometric muscle contractions. When pain abates, dynamic muscle and flexibility exercises can be resumed, together with a conditioning program. If possible, eccentric exercises should be performed.

Overuse injuries are a great diagnostic and therapeutic problem because the symptoms are often diffuse and uncharacteristic. An appropriate diagnosis followed by adequate treatment can improve or eliminate most of these conditions. But physicians can gain most by understanding overuse syndromes better, thus permitting them to assist athletes, trainers, and coaches in preventing the injuries.

▶ An excellent review of overuse injuries. The interested reader is referred to the original article. Notably, the authors point out that even though most of these injuries do not cause problems in everyday life, physicians must understand the importance of physical activity to a large segment of the population whether they are professional, amateur, or recreational athletes. Also emphasized is that scientific knowledge about these injuries is limited and that there is an empirical nature of prevailing treatment methods. The statements that "The education of young physicians concerning these injuries varies in quality and is often very superficial" and "that overuse injuries are unnecessary and can usually be prevented" serves as a challenge.—Joseph S. Torg, M.D.

---

**Three-Phase Radionuclide Bone Imaging in Sports Medicine**
Harendra D. Rupani, Lawrence E. Holder, Danilo A. Espinola, and Semra I. Engin (Johns Hopkins Med. Inst.)
Radiology 156:187–196, July 1985                                          3–97

---

Between May 1978 and February 1982, 238 patients (136 males), aged 11 to 72 years, with sports-related injuries were referred for three-phase radionuclide bone (TPB) imaging. Final diagnoses were based on clinical follow-up in 232 patients, 14 of whom had follow-up roentgenograms and 6 of whom had been operated on. Follow-ups ranged from 6 to 24 months. For 145 patients in whom the diagnosis was made and successful therapy begun after only one or two visits, follow-up of 6 months or longer was not documented in their records. Of these patients, 106 responded to a detailed letter questionnaire, and the other 39 were interviewed by telephone.

The TPB imaging was performed predominantly because of a confusing clinical picture with normal roentgenograms (149 cases). Of the 238 patients examined, 192 had focal pain and 46 had diffuse pain. Of the 238 TPB images, 185 (77.7%) were abnormal in at least one phase; 38 radionuclide angiograms, 83 blood pool images, and 184 delayed images were abnormal. Abnormal TPB images were obtained from 110 of the 149 patients who had normal roentgenograms, 31 of 37 who had x-ray findings of uncertain clinical significance, and all 28 with abnormal x-ray films. Ninety-five percent of the patients had recovered from their injuries and were asymptomatic at follow-up.

Three distinct lesions were seen in the tibia and fibula: stress fractures (79 cases), shin splints (44), and "indeterminate bone stress" lesions (15). On delayed images, stress fractures appeared as solitary, focal, fusiform, longitudinal areas of increased uptake (2+ and 3+) most often involving the posterior tibial cortex. Radionuclide angiograms and blood pool images were focally positive (1+ to 2+) in relation to the severity of the lesion. The most frequent lesion site in the tibia was at the junction of the middle and distal thirds (42 cases); the distal part of the tibia (26) and the junction of the proximal and middle parts of the tibia (11) were also involved. Lesions were unilateral in 44 patients and bilateral in 13; in 3 patients, three sites were involved. Forty-four shin splint lesions appeared as linear, longitudinal areas of increased tracer accumulation confined mainly to the posterior tibial cortex (82%) and varying in intensity of uptake from 1+ to 2+ along its length. Shin splints involved longer bone segments, with ratios of lesion to bone length ranging from 1:3 to 3:4. Radionuclide angiograms and blood pool images were always normal. The third type of lesion, found only in the tibia, was indeterminate bone stress. On delayed images, focal areas of 1+ and 2+ uptake were seen that had neither the fusiform appearance of stress fractures nor the linear longitudinal uptake of varying intensity characteristic of shin splints. Seven lesions were symptomatic and 8 were asymptomatic. The radionuclide angiograms and blood pool images for all these lesions and the roentgenograms obtained to correlate with 5 of these lesions were normal.

Stress fractures of the metatarsal shaft (19 cases) appeared as solitary, focal areas of 2+ to 3+ uptake involving the entire width and varied lengths of the shaft. Radionuclide angiograms and blood pool images showed 1+ to 2+ focal uptake in relation to the severity of the lesion. The most commonly involved sites were the second (10 cases) and third (7) metatarsal shafts. On the TPB images, there were no differences in the appearance of the 10 lesions with abnormal and the 9 with normal roentgenograms.

▶ The radionuclide bone scan, even if only single phase is available, is an extremely sensitive, painless test that should be utilized any time the diagnosis of an athlete's pain is elusive.—Joseph S. Torg, M.D.

## MR Imaging of Intramuscular Hemorrhage

Georges C. Dooms, Madeleine R. Fisher, Hedvig Hricak, and Charles B. Higgins (Univ. of California, San Francisco)
J. Comput. Assist. Tomogr. 9:908–913, September–October 1985      3–98

A retrospective study was performed to analyze the appearance of normal striated muscle using the spin echo technique and to evaluate the potential of magnetic resonance (MR) imaging for demonstrating intramuscular bleeding. Magnetic resonance examinations were performed in 17 males and 13 females aged 14 to 81 years for reasons other than muscular disorders. Normal striated muscle was always imaged with a lower intensity than fat because muscle had a longer longitudinal relaxation time (T1) and a shorter transverse relaxation time (T2) than fat had; the spin density of muscle was less than that of fat. The best contrast between the two tissues was obtained with a short repetition time (TR) of 0.5 second and a long echo time (TE) of 56 msec. Results of five MR examinations of three males aged 15 to 29 years with intramuscular bleeding also were assessed. In one case the CT examination was available for comparison.

In every case MR permitted the diagnosis and revealed the precise extent of intramuscular bleeding and its regression after therapy. The MR diagnosis of intramuscular bleeding was readily performed because of the excellent contrast resolution of the technique. The lesions were always brighter than the surrounding normal muscle. The optimum spin echo technique, which enhanced the contrast between muscle and site of bleeding, was a long TR of 2.0 seconds and a long TE of 56 msec. The T1 and T2 relaxation times of intramuscular bleeding were always longer than those of normal striated muscle.

A CT diagnosis of intramuscular bleeding is based mainly on the demonstration of asymmetric enlargement of the involved muscle. On occasion, a high CT density lesion is present because of acute hemorrhage. Magnetic resonance, because of its inherent and excellent soft tissue contrast resolution, can readily demonstrate intramuscular bleeding and differentiate it from the normal surrounding striated muscle. Not only is the asymmetric enlargement of the muscle demonstrated, but the site of intramuscular bleeding is visualized as a higher intensity than the normal muscle, particularly with certain imaging parameters, e.g., a long TR and a long TE. The direct multiplanar imaging capability of MR is helpful when the precise extent of intramuscular bleeding is needed. Regression of intramuscular bleeding after therapy is well demonstrated by MR; like CT, it is based mainly on size reduction of the hematoma.

Two spin echo imaging sequences are recommended. The short TR and TE sequence is useful in revealing the extension of hemorrhage into the perimuscular fatty tissues and also in differentiating between fatty muscular infiltration and intramuscular hemorrhage. A long TR and TE sequence is also necessary because it provides optimal contrast between intramuscular hemorrhage and normal striated muscle, and demonstrates hemorrhage and its extent.

▶ The potential of MR imaging is apparent. However, only one case had surgical documentation, and it is premature to conclude the precise accuracy of the MR image. Because of the expense and limited availability of the MRI equipment, this diagnostic tool must not replace the clinical history and physical examination.—Joseph S. Torg, M.D.

## Rib Perichondrial Grafts for the Repair of Full-Thickness Articular-Cartilage Defects: A Morphological and Biochemical Study in Rabbits

David Amiel, R. D. Coutts, Mark Abel, Will Stewart, Fred Harwood, and W. H. Akeson (Univ. of California, San Diego)

J. Bone Joint Surg. [Am.] 67-A:911–920, July 1985                3–99

This study investigated the use of perichondrial grafts in articular cartilage defects and attempted to characterize the newly formed cartilage. In a rabbit model, rib perichondrium was used to repair full-thickness defects in the femoral condyle. The quality of repair was then evaluated histologically and biochemically at 6 and 12 weeks after grafting in 50 animals.

Repair was classified as satisfactory in specimens where the defect had filled with cartilaginous tissue. Overall, the result was satisfactory in 48% (12) of 25 animals in the 6-week group and in 51% (13) of 25 animals in the 12-week group. Failure was due to medial condylar fracture in 10 (20%) of the 50 animals, to wound infection and failure of the animal to thrive after surgery in 5 (10%), and to a failed graft due to detachment and failure to proliferate in 10 (20%). These problems occurred because of the large size of the coring device. Grossly, all defects that were graded satisfactory and biologically acceptable were filled with glistening, smooth, firm cartilaginous tissue at 6 and 12 weeks. All medial condyles showed degenerative changes, as evidenced by osteophyte formation and focal areas of fibrillation. All contralateral control defects at 6 and 12 weeks contained a very thin layer of soft repair tissue that partially covered the bone core. Histologic assessment of the perichondrial tissue from the rib of the rabbit revealed that it is a membrane with two cellular regions. The inner cell layer is composed of elongated cells with round nuclei and the outer cell layer has fibrous tissue containing flat fibrocytic-like cells. Six weeks after transplantation of the perichondrial graft, a marked change in thickness, cell morphology, and safranin-O staining was observed. The grafts grew to a thickness about two times that of the normal adjacent cartilage. In sagittal sections the edge of the bone plug was still clearly demarcated from the surrounding osseous bed.

Thus, perichondrial grafts have the capacity to generate cartilage, but the differentiation of this basic tissue into hyaline cartilage depends on extrinsic influences. The presence of motion, low oxygen tension, and absence of vascularity of the synovial environment could favor and maximize its development.

▶ The potential clinical applications of this study are exciting. Treatment by grafting with perichondrium of localized articular cartilage lesions such as those that occur with osteochondritis dissecans or traumatic full-thickness chondral fractures awaits further development of this technique in humans.—Joseph S. Torg, M.D.

### Treatment of Recalcitrant Non-Union With a Capacitively Coupled Electrical Field: A Preliminary Report

Carl T. Brighton and Solomon R. Pollack (Univ. of Pennsylvania)
J. Bone Joint Surg. [Am.] 67-A:577–585, April 1985                          3–100

Twenty-two well-established nonunions in 20 patients have been treated with a capacitively coupled electrical signal, applied noninvasively via stainless steel capacitor plates on the skin overlying the site of nonunion. The 11 women and 9 men had an average age of 38 years. The average duration of nonunion was 3½ years. Seventeen nonunions had failed to heal after bone grafting or another type of electrical stimulation or both. Tibial nonunions were most frequent. A constant 5-volt peak-to-peak, 60-kH, symmetrical sine-wave signal was used. Current ranged from 7 to 10.5 mA. The electrodes were placed through windows cut in the cast (Fig 3–34). Treatment continued for 25 weeks on average.

Seventeen nonunions (77%) achieved solid bony union. The success rate in recalcitrant cases was 76%. It did not seem to matter whether a patient bore full weight on the casted extremity during treatment for tibial or femoral nonunion. Cast immobilization alone for another 5–12 weeks was necessary after electrical field treatment in 7 cases. No complications were noted, except for a slight skin rash in 1 case.

This preliminary study showed healing of recalcitrant nonunions in three fourths of the cases on treatment with a capacitively coupled electrical field. Patients awaiting amputation have been successfully treated by this method. The system is portable and allows full weight-bearing on the casted lower extremity. Capacitative coupling would appear to have distinct advantages over other methods of treating nonunions with electricity.

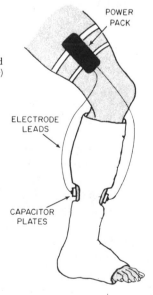

**Fig 3–34.**—Drawing showing the placement of the capacitor plates (electrodes) on the skin through windows in the cast in a patient with nonunion of the tibia. (Courtesy of Brighton, C.T., and Pollack, S.R.: J. Bone Joint Surg. [Am.] 67-A:577–585, April 1985.)

## Malignant Hyperthermia

Henry Rosenberg (Hahnemann Univ.)
Hosp. Practice 20:139–152, March 15, 1985                3–101

Malignant hyperthermia can occur explosively during induction of anesthesia, or develop insidiously after several hours of anesthesia or even postoperatively. More than half of the initially reported cases were fatal. Incidence figures vary widely, but a recent provocactive study suggested that malignant hyperthermia may occur in 1 in 100 or 200 pediatric anesthesias. Not all susceptible patients develop the syndrome whenever exposed to triggering anesthetics. The diagnosis may be very difficult. The most definitive test has been exposure of a skeletal muscle biopsy to incremental doses of caffeine and to halothane in vitro. Studies in genetically susceptible swine implicate skeletal muscle as the site of the primary defect in malignant hyperthermia. A basic defect in intracellular calcium movement may result in muscle contraction and activation of metabolic paths on exposure to halogenated anesthetics or succinylcholine.

Susceptible patients can be safely anesthetized with major conduction anesthetics such as spinal, epidural, and nerve blocks. If general anesthesia is necessary, $N_2O$, narcotic, or barbiturate anesthesia may be employed. Muscle relaxation is safely obtained with pancuronium. Patients are premedicated with dantrolene sodium. The resting creatine kinase may help identify susceptible patients. Relatives with scoliosis, recurrent muscle cramps, or chronic subluxations probably are at risk. The neuroleptic malignant syndrome has many similarities to malignant hyperthermia. A relationship with heatstroke or sudden infant death syndrome also has been suggested.

Local anesthetics may be dangerous in persons susceptible to malignant hyperthermia. Practitioners of anesthesia in any setting must be prepared to deal with the disorder.

▶ An excellent review of the subject that emphasizes several points. The syndrome can appear explosively during the induction of anesthesia, develop insidiously after several hours of anesthesia, or develop in the early postoperative period. Trismus or masseter muscle spasm after administering succinylcholine has been associated with malignant hyperthermia. If anesthesia with a hologenetic agent is continued after this sign, the full syndrome is likely to develop. Of interest, a causal relationship between malignant hyperthermia and heatstroke and sudden infant death syndrome has been postulated. The association with heatstroke is suggestive because of the beneficial therapeutic effect on dantrolene. A greater than chance incidence of sudden infant death has been noted in families with malignant hyperthermia.—Joseph S. Torg, M.D.

# 4 Pediatric Sports Medicine

**Sudden and Unexpected Natural Death in Childhood and Adolescence**
Daniel R. Neuspiel and Lewis H. Kuller (Univ. of Pittsburgh)
JAMA 254:1321–1325, Sept. 13, 1985                                    4–1

The descriptive epidemiology of sudden nontraumatic death from persons, aged 1 to 21 years, was studied among residents of the greater Pittsburgh area during 1972–1980. During the 9-year period, the 207 deaths in this group (4.6/100,000 population per year) comprised 22% of nontraumatic mortality. Age-specific rates were highest at ages 1 to 4 (mainly infections and undetermined causes) and 14 to 21 years (mainly cardiovascular causes, epilepsy, intracranial hemorrhage, and asthma) (Fig 4–1). Nonwhite rates were higher than whites, and white men had higher rates than white women. Referral for medicolegal evaluation was inconsistent. Only 18% died at university hospitals. Infections included septic shock and those of the lower respiratory tract. The main cardiac diagnosis was myocarditis. Most epilepsy deaths were unwitnessed and had absent or low anticonvulsant levels. Eighty-five cases had a known associated chronic illness and 111 reported prodromal symptoms.

A previous medicolegal study calculated a mortality rate for sudden and unexpected natural death (ages 1 to 20 years) of 1.1 per 100,000 per year. The present rate of 4.6 per 100,000 per year includes both coroner and noncoroner cases. An early study found that sudden and unexpected natural death was less common beyond age 2 years, was lowest at ages 10 to 14 years, and then increased steadily during ages 15 to 20 years.

The major role of respiratory tract infection in sudden cardiac arrest in young children has been previously suggested. Septic shock has also been noted among sudden deaths in children and adolescents. Many patients with infections received prodromal care, suggesting that warning signs for acute deterioration may be identifiable at an earlier phase. Myocarditis has been reported in many sudden deaths. As some pneumonia, myocardial fibrosis, cardiomyopathy, and undetermined cases may also be related to myocarditis, this disease may have an even greater impact than initially evident. The incidence of subclinical myocarditis accompanying viral prodromes is unknown, although an uncontrolled study supports this association. The avoidance of strenuous physical activity for some period after upper respiratory tract illness has been suggested to prevent myocarditis-related dysrhythmias and sudden death. In addition, cardioactive "cold" medications may be hazardous during these prodromes. Asthma deaths occur in both mild and severe attacks, and have been attributed to both drug toxicity and undertreatment. At particular risk may be those with

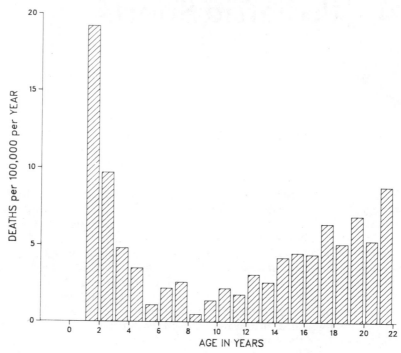

Fig 4–1.—Age-specific mortality rates. (Courtesy of Neuspiel, D.R., and Kuller, L.H.: JAMA 254:1321–1325, Sept. 13, 1985. Copyright 1985, American Medical Association.)

either marked bronchiolar obstruction but few signs and symptoms, extreme sensitivity to inhaled agents, or recently decreased medications. The reported increase in asthma deaths at night was not observed.

School health education is important in the management of the chronic conditions that cause disability and death in this age group. Effective cardiopulmonary resuscitation by trained school personnel may improve some outcomes. The incidence, severity, and management of conditions predisposing to sudden death may vary with race and sex, as reflected in the differences noted here.

Potential sources of bias in this study include possible omission of cases inappropriately classified as traumatic, improper elimination of cases that were truly sudden and unexpected, and lack of uniformity in collection and recording of data in clinical and pathologic records. Autopsy data may not be equivalent in the extent of investigation by different pathologists. Because of the retrospective nature of the study and the lack of interviews of next of kin, there were incomplete data on many variables. There was no test of reliability or quality control of case ascertainment, coding, or diagnostic determination.

Many nontraumatic deaths in childhood and adolescence are sudden and unexpected, varying with age, race, and sex. Medicolegal investigation is not uniform, and depends on location of death, duration of survival, and whether the event was witnessed. Because most deaths occur away from tertiary medical centers, an emphasis on community-based prevention seems appropriate. Many are preceded by chronic or prodromal symptoms, and they may be expected and preventable by attention to early warning signals.

▶ The tragedy of death in the apparently healthy is always disquieting, and more so in a child or adolescent. This study population excludes trauma. Myocarditis may be a common denominator for some of these deaths, and the relationship of myocarditis to viral prodromes remains unknown. This study does argue that with viral disease, and in particular respiratory disease, there may be a place for rest, which has been the cultural habit. Those deaths attributed to asthma are truly tragic. This, in theory, should be capable of prevention by adequate treatment and access to emergency medical centers.

Sudden death from undetermined cause can occur at any age. Some deaths are inevitable. As the authors suggest, some may represent an etiologic continuum with the sudden infant death syndrome.—Lewis J. Krakauer, M.D., F.A.C.P.

---

**Physical Activity and Adiposity: A Longitudinal Study From Birth to Childhood**
Robert I. Berkowitz, W. Stewart Agras, Anneliese F. Korner, Helena C. Kraemer, and Charles H. Zeanah (Stanford Univ.)
J. Pediatr. 106:734–738, May 1985                                                  4–2

---

Sedentary habits may be more important than overeating is in the development of obesity in childhood. Physical activity was assessed in a cohort of children aged 4 to 8 years who first were studied within 3 days of birth. All 52 children had been born at term with adequate Apgar scores; all had normal prenatal courses. The 25 boys and 27 girls had a mean birth weight of 3.4 kg. Neonatal physical activity was measured with an electronic activity monitor; activity in childhood was determined by a solid-state ambulatory microcomputer connected to a motion sensor.

Little relationship was apparent between the adiposity index at birth and activity in the neonatal period. Activity levels in the neonatal period did not predict adiposity in childhood, and the birth and child adiposity indices were not significantly correlated. There was some stability in physical activity in the two assessments. Childhood adiposity tended to increase with parental adiposity and with decreasing day high activity. Neither birth adiposity nor child adiposity correlated with socioeconomic status, but the range was narrow.

Childhood activity may be related to fat cell physiology during development. High physical activity may reduce the risk of adiposity developing, and greater efforts to increase exercise levels may be warranted. Longitudinal studies with repeated measurements of activity and indices of adiposity could provide a basis for early efforts at preventing obesity.

▶ If these data are correct, childhood obesity appears to correlate primarily with levels of childhood activity and with parental patterns of obesity. The option of intervention with regard to the first point is present as a cultural or personal pattern of choice. The second factor of parental obesity suggests a genetic factor, not studied in this particular paper, and possibly not subject to corrective measures. The connecting link may be that patterns of activity, determined in childhood, tend to be perpetuated through one's lifetime. (This theoretical point is not claimed by the authors of this study).—Lewis J. Krakauer, M.D., F.A.C.P.

---

**Physiological Alterations in 7- to 9-Year-Old Boys Following a Season of Competitive Wrestling**
David H. Clarke, Paul Vaccaro, and Nancy M. Andresen (Univ. of Maryland)
Res. Q. Exerc. Sport. 55:318–322, December 1985                                    4–3

---

Relatively little attention has been given to young boys who participate in sports emphasizing muscular endurance and strength, e.g., wrestling. Changes in muscular and aerobic capacity resulting from 3 months of wrestling training were examined in 23 normally active members of a boys' club athletic league aged 7 to 9 years. The boys participated in a highly competitive wrestling season. They were not encouraged to lose weight. Warm-up stretching exercises and partly aerobic activities preceded work on wrestling skills and games related to wrestling. Twenty-two boys of similar age and size served as controls.

The study and control groups were well matched at the outset, but the wrestlers had considerably smaller skinfold thicknesses before and after training. Leg press values increased significantly by about 17% after training, but no significant difference in back lift occurred. Arm endurance improved by 43% in the study group and by 7% in the controls. The maximal oxygen uptake did not differ significantly in the two groups after 12 weeks of training, and maximal heart rates also were similar after training.

Muscle strength and endurance improve in young boys who participate in training for wrestling and in age-group competition. Aerobic capacity, however, did not improve more than in matched control children in the present series.

▶ There is a certain self-selection in those that enter the wrestling program vs. the control group. This is clear in the description of their body build as more ectomorphic vs. endomorphic, although equal in mesomorphy. The conclusion that wrestling training in young boys may improve strength, but not aerobic capacity any more than one would expect in the normal, parallels the data from older athletes involved in this sport. This paper does not deal with the question of risk to the joints and muscles in this young athlete group.—Lewis J. Krakauer, M.D., F.A.C.P.

---

**Kinematics and Kinetics of the Dead Lift in Adolescent Power Lifters**
Eugene W. Brown and Kaveh Abani (Michigan State Univ. and Central Michigan Univ.)
Med. Sci. Sports Exerc. 17:554–566, October 1985                                    4–4

Weight lifting by adolescents has been associated with various medical problems, but little research has been done on the kinematics and kinetics of lifting by adolescents. The dead lift, in which a weighted bar is raised in front of the lifter as shown in Figure 4–2, was investigated in 10 skilled and 11 unskilled contestants in a teen-age power lifting championship. Equations of motion, force, and moments were developed for a multi-segment model of movement in the sagittal plane and applied to film data. The analysis included body segment orientations, vertical bar acceleration, vertical joint reaction forces, segmental angular acceleration, horizontal moment arms of the bar to selected joints, and intersegmental resultant motions.

Significant differences in body segment orientation between the skilled and the unskilled subjects indicated a more upright posture at lift-off in the former. Maximum vertical bar acceleration and angular acceleration of the trunk tended to occur near lift-off in this group. Unskilled subjects had more variable linear and angular acceleration measurements. Maximum vertical force occurred at the ankle in all lifters. The hip was the site of greatest torque because of the relatively large horizontal moment arm of the bar to this joint. Hip moment and vertical ankle, knee, and hip forces depended chiefly on the amount of mass lifted rather than on technique.

Increasing skill by adolescent weight lifters is likely to result in exposure of the hips to greater intersegmental resultant moments and in increased vertical force at the ankle, knee, and hip.

▶ As with anything, common sense must be applied when adolescents be-

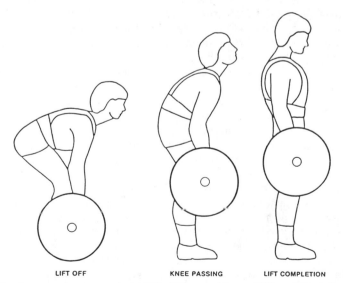

LIFT OFF          KNEE PASSING          LIFT COMPLETION

Fig 4–2.—Sequence of movements in dead lift. (Courtesy of Brown, E.W., and Abani, K.: Med. Sci. Sports Exerc. 17:554–566, October 1985. Copyright 1985, the American College of Sports Medicine. Reprinted by permission.)

come involved with weight lifting. An activity such as the dead lift should not normally be considered dangerous if proper techniques are used. The weight begins on the ground and if the lifter does not have the strength to lift it, the activity is relatively safe. Improved technique may allow a lifter to lift the same weight without an increase in strength and, once lifted, it can become dangerous, especially if it is dropped and not kept under control at all times. Other weight lifter activities such as the bench press can be more dangerous because the weight must be lowered and then lifted. A loss of control of a weight by the lifter can then be dangerous.—Col. James L. Anderson, PE.D.

**Mechanical Power Output in Children Aged 11 and 14 Years**
C. T. M. Davies and K. Young (Queen's Med. Ctr., Nottingham, England)
Acta Paediatr. Scand. 74:760–764, September 1985          4–5

The plasticity of young muscle suggests that short-term mechanical power output should be similar in boys and girls of different ages, and should approximate values found for young adults. Power output in vertical jumping off a height of two feet and in cycling at constant velocity was quantified in 24 boys and 32 girls, aged 11 to 14 years. All were normally active children. Measurements were made three times on the force platform and at six speeds on the force bicycle.

Peak power output in cycling and jumping was closely associated but, in absolute terms, output during cycling was about 34% greater than that during jumping. No significant sex differences were found in 11-year-old children, but boys aged 14 years had power output values in both tests about 25% higher than did girls of the same age. The older boys were about twice as powerful as the younger ones. Velocity of movement in both tests at a given age was independent of sex in younger children. When power output was related to anthropometric estimates of leg muscle plus bone volume, differences in absolute power output were eliminated.

Differences between power output in various activities and the increase in absolute mechanical power output with advancing age are mainly functions of size and the force exerted at the optimal movement frequency in children. The findings accord with previous evidence suggesting that the muscle of pre- and postpubertal children is physiologically similar. As in adults, the force and velocity at which peak power is reached in children corresponded to about half of maximal values.

▶ The fact that prepubescent boys and girls have similar levels of strength and power while postpubescent boys are significantly stronger and more powerful than postpubescent girls tends to show that the differences are more physiologic than sociocultural. Although it is true that when absolute power output is corrected to account for lean body mass the power output differences between the sexes disappear, in practical terms, the lean body mass differences are there and they do cause increases in absolute power output. That is true whether one is comparing a large man with a small man or a man with a woman. I am certain that there are women weight lifters who can generate a higher absolute power output than some men. However, on the average, the man, with a higher lean body mass, will generate a higher absolute power output.—Col. James L. Anderson, PE.D.

## Predictive Leg Strength Values in Immediately Prepubescent and Post-pubescent Athletes

Geoffrey C. Tabin, John R. Gregg, and Tina Bonci (Univ. of Pennsylvania)
Am. J. Sports Med. 13:387–389, November–December 1985          4–6

Muscle strength development is closely related to sexual maturation. An attempt was made to obtain data that would be of use in evaluating a young athlete's progress in leg training and rehabilitation programs. Thirty subjects of each sex aged 10 to 15 years, in the fourth to seventh grades, were selected from a suburban parochial school. Half were immediately prepubescent, in Tanner stage I, while half were postpubescent, in Tanner stage IV or more. The subjects were among the best in their gym classes.

The maximal torque force generated correlated well with lean body weight. Percent body fat averaged just below 10% for both prepubescent and postpubescent boys. Athletic girls increased in average percent body fat from 11.5% in the prepubescent period to nearly 15% after puberty. Maximal quadriceps torque force was 70% of lean body weight in prepubescent subjects of both sexes. Following puberty, the torque force equalled 80% of lean body weight in girls and 90% in boys. Hamstring strength was about 40% of lean body weight in prepubescent subjects. It was 50% of lean body weight in postpubescent girls, and 55% in boys.

Ideal strength in lower extremity muscle groups at the time of the pubertal growth spurt can be predicted from lean body weight. Correlations between peak torque force and lean body weight can be used to plan training and rehabilitation programs and determine when an injured athlete can safely return to sports activity.

▶ We should not be surprised to learn that there are significant strength differences between immediate prepubescent and postpubescent boys and girls. It is well known that strength measures for prepubescent boys and girls are quite similar and that the significant differences between the sexes begin to show up after puberty. The boys begin to show a large increase in lean body mass, and girls have a significant increase in percent body fat. It is after puberty that performance differences also become more significant and appear to be linked with increased strength, speed, and power.—Col. James L. Anderson, PE.D.

## Secondary School Athletic Injury in Boys and Girls: A Three-Year Comparison

Thomas A. Chandy and William A. Grana
Physician Sportsmed. 13:106–111, March 1985          4–7

Female participation in organized sports is increasing, making it necessary to determine injury patterns in this group. The rates of injury in secondary school athletes in Oklahoma were analyzed for 3 school years (1978–1981). In all, 24,485 boys and 18,289 girls participated in track, cross-country running, swimming, tennis, volleyball, basketball, and baseball or softball.

The overall injury rates were 26/1,000 for boys and 36/1,000 for girls. Excluding basketball, the respective rates were 14/1,000 and 13/1,000. Basketball injuries were significantly more frequent in girls. A similar but less pronounced difference was apparent in volleyball. Injury rates when more than 7 days were lost were 13/1,000 for boys and 21/1,000 for girls. Girls had more knee injuries than boys had, and boys had more shoulder injuries. Most students out for the season because of injury were basketball players, and knee injuries were most often responsible. Significantly more girls had surgical treatment. Again, knee injuries from basketball participation were chiefly responsible.

This large survey found no unique gender differences in sports injuries, but knee injuries were prominent in female basketball players. This finding suggests the importance of preparticipation evaluation of fitness, especially quadriceps and hamstring function. A conditioning program must be preceded by an adequate baseline evaluation to document the status of the muscles and develop appropriate conditioning activities.

▶ In a comparison of 24,000+ male and 18,000+ female athletes, only with basketball was there a major difference in the rate of injury. In that sport, female basketball players were at significantly greater risk. The presumptive logic is that they entered the activity with a lesser quadriceps and hamstring mass to protect the knee, the primary joint at risk. More girls than boys had knee surgery. The recommendation has merit that a prospective evaluation of girls' basketball be carried out as confirmatory study.—Lewis J. Krakauer, M.D., F.A.C.P.

---

**Cardiorespiratory Status in Relation to Mild Deformity in Adolescent Idiopathic Scoliosis**
J. A. Leech, P. Ernst, E. J. Rogala, J. Gurr, I. Gordon, and M. R. Becklake (Univ. of Illinois Hosp., Chicago, and McGill Univ.)
J. Pediatr. 106:143–149, January 1985                                    4–8

---

The cardiorespiratory function was assessed in young persons with adolescent idiopathic scoliosis as they entered adulthood. The condition was detected and managed through a Montreal area school screening program between 1975 and 1979, and all patients had been discharged from the hospital in stable condition. Of 11,814 students screened, 646 were discharged from the referral clinic by August 1, 1982.

Complete results were obtained in 32 boys (average age, 17.7 years) with Cobb angles from 3 to 32 degrees, 93 girls (average age, 17.3 years) with angles from 3 to 46 degrees, and 22 male controls and 32 female controls (average ages, 17.9 and 17.5 years, respectively). The mean values in white children were similar to those in controls. Certain values differed clearly from predicted. There was no relationship between percent predicted vital capacity and angle of deformity in the young women; however, a significant effect of smoking on peak flow and forced vital capacity at the 0.05 level was detected. By history, fewer than 10% of patients and fewer than 20% of controls participated in daily exercise, and average maximal power outputs were similar. In the 20 girls who completed more detailed exercise tests, the mean maximal oxygen uptake was 87% of predicted. There was no significant relationship among the various indices of performance and angle of curvature.

Justification for the treatment of scoliosis is provided not by present status but by the risk of future deterioration. Demonstration of normal cardioerespiratory function associated with mild deformity at the end of adolescence should not be allowed to diminish efforts to investigate screening outcomes until it is possible to identify those patients at future risk for progression and potential cardiopulmonary compromise.

▶ No cardiorespiratory abnormality was found in young adults with the milder degrees of idiopathic scoliosis (angles up to 46 degrees). There is concern because in advanced adolescent scoliosis there may be a pathway leading to compromised cardiorespiratory function. This is a consequence of mechanical factors on the chest wall that can lead to disability, cardiorespiratory failure, and premature death. Whether the milder adolescent variant will progress to significant extent in adult life will require a prolonged prospective study of a group, with this disease. It is of some comfort to know that people are not at immediate risk in adolescence.—Lewis J. Krakauer, M.D., F.A.C.P.

---

**Osgood-Schlatter's Disease in Adolescent Athletes: Retrospective Study of Incidence and Duration**
Urho M. Kujala, Martti Kvist, and Olli Heinonen (Univ. of Turku, Finland)
Am. J. Sports Med. 13:236–241, July–August 1985          4–9

---

Participation in sports training at an early age often leads to overexertion injuries, e.g., apophysitides. Osgood-Schlatter disease (OSD) tends to occur when there are separate ossification centers in the apophysis of the tibial tuberosity. Radiographs show soft tissue swelling anterior to the tibial tuberosity. The occurrence of OSD was examined in 405 randomly selected students aged 16 to 21 years; 66 male ice hockey players aged 16 to 19 years; 68 athletes who had OSD; and 40 athletes with Sever's disease, or calcaneal apophysitis. Responses were obtained from 50 athletes with OSD and 22 of those with Sever's disease.

Overall, OSD-like symptoms were found in 13% of the students. The incidence in those active in sports at age 13 years was 21%, compared with an incidence of 4.5% in inactive individuals. The disease was identified in 24% of the ice hockey players, and was the most frequent specific complaint of athletes less than 16 years of age in the outpatient sports clinic series. Osgood-Schlatter disease was present in the preferred takeoff leg for jumping in 68% of the patients. The disease interfered with full training for almost 7½ months on average. Two thirds of the athletes who previously had Sever's disease also had OSD.

A conservative approach to the treatment of OSD is preferred, because complete healing and relief of symptoms usually occur when training is interrupted. If rest is neglected, however, a prolonged and exacerbated course can be expected. The use of steroids locally should be avoided. Excision of loose fragments of the tibial tuberosity is indicated to relieve symptoms after ossification of the tuberosity and when separate ossicles persist and cause symptoms.

▶ The background for this disease should be given: in 1903, Osgood and Schlatter described a traumatic disturbance in the development of the tibial tuberosity. According to present knowledge, OSD is then a consequence of microavulsions caused by repeated traction on the anterior portion of the developing ossification center of the tibial tuberosity, leaving the growth plate intact. In children and adolescents, the apophysis is weaker than the surrounding tissues. This is an overuse syndrome of vigorous sports training at an early age, or particularly vigorous single-episode activity such as ski jumping. As many as 15%–20% of a young group of athletes may have the condition in adolescence. The distinction is radiographic for a differential diagnosis, which includes patellar peritendinitis and patellar apicitis.

The treatment, admittedly difficult in adolescents, is to avoid all physical activity causing pain for approximately 60 days, particularly in the beginning of the condition. With rare exceptions, the treatment is conservative and non-surgical. Corticosteroids, while tempting in the setting of swelling and tenderness in this area, are relatively contraindicated because of the side effects of injected corticosteroid preparations on connective tissue.—Lewis J. Krakauer, M.D., F.A.C.P.

---

**Osgood-Schlatter Disease: Review of Literature and Physical Therapy Management**
T. J. Antich and Clive E. Brewster (Southwestern Orthopaedic Med. Group, Inglewood, Calif.)
J. Orthop. Sports Phys. Ther. 7:5–10, July–August 1985                    4–10

---

Osgood-Schlatter disease is defined as a separation of the tibial tubercle apophysis from the proximal end of the tibia. Patients with this lesion may have a history of trauma or may have no significant recognizable injury. Increased stress on the weak link of the adolescent knee extensor mechanism accounts for the symptoms. Based on microscopic examination of bony ossicles removed at surgery, the separation results from increased tension over a small area of tendon insertion. Osgood-Schlatter disease is easily recognized in the adolescent with complaints of pain localized to the area of the tibial tubercle that usually occurs on running, kneeling, or stair climbing. Radiographic examination is needed to confirm the diagnosis.

A wide range of treatment philosophies exists, with some authors believing that no treatment is needed other than pain relief. Improvement occurs spontaneously within 1–2 years with or without treatment, the only sequela being residual deformity of the tibial tubercle. Limitation of activity is recommended, specifically restricting running and climbing stairs for 12 weeks and walking barefoot before the age of 15 years. Wearing special shoes, using salicylates, and applying ice locally have all been recommended. Injection of the tubercle with hydrocortisone or with lidocaine HCl combined with steroids may be used if activity restriction and immobilization are not successful. Use of an infrapatellar strap to decrease the pull of the quadriceps against the tibial tubercle has been suggested.

Physical therapy includes measuring knee flexion range of motion with the patient prone, if pain is felt in the area of the infrapatellar tendon or tubercle area, stretching the quadriceps is contraindicated. Iontophoresis is the preferred treatment, but the trial period should consist of no more than three sessions. Applying hot packs to the anterior and posterior thigh is followed by quadriceps stretching performed prone or by hamstring stretching. When there is extreme tightness, a belt may be needed around the dorsal foot. Strengthening the involved limb quadriceps is attempted in patients with atrophy secondary to disuse. Isometric quadricep sets, straight leg raises, and short arc quadricep exercises are standard if the patient is pain free. Perhaps the most important part of rehabilitation is education of the adolescent and his parents to reassure them that the condition is temporary.

▶ There are many proposed treatments for Osgood-Schlatter disease. The authors stress that when evaluating or treating this disease by stretching the knee extensors, caution must be used. If there is pain in or about the infrapatellar tendon or tubercle, stretching must not be done. If there is a strain only in the muscle belly, then stretching should be done to alleviate stress on the tibial tubercle.—Frank George, A.T.C., P.T.

---

**Back Pain and Vertebral Changes Simulating Scheuermann's Disease**
Thomas L. Greene, Robert N. Hensinger, and Letha Y. Hunter (Univ. of Michigan)
J. Pediatr. Orthop. 5:1–7, January–February 1985                    4–11

Classic Scheuermann's disease involves the thoracic spine, but lumbar and dorsolumbar forms of Scheuermann's juvenile kyphosis have also been described. Nineteen adolescents were seen at the University of Michigan Hospitals with mechanical-type back pain and vertebral changes simulating Scheuermann's disease, primarily at the dorsolumbar junction. Intervertebral disk herniation, disk space narrowing, and minimal wedge deformity were observed. Twelve patients were among 100 consecutive children seen in 1979 with a chief complaint of back pain. Four others had classic Scheuermann's disease of the thoracic spine.

The study group included 13 boys and 6 girls whose average age was

14 years at the onset of back pain. The average duration of symptoms was 1 year. All but 3 had a definite history of injury or athletic effort coinciding with the onset of pain. Weight lifting was most often implicated. Back pain, typically located at the dorsolumbar junction, was usually described as an intermittent aching. No patient had a neurologic deficit. Radiography showed anterior wedging, Schmorl node formation, and septation of an apophyseal fragment. Associated abnormalities (e.g., scoliosis and 6 lumbar vertebrae) were frequent. Sixteen patients were followed after medical treatment for an average of 20 months. Simple measures (e.g., rest and aspirin therapy) were used in most cases. No patient became worse, and no progressive spinal deformity developed. Seven patients were treated with an orthosis. No patient required surgery for control of symptoms or to correct spinal deformity.

Excessive loading of the immature spine may lead to localized dorsolumbar vertebral changes and back pain in adolescents engaging in strenuous activities. However, the vertebral abnormalities appear not to be progressive.

▶ This disease is a fixed kyphosis of the thoracic spine with radiographic changes of vertebral wedging, endplate irregularity, and narrowing of the disk space with or without disk herniation. Less common are the lumbar and dorsolumbar variants. These particular forms of this disease characteristically are associated with more pain than the thoracic variant. There appears to be a correlation with strenuous physical activity, although not universal.

This study population presented with pain at the dorsolumbar region. In 16 of the 19 patients there was a traumatic event or a specific activity of strenuous nature associated with onset. None progressed to the true kyphotic deformity. The common denominator appears to be increased stress applied to an immature spine, particularly in a pre-flexed posture.—Lewis J. Krakauer, M.D., F.A.C.P.

---

**Fracture of the Pars Interarticularis in Adolescent Athletes: A Clinical-Biomechanical Analysis**
Merv Letts, Tom Smallman, Ron Afanasiev, and Gerard Gouw (Univ. of Manitoba)
J. Pediatr. Orthop. 6:40–46, January–February 1985                4–12

---

Stress fracture of the pars interarticularis is an increasing cause of disability in competitive adolescent athletes. A review was made of the findings in 14 adolescent athletes engaged in repetitive training and competition involving flexion-extension of the lumbar spine. All had defects in the pars interarticularis that were thought to represent stress fractures. Hockey and gymnastics were most commonly represented. Most patients were aged 10 to 14 years. Eleven healthy adolescent girls were studied for muscle torque output during extension and lateral spine flexion. Their mean age was 15 years.

Mean torque values in the normal girls were 22.6 nmole for left lateral flexion and 27.4 nmole for hyperextension. All but 1 of the clinical defects involved the pars interarticularis at L-5. Bone scans were useful in showing the site of symptomatic spondylolysis, especially in the 4 subjects with bilateral pars defects. A thoracolumbar spinal orthosis of the Boston type has proved useful for protecting these athletes. Symptoms usually subside over 4–6 weeks, but use of the brace must continue for the lesion to heal. Full activity is resumed without the orthosis after 3 months if symptoms have resolved and there is evidence of healing. Five of the 10 unilateral lesions have healed, but no bilateral defects healed on immobilization. Two of the latter patients progressed to grade I spondylolisthesis but were asymptomatic. Two patients with unilateral defects developed lucent pars defects on the other side.

Acute spondylolysis from stress fracture should be considered in adolescent athletes with persistent back pain. Rest in a thoracolumbar spinal orthosis is symptomatically effective. A subject with a nonhealing unilateral lesion may return to sports activity, but those with bilateral defects should avoid weight lifting and contact sports. Diagnosis is aided by bone scanning with $^{99m}$Tc.

▶ Back pain is always a serious problem in childhood and demands the exclusion of serious underlying pathology. In the adolescent athlete, the possibility of underlying fatigue fracture of the pars interarticularis must always be considered because healing of the lesion may be possible. Spondylolysis occurs in the adolescent athlete as a result of repetitive stress in the L-5 vertebrae secondary to flexion-extension exercising. The lesions can be healed if recognized early, and spine placed at rest in thoracolumbar spinal orthosis. Some return to activity is possible with unilateral lesions. The pre-spondylolytic lesion that occurs on the contralateral side to an established radiographically visible lesion can only be identified by $^{99m}$Tc bone scan.

These authors should be commended for an excellent prospective study and review of the problem.—Lewis J. Krakauer, M.D., F.A.C.P.

---

**Soccer Injuries of Youth**
S. Schmidt-Olsen, L. K. H. Bünemann, V. Lade, and J. O. K. Brassøe (Hjørring Central Hosp., Hjørring, Denmark)
Br. J. Sports Med. 19:161–164, September 1985                    4–13

---

Soccer is probably the most popular organized sport in the world, but little is known of soccer-related injuries in children. Injury patterns were examined in two large international soccer tournaments for youths held in the summer of 1984. The participants were aged 9 to 19 years. A total of 6,600 players participated in 945 matches in more than 800 hours.

About 5% of active players had soccer injuries, and 0.4% had serious injuries. The overall injury rate was 19 per 1,000 playing hours. Older girls had the highest injury rate, and younger girls had the lowest incidence. Injuries to the lower extremity predominated, but severe injuries tended to occur in the upper extremity. Injuries to the head and face were few.

Contusion accounted for one third of all cases. Few overuse injuries were seen. There were 14 fractures and 3 ligament ruptures. Three of 4 concussions were considered fairly serious.

Soccer injuries appear to be less frequent in children than in adults. Injuries become more prevalent with advancing age, and occur more often in girls. The lower extremities, especially the feet and ankles, are involved most often. Fractures occur most often in the upper extremities. Severe injuries were rare in the present survey. About 5% of participants at youth soccer tournaments were injured.

▶ The observation that soccer injuries in children seem relatively rare and mostly of a nonsevere nature coincides with that of other contact sports. However, the age range of this population was 9 to 19 years. Generally, injury rates and severity increase with the onset of adolescence. The authors did not correlate the injury pattern with age.—Joseph S. Torg, M.D.

---

**Stress Changes of the Distal Radial Epiphysis in Young Gymnasts: A Report of Twenty-One Cases and a Review of the Literature**
Steven Roy, Dennis Caine, and Kenneth M. Singer (Sports Injuries and Running Clinic, and Orthopaedic and Fracture Clinic, Eugene, Ore.)
Am. J. Sports Med. 13:301–308, September–October 1985                4–14

---

During 1980–1983, gymnasts (19 girls and 2 boys; aged 10 to 17 years; mean age, 12), all of whom were from a nationally known academy of artistic gymnastics, presented with complaints of wrist pain. Clinical and radiologic evaluation indicated stress-related changes of the distal radial epiphysis. All cases of acute wrist fracture, acute sprains, tendinitis, synovial cysts, and joint dysfunction were excluded from the study. Of the 21 gymnasts, 17 worked out at least 6 hours a day, 6 days a week; the other 4 participated an average of 3 hours, 3 days a week. Of the gymnasts injured, 8 had involvement of both wrists, 7 had symptoms of the right wrist alone, and in 6 only the left wrist was symptomatic. The symptomatic gymnasts were followed for a period of 6–42 months (mean, 24 months).

Review of the roentgenograms of the survey group (controls) revealed 3 gymnasts with changes related to the distal radial epiphysis, one of whom became symptomatic 4 months later. There were no other major abnormalities of the distal radial epiphyseal plate or metaphysis, although some variations, which were considered to be adaptive changes, were seen. These changes included sclerosis of either side of the growth plate (although mainly of the metaphyseal side), calcific lines within the growth plate, and minimal widening of the radial aspect of the distal radial epiphysis, which was seen in the wrists of 8 of the gymnasts.

A number of roentgenographic changes were present in 11 of the gymnasts. They were (1) widening of the growth plate of the distal radial epiphysis, predominantly on the radial side, but also on the volar aspect of the epiphysis, (2) cystic changes usually of the metaphyseal aspect of the epiphyseal plate, and associated with an increase of irregularity of the metaphyseal margin, (3) a beaked effect of the distal aspect of the epiphysis (although sometimes of the proximal aspect), usually on the radial and volar side, and pointing toward the epiphyseal plate, (4) occasional haziness within the usually radiolucent area of the epiphyseal plate.

The clinical course appeared to be related mainly to the radiologic changes noted. If the changes previously outlined were present, the prognosis for a speedy recovery was slim. Five of the gymnasts with roentgenographic changes required at least 6 months to become asymptomatic (one had recurring relapses over the course of a year, and finally retired). Three others could only return after a period of 3 months of inactivity. Ten gymnasts had the clinical findings of stress involvement of the distal radial epiphysis, but did not develop roentgenographic changes. Seven were able to return to gymnastics symptom-free within 2–4 weeks without a recurrence of symptoms; 2 returned after a 4-week layoff.

When a gymnast presents with wrist pain and has radiologic evidence of widening, cystic changes, irregularity, or haziness of the distal radial epiphysis, a diagnosis of a stress fracture of the distal radial epiphyseal plate should be considered. Once these changes are present, it may be many weeks or even months before healing is sufficient to allow the gymnast to continue with workouts.

The long-term effect of these stress-related changes on bony growth and maturation is unknown. Within the short follow-up available (6–42 months), premature epiphyseal closure or abnormal bone growth have not been documented. However, gymnasts should be kept under medical supervision and observed for growth abnormalities affecting the wrist or forearm. Physicians associated with gymnastic clubs should educate coaches in the existence of the condition of stress fractures and related changes of the wrist in gymnasts.

▶ The upper extremities are used as weight-bearing limbs in gymnastics and it is surprising that acute wrist injuries present as infrequently as they do. The authors comment that overuse injuries are rarely described. However, there seems to be an increasing pattern of these injuries in the past few years and the distinction to be made is whether there is radiographic change involving distal radial epiphysis as opposed to a simple stress phenomenon alone as a cause for the symptoms of wrist pain. The x-ray appearance determines the duration of therapy, which is important in this instance, 3 months vs. 4 weeks.

The authors argue that an overuse injury to the distal radial epiphysis probably represents a stress fracture of the epiphyseal plate. The best prognosis is then in those in whom roentgenographic changes have not yet occurred and who can reduce the intensity of their participation for the 2–4 week interval or until asymptomatic.—Lewis J. Krakauer, M.D., F.A.C.P,

---

**The Three Wheeler: A Menace to the Preadolescent Child**
E. Stevers Golladay, James W. Slezak, Daniel L. Mollitt, and Robert W. Seibert (Univ. of Arkansas and Arkansas Children's Hosp., Little Rock)
J. Trauma 25:232–233, March 1985                                    4–15

---

Trauma continues to be the most frequent cause of death in childhood.

Sales of 3-wheeled motorcycles have increased markedly in Arkansas, and at the Arkansas Children's Hospital 12 children with serious or fatal injuries from 3-wheeler accidents were seen during a 1-year period. The group included 10 boys and 2 girls whose mean age was 8½ years. Ten children were drivers and 2 were passengers. None of the injured children wore a helmet. Six ran into a branch or wire and 3 flipped over. One child was struck by a car, 1 fell off, and 1 stopped abruptly and struck the handlebars. Ten children had upper chest or head injuries, 1 child had upper abdominal injury, and 1 drowned.

These vehicles can be driven without a license in Arkansas. Typically, rural preadolescent boys from relatively affluent families are affected. Many parents allowed their children to drive alone believing that the vehicle was safe because of its wide tripod base. Accidents most often resulted not from instability, but from the rider being struck by a wire or branch in the upper body while traveling fast. In other cases the driver swerved to avoid an obstruction and the vehicle overturned.

Regulation of the 3-wheeled motorcycle obviously is needed. Most of the injuries in the present series would have been prevented if a helmet had been worn; also, a bar to knock aside obstructions would be helpful. A 4-wheeled, caged vehicle having a throttle to limit the top speed would be safer if used under adequate supervision.

▶ The three-wheeled motorcycle was introduced into this country in 1971. A rapid increase in sales correlated with a rapid increase in childhood trauma. The authors report on 12 children who sustained serious or fatal injuries while using such vehicles. This small case number from a limited area is cited against the larger background that trauma continues to be the most frequent cause of death in childhood. This remains a nonlegislated area of recreation at this moment, to my knowledge. Some restrictions on age-related use would seem appropriate.—Lewis J. Krakauer, M.D., F.A.C.P.

# 5 Women in Sports

**Iron Status of Adolescent Female Athletes**
Robert T. Brown, Susan M. McIntosh, Vicki R. Seabolt, and William A. Daniel, Jr. (Univ. of Alabama in Birmingham)
J. Adolesc. Health Care 6:349–352, September 1985                5–1

The authors assessed 63 female high school students for iron status. Thirty-two were track athletes from 5 high schools in the midst of their track season; 31 were nonathletes from physical education classes in the same schools. None in the latter group was involved in an organized sports program or was training for any athletic endeavor.

There was no significant difference in blood hemoglobin or transferrin saturation between athletes and nonathletes. Nonathletes had significantly higher serum ferritin levels than did the athletes. White subjects had higher hemoglobin levels, higher transferrin saturation values, and higher serum ferritin concentrations than black subjects. A comparison of the percentages of girls whose values for hemoglobin, transferrin saturation, and serum ferritin fell below the lower limits of normal was conducted; there was no difference between athletes and nonathletes in hemoglobin and serum ferritin levels, but more athletes had low transferrin saturation than did nonathletes. Equivalent numbers of black and white girls were deficient in hemoglobin and transferrin saturation, but more black girls were deficient in serum ferritin. There were no differences among the groups in the estimated amount of dietary iron intake. Bioavailability of dietary iron was not determined.

These findings suggest that adolescent female athletes are more iron depleted than their nonathletic counterparts, thus having a greater risk for iron deficiency anemia. Iron deficiency anemia has been shown to produce decreased work ability in muscle; therefore, these girls are at greater risk for decreased athletic performance. While not necessarily suggesting that all adolescent female athletes should routinely receive iron supplementation, the data suggest that greater efforts are necessary to detect the early stages of iron depletion, which are not revealed by hemoglobin or Hct values. Although the costs of obtaining serum iron, iron-binding capacity, and serum ferritin determinations are significant, their value in detecting iron-depleted girls is substantial. When these tests become more economically feasible, they should be added to the routine screening tests performed on prospective and participating adolescent female athletes.

The finding of lower transferrin saturation and serum ferritin values in black girls suggests that they may be at greater risk for iron deficiency. In support of this impression is the observation that a greater number of black girls were below the lower limit of normal for serum ferritin as compared with their white counterparts. A low serum ferritin level reflects decreased body iron stores, a stage of iron depletion that precedes iron deficiency anemia. Since all of these girls were regularly menstruating, differences in menstrual status do not appear to have been a factor. Dietary iron intake, another possible cause of this black-white disparity, was not found to be a factor, although dietary iron bioavailability was not quantitated. Black adolescent girls require more careful screening for iron depletion than white girls, and should be educated in this area of nutrition.

▶ In an ordinary high school or college population, it has been stated that as high as 30%–40% of the female population may be borderline or true iron deficient. This paper looks at females athletes vs. nonathletes and makes the additional observation that athletes are at greater risk still of iron deficiency anemia. Then to go one step further, black adolescents have an increased prevalence for iron deficiency vs. nonblacks.

The clue to potential deficiency is the level of serum ferritin, not hemoglobin alone. If 20%–50% of this total population of athlete, nonathlete, black and white, is potentially iron deficient, why would iron not be a routine supplement in the adolescent years? This is a safe and inexpensive drug.—Lewis J. Krakauer, M.D., F.A.C.P.

---

**Athletic Amenorrhea: A Review**
Anne B. Loucks and Steven M. Horvath (Univ. of California, Santa Barbara)
Med. Sci. Sports Exerc. 17:56–72, February 1985                                  5–2

---

The very existence of athletic amenorrhea remains controversial. Higher rates have been reported in highly trained, younger athletes, while a low incidence is reported in older recreational participants, using a more conservative definition of amenorrhea. It is unclear whether any induced amenorrhea is a direct effect of exercise, or results indirectly from elevated body temperature, psychological stress, malnutrition, or other factors. Lack of a standard definition of amenorrhea has been a problem, and subject selection has been poor in some studies. Many investigations have used undertrained or recreational athletes, and training often is not adequately quantified. Preexisting amenorrhea or menstrual irregularity is not always controlled for. Body composition measurements have been inadequate and blood sampling poorly controlled.

Further work is needed on the psychological status of amenorrheic athletes. There is evidence for hypothalamic dysfunction in amenorrheic athletes, but the specific mechanism by which the hypothalamus may be disrupted is not clear. Neurotransmitter synthesis might be altered by an inadequate diet. Signs of hyperprolactinemia are not a consistent finding in amenorrheic athletes. Peripheral steroid metabolism has been suggested as a mechanism for altering steroid feedback to the hypothalamus or pituitary. The clinical significance of athletic amenorrhea also is obscure; data on reversibility are unavailable. Many physicians believe that exercise-associated changes in reproductive function can be reversed by changes in life-style. Management depends on whether the subject wishes to become pregnant. Clomiphene citrate has been used to induce ovulation.

▶ This paper reports that the mechanisms that induce athletic amenorrhea have not been determined. It is not known whether the amenorrhea is some direct effect of exercise itself or an indirect consequence of some conditions such as elevated body temperature, psychological stress, or malnutrition. From our experience here at West Point, I feel certain that when the answers are discovered the psychological stress will be at least one of the conditions that may cause secondary amenorrhea. The physical stress that the young women face in their first 2 months does not approach that of a marathon runner. However, the psychological stress is more significant than any they have ever experienced, and over 85% of them will develop symptoms of secondary amenorrhea within 2 months. However, as they adapt to the stress, the symptoms eventually disappear. Approximately 15% will take more than 9 months to adapt.—Col. James L. Anderson, PE.D.

---

**Menstrual Function and Bone Mass in Elite Women Distance Runners: Endocrine and Metabolic Features**
Robert Marcus, Christopher Cann, Philip Madvig, Jerome Minkoff, Mary Goddard, Monika Bayer, Mary Martin, Linda Gaudiani, William Haskell, and Harry Genant (VA Med. Ctr., Palo Alto, Calif.; Stanford Univ.; and Univ. of California, San Francisco)
Ann. Intern. Med. 102:158–163, February 1985                    5–3

---

Intense physical training may alter menstrual function, and there is concern that amenorrheic athletes may prematurely lose bone mass and incur risks of fracture from osteoporosis. However, there is evidence that weight-bearing exercise protects skeletal mass. Bone mass and metabolism were assessed in 17 female distance runners from track teams and running organizations. They could run a marathon in 3 hours, and trained for more than 65 km per week. Eleven women had had secondary amenorrhea for 1 to 7 years, while 6 had had regular menses without interruption. Thyroid function also was studied in 20 women who did not exercise intensively.

The amenorrheic women were younger and lighter than those with regular menstrual cycles. They had begun intensive training very close to the onset of menses, while the cycling women had started an average of 5 years after menarche. Four amenorrheic women had begun training before menarche. Spine density was lower in amenorrheic women compared with both cycling women and age-matched nonathletic control women. Forearm mineral density was normal in both study groups. Plasma estradiol was low in the amenorrheic group. Both groups had normal serum calcium, phosphorus, parathyroid hormone, and calcifediol levels. Free thyroxine and serum triiodothyronine were lower in amenorrheic women than in sedentary controls. Four amenorrheic women took less than the recommended amount of dietary protein.

Superior female athletes apparently can exercise enough to partly compensate for the adverse skeletal effects of amenorrhea, but casual athletes are not likely to do so. Most women should not train to the point where menstrual function is compromised. Estrogen replacement may be useful for those who elect to train intensively, although this remains to be demonstrated. The calcium intake should be 1,500 mg daily.

▶ A few years ago, about the time that athletic amenorrhea was becoming a subject for discussion and before much research was being done in this area, the general wisdom was that it had only short-term effects and there didn't appear to be too much to worry about. Within the past 10 years, when more research and study has been done, we are beginning to have more questions asked and more concerns being expressed. Much work remains to be done. The long-term effects of strenuous and continuous prepubertal exercise is still not understood. The use of nutritional supplements such as calcium for young athletes must be studied. Larger studies to determine whether intense exercise does in fact reduce the impact of amenorrhea on bone mass, as this study suggests, should be done. Over the past 10 years we have moved from darkness into the twilight and hopefully we are now moving toward daylight and a more complete understanding of these complicated problems.—Col. James L. Anderson, PE.D.

---

**Altered Neuroendocrine Regulation of Gonadotropin Secretion in Women Distance Runners**
J. D. Veldhuis, W. S. Evans, L. M. Demers, M. O. Thorner, D. Wakat, and A. D. Rogol (Univ. of Virginia and Pennsylvania State Univ.)
J. Clin. Endocrinol. Metab. 61:557–563, September 1985          5–4

---

The endocrine mechanisms underlying secondary amenorrhea in women who exercise strenuously are not completely understood. The possibility that physiologic patterns of pulsatile gonadotropin secretion are altered in severely oligomenorrheic and amenorrheic long-distance runners was examined in nine women who had definitely abnormal menstruation associated with strenuous training. All had run at least 20 miles a week for the past 6 months. Seven women had had normal cycles before starting training, while two had a delayed menarche after starting vigorous exercise.

All subjects had normal hepatorenal, hematologic, and thyroid function. The average time of training was 5½ years. Body mass index averaged 21, compared with 22.4 for control women who had normal cycles. The runners had up to three spontaneous menstrual cycles per year. Estradiol and testosterone levels were normal, and serum luteinizing hormone (LH) levels resembled those of normal women in the early follicular phase. Six runners had a reduced LH pulse frequency, but spontaneous pulse amplitude was normal. Responses to gonadotropin-releasing hormone (GnRH) in lower dosage were higher in runners than in control women. Estradiol responses to GnRH were normal. The mean serum prolactin in the runners with a reduced LH pulse frequency was 10 ng/ml.

Some female distance runners with secondary amenorrhea or marked oligomenorrhea have decreased pulsatile LH secretion despite normal or increased pituitary responsiveness to GnRH. An alteration in central neural regulation of pulsatile LH secretion is a possibility. This may represent an adaptive response of the hypothalamic pulse generator controlling the intermittent GnRH signal to the pituitary.

▶ An excellent and thorough study of the endocrine mechanisms underlying secondary amenorrhea that adds considerably to the body of knowledge. What a change since the YEAR BOOK OF SPORTS MEDICINE was first published in 1979, when very little information was available concerning athletic amenorrhea. We are well on our way to gaining an understanding of this phenomenon.—Col. James L. Anderson, PE.D.

---

**Defects in Pulsatile LH Release in Normally Menstruating Runners**
D. C. Cumming, M. M. Vickovic, S. R. Wall, and M. R. Fluker (Univ. of Alberta)
J. Clin. Endocrinol. Metab. 60:810–812, April 1985                                5–5

---

Abnormal hypothalamic-pituitary-gonadal function appears to be expressed as secondary amenorrhea in susceptible women who exercise intensively. An attempt was made to determine whether endurance training can modify the pattern of spontaneous pulsatile luteinizing hormone (LH) release by comparing LH release in female runners and sedentary women over a standardized 6-hour interval in the early follicular phase of the menstrual cycle. Six runners training at least 32 km weekly and 4 sedentary women, all with normal menstrual cycles, were evaluated. The respective mean ages were 25 and 27 years. The groups were similar in mean height and weight. Blood sampling was carried out on cycle days 3 to 6.

All control women had LH pulse patterns typical of the early follicular phase of the menstrual cycle. In the eumenorrheic runners, however, both pulsatile LH release and serum LH levels themselves appeared to be decreased. Pulse frequency, amplitude, and area under the LH curve all were significantly decreased in the runners. Baseline serum estradiol levels were comparable in the two groups of women.

Pulsatile LH secretion appears to be impaired in eumenorrheic female runners. The findings support the view that a high volume of endurance activity exerts a central inhibitory effect on the hypothalamic-pituitary axis. This could be related to the minor changes in menstrual function described in some runners who continue to menstruate. In contrast to hypothalamic amenorrhea, the central inhibition may be mediated by specific dopaminergic inhibition, without involvement of endogenous opiates.

▶ This paper is interesting in demonstrating that prolonged distance running (32 km/wk) produces some changes of the menstrual cycle, even in ostensibly eumenorrheic women. While it is not yet established that this has any permanent adverse consequences, there have been reports linking abnormal LH pulses to polycystic ovaries (Rebar R. W., et al.: *J. Clin. Invest.* 57:1320, 1976) and luteal phase deficiency (Soules M. R., et al.: *Obstet. Gynecol.* 63:626, 1984).

The primary cause of the altered LH pulses continues to be the subject of vigorous debate. While some authors have postulated a role for increased output of prolactin and/or testosterone, the present authors argue that this is unlikely, given the prolonged nature of the LH disturbance. A role of endorphins has been suggested in hypothalamic amenorrhea, but this is also unlikely in exercise-induced menstrual disturbances, since LH levels cannot be increased by administration of the opiate antagonist naloxone (Cumming D.C., et al.: *Am. J. Ind. Med.* 4:113, 1983). Cumming and associates thus argue for a dopamine-mediated effect, amenorrhea arising in those subjects who are most sensitive to an inhibition of the hypothalamic/pituitary-gonadal axis.—Roy J. Shephard, M.D., Ph.D.

---

**Endorphins and Exercise in Females: Possible Connection With Reproductive Dysfunction**
Janet W. McArthur (Harvard Univ.)
Med. Sci. Sports Exerc. 17:82–88, February 1985                    5–6

---

The endorphins are considered to be critically involved in hypothalamic mechanisms regulating the release of several pituitary hormones. Available estimates of β-endorphin and β-lipotropin in exercising women indicate a two to three-fold increase over baseline. It seems unlikely that this can immediately inhibit luteinizing hormone (LH) levels. Studies with dyes suggest that exercise may make the blood-brain barrier more permeable to certain molecules. It remains uncertain whether a temporal connection exists between exercise-associated increases in humoral endorphin and activation of central nervous system endorphin and enkephalin systems. Steady-state gonadotropin levels must be better defined in female athletes in order to elucidate exercise-related disorders of reproduction. Normative studies are needed on subjects with exercise-related oligo-amenorrhea in its most uncomplicated form.

Relatively low gonadotropin levels may be attributable to repeated activation of the corticotropin-releasing hormone-ACTH-proopiomelanocortin axis. This hypothesis is supported by naloxone studies and by the changes in endogenous opioid metabolism induced by exercise training. Selye described LH deficiency as characteristic of the general adaptation syndrome. The adverse effects of stress on reproductive function and behavior in general are well known, and are simulated by administering ACTH, corticoids, or β-endorphin to experimental animals. Possible mechanisms of the antireproductive actions of stress include inhibition at the gonadal level; decreased pituitary responsiveness to Gn-RH; axo-axonic interaction between endogenous opioid peptides and Gn-RH terminals; and a direct action of corticotropin releasing hormone on central mechanisms regulating LH secretion.

▶ This report is included in to provide to women and doctors who treat them for reproductive dysfunction some interesting information concerning the possible effects of exercise on endorphin levels and the possible consequences. I am not qualified to make critical comment on the information provided.—Col. James L. Anderson, PE.D.

## Induction of Menstrual Disorders by Strenuous Exercise in Untrained Women

Beverly A. Bullen, Gary S. Skrinar, Inese Z. Beitins, Gretchen von Mering, Barry A. Turnbull, and Janet W. McArthur (Boston Univ.)

N. Engl. J. Med. 312:1349–1353, May 23, 1985                    5–7

High-intensity athletic performance is associated with an increased risk of menstrual disorders. A prospective study was carried out in 28 initially untrained women to assess the effects of two consecutive 4-week periods of strenuous but noncompetitive exercise. Subjects in weight-maintenance and weight-loss groups were asked to run 4 miles a day, progressing to 10 miles daily by the fifth week, and to engage in 3½ hours of moderate-intensity sports activity daily. University students with established menstrual function participated in the study. Weight loss was limited to 0.45 kg per week.

Only 4 subjects had a normal menstrual cycle during exercise training. All but 1 of the 5 normal cycles were in weight maintenance subjects. Delayed menses and loss of the luteinizing hormone surge occurred more often in weight-loss subjects. Distances run were similar in the weight maintenance and weight-loss groups. Of the 53 training cycles, 60% were clinically abnormal, while 89% were abnormal on hormonal evaluation.

Menstrual function was consistently disrupted by strenuous exercise training in these women, but all had normal function within 6 months of the end of the study. Vigorous exercise apparently can impair reproductive function in women, especially if weight loss occurs. Hormonal study may be necessary to appreciate this dysfunction.

► Another excellent study that is limited only by the size of the study sample. What makes this subject so different to study is the large number of variables that must be controlled and studied. I am personally convinced that we still do not understand the psychological effects impact on amenorrhea. For instance, what are the psychological effects of being in a weight loss group vs. being in a weight maintenance group? And, what is the impact of those psychological effects? Our experiences at West Point showed that the women who lost weight did not differ significantly from the women who maintained or gained weight when incidence of amenorrhea were measured.—Col. James L. Anderson, PE.D.

## The Effects of Menstruation on Performance of Swimmers

Peter Bale and Gillian Nelson (Chelsea School of Human Movement Brighton Polytechnic, England)

Aust. J. Sci. Med. Sport 17:19–22, March 1985                    5–8

Past studies on physiologic responses to exercise during menstruation have given conflicting results. The effects of periodic variation of the menstrual cycle on swimming performance were studied in 20 female team swimmers aged 18 to 22 years who were not on oral contraceptives. They

SWIMMING RESULTS

| Subject | Time for swimming 50m (secs) | | | | Are your performances affected by your menstrual period? |
|---|---|---|---|---|---|
| | 1st day | 8th day | 15th day | 21st day | |
| 1 | 40.20 | 36.12 | 37.72 | 38.51 | Yes |
| 2 | 35.50 | 34.22 | 34.81 | 35.00 | Yes |
| 3 | 34.00 | 32.91 | 33.29 | 33.64 | Yes |
| 4 | 30.35 | 30.29 | 30.34 | 30.35 | Yes |
| 5 | 33.97 | 31.82 | 32.00 | 33.01 | Yes |
| 6 | 35.61 | 34.09 | 34.90 | 35.42 | Yes |
| 7 | 37.11 | 34.81 | 35.78 | 36.62 | No |
| 8 | 36.99 | 37.29 | 37.35 | 38.00 | Yes |
| 9 | 38.07 | 36.52 | 37.00 | 37.64 | Yes |
| 10 | 33.91 | 30.35 | 32.47 | 33.07 | No |
| 11 | 32.07 | 32.10 | 32.11 | 32.15 | Yes |
| 12 | 32.60 | 31.09 | 31.87 | 32.06 | Yes |
| 13 | 34.49 | 32.27 | 32.99 | 33.65 | Yes |
| 14 | 34.98 | 33.91 | 34.00 | 34.31 | No |
| 15 | 35.17 | 34.07 | 34.57 | 34.99 | Yes |
| 16 | 32.98 | 32.72 | 32.89 | 33.10 | Yes |
| 17 | 31.79 | 30.54 | 30.84 | 31.24 | Yes |
| 18 | 33.04 | 31.79 | 32.01 | 32.56 | No |
| 19 | 33.84 | 33.85 | 33.88 | 33.87 | Yes |
| 20 | 36.43 | 34.64 | 35.02 | 35.76 | Yes |
| Mean | 34.66 | 33.27 | 33.79 | 34.25 | |
| Standard deviation | 2.34 | 2.04 | 2.10 | 2.24 | |

(Courtesy of Bale, P., and Nelson, G.: Aust. J. Sci. Med. Sport 17: 19–22, March 1985.)

swam 50 meters as fast as possible at various points of the menstrual cycle. Menstrual function appeared to be normal. The women trained for nearly an hour, mainly by 50–100-meter interval swims after a 600-meter warm-up segment. Studies were done on the first day of menstrual flow, at 8 days, 12–15 days after the cessation of flow, and 6–7 days before the onset of a new cycle.

Swimming times generally were best on cycle day 8 and poorest at the onset of menstruation (table). Swim times at the different phases of the menstrual cycle differed at the 1% level of significance. Eighteen subjects reported menstrual problems of some time. Fatigue or weakness was most frequent, followed by backache and stomachache. About half of the subjects reported breast soreness, especially premenstrually. Nine subjects described skin problems. Two swimmers noted loss of coordination during the menstrual period. The subjects' views of the effect of menstruation on performance were unrelated to actual performance. Most subjects felt that exercise lessened their menstruation-related problems.

Swimming performance was best in the postmenstrual period in this study. It would be of interest to repeat the study with hormonal analyses.

▶ It appears that women swimmers' times for sprint swimming can be affected by their menstrual cycle. However, it is not understood whether the effects are the result of psychological or physiological factors. Sixteen of the 20 subjects felt that their menstrual period did affect their performance. Their times for the 50-meter swim proved that they were right. What psychological import can we expect if we think something will adversely affect our performance? Can we use some psychological training with women to change their expectations?—Col. James L. Anderson, PE.D.

### Relationship of Exercise, Oral Contraceptive Use, and Body Fat to Concentrations of Plasma Lipids and Lipoprotein Cholesterol in Young Women

Daniel R. Merians, William L. Haskell, Karen M. Vranizan, James Phelps, Peter D. Woods, and Robert Superko (Stanford Univ. and Case Western Reserve Univ.)
Am. J. Med. 78:913–919, June 1985                                              5–9

To investigate the relationship of exercise and oral contraceptive use to plasma lipids and lipoproteins, a cross-sectional study was designed to compare lipid levels in 96 exercising and nonexercising women who used or did not use oral contraceptives. Women between the ages of 21 and 35 years were studied. Eligible subjects were divided into four groups of 24 subjects each: exercising oral contraceptive users, exercising oral contraceptive nonusers, nonexercising oral contraceptive users, and nonexercising oral contraceptive nonusers.

Two-way analysis of variance revealed no significant differences in demographic or anthropometric parameters. The exercisers had significantly less body fat than nonexercisers $(P < .005)$ when results were controlled for oral contraceptive use. Oral contraceptive groups had significantly lower mean maximal oxygen consumption $(P < .01)$ and significantly higher mean resting heart rate $(P > .0001)$, maximal heart rate $(P < .01)$, and resting systolic $(P < .0001)$ and diastolic $(P < .05)$ blood pressures than nonoral contraceptive users. The exercising groups had significantly higher mean maximal oxygen consumption $(P < .0001)$ and significantly lower resting heart rate $(P < .0001)$ than the nonexercising groups. The 24-hour dietary recall results revealed no significant differences among the four groups. Results of plasma lipid analyses appear in the table. Oral contraceptive use was significantly associated with elevated plasma triglyceride levels $(P < .0001)$, whereas exercise was significantly associated with reduced triglyceride levels $(P < .03)$. When results were controlled for pill type differences, there were significant associations of pill use with triglyceride $(P < .0001)$ and high-density lipoprotein $(P < .02)$ levels and low-density/high-density lipoprotein ration $(P < .01)$, and also for exercise with triglyceride $(P < .06)$ and low-density/high-density lipoprotein ratio $(P < .03)$.

CONCENTRATION (MG/DL) OF LIPID/LIPOPROTEINS BY ORAL CONTRACEPTIVE AND EXERCISE STATUS (MEAN ± SD)

| | Oral Contraceptive Users | | Oral Contraceptive Non-Users | | p Values | |
| --- | --- | --- | --- | --- | --- | --- |
| | Non-Exercisers (n = 22) | Exercisers (n = 25) | Non-exercisers (n = 24) | Exercisers (n = 25) | Oral Contraceptive | Exercise |
| Triglycerides | 94.9 ± 31.7 | 82.8 ± 17.9 | 70.4 ± 23.7 | 62.8 ± 17.5 | 0.0001 | 0.03 |
| Total cholesterol | 186.7 ± 23.2 | 193.8 ± 27.6 | 189.0 ± 25.2 | 176.5 ± 29.2 | NS* | NS |
| High-density lipoprotein | 66.5 ± 15.7 | 70.4 ± 15.8 | 66.7 ± 13.2 | 66.5 ± 10.4 | NS | NS |
| Low-density lipoprotein | 112.4 ± 27.4 | 116.0 ± 22.2 | 117.5 ± 23.3 | 104.4 ± 25.8 | NS | NS |
| Low-density/high-density lipoprotein ratio | 1.79 ± 0.60 | 1.72 ± 0.53 | 1.82 ± 0.50 | 1.59 ± 0.44 | NS | NS |

*NS > 0.1.
(Courtesy of Merians, D.R., et al.: Am. J. Med. 78:913–919, June 1985.)

The authors conclude that exercise, together with reduced body fat, was associated with favorable plasma lipid and lipoprotein concentrations, and partially compensated for the lipid changes associated with oral contraceptive use. Clinicians should use caution when prescribing oral contraceptives since their use may interact synergistically with other cardiovascular risk factors such as cigarette smoking. Direct causal relationships cannot be inferred from these findings because of their cross-sectional nature.

▶ One important objection to oral contraceptives has been an increased risk of ischemic heart disease in users of these preparations. The present cross-sectional study suggests that regular exercise may help to reverse the risk, since in both progestin-dominant and estrogen/progestin balanced users, regular physical activity was associated with higher levels of HDL cholesterol. There are two caveats: (1) with the number of subjects tested, exercise did not lead to a higher HDL in nonusers of the drugs, and (2) all subjects were nonsmokers. It would be interesting to repeat observations in a large group of smokers, where the risk of oral contraceptives is much greater.—Roy J. Shephard, M.D., Ph.D.

---

### Exercise During Pregnancy: Maternal and Fetal Responses: A Brief Review
Jan Gorski
Med. Sci. Sports Exerc. 17:407–416, August 1985                           5–10

---

Many physiologic, metabolic, and endocrine changes that occur during pregnancy are evident even at rest, and exercise-induced alterations may not necessarily be the same as those found in the normal population. The exercise-induced cardiopulmonary changes are essentially normal or slightly exaggerated during pregnancy, and the energy cost of cycle exercise is unchanged. However, the increased weight-bearing, especially evident in late pregnancy, adds to the exercise effort during walking, climbing, or jogging. Aerobic work capacity remains unchanged during pregnancy, and typical training adaptations can be found. Hypoglycemia occurs more easily during exercise in pregnant women, even though lipid provision is exaggerated during late pregnancy.

Cardiac output (CO) during rest increases in the first trimester of pregnancy, reaches a maximum of about 40% above the nonpregnant value in the second trimester, and then remains stable. This increase in resting CO is due to an increase in both stroke volume and heart rate. The increased CO is not uniformly distributed throughout the mother's body. Hepatic and cerebral blood flow remain unchanged, while blood flow to the uterus is increased. Renal blood flow is elevated throughout pregnancy, especially in the early phase. The increase in CO is accompanied by an increase in blood volume of about 40% above the nonpregnant volume. The effects of exercise on CO in pregnant women are not well known. Bader et al. found CO during exercise on a cycle ergometer to be similar to a reference control response and to be stable throughout pregnancy.

Knuttgen and Emerson also noted that CO after cycle exercise at 375 kpm/ minute was similar in prepartum and postpartum subjects. However, Ueland et al. found that the increased CO during cycle exercise at 100 kpm/ minute was higher in prepartum subjects and was elevated throughout pregnancy.

Minute ventilation in pregnant women is higher than in nonpregnant control women during cycle and treadmill exercise. Alveolar ventilation during exercise has been found to be higher in pregnant women than in postpartum subjects only during the second half of pregnancy. The ventilatory equivalent, which is already increased at rest, did not change during exercise. The increase in respiratory frequency in response to a given exercise task during pregnancy has been repeatedly shown to be no different from that observed postpartum. Thus, the rise in minute ventilation in exercising pregnant women is due to a rise in tidal volume. The rate of change in minute ventilation at the onset of exercise is greater than normal during late pregnancy.

The influence on delivery of being a female athlete remains controversial. Some obstetricians feel that intensive sports activities stiffen the pelvic floor and perineum, thereby making labor more difficult than for the normal population. Others consider that the strengthened abdominal muscles in athletes are beneficial during the second stage of labor (i.e., expulsion of the fetus). The latter view is supported by Zaharieva; however, this conclusion was not substantiated statistically.

The influence of maternal exercise on the fetus is evident in changed heart rhythm and breathing patterns of the fetus. Pregnant patients with uteroplacental insufficiency are more likely to have those fetal changes during exercise. Severe hyperthermia should be avoided during pregnancy. Animal studies indicate that some aspects of fetal metabolism are affected by maternal exercise. It is not known whether the reduction in uterine blood flow found during heavy exercise exacerbates this response. Birth weight is unaffected when healthy, well-nourished mothers participate in mild to moderate exercise programs during pregnancy. However, more intense exercise programs during pregnancy in animals can cause changes in fetal growth and litter size.

▶ There is a general belief in the medical community that "fitness" for delivery is an asset to the mother. The typical adjustments to exercise are essentially those observed in the nonpregnant group. Thus, mild to moderate exercise tasks are well tolerated. The debate heats up when it comes to the more stressful physical activity.

There are some adverse factors with extreme activity. Thus, fetal growth may be effected by demanding physical work, especially if caloric intake is inadequate. Birth weights of babies born to mothers characterized as performing heavy physical work are significantly lower than the birth weights of babies born to mothers performing only light work. Structured activity programs coupled with adequate nutrition do not pose such a risk.

Scuba diving definitely interrelates, and there will be increased birth defects in a scuba population. The present recommendation would be that strenuous dives, hypoventilation, and chilling should be avoided. Depth should be held to no more than 60 feet and the duration of diving time to one-half of the limits of the standard Navy no-decompression tables. A study group of humans that will provide further information is difficult to obtain. Animal research will continue at a vigorous pace, but the correlation is always difficult between animal studies and human pregnancy.

What if you are signed up for a glorious dive trip to Cayman, and don't know if you are pregnant? No answer.

For the moment, common sense, moderation, and the particular specific interdictions that apply to diving would seem a reasonable recommendation.—Lewis J. Krakauer, M.D., F.A.C.P.

---

**The Effect of Exercise on Uterine Activity in the Last Eight Weeks of Pregnancy**
Jean-Claude Veille, A. Roger Hohimer, Kathy Burry, and Leon Speroff (Oregon Health Sciences Univ.)
Am. J. Obstet. Gynecol. 151:727–730, March 15, 1985                    5–11

---

Lower birth weights in women who work while standing raise questions regarding the effects of exercise on uterine activity late in pregnancy. The effects of exercise raising the maternal heart rate to 70% of predicted maximum on uterine activity were studied in 17 healthy pregnant women having a mean age of 31 years. Six were nulliparous. The mean gestational age at the time of study was 35 weeks. Most women had exercised regularly before conceiving. Subjects exercised by walking on the level for 30 minutes or by operating a bicycle ergometer at 50–60 rpm and 50 W for 10–15 minutes.

The fetal heart rate rose significantly early in the postexercise recovery period. No significant changes in mean maternal blood pressure or mean uterine activity were noted. Delivery occurred at a mean gestational age of 40 weeks. The average birth weight was 3802 gm. Labor averaged 12 hours in length. Few differences were found in the groups performing weight-bearing and nonweight-bearing exercise.

Moderate prenatal exercise by highly motivated, trained women does not increase uterine activity in the immediate postexercise period. The findings of this study encourage women who wish to engage in physical fitness activities during pregnancy.

▶ This study is an encouragement to all women who exercise and then become pregnant. They know that they can continue to exercise at a moderate level of intensity. This is not new information, but it does confirm the positive findings of other investigators.—Col. James L. Anderson, PE.D.

---

**Fetal Heart Rate Response to Maternal Exercise**
Catherine Collings and Luis B. Curet (Univ. of Wisconsin–Madison)
Am. J. Obstet. Gynecol. 151:498–501, Feb. 15, 1985                    5–12

Twenty-five pregnant women without complications underwent fetal heart rate evaluation during a program involving exercise at a relative intensity of 61% to 73% of maximal capacity during the course of the pregnancy. Assessment of the influence of gestational age on the fetal heart rate response to exercise and evaluation of the course of fetal heart rate recovery were the main goals of the study. The subjects were aged 25 to 33 years and 24 were primiparous.

Eleven subjects had complete serial data for gestational weeks 28, 32, 34, 36, and 38. There were no significant differences between weeks of gestation in fetal heart rate response to exercise. All values from these 11 subjects plus the remaining 14 subjects were averaged. The baseline fetal heart rate after exercise was significantly greater than the fetal heart rate before exercise ($P < .001$). Mid-range fetal heart rate values for each minute after exercise were significantly greater than the final value before exercise. Fetal heart rate declined at a rate of about 1.8 bpm over the 10-minute recovery period after exercise. Less than 1% of the responses before exercise were found to be in the moderate tachycardia range of 161–180 bpm. In contrast, almost 10% of the responses after exercise were found to be in the moderate tachycardia range. Twenty-four women delivered normal infants with a 5-minute Apgar score of 9. One subject delivered a postterm infant who suffered severe perinatal asphyxia and died 1 week later.

The results of the study confirmed previous findings that fetal heart rate is accelerated after maternal exercise. However, contrary to other studies, no effect of gestational age on fetal heart rate response to exercise was found. Neonatal findings provided further evidence that quantitated maternal exercise up to 70% of maximal capacity does not interfere with normal fetal growth and development.

▶ The present report confirms earlier papers indicating that maternal exercise gives rise to a fetal tachycardia that persists into the immediate postexercise period. No evidence was obtained that this was a compensation for bradycardia during exercise (Hauth et al.: *Am. J. Obstet. Gynecol.* 142:545, 1982); it could reflect fetal arousal, placental transfer of catecholamines, or an increase of fetal temperature. The immediate outcome of pregnancy was good in 24 of 25 pregnancies where an effect of this type was allowed.—Roy J. Shephard, M.D., Ph.D.

---

**Thermoregulation During Aerobic Exercise in Pregnancy**
Robert I. Jones, John I. Botti, William M. Anderson, and Nancy L. Bennett (Pennsylvania State Univ. and Harrisburg Hosp.)
Obstet. Gynecol. 65:340–345, March 1985                                5–13

---

To characterize maternal thermal balance during pregnancy, the authors recorded the thermal response to moderate weight-bearing exercise stress in 4 aerobically conditioned pregnant women. Studies were performed in a climate-controlled environment in each trimester of pregnancy and postpartum after modifying the exercise protocol for changes in maternal exercise condition. Core, vaginal, and mean skin temperatures were recorded at rest and during maximum exercise.

Core temperature response to a moderate exercise stress at each 5-minute interval was similar in each trimester as well as in the postpartum period. Core temperature increased gradually to a maximum of 0.6 to 1.0 C above basal levels and never exceeded 39 C. Reductions in exercise velocity were associated with a tendency for core temperature to decrease also. Mean skin temperature responses were variable, showing a tendency to decrease early during exercise. Mean maximum core temperature did not change during pregnancy. Resting heat storage (heat content) increased only slightly during pregnancy and could be accounted for by increased maternal mass. Although there was no significant difference in the mean distance covered, one women increased her exercise distance, whereas others reduced it. The work required to cover a unit distance increased in the third trimester when compared with the first trimester ($P < .05$) and post partum ($P < .025$). Sweat production from exercise did not change throughout pregnancy.

According to these findings, thermal balance can be maintained with advancing gestation when exercise prescriptions are appropriately modified for conditioned women.

▶ Moderate exercise is increasingly recommended to pregnant women. However, one note of caution has been a possible link between fetal hyperthermia and teratogenic changes (Smith et al.: *J. Pediatr.* 92:878, 1978). The present report suggests that the increase of core temperature produced by exercising at a given percentage of current maximum oxygen intake does not change during pregnancy. Nevertheless, maximal increments of core temperature were 1.5 C. There is need for further research to see what fetal temperatures were, and to define the safe limits of temperature increment.—Roy J. Shephard, M.D., Ph.D.

---

**Bone Density in Women: College Athletes and Older Athletic Women**
P. C. Jacobson, W. Beaver, S. A. Grubb, T. N. Taft, and R. V. Talmage (Univ. of North Carolina at Chapel Hill)
J. Orthop. Res. 2:328–332, 1985                                   5–14

---

Bone mineral loss is considered a natural process in women, especially after menopause. However, an excessive rate of bone loss can lead to osteopenia and fractures with minimal trauma. There is considerable interest in the potential of exercise for increasing or maintaining bone mass, or at least reducing the rate of age-related bone mineral loss. The effects of exercise on women aged 18 to 70 years were assessed by bone densitometry in college varsity athletes engaged in intense activity, and older women in less strenuous exercise programs. Eleven tennis players and 23 swimmers aged 18 to 22 years and 86 women aged 22 to 70 years who had exercised at least three times a week for 3 years or longer were studied. Some of the latter subjects had exercised regularly since childhood, while others had begun regular exercise as adults, sometimes as late as age 50.

In tennis players the dominant arm had a 16% higher bone mineral content (BMC) than the nondominant arm. Radial BMC increased in both arms of swimmers, and bone width also was increased. Bone density was not increased in the athletes. Lumbar vertebral density increased only in the tennis players. Differences between athletic and control subjects were most marked in the elderly. Radial and lumbar spinal bone measurements in older athletic women were in the same range as for younger subjects, whereas in control subjects they decreased at a rate of 0.7% a year.

Regular exercise may reduce the rate of bone mass loss with advancing age in women, especially after the menopause. Whether this will reduce the risk of nontraumatic fractures in later life remains to be determined, but sustained exercise can be expected to improve both skeletal and cardiovascular health.

▶ This study does tend to show that participation in a regular athletic program by adult women may increase bone mass, or at least prevent or reduce the rate of bone loss after menopause, even if the exercise program is initiated as late as the fifth decade of life. However, I agree with the authors that it is still too early to make a definite positive statement from this cross-section of study. There is, however, a strong indication that this is true, and we must conduct more longitudinal investigations, properly controlled, before more definite statements can be made. We can say that adult women should continue or initiate sustained exercise programs because of the likelihood of the benefits, both cardiovascular and skeletal.—Col. James L. Anderson, PE.D.

---

**Responses of Pre- and Post-Menopausal Females to Aerobic Conditioning**
Mary M. Cowan and Larry W. Gregory (Western New Mexico Univ.)
Med. Sci. Sports Exerc. 17:138–143, February 1985                5–15

---

If the menopause involves adverse changes in aerobic functional capacity and body composition, the trainability of older and postmenopausal females may be compromised. The responses of pre- and postmenopausal women to aerobic conditioning were compared during a program of aerobic exercise including warmup exercises and walking 4 days a week over 9 weeks. The goal was a heart rate 80% of the age-adjusted maximum. Walking progressed to 2.7 miles in 44 minutes during the program. Sixteen premenopausal women with a mean age of 41 years and 14 postmenopausal women with a mean age of 57 years participated in the program. Four other older women and 4 younger ones did not exercise.

Compliance with the exercise program was excellent. Cardiorespiratory endurance was greater in the premenopausal group. Percent body fat and lean body weight improved significantly in the younger women, and percent body fat and total body weight in the older women. The changes were not marked, and the main effects of menopause on total body weight, percent body fat, and lean body weight were not significant. Exercise did reduce percent body fat significantly compared with the control situation. Both exercise groups had significant increases in all measures of cardiorespiratory endurance. Menopause did not influence the cardiorespiratory response to training to a significant degree.

Menopausal status appears not to impair the abilities to favorably alter body composition or cardiorespiratory endurance through exercise training. Pre- and postmenopausal women have comparable training responses to an aerobic conditioning program.

▶ The more research that I read about postmenopausal women the more excited I become about the total possible benefits for our over-50 population if they will stay involved in well-balanced exercise programs. I am convinced that exercise will help our over-50 population to live a quality life and, overall, should reduce health costs for our society.—Col. James L. Anderson, PE.D.

**The Effects of Age on Muscle Strength and Anthropometric Indices Within a Group of Elderly Men and Women**
M. B. Pearson, E. J. Bassey, and M. J. Bendall (Queen's Med. Ctr., Nottingham, England)
Age Ageing 14:230–234, July 1985                                     5–16

A decline in muscle strength generally has been associated with advancing age. The effects of age were examined within a group of 100 women and 84 men older than age 65 years. The mean ages were 73 and 71 years, respectively. Triceps surae and biceps brachii strength was assessed, and skin-fold thicknesses measured.

The strength of both muscle groups except the biceps in the women declined significantly with advancing age. Muscle area decreased only in men. Strength per area decreased only in women, and only in the calf. Weight decreased significantly with age in women at a rate of 0.9% per year, but not in men. No changes in superficial fat measurements or calculated fat cross-sectional area were noted. Height decreased significantly with aging in the population as a whole, but not in men or women separately. Calf strength related to body weight decreased with advancing age in both sexes. Sex, age, and weight all had independent effects on calf or biceps strength. Sex accounted for 23% of the variance.

Loss of strength in relation to body weight with advancing age is viewed as a decline in the "power to weight" ratio. It is relevant to locomotion, stair-climbing, and balance, and therefore influences safe movement in old age. Factors other than age itself also influence the course of power-to-weight ratio in the elderly.

▶ This study is valuable in that it tells us some of the information we need to know about the effects of aging as aging is commonly practiced today. For instance, today most people who no longer work are expected to simply take it easy and wait for the remaining years to pass them by. It should not surprise us that aging brings about loss of strength, loss of muscle, and loss of flexibility when aging is accompanied by general inactivity. At any age the cliche "use it or lose it" is applicable, so why should that be different as we get older? What we need to know is can exercise slow down the aging process? I think we already have intuitive answers to that, but we need a good longitudinal study that will give us better data on the effects of exercise on the aging process. This study gives us some baseline data that will be useful in the future.—Col. James L. Anderson, PE.D.

---

**Muscle Strength and Anthropometric Indices in Elderly Men and Women**
M. B. Pearson, E. J. Bassey, and M. J. Bendall (Queen's Med. Ctr. and Sherwood Hosp., Nottingham, England)
Age Ageing 14:49–54, January 1985                    5–17

---

Relatively little is known about strength in older persons, particularly women, and those older than 75 years of age. Triceps surae and biceps brachii strength was measured in a large, relatively unselected sample of elderly persons living in private households. Cross-sectional muscle area was estimated anthropometrically. Eight-four men and 100 women were studied; the age range was 65 to 90 years.

The subjects appeared to be well-nourished, but the women were shorter, lighter, weaker, and fatter than the males, and had less muscle bulk. Strength per area in the arm and the ratio of calf muscle strength to body weight were significantly less in females. Quetelet indices did not differ between men and women. Close correlation was found between strength and cross-sectional area for both the arm and calf. Arm and calf strength were highly correlated, as were the arm and calf areas. Weight was not associated with arm muscle area or strength, but it was related to calf muscle area and strength.

Muscle strength and area were low in these healthy older subjects than in younger subjects. Strength related to muscle area was lower than in younger subjects, and less in older women than in men. Several subjects had ratios of strength to weight below unity. The safety margins for such activities as stepping up a stair or a bus platform frequently are low in older persons.

▶ It is true that as people get older they lose strength. However, the rate of strength loss can be lessened by a balanced exercise program. Much work needs to be done in order to establish baseline strength data for our elderly population. A few years ago the fitness programs concentrated primarily on aerobic fitness or developing a healthy cardiovascular system. Today the realization has hit that fitness programs must be balanced to include muscular strength and endurance and flexibility exercises as well as aerobic work. I predict that the next big fitness boom will be with the over-50 population, and they must have balanced fitness programs.—Col. James L. Anderson, PE.D.

### Age-Related Differences in Muscular Strength and Muscular Endurance Among Female Masters Swimmers

Gail M. Dummer, David H. Clarke, Paul Vaccaro, Lee Vander Velden, Allan H. Goldfarb, and James M. Sockler (Michigan State Univ.; Univ. of Maryland; and Colorado State Univ.)

Res. Q. Exerc. Sports 56:97–102, June 1985                    5–18

Relatively little is known of the physical fitness attributes of active adult women. Age-related differences in muscle strength and endurance were examined in a series of 73 female swimmers aged 24 to 71 years. They had trained 4 days a week for about an hour on average in the past year, individually or with masters swim teams. Subjects of varying age were similar in height, weight, and lean body mass. Twenty-six subjects ranged in the top 10 nationally in at least one competitive swimming event.

Grip strength peaked at ages 30 to 39 years, but age-related differences were not significant for either dominant or nondominant grip strength. Higher torque values were found for younger than for older subjects. Swimmers aged 20 to 29 years had greater muscle strength than those aged 60 and older on all tests of peak torque. Strength declined as a function of chronologic age. No such age-related pattern was found for muscular endurance of knee and shoulder movements. Height, weight, and lean body mass did not predict performance on any muscle strength or endurance variables. There was little relation between levels of performance on strength and endurance tests for the group as a whole.

Competitive swimming training helps adult women maintain relatively high levels of muscle strength and endurance, but it does not halt an age-related loss of muscle strength. Data from adult participants in other sports and longitudinal observations would help elucidate the influence of activity on the maintenance of muscle strength and endurance.

▶ It is of interest that the grip strength of women swimmers aged 60 years and older from this study was equivalent to that of less active women 30 to 40 years younger. Although there appears to be an age-related decline in strength for the subjects in this group of adult swimmers, the decline is much more gradual than for women who do not exercise. What better reason do we have to help people to age slower and more gracefully—for encouraging people to develop an active life-style and continue it into their eighth decade, and longer, of their life. We need more data to see how other activities contribute to helping us maintain our quality of life.—Col. James L. Anderson, PE.D.

### Muscular Strength and Flexibility of Two Female Masters Swimmers in the Eighth Decade of Life

Gail M. Dummer, Paul Vaccaro, and David H. Clarke (Michigan State Univ. and Univ. of Maryland)

J. Orthop. Sports Phys. Ther. 6:235–237, January–February 1985        5–19

Few older women participated in competitive athletic programs in the past, and many older women were told by physicians not to initiate vigorous sports programs. Two well-trained female swimmers in their 70s were evaluated. Neither was a notable athlete earlier in life, but both were generally active in recreational sports and activities. Competitive swimming had been started in the mid-60s. The subjects currently trained four

TABLE 1.—Physical Characteristics and Muscular Strength

| Parameter | Subject 1 | Subject 2 |
|---|---|---|
| Age (years) | 71 | 70 |
| Height (inches) | 62.9 | 64.5 |
| Weight (lb) | 124 | 147 |
| Grip strength, dominant arm (lb) | 59.4 | 63.8 |
| Grip strength, nondominant arm (lb) | 63.8 | 57.2 |
| | peak torque | peak torque |
| Shoulder extension strength at 180°/sec (ft lb) | 21 | 18 |
| Shoulder flexion strength at 180°/sec (ft lb) | 16 | 12 |
| Knee extension strength at 30°/sec (ft lb) | 68 | 72 |
| Knee flexion strength at 30°/sec (ft lb) | 40 | 26 |
| Knee extension strength at 180°/sec (ft lb) | 33 | 41 |
| Knee flexion strength at 180°/sec (ft lb) | 22 | 16 |

(Courtesy of Dummer, G.M., et al.: J. Orthop. Sports Phys. Ther. 6:235–237, January–February 1985. Copyright by Williams and Wilkins, 1985.)

TABLE 2.—Flexibility Characteristics

| Movement | Subject 1 | Subject 2 | Normal |
|---|---|---|---|
| Shoulder forward flexion | 165 degrees | 160 degrees | 150–180 degrees |
| Shoulder extension | 0 degrees | 0 degrees | 0 degrees |
| Shoulder hyperextension | 70 degrees | 75 degrees | 40–80 degrees |
| Shoulder abduction | 140 degrees | 160 degrees | 150–180 degrees |
| Shoulder internal rotation | 70 degrees | 70 degrees | 70 degrees |
| Shoulder external rotation | 100 degrees | 105 degrees | 90 degrees |
| Elbow flexion | 155 degrees | 160 degrees | 135–150 degrees |
| Elbow extension | 0 degrees | 0 degrees | 0 degrees |
| Elbow hyperextension | 0 degrees | 0 degrees | 0–10 degrees |
| Wrist palmarflexion | 70 degrees | 70 degrees | 70–80 degrees |
| Wrist dorsiflexion | 125 degrees | 55 degrees | 60–90 degrees |
| Hip flexion | 145 degrees | 145 degrees | 100–120 degrees |
| Hip extension | 0 degrees | 0 degrees | 0 degrees |
| Hip hyperextension | 10 degrees | 10 degrees | 20–30 degrees |
| Hip abduction | 70 degrees | 60 degrees | 40–55 degrees |
| Internal hip rotation | 30 degrees | 35 degrees | 45 degrees |
| External hip rotation | 55 degrees | 40 degrees | 45 degrees |
| Knee flexion | 145 degrees | 145 degrees | 120–145 degrees |
| Knee extension | 0 degrees | 0 degrees | 0 degrees |
| Knee hyperextension | 0 degrees | 0 degrees | 0–10 degrees |
| Ankle plantarflexion | 25 degrees | 35 degrees | 40–50 degrees |
| Ankle dorsiflexion | 20 degrees | 20 degrees | 15–20 degrees |
| Spinal lateral flexion | 35 degrees | 45 degrees | 40–45 degrees |
| Spinal flexion | 10.0 cm | 12.0 cm | 8.0–8.5 cm |

Courtesy of Dummer, G.M., et al.: J. Orthop. Sports Phys. Ther. 6:235–237, January–February 1985.)

or five times a week for up to an hour, swimming 1,000 to 1,500 yards or more per session.

The women had greater muscular strength than less active women of the same age. Grip strength was comparable to that of moderately active women aged 30 to 39 years (Table 1). Both subjects gave maximum voluntary efforts and completed all strength tests at maximal levels through a complete range of motion. Good levels of flexibility were maintained (Table 2).

Active persons can maintain optimal flexibility and good muscle strength well into old age. Swimming may be ideal for maintaining flexibility, since most body parts must be moved through a wide range of motion. Longitudinal studies of many women who remain active throughout their lives are required.

▶ This study had only two subjects, so why include it here? First, it is my prime interest to see people continue to exercise regardless of their age. These two subjects did not begin to swim competitively until they reached their middle sixties. Now they are continuing into their seventies. By all measures available, their strength and flexibility are excellent. It happens that their activity is swimming, but it could be something else, such as exercises to music to include walking/running. Another reason this study is included here is because we need more studies involving subjects into their fifth decade of life and beyond. We need to encourage our elderly to continue to exercise and not expect them to sit down and take it easy once they reach retirement. We need to help them to improve the quality of their retirement life and convince them to stay active.—Col. James L. Anderson, PE.D.

## Strength Training Effect in Young and Aged Women
Timothy L. Kauffman (Virginia Commonwealth Univ.)
Arch. Phys. Med. Rehabil. 66:223–226, April 1985                    5–20

Several studies have shown a loss of muscle strength with advancing age, and older persons can improve their muscle strength by training. The isometric strength gained in 6 weeks of training was compared in 10 women aged 65 to 73 years and 10 others aged 20 to 26 years. Several of the older subjects had such maladies as arthritis and angina. The abductor digiti minimi muscle was trained three times weekly over 6 weeks on an individual basis. Two sets of ten maximal isometric contractions of the nondominant muscle were performed, each contraction lasting 6 seconds. A 10-second interval was allowed between contractions, and 5 minutes between sets.

Highly significant increases in strength were found in both groups, the mean gain being 819 gm in the younger subjects and 607 gm in the older ones. There were no significant differences between the two groups in weekly strength changes or in cumulative change in strength (Fig 5–1).

These findings conflict with reports of an age-dependent loss of muscle strength. Both pretest strength and increase in muscle strength with training

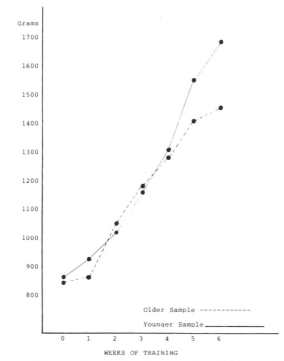

**Fig 5–1.**—The cumulative strength gains for each week are shown for each sample. Strength in grams is on the left. (Courtesy of Kauffman, T.L.: Arch. Phys. Med. Rehabil. 66:223–226, April 1985.)

were comparable in younger and older subjects. Further work is needed on the effects of various types of muscle contraction and training on muscle performance and response in an aging population.

▶ This study should generate considerable excitement among people who are working with the elderly. However, as the investigator cautioned, their results should not be extrapolated to other muscles or to the general population. The peculiarity of the abductor digiti minimi muscle may have been a factor in the outcome of this study. I have seen some great things that people are doing in working with the elderly, and it appears to me that loss of strength and muscle mass may well be the result of disuse and atrophy as much as from aging. We need more research on the effects of strength training for both elderly men and women.—Col. James L. Anderson, PE.D.

---

**Relationships Among Physique, Strength, and Performance in Women Students**
P. Bale, E. Colley, and J. L. Mayhew (Brighton Polytechnic, Eastbourne, England, and Northeast Missouri State Univ.)
J. Sports Med. 25:98–103, September 1985                                    5–21

A previous study of male students showed strength and power to be greatest in endomesomorphic subjects with relatively high fat and lean weight. Subjects with greater aerobic capacity in relation to weight had more ectomorphic physiques. Similar relations have now been studied in 206 female students in a fitness concepts class. Somatotypes were plotted on a somatochart.

Endomorphy and mesomorphy correlated positively with weight, whereas ectomorphy was negatively related to both weight and the other somatotype components. Significant numbers of women were in the dominant endomorphic and endoectomorphic classes, in contrast to men. No women were dominant mesomorphs. Some women were high in endomorphy combined with mesomorphy. The endomesomorphic group, who were heaviest, had the highest scores in measures of dynamic strength. The lightest students had the worst performance. The dominant ectomorphs had the highest aerobic capacities related to body weight, whereas the heaviest groups did the worst in this respect. Like the men, women in the central balanced group had strength and physiologic performance between subjects high in fat and lean body weight and those with more linear physiques.

These women students were found to be more endomorphic and less mesomorphic than men students of similar age. Their strength and performance scores were lower, and single measures of physique seemed to have little effect. Somatotype groups were best distinguished by grip strength, total strength, maximal oxygen uptake, and work capacity at a heart rate of 170 beats per minute.

▶ There is little that is very surprising in this study because most of us realize that larger untrained people are normally stronger than smaller untrained people, even if larger also means they are fatter. We also know that taller, slender people can normally run further and faster than overweight people. The fact that there were more overweight (meaning overfat) women in the study than overweight (because of muscle) than slender women has more to do with our social values than anything else. That is because until recently we have not encouraged women to exercise and compete and to train so that they strengthen themselves through weight training. We have told them that fat is good and necessary for women but bad for athletic men. In fact, everyone needs fat, we just aren't certain how much. However, it appears that men have an easier time shedding unwanted fat. We need to learn more about fat to be able to teach both men and women how much they need in order to meet their life goals.—Col. James L. Anderson, PE.D.

**Strength Comparisons in Untrained Men and Trained Women Body Builders**
Vernon Bond, Jr., Kermit E. Gresham, Laverne E. Tuckson, and Basedo Balkissoon (Howard Univ.)
J. Sports Med. 25:131–134, September 1985                              5–22

It has been proposed that trained female athletes may be as strong as untrained men in absolute terms, but studies of relative strength differences between the sexes have yielded conflicting findings. Eight trained women body builders were compared with 8 untrained college-age men randomly selected from elective physical education classes. The men had not participated in regular exercise or sport for the past 3 years. Maximum dynamic strength was tested using a Cybex II dynamometer.

The men were significantly taller and heavier than the women. The men produced larger absolute strength values when testing flexion and extension for the arm at 30 degrees/second. No significant differences were found between absolute strength of leg flexion or extension. The untrained men and trained women did not differ significantly in upper and lower body strength when body composition characteristics were controlled.

Untrained men in this study had greater upper body strength than trained women in absolute terms, but no difference in lower body strength was apparent. No significant differences in relative strength were found, but men tended to have greater upper body strength, and women to have stronger leg flexors. Further studies are needed on women trained in other strength-oriented sports events.

▶ This study is probably interesting to some but should not be surprising because the untrained men tested were significantly taller and heavier than the women. Maybe the study should be repeated with the height, weight, or at least the weight controlled.—Col. James L. Anderson, PE.D.

---

**Distribution, Number and Size of Different Types of Fibers in Whole Cross-Sections of Female M Tibialis Anterior: An Enzyme Histochemical Study**
K. Henriksson-Larsén (Univ. of Umeå, Sweden)
Acta Physiol. Scand. 123:229–235, March 1985                    5–23

---

Sex differences in fiber size and distribution were examined by estimating the number, size, and distribution of fibers in whole cross-sections of the female tibialis anterior muscle and comparing them with data obtained previously from male skeletal muscles. Samples were taken 100 mm from the muscle origin in 5 previously healthy women who died suddenly at ages 25 to 35 years. A modified enzyme histochemical technique for myofibrillar ATPase was used. Fibers of each type were quantified in three areas of each muscle (Fig 5–2).

The mean proportion of type 2 fibers was 31% in 4 of the subjects, and 70% in 1 without other "abnormality." The overall mean number of fibers per muscle was about 125,000. Type 2 fibers were most prevalent at the ventral surface of the muscle and also deep in the muscle. The cross-sectional area of type 2 fibers was significantly greater than that of type 1 fibers. The mean combined area of all muscle fibers was 335 sq m, or 44% of the entire muscle cross-sectional area in dehydrated sections.

There are a number of differences between the tibialis anterior muscle in males and females, but it is not clear to what extent they are related to different activity patterns, hormonal influences, or other factors. Differing

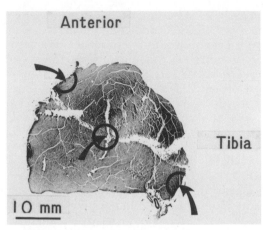

**Fig 5–2.**—Macrograph of a whole cross-section of human m tibialis anterior. Fiber area measurements were performed at the superficial, central, and deep sites indicated by *arrows*. (Courtesy of Henriksson-Larsén, K.: Acta Physiol. Scand. 123:229–235, March 1985.)

functional demands on various parts of the muscle may explain some of the gender differences. In men, for instance, both type 1 and type 2 fibers are larger in the deeper parts of the muscle, while in women this is true only for type 2 fibers. Both the total number and size of muscle fibers are smaller in females, and the total muscle fiber area is 30%–40% less than in male muscles.

▶ This study is another indication of differences between men and women for which cause and effect cannot be explained. The differences outlined in this study that exist between the man's and woman's tibialis anterior muscle cannot be explained at this time as to whether they are the result of different patterns of activity or to hormonal or other unknown influences. We must continue to study these differences.—Col. James L. Anderson, PE.D.

---

**Velocity, Stroke Rate, and Distance per Stroke During Elite Swimming Competition**
Albert B. Craig, Jr., Patricia L. Skehan, James A. Pawelczyk, and William L. Boomer (Univ. of Rochester)
Med. Sci. Sports Exerc. 17:625–634, December 1985                    5–24

---

World records in swimming have increased 3% for women's events and 2.3% for men's events since 1976. Performance in the 1984 Olympic trials in the United States was analyzed and compared with 1976 data. Velocity, stroke rate, and distance per stroke were compared in the 8 swimmers in the finals in each event and competitors whose velocities were 3% to 7% lower than those of the finalists.

Mean velocity was greater in 1984 for nine of 10 women's events and for three of 10 men's events. In nine of these 12 events, increased velocity was explained by increased distance per stroke. Stroke rate declined in 8

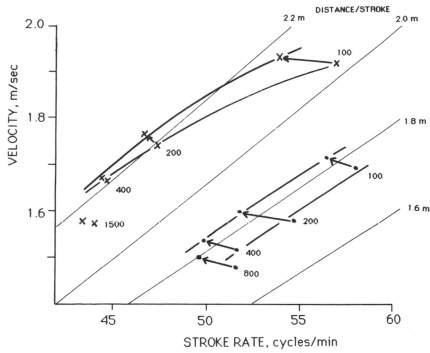

**Fig 5–3.**—Average stroke rates and velocities of freestyle events for men (*x*) and women (*solid circles*) for 1984 and 1976. Numbers near sets of data points indicate length of race in meters. In events in which there was significant increase of velocity between the 2 years, vectors indicate manner in which change occurred. Lines connecting events of different distances represent small portions of stroke rate-velocity curves that characterize these swimmers. (Courtesy of Craig, A.B., Jr., et al.: Med. Sci. Sports Exerc. 17:625–634, December 1985. Copyright 1985, the American College of Sports Medicine. Reprinted by permission.)

instances. In freestyle events for men, swum using the front crawl stroke, the increased velocity of shorter races was associated with a lesser distance per stroke and an increased stroke rate (Fig 5–3). In women an increased stroke rate was chiefly responsible. Faster stroking was also responsible for increased velocity in the women's 100-m butterfly and 100-m backstroke events. Finalists had greater distances per stroke than slower swimmers in nearly all events. A decreased stroke rate was also evident in most men's events. The faster women swimmers were more dependent than men on faster stroke rates to swim faster. Distance per stroke declined in longer events and was compensated for by a maintained or higher stroke rate by the faster swimmers.

The stroke rate and distance per stroke reflect differences in performance in various swimming events. A greater emphasis on improving the biomechanics of swimming rather than merely swimming long distances might lead to improved competitive swimming performance.

▶ I find these differences between the Olympic finalists in 1976 and 1984 to be quite intriguing. For instance, I wonder if our coaches were aware that the

**390** / Sports Medicine

stroke rates were changing and stroking was becoming more efficient. Also, what about the differences between the men and women? Was that caused by differences in coaching philosophies or because the swimmers adapted themselves to what made them go faster? Is it possible that men are reaching their physiologic limit in generating faster and faster stroke rates and must now count on more efficient strokes to continue to improve? Will women eventually reach their own physiologic limit and begin the same reduction in stroke rate for more efficient strokes? How does one develop a more efficient stroke? By swimming more and more or by biomechanical analysis? I am not certain our analytical techniques are that well defined at this time.—Col. James L. Anderson, PE.D.

**The Mechanics of Batting: Analysis of Ground Reaction Forces and Selected Lower Extremity Kinematics**
Stephen P. Messier and Marjorie G. Owen (Wake Forest Univ. and Temple Univ.)
Res. Q. Exerc. Sports 56:138–143, June 1985　　　　　　　　　5–25

A baseball batter moves body segments by exerting ground reaction

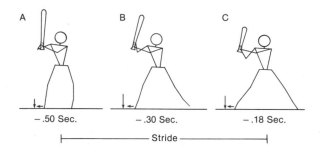

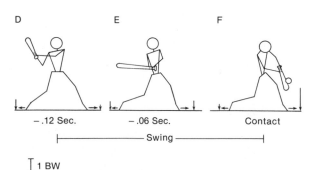

**Fig 5–4.**—Depiction of the mean vertical (F$_z$) and mediolateral (F$_x$) forces for all subjects for both feet at six instants of time during the stride and swing phases. The times shown for each position (A–F) were recorded for one subject (shown above). The timing varied slightly among subjects. Forces less than .1 BW are not shown. (Courtesy of Messier, S.P., and Owen, M.G.: Res. Q. Exerc. Sports 56:138–143, June 1985. Reprinted by permission of the American Alliance for Health, Physical Education, Recreation and Dance, 1900 Association Drive, Reston, Virginia 22901)

forces, which cause translation and rotation of the body and bat. Variations in ground reaction forces and in selected lower extremity kinematics were assessed during the stride and swing phases of batting in 7 female intercollegiate softball players, each currently playing fast pitch softball in an amateur summer league. All were considered above-average hitters. The mean age was 23 years. A pitching machine delivered balls at a mean velocity of 85 km/hour. High-speed photography using direct linear transformation methodology and a force plate were used to record three-dimensional kinematic and kinetic data.

Mean vertical and mediolateral forces in the stride and swing phases are shown in Figure 5–4. Mean vertical forces of the rear foot increased to about 1 BW (body weight) during stride, decreasing when the forward foot made contact with the ground. The mean reduction in rear-foot vertical force was 55%. Mediolateral force of the rear foot was exerted laterally away from the batter, and initiated movement of the body toward the ball. Force of the front foot was exerted laterally toward the pitched ball. Reaction to these forces retarded forward momentum, increased stability, and caused the forward hip and knee to extend as contact approached. Anteroposterior forces acted to rotate the hips and upper body counterclockwise toward the pitched ball. Decreased forces contributed to horizontal angular deceleration of both thighs just before contact.

These data may help identify atypical batting patterns, and in improving shoe design. Force production and stability might be enhanced by aligning the cleats along the lines of action of applied shear forces.

▶ This cinematographic analysis of the woman softball batter is an excellent way to study and develop the proper biomechanical patterns. However, before any definite conclusions can be drawn, more subjects must be studied. One of the weaknesses that I have noticed in many women when swinging a bat is the lack of adequate strength in their hands and lower arms, or grip strength. This causes them not to be able to hold onto the bat firmly enough to cause the bat to swing through the ball, and considerable power is lost.— Col. James L. Anderson, PE.D.

---

**Physiologic Changes in Rowing Performance Associated With Training in Collegiate Women Rowers**
D. A. Mahler, H. W. Parker, and D. C. Andresen (Dartmouth College)
Int. J. Sports Med. 6:229–233, August 1985                    5–26

---

Training in rowing has emphasized aerobic conditioning in the fall and winter and anaerobic exercise in the spring and summer in conjunction with competitive rowing. Physiologic changes in rowing performance were assessed at 3-month intervals in 7 collegiate women rowers during incremental exercise on a rowing ergometer. The average age was 20 years. Four subjects rowed in the first varsity boat and 3 in the junior varsity boat. The test instrument closely simulates competitive rowing (Fig 5–5).

Body weight did not change throughout the season. There were no significant changes in heart rate or oxygen consumption during steady-

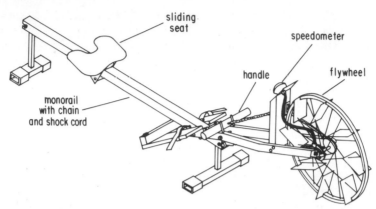

**Fig 5–5.**—Variable-resistance rowing ergometer used for exercise testing. (Courtesy of Mahler, D.A., et al.: Int. J. Sports Med. 6:229–233, August 1985.)

state exercise at 35 km per hour. Peak power production increased 18% during the 6-month study period, and maximal oxygen consumption increased 14%. Maximal heart rate was unchanged during training. Oxygen pulse increased significantly by 14%, whereas the ventilatory equivalent for oxygen did not change. Oxygen consumption as a proportion of peak oxygen uptake and heart rate at anaerobic threshold rose significantly in the latter part of training, when anaerobic conditioning was emphasized.

Serial measurement of maximal oxygen uptake and anaerobic threshold can be used to evaluate the benefits of specific training and to develop personal outlines for aerobic and anaerobic conditioning. Further experience is needed to determine whether serial testing can augment crew performance.

▶ This is an example of how the exercise sciences can be used to help a coach be certain that his training program is accomplishing what he wants it to accomplish. Many coaches, however, do not use all of the knowledge that is available because they do not have an adequate understanding of what it all means. More and more, coaches are graduated athletes with on-the-job training with a head coach and maybe no background in exercise physiology. I am concerned that if we continue in the direction we are now heading, American athletes may no longer be the best coached athletes in the world, at least not at the high school and college levels.—Col. James L. Anderson, PE.D.

**Isokinetic Leg Flexion and Extension Strength of Elite Adolescent Female Track and Field Athletes**
Terry J. Housh, William G. Thorland, Gerald D. Tharp, Glen O. Johnson, and Craig J. Cisar (Portland State Univ. and Univ. of Nebraska at Lincoln)
Res. Q. Exerc. Sport 55:347–350, December 1984                          5–27

Critical levels of muscle strength are necessary in successfully performing many athletic events, and peak torque levels in dissimilar sports may be useful discriminators of athletic ability. Isokinetic strength of leg flexion and extension was measured in 62 elite adolescent female track and field athletes with a mean age of 16½ years. Throwers, jumpers, middle-distance runners, and sprinters participated in the study. Dominant leg strength for flexion and extension through the knee were measured by a Cybex II isokinetic dynamometer.

The throwers and jumpers were taller than the other athletes. The throwers had relatively high body weight, fat weight, and lean body weight. Peak torque correlated with body weight and lean body weight with coefficients of .85 and .88, respectively, and body weight and lean body weight correlated at .94. The throwers were significantly stronger than the other athletes for both flexion and extension movements, although the jumpers had comparable flexion strength. When extension strength was related to body weight, the jumpers were stronger than the middle-distance runners.

Few differences in leg strength were found between groups of adolescent female track and field athletes in this study when leg flexion and extension strength were related to body weight. Relative strength may be preferable to absolute strength when comparing female competitors in certain settings.

▶ Although these data are useful and valuable, they are not surprising. What would be even more valuable would be for this type study to be continued and to see what happens to the strength levels as life-styles and activity levels change. What level of activity would it take to maintain strength levels at a given desired limit? What will happen to bone density later in life if we could compare the subjects who remain active with those who stop exercising when they leave school? We need more data to help us answer some of the questions being asked in our studies of aging and osteoporosis.—Col. James L. Anderson, PE.D.

---

**Anthropometric and Training Characteristics of Female Marathon Runners as Determinants of Distance Running Performance**
Peter Bale, Sarah Rowell, and Elizabeth Colley (Brighton Polytechnic, Eastbourne, England)
J. Sports Sci. 3:115–126, Summer 1985                                          5–28

---

Anthropometric measurements were compared in elite, good, and moderate British women marathoners, and multivariate analysis was carried out to find potential predictors of long distance running performance. Thirty-six participants in a 10-mile road race were evaluated. Eleven elite runners with marathon times of 175 minutes or less were compared with 12 good runners, with times of 175 to 188 minutes, and 13 moderate marathoners, with times of 198 to 210 minutes.

Runners in all three groups had body weights of about 53 kg. Each had a lower percent body fat than sedentary women, as assessed from skin fold thicknesses, but the elite runners had lower values than the other groups. Triceps skin fold differences were most marked. The elite runners

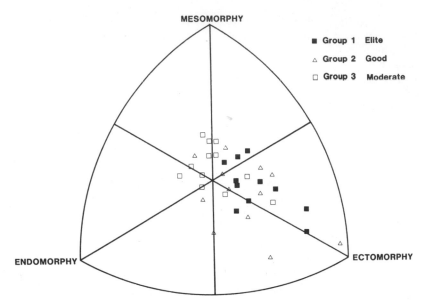

Fig 5–6.—Personal somatotype ratings of marathon runners. (Courtesy of Bale, P., et al.: J. Sports Sci. 3:115–126, Summer 1985.)

tended to be more ectomorphic and less endomorphic than the other groups (Fig 5–6). The more accomplished runners had run longer and more strenuously than the others. The number of weekly training runs and the years of training were the best predictors of competitive performance at both 10 miles and the marathon distance. Better runners also had low body weight related to height.

Female long distance runners who are slim and relatively ectomorphic are likeliest to succeed, if they train intensively over a long period. A combination of structural and physiologic factors can be used to provide guidelines for competitive standards and permit better predictions of running performance.

▶ This study confirms that which many would say is common sense. That is, of the variables analyzed by multiple regression and discriminant function analysis, the best predictor of success at racing 10 miles and the marathon were the number of training sessions per week and the number of years the runner had been training. Also, women runners with a slim physique high in ectomorphy have the greatest potential for success. Although we can be fairly accurate in identifying the elite runners from the good or moderate runners, I am not certain that is much good except as an academic exercise. Elite runners normally compete against elite runners and then it comes down to who runs the prescribed distances the fastest. That is when the intangibles that we often call "heart" or "guts" comes in. But, isn't that the way it should be? If we can pick the winners in the laboratory, then why have the race?—Col. James L. Anderson, PE.D.

## Psychological Characteristics of the Average Female Runner
Kay Porter (Eugene, Ore.)
Physician Sportsmed. 13:171–175, May 1985                              5–29

Most past studies on exercise and its effects on mood have involved college-agcd subjects or world-class athletes. Several studies were carried out on women competing in races in the Northwest in 1979–1981. A wide age range was represented. Respondents, who ran an average of 6 miles or more a day, usually 3 or 4 days in succession, reported a lower intake of meat and sugar and often, substantial weight loss since the start of running. Most subjects felt that running had improved their self-image. Weight control and feelings of achievement were prominently mentioned. Most women felt that running helped them cope with stress and, relieved tension and depression. Marathon runners consistently felt that running had improved their self-confidence and self-image. Characteristics of faster and slower runners are compared in the table. Profile of Mood States scores indicated less tension, anger, and depression than in the general population.

Studies of both men and women have found substantial psychologic benefit from running. Running appears to promote psychological well-being with respect to anxiety, depression, mood, and satisfaction with relationships. These effects are apparent in women older than age 35 years. Exercise also may promote acceptance of aging and increase enjoyment of life. The experiences of women who run and compete can serve to inspire others who are pessimistic about reaching age 35 and being over-weight.

▶ We should not be surprised by these findings because similar ones were discovered with men runners. There is no reason to expect significant differences between men and women when comparing the psychological factors of

COMPARISON OF FEMALE MARATHON RUNNERS BY TIME

| Related Variable | Under 3:20(%) | Over 3:20 (%) |
|---|---|---|
| Sick during training | 15 | 30 |
| Injured during training | 47 | 42 |
| Train with weights | 42 | 28 |
| Use a coach | 47 | 15 |
| Developed amenorrhea | 67 | 28 |
| Use birth control | 32 | 51 |
| Have time for intimate relationship | 76 | 95 |
| Running interfered with relationship | 47 | 43 |
| Disagree with partner about running | 15 | 13 |
| Partner felt neglected at some time | 20 | 21 |

(Courtesy of Porter, K.: Physician Sportsmed. 13:171–175, May 1985. Preprinted by permission. A McGraw-Hill publication.)

running. I am certain we have all known some women who have demonstrated more self-confidence and a better self-image as a result of their running. I have seen the same reaction with some men.—Col. James L. Anderson, PE.D.

**Sex Differences in Achievement Cognitions and Performance in Competition**
Diane L. Gill, John B. Gross, Sharon Huddleston, and Bethany Shifflett (Univ. of Iowa)
Res. Q. Exerc. Sport 55:340–346, December 1984                           5–30

Perceived ability and expectancies influence athletic performance and also mediate interpretations of success and failure. Females may have a relatively low-expectancy cognitive pattern, but this seems to be less consistent than the literature would suggest. Gender differences in achievement cognition were examined in 20 subjects of each sex from physical education skills classes. Five trials of a pegboard task were performed in a noncompetitive session, and pairs of same- and opposite-sex opponents of similar ability then were tested. The task required subjects to move blocks between pegs as rapidly as possible.

Males were likelier than females to predict a win in competition, but actual performance measures, postcompetition ability ratings, and attributions showed more positive responses to competition by females than by males. Females improved their performance times and increased their ability ratings from the initial noncompetitive session more than did males.

Competition can have a positive influence on achievement cognition and behavior in females where the competitive task and situation are clearly gender-appropriate. Females in the present study improved their performance, stressed effort attributions, gave higher postcompetition ability evaluations, and generally responded more positively than males to a competitive situation. The tendency for males to predict more success did not translate into better performance. The pegboard task used, however, may be better suited to female achievement orientations than typical sports tasks.

▶ In the past we have encouraged boys to be competitive from a very young age and girls have been somewhat discouraged from competing. It is not surprising that the males are more likely than females to predict success even though they are competing at a new task that may well be more suited to females. Now and in the future, we may see a change in the patterns of females as they are being encouraged to compete more. It may take several generations for the changes to become measurable, however. In 10 years since women have been admitted to West Point, I have noticed few changes in their performance abilities and patterns. I have come to believe that it is too soon to expect to see measurable changes.—Col. James L. Anderson, PE.D.

**Estimation of Fitness and Physical Ability, Physical Performance, and Self-Concept Among Adolescent Females**
Mary L. Young (Univ. of Minnesota)
J. Sports Med. 25:144–150, September 1985                                    5–31

A model in which involvement in physical activity increases ability and, in turn, influences self-concepts of ability has proved generalizable for adolescent males, but there is no supporting evidence for females. Seventy-five grade 7 and 75 grade 9 female students were randomly selected from a chiefly white, suburban junior high school; 57 and 65 young women respectively, completed all tests. The Tennessee Self Concept Scale was used. Sit-ups and a 600-yard run were used to assess physical performance. Seventy-one grade 10 females also were evaluated.

Significant positive relationships were found between both items of physical performance and self-esteem for the oldest group, and between the run and self-esteem for grade 7 females. Estimated fitness correlated positively with overall self-esteem for all groups, and with estimated physical ability for subjects in grades 7 and 10. Subjects who believed it important to be good at physical activities and who also rated their ability as high, had greater overall levels of self-esteem than other subjects.

These findings support Sonstroem's physical activity model for adolescent females, as has been established for males. Relations between physical ability and performance and self-concepts are relevant to program development in physical education and sports. Regardless of whether development of fitness or improvement in specific performance items enhances self-esteem, or the development of a positive self-concept disposes one to engage in activity, both are desirable, and provision should be made for positive developments in both areas.

▶ We should all be pleased to know that young women's estimation of their physical fitness is significantly and positively related to overall self-esteem. Let's hope that school physical education programs will take advantage of that finding. Too often our physical education teachers are also coaches, and they spend more time working with a few athletes than they do working with the rest of the student body and teaching them how to get in shape and why it is important. They hardly have time to design programs that will help the students develop their physical fitness and their self-esteem.—Col. James L. Anderson, PE.D.

**The Adolescent Ballet Dancer: Nutritional Practices and Characteristics Associated With Anorexia Nervosa**
Jacquelyn R. Braisted, Laurel Mellin, Elizabeth J. Gong, and Charles E. Irwin, Jr.
J. Adolesc. Health Care 6:365–371, September 1985                           5–32

The physical requirements for ballet are usually extraordinary. Beginning at an early age (4 to 8 years), female ballet students often exercise in class for 5–7 hours a day. Intensive training and optimal performance require sufficient calories to maintain adequate body protein and fat reserves, as well as sufficient water and electrolytes to replace fluid losses. A questionnaire was administered to 45 female ballet dancers aged 12 to 21 years and 44 nonathletic female subjects aged 14 to 16 years. Dietary practices and nutrition beliefs of the dancers were assessed, and a comparison was made of the prevalence of anorexia nervosa (AN) characteristics in the two groups.

Characteristics used to differentiate between the groups were underweight, distorted body image, amenorrhea, and binge eating. Nutritional practices and beliefs among adolescent ballet dancers included frequent use of weight-reduction strategies such as fasting, binge eating, and selective food restriction. Supplements were used by 60% of the dancers, primarily multivitamin or vitamin C supplements. Fluids or carbohydrates were not viewed as an important aid to performance by most dancers.

This group of ballet dancers exhibited several areas of nutritional concern associated with both nutritional beliefs and the practices and characteristics of AN. Ballet dancers reported characteristics of AN significantly more often than did nonathletic controls. The incidence of amenorrhea, oligomenorrhea, and delayed menarche among the ballet dancers was similar to that in studies by other authors. The mean age at menarche was higher in the dancers than the mean of 13.7 years found by Frisch et al., yet lower than the 15.4 years observed by Warren. The control mean age at menarche matched the 12.9 years for average American girls. Irregular cycles or secondary amenorrhea was reported more frequently than regular cycles among dancers with lower weight for height.

Exhaustive training and low calorie intake both contribute to the high prevalence of amenorrhea found in dancers. It is also possible that delayed menarche in the dancers merely reflects that late maturers choose to become ballet dancers. Since the incidence of irregular cycles was high in this sample, it may be that strenuous training and low food intake brought about the extreme thinness that contributes to menstrual irregularity. The dancers' reports supported this contention; several mentioned that their menstrual cycle resumed when they weighed more or reduced training after injury.

There was a significantly higher prevalence of body image distortion among ballet dancers than among controls. Patients with AN usually exhibit concern over their physical size and weight and markedly overestimate the width of their bodies. Studies have not been conducted to assess this phenomenon in underweight female athletes, although it has been described. Dancers complained more frequently of stomachaches, constipation, and diarrhea than did controls. These problems may have had an influence on appetite and intake. Constipation has been commonly reported for ballet dancers in the literature, but a high occurrence of diarrhea has not. Self-reported weights and heights were used for both dancers and controls, and they may have been a source of error.

Nutrition beliefs and practices among adolescent ballet dancers are also problematic. Only 2 subjects reported taking supplemental iron, and 1 reported taking a calcium supplement. Given the low iron intakes of women athletes and the high risk of bone loss in this population, these supplements may be beneficial. The severe restriction of food and the low body weight may also warrant consideration of a multivitamin supplement as an adjunct to the dancers' food intake.

▶ Studies have shown that, in looking at 61 different athletic events, ballet is second only to football in terms of physical, mental, and environmental demands on the individual. This is in turn reflected in the need for sufficient calories to maintain an adequate protein and fat reserve, as well as to monitor fluid replacement and electrolytes. In addition, since this involves the years of pubertal growth and development, the dietary need for both macro- and micronutrients is higher with regard to calories, protein, calcium, phosphorus, thiamine, riboflavin, niacin, and vitamin D. All of these are potential deficiencies in this group.

Amenorrhea in this circumstance is hardly surprising and has been found in the general population as well, reversible with an increase in weight and caloric consumption. This parallel to anorexia nervosa is also present. In the psychological sense, whether a tendency to AN predisposes to choosing ballet, or whether ballet may lead to overt anorexia nervosa remains an intriguing question.—Lewis J. Krakauer, M.D., F.A.C.P.

---

**Inadequate Nutrition and Chronic Calorie Restriction in Adolescent Ballerinas**
Joan Benson, Donna M. Gillien, Kathy Bourdet, and Alvin R. Loosli (Saint Francis Mem. Hosp., San Francisco)
Physician Sportsmed. 13:79–90, October 1985                5–33

---

Studies show that adult ballerinas practice poor nutrition habits, but little research has been done on adolescent dancers. The authors analyzed the diets of 92 female ballet dancers aged 12 to 17 years enrolled in six professional schools. Three-day diet histories were used to compile data, and a dietician worked with the dancers to ensure accuracy in record keeping.

The table shows mean intake plus or minus SD and the percentage of dancers who consumed less than two thirds of the RDA (recommended daily allowance) for each vitamin or mineral. Of special concern was the percentage of dancers below two thirds of the RDA in B6, folacin, calcium, iron, and zinc. Each rehearsal period of choreographed dance requires only a few minutes, with a high energy demand. Average daily calorie intake of the subjects was 1,890 kcal. However, 48.1% consumed less than 1,800 kcal/day, 28.9% consumed less than 1,500 kcal/day, and 10.8% consumed less than 1,200 kcal/day. For the dancer subjects, the recommended calorie intake is 2,243 kcal/day (mean age, 14.6 years). A high proportion of the diet came from fats (mean 34.6%); an average of 49.8% was derived from carbohydrates, and 15.6% from protein. All 92 dancers were well above

VITAMIN/MINERAL INTAKE OF BALLET DANCERS

| Vitamin/Mineral | Mean Intake | SD | No. Consuming <2/3 of RDA (%) |
|---|---|---|---|
| Vitamin E (mg a-TE) | 9.4 | 11.4 | 38.0 |
| Vitamin A (µgRE) | 1,410.0 | 1,067.7 | 9.7 |
| Vitamin C (mg) | 148.3 | 108.9 | 7.6 |
| Thiamine (mg) | 1.65 | 1.90 | 11.9 |
| Riboflavin (mg) | 1.95 | .99 | 2.1 |
| Niacin (mgNE) | 20.2 | 10.5 | 7.6 |
| Vitamin $B_6$ (mg) | 1.56 | 1.04 | 4.23 |
| Vitamin $B_{12}$ (µg) | 5.13 | 5.6 | 14.3 |
| Folacin (µg) | 266.0 | 179.3 | 58.6 |
| Calcium (mg) | 932.8 | 458.9 | 40.2 |
| Phosphorus (mg) | 1,214.2 | 415.4 | 17.3 |
| Magnesium (mg) | 227.6 | 89.1 | 43.4 |
| Iron (mg) | 13.4 | 7.6 | 48.9 |
| Zinc (mg) | 7.65 | 3.4 | 75.0 |

(Courtesy of Bensen, J., et al.: Physician Sportsmed. 13:79–90, October 1985. Reprinted by permission. A McGraw-Hill publication.)

the RDA for protein. Few complex carbohydrates (fruits, vegetables, pasta, potatoes, and whole grains) were found among the dancers' diets. Some 40.2% of the 92 dancers consumed less than two thirds of the RDA for calcium; and 42.3% consumed less than two thirds of the RDA for vitamin B6. Of these subjects, 58.6% were at risk for folate hypovitaminosis. Sixty-percent of the subjects routinely took vitamin or mineral supplements but rarely consumed the proper types or amounts of them to cover nutrition inadequacies.

When counseling the adolescent ballet dancer one must remember that the dancer must maintain a body weight well below the standard for height to compete realistically in the dance world, and that the schedule of the dancer makes it difficult to eat regular meals. At such a critical time of growth, when skeletal mass and height are of major concern, the dietary habits of these dancers warrant attention.

▶ Garner and Garfinkel have noted that the incidence of anorexia nervosa is up to 100 times the anticipated adolescent figure in aspiring ballet dancers (*Lancet* 2:674, 1978). The authors of the present report trace the problem to the mid-19th century romantic period of dance, and suggest the search for a willowy, sylph-like body is not going to change soon. However, it seems a counsel of despair for nutritionists to advise young girls who are doing vigorous exercise several hours a day on methods to eat only 4 MJ (1,000 kcal) per day "safely." A massive education campaign is needed to disabuse both ballet instructors and the general public of such absurd concepts of feminine beauty.—Roy J. Shephard, M.D., Ph.D.

**Maximal Oxygen Uptake, Nutritional Patterns and Body Composition of Adolescent Female Ballet Dancers**

Priscilla M. Clarkson, Patty S. Freedson, Betsy Keller, David Carney, and Margaret Skrinar (Univ. of Massachusetts)
Res. Q. Exerc. Sport 56:180–185, June 1985                          5-34

Classical ballet is as physically strenuous and demanding as most sports activities, and the effects on young preprofessional dancers are of concern. Fourteen classically trained dancers aged 12 to 17 years were evaluated. They averaged 17 hours a week in class or rehearsal, and were tested before attending a highly competitive dance program.

The mean maximal oxygen uptake was 49 ml/kg/minute, compared with 36–41 ml/kg/minute for untrained girls of similar age. Elite high school female tennis players and nonelite cross-country runners have reported values of 48–51 ml/kg/minute. The mean percent body fat was 16% for the dancers. Skin-fold thicknesses were greater than are reported for professional dancers. Somatograms resembled those of reference college-age women except for biceps and ankle measurements. Nutrient intake levels were less than adequate in some instances. Mean total daily calories were 37 kcal/kg.

Adolescent female ballet dancers are characterized by a high maximal oxygen uptake and a percent body fat substantially lower than in nonathletic girls of similar age. Caloric intake was normal for body weight but lower than recommended. Mineral intake was lower than recommended, though normal when iron and calcium intakes were related to body weight.

▶ It would have been interesting to have used these subjects in a secondary amenorrhea study and to have included a bone density check at the same time. The mean maximum oxygen uptake of 49 ml/kg/minute is really quite high because ballet dancing is considered to be more anaerobic than aerobic. At least I am quite surprised with that level.—Col. James L. Anderson, PE.D.

---

**Pathogenic Weight-Control Behavior in Female Athletes**
Lionel W. Rosen, Douglas B. McKeag, David O. Hough, and Victoria Curley (Michigan State Univ.)
Physician Sportsmed. 14:79–86, January 1986                          5-35

Most coaches and trainers set weight goals for their athletes, but most know little about nutrition as it relates to athletic performance, and little controlled research has addressed the issue of optimal weight/height ratios for peak performance. Idiosyncratic weight control measures were investigated in a series of 182 competitive intercollegiate women athletes, aged 17 to 23 years, from two universities.

Self-induced vomiting was found in 14% of cases, and laxative abuse in 16%. One fourth of subjects routinely used diet pills. One third of all subjects practiced some pathogenic weight-control behavior. Half the athletes who reported a history of obesity exhibited pathogenic weight control behavior. More than half the 32 subjects who lost more weight dieting than they had initially intended resorted to pathogenic behavior. Most acknowledged that they feared losing control of their eating habits if they ended their diets. Most of the 30 subjects followed up indicated a primary concern over athletic performance, rather than their appearance. Older athletes and even coaches and trainers often encouraged the younger competitors to use pathogenic methods, reassuring them that no harm could result.

Athletes who have previously considered themselves obese are especially likely to practice pathogenic weight control methods. Athletes, coaches, and trainers should have access to education in nutrition and proper weight control methods, and on the management of pathogenic weight-control behavior.

▶ Too often coaches today are not properly educated to do the job of coaching young athletes. Many have little knowledge of the human body because they have not studied it. There is no requirement that coaches understand anatomy or physiology, only that they understand the strategy of the sport and how to win. Any coach that encourages young athletes to use pathogenic methods to control weight should be fired. The fact that this is going on is a certain indication that we need to certify our coaches.—Col. James L. Anderson, PE.D.

# 6 Athletic Training

## Introduction

The lead article in this chapter (Digest 6–1) was selected because it will help high school administrators answer the problem of providing adequate medical care for their athletes. The least expensive and most proficient manner of doing this is to hire a faculty athletic trainer. The qualified person (certified or licensed) will teach classes during the school day and serve as an athletic trainer after school hours. The benefits to the athletes and the total athletic program will be tremendous. The method of payment is similar to the manner in which coaches are paid; that is, a regular teacher salary for the courses taught and a stipend from the athletic budget, usually a salary equivalent to that of a head coach. It is expected that the athletic trainer will be paid for each of the seasons he or she works. Some school systems provide release or compensatory time during the school day rather than an additional salary.

The presence of a qualified athletic trainer will relieve the coaches of a tremendous responsibility. It will provide legal protection for the school system. Most importantly, however, it will improve the health care of the athletes. High school athletes deserve proper medical attention for their injuries. School systems that provide athletic programs are responsible for proving proper health care.

The second article in this chapter (Digest 6–2) provides statistical evidence that hiring the qualified athletic trainer will improve the health care of the athlete.

---

**How to Acquire an Athletic Trainer on the High School Level**
Phillip Hossler (East Brunswick High School, N.J.)
Athletic Training 20:199–229, Fall, 1985                                    6–1

---

The fitness boom that is sweeping the United States has made persons involved in medical care aware of three facts: (1) There is a shortage of qualified physicians to manage athletic injuries; (2) increased knowledge of athletic injuries is needed; and (3) individuals are becoming involved in sports activities at a much younger age. Many school systems operate their athletic programs in the hope that none of the participants will be injured. In the absence of a qualified athletic trainer, the school is faced with the following options for managing an athletic injury. (1) the coach can determine the severity of the injury; (2) the coach can have the athlete transported to a hospital for evaluation; (3) the athlete can be sent home with the recommendation to see a physician; or (4) the coach can make an appointment for the athlete to see the appropriate specialist.

A properly accredited athletic trainer should be available to treat athletic injuries. School administrators should be aware of the medical as well as the possible legal ramifications of hiring persons who are not certified or state licensed to provide the service for which they are hired. The number of states adopting licensure for athletic trainers is increasing (15 states now have such requirements). Licensure is not meant to eliminate the care provided by high school coaches, e.g., initiating first aid. Rather, it sets limits so that, to be within the law, the person providing the services must have met the requirements necessary to be licensed or registered within that state.

▶ How can our high school have an athletic trainer? A number of solutions are presented from the very best to adequate, along with salary recommendations. The time has come for administrators to seriously look at the problem of proper health care for the high school athlete and hire the person who can help solve the problem.—Frank George, A.T.C., P.T.

## The Utilization of Athletic Trainer-Team Physician Services and High School Football Injuries

Daniel T. Lackland, James M. Testor, Paul C. Akers, Isao Hirata, Jr., Roland M. Knight, and J. Lorin Mason (South Carolina Dept. of Health and Environmental Control; South Carolina Governor's Council on Physical Fitness; Univ. of South Carolina; and Clemson Univ.)
Athletic Training 20:20–23, Spring 1985                                   6–2

The South Carolina High School Injury Reporting System, implemented in 1980, attempts to provide administrators and coaches with an accurate medical history of their players. Consequently, it generates an epidemiologic review of all injuries from football. The overall success of the program in its first 2 years has provided strong statistical evidence of the importance of a strong medical support team.

Overall, 1,079 injuries were reported by 36 schools during the two seasons. Defensive linemen had the largest number of injuries, followed by offensive backs. Offensive players incurred 56% of the injuries, defensive players 43%, and specialty squad members 1%. The most predominant injuries were of the knee, ankle, and arm, respectively.

Of the 36 schools, 9 had neither a trainer nor a team physician, 3 had a trainer but no physician, 9 had a physician but no trainer, and 15 had both a trainer and a physician. The clinical specialties represented by physicians were: 8, orthopedic; 12, family practice; 1, emergency medicine; 2, pediatrics; and 1, occupational medicine. A significant difference was found in the severity distribution. Teams with trainers assessed injuries as less severe than nontrainer teams (table). Significantly more injuries were recognized by nontrainer schools as occurring during games. Trainers thus recognized substantially more injuries during practices. The physician and physician-trainer teams also reported a significantly greater number of physician-examined injuries.

Injuries incapacitating a player for less than a week constituted 78% of the total. These appear to be the injuries that should be treated by a certified trainer and reviewed by a physician, leaving only 22% that would require more attention by the team physician. Severe injuries (those resulting in

FOOTBALL INJURIES BY TYPE OF MEDICAL SERVICE

| | Trainer/Doctor Service | | | | Trainer Service | | Doctor Service | |
|---|---|---|---|---|---|---|---|---|
| | No Trainer No Doctor N#226 | Trainer No Doctor N#160 | No Trainer Doctor N#241 | Trainer Doctor N#414 | No Trainer N#484 | Trainer N#594 | No Doctor N#389 | Doctor N#690 |
| **Severity of Injury** | | | | | | | | |
| 1 | 35% | 30% | 15% | 28% | 25% | 29% | 33% | 23% |
| 2 | 13 | 25 | 14 | 17 | 13 | 19 | 18 | 16 |
| 3 | 27 | 29 | 47 | 32 | 38 | 31 | 27 | 38 |
| 4 | 12 | 11 | 12 | 10 | 12 | 10 | 12 | 11 |
| 5 | 5 | 1 | 3 | 6 | 4 | 4 | 3 | 5 |
| 6 | 8 | 3 | 9 | 7 | 8 | 6 | 6 | 7 |
| 7 | 0 | 1 | 0 | 0 | 0 | 1 | 1 | 0 |
| Level of Significance | | $P<.01$ | | | | $P<.01$ | | $P<.01$ |
| Injury Occurred During Game | 72.2% | 65.6% | 65.8% | 57.9% | 69% | 60% | 69% | 61% |
| Level of Significance | | $P<.01$ | | | | $P<.01$ | | $P<.01$ |
| Injury Examined By Physician | 50.7 | 43.8 | 57.9 | 60.2 | 54 | 56 | 48 | 59 |
| Level of Significance | | $P<.01$ | | | | $P<.05$ | | $P<.01$ |
| Repeat Injury in One Season | 2.6 | 6.9 | 3.3 | 4.8 | 3.0 | 5.4 | 4.4 | 4.3 |
| Level of Significance | | not significant | | | | not significant | | not significant |
| Average Number of Injuries/School | 25.1 | 53.3 | 26.8 | 27.6 | 25.1 | 31.9 | 32.2 | 27.3 |
| Level of Significance | | $P<.01$ | | | | $P<.01$ | | $P<.01$ |

(Courtesy of Lackland, D.T., et al.: Athletic Training 20:20–23, Spring 1985.)

operations, loss of the player for the season or longer, or both) comprised 7% of the total. All of these were musculoskeletal. Thus the orthopedist, certified trainer, and family practitioner are essential members of the medical care team in dealing with these less numerous but potentially more catastrophic injuries.

Few if any teams can have the physician attend practices. Therefore the triage performed by the trainer is valuable to the team physician. The success of this triage is demonstrated by the trainer-physician team reporting the greatest number of injuries during practice, the greatest number of less severe injuries, and the greatest number of injuries examined by a physician. In these circumstances, players are recognized, treated, and resume playing with less chance of reinjury because medical services are provided all injured players, not just those with injuries that would keep them from practice or a game.

▶ It is truly encouraging to find that 18 of the 36 high schools in this study in South Carolina have an athletic trainer. This percentage is much higher than the national average. As would be expected, more injuries were recognized and treated in those schools with athletic trainers. This proves that an athletic trainer can improve the health care of the high school athlete a great deal.— Frank George, A.T.C., P.T.

---

**An Examination of Health Counseling Practices of Athletic Trainers**
Steven R. Furney and Bobby Patton (Southwest Texas State Univ.)
Athletic Training 21:294–297, Winter 1985

6–3

The athletic trainer may serve as a resident counselor and advisor on health-related matters. Health-oriented counseling practices were studied in a sample of 310 active athletic trainers, 48% of whom responded to a mailed survey. The subjects had an average of 10½ years of experience. Their average age was 33½ years. Ten percent of the group were females. Two thirds held a master's degree.

Ninety percent of the respondents felt that counseling in health-related areas is an important part of their work as trainers, but few spent much time counseling. Injury prevention and treatment were the most frequent subjects of counseling, followed by nutrition and weight control. The least frequent subjects were death or bereavement, child abuse, and suicide. Trainers did not feel adequate in the latter areas. Respondents felt strongly that education in counseling should be part of academic preparation. Most respondents reported being willing to participate in continuing education in various areas of counseling.

Athletic trainers consider counseling in health-related topics to be an important part of their work. Training institutions should recognize this aspect of training and provide appropriate curriculum. Trainers are increasingly recognizing that the pain or problems presented by student athletes are not always physical.

▶ Everyone needs someone to talk to. The athlete often chooses the athletic trainer because of his medical and health knowledge. The athletic trainer is the one who explains to the athlete and the coach the diagnosis or prognosis the examining physician has made. A close relationship may develop between athlete and athletic trainer, one of both trust and friendship. When the athlete needs to talk to someone about an injury, the athletic trainer is the one most often turned to.—Frank George, A.T.C., P.T.

---

**The Effects of Oscillating Inversion on Systemic Blood Pressure, Pulse, Intraocular Pressure, and Central Retinal Arterial Pressure**
Robert M. Goldman, Robert S. Tarr, Burton G. Pinchuk, and Robert E. Kappler (Chicago College of Osteopathic Medicine)
Physician Sportsmed. 13:93–96, March 1985                                    6–4

---

The effects of gravity inversion oscillation procedures on systemic blood pressure (BP), pulse rate, intraocular pressure, and central retinal arterial pressure were studied. Twenty healthy men with a mean age of 25 years, oscillated between the upright and inverted state 80 to 150 times during a 15-minute period. Measurements were made in the completely inverted stage of a cycle at 5, 10, and 15 minutes.

Systemic BP fell throughout the 15-minute oscillation period. Both systolic and diastolic pressures were significantly reduced in each measurement period (table). Pulse rate also decreased on inversion and throughout the oscillation period. Intraocular pressure rose initially, then fell slightly, but was still elevated above preinversion values.

SYSTOLIC AND DIASTOLIC SYSTEMIC BLOOD PRESSURE (BP) AND PULSE RATE IN 20
MEN BEFORE AND DURING INVERSION (MEAN ± SE)

|  | Preinversion (Upright) | Inverted 5 Minutes | Inverted 10 Minutes | Inverted 15 Minutes |
|---|---|---|---|---|
| Systolic BP (mm Hg) | 123 ± 1.6 | 121 ± 1.2* | 120 ± 1.0* | 118 ± 1.0* |
| Diastolic BP (mm Hg) | 81 ± 0.7 | 80 ± 0.6* | 79 ± 0.5* | 78 ± 0.5* |
| Pulse rate | 69 ± 1.8 | 66 ± 1.9* | 65 ± 1.8† | 64 ± 1.9† |

*Significantly different ($P < .05$) from both preinversion and adjacent time columns.
†Significantly different ($P < .05$) from preinversion only.
(Courtesy of Goldman, R.M., et al.: Physician Sportsmed. 13:93–96, March 1985. Reprinted by permission. A McGraw-Hill publication.)

Studies in both normotensive and hypertensive subjects in which static inversion was used showed increases in BP, pulse rate, intraocular pressure, and central retinal arterial pressure. Analysis, however, suggested that the BP elevations resulted from centrally mediated neural events, probably the anxiety attendant on inversion. Tilt-table experiments have shown that tilting does not cause an increase in BP because the increase in venous return observed in tilted subjects is offset by a reflex-mediated decrease in heart rate. Thus in the static inversion studies, the rise in both heart rate and BP suggests some process other than the increase in cardiac preload caused by inversion.

In this study the subjects reported a relaxed feeling of well-being while operating the oscillation equipment. Their ability to control the degree and duration of inversion and avoid a prolonged (static) inversion posture resulted in a relatively anxiety-free situation. The decreases in systemic BP and pulse rate observed presumably reflect this feeling of tranquility. That BP continued to fall throughout the 15-minute inversion period is especially significant, because it suggests that the procedure can relax subjects even beyond resting levels.

The increases in intraocular pressure and central retinal arterial pressure reported here, as in previous studies on static inversion, are hydrostatic effects. In the inverted position, the column of blood between the heart and the head causes an increase in pressure in the vessels of the head. Venous distention allows accumulation of blood in the extracranial vessels. The increase in intraocular pressure presumably results from increased resistance to aqueous outflow due to elevation of episcleral venous pressure similar to that found in a change from a sitting to a supine position. It is well documented that the increase in cerebral (intracranial) BP is balanced by increased interstitial hydrostatic pressure. Even in the vessels of the eye, however, the increased BP is balanced by increases in intraocular pressure.

The risk of stroke expressed in previous studies appears to be exaggerated. There have been no reports of stroke, cerebrovascular accident, or any serious injury with properly functioning gravity inversion equipment. Protection against brain hemorrhage may be due to the concomitant increase in cerebrospinal fluid (CSF) and the "closed box" system of the skull. The risk of stroke may be greater during strenuous weight training or severe anxiety in the upright posture, which would not provide this protective CSF increase. The unexpected finding of a progressive decrease in intraocular pressure as the oscillation period continued may reflect the decrease in systemic BP.

▶ Oscillating inversion appears to be a safe procedure regarding blood pressure and heart rate. We do screen our patients very carefully before we introduce static gravity inversion into their treatment regimen. Initially, patients are in the inverted position for short periods (30–60 seconds) and the time is gradually increased over a 3-week period.—Frank George, A.T.C., P.T.

---

**The Effect of Local Cold Application on Intramuscular Blood Flow at Rest and After Running**
Ola Thorsson, Bo Lilja, Lars Ahlgren, Bengt Hemdal, and Nils Westlin (Univ. of Lund)
Med. Sci. Sports Exerc. 17:710–713, December 1985                     6–5

---

Local cold application reduces pain from soft tissue injury and minimizes inflammatory enzyme activity, but its effects on intramuscular blood flow are uncertain. The effects of therapeutic cooling on blood flow were examined in 8 male middle-distance runners of varying ability, aged 17 to 27 years. Muscle blood flow was determined by the radioxenon clearance technique, in conjunction with application of cold packs and "dummy" packs to the skin for 20 minutes. The study was repeated after 15 minutes of treadmill running.

Minimum skin temperatures after cooling for 4½ minutes were 15.7 C at rest and 17.5 C after running. Mean intramuscular blood flow before cooling was significantly greater in exercised legs, when estimated 10 minutes after running. Maximal reductions in blood flow 10 minutes after the end of cooling were 66% at rest and 69% after running, compared with control legs.

The delayed effect of cryotherapy on intramuscular blood flow suggests that cold application not be the primary treatment of acute injury with intramuscular bleeding, unless the chief goal is pain relief. Immediate external compression of the injured area is the best means of limiting the size of the hematoma.

---

**External Compression for Controlling Traumatic Edema**
Gary B. Wilkerson (Centre College, Danville, Ky.)
Physician Sportsmed. 13:97–106, June 1985                     6–6

---

Compression appears to be the most effective deterrent to swelling after acute musculoskeletal injury. External compression inhibits seepage of fluid into underlying tissue spaces and disperses excess fluid. Ice application may increase swelling and must be combined with compression and elevation. Edema at an injury site compounds tissue damage, delays healing, and may result in chronic disability. Congestion of the interstitium impedes the delivery of oxygen and nutrients to surviving cells, and promotes hypoxic tissue death, adding to necrotic debris and further increasing the osmolarity of the interstitial fluid. Fluid accumulation between damaged ligaments may lead to separation of torn tissue ends and prevent primary healing. Edema also contributes to pain from trauma, and the resultant muscle spasm in turn enhances pain. Lack of use from excess edema leads to muscle atrophy and fluid stasis, and promotes coagulation that inhibits the removal of edema fluid.

Complications from fluid accumulation can be minimized by the early and continuous use of external compression. Elevation of the affected extremity lowers the hydrostatic pressure of blood and decreases interstitial osmolarity through facilitating lymphatic drainage. Active exercise increases lymph flow and therefore the drainage of protein-containing fluid from the interstitium. This is the rationale for using high-voltage galvanic muscle stimulation and intermittent pneumatic compression to mobilize edema.

▶ The two previous articles (Digests 6–5 and 6–6) have significant meaning to the clinician. We have argued among ourselves and I have changed my mind more than once when deciding if ice or compression is a more important aspect of first aid for athletic injuries. I do believe that there is nothing like compression to prevent swelling and edema. However, because of compromised blood flow, ice must be used to prevent secondary tissue necrosis of uninjured tissue.

The use of rest, ice, compression, and elevation (RICE) is agreed by many to be the best first aid treatment for athletic injuries.

▶ ↓ Please read the following article as well as the two previous articles — Frank George, A.T.C., P.T.

---

**Inflammation in Connective Tissue: Etiology and Management**
Gary B. Wilkerson (Centre College, Danville, Ky.)
Athletic Training 21:298–301, Winter 1985                                        6–7

---

Inflammation ranges from a localized, transient response to a sustained response involving the entire body. Both histamine and serotonin are important in the early stages of inflammation; bradykinin is also involved. Preformed inflammatory substances may be released suddenly or gradually from cells, producing local vasodilation and increased capillary permeability. Several classes of prostaglandins with diverse, sometimes opposed effects have a role in inflammatory responses. Inflammatory substances can cause marked stimulation of nerve fibers and severe pain without necessarily damaging the fibers. Edema can produce pain through pressure on mechanosensitive receptors. Muscle spasm has a similar effect and also acts indirectly by stimulating chemosensitive receptors. A cycle of pain-spasm-ischemia-hypoxia-pain may be established. Hypoxic pain can be relieved by measures that improve oxygen delivery to the tissues.

Nonsteroidal anti-inflammatory agents can be used to combat inflammatory responses without adverse corticosteroid effects on the structural protein of collagen fibers. They act chiefly by inhibiting prostaglandin synthesis, but other actions are also possible. Synthesis of all classes of prostaglandins is inhibited by nonsteroidal drugs. Cryotherapy is helpful in all acute and some chronic states. Cold has an anesthetic effect and directly inhibits inflammation by slowing chemical reactions in cells and inhibiting enzyme activity. Cold is widely used to minimize posttraumatic swelling, and there is evidence that it does reduce recovery time. The value of heat depends on the prevailing conditions in the tissue to be treated. Thermotherapy is helpful in resolution of the late stages of inflammation, but in the acute phase the inflammatory response may be intensified by heat application.

▶ This article should be read carefully with the two previous articles (Digests 6–5 and 6–6). The author states "Although there is little evidence to indicate that cold reduced swelling, there is convincing evidence that cryotherapy reduces recovery time." The author goes on to state that "It has been suggested that the most beneficial effect of cryotherapy use is decreased tissue metabolism rather than decreased circulation. Reduction of oxygen requirements allows cells to survive the hypoxic condition that exists after trauma until greater amounts of oxygen become available. Prevention of hypoxic damage to tissue minimizes additional release of inflammatory substances beyond that caused directly by trauma."

It is very important to use ice as well as compression on acute athletic injuries.—Frank George, A.T.C., P.T.

---

**Isokinetic Testing of Shoulder Strength: Normal Values**
Frank M. Ivey, Jr., Jason H. Calhoun, Ken Rusche, and Jane Bierschenk (Univ. of Texas, Galveston)
Arch. Phys. Med. Rehabil. 66:384–386, June 1985                    6–8

---

The Cybex II isokinetic dynamometer, a variable-speed, accommodating resistance control device, allows dynamic torsional forces to be recorded at set velocities throughout the range of motion (ROM). The torque applied to the input shaft is recorded in foot-pounds on a chart recorder and can be compared with time and ROM. The Cybex Upper Body Exercise and Testing Table stabilizes the trunk and permits testing of the shoulder, elbow, and wrist. Normal values are necessary for proper interpretation of results concerning dominant and nondominant extremities, strength ratios for coupled motions (flexion-extension, abduction-adduction), and strength matched for lean body weight.

To date, no normal values or ratios have been available for shoulder strength testing. Isokinetic muscle testing was performed on the shoulders of 31 normal volunteers (18 men), aged 21 to 50 years, of whom 12 did no upper extremity exercise, 7 exercised occasionally, and 12 exercised regularly. In 24 subjects the right was the dominant shoulder. No statistical

NORMAL VALUES FOR ISOKINETIC TESTING OF SHOULDER STRENGTH*

| Sex | Freq | Result | IR-S | IR-F | ER-S | ER-F | AB-S | AB-F | AD-S | AD-F | EX-S | EX-F | FL-S | FL-F |
|---|---|---|---|---|---|---|---|---|---|---|---|---|---|---|
| **A. Average strength, males and females (foot pounds)** | | | | | | | | | | | | | | |
| M | 36 | Mean | 33.2 | 30.2 | 21.8 | 19.9 | 37.5 | 28.4 | 61.0 | 52.6 | 53.9 | 44.2 | 43.0 | 34.1 |
| M | 36 | SD | 11.8 | 10.9 | 5.7 | 6.0 | 11.4 | 9.9 | 15.2 | 16.7 | 14.3 | 12.8 | 9.3 | 7.4 |
| F | 26 | Mean | 17.9 | 16.0 | 13.0 | 10.8 | 19.5 | 13.9 | 34.2 | 27.8 | 28.4 | 22.9 | 24.0 | 18.6 |
| F | 26 | SD | 2.6 | 3.0 | 2.0 | 2.1 | 5.9 | 4.6 | 6.7 | 4.2 | 4.3 | 5.0 | 4.5 | 4.4 |
| **B. Maximum strength, males and females (foot pounds)** | | | | | | | | | | | | | | |
| M | 36 | Mean | 36.4 | 32.7 | 23.8 | 21.1 | 41.6 | 31.2 | 65.9 | 55.5 | 59.1 | 47.6 | 45.8 | 37.5 |
| M | 36 | SD | 12.2 | 11.0 | 5.8 | 6.8 | 11.4 | 10.3 | 16.4 | 17.0 | 14.8 | 13.0 | 9.2 | 8.4 |
| F | 26 | Mean | 19.6 | 17.1 | 13.9 | 11.2 | 21.6 | 15.5 | 37.2 | 30.7 | 31.6 | 24.8 | 26.2 | 28.8 |
| F | 26 | SD | 2.9 | 3.0 | 2.3 | 2.3 | 6.6 | 5.1 | 6.7 | 5.3 | 4.7 | 5.5 | 5.5 | 4.1 |
| **C. Angles at maximum strength (degrees)** | | | | | | | | | | | | | | |
| M | 36 | Mean | 26.2 | 16.5 | -14.1 | -39.6 | 51.5 | 49.6 | 100.8 | 115.9 | 83.6 | 95.4 | 97.5 | 88.0 |
| M | 36 | SD | 26.6 | 23.6 | 46.7 | 39.7 | 47.3 | 31.1 | 33.4 | 25.0 | 34.5 | 25.8 | 48.7 | 44.3 |
| F | 26 | Mean | -2.9 | 1.8 | 16.9 | 5.8 | 43.2 | 57.2 | 113.6 | 124.4 | 57.6 | 65.7 | 110.8 | 98.0 |
| F | 26 | SD | 27.2 | 17.8 | 40.7 | 36.9 | 44.6 | 38.9 | 39.9 | 27.4 | 19.7 | 19.6 | 48.3 | 42.7 |
| **D. Individual strength divided by weight** | | | | | | | | | | | | | | |
| M | 36 | Mean | 19.6 | 17.7 | 12.9 | 11.7 | 21.9 | 16.5 | 35.9 | 30.9 | 32.0 | 26.2 | 25.4 | 20.2 |
| M | 36 | SD | 6.0 | 5.5 | 2.8 | 2.9 | 4.5 | 4.5 | 6.6 | 8.2 | 7.7 | 6.7 | 4.1 | 3.9 |
| F | 26 | Mean | 13.9 | 12.5 | 10.0 | 8.4 | 15.0 | 10.7 | 26.5 | 21.5 | 22.0 | 17.9 | 18.6 | 14.4 |
| F | 26 | SD | 2.0 | 2.4 | 1.1 | 1.5 | 3.9 | 3.4 | 4.9 | 3.0 | 3.1 | 4.1 | 3.4 | 3.1 |
| **E. Individual strength divided by lean body mass (foot pounds)** | | | | | | | | | | | | | | |
| M | 36 | Mean | 23.0 | 20.8 | 15.2 | 13.7 | 25.9 | 19.4 | 42.2 | 36.2 | 32.0 | 30.6 | 29.9 | 23.7 |
| M | 36 | SD | 7.1 | 6.4 | 3.2 | 3.4 | 5.9 | 5.4 | 7.7 | 9.1 | 7.7 | 7.2 | 5.0 | 4.1 |
| F | 26 | Mean | 18.2 | 16.4 | 13.2 | 11.0 | 19.6 | 14.0 | 34.7 | 28.2 | 22.0 | 23.3 | 24.4 | 18.9 |
| F | 26 | SD | 2.7 | 3.1 | 1.5 | 2.2 | 5.2 | 4.3 | 6.1 | 3.8 | 3.1 | 5.1 | 4.7 | 4.1 |

*IR-S: internal rotation, slow; IR-F: internal rotation, fast; ER: external rotation; AB: abduction; AD: adduction; EX: extension; and FL: flexion.
(Courtesy of Ivey, F.M., Jr., et al.: Arch. Phys. Med. Rehabil. 66:384–386, June 1985.)

difference was found between dominant and the nondominant shoulder, though there was a consistent pattern of greater strength in the dominant shoulder. Internal rotation strength was significantly greater than external rotation strength by 3:2 for both fast- and slow-torque arm speeds. Extension strength was significantly greater than flexion by 5:4 at both speeds. Adduction strength was significantly greater than abduction by 2:1 for both speeds. Overall, adduction strength was greatest, followed by extension, flexion, abduction, internal rotation, and external rotation.

Male strength was greater than female, but the advantage decreased when normalized for lean body mass and exercise activities (table).

The shoulder is vulnerable to injury because of its global ROM and reliance upon soft tissue structures for stability. Since the acromioclavicular, sternoclavicular, glenohumeral, and scapulothoracic articulations generally move as a unit, isolation of a single segment is not easy nor would it provide useful information with regard to function of the whole. Therefore, shoulder testing for extent of rehabilitation or before participation or training cannot eliminate elevation, depression, retraction, or protraction of the shoulder girdle. Full rehabilitation after injury requires attention to flexibility, strength, power, aerobic conditioning, and neuromuscular coordination. Some objective measure of strength training is helpful in assessing the degree of recovery before return to full activity.

When women are compared with men after normalization for lean body mass, shoulder girdle strength difference is much less. This appears to be due to the dissimilarity in upper body use, rather than to a difference in fiber type or muscle distribution. Preparticipation or pretraining objective evidence of strength deficits about the shoulder may help identify areas in which to concentate strength training. This would theoretically decrease the chance of injury and might improve performance.

▶ We have been waiting for normal values and ratios for isokinetic shoulder testing to be published. The authors have given us a beginning with a study of 31 subjects. More studies need to be done; however, the authors have presented the following ratios, which we have begun to use with our patients:
Internal Rotation: External Rotation 3:2
Extension: Flexion 5:4
Adduction: Abduction 2:1
    All ratios were the same at both slow and fast speeds.—Frank George, A.T.C., P.T.

---

**Rehabilitation of the Pitching Shoulder**
Arthur M. Pappas, Richard M. Zawacki, and Claire F. McCarthy (Univ. of Massachusetts)
Am. J. Sports Med. 13:223–235, July–August 1985                6–9

---

Shoulder pain is a common complaint among baseball pitchers. The nature of shoulder problems often can be traced to a lack of flexibility and muscular imbalance. The following are described: (1) the normal biomechanical properties of a properly functioning shoulder during a baseball pitch; (2) pathomechanics of shoulder problems; (3) flexibility requirements of the throwing shoulder; and (4) the muscular balance necessary for an effective throwing shoulder.

The demand and overload of pitching more than likely leads to injury and inflammation of many of the muscles involved with the shoulder girdle complex. Pain associated with shoulder problems has a secondary effect of inhibiting muscle action. It is important to maintain the humeral head in a central location within the glenoid. Weakness of the rotator cuff precludes the stabilization necessary for glenohumeral movement.

Physical examination of the pitching shoulder should include a visual assessment of synchrony of motion. Synchronous motion refers to bilaterally identical movements of the shoulder girdle complex, assuming lack of problems in the nonthrowing arm. It is best observed by having the pitcher simultaneously and sequentially abduct to 90 degrees, horizontally extend, and then externally rotate his shoulders while seated. The posterior shoulder girdle musculature must be palpated to locate changes in muscle tissue integrity, changes in muscle volume, and nodules. Loss of flexibility in the pitching shoulder with chronic discomfort tends to occur in the glenohumeral joint. Glenohumeral inflexibility is best demonstrated during horizontal flexion and combined abduction.

A detailed manual muscle examination provides a good data base for assessing the timing and synchrony of shoulder musculature. The posterior deltoid, infraspinatus, teres minor, rhomboids, and middle trapezius can be tested by having the pitcher externally rotate and horizontally extend his pitching shoulder.

The sequential goals of rehabilitation are as follows: (1) return to normal passive and active range of motion; (2) re-establish synchrony of motion; (3) increase strength and endurance in integrated muscle action; and (4) progressively return to pitching.

▶ The authors stressed a very important aspect of shoulder rehabilitation, i.e., "It is important not to start strengthening exercises until flexibility, synchrony of motion of the shoulder girdle complex, and distinct contractions in all shoulder musculature through a normal range have been achieved." Too often the young athlete wants to begin lifting weights in the rehabilitation program and this may lead to a loss of motion and subsequently a loss of strength. The authors also recommend using no more than 5 lbs of weight.—Frank George, A.T.C., P.T.

**Swimmer's Shoulder: The Influence of Flexibility and Weight Training**
Joseph F. Greipp (Fitness Counsel, Inc., Moorestown, N.J.)
Physician Sportsmed. 13:92–105, August 1985                          6–10

The incidence of shoulder pain was studied in 82 males and 86 females aged 12 to 23 years who represented four universities and two clubs. A simple test of shoulder flexibility was conducted in October, and the team-wide incidence of swimmer's shoulder developing in the coming winter season was predicted.

TECHNIQUE.—The swimmer assumed the supine position on an inclined bench. The swimmer then allowed gravity to pull the straightened arms toward the floor as far as possible without undue pain. In tests on nearly 300 swimmers, shoulder pain was never a limiting factor. To increase the tension on the biceps and supraspinatus muscles and tendons, the hands were pronated, palms toward the ground. The top of the individual's head was level with the higher end of the bench. For uniformity, the straightened arms were kept perpendicular to the torso. When the swimmer stated that the arms could not approach the ground further, the distance between the centers of the styloid processes at the wrists was measured. To compensate for varying arm lengths, the distance between the wrists was divided by the athlete's height. The resulting value is termed the shoulder flex factor, which usually is 0.300–0.800. Clinically, a goniometer is preferred for measurement, especially if unusual arm length is suspected. When using a goniometer, the angle formed by the two arms in the test position is calculated and converted to a flex factor value using the formula: angle + 74.23/264. The validation study also revealed a positive correlation between swimmers with poor flexibility (high flex factor) and those who had shoulder pain in the preceding season.

The predictions were about 93% accurate, clearly showing a strong correlation between lack of flexibility and the incidence of swimmer's shoulder. In males, an increased incidence of shoulder pain was also related to increased intensity and duration of weight training. This study suggests that, consistent with animal studies, tendon hypertrophy was the reason for the increased number of shoulder problems in male weight trainers. The incidence of shoulder pain was not directly dependent on stroke, distance, or sex, with one exception: At a given level of ability, butterfly swimmers had shoulder pain more frequently than other swimmers did.

In this series, with few exceptions, the incidence of shoulder pain was related to flexibility. The flex factor is most severely tested in the butterfly stroke; in the freestyle and backstroke, a swimmer can compensate for lack of shoulder flexibility by using a commensurate amount of body roll, which is not possible when doing the butterfly stroke. If swimmers do not use a compensatory roll in the freestyle and backstroke, they could possibly have the higher incidence of shoulder pain observed in butterfly stroke swimmers.

The correlation between flexibility and subsequent shoulder pain suggests that flexibility should be considered when conducting research on shoulder pain. Flexibility has probably been a confounding variable in previous studies to determine which swim strokes have the greatest capacity to produce shoulder pain. The same might be said for previous studies to evaluate the role of distance swimming, or future attempts to reassess the role of resistance training.

▶ The author has described a good field test for anterior shoulder flexibility. (There is a relationship between anterior shoulder inflexibility and shoulder pain in swimmers.) This test will help discover those swimmers who need flexibility training to prevent shoulder pain. The author also describes weight training exercises that should be performed and those that should be avoided by swimmers.—Frank George, A.T.C., P.T.

---

**High Voltage Galvanic Stimulation: Can There Be a "State of the Art"?**
David J. Ralston (Univ. of Michigan)
Athletic Training 21:291–293, Winter 1985                                    6–11

High-voltage galvanic stimulation (HVGS) is a continuous, waveless, unidirectional current of chemical nature that is being evaluated in the management of athletic injuries. A survey of 19 Certified Athletic Trainers showed that the modality is used by many intercollegiate programs, but in widely varying ways. Persons with acute pain are treated with the positive pole over the site of pain, at a frequency of about 100 pulses per second (pps) for 15–20 minutes. The negative pole is more effective in chronic disorders, used at a relatively low frequency for 15–20 minutes. Persons with swelling and edema are treated at low intensity, regardless of frequency. Many trainers use the four-pad system for treatment of a large area such as the lower part of the back. Some trainers use the continuous high-frequency current to relieve muscle spasm. High-voltage galvanic stimulation is often used to treat persons with acute contusions, often in conjunction with cold immersion.

Much more work is needed to obtain definitive indications for using HVGS in treatment of injuries. It is recommended that positive polarity be used over sites of acute pain, at high frequency, and that for chronic states, negative polarity, at low frequency, be used. Either a high-or a low-frequency current can be used for swelling and edema. Negative polarity is used at low frequency to increase blood flow. Persons with muscle spasm are treated with negative polarity at 20–120 pps. The use of cold immersion or a cold whirlpool in conjunction with HVGS may help relieve acute pain and edema. The adjunctive use of ultrasound may help increase blood flow.

▶ This article was answered by a very interesting letter to the editor in the Spring *Journal of Athletic Training.* The author of the letter is Francy Rubin, M.S., R.P.T., A.T.C., from Boulder Creek, California. The letter states that the high-voltage galvanic stimulators found in most training rooms are really TENS units and not what is classically considered as Galvanic units. Therefore, she states that polarity is of very little importance, with the exception of HVGS for wound healing. Both the author of the letter and the author of the article agree that a great deal more research needs to be published on this subject.— Frank George, A.T.C., P.T.

▶ ↓ There have been many articles published in recent years regarding strength responses to electrical muscle stimulation. The stimulus for these studies came from reports of Russian experiments claiming tremendous increase in strength using electrical muscle stimulation. When these effects could not be reproduced in American and other European studies, it was suggested that the stimulators used did not have the same wave length, amplitude, or frequency as the Russian stimulators. There have been a number of studies done in this country that have shown significant increases in strength using electrical muscle stimulation. There have been an equal number of studies showing very little or no significant increases in strength. All in all it has become confusing to the clinician in attempting to evaluate both the studies and the effects of electrical stimulation (ES) on our patients.

When attempting to evaluate these studies, a number of factors must be considered. The first consideration must be the stimulator that is being used. It appears, from the studies and from my own experience, that ES units that are designed to produce a forceful muscle contraction, as opposed to those designed to reduce spasticity and edema and for pain relief, produce better increases in strength. Secondly, the design of the study must be closely examined. What is being measured? Is isometric strength being measured? Is isokinetic strength being measured? Where in the joint range was the strength tested? Where in the joint range was the ES administered? Are the subjects being tested healthy or are they postoperative or postinjury? The frequency, the intensity, and the length of treatment must also be considered. An equally important consideration is electrode type, size, and placement. Another factor is how many weeks or months was the study done?

As you can see, many questions must be looked into when evaluating the effectiveness of ES to improve strength. Also keep in mind my comments after Digest 6–11 where Rubin states that we are really using TENS units and not true galvanic muscle stimulators.

Many clinicians say, "Why not try ES, because at least no harm can be done?" I don't agree with that statement, especially when treating a patient who has had anterior cruciate ligament repair. An overzealous stimulation of the quadriceps muscles too soon after the repair may stretch some of the healing tissue and cause increased laxity in the knee joint. I do use ES to increase strength in the injured or surgical knee. I do use it with chondromalacia patients to increase vastus medialis obliquus strength. I do believe it has helped some, not all, of my patients. I know that a great deal more research needs to be done on the subject. Please keep in mind the previous stated questions when evaluating the following articles (Digests 6–12, 6–13, 6–14, 6–15, and 6–16).

---

### A Strength Study Utilizing the Electro-Stim 180
David Boutelle, Brad Smith, and Terry Malone (Indianapolis)
J. Orthop. Sports Phys. Ther. 7:50–53, September 1985                6–12

---

Interest has increased in the use of electrical stimulation as either an adjunct or a substitution for voluntary muscle contraction to improve strength in normal individuals. This study evaluated whether electrical stimulation does significantly increase the strength of normal musculature. A sample was obtained using 17 normal subjects (10 men, 7 women) with an average mean age of 26 years. Subjects were divided into two groups. Three different speeds (0, 60, 240 degrees per second), with three to five contractions at each speed, were used to determine the maximum strength of each subject's nondominant leg as measured by a Cybex II dynamometer. Group A consisted of 8 subjects used as controls. Group B consisted of 9 subjects who received electrical stimulation to the nondominant leg for 20 treatment sessions (5 days per week for 4 weeks).

Results presented in the table showed that group B obtained a statisti-

| | DESCRIPTIVE STATISTICS* | | | | | |
| | 0°/sec (30° knee flexion) | | 60°/sec (peak torque) | | 240°/sec (peak torque) | |
| | Mean | SD | Mean | SD | Mean | SD |
|---|---|---|---|---|---|---|
| **Group A** | | | | | | |
| Pretest | 60.9 | 10.9 | 126.9 | 29.8 | 79.6 | 17.4 |
| Post-test | | | | | | |
| 4 weeks | 56.4 | 14.2 | 149.8 | 29.1 | 99.0 | 17.1 |
| | | | | | | |
| **Group B** | | | | | | |
| Pretest | 60.3 | 17.0 | 144.6 | 25.7 | 92.0 | 23.1 |
| Post-test | | | | | | |
| 4 weeks | 78.9 | 30.0 | 149.8 | 28.6 | 99.0 | 14.4 |
| 8 weeks | 70.5 | | | | | |

*Means, standard deviations, and changes of group torque (ft–lb).
(Courtesy of Boutelle, D., et al.: J. Orthop. Sports Phys. Ther. 7:50–53, September 1985. Copyright by Williams and Wilkins, 1985.)

cally significant 32% increase after 4 weeks of stimulation. This increase in strength was only apparent in the zero degrees per second phase, and did not show any significant change at the 60 or 240 degrees per second phases. The results of a one-month poststimulation post-test showed an average quadriceps strength, or 70.5 foot-pounds. This represents only a 4% decrease in quadriceps strength over the 31 days without stimulation. Cutaneous discomfort and cramping were the primary complaints of the subjects.

The 30% gain in strength was seen only in an isometric mode, not dynamically, when assessed. The application of the Electro-Stim 180 at various consecutive joint angles of full knee extension—with subsequent dynamic testing, as well as long-term poststimulus testing at 1, 2, and 4 months—requires further research.

▶ See editor's comments preceding Digest 6–12.—Frank George, A.T.C., P.T.

**Improvement in Isometric Strength of the Quadriceps Femoris Muscle After Training With Electrical Stimulation**
David M. Selkowitz (Merritt/Peralta Med. Ctr., Oakland, Calif.)
Phys. Ther. 65:186–196, February 1985                                      6–13

Exogenous electrical stimulation (ES) of nerve and muscle is used for muscle re-education, to delay atrophy, to reduce spasticity temporarily, and to reduce contractures and edema. The use of ES for muscle strengthening in research and clinical practice has become increasingly popular. Isometric training with ES is reported to increase isometric and isokinetic quadriceps femoris strength in healthy subjects. Patients recovering from knee ligament operations and patients with chondromalacia patellae have also shown increases in isometric strength of the quadriceps after ES training.

The author studied 24 volunteers (16 females), aged 18 to 32 years, to determine if isometric training with ES alone would significantly increase isometric strength of the quadriceps. The relations between the strength changes and the relative force and duration of training contractions were also studied. An experimental group of 12 subjects (group 1) and a control group of 12 (group 2) underwent pretesting and posttesting to determine their maximum voluntary isometric contractions (MVICs). Group 1 trained with maximally tolerable isometric contractions induced by ES, 3 days a week for 4 weeks.

Subjects were instructed not to add a voluntary component to the ES contractions. The training protocol included ten 10-second tetanic, maximally tolerable, isometric contractions, with a 2-minute rest between contractions. The electrical stimulus was provided by a unit that delivers a current with an unalterable frequency, pulse width, and wave form. Oscilloscope analysis relealed an ac with a frequency of 2,200 Hz and a 0.45-msec pulse width. The wave form has been reported to be sinusoidal. Sinusoidal waves at such high frequencies, however, take on the characteristics of a pulse wave. The current amplitude delivered was to subject tolerance (as verbally indicated) and varied from 28 to 90 mamp. The time for the current to rise to peak amplitude also varied according to tolerance, from 0.6 second to 3 seconds.

Although both groups demonstrated increases in isometric strength of the quadriceps, isometric training with ES produced a significantly greater increase. The relative strength improvement in group 1 was postitively and significantly correlated with training contraction intensity and duration.

Strength training with ES may be useful in decreasing the time for rehabilitation and maximizing the recovery potential of patients with decreased quadriceps femoris strength. It may permit earlier initiation of vigorous strength training while a patient is immobilized in a cast, or if there are relative contraindications to dynamic strengthening techniques.

▶ See editor's comments preceding Digest 6–12.—Frank George, A.T.C., P.T.

## The Effects of Electrical Stimulation on the Quadriceps During Postoperative Knee Immobilization

Matthew C. Morrissey, Clive E. Brewster, Clarence L. Shields, Jr., and Mark Brown (Southwestern Orthopedic Med. Group, Inglewood, Calif.)
Am. J. Sports Med. 13:40–45, January–February                                    6–14

Decreased quadriceps muscle strength can result from knee immobilization following reconstruction of the anterior cruciate ligament (ACL). The efficacy of surface electrical stimulation of the quadriceps in minimizing the decrease in quadriceps isometric strength was examined in 15 male patients scheduled for ACL reconstruction using part of the patellar tendon. The mean age was 24 years. Patients were immobilized for 6 weeks in a cylinder cast at −45 degrees of knee extension, with weight-bearing to tolerance. Study patients used the Respond II neuromuscular stimulation system. The electrodes were applied to the middle of the quadriceps muscle and to the vastus medialis motor point. Initial stimulation was at 40 milliamperes.

Six patients applied stimulation to the affected quadriceps for an average of 216 hours during immobilization, for an average of 6 hours a day at 52 milliamperes. Isometric quadriceps torque production declined 80% in control subjects and 60% in those who used stimulation. Change in thigh circumference did not differ significantly in the two groups, and there was no substantial difference in pain on maximum quadriceps contraction.

The reduction in quadriceps isometric torque on immobilization after ACL reconstruction can be lessened by electrically stimulating the affected muscle, but thigh circumference changes are not significantly altered. There is no significant difference in quadriceps strength 12 weeks postoperatively in stimulated and control subjects.

▶ See editors's comments preceding Digest 6–12.—Frank George, A.T.C., P.T.

---

**Comparison of Isometric Exercise and High Volt Galvanic Stimulation on Quadriceps Femoris Muscle Strength**
Thomas Mohr, Barbara Carlson, Cathy Sulentic, and Richard Landry (Univ. of North Dakota)
Phys. Ther. 65:606–612, May 1985                                      6–15

---

The effectiveness of high-volt galvanic current (HVG) was compared with isometric exercise in strengthening the quadriceps femoris muscles in 17 healthy subjects. The subjects were divided into three groups: the control group (n = 6) received no exercise or stimulation; the isometric exercise group (n = 5) performed 15 sessions of maximum isometric contractions; and the electrical stimulation group (n = 6) engaged in 15 sessions of electrically stimulated isometric contractions. Subjects ranged in age from 21 to 29 years.

The largest net change was found in the isometric exercise group (14.7%); both the control and electrical stimulation groups had strength increases of only about 1 percent. Scheffe's method of post-hoc analysis showed a significantly greater increase in strength of the isometric exercise group than in either the control or electrical stimulation group. Within 3 stimulation sessions, all of the subjects in the electrical stimulation group could tolerate a full-scale current reading of 2,500 milliamperes. None of the subjects in either the isometric-exercise or electrical stimulation groups experienced any long-lasting discomfort after the training sessions. Most of the subjects in the electrical stimulation group did, however, report some discomfort during the stimulation sessions.

Three weeks (15 sessions) of HVG stimulation are not an effective method of increasing strength in healthy subjects. Further investigation is required with HVG stimulation in comparable subjects, as well as in patients with muscle atrophy, to establish it as an efficient means of muscle strengthening.

▶ See editor's comments preceding Digest 6–12.—Frank George, A.T.C., P.T.

---

**Influence of Sex Differences and Knee Joint Position on Electrical Stimulation-Modulated Strength Increases**
Thomas D. Fahey, Michael Harvey, Richard V. Schroeder, and Frank Ferguson (California State Univ.)
Med. Sci. Sports Exerc. 17:144–147, February 1985                                          6–16

---

Electrical stimulation is widely used to strengthen skeletal muscle in both healthy and injured persons. It is possible that stimulating the muscles in a lengthened rather than in a shortened position may create more tension and require a greater training effort. Increased tension may be generated in the electrically stimulated lengthened muscles as a result of preloading caused by stretching the muscular elastic components and by placement of individual sarcomeres in positions conducive to a greater degree of internal shortening during isometric contraction. Sex differences in responsiveness to electrical stimulation may be due to factors such as the greater electrical impedance in women (caused by a larger subcutaneous fat layer) and relative differences in the training state.

The authors analyzed 55 subjects (28 men and 27 women; mean age, 27 years), who were assigned to either a control group (C) that received no electrical stimulation, to an experimental group receiving stimulation of the quadriceps with the knee flexed at 65 degrees (EF), or to an experimental group receiving this stimulation with the knee fully extended (EE). Experimental subjects received 15 minutes of electrical stimulation 3 times a week for 6 weeks. Before and after the study, knee extension strength was measured with a Cybex II, isometrically at 65 degrees of knee flexion and isokinetically at 30, 60, 90, and 120 degrees per second.

Multivariate analysis of covariance, using the pretests as the covariate, revealed no sex differences in responsiveness to electrical stimulation. The EF was superior to EE at 30 and 120 degrees/second in women, and at 120 degrees/second in men. Male and female EF was superior to C in all tests. The EE was higher than C at isometric, 30, 90, and 120 degrees/ second in women, and at isometric and 30 degrees/second in men.

These results agree with Romero et al., who showed that electrical stimulation is effective in increasing isometric strength. The present study also revealed consistent increases in isokinetic strength in the EF groups. The practical significance of this modality is questionable in healthy individuals. The strength increases shown are relatively small and do not exceed those that can be achieved by traditional forms of resistive exercise. However, electrical muscle stimulation may be useful in increasing or maintaining strength when normal joint mobility is impaired.

The data suggest that electrical stimulation of the quadriceps muscle may be more effective in increasing strength, particularly at faster speeds of motion, if the knee joint is flexed during treatment. While the EF torques of men and women were statistically superior in only 3 of 10 comparisons, the EF torque was more consistently superior to controls than EE torques. This trend was more evident in men than in women.

The quadriceps of the EF subjects were slightly stretched, which may have caused greater tension during electrical stimulation than occurred in the EE group. Tension is one of the most important factors causing changes in the contractile characteristics of skeletal muscle. The possibility that greater tension was produced in the EE group may explain the trend toward a superior training responsiveness to isokinetic strength tests conducted at higher angular velocities. The selective effect of a training program is due to the selective recruitment of muscle fibers. Increased tension produced in the EE subjects may have caused greater training effects in muscle fibers recruited for faster motions.

▶ See editor's comments preceding Digest 6–12.—Frank George, A.T.C., P.T.

---

**Isometric Torque of the Quadriceps Femoris After Concentric, Eccentric, and Isometric Training**
Eugene Pavone and Marilyn Moffat (Helen Hayes Hosp., West Haverstraw, N.Y. and New York Univ.)
Arch. Phys. Med. Rehabil. 66:168–170, March 1985                        6–17

---

Twenty-seven healthy women, aged 22 to 39 years, underwent a 6-week training program of eccentric, concentric, and isometric exercises to increase quadriceps isometric strength. The peak isometric torque of the quadriceps femoris was determined on the Cybex II Isokinetic Dynamometer before and after training. Eighteen exercise sessions per subject were held.

Two-way analysis of variance with repeated measures revealed that although all three exercise types significantly increased isometric strength, none was superior. There was no interaction between the effects of pretraining and posttraining scores and the type of training. The relation between experimental design and knee biomechanics may have precluded significant differences in strength gain among the training groups.

Although eccentric muscle contractions have been shown to be less costly than concentric concentrations in terms of oxygen consumption, results of previous studies of concentric, eccentric, and isometric training programs have been contradictory. The present study showed that significant strength gain was achieved through any training modality. "Specificity of training" did not appear to influence the results, since both concentric and eccentric exercise resulted in equivalent isometric strength gain.

The results are surprising since eccentric contractions have been shown to produce the greatest muscular tension. Also, most subjects in other studies found eccentric contractions more comfortable than concentric. A muscle that contracts eccentrically produces greater tension than a muscle that contracts isometrically or concentrically. Thus, it would have been expected that the resultant strength increase in isometric tension with eccentric contraction would have been greater than demonstrated.

It has been suggested that plateaus may result from normal variations in strength. In this study, it was more likely that training plateaus could be explained by the finding of Lieb and Perry that a 60% greater quadriceps force is required to move the knee through 15 degrees of terminal extension. This observation agrees with the subjective reports of the persons in the eccentric and concentric groups. Subjects in the former reported difficulty in resisting a "dropping" of the load through the initial 15 degrees of flexion. Subjects in the concentric group reported difficulty in completing terminal knee extension.

Although the use of peak torque as a measure of strength is convenient and widespread, it may not accurately indicate a person's functional abilities. As Sapega et al. stated: "The validity of using peak torque values for the determination of strength deficits or imbalances is based on the assumption that comparing extremities at the strongest point in the range of motion will give an accurate indication of comparative strength throughout the entire range of motion."

▶ There are a couple of surprises in this study. The results did not support "specificity of training," nor did eccentric contractions produce superior results. I have been a strong supporter of "specificity of training" and will continue to be one. I do agree with the authors' statement that peak torque may not be the best measure of functional capability. That is why on-the-field testing should be done with all athletes in a rehabilitation program before they return to full activity.—Frank George, A.T.C., P.T.

---

### Quadriceps Torque and Integrated Electromyography

Bruce A. Brownstein, Robert L. Lamb, and Robert E. Mangine (Cincinnati Sportsmedicine and Orthopedic Ctr. and Medical College of Virginia)
J. Orthop. Sports Phys. Ther. 6:309–314, May–June 1985                6–18

---

The myoelectric activity and torque of the quadriceps were recorded under isometric conditions by electromyography (EMG) to identify the optimal angle of knee flexion for normalization. The behavior of the quadriceps as the knee was flexed was also investigated. The left quadriceps of 4 men, aged 24 to 36 years, and 7 women, aged 25 to 36, were tested. Separate motor points for the vastus medialis obliquus (VMO) and vastus medialis longus (VML) were found in 6 of the 11 subjects.

Mean peak torque occurred at 50 degrees for the entire group as well as for men alone. Mean peak torque for women occurred at 70 degrees. The mean torque for men was greater than that for women. Integrated EMG results varied according to muscle. Overall, only the VMO and the VML showed significant variation throughout the tested range of motion. The variation occurred between contractions at flexion angles greater than or equal to 50 degrees and those less than 50 degrees. Men showed no significant variation in the normalized integrated EMG for any of the quadriceps muscles. As a whole, peak torque and maximal integrated EMG showed no clear relation. When examined by subject gender, maximal integrated EMG tended to occur with peak torque. Three of the four muscles in each group followed this pattern; the VMO was the exception in men and the rectus femoris in women.

All four muscles exhibited similar patterns of normalized myoelectric activity, supporting previous findings in leg extension and isometric contractions. The relation between peak torque and myoelectric activity seen in both men and women reinforces the close interaction between muscle physiology and joint biomechanics at the knee.

The finding that both maximal myoelectric activity and peak torque occur in flexion rather than extension may have clinical implications. Classic treatment protocols for knee rehabilitation often include terminal extension and straight-leg raising exercises. Adduction straight-leg raises should be performed, since it may be possible selectively to strengthen the VMO because of its attachment to the adductor magnus. Short arc quadriceps exercises may be more effective in the 90–60-degree range for two reasons. (1) The myoelectric activity of the quadriceps is greater. Lieb and Perry state that the quadriceps is more efficient in that range. (2) The area of the patella that is in contact with the femur is greater in the 90–60-degree range. This increased contact area reduces tensile stress in the patella, which occurs when the patella is not in contact with the femur. Short arc quadriceps exercises in the flexed position should not be performed in the presence of pain or crepitus.

▶ The authors have made some very good recommendations for rehabilitation of injured knees. They stress the need for doing straight leg adduction exercises to increase VMO strength. They also recommend doing short arc exercises in the 90–60 degree range rather than in terminal extension. This will help alleviate patella-femoral joint irritation and hopefully prevent chondromalacia patella.—Frank George, A.T.C., P.T.

---

**Maintenance of Hamstring Strength Following Knee Injury**
Joseph J. Vegso, Susan E. Genuario, and Joseph S. Torg (Univ. of Pennsylvania)
Med. Sci. Sports Exerc. 17:376–379, June 1985                                    6–19

Clinical observations of routine postoperative isokinetic strength-testing show that the hamstring muscle group loses less strength than the quadriceps group after knee surgery for a variety of pathologic conditions. To quantify this observation and to determine if the condition was produced by a particular surgery, the Cybex isokinetic strength tests from two groups of postsurgical patients were evaluated. Group I consisted of 15 patients who had undergone arthrotomy and medial meniscectomy; group II consisted of 20 patients who had had extra-articular anterior cruciate ligament substitution.

The average percent deficits of quadriceps and hamstring strength were analyzed by three-way analysis of variance (ANOVA). A significant difference ($P < .001$) was found between the two surgical groups. Regardless of the surgical procedure, the hamstring deficit was significantly lower ($P = .041$) than the quadriceps deficit. No significant difference in the percent strength deficit was found at the various joint angles (30, 60, and 90 degrees) in either group.

After knee surgery, not all muscle groups need to be rehabilitated with equal emphasis. Further research is warranted into the causes of selective strength loss in various muscle groups acting on the same joint.

▶ The authors bring out an important aspect of knee rehabilitation—that is, after surgery certain muscle groups require more emphasis for strengthening than others. The diagnosis and surgical repair must control the type of rehabilitation program that is adhered to.—Frank George, A.T.C., P.T.

### Rehabilitation of the Knee Following Arthroscopic Surgery

Joseph S. Sutter (Tuckahoe Orthopaedic Associates, Ltd., Richmond, Va.)
Contemp. Orthop. 11:29–41, September 1985                          6–20

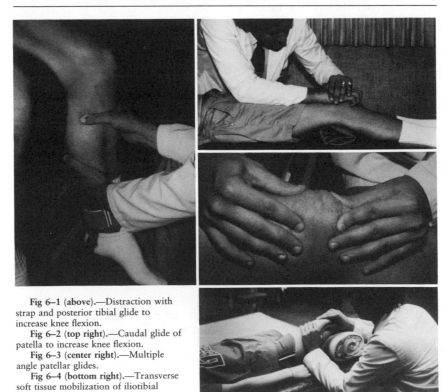

Fig 6–1 (above).—Distraction with strap and posterior tibial glide to increase knee flexion.

Fig 6–2 (top right).—Caudal glide of patella to increase knee flexion.

Fig 6–3 (center right).—Multiple angle patellar glides.

Fig 6–4 (bottom right).—Transverse soft tissue mobilization of iliotibial band.

(Courtesy of Sutter, J.S.: Contemp. Orthop. 11:29–41, September 1985.)

The goal of rehabilitation after arthroscopic knee surgery is to restore as normal a level of function as possible. Rehabilitation generally is easier and more rapid after arthrotomy because the adverse effects of immobilization are reduced or eliminated. In some instances, simple instructions to the patient on exercises and gentle range of motion will suffice, but high-performance athletes require a more formal program. Strengthening of the quadriceps should be begun immediately after patella surgery. Similar measures are taken after surgery for chondral disorders, with an emphasis on passive and low-load exercises. Meniscal repair requires a period of immobilization before exercises are begun. Aggressive mobilization is necessary after the release of synovial adhesions.

Active range-of-motion exercises usually can be instituted the first or second day after surgery. Various techniques to increase flexion and mobilize the patella are illustrated in Figures 6–1, 6–2, 6–3, 6–4. A frequently used sequence of strengthening modes is isometric, manual resistance, isokinetic, isotonic, and variable resistance. Total limb strength is incorporated into most rehabilitation programs. Electric stimulation is an effective adjunct in muscle re-education and pain reduction. Electromyographic feedback can help improve strength and knee function. Proprioception training is begun when the patient has good control of the limb in terminal knee extension and a normal gait pattern.

Running can begin when healing is adequate, symptoms have resolved, and isokinetic study shows about 75% of function compared with the uninvolved side. Isokinetic assessment should show function in the 80%–90% range before a return to controlled activities is permitted. A return to full activity is allowed when isokinetic assessment shows function of 90% or better and torque curves are nearly normal. Any necessary changes in life-style should be discussed before discharge.

▶ The accompanying illustrations were selected because of the problems that may arise in the patella femoral joint when the knee is immobilized. The author states that patella mobilization should be done during cast changes "to nourish the articular cartilage and to help restrict adhesion formation." We have also used these exercises before our standard range of motion and muscular strengthening exercises. The author has included a number of very helpful do's and don't's in this article. One example is, after meniscus repair monitor flexion carefully with posterior tears and extension for anterior tears to avoid "pinching." He also states "Strenuous resistive flexion exercises should be avoided initially, especially with medial meniscal repairs due to the insertion of the semimembranosus."—Frank George, A.T.C., P.T.

---

**Knee Rehabilitation Following Arthroscopic Meniscectomy**
Bertram Zarins, John Boyle, and Bette Ann Harris (Massachusetts Gen. Hosp., Boston)
Clin. Orthop. 198:36–42, September 1985                    6–21

---

Arthroscopic surgery often allows an earlier return to sports activity

PHASES OF POSTOPERATIVE KNEE REHABILITATION

| Phase | Description | Characteristics | Exercises |
|-------|-------------|-----------------|-----------|
| I | Immediate postoperative period | Incision, bleeding, pain, quadriceps inhibition | Quadriceps setting, straight-leg raising, hamstring resistance, ambulation ± external support |
| II | Early healing phase | Less pain, effusion, muscles weak, 90° of motion | Active range of motion, continue isometrics, ambulate, bicycle |
| III | Late healing phase | No pain, Effusion ± weakness, 120° of motion | Walk, bicycle, swim, functional exercise, isokinetics—high speed |
| IV | Late rehabilitation and conditioning phase | Full range of motion, no effusion, muscle weakness, not back to sports | Isokinetics—all speeds, isotonic, functional activities, run, jump, gradual return to sport |

(Courtesy of Zarins, B., et al.: Clin. Orthop. 198:36–42, September 1985.)

than conventional arthrotomy, particularly in young athletes who undergo partial meniscectomy but have no other pathologic changes in the knee. The immediate postoperative period, lasting 3–5 days, usually is followed by an early healing phase 5–14 days after arthroscopy (table). The late healing phase usually occurs by 2–3 weeks after arthroscopy, and is followed by a conditioning phase at 3–5 weeks. The rate of progression through these phases depends on the amount of soft tissue dissection; the presence of coexisting knee lesions, such as chondromalacia; and the extent of meniscectomy. The preoperative status of the knee and the motivation and expectations of the patient also are important factors. The degree of periarticular dissection is the most important difference between arthroscopic and open meniscectomy. Degenerative changes substantially prolong the time of rehabilitation.

No uniform guidelines exist for knee rehabilitation after arthroscopic meniscectomy. The program should be individualized. Patients who have minimal pain, no effusion, and no quadriceps inhibition and who maintain a full range of motion after surgery can return to sports or work rapidly; those who do poorly after meniscectomy are at the other end of the spectrum. The initial phase of rehabilitation may be prolonged by bleeding, low pain tolerance, or wound problems, such as hematoma or infection. Reflex sympathetic dystrophy is less frequent after arthroscopic meniscectomy than after open meniscectomy. Progress in rehabilitation should be dependent on objective knee findings. A return to sports is possible when a full range of painless motion and adequate dynamic muscular control are recovered.

▶ Because of newspaper reports and sensationalized stories of professional athletes, many patients expect to return to activity in an unrealistic amount of time after an arthroscopic meniscectomy. The authors stress the need for individualizing each knee rehabilitation program. The important factors stated by the authors that must be considered are pain, effusion, quadriceps function, and range of motion. Total rehabilitation is imperative before a return to full activity is allowed.—Frank George, A.T.C., P.T.

**Anteroposterior Tibiofemoral Displacements During Isometric Extension Efforts: The Roles of External Load and Knee Flexion Angle**
Kenneth A. Jurist and James C. Otis (New York Hosp.–Cornell Univ.)
Am. J. Sports Med. 13:254–258, July–August 1985                    6–22

Rehabilitation of knee extensors is a major consideration in patients with cruciate injuries and repairs. Extension exercises can produce undesirable loads on the injured or replaced anterior cruciate ligament (ACL), resulting in the permanent stretching of this restraint. This study measured the tibiofemoral displacements associated with proximal, middle, and distal locations of the external resisting force—and with knee flexion angles of 30, 60, and 90 degrees. The left knees of 15 male volunteers (mean age, 26.7 years; mean weight, 77.3 kg; and mean height, 179 cm) were used in the study.

As the external load was moved proximally on the tibia and the mean displacements became increasingly negative, the tibia was displaced more posteriorly. Results of the one-way analyses of variance between tibiofemoral displacement and external load location at each of the flexion angles demonstrate statistically significant ($P < .01$) differences in displacement. These were for the different external load locations at each of the flexion angles studied. There were also statistically significant ($P < .01$) differences noted in displacment over the three flexion angles used for middle and distal positions of the external load. However, when the external force was applied at the proximal position, tibiofemoral displacement was independent of the knee flexion angle, consistently resulting in posterior displacement of the tibia.

At present, there is considerable controversy as to the appropriate treatment of ACL injuries. The spectrum of opinions runs from primary repair in acute injury to muscle-strengthening exercises in chronic injury. A dual-pad system has no advantage over a single pad in reducing shear loads at the knee during extension exercise. The joint force will depend on the center of the force on the tibia, which is found at the pad in a single-pad system. Quadriceps muscle strengthening can be started safely between 90 and 30 degrees of flexion. This method avoids jeopardizing the integrity of the cruciate ligament or its replacement by using a proximally placed resistance to active extension. Further work is needed to record tibiofemoral displacements near full extension.

▶ The dual pad system was designed to prevent anterior displacement of the tibia and protect the anterior cruciate ligament and its supporting structures. The authors feel the same amount of protection can be provided if a single pad is used where the fulcrum of the dual pad system is, and the knee is exercised from 90 degrees to 30 degrees. I have the dual pad system and will continue to use it because I feel safe using it. If I didn't have it I would try what the authors recommend.—Frank George, A.T.C., P.T.

## Quadriceps Strengthening With the DAPRE Technique: Case Studies With Neurological Implications

Kenneth L. Knight (Indiana State Univ.)
Med. Sci. Sports Exerc. 17:646–650, December 1985                    6–23

Variations of Delorme's progressive resistive exercise (PRE) technique have been used in rehabilitation for four decades. The daily adjustable PRE (DAPRE) technique was developed to objectively determine the best time to increase resistance and the optimal amount of weight to use. The results of this method were assessed in 8 patients undergoing knee rehabilitation, all male athletes who had repair of simple collateral ligament or meniscal tears. They were immobilized in plaster for 3–6 weeks postoperatively. Thirteen other subjects, also with a mean age of 20 years, were immobilized for at least 3 weeks but had not been operated on. The DAPRE method is outlined in Tables 1 and 2. A Universal Gym knee-thigh machine was used. In 13 cases, both lower extremities were exercised independently with individual working weights.

The average ending working weight in both groups of athletes was about 41 kg, or 230% of the adjusted working weight on the first day. The average number of days exercised was 6½ for each group. Strength gain was greater in surgical cases because these subjects were weaker at the outset. The average increase in strength was 24% of initial strength. In the patients who exercised both limbs, the injured limb had a 141% increase in strength, compared with 69% for the uninjured extremity.

Strength gains with the DAPRE technique are impressive, and occur more rapidly than with the Delorme method. Strength rehabilitation after immobilization may depend on an ability to activate morphological components. Efforts toward re-establishing the neural component are neces-

### TABLE 1.—THE DAPRE TECHNIQUE*

| Set | Portion of Working Weight Used | No. of Repetitions |
|-----|-------------------------------|--------------------|
| 1 | ½ | |
| 2 | ¾ | 6 |
| 3 | Full | Maximum† |
| 4 | Adjusted | Maximum§ |

*Adapted from Knight, K.L.: Am. J. Sports Med 7:336–337, 1979.

†Number of repetitions performed during the third set is used to determine the adjusted working weight for the fourth set according to the guidelines in Table 2.

§Number of repetitions performed during the fourth set is used to determine the adjusted working weight for the next day according to the guidelines in Table 2.

(Courtesy of Knight, K.L.: Med. Sci. Sports Exerc. 17:646–650, December 1985. Copyright 1985, the American College of Sports Medicine. Reprinted by permission.)

*Chapter 6–Athletic Training* / **429**

TABLE 2.—General Guidelines for
Adjustment of Working Weight*

| No. of Repetitions Performed During Set | Adjustment to Working Weight for the: | |
| --- | --- | --- |
| | Fourth Set† | Next Day§ |
| 0–2 | Decrease 2–5 kg and repeat the set | |
| 3–4 | Decrease 0–2 kg | Keep the same |
| 2–7 | Keep the same | Increase 2–5 kg |
| 8–12 | Increase 2–5 kg | Increase 2–7 kg |
| 13+... | Increase 5–7 kg | Increase 5–10 kg |

*Adapted from Knight, K.L.: Am. J. Sports Med 7:336–337, 1979.
†Number of repetitions performed during the third set is used to determine the adjusted working weight for the fourth set according to the guidelines in this column.
§Number of repetitions performed during the fourth set is used to determine the adjusted working weight for the next day according to the guidelines in this column.
(Courtesy of Knight, K.L.: Med. Sci. Sports Exerc. 17:646–650, December 1985. Copyright 1985, the American College of Sports Medicine. Reprinted by permission.)

sary. It is possible that strength is developed by different processes during conditioning and during rehabilitation.

▶ I was amazed the first time I heard Ken Knight lecture on the DAPRE technique. I couldn't believe the strength gains in the relatively short amount of time he was reporting. However, after reading some of his studies and talking with others who have used this program, I found that it is not unusual to encounter significant strength gains in short periods of time after knee immobilization. The author postulates "that strength redevelopment following immobilization involves changes in neural pathways and/or overcoming possible neural inhibitors."—Frank George, A.T.C., P.T.

## Knee Braces: Questions Raised About Performance
Carol Potera (Ketchum, Idaho)
Physician Sportsmed. 13:153–155, September 1985                6–24

Use of the knee brace offers the promise of rigid immobility, rotational control, and resistance to combinations of instability. But after nearly 6 months of study the Sports Medicine Committee (SMC) of the American Academy of Orthopedic surgeons concluded that the effectiveness of knee braces is a controversial area that needs further biomechanical and epidemiologic study to aid in better designs. These conclusions were based, in part, on the information gathered at a knee brace seminar held in Chicago in August 1984. The SMC categorized braces as prophylactic, rehabilitative, or functional.

Data from two unpublished studies showed that prophylactic braces are not effective in decreasing the risk of injury. Another study found that not only was a brace ineffective, but that wearing one could increase the chance of injury. Researchers were concerned that false claims have convinced coaches, trainers, and player organizations that every high school, college, and professional football player should wear prophylactic braces as standard equipment.

In the past 5 years, rehabilitative braces have largely replaced casts for more than esthetic reasons. However, questions remain as to whether braces can control medial, lateral, anterior, and posterior displacement as well as control rotation. Most functional braces were designed by benchtop biomechanics; whereas these braces may provide a degree of support, it is questionable whether a significant difference results with their use. The SMC concluded that functional braces do not control knee laxity or restore it to normal under the forces encountered in sports. Further, if the brace had a viscoelastic component, the average recovery time for an injured ligament could be reduced from a year to 6 months.

▶ To wear a brace or not, that is the question. We will probably know in another 3 years if knee braces are effective in preventing knee injuries in football. My team has been wearing them for the past 2 years. There is an indication that they have reduced both the number and severity of knee injuries sustained. However, there was also a coaching change two years ago, and I'm not sure how much effect that has had. When we have 5 years of statistics to compare among many schools, then we will know if the braces are helpful.

A recent article has warned about braces causing a "pre loading" effect on the varus knee. This will have to be examined closely, and such knees should have a modified brace if braced at all. As I said, talk to me in 3 more years, and I will have a more definite opinion on the value of these braces. Until then the football players at my school will continue to wear knee braces to prevent injuries.—Frank George, A.T.C., P.T.

---

**Cybex Evaluation of the Relationship Between Anterior and Posterior Compartment Lower Leg Muscles**
Pierce E. Scranton, Jr., James P. Whitesel, and Vern Farewell (Seattle)
Foot Ankle 6:85–89, October 1985　　　　　　　　　　　　　　　　6–25

---

Popular running magazines and symposia for runners have offered speculation concerning a possible imbalance between the anterior compartment and posterior compartment lower leg muscles as related to overuse syndromes. Posterior stretching and anterior strengthening exercises have been advocated to correct anterior compartment muscle weakness. In this study, 20 men aged 21–28 tested with the Cybex II isokinetic dynamometer to compare the torque in each leg produced by the anterior and posterior muscle compartments. All 20 participants had normal lower extremities and no previous injury or surgery on the knee or ankle.

There was no difference in peak torque between the right and left leg as correlated with "handedness." When the knee was bent 90 degrees, the plantar flexion torque declined by 20% and 15% for the 30 degree per second and 180 degree per second measurements, respectively. The dorsiflexion torque was also significantly greater at 0 degrees of knee extension vs. 90 degrees for both the 30 degrees per second and 180 degrees per second. The anterior compartment muscles do not cross the knee. The average differences in torque measurements between the ectomorphic and mesomorphic legs were significant the 5% level, at least, for all measurements except for dorsiflexion strength at 30 degrees per second with the knee bent 90 degrees. Leg length correlated only with dorsiflexion strength measurements at 30 degrees per second, and calf girth correlated only with these measurements when the knee was extended.

The finding of no relationship between "handedness" and leg power supports the concept that lower leg muscle function is predominantly postural. The Cybex measurements of voluntary lower leg muscle torque represent only a small portion of the potential for torque generation. The baseline values of anterior and posterior compartment torque generated on a voluntary basis represent a fraction of the reserve in terms of total functional torque available in an individual.

▶ We have come to rely heavily on peak torque value when testing the quadriceps and hamstrings in our knee screening and rehabilitation programs. A number of articles have supplied us with normal values to follow. Earlier in this chapter there is an article which reports normal values for shoulder musculature (Digest 6–8). It is a beginning. The above digest is also a beginning to establish normal values for the musculature of the lower leg.

The authors report finding the following ratios: ". . . dorsiflexion torque is approximately one-third that of plantarflexion torque at slow speeds and half that of plantarflexion at fast speeds." The authors stress that the torque values generated on a voluntary basis are only a fraction of the available power.— Frank George, A.T.C., P.T.

---

**Prevention of Ankle Sprains**
Hans Tropp, Carl Askling, and Jan Gillquist (Univ. of Linköping, Sweden)
Am. J. Sports Med. 13:259–262, July–August 1985          6–26

---

This study investigated the efficiency of a semi-rigid ankle orthosis and ankle-disk training in reducing the incidence of ankle sprains in soccer players. Twenty-five male senior soccer teams were studied in division VI of the Swedish national league. Eighteen players in each team (n = 450) were selected, with all players randomly divided into three groups. Group 1 served as control and comprised 10 teams, each with 18 players. Group 2 comprised 7 teams that used a special orthosis as an alternative to ankle taping. Group 3 included 65 men with previous ankle problems who received ankle disk training and 71 men with no previous ankle problems and no ankle disk training.

Forty-eight of the 439 players had had previous problems with one or both ankles. In group 1, 30 players (17%) sustained an ankle sprain during the study period, with 19 sprains occurring among 75 men who had a history of previous problems (25%) and 11 among 96 (11%) with no such history ($P < .05$). Of the 60 players in group 2 using the ankle orthosis, there were 2 sprains (3%), which was significantly lower than among the controls ($P < .05$). The corresponding figure for group 3 (n = 142), of whom 65 were receiving ankle-disk training was 7 sprains (5%), which was also significantly lower than in controls ($P < .01$). Among controls, 75 men with previous ankle problems sustained 19 sprains (25%), as compared with 3 of 65 (5%; ($P < .01$) in group 3 and 1 of 45 (2%; ($P < .01$) in group 1. In group 3, the incidence of injury was 5% both in players with a history of problems (n = 65, all training) and in those without previous problems (n = 77, not training).

The ankle orthosis should be used during the rehabilitation period before coordination training has achieved its prophylactic effect in ankle injuries. The device has also proved valuable when playing on uneven ground and in special situations when the risk of injury is considered greater than usual. In this study overall, however, ankle-disk training reduced the incidence of ankle sprains among players with a history of related problems to that of players without any history of sprains—and to that of those using the orthosis.

▶ The ankle-disk exercises are a major component of our ankle rehabilitation program. We feel these exercises are necessary to restore normal proprioception in any ankle that has been immobilized. We also require all our athletes who wish to have their ankles taped to first spend 1 minute doing flexibility exercises, 1 minute of strengthening exercises, and 1 minute on the ankle disk.

The ankle-disk exercises are a must for the patient with normal strength and no ankle joint laxity who complains of the ankle "giving way" when walking. The cause is probably loss of proprioception. The cure is exercise with the disk.—Frank George, A.T.C., P.T.

---

### Comparative Radiological Study of the Influence of Ankle Joint Strapping and Taping on Ankle Stability

P. Vaes, H. De Boeck, F. Handelberg, and P. Opdecam (Free Univ. of Brussels)

J. Orthop. Sports Phys. Ther. 7:110–114, November 1985                    6–27

---

Trauma in ankle varus appears to be the most frequent sports injury, but its proper management remains in dispute. With many methods, strapping or taping is used at some stage to support the ankle and relieve tension on the lateral ligaments. The effects of strapping and taping on talar tilt (TT) were compared in 51 subjects with ankle instability related to sports activities. The average age was 21 years. Talar tilt was demonstrated by applying varus stress manually during video monitoring. A 15-kg torque force was applied with the leg fixed and the foot in 40 degrees of plantar flexion.

A mean TT of 13 degrees was found without bandaging. With strapping the mean TT was 13 degrees; with taping, it was 5 degrees. After 30 minutes of activity with tape in place, the mean TT was 7 degrees. The reduction in TT with taping was highly significant, and it remained significant after activity.

Strapping provides inadequate support to the ankle to eliminate TT, but taping has a significant effect in reducing tibiotalar instability. Further study of taping of the ankle joint for therapeutic purposes is warranted.

▶ A number of studies have been done to indicate the effectiveness of ankle taping. The authors use the term "strapping" to describe a "figure of eight" WRAP with an elastic bandage. Elastic bandages are not commonly used on ankles for athletic activity. If we want to provide support and stability, we agree with the authors that a nonelastic adhesive tape must be used. It was very encouraging to see how much support was provided to the ankle by taping in both the pre- and post-exercise state. Reducing the talar tilt from 13 degrees to 5 degrees and 7 degrees, respectively, is a significant accomplishment. I will continue to tape ankles that need it. We tape those ankles that have been recently sprained or have a history of recurrent sprain, or the lax ankle to prevent reinjury. We also use adhesive tape for support in our ankle treatment and rehabilitation program.—Frank George, A.T.C., P.T.

---

**Ankle Joint Support: A Comparison of Reusable Lace-on Braces With Taping and Wrapping**
Richard P. Bunch, Kathryn Bednarski, D. Holland, and Raymond Macinanti
Physician Sportsmed. 13:59–62, May 1985                                    6–28

---

Prophylactic taping and cotton wrapping were compared with five lace-on braces to determine the best way to provide ankle support. An instrumented fixture applied an inversion torque to the ankle of a polyurethane foot form molded from castings taken from a man's size 9 foot. A hybrid form was constructed by blending the foot portion of the last mold with the ankle portion of the foot mold. Soft polyurethane was injected into the mold cavity, which had been fitted with a ball joint positioned along the axis defined by the centers of the two malleoli. This produced an anatomically correct foot form that could be easily articulated into inversion and eversion about the ankle.

Baseline measurements were made on the amount of torque required to flex only the foot form (mounted in the modified oxford shoe). Checks were made during the study to ensure that no change occurred in the resistance offered by the raw form, e.g., from heat buildup. A certified athletic trainer applied 1.5-in. tape directly to the form. Adhesion was regarded as excellent. A Gibney basket weave and heel lock was selected as a representative taping and wrapping style; 25 cycles of inversion and return to neutral were used to allow the tape, form, and shoe to seat themselves together. Data for the next 5 cycles were collected and averaged for a test result. The mean of five separate tape applications was used to evaluate overall support. Similar procedures were used to evaluate the support from a 1.5-in. bias-ply cotton wrap and lace-on braces from four manufacturers.

The tape provided the highest level of support. It was about 25% stiffer than the best laced support and 70% stiffer than the cotton wrap. There were marked differences among the lace-on braces. Three were not statistically different from the cotton wrap, and the other two were about midway between the cottom wrap and the tape. After the 20-minute period of inversion cycles, the greatest change in support was in the tape (21%). The changes in support of the lace-on braces ranged from 4.5% to 8.5%. At the end of 20 minutes there was no difference in the level of support given by the tape and the best two lace-on braces.

The results from the freshly applied support systems might lead to the conclusion that the professionally applied athletic tape provided the best support. However, preliminary laboratory studies indicate that more than 33% of the ankle support can be lost when inexperienced personnel apply the tape. Although tape provided the best support initially, it is more useful to find out how much support is available during activity. The 20-minute cycle used in this study simulated a postexercise condition. The change in the tape support measured is probably conservative compared with that which occurs in practice. The weakening of tape support is a combined process of mechanical breakdown caused by excessive strain on the tape fibers and loss of adhesion caused by moisture on the skin surface. The fixture used was able to reproduce only the mechanical contribution to the loss of support of the tape. Studies have reported 18% to 40% losses of support for taped ankles of subjects after exercise. The change in support of the lace-on braces was most likely caused by the laces becoming loose. The original level of support was restored by replacing the braces. The change in the study should represent the change that would occur on a human subject, because support is not dependent on skin adhesion.

▶ Another digest concerning the effectiveness of adhesive tape on ankle stabilization. The original article also includes figures on lace-on ankle supports. Preexercise states show the adhesive tape to be the most supportive. Postexercise states indicate that two of the five braces tested provide support equal to that of adhesive tape.

I have tried a number of different ankle supports. Some athletes like them, they wear them, they feel safe with them. Others state "they are uncomfortable," and they will not use them. It is really a matter of choice. There is no choice, however, if the athlete needs assistance for ankle stability and is unable to be taped by someone who knows how to tape.—Frank George, A.T.C., P.T.

---

**Strength Development: Using Functional Isometrics in an Isotonic Strength Training Program**
Allen Jackson, Timothy Jackson, Jan Hnatek, and Jane West (North Texas State Univ.)
Res. Q. Exerc. Sport 56:234–237, September 1985                        6–29

---

In a given range of motion of an isotonic contraction, there is a "sticking point" where muscle torque is at its lowest level. An attempt was made

DESCRIPTIVE STATISTICS OF VARIABLES MEASURED*

| Condition | Pretest Mean | SD | Post Test Mean | SD | Body Weight Mean | SD |
|---|---|---|---|---|---|---|
| Experimental | 183.18 | 23.97 | 218.64 | 23.39 | 164.27 | 19.14 |
| Control | 177.69 | 29.37 | 198.85 | 32.35 | 164.57 | 19.84 |

| | Absolute gain | Percentage Improvement |
|---|---|---|
| Experimental | 35.46 | 19.4 |
| | 21.16 Control | 11.9 |

*Measured in pounds.
(Courtesy of Jackson, A., et al.: Res. Q. Exerc. Sport 56:234–237, September 1985. Reprinted by permission of the American Alliance for Health, Physical Education, Recreation and Dance, 1900 Association Drive, Reston, Virginia 22901.)

to determine whether maximum voluntary isometric contractions at isotonic sticking points would enhance isotonic strength expression. College males in four weight training classes were studied. Two classes were in an experimental group performing maximum voluntary isometric contractions in sets of two or three, at a bar height at which the previous attempt had failed. All groups performed bench press exercise over 10 weeks of training, 3 days a week.

The results are compared in the experimental and control groups in the table. Significant improvement was evident in both groups, but experimental subjects were significantly stronger than controls on testing after training.

The findings support a role for functional isometrics in enhancing standard isotonic training regimens where achievement of maximal strength is desired. The approach could be extended to other isotonic exercise, and females could become a population of interest. Competitive weight lifters could use this technique to move past previously limiting weight loads. The dependent variable might be the time or the speed of improvement rather than the maximum strength.

▶ The authors have presented a very interesting method of strength training to overcome the "sticking point." Isometric exercises are performed at the "sticking point," with a goal of increasing muscle strength enough to pass this point. This method of strength training may be utilized in rehabilitation programs. I am anxious to try this in knee rehabilitation programs where "extensor lag" may be a problem.—Frank George, A.T.C., P.T.

**Free Weights: A Review Supporting Their Use in Training and Rehabilitation**
Larry J. Nosse and Gary R. Hunter (Marquette Univ. and Univ. of Alabama in Birmingham)
Athletic Training 20:206–209, Fall 1985                    6–30

The functional morphological benefits of free-weight use can increase performance capacity and prevent injury. Free weights can also be used in rehabilitation of the injured athlete. Specific strength development is one important aspect in improving performance capacity for many athletes. Both isokinetic and variable-resistance apparatuses may have serious lim-

TABLE 1.—General Progression for Strengthening in Nonsurgical Cases

| Rehabilitation Stages | Strengthening Modes |
|---|---|
| Advanced | Unrestricted free weights for overall strengthening |
| | Resistive machines for specific muscle groups |
| | Isokinetics for specific muscle groups at all speeds |
| Intermediate | Moderate free weights |
| | High speed isokinetics maximal effort |
| | Various traditional strengthening machines |
| Late Acute | Light free weights |
| | Elastic straps |
| | High speed isokinetics, less than maximal effort |
| | Manual resistance |
| | Active exercise |
| Early Acute | Active assistive exercise |
| | Isometrics |

(Courtesy of Nosse, L., and Hunter, G.: Athletic Training 20:206–209, Fall 1985.)

TABLE 2.—General Progression for Strengthening in Postsurgical Cases

| Rehabilitation Stages | Strengthening Modes |
|---|---|
| Advanced | Unrestricted free weights for overall strengthening |
| | Resistive machines for specific muscle groups |
| | Isokinetics for specific muscle groups at all speeds |
| | Moderate free weights |
| | High speed isokinetics moderate effort |
| Intermediate | Light free weights |
| | Elastic straps |
| | High speed isokinetics, minimal effort level |
| | Manual resistance |
| Late Acute | Active movements |
| | Active movements in controlled ranges |
| Early Acute | Assisted movements in controlled ranges |
| | Isometrics |

(Courtesy of Nosse, L., and Hunter, G.: Athletic Training 20:206–209, Fall 1985.)

itations. Research indicates that eccentric training may cause more hypertrophy than concentric training. All variable-resistance apparatuses cause the resistance to change throughout the range of motion. The scientific literature on the development of strength has largely been inconclusive, indicating that there is no advantage in variable-resistance or isokinetic training over isotonic training.

Free weights are often believed to have an advantage in developing specific strength because increases in strength are specific to muscle length. Moreover, movement in most sports does not occur in only one joint at a time, and muscles that stabilize joints and are active in balance also need to be trained. Power is also an important component in many sports. Recent research indicates that training adaptations are probably at least partially specific to the velocity at which training occurs. Acceleration is an important factor, too.

Rehabilitation of a limb after soft-tissue injury or surgery involves many activities over time. Table 1 summarizes a typical strengthening progression of an injured limb (no surgery). Table 2 presents such a progression in postsurgical cases. Many movements are not easily learned without the use of some form of weight machine. Isokinetic apparatuses offer the opportunity to choose speeds of contraction that are comparable to segment speeds in particular sports. The intermediate and later stages of rehabilitation may incorporate isokinetic exercise if done judiciously.

▶ I feel this is a good article supporting the use of free weights. The authors state that "free weights are felt to have an advantage in developing specific usable strength and neuromuscular coordination." I agree with the authors' statement" . . . that, as yet, there is insufficient evidence to conclude that the use of strengthening machines result in superior performance, fewer injuries or shortened rehabilitation periods compared to traditional weight strengthening." Both the free weights and the machines the authors describe have a place in rehabilitation. We use a combination of free weights and the isokinetic, variable resistance, and multiaxial machines. The type of weight or machine used does not compare in importance to the amount of time and effort the athlete is willing to expend. The hard-working athlete will derive benefit from weights or machines; the athlete who is unwilling to expend the effort will benefit from neither. Depending on the body part being rehabilitated, there are, at times, advantages to certain machines and at times advantages to free weights.—Frank George, A.T.C., P.T.

---

## Acquisition and Retention of Golf Putting Skill Through the Relaxation, Visualization and Body Rehearsal Intervention

William G. Meacci and Eldon E. Price (Pennsylvania State Univ.)
Res. Q. Exerc. Sport 56:176–179, June 1985                                                6–31

---

Price and Braun (1983) used undergraduate college students to compare three methods for acquiring basketball foul-shooting skill: (1) relaxation, visualization, and body rehearsal intervention (RVR); (2) traditional rep-

**438** / Sports Medicine

etition; and (3) a combination of these two. This study replicates the task variables in the 1983 report to evaluate the effectiveness of RVR intervention for learning aggressive golf-putting skill. A total of 77 undergraduate students, aged 18 to 21 years, participated. Three experimental groups were used, composed of students registering for one of three golf classes, and a tennis class was used as a control group. Group 1 used RVR (15 students); group 2 used repetition (25 students); and group 3 used a combination of RVR and repetition (15 students).

The distribution of group means for Learning Acquisition × Testing Sessions is shown in Figure 6–5. Results indicated that the 30th-session test mean for the RVR-repetition group was significantly higher ($P < .01$) than for the other three groups. The RVR and repetition groups were not significantly different ($P < .05$) from each other in acquisition on the 30th-session test mean, but were significantly different ($P < .01$) from the control. Figure 6–6 illustrates the comparison of acquisition- (session 30) with retention-test means. There were no significant differences between experimental groups on these test means, but the experimental groups did significantly differ from the controls ($P < .01$).

The RVR-type of cognitive intervention was as effective as traditional practice in acquiring a motor skill, and a combination of the two methods was superior when compared with using the methods separately. The retention results indicate that a properly administered cognitive intervention could be incorporated with physical practice to provide meaningful activity in physical education classes. Cognitive intervention would be of

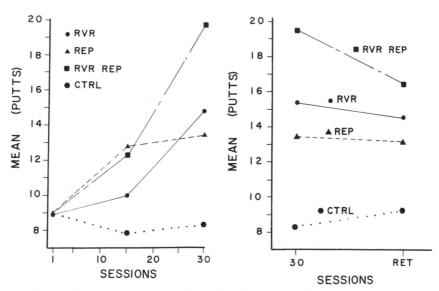

Fig 6–5.—Group test means × session for evaluating learning acquisition.
Fig 6–6.—Group test means × session for evaluating learning retention. (Courtesy of Meacci, W., and Price, E.: Res. Q. Exerc. Sport 56:176–179, June 1985. Reprinted by permission of the American Alliance for Health, Physical Education, Recreation and Dance, 1900 Association Drive, Reston, Virginia 22901. Photography by the Pennsylvania State University Instructional Services, Jim Luce.)

particular value in crowded classes, classes with short time periods, and in limited-equipment situations.

▶ My annual selection to help improve our golf games. Many athletes are using the relaxation, visualization, and body rehearsal technique to improve their skill. Many have been successful. Why can't I break 100?—Frank George, A.T.C., P.T.

# Subject Index

## A

Acetazolamide
  exercise and, in sojourners to 6,300 meters, 183
Achievement
  cognitions in competition, sex differences in, 396
Achilles tendon
  CT demonstration, 266
  rupture
    magnetic resonance imaging of, 267
    review of, 268
ACL (*see* Ligament, cruciate, anterior)
Acromioclavicular
  injury, shoulder strength after, 215
Acromioplasty
  anterior, shoulder impingement syndrome after, 250
Adiposity
  physical activity and, in children, 351
Adolescence
  ballet dancer (*see* Ballet dancer, adolescent)
  female, fitness, physical ability, physical performance and self-concept during, 397
  lifting during, power, study of dead lift, 352
  prepubescent and postpubescent athletes, predictive leg strength in, 355
  scoliosis in, idiopathic, cardiorespiratory status and mild deformity in, 356
  sudden death during, unexpected natural, 349
  track and field events during, in female, 392
Adolescent athletes (*see* Athletes, adolescent)
Adrenaline
  airway responses to, 59
  during mental stress and isometric exercise, 79
Adrenergic, beta (*see under* Beta, adrenergic)
Adrenoceptor (*see* Beta, adrenoceptor)
Aerobic
  conditioning of pre- and post-menopausal females, 379
  exercise, thermoregulation during pregnancy, 377
Age
  differences in muscle strength and muscle endurance of female masters swimmers, 382
  muscle strength and anthropometric indices, 380

-related augmentation of catecholamines during dynamic exercise, 81
Aged
  female masters swimmers, muscular strength and flexibility of, 382
  muscle strength and anthropometric indices, 380, 381
  strength training effect in, in women, 384
Air
  embolism in sport divers, 127
Airway, 58 ff.
  obstruction, ventilatory changes during exercise and, 58
  pressure, positive for high altitude pulmonary edema, 187 ff.
  responses to adrenaline and noradrenaline, 59
Alignment
  of body in standing, 203
Allergy
  nasal, nasal mucosal responses in, after cold exposure and exercise, 176
  physical, and mast cell degranulation, 161
Altitude
  high (*see* High altitude)
  moderate, exposure and the heart patient, 191
  mountain, splenic syndrome at, in sickle cell trait, 190
Amenorrhea
  athletic, 366
Anabolic (*see* Steroids, anabolic)
Anaphylaxis
  exercise causing, 161
Androgen
  after exercise, physical, 85
  $HDL_2$-cholesterol reduced by, 146
  hormone response to, in power athletes, 149
  after sleep deprivation, 85
  triglyceride lipase increase due to, 146
Androgenic
  response to exercise and endurance training, 155
  steroid effects on liver and red cells, 152
Anemia
  at high altitude, and hemoglobin distribution, 181
Anesthesia
  local, for arthroscopic surgery of knee, 315
Angina pectoris
  exercise in coronary artery disease causing, and coffee drinking, 142
  nitroglycerin failure to improve exercise capacity and, 160

441

capacity
maximal short term, 167
nitroglycerin failure to improve, and
angina pectoris, 160
cold exposure and, nasal mucosal
responses in nasal allergy and, 176
consequence to continuous, and ozone
inhalation, 65
dynamic, age-related augmentation of
catecholamines during, 81
endorphins and, in females, 370
endurance, water intoxication
complicating, 108
of Enduro athletes, gastrointestinal
symptoms during, 173
exhausting, maximal ventilation after,
57
fat utilization enhanced by, in cold
environment, 86
fructose before, 70
glucose before, 70
in hypertension, learned control of heart
rate during, 55
hyperthermia due to, aspirin in, 98
impact on medical cost, 192
interferon levels after, plasma, 165
ischemia due to, revascularization in, 23
isometric
adrenaline and noradrenaline during,
79
quadriceps femoris muscle strength
and, 419
lipids and lipoprotein cholesterol, in
women, 373
lipids in obesity and, 66
magnesium and, 78
maternal, response of fetal heart rate to,
376
muscle, and fatigue, 105
muscle glycogen during, and fructose
ingestion, 113
muscle metabolism during, in heat, 88
myocardial injury after, diagnosis, 20
occupational, and colonic cancer, 196
oxygen transport and metabolism
during, and nifedipine, 42
oxygen uptake in, 83
minimal renal disease and, 75
performance after passive cigarette
smoking, 64
potassium shifts during, catecholamine
modulation of, 38
during pregnancy, responses to, 374
progressive, plasma volume and protein
content in, 114
prolonged, circulating immune
complexes after, assessment, 164
pulmonary edema and, high altitude, on
Mount McKinley, 188

recovery after, energy metabolism
during, 72
renin during, and beta adrenoceptors,
29
resistance, hydraulic, cardiorespiratory
responses to, 54
response
beta blockade and, 30
physiological, beta$_1$ adrenoceptor
blockade in, 28
ST depression due to, and R wave
amplitude, 44
strength and, 83
strengthening, for sequelae of
poliomyelitis, 172
strenuous
menstrual disorder induction in, in
untrained women, 371
myocardial blood flow after, 19
submaximal, heart response to,
reliability of, 26
temperature control and performance,
89
testing
arm, in coronary artery disease
detection, 48
during coronary artery disease and
beta-adrenergic blockade, 31
limitations of, 43
responses in coronary artery disease,
and prajmaline bitartrate, 52
tolerance in rheumatoid arthritis and
osteoarthritis, 170
training (*see* Training, exercise)
treadmill, score vs. ECG in coronary
artery disease screening, 46
uterine activity and late pregnancy,
376
vapor permeation through garments
during, 91
ventilatory changes during, $P_{CO_2}$ and
airway obstruction, 58
in water, thermal responses to, 101
Extension
isometric, anteroposterior tibiofemoral
displacements during, 427
Extremities
injury and muscle imbalance, 199
lower
biomechanics, load analysis and
sports injuries in, 218
edema in, physiological, 24
kinematics in baseball batting, 390
loading during running, 208
masculature in cruciate ligament
instability, 304
stretching in soccer training, 225
upper, rhabdomyolysis, and weight
lifting, 136

# Index to Authors

## A

Åkerström, G., 78
Aarli, J. A., 129
Abani, K., 352
Abel, M., 345
Abouantown, S., 160
Adams, W. C., 65
Adeniran, S. B., 67
Afanasiev, R., 360
Aglietti, P., 323
Agras, W. S., 351
Agre, J. C., 279
Aharonson, Z., 275
Ahlgren, L., 408
Akers, P. C., 404
Akeson, W. H., 345
Albers, J. J., 67
Albers, J. W., 170
Albright, J. P., 230, 306
Aldercreutz, H., 85
Alén, M., 71, 149, 151, 152
Almi, A., 165
Amery, A., 29, 77
Amiel, D., 345
Amis, A. A., 298
Amsterdam, J. T., 96
An, K. N., 245
Anderson, J. T., 66
Anderson, M. E., 338
Anderson, W. M., 377
Andree, R. A., 315
Andresen, D. C., 391
Andresen, N. M., 352
Andrews, J. R., 241, 260, 261, 300, 334
Andrish, J. T., 303
Angel, D., 297, 299
Antich, T. J., 358
Aquiar, C. A., 67
Araujo, J., 86
Arfors, K.-E., 143
Armao, J. C., 96
Armstrong, L. E., 93
Arnaud, M.-J., 70
Askew, L. J., 245
Askling, C., 431
Atha, J., 227
Austen, K. F., 161

## B

Bach, D. K., 201
Bailey, P., 264
Baker, B. E., 240, 244, 246
Balady, G. J., 48
Bale, P., 371, 358, 393
Balkissoon, B., 386
Ball, S. G., 59
Banta, G., 84
Banwell, B. F., 170

Barber, F. A., 278, 318
Bares, C., 130
Barker, W. J., 96
Barnes, R. E., 196
Bartlett, J. C., 136
Bassett, D. R., 68
Bassett, F. H., III, 309
Bassey, E. J., 380, 381
Bassi, P. B., 323
Bates, P., 271
Bauer, M., 324, 337
Bayer, M., 367
Beals, C. A., 170
Beard, J. L., 181
Beaver, W., 378
Becker, G. D., 133
Becklake, M. R., 356
Bednarski, K., 433
Bedu, M., 155
Bedynek, J. L., 46
Beisel, W. R., 169
Beitins, I. Z., 371
Bendall, M. J., 380, 381
Bender, P. R., 57
Ben-Ezra, V., 74
Bennett, N. L., 377
Benson, J., 399
Berasi, C. C., 322
Berg, K., 62
Bergfeld, J. A., 303
Bergström, B., 337
Berkin, K. E., 59
Berkowitz, R. I., 351
Bernier, D., 146
Bernier-Cardou, M., 227
Bianchini, A., 146
Bielinski, R., 72
Bierschenk, J., 410
Bierwagen, D., 246
Bills, G. L., 96
Binkhorst, R. A., 218
Bishop, P. J., 237
Bittar, E. S., 293
Björk, J., 143
Blankstein, A., 117
Block, W. D., 68
Bocci, V., 165
Bohannon, R. W., 204
Bonanni, G., 287
Bonci, T., 355
Bond, V., Jr., 386
Bongaerts, M. C. M., 124
Bönlökke, L., 79
Boomer, W. L., 388
Booth, R. F., 251
Boss, J., 299
Botti, J. J., 377
Boucher, D., 155
Bourdet, K., 399
Boutelle, D., 416
Bove, A. A., 19, 36
Boyle, J., 425
Bradwell, A. R., 183
Braisted, J. R., 397

Braly, W. G., 256
Branken, T., 108
Brassøe, J. O. K., 361
Braunstein, E. M., 170
Brewster, C. E., 59, 358, 418
Brighton, C. T., 347
Brooks, G. A., 178, 180
Broome, A. E. A., 282
Brotherhood, J. R., 119
Broussard, T. S., 260
Brown, E. W., 352
Brown, M., 418
Brown, R. T., 365
Brownstein, B. A., 422
Brubakk, O., 129
Bühlmann, A. A., 128
Bullen, B. A., 371
Bunch, R. P., 433
Bünemann, L. K. H., 361
Burks, R., 283
Burman, K. D., 37
Burrows, B. A., 83
Burry, K., 376
Burton, G. R., 62
Butman, S. M., 142
Buzzi, R., 323

## C

Cabaud, H. E., 296
Caine, D., 362
Calhoun, J. H., 410
Campbell, J. R., 298
Cann, C., 367
Cardou, A., 227
Carey, R. A., 36
Carleton, R. A., 60
Carlson, B., 419
Carmichael, S. W., 212
Carney, D., 401
Caron, J., 157
Carroll, J. D., 23
Carson, W. G., 241, 260, 334
Carson, W. G., Jr., 261
Carter, V. S., 250
Casal, D., 66
Castor, C. W., 170
Celliers, C. P., 28
Cena, K., 91
Chandy, T. A., 355
Chantraine, A., 137
Chapman, P. J., 232
Charalambakis, A., 52
Chen, G., 272
Chen, H., 272
Chisin, R., 275
Choong, C. Y. P., 42
Christensen, N. J., 79
Christiaanse, J. C., 124
Cilliers, J. F., 28, 94
Cisar, C. J., 392
Claasen, H., 304

461